American Politics

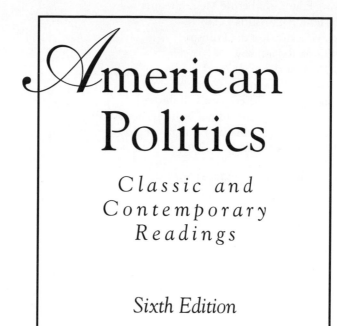

American Politics

Classic and Contemporary Readings

Sixth Edition

Allan J. Cigler
University of Kansas

Burdett A. Loomis
University of Kansas

Houghton Mifflin Company   Boston   New York

Publisher: Charles Hartford
Sponsoring Editor: Katherine Meisenheimer
Assistant Editor: Christina Lembo
Editorial Associate: Kendra Johnson
Project Editor: Reba Libby
Editorial Assistant: Rachel Zanders
Manufacturing Coordinator: Carrie Wagner
Senior Composition Buyer: Sarah Ambrose
Senior Art and Design Coordinator: Jill Haber Atkins
Executive Marketing Manager: Nicola Poser
Marketing Assistant: Kathleen Mellon

Front cover photography: Terry Heffernan, Inc.

Printed in the U.S.A.

Library of Congress Control Number: 2003115593

ISBN: 0-618-45323-7

23456789-QF-08 07 06 05

Contents

Topic Correlation Chart

Although the chapters of this book of readings have been organized to mesh with the coverage of most American government textbooks, many subjects receive attention in more than one chapter. The following chart permits students and instructors to locate relevant readings for twenty-four subjects, ranging (in alphabetical order) from bureaucracy to the Washington establishment.

Topic:	Covered In:
Bureaucracy	Chapter 12; 2.4, 14.1
Campaigns and Elections	Chapter 7; 4.3, 6.2, 6.3
Bush Administration	2.4, 3.6, 11.3, 14.5
Congress	Chapter 10; 6.2, 7.3
Constitution	Chapters 1, 3, 13; 2.1, 2.2, 7.2, 9.1
Domestic Policy	Chapter 14; 2.3, 2.4, 3.8, 3.9, 4.2, 10.2, 12.1, 13.4
Federalism	Chapter 2; 1.1, 6.2, 9.1, 14.3
The Founding	Chapter 1; 9.1
Interest Groups	Chapter 9; 14.1, 14.2
Leadership	Chapter 11; 5.4, 8.1, 10.3, 10.4, 13.4, 14.1
Money and Politics	7.2, 7.3, 9.2, 9.4, 10.3, 10.4
Participation	Chapter 5; 4.2, 6.3, 7.4, 9.3
Policy Making Process	Chapter 14; 2.4, 7.3, 9.4, 10.4, 11.3
Political Culture	3.5, 5.2, 5.3, 5.4, 6.3, 9.3
Political Parties	Chapter 6; 5.1, 7.1, 7.2, 7.3, 10.3, 12.1
Post 9/11 and the War on Terrorism	2.4, 3.6, 5.4, 8.2, 8.3, 14.4, 14.5
Presidency	Chapter 11; 8.1, 14.5
Public Opinion	Chapter 4; 3.6, 5.4, 7.1, 8.3, 14.4, 14.5
Reform	5.2, 6.2, 7.1, 7.2, 9.3
Representation	Chapter 9; 4.2, 6.3, 10.1, 10.3, 10.4, 13.4
Separation of Powers	1.4, 10.2, 11.1, 11.4, 13.1
Supreme Court and the Judiciary	Chapters 3 and 13; 6.2, 7.2
Technology and Politics	4.3, 7.4, 8.3, 12.3, 12.4
Washington Establishment	1.3, 9.2, 10.3, 10.4, 11.1, 11.4

PREFACE

Since this book was first conceived more than fifteen years ago, we have hewed to the dual themes of continuity and change in American politics. We offer a core of classic articles and complement them with up-to-date explorations of various elements of political life. This has proved a useful pedagogical approach, but in 2004 the continuity-change dualism is more important, and more timely, than in any of the book's previous editions.

Consider what has happened in American politics in recent years. With fewer than nine months in office, President Bush had to confront the most devastating attack on the United States since Pearl Harbor. In the aftermath of the 9/11 events, the president and the Congress had to address both domestic and international security issues that would change long-established practices and basic assumptions about many policies, ranging from civil liberties to the use of military force. At the same time, some facets of American politics have remained remarkably stable. Indeed, 2004 represents the fiftieth anniversary of *Brown* v. *Board of Education*, a landmark decision whose core issues have remained relevant over many decades.

In light of the simultaneous continuity and change that characterizes American politics, we remain committed to assembling a mix of articles that combines well-established classics with the best of contemporary analyses. The sixty articles in this edition include twenty-eight new articles and two (Richard Hofstadter on the founding and the text of the *Brown* decision) that appeared in the fourth edition and other earlier editions of the text.

The articles selected for this edition include a large number of true "classics," including John P. Roche's "The Founding Fathers: A Reform Caucus in Action," and Richard E. Neustadt's essential analysis of presidential power. Other articles focus on the contemporary, as with Richard E. Cohen's profile of House Majority Leader Tom DeLay (R-Texas), perhaps the most important legislator of his generation. Finally, we have strived to identify articles that we see as "contemporary classics," such as Kenneth A. Shepsle's "The Changing Textbook Congress," and Federal Judge Richard A. Posner's "What Am I? A Potted Plant?" In addition, we have included more key court cases in this edition, ranging from *Brown* to the 2003 rulings on the right to privacy (*Lawrence and Garner* v. *Texas*) and the constitutionality of the Bipartisan Campaign Finance Act (*McConnell* v. *The Federal Election Commission*).

American Politics: Classic and Contemporary Readings, Sixth Edition, is divided into fourteen chapters that correspond to the organization of most American government texts. Each chapter starts with an essay that lays out the major themes of the particular subject at hand and links the readings to those themes. In addition, each article begins with a headnote that introduces the selection and provides some context for the selection. Following each article are questions for discussion that address major issues raised by the piece.

American Politics includes two other, useful features. First, each selection is annotated, so that difficult terms and obscure historical references are clarified. Second, we have produced an extensive topic correlation chart that follows the table of contents. This chart provides cross references for twenty-four subjects, including "post 9/11 and the war on terrorism" and "money and politics." Complementing the collection of readings is an *Instructor's Resource Manual with Test Items*, written by Professor Joel Paddock of Southwest Missouri State University. This manual includes article summaries, suggestions for classroom use, and sets of both multiple-choice and essay questions for all readings.

Over the years, Houghton Mifflin has recruited excellent reviewers who have made numerous suggestions for strengthening this book; without question, we have benefited from these suggestions. Once again, we are in their debt. They include:

David Gray Adler, Idaho State University

Cary R. Covington, University of Iowa

Vida Davoudi, Kingwood College

Gerard P. Heather, San Francisco State University

Roberta Herzberg, Utah State University

Donna R. Hoffman, University of Northern Iowa

Jeremy Walling, Southeast Missouri State University

As always, the Houghton Mifflin editors have worked hard to publish the best book possible. Our thanks go to Christina Lembo, Reba Libby, Rachel Zanders, and, of course, the indefatigable Jean Woy.

Though not as funny as Martin and Lewis, we've lasted longer, with fewer spats. In the end, we're two Western Pennsylvania boys, united in Kansas, whose friendship and mutual respect has grown through twenty years of collaboration. Beth Cigler and Michel Loomis remain our greatest supporters and most trenchant critics. We wouldn't have it any other way.

A.J.C.
B.A.L.

American
Politics

Chapter 1

THE CONSTITUTION AND FOUNDING

The framing of the Constitution serves as one of the anchors of American politics. The Constitution was written, under pressure, by an extraordinary band of political leaders, whose accomplishments at the Philadelphia convention have proven so workable and lasting that it is difficult not to see them as mythical figures. Still, with the possible exception of George Washington, these were people, not demigods. And Washington's elevated status proved useful to the framers: As they devised the presidency and later pushed for ratification, they, along with the great body of citizens, could easily envision Washington as the first incumbent of the office.

It is difficult to exaggerate the scope of the problems the framers faced. They confronted a system of government under the Articles of Confederation that emphasized the sovereignty of the individual states at the expense of a coherent national identity and that hindered the development of the nation. An armed insurrection in Massachusetts (Shays's Rebellion) demonstrated the weakness of the states in coming to terms with problems of commerce, currency, and credit. In addition, this uprising brought home the supposed dangers of the masses within a democratic state. The possible "tyranny of the majority" was a real fear. Domestic challenges were no greater than those from abroad. The United States may have won its war of independence, but European powers certainly did not see American sovereignty as immutable. Throughout the country's first few decades, there were numerous plots to compromise American independence, such as the XYZ Affair and Aaron Burr's plan for a separatist state in the Southwest.

In writing the Constitution and securing its ratification, the framers proved themselves skillful political engineers and propagandists. As Jack Rakove points out, the framers had to "reconstitute" the government of the new nation by the very act of writing a constitution, and Rakove argues that they learned well from the Massachusetts experience of including "broad statements on the first principles of government" within the document. John P. Roche sees these individuals as a "reform caucus," a label that aptly captures the essentially political nature of their task. Nevertheless, their purposes were more radical than merely carrying out a set of reforms. As Roche notes, "The Constitutionalists went forth to subvert the Confederation," not to enact some modest changes.

Just as the American Revolution has been characterized as conservative, the same can be said of the writing of the Constitution. As historian Richard Hofstadter emphasizes, protecting property rights played a central role in the framers' thinking. Given their status as part of the new nation's elite, this is understandable. Still, protecting property rights represented more than a simple appeal to self-interest; for the framers, such safeguards were important guideposts in assessing the reach of governmental power. Property rights could best be protected by the creation of a central government that was strong enough to ensure orderly commerce but not so strong that it impinged on the rights of the minority.

A governmental structure that could protect property rights without becoming oppressive would not only have to make sense theoretically; it would have to win the approval of the states in the ratification process. To address these necessities, the framers created a series of checks and balances, most notably federalism (see Chapter 2) and the separation of powers. In *The Federalist,* No. 51, James Madison argues that liberty can be protected only where the executive, legislative, and judicial functions are divided. The division, however, need not be, and cannot be, complete; there will always be some sharing of powers. Indeed, Madison notes in *The Federalist,* No. 47, "where the *whole* power of one department is exercised by the same hands which possess the *whole* power of another department, the fundamental principles of a free constitution are subverted."

One test of a "fundamental principle" of any constitution is its staying power. The separation of powers has not gone unchallenged over the course of the American republic. The most common conflict has arisen between the executive and the legislature, with critics often arguing that the executive branch needs more power to carry out its electoral mandate and to implement a coherent foreign policy.

In the 2000 election between Vice President Al Gore and Governor George W. Bush of Texas, the staying power of one fundamental element of the American political system—the Electoral College—was challenged by the closest election in more than a century. This jerrybuilt system, the product of political compromises in the 1787 convention, survived and produced a legitimate winner, even though Gore received about 500,000 more votes than Bush.

Still, as we proceed well into our third century as a nation, eighteenth-century solutions developed by the framers may require re-evaluation, especially in highly partisan times. The impeachment of Bill Clinton, the contentiousness of Senate judicial confirmations, and the lack of effective legislative deliberation all demonstrate the costs of seeking partisan advantage, which often overwhelms the willingness of national politicians to work together. Much as the Supreme Court continues to reassess the meaning of federalism in the twenty-first century, so too must legislators and presidents wrestle with the fundamental issues of governance addressed by the framers almost 220 years ago.

A Tradition Born of Strife

Jack N. Rakove

When the framers decided to write a new constitution rather than attempt to re-structure the Articles of Confederation, they were setting out for unknown territory. Some of them, however, had experience with state constitutions that had been written after 1776. In addition, the framers could reflect on how well these documents had done in establishing a balance of liberty and order. In particular, the Massachusetts delegates to the 1787 Constitutional Convention benefited from their four years of efforts to craft a suitable constitution.

In this article, Jack N. Rakove argues that in writing a new constitution the framers concluded that the Union needed to be completely reconstituted and that the states' constitution-building experiences offered a series of practical lessons for them to draw on. Most important, the state experiences taught the framers to think of a constitution as specifying the broad nature and powers of government, an integral step to making it the supreme law of the land. Their preliminary efforts at writing state documents gave the framers a base of understanding for their more difficult task of constructing a national constitution.

Traditions, by nature conservative, may sometimes have revolutionary origins. So it is with America's constitutional tradition. It was shaped not only by the decade of controversy that carried Americans to independence, but also—and more importantly—by the process of writing a series of innovative governing documents for the states and observing their effectiveness over the decade that followed.

For much of the 18th century, the American colonies and Great Britain had shared a constitutional tradition, though each emphasized different aspects. England, of course, had no single written constitutional document; its "constitution" was the totality of its governing laws and customs. The British held that the Glorious Revolution of 1688–89, which limited the King's authority over Parliament and confirmed that he was bound by constitutional principles, had

Jack N. Rakove is the Coe Professor of History and American Studies at Stanford University.

"A Tradition Born of Strife." From *Constitution*, Volume 7, Number 1, pp. 4–10. Reprinted by permission from Jack Rakove.

also made parliament the supreme source of law within the British Empire. But during the Stamp Act crisis of 1765, when Parliament took the position that it had the power to legislate for America "in all cases whatsoever," a grave and prophetic constitutional dispute erupted between the two countries.

In the American view, the Glorious Revolution restrained all arbitrary power, Parliament's as well as the King's. Americans were seeking for their own legislative assemblies the same rights and privileges that Parliament had secured for itself—including the exclusive power to enact laws and taxes for the people whom these bodies represented. That right rested on an ancient and hallowed constitutional principle: that law was binding only when enacted through popular consent.

Each crisis that followed the Stamp Act brought Britain's and the colonies' views of their rights and obligations toward each other into greater conflict. In Massachusetts in 1768, for example, the colony's General Court denied Parliament's authority to impose the Townshend duties. Britain's movement of troops into Boston that year was denounced as an occupation by a standing army. It begat the Boston Massacre in 1770. After the 1773 Tea Party, Parliament closed Boston's port, restructured the General Court, forbade town meetings without the governor's consent and decreed that Americans might be taken to England to stand trial. These actions brought on the convocation of the First Continental Congress and, eventually, the open hostilities at Lexington and Concord.

In the aftermath of these events, Americans were forced to think creatively about constitutionalism. Legal government collapsed in nearly every colony. Governors and officials acting under royal commission could hardly allow the colonial assemblies to enact laws mobilizing arms and men to defy Parliament and the King; colonists, on the other hand, had to reconsider their allegiance to a crown that made war on them. In the traditional view, government meant a contract under which subjects pledged fealty in exchange for the King's protection. Many Americans thus felt they were now absolved of any obligation to George III.

These colonists concluded that war and the collapse of lawful government had placed them in something like the state of nature described by the philosophers Thomas Hobbes and John Locke. It was impossible simply to restore the old colonial government: The judges, councillors and governors who ran it had resigned or fled. Government itself must be reconstituted. Americans had to replace elements of the monarchy under which they'd lived with new institutions appropriate to a republican people.

But how does one reconstitute government? Obviously a new executive must replace the old imperial governors, but the enterprise did not stop there. In the months preceding and after the Declaration of Independence, then, 11 of the 13 colonies decided to write constitutions that would bring their citizens out of the state of nature and give them the benefits of government by consent. These constitutions were revolutionary not only because of the circumstances that gave them birth, but also because the process of writing them enabled Americans to break from the constitutional tradition inherited from England. No longer did the colonists think of a constitution as a set of norms and customs descended from a distant past, or use the word to describe the current practices of a government. Americans gave the concept an entirely new meaning. As they now defined it, *constitution* referred to a single document that specified the nature and powers of the government, written and adopted at a specific moment in time. A later innovation would give the document revolutionary authority: It would be adopted under conditions establishing it as the supreme and fundamental law of the land, limiting government and unalterable by it.

In reconstituting government through written constitutions, the colonists did not consider how to distinguish an act establishing government from statutes or ordinary legislative acts. Although several states had held new elections so that the drafters of these constitutions could come with fresh authority from their citizenry, some observers—notably in Massachusetts—began to think that more might be needed.

In the often contentious Bay State, the legislature's efforts to draft a constitution under its own authority sparked a popular revolt that led to a critical constitutional breakthrough. For a constitution to become supreme law, a number of communities insisted, two conditions had to be met. First, the document had to be drafted by a body appointed for that purpose alone; and second, the proposed constitution then had to be submitted to the people for approval. It took the citizens of Massachusetts four years to reach agreement on these points, but when they adopted the constitution of 1780 on this basis, they had discovered a principle that would be of critical importance to the framers of the federal Constitution.

The precise legal authority of the other state constitutions was in doubt. These constitutions and their accompanying declarations of rights were more than statutes but less than supreme, fundamental law. To a modern reader, these declarations of rights are strange but exciting documents. They are not merely compendiums of legally enforceable rights; they also include broad statements on the first principles of government, the moral obligations and political rights of citizens and the importance of freedom of the press and religious conscience, as well as rules relating to specific issues such as search-and-seizure and compensation for property taken for public use. But rather than compel government to follow their dictates, these statements typically said that such rights "ought to" (not "shall") be respected.

But it is one thing to declare rights and another to set them beyond the reach of politics. To observers like Thomas Jefferson and James Madison, the experience of the states after 1776 offered a continuing lesson in the errors of the "compilers"—as Madison called them—of the first constitutions. Two errors were critical. First, the defective procedures used to adopt those constitutions prevented the documents from becoming fundamental law, unalterable by later legislatures. And second, the real danger to balanced government that a well-constructed constitution should guard against came from the people's own legislative representatives. As Jefferson observed in his *Notes on the State of Virginia* (1785), "An elective despotism was not the government we fought for."

Madison kept these problems in mind as he worked to bring about the Constitutional Convention of 1787. The Articles of Confederation, America's first governing document, had often been denounced as an "imbecility" because of its want of power. Its single-chambered Congress had no authority to legislate or tax in its own right; instead it proposed measures that the state legislatures were expected to carry out. The failure of the states to do so had convinced Madison and others that the national government had to be given the authority to enact, execute and adjudicate law in its own right, without relying on the intermediary authority of the states.

Had the framers simply wished to give the existing Congress a few modest additional powers, the convention could have wrapped up its business in a fortnight or so and headed home. But many of them realized that the Union must be reconstituted as a government in the full sense of the term, and with this insight they embarked on a more ambitious and difficult project. Now they could ask what a well-constructed republican government should look like. And in answering this question, they drew time and again on the past decade of constitutional experience within the states. There were many sources for the framers' ideas of government—from the writers of classical antiquity to the luminaries of the European Enlightenment—but the lessons that mattered most were those they had learned on native ground.

The framers were expected to present the results of the convention's work to the Confederation Congress, which presumably would submit the Constitution to the states for approval. Under the Articles of Confederation, all 13 legislatures had to accept any amendments; but one of those states, Rhode Island, had not even sent a delegation to Philadelphia. Nor were the framers at all confident that the other 12 states, as net losers of power, would comply with so radical a restructuring of the Union and sanction the Constitution.

Obviously, the rule of unanimity had to go. But even if the Constitution won approval, how was its supremacy over state constitutions to be confirmed? Now Madison, James Wilson and other nationalists invoked the Massachusetts discovery, which became a guiding rule of American constitutionalism. They asked Congress to suggest that the state legislatures lay the proposed Constitution before special, popularly elected ratification conventions. Approval by these conventions would establish grounds for making the Constitution the supreme and fundamental law of the land. Ratification by the people would create a Constitution superior in authority to the constitutions and laws of the states, and would give the federal government a persuasive argument for countermanding state measures that ran contrary to national law. Popular ratification would also convey this benefit within the national government. Each of the three federal branches—particularly the weaker executive and the judiciary—would have a rationale for opposing the "encroachments" of the others, especially Congress's.

The possibility, however, that a powerful national government would run roughshod over the states alarmed anti-Federalists, who opposed the Constitution. One of the most vociferous, Maryland Attorney General Luther Martin, left the convention early to organize opposition to the new government. In his view, and those of many states'-rights advocates since, no national constitution can abridge the immutable sovereignty of the Union's original members—the states. This tension between national supremacy and state sovereignty has been a continuing part of America's constitutional tradition. It dominated constitutional discourse for much of the 19th century, and has been revived periodically in the 20th, most recently in the wake of the 1994 congressional elections.

George Mason of Virginia, a delegate to the convention who would refuse to sign the Constitution, opposed it for other reasons. High on his list of objections was his colleagues' refusal to add a declaration of rights such as the one he had drafted for Virginia in 1776. Their failure to do so is often regarded as a political error—and perhaps it was. But the omission also reflected the reexamination of constitutionalism that was going on. Before 1787, a bill of rights recognized those rights existing from time immemorial that had become part of the social contract, a pact formed in some mythic past when people first agreed to live in society. But Americans were writing real compacts of government, and this process raised disturbing questions: Must rights be explicitly stated in these new constitutions to retain their authority? Or would fundamental rights remain intact whether stated or not?

Anti-Federalists had a plain answer to these questions: adopt a bill of rights no matter what. But Federalists were less certain. Suppose you wrote a bill of rights, Madison asked, and failed to enumerate all rights worth protecting? Would those unenumerated rights lose influence? Or suppose you used an ambiguous or watered-down text to secure adoption of an unpopular right. Wouldn't you risk weakening the authority of that right?

Despite these concerns, Madison conceded that a bill of rights should be added to the Constitution—more to allay the fears of moderate anti-Federalists than because he believed it important in itself. In 1789, at the first session of the new Congress, he persuaded his colleagues to propose 12 amendments; of these, the 10 we know as the Bill of Rights were ratified by the states. For more than a century afterward, the seeming irrelevance of these amendments suggested that Madison's doubts about their utility were well founded. Only early in the 20th century did the courts begin to interpret parts of the Bill of Rights to protect individual rights and liberties from abuse by both state and national governments. In the past 50 years, the interpretation and reinterpretation of the Bill of Rights and its great descendant, the 14th Amendment, have generated many of the serious controversies of law and politics that have shaped the American constitutional tradition.

Despite two centuries of debate, urgent political or legal questions repeatedly call the meaning of one or another constitutional provision into doubt. That the Constitution can be continually enlarged and invigorated in this way tells us something important. When Americans began writing constitutions, they did not foresee that these texts—especially the national charter—would acquire such profound authority. Constitutionalism was an experiment; even its greatest adherents—men like Madison, Jefferson and Alexander Hamilton—brooded about its likely success. Both Madison and Hamilton were privately skeptical whether the federal Constitution would last, and Jefferson mused that constitutions should be replaced every generation. Each would be surprised by how deep a hold the Constitution has acquired and retained over our political culture. Revolutionary in its origins, the American constitutional tradition may have grown more conservative in its workings—yet what is most striking about it is its vitality.

Questions for Discussion

1. How did the framers' experiences within the colonies and states (under the Articles of Confederation) shape their approaches to constructing a new constitution?
2. Why did Madison oppose the listing of a particular "Bill of Rights"? You might return to this question in light of the reasoning in *Griswold* v. *Connecticut* (see selection 3.4), which establishes a "right of privacy."

 1.2

The Founding Fathers: An Age of Realism

Richard Hofstadter

If the framers were, in John P. Roche's words (see selection 1.3), "a reform caucus," they were also realists who had witnessed more than a decade of severe economic, social, and political turbulence. They wanted some greater certainty

---

Probably the pre-eminent American historian of his time, Richard Hofstadter (1916–1970) was DeWitt Clinton Professor of American History at Columbia University.

for themselves and their new nation. At the same time, they remained steadfast in their desire to retain the liberty they had so recently won.

Historian Richard Hofstadter examines the interplay among liberty, stability, and property rights in this brief essay. As the framers saw it, the key to the long-term success of a democratic state (if it was to be possible) was to ensure that substantial numbers of citizens had a stake in the government and in the state. If that were so, people's "rapacious self-interest" might well be reconciled with freedom. This tenuous balance of self-interest and property rights seems an unlikely brace for a government, but it has proven adequate for more than two hundred years.

It is ironical that the Constitution, which Americans venerate so deeply, is based upon a political theory that at one crucial point stands in direct antithesis to the main stream of American democratic faith. Modern American folklore assumes that democracy and liberty are all but identical, and when democratic writers take the trouble to make the distinction, they usually assume that democracy is necessary to liberty. But the Founding Fathers thought that the liberty with which they were most concerned was menaced by democracy. In their minds liberty was linked not to democracy but to property.

What did the Fathers mean by liberty? What did Jay mean when he spoke of "the charms of liberty"? Or Madison when he declared that to destroy liberty in order to destroy factions would be a remedy worse than the disease? Certainly the men who met at Philadelphia were not interested in extending liberty to those classes in America, the Negro slaves and the indentured servants, who were most in need of it, for slavery was recognized in the organic structure of the Constitution and indentured servitude was no concern of the Convention. Nor was the regard of the delegates for civil liberties any too tender. It was the opponents of the Constitution who were most active in demanding such vital liberties as freedom of religion, freedom of speech and press, jury trial, due process, and protection from "unreasonable searches and seizures." These guarantees had to be incorporated in the first ten amendments because the Convention neglected to put them in the original document. Turning to economic issues, it was not freedom of trade in the modern sense that the Fathers were striving for. Although they did not believe in impeding trade unnecessarily, they felt that failure to regulate it was one of the central weaknesses of the Articles of Confederation, and they stood closer to the mercantilists than to Adam Smith.* Again, liberty to them did not mean free access to the nation's

---

*Mercantilist theory emphasized state control of the economic process to accumulate as much of value as possible. Achieving positive trade balances became a principal element of national policy. Scottish economist Adam Smith, in *The Wealth of Nations* and other writings, opposed this theory and developed his own ideas on the division of labor, laissez-faire (free market) economics, and the ultimate increase in value as more labor is expended in the production process.

unappropriated wealth. At least fourteen of them were land speculators. They did not believe in the right of the squatter to occupy unused land, but rather in the right of the absentee owner or speculator to pre-empt it.

The liberties that the constitutionalists hoped to gain were chiefly negative. They wanted freedom from fiscal uncertainty and irregularities in the currency, from trade wars among the states, from economic discrimination by more powerful foreign governments, from attacks on the creditor class or on property, from popular insurrection. They aimed to create a government that would act as an honest broker among a variety of propertied interests, giving them all protection from their common enemies and preventing any one of them from becoming too powerful. The Convention was a fraternity of types of absentee ownership. All property should be permitted to have its proportionate voice in government. Individual property interests might have to be sacrificed at times, but only for the community of propertied interests. Freedom for property would result in liberty for men—perhaps not for all men, but at least for all worthy men. Because men have different faculties and abilities, the Fathers believed, they acquire different amounts of property. To protect property is only to protect men in the exercise of their natural faculties. Among the many liberties, therefore, freedom to hold and dispose property is paramount. Democracy, unchecked rule by the masses, is sure to bring arbitrary redistribution of property, destroying the very essence of liberty.

The Fathers' conception of democracy, shaped by their practical experience with the aggressive dirt farmers in the American states and the urban mobs of the Revolutionary period, was supplemented by their reading in history and political science. Fear of what Madison called "the superior force of an interested and overbearing majority" was the dominant emotion aroused by their study of historical examples. The chief examples of republics were among the city-states of antiquity, medieval Europe, and early modern times. Now, the history of these republics—a history, as Hamilton said, "of perpetual vibration between the extremes of tyranny and anarchy"—was alarming. Further, most of the men who had overthrown the liberties of republics had "begun their career by paying an obsequious court to the people; commencing demagogues and ending tyrants."

All the constitutional devices that the Fathers praised in their writings were attempts to guarantee the future of the United States against the "turbulent" political cycles of previous republics. By "democracy," they meant a system of government which directly expressed the will of the majority of the people, usually through such an assemblage of the people as was possible in the small area of the city-state.

A cardinal tenet in the faith of the men who made the Constitution was the belief that democracy can never be more than a transitional stage in government, that it always evolves into either a tyranny (the rule of the rich demagogue who has patronized the mob) or an aristocracy (the original leaders of the democratic elements). "Remember," wrote the dogmatic John Adams in one of his letters to John Taylor of Carolina, "democracy never lasts long. It soon wastes, exhausts, and murders itself. There never was a democracy yet that did not commit suicide." Again:

> If you give more than a share in the sovereignty to the democrats, that is, if you give them the command or preponderance in the . . . legislature, they will vote all property out of the hands of you aristocrats, and if they let you escape with your lives, it will be more humanity, consideration, and generosity than any triumphant democracy ever displayed since the creation. And what will follow? The aristocracy among the democrats will take your place, and treat their fellows as severely and sternly as you have treated them.

Government, thought the Fathers, is based on property. Men who have no property lack the necessary stake in an orderly society to make stable or reliable citizens. Dread of the propertyless masses of the towns was all but universal. George Washington, Gouverneur Morris, John Dickinson, and James Madison spoke of their anxieties about the urban working class that might arise some time in the future—"men without property and principle," as Dickinson described them—and even the democratic Jefferson shared this prejudice. Madison, stating the problem, came close to anticipating the modern threats to conservative republicanism from both communism and fascism:

> In future times, a great majority of the people will not only be without landed but any other sort of property. These will either combine, under the influence of their common situation—in which case the rights of property and the public liberty will not be secure in their hands—or, what is more probable, they will become the tools of opulence and ambition, in which case there will be equal danger on another side.

What encouraged the Fathers about their own era, however, was the broad dispersion of landed property. The small landowning farmers had been troublesome in recent years, but there was a general conviction that under a properly made Constitution a *modus vivendi* could be worked out with them. The possession of moderate plots of property presumably gave them a sufficient stake in society to be safe and responsible citizens under the restraints of balanced government. Influence in government would be proportionate to property; merchants and great landholders would be dominant, but small property-owners would have an independent and far from negligible voice. It was "politic as well as just," said Madison, "that the interest and rights of every class should be duly represented and understood in the public councils," and John Adams declared that there could be "no free government without a democratical branch in the constitution."

The farming element already satisfied the property requirements for suffrage in most of the states, and the Fathers generally had no quarrel with their enfranchisement. But when they spoke of the necessity of founding government upon the consent of "the people," it was only these small property-holders that they had in mind. For example, the famous Virginia Bill of Rights, written by George Mason, explicitly defined those eligible for suffrage as all men "having sufficient evidence of permanent common interest with and attachment to the community"—which meant, in brief, sufficient property.

However, the original intention of the Fathers to admit the yeoman into an important but sharply limited partnership in affairs of state could not be perfectly realized. At the time the Constitution was made, Southern planters and Northern merchants were setting their differences aside in order to meet common dangers—from radicals within and more powerful nations without. After the Constitution was adopted, conflict between the ruling classes broke out anew, especially after powerful planters were offended by the favoritism of Hamilton's policies to Northern commercial interests. The planters turned to the farmers to form an agrarian alliance, and for more than half a century this powerful coalition embraced the bulk of the articulate interests of the country. As time went on, therefore, the mainstream of American political conviction deviated more and more from the antidemocratic position of the Constitution-makers. Yet, curiously, their general satisfaction with the Constitution together with their growing nationalism made Americans deeply reverent of the founding generation, with the result that as it grew stronger, this deviation was increasingly overlooked.

There is common agreement among modern critics that the debates over the Constitution were carried on at an intellectual level that is rare in politics, and that the Constitution itself is one of the world's masterpieces of practical statecraft. On other grounds there has been controversy. At the very beginning contemporary opponents of the Constitution foresaw an apocalyptic destruction of local government and popular institutions, while conservative Europeans of the old regime thought the young American Republic was a dangerous leftist experiment. Modern critical scholarship, which reached a high point in Charles A. Beard's *An Economic Interpretation of the Constitution of the United States*, started a new turn in the debate. The antagonism, long latent, between the philosophy of the Constitution and the philosophy of American democracy again came into the open. Professor Beard's work appeared in 1913 at the peak of the Progressive Era, when the muckraking fever was still high;* some readers tended to conclude from his findings that the Fathers were selfish reactionaries who do not deserve their high place in American esteem. Still more recently, other writers, inverting this logic, have used Beard's facts to praise the Fathers for their opposition to "democracy" and as an argument for returning again to the idea of a "republic."

In fact, the Fathers' image of themselves as moderate republicans standing between political extremes was quite accurate. They were impelled by class motives more than pietistic writers like to admit, but they were also controlled, as Professor Beard himself has . . . emphasized, by a statesmanlike sense of moderation and a scrupulously republican philosophy. Any attempt, however, to tear their ideas out of the eighteenth century context is sure to make them seem

---

*The Progressive era, from roughly 1900 to 1920, was marked by reformist movements against governmental corruption and political machines. Crusading journalists (muckrakers) and insurgent mayors and governors attempted to inject professionalism and merit into government.

starkly reactionary. Consider, for example, the favorite maxim of John Jay: "The people who own the country ought to govern it." To the Fathers this was simply a swift axiomatic statement of the stake-in-society theory of political rights, a moderate conservative position under eighteenth-century conditions of property distribution in America. Under modern property relations this maxim demands a drastic restriction of the base of political power. A large portion of the modern middle class—and it is the strength of this class upon which balanced government depends—is propertyless; and the urban proletariat, which the Fathers so greatly feared, is almost one half the population. Further, the separation of ownership from control that has come with the corporation deprives Jay's maxim of twentieth century meaning even for many propertied people. The six hundred thousand stockholders of the American Telephone & Telegraph Company not only do not acquire political power by virtue of their stock-ownership, but they do not even acquire economic power; they cannot control their own company.

From a humanistic standpoint there is a serious dilemma in the philosophy of the Fathers, which derives from their conception of man. They thought man was a creature of rapacious self-interest, and yet they wanted him to be free— free, in essence, to contend, to engage in an umpired strife, to use property to get property. They accepted the mercantile image of life as an eternal battleground, and assumed the Hobbesian war of each against all; they did not propose to put an end to this war, but merely to stabilize it and make it less murderous. They had no hope and they offered none for any ultimate organic change in the way men conduct themselves. The result was that while they thought self-interest the most dangerous and unbrookable quality of man, they necessarily underwrote it in trying to control it. They succeeded in both respects: under the competitive capitalism of the nineteenth century America continued to be an arena for various grasping and contending interests, and the federal government continued to provide a stable and acceptable medium within which they could contend; further, it usually showed the wholesome bias on behalf of property which the Fathers expected. But no man who is as well abreast of modern science as the Fathers were of eighteenth century science believes any longer in unchanging human nature. Modern humanistic thinkers who seek for a means by which society may transcend eternal conflict and rigid adherence to property rights as its integrating principles can expect no answer in the philosophy of balanced government as it was set down by the Constitution-makers of 1787.

Questions for Discussion

1. What is the connection between property and liberty? Does it still hold true today?
2. How would widespread property ownership contribute to the stability of government?

1.3

The Founding Fathers: A Reform Caucus in Action

John P. Roche

After two hundred years, the American Constitution remains a vital document, subject to continuing reinterpretation in the courts. At the same time, its status in American mythology has become more firmly enshrined. A balance between tangible and symbolic elements has been central to the success of the Constitution, but we need to put down our rose-colored glasses to view its creation in ways that contribute to both our contemporary and our historic understanding of it.

In this selection, John P. Roche argues that the framers of the Constitution were above all "superb democratic politicians" who constituted an elite—but a democratic elite. Roche objects to viewing the framers solely through the lens of *The Federalist,* the collection of articles in support of ratification, which he regards as a brilliant set of post hoc rationalizations. Instead, James Madison should be seen as a clever tactical politician and an "inspired propagandist," whose writing in *The Federalist* only incidentally emerges as brilliant political theory. We might well wonder what our political system would have looked like, absent the framers' political acumen.

◆ ◆ ◆ The Convention has been described picturesquely as a counter-revolutionary junta and the Constitution as a *coup d'état,* but this has been accomplished by withdrawing the whole history of the movement for constitutional reform from its true context. No doubt the goals of the constitutional elite were "subversive" to the existing political order, but it is overlooked that their subversion could only have succeeded if the people of the United States endorsed it by regularized procedures. Indubitably they were "plotting" to establish a much stronger central government than existed under the Articles, but only in the sense in which one could argue equally well

John P. Roche was formerly a professor of political science at Tufts University.

From *American Political Science Review* 55 (1961): 799–816. Copyright © 1961 by the American Political Science Association. Reprinted with permission.

that John F. Kennedy was, from 1956 to 1960, "plotting" to become President. In short, on the fundamental *procedural* level, the Constitutionalists had to work according to the prevailing rules of the game. . . .

I

The history of the United States from 1786 to 1790 was largely one of a masterful employment of political expertise by the Constitutionalists against bumbling, erratic behavior by the opponents of reform. Effectively, the Constitutionalists had to induce the states, by democratic techniques of coercion, to emasculate themselves. To be specific, if New York had refused to join the new Union, the project was doomed; yet before New York was safely in, the reluctant state legislature had . . . to take the following steps: (1) agree to send delegates to the Philadelphia Convention; (2) provide maintenance for these delegates . . . ; (3) set up the special *ad hoc* convention to decide on ratification; and (4) concede to the decision of the *ad hoc* convention that New York should participate. New York admittedly was a tricky state, with a strong interest in a *status quo* which permitted her to exploit New Jersey and Connecticut, but the same legal hurdles existed in every state. . . . [T]he *only* weapon in the Constitutionalist arsenal was an effective mobilization of public opinion.

The group which undertook this struggle was an interesting amalgam of a few dedicated nationalists with the self-interested spokesmen of various parochial bailiwicks. The Georgians, for example, wanted a strong central authority to provide military protection for their huge, underpopulated state . . . ; Jerseymen and Connecticuters wanted to escape from economic bondage to New York; the Virginians hoped to establish a system which would give that great state its rightful place in the councils of the republic. . . . There was, of course, a large element of personality in the affair: There is reason to suspect that Patrick Henry's opposition to the Convention and the Constitution was founded on his conviction that Jefferson was behind both, and a close study of local politics elsewhere would surely reveal that others supported the Constitution for the simple (and politically quite sufficient) reason that the "wrong" people were against it.

To say this is not to suggest that the Constitution rested on a foundation of impure or base motives. It is rather to argue that in politics there are no immaculate conceptions, and that in the drive for a stronger general government, motives of all sorts played a part. Few men in the history of mankind have espoused a view of the "common good" or "public interest" that militated against their private status; even Plato with all his reverence for disembodied reason managed to put philosophers on top of the pile. Thus it is not surprising that a number of diversified private interests joined to push the nationalist public interest; what would have been surprising was the absence of such a pragmatic united front. And the fact remains that, however motivated, these men did demonstrate a willingness to compromise their parochial interests on behalf of an ideal which took shape before their eyes and under their ministrations.

As Stanley Elkins and Eric McKitrick have suggested in a perceptive essay, what distinguished the leaders of the Constitutionalist caucus from their enemies was a "Continental" approach to political, economic and military issues. To the extent that they shared an institutional base of operations, it was the Continental Congress (thirty-nine of the delegates to the Federal Convention had served in Congress), and this was hardly a locale which inspired respect for the state governments. . . . "Continental" ideology developed which seems to have demanded a revision of our domestic institutions primarily on the ground that only by invigorating our general government could we assume our rightful place in the international arena. Indeed, an argument with great force—particularly since Washington was its incarnation—urged that our very survival in the Hobbesian* jungle of world politics depended upon a reordering and strengthening of our national sovereignty. . . .

The great achievement of the Constitutionalists was their ultimate success in convincing the elected representatives of a majority of the white male population that change was imperative. A small group of political leaders with a Continental vision and essentially a consciousness of the United States' *international* impotence, provided the matrix of the movement. To their standard other leaders rallied with their own parallel ambitions. Their great assets were (1) the presence in their caucus of the one authentic American "father figure," George Washington, whose prestige was enormous; (2) the energy and talent of their leadership (in which one must include the towering intellectuals of the time, John Adams and Thomas Jefferson, despite their absence abroad), and their communications "network," which was far superior to anything on the opposition side; (3) preemptive skill which made "their" issue The Issue and kept the locally oriented opposition permanently on the defensive; and (4) the subjective consideration that these men were spokesmen of a new and compelling credo: *American* nationalism, that ill-defined but nonetheless potent sense of collective purpose that emerged from the American Revolution. . . .

The Constitutionalists got the jump on the "opposition" (a collective noun: oppositions would be more correct) at the outset with the demand for a Convention. Their opponents were caught in an old political trap: They were not being asked to approve any specific program of reform, but only to endorse a meeting to discuss and recommend needed reforms. If they took a hard line at the first stage, they were put in the position of glorifying the *status quo* and of denying the need for *any* changes. Moreover, the Constitutionalists could go to the people with a persuasive argument for "fair play"—"How can you condemn

---

*Thomas Hobbes (1588–1679) was an English philosopher who viewed human nature as brutish and self-seeking to the point of anarchy. The state, with an absolute ruler, thus becomes an agency for maintaining peace and order.

reform before you know precisely what is involved?" Since the state legislatures obviously would have the final say on any proposals that might emerge from the Convention, the Constitutionalists were merely reasonable men asking for a chance. Besides, since they did not make any concrete proposals at that stage, they were in a position to capitalize on every sort of generalized discontent with the Confederation.

Perhaps because of their poor intelligence system, perhaps because of over-confidence generated by the failure of all previous efforts to alter the Articles, the opposition awoke too late to the dangers that confronted them in 1787. Not only did the Constitutionalists manage to get every state but Rhode Island . . . to appoint delegates to Philadelphia, but when the results were in, it appeared that they dominated the delegations. Given the apathy of the opposition, this was a natural phenomenon: In an ideologically nonpolarized political atmosphere those who get appointed to a special committee are likely to be the men who supported the movement for its creation. Even George Clinton, who seems to have been the first opposition leader to awake to the possibility of trouble, could not prevent the New York legislature from appointing Alexander Hamilton—though he did have the foresight to send two of his henchmen to dominate the delegation. Incidentally, much has been made of the fact that the delegates to Philadelphia were not elected by the people; some have adduced this fact as evidence of the "undemocratic" character of the gathering. But put in the context of the time, this argument is wholly specious: The central government under the Articles was considered a creature of the component states and in all the states but Rhode Island, Connecticut and New Hampshire, members of the national Congress were chosen by the state legislatures. This was not a consequence of elitism or fear of the mob; it was a logical extension of states'-rights doctrine to guarantee that the national institution did not end-run the state legislatures and make direct contact with the people.

II

With delegations safely named, the focus shifted to Philadelphia. While waiting for a quorum to assemble, James Madison got busy and drafted the so-called Randolph or Virginia Plan with the aid of the Virginia delegation. This was a political master-stroke. Its consequence was that once business got underway, the framework of discussion was established on Madison's terms. There was no interminable argument over agenda; instead the delegates took the Virginia Resolutions—"just for purposes of discussion"—as their point of departure. And along with Madison's proposals, many of which were buried in the course of the summer, went his major premise: a new start on a Constitution rather than piecemeal amendment. This was not necessarily revolutionary—a little exegesis could demonstrate that a new Constitution might be formulated as "amendments" to the Articles of Confederation—but Madison's proposal that this "lump sum" amendment go into effect after approval by nine states (the Articles required unanimous state approval for any amendment) was thoroughly subversive. . . .

Basic differences of opinion emerged, of course, but these were not ideological; they were *structural*. If the so-called "states'-rights" group had not accepted the fundamental purposes of the Convention, they could simply have pulled out and by doing so have aborted the whole enterprise. Instead of bolting, they returned day after day to argue and to compromise. An interesting symbol of this basic homogeneity was the initial agreement on secrecy: These professional politicians did not want to become prisoners of publicity; they wanted to retain that freedom of maneuver which is only possible when men are not forced to take public stands in the preliminary stages of negotiation. There was no legal means of binding the tongues of the delegates: At any stage in the game a delegate with basic principled objections to the emerging project could have taken the stump (as Luther Martin did after his exit) and denounced the convention to the skies. Yet Madison did not even inform Thomas Jefferson in Paris of the course of the deliberations and available correspondence indicates that the delegates generally observed the injunction. Secrecy is certainly uncharacteristic of any assembly marked by strong ideological polarization. This was noted at the time: The *New York Daily Advertiser*, August 14, 1787, commented that the ". . . profound secrecy hitherto observed by the Convention [we consider] a happy omen, as it demonstrates that the spirit of party on any great and essential point cannot have arisen to any height."

Commentators on the Constitution who have read *The Federalist* in lieu of reading the actual debates have credited the Fathers with the invention of a sublime concept called "Federalism." Unfortunately *The Federalist* is probative evidence for only one proposition: that Hamilton and Madison were inspired propagandists with a genius for retrospective symmetry. Federalism, as the theory is generally defined, was an improvisation which was later promoted into a political theory. . . .

It is indeed astonishing how those who have glibly designated James Madison the "father" of Federalism have overlooked the solid body of fact which indicates that he shared Hamilton's quest for a unitary central government.* To be specific, they have avoided examining the clear import of the Madison-Virginia Plan, and have disregarded Madison's dogged inch-by-inch retreat from the bastions of centralization. The Virginia Plan envisioned a unitary national government effectively freed from and dominant over the states. The lower house of the national legislature was to be elected directly by the people of the states with membership proportional to population. The upper house was to be selected by the lower, and the two chambers would elect the executive

---

*Unitary governments such as that of Great Britain minimize the importance of local or regional units. Most major decisions are made at the national level.

and choose the judges. The national government would be thus cut completely loose from the states.

The structure of the general government was freed from state control in a truly radical fashion, but the scope of the authority of the national sovereign as Madison initially formulated it was breathtaking. . . . The national legislature was to be empowered to disallow the acts of state legislatures, and the central government was vested, in addition to the powers of the nation under the Articles of Confederation, with plenary authority wherever ". . . the separate States are incompetent or in which the harmony of the United States may be interrupted by the exercise of individual legislation." Finally, just to lock the door against state intrusion, the national Congress was to be given the power to use military force on recalcitrant states. This was Madison's "model" of an ideal national government, though it later received little publicity in *The Federalist*.

The interesting thing was the reaction of the Convention to this militant program for a strong autonomous central government. Some delegates were startled, some obviously leery of so comprehensive a project of reform, but nobody set off any fireworks and nobody walked out. Moreover, in the two weeks that followed, the Virginia Plan received substantial endorsement *en principe;* the initial temper of the gathering can be deduced from the approval "without debate or dissent," on May 31, of the Sixth Resolution which granted Congress the authority to disallow state legislation ". . . contravening *in its opinion* the Articles of Union." Indeed, an amendment was included to bar states from contravening national treaties.

The Virginia Plan may therefore be considered, in ideological terms, as the delegates' Utopia, but as the discussions continued and became more specific, many of those present began to have second thoughts. After all, they were not residents of Utopia or guardians in Plato's Republic who could simply impose a philosophical ideal on subordinate strata of the population. They were practical politicians in a democratic society, and no matter what their private dreams might be, they had to take home an acceptable package and defend it—and their own political futures—against predictable attack. On June 14 the breaking point between dream and reality took place. Apparently realizing that under the Virginia Plan, Massachusetts, Virginia and Pennsylvania could virtually dominate the national government—and probably appreciating that to sell this program to "the folks back home" would be impossible—the delegates from the small states dug in their heels and demanded time for a consideration of alternatives. One gets a graphic sense of the inner politics from John Dickinson's reproach to Madison: "You see the consequences of pushing things too far. Some of the members from the small States wish for two branches in the General Legislature, and are friends to a good National Government; but we would sooner submit to a foreign power than . . . be deprived of an equality of suffrage in both branches of the Legislature, and thereby be thrown under the domination of the large States."

. . . Now the process of accommodation was put into action smoothly—and wisely, given the character and strength of the doubters. Madison had the votes, but this was one of those situations where the enforcement of mechanical majoritarianism could easily have destroyed the objectives of the majority: The Constitutionalists were in quest of a qualitative as well as a quantitative consensus. This was hardly from deference to local Quaker custom; it was a political imperative if they were to attain ratification.

III

According to the standard script, at this point the "states'-rights" group intervened in force behind the New Jersey Plan, which has been characteristically portrayed as a reversion to the *status quo* under the Articles of Confederation with but minor modifications. A careful examination of the evidence indicates that only in a marginal sense is this an accurate description. It is true that the New Jersey Plan put the states back into the institutional picture, but one could argue that to do so was a recognition of political reality rather than an affirmation of states' rights. A serious case can be made that the advocates of the New Jersey Plan, far from being ideological addicts of states' rights, intended to substitute for the Virginia Plan a system which would both retain strong national power and have a chance of adoption in the states. The leading spokesman for the project asserted quite clearly that his views were based more on counsels of expediency than on principle; said Paterson on June 16: "I came here not to speak my own sentiments, but the sentiments of those who sent me. Our object is not such a Governmt. as may be best in itself, but such a one as our Constituents have authorized us to prepare, and as they will approve." This is Madison's version; in Yates' transcription, there is a crucial sentence following the remarks above: "I believe that a little practical virtue is to be preferred to the finest theoretical principles, which cannot be carried into effect." . . .

This was a defense of political acumen, not of states' rights. In fact, Paterson's notes of his speech can easily be construed as an argument for attaining the substantive objectives of the Virginia Plan by a sound political route, *i.e.*, pouring the new wine in the old bottles. With a shrewd eye, Paterson queried:

> Will the Operation and Force of the [central] Govt. depend upon the mode of Representn.—No—it will depend upon the Quantum of Power lodged in the leg. ex. and judy. Departments—Give [the existing] Congress the same Powers that you intend to give the two Branches [under the Virginia Plan], and I apprehend they will act with as much Propriety and more Energy. . . .

In other words, the advocates of the New Jersey Plan concentrated their fire on what they held to be the *political liabilities* of the Virginia Plan—which were matters of institutional structure—rather than on the proposed scope of national authority. Indeed, the Supremacy Clause of the Constitution first saw the light of day in Paterson's Sixth Resolution; the New Jersey Plan contemplated the use of military force to secure compliance with national law; and finally Paterson made clear his view that under either the Virginia or the New Jersey systems, the general government would ". . . act on individuals and not on states." From the states'-rights viewpoint, this was heresy: the fundament of that doctrine was the proposition that any central government had as its contituents the states, not the people, and could only reach the people through the agency of the state government.

Paterson then reopened the agenda of the Convention, but he did so within a distinctly nationalist framework. Paterson's position was one of favoring a strong central government in principle, but opposing one which in fact *put the big states in the saddle*. (The Virginia Plan, for all its abstract merits, did very well by Virginia.) As evidence for this speculation, there is a curious and intriguing proposal among Paterson's preliminary drafts of the New Jersey Plan:

> Whereas it is necessary in Order to form the People of the U.S. of America in to a Nation, that the States should be consolidated, by which means all the Citizens thereof will become equally intitled to and will equally participate in the same Privileges and Rights . . . it is therefore resolved, that all the Lands contained within the Limits of each state individually, and of the U.S. generally be considered as constituting one Body or Mass, and be divided into thirteen or more integral parts.
> Resolved, That such Divisions or integral Parts shall be styled Districts.

This makes it sound as though Paterson was prepared to accept a strong unified central government along the lines of the Virginia Plan if the existing states were eliminated. He may have gotten the idea from his New Jersey colleague Judge David Brearley, who on June 9 had commented that the only remedy to the dilemma over representation was ". . . that a map of the U.S. be spread out, that all the existing boundaries be erased, and that a new partition of the whole be made into 13 equal parts." According to Yates, Brearley added at this point, ". . . then a government on the present [Virginia Plan] system will be just."

This proposition was never pushed—it was patently unrealistic—but one can appreciate its purpose: It would have separated the men from the boys in the large-state delegations. How attached would the Virginians have been to their reform principles if Virginia were to disappear as a component geographical unit (the largest) for representational purposes? Up to this point, the Virginians had been in the happy position of supporting high ideals with that inner confidence born of knowledge that the "public interest" they endorsed would nourish their private interest. Worse, they had shown little willingness to compromise. Now the delegates from the small states announced that they were unprepared to be offered up as sacrificial victims to a "national interest" which reflected Virginia's parochial ambition. Caustic Charles Pinckney was not far off when he remarked sardonically that ". . . the whole [conflict] comes to this"[:] "Give N. Jersey an equal vote, and she will dismiss her scruples, and concur in the Natil. system." What he rather unfairly did not add was that the Jersey delegates were not free agents who could adhere to their private convictions; they had to take back, sponsor and risk their reputations on the reforms approved by the Convention—and in New Jersey, not in Virginia. . . .

IV

On Tuesday morning, June 19, . . . James Madison led off with a long, carefully reasoned speech analyzing the New Jersey Plan which, while intellectually vigorous in its criticisms, was quite conciliatory in mood. "The great difficulty," he observed, "lies in the affair of Representation; and if this could be adjusted, all others would be surmountable." (As events were to demonstrate, this diagnosis was correct.) When he finished, a vote was taken on whether to continue with the Virginia Plan as the nucleus for a new constitution: seven states voted "Yes"; New York, New Jersey, and Delaware voted "No"; and Maryland, whose position often depended on which delegates happened to be on the floor, divided. Paterson, it seems, lost decisively; yet in a fundamental sense he and his allies had achieved their purpose: From that day onward, it could never be forgotten that the state governments loomed ominously in the background and that no verbal incantations could exorcise their power. Moreover, nobody bolted the convention: Paterson and his colleagues took their defeat in stride and set to work to modify the Virginia Plan, particularly with respect to its provisions on representation in the national legislature. Indeed, they won an immediate rhetorical bonus; when Oliver Ellsworth of Connecticut rose to move that the word "national" be expunged from the Third Virginia Resolution ("Resolved that a *national* Government ought to be established consisting of a *supreme* Legislative, Executive and Judiciary"), Randolph agreed and the motion passed unanimously. The process of compromise had begun.

For the next two weeks, the delegates circled around the problem of legislative representation. The Connecticut delegation appears to have evolved a possible compromise quite early in the debates, but the Virginians and particularly Madison (unaware that he would later be acclaimed as the prophet of "federalism") fought obdurately against providing for equal representation of states in the second chamber. There was a good deal of acrimony and at one point Benjamin Franklin—of all people—proposed the institution of a daily prayer; practical politicians in the gathering, however, were meditating more on the merits of a good committee than on the utility of Divine intervention. On July 2, the ice began to break when through a number of fortuitous events—and one that seems deliberate—the majority against equality of representation was converted into a dead tie. The Convention had reached the stage where it was "ripe" for a solution (presumably all the therapeutic speeches had been made), and the South Carolinians proposed a committee. Madison and James Wilson wanted none of it, but with only Pennsylvania dissenting, the body voted to establish a working party on the problem of representation.

The members of this committee, one from each state, were elected by the delegates—and a very interesting committee it was. Despite the fact that the Virginia Plan had held majority support up to that date, neither Madison nor Randolph was selected (Mason was the Virginian) and Baldwin of Georgia, whose shift in position had resulted in the tie, was chosen. From the composition, it was clear that this was not to be a "fighting" committee: The emphasis in membership was on what might be described as "second-level political entrepreneurs." On the basis of the discussions up to that time, only Luther Martin of Maryland could be described as a "bitter-ender." Admittedly, some divination enters into this sort of analysis, but one does get a sense of the mood of the delegates from these choices—including the interesting selection of Benjamin Franklin, despite his age and intellectual wobbliness, over the brilliant and incisive Wilson or the sharp, polemical Gouverneur Morris, to represent Pennsylvania. His passion for conciliation was more valuable at this juncture than Wilson's logical genius, or Morris' acerbic wit.

. . . It should be reiterated that the Madison model had no room either for the states or for the "separation of powers": Effectively *all* governmental power was vested in the national legislature. The merits of Montesquieu did not turn up until *The Federalist*; and although a perverse argument could be made that Madison's ideal was truly in the tradition of John Locke's *Second Treatise of Government*, the Locke whom the American rebels treated as an honorary president was a pluralistic defender of vested rights, not of parliamentary supremacy.*

It would be tedious to continue a blow-by-blow analysis of the work of the delegates; the critical fight was over representation of the states and once the Connecticut Compromise[†] was adopted on July 17, the Convention was over the hump. . . . Moreover, once the compromise had carried (by five states to four, with one state divided), its advocates threw themselves vigorously into the job of strengthening the general government's substantive powers—as might have been predicted, indeed, from Paterson's early statements. It nourishes an increased respect for Madison's devotion to the art of politics, to realize that this dogged fighter could sit down six months later and prepare essays for *The Federalist* in contradiction to his basic convictions about the true course the Convention should have taken. . . .

---

*John Locke (1632–1704) was an English philosopher whose writings served as a basis for government rooted in a social contract between citizens and their rulers. Montesquieu (1689–1755) was a French political philosopher whose work emphasized checks and balances in the exercise of authority.

[†]The Connecticut Compromise advanced the solution of a two-chamber legislature, with each state receiving two senators and House representation in proportion to its population.

VI

Drawing on their vast collective political experience, utilizing every weapon in the politician's arsenal, looking constantly over their shoulders at their constituents, the delegates put together a Constitution. It was a makeshift affair; some sticky issues (for example, the qualification of voters) they ducked entirely; others they mastered with that ancient instrument of political sagacity, studied ambiguity (for example, citizenship), and some they just overlooked. In this last category, I suspect, fell the matter of the power of the federal courts to determine the constitutionality of acts of Congress. When the judicial article was formulated (Article III of the Constitution), deliberations were still in the stage where the legislature was endowed with broad power under the Randolph formulation, authority which by its own terms was scarcely amenable to judicial review. In essence, courts could hardly determine when ". . . the separate States are incompetent or . . . the harmony of the United States may be interrupted"; the National Legislature, as critics pointed out, was free to define its own jurisdiction. Later the definition of legislative authority was changed into the form we know, a series of stipulated powers, *but the delegates never seriously reexamined the jurisdiction of the judiciary under this new limited formulation*. All arguments on the intention of the Framers in this matter are thus deductive and *a posteriori*, though some obviously make more sense than others.

The Framers were busy and distinguished men, anxious to get back to their families, their positions, and their constituents, not members of the French Academy devoting a lifetime to a dictionary. They were trying to do an important job, and do it in such a fashion that their handiwork would be acceptable to very diverse constituencies. No one was rhapsodic about the final document, but it was a beginning, a move in the right direction, and one they had reason to believe the people would endorse. In addition, since they had modified the impossible amendment provisions of the Articles (the requirement of unanimity which could always be frustrated by "Rogues [Rhode] Island") to one demanding approval by only three-quarters of the states, they seemed confident that gaps in the fabric which experience would reveal could be rewoven without undue difficulty. . . .

Madison, despite his reservations about the Constitution, was the campaign manager in ratification. His first task was to get the Congress in New York to light its own funeral pyre by approving the "amendments" to the Articles and sending them on to the state legislatures. Above all, momentum had to be maintained. The anti-Constitutionalists, now thoroughly alarmed and no novices in politics, realized that their best tactic was attrition rather than direct opposition. Thus they settled on a position expressing qualified approval but calling for a second Convention to remedy various defects (the one with the most demagogic appeal was the lack of a Bill of Rights). Madison knew that to accede to this demand would be equivalent to losing the battle, nor would he agree to conditional approval (despite wavering even by Hamilton). This was an all-or-nothing proposition: national salvation or national impotence with no intermediate positions possible. Unable to get congressional approval, he settled for second best: a unanimous resolution of Congress transmitting the Constitution to the states for whatever action they saw fit to take. . . .

VII

. . . Victory for the Constitution meant simultaneous victory for the Constitutionalists; the anti-Constitutionalists either capitulated or vanished into limbo—soon Patrick Henry would be offered a seat on the Supreme Court and Luther Martin would be known as the Federalist "bull-dog." And irony of ironies, Alexander Hamilton and James Madison would shortly accumulate a reputation as the formulators of what is often alleged to be our political theory, the concept of "federalism." Also, on the other side of the ledger, the arguments would soon appear over what the Framers "really meant"; while these disputes have assumed the proportions of a big scholarly business in the last century, they began almost before the ink on the Constitution was dry. One of the best early ones featured Hamilton versus Madison on the scope of presidential power, and other Framers characteristically assumed positions in this and other disputes on the basis of their political convictions.

Probably our greatest difficulty is that we know so much more about what the Framers *should have meant* than they themselves did. We are intimately acquainted with the problems that their Constitution should have been designed to master; in short, we have read the mystery story backward. If we are to get the right "feel" for their time and their circumstances, we must, in Maitland's phrase, ". . . think ourselves back into a twilight." Obviously, no one can pretend completely to escape from the solipsistic web of his own environment, but if the effort is made, it is possible to appreciate the past roughly on its own terms. The first step in this process is to abandon the academic premise that because we can ask a question, there must be an answer.

Thus we can ask what the Framers meant when they gave Congress the power to regulate interstate and foreign commerce, and we emerge, reluctantly perhaps, with the reply that . . . they may not have known what they meant, that there may not have been any semantic consensus. The Convention was not a seminar in analytic philosophy or linguistic analysis. Commerce was *commerce*—and if different interpretations of the word arose, later generations could worry about the problem of definition. The delegates were in a hurry to get a new government established; when definitional arguments arose, they characteristically took refuge in ambiguity. If different men voted for the same proposition for varying reasons, that was politics (and still is); if later generations were unsettled by this lack of precision, that would be their problem. . . .

The Constitution, then, was not an apotheosis of "constitutionalism," a triumph of architectonic genius; it was a patch-work sewn together under the pressure of both time and events by a group of extremely talented democratic politicians. They refused to attempt the establishment of a strong, centralized sovereignty on the principle of legislative supremacy for the excellent reason that the people would not accept it. They risked their political fortunes by opposing the established doctrines of state sovereignty because they were convinced that the existing system was leading to national impotence and probably foreign domination. For two years, they worked to get a convention established. For over three months, in what must have seemed to the faithful participants an endless process of give-and-take, they reasoned, cajoled, threatened, and bargained amongst themselves. The result was a Constitution which the people, in fact, by democratic processes, did accept, and a new and far better national government was established. . . .

To conclude, the Constitution was neither a victory for abstract theory nor a great practical success. Well over half a million men had to die on the battlefields of the Civil War before certain constitutional principles could be defined—a baleful consideration which is somehow overlooked in our customary tributes to the farsighted genius of the Framers and to the supposed American talent for "constitutionalism." The Constitution was, however, a vivid demonstration of effective democratic political action, and of the forging of a national elite which literally persuaded its countrymen to hoist themselves by their own boot straps. American pro-consuls would be wise not to translate the Constitution into Japanese, or Swahili, or treat it as a work of semi-Divine origin; but when students of comparative politics examine the process of nation-building in countries newly freed from colonial rule, they may find the American experience instructive as a classic example of the potentialities of a democratic elite.

Questions for Discussion

1. How does Roche's approach to the framers affect our contemporary understanding of the Constitution? How might the framers have confronted difficult problems such as abortion and affirmative action?

2. What does Roche mean by a "democratic elite"? Is this phrase a contradiction in terms, or does it have real meaning?

The Federalist, No. 51

James Madison

As we have seen, among the formidable tasks the framers faced in writing the Constitution was establishing a strong central government while minimizing the possibility that this authority would be abused. The resulting system of checks and balances relies heavily on the separation of powers and a multiple-level, federal relationship between the states and the national government.

James Madison, Alexander Hamilton, and John Jay led the fight for ratification through a series of newspaper articles, *The Federalist*. In the following selection from these papers, Madison articulates a sophisticated understanding of the actual operation of central authority divided into legislative, executive, and judicial branches. Madison observes that regardless of the formal separations embodied within a constitution, the different branches in fact will share powers. Such a realistic assessment is reflected today in continuing arguments over the legislature's role in foreign policy (for example, passing legislation to implement the North American Free Trade Agreement) and the Supreme Court's willingness to range beyond narrow constitutional interpretations, as in its 1973 *Roe* v. *Wade* abortion decision.

To the People of the State of New York: To what expedient, then, shall we finally resort for maintaining in practice the necessary partition of power among the several departments as laid down in the Constitution? The only answer that can be given is, that as all these exterior provisions are found to be inadequate, the defect must be supplied by so contriving the interior structure of the government as that its several constituent parts may, by their mutual relations, be the means of keeping each other in their proper places. Without presuming to undertake a full development of this important idea, I will hazard a few general observations, which may perhaps place it in a clearer light, and enable us to form a more correct judgment of the principles and structure of the government planned by the convention.

James Madison, who was the chief drafter of the Constitution, became the fourth president of the United States.

In order to lay a due foundation for that separate and distinct exercise of the difficult powers of government, which to a certain extent is admitted on all hands to be essential to the preservation of liberty, it is evident that each department should have a will of its own; and consequently should be so constituted that the members of each should have as little agency as possible in the appointment of the members of the others. Were this principle rigorously adhered to, it would require that all the appointments for the supreme executive, legislative, and judiciary magistracies should be drawn from the same fountain of authority, the people, through channels having no communication whatever with one another. Perhaps such a plan of constructing the several departments would be less difficult in practice than it may in contemplation appear. Some difficulties, however, and some additional expense would attend the execution of it. Some deviations, therefore, from the principle must be admitted. In the constitution of the judiciary department in particular, it might be inexpedient to insist rigorously on the principle: first, because peculiar qualifications being essential in the members, the primary consideration ought to be to select that mode of choice which best secures these qualifications; secondly, because the permanent tenure by which the appointments are held in that department must soon destroy all sense of dependence on the authority conferring them.

It is equally evident, that the members of each department should be as little dependent as possible on those of the others for the emoluments annexed to their offices. Were the executive magistrate or the judges not independent of the legislature in this particular, their independence in every other would be merely nominal.

But the great security against a gradual concentration of the several powers in the same department, consists in giving to those who administer each department the necessary constitutional means and personal motives to resist encroachments of the others. The provision for defence must in this, as in all other cases, be made commensurate to the danger of attack. Ambition must be made to counteract ambition. The interest of the man must be connected with the constitutional rights of the place. It may be a reflection on human nature, that such devices should be necessary to control the abuses of government. But what is government itself, but the greatest of all reflections on human nature? If men were angels, no government would be necessary. If angels were to govern men, neither external nor internal controls on government would be necessary. In framing a government which is to be administered by men over men, the great difficulty lies in this: you must first enable the government to control the governed; and in the next place oblige it to control itself. A dependence on the people is, no doubt, the primary control on the government; but experience has taught mankind the necessity of auxiliary precautions.

The policy of supplying, by opposite and rival interests, the defect of better motives might be traced through the whole system of human affairs, private as well as public. We see it particularly displayed in all the subordinate distributions of power, where the constant aim is to divide and arrange the several offices in such a manner as that each may be a check on the other—that the private interest of every individual may be a sentinel over the public rights. These inventions of prudence cannot be less requisite in the distribution of the supreme powers of the state.

But it is not possible to give to each department an equal power of self-defence. In republican government the legislative authority necessarily predominates. The remedy for this inconveniency is to divide the legislature into different branches; and to render them, by different modes of election and different principles of action, as little connected with each other as the nature of their common functions and their common dependence on the society will admit. It may even be necessary to guard against dangerous encroachments by still further precautions. As the weight of the legislative authority requires that it should be thus divided, the weakness of the executive may require, on the other hand, that it should be fortified. An absolute negative on the legislature [i.e., veto] appears, at first view, to be the natural defence with which the executive magistrate should be armed. But perhaps it would be neither altogether safe nor alone sufficient. On ordinary occasions it might not be exerted with the requisite firmness, and on extraordinary occasions it might be perfidiously abused. May not this defect of an absolute negative be supplied by some qualified connection between this weaker department and the weaker branch of the stronger department, by which the latter may be led to support the constitutional rights of the former, without being too much detached from the rights of its own department?

If the principles on which these observations are founded be just . . . and they be applied as a criterion to the several state constitutions and to the federal Constitution, it will be found that if the latter does not perfectly correspond with them, the former are infinitely less able to bear such a test.

There are, moreover, two considerations particularly applicable to the federal system of America, which place that system in a very interesting point of view.

First. In a single republic, all the power surrendered by the people is submitted to the administration of a single government; and the usurpations are guarded against by a division of the government into distinct and separate departments. In the compound republic of America,* the power surrendered by the people is first divided between two distinct governments, and then the portion allotted to each subdivided among distinct and separate departments. Hence a double security arises to the rights of the people. The different governments will control each other, at the same time that each will be controlled by itself.

Second. It is of great importance in a republic not only to guard the society against the oppression of its rulers, but to guard one part of the society against the injustice of the other part. Different interests necessarily exist in different

---

*For the framers, a republic was essentially a representative democracy. A compound republic placed representative authority at two levels, state and national.

classes of citizens. If a majority be united by a common interest, the rights of the minority will be insecure. There are but two methods of providing against this evil: the one by creating a will in the community independent of the majority—that is, of the society itself; the other by comprehending in the society so many separate descriptions of citizens as will render an unjust combination of a majority of the whole very improbable, if not impracticable. The first method prevails in all governments possessing an hereditary or self-appointed authority. This, at best, is but a precarious security; because a power independent of the society may as well espouse the unjust views of the major, as the rightful interests of the minor party, and may possibly be turned against both parties. The second method will be exemplified in the federal republic of the United States. Whilst all authority in it will be derived from and dependent on the society, the society itself will be broken into so many parts, interests and classes of citizens, that the rights of individuals or of the minority will be in little danger from interested combinations of the majority. In a free government the security for civil rights must be the same as that for religious rights.* It consists in the one case in the multiplicity of interests and in the other in the multiplicity of sects. The degree of security in both cases will depend on the number of interests and sects; and this may be presumed to depend on the extent of country and number of people comprehended under the same government. This view of the subject must particularly recommend a proper federal system to all the sincere and considerate friends of republican government, since it shows that in exact proportion as the territory of the Union may be formed into more circumscribed confederacies or states, oppressive combinations of a majority will be facilitated; the best security under the republican forms for the rights of every class of citizens will be diminished; and consequently the stability and independence of some member of the government, the only other security, must be proportionally increased. Justice is the end of government. It is the end of civil society. It ever has been and ever will be pursued until it be obtained, or until liberty be lost in the pursuit. In a society under the forms of which the stronger faction can readily unite and oppress the weaker, anarchy may as truly be said to reign as in a state of nature, where the weaker individual is not secured against the violence of the stronger; and, as in the latter state even the stronger individuals are prompted, by the uncertainty of their condition, to submit to government which may protect the weak as well as themselves; so, in the former state will the more powerful factions or parties be gradually induced by a like motive to wish for a government which will protect all parties, the weaker as well as the more powerful. It can be little doubted that if the state of Rhode Island was separated from the Confederacy

---

*Madison and his colleagues did not incorporate a separate bill of rights into the Constitution; rather, they relied on the "multiplicity of interests" to protect these rights. In part, a guarantee that a bill of rights would be passed was essential to ratification, especially at New York's convention, where the document won a narrow 30-to-27 victory.

and left to itself, the insecurity of rights under the popular form of government within such narrow limits would be displayed by such reiterated oppressions of factious majorities that some power altogether independent of the people would soon be called for by the voice of the very factions whose misrule had proved the necessity of it. In the extended republic of the United States and among the great variety of interests, parties, and sects which it embraces, a coalition of a majority of the whole society could seldom take place on any other principles than those of justice and the general good; and there being thus less danger to a minor from the will of a major party, there must be less pretext, also, to provide for the security of the former, by introducing into the government a will not dependent on the latter, or, in other words, a will independent of the society itself. It is no less certain than it is important, notwithstanding the contrary opinions which have been entertained, that the larger the society, provided it lie within a practical sphere, the more duly capable it will be of self-government. And happily for the *republican cause*, the practicable sphere may be carried to a very great extent by a judicious modification and mixture of the *federal principle*.

Questions for Discussion

1. Could governmental powers ever be completely separated into three distinct branches?
2. Madison claims that the legislative branch will be the strongest. Why would this be so? Does such a contention hold true today?

Chapter 2

FEDERALISM AND INTERGOVERNMENTAL RELATIONS

Federalism is a way of organizing a political system so that authority is shared between a central government and state or regional governments. Individuals living in Pennsylvania, for example, are citizens of both that state and the United States, are under the legal authority of both governments, and have obligations (such as paying taxes) to each government.

A country is federal only if the subnational units exist independently of the national government and can make some binding decisions on their own. Some nations, like Britain and France, have unitary forms of government, in which regional and local units exist only to aid the national administration. Such subnational units can be abolished or altered at any time by the national government. In contrast, the central government in the United States (commonly referred to as the federal government) can never abolish a state. Also, the Constitution protects states by providing for two senators and at least one member of the House of Representatives from each state.

The United States embraced the concept of federalism in the Constitution more than two hundred years ago, amid much debate. The Articles of Confederation had proved inadequate because of the weakness of the central government and the almost total autonomy of the states. The nation's domestic economy was chaotic, as individual states' trade restrictions, tariff barriers, and currency weaknesses led to local depressions and encouraged citizens to move from state to state to escape debt obligations. At the same time, neither the central government nor the states could protect citizens from foreign threats or even from domestic insurrection. At the Constitutional Convention in 1787, the founders agreed that the existing government was inadequate; debate arose over the amount of power the central government should be given and how certain aspects of state autonomy could be ensured.

Federalism resulted from a compromise between those seeking a more powerful and efficient central government and those who feared such a government and valued state independence. The founders hoped the national government would act on matters concerning the common good, such as defense, trade, and financial stability, yet not become so strong that it threatened individual liberty and reduced diversity among the states. Federalism as it was understood then, and as it operated until the twentieth century, essentially meant dual federalism: Governmental functions were divided between the state and the national government, each of which was autonomous in its own sphere. For example, the national government had a monopoly on delivering the mail and conducting foreign relations, whereas state governments were in charge of areas such as education and law enforcement.

The framers tried to be as clear as possible in defining the powers possessed by the national government (Article I, Section 8 of the Constitution). But with some exceptions, such as state control of the conduct of elections, they said little about state powers or about what should happen when national and state authorities collide.

In general, the trend has been to expand the central government's powers beyond those enumerated in the Constitution and thus to erode state power and independence. Supreme Court decisions have played a crucial role here, opening the door for the federal government's involvement in many traditionally state functions. In the landmark case of *McCulloch* v. *Maryland* (1819), the Court affirmed the supremacy of the national government over the states and introduced the notion of implied powers. The Court ruled that the purpose of the Constitution is not to prevent Congress from carrying out the enumerated powers; Congress has the authority to use all means "necessary and proper" to fulfill its obligations. For example, broad interpretations of the commerce clause not only have given Congress the authority to regulate commerce with foreign nations and among the states but also have provided it with a basis for intervention within state boundaries on matters such as racial relations.

The variety and scale of the federal government's actions have changed over the years. Since the Civil War (which definitively settled the question of national supremacy), the relationships between the states and the federal government have become increasingly characterized by cooperative federalism, in which governmental powers and policies are shared. Cooperative federalism often involves sharing the costs of needed programs or projects, which requires state and local officials to adhere to federal guidelines. Franklin Roosevelt's New Deal, with its expanded national economic and social agenda, had an especially marked impact on intergovernmental relations. Both states and citizens became dependent on Washington for aid, for many states were incapable of dealing with poverty on their own. In addition, the problems of an industrial society that did not stop at state boundaries, such as water and air pollution, necessitated federal government action.

By the 1960s, American citizens seemed unwilling to let states and localities thwart the national will, and the central government was viewed as an entity to be encouraged rather than feared. Perhaps the greatest cost of federalism has been the systematic oppression of African Americans by localities and states, first as slaves and then as a separate class. The Great Society programs of the Johnson years attempted to eliminate racism and poverty through national initiatives, and federal aid to the states rose greatly during the 1960s and 1970s. By 1980, Daniel Elazar, a leading scholar of federalism, concluded that

> we have moved to a system in which it is taken as axiomatic that the federal government shall initiate policies and programs, shall determine their character, shall delegate their administration to the states and localities according to terms that it alone determines, and shall provide for whatever intervention on the part of its administrative agencies it deems necessary to secure compliance with those terms.

Still, the boundaries between state and national authority, originally inspired by a fear of a strong central government, have never been fixed, and political conflict between national and state governments has existed since the nation's founding.

There is a great deal of evidence to support the notion that the role of the states was enhanced during the 1980s. But forces such as the mass media and economic interdependence among nations are leading to an increasingly national culture. Further, it is unlikely that the states will have the protection of the courts in defending their rights, as has often been the case in the past. In *Garcia* v. *San Antonio Metropolitan Transit Authority* (1985), the Supreme Court ruled that no constitutional limits contained in the Tenth Amendment or any other section of the Constitution may limit the national government's power over commerce. States' rights, therefore, are to be found only in the structure of the government, such as equal state representation in the Senate. In a sense, states are now considered equivalent to other special-interest groups asking for favors and protection from the national government in Washington.

By the 1990s, however, the political winds were blowing in favor of returning power on many matters back to the states, and "devolution" became the rage among Washington policymakers. The Clinton administration sought to "reinvent" federalism, while congressional Republican majorities aggressively pursued a states'-rights agenda. One consequence was that in a number of program areas, such as welfare, states became more influential.

The four readings in this chapter illustrate various aspects of the controversy over the meaning and changing nature of federalism. *The Federalist,* No. 39, reflects James Madison's views on the relations between states and the national government under the new Constitution and on the importance of the governmental structure as an American innovation. The landmark case *McCulloch* v. *Maryland* resolved two key issues left open by the Constitution: which level of government is supreme when state and national policies clash and whether the federal government is limited by the Tenth Amendment to those powers explicitly enumerated in the Constitution.

The final two selections look at federalism in practice. John Donahue argues that "devolution" has tremendous costs and may be ill suited for a period in history when economic and cultural lines across states are becoming stronger. In the final selection, Sydney J. Freedberg and Marilyn Werber Serafini examine the challenges domestic terrorism poses for the U.S. federal system. Focusing on the anthrax scare in the aftermath of 9/11, they find that the very decentralized, heavily privatized public health sector had a difficult time responding in a coordinated, unified manner to the homeland security threat.

The Federalist, No. 39

James Madison

At the time of the framing of the Constitution, the founders were aware of two basic forms of government: a national government, with total central domination, and a confederation, a loose alliance of states in which the central government has virtually no power. When the Constitution and *The Federalist* were written, a "federal" government and a "confederation" were synonymous. The governmental form that has come to be called *federalism,* in which authority is divided between two independent levels, was the invention of the founders, though the label came later.

Critics of the Constitution believed the document gave so much power to the central government that it was in fact "national" in character. In *The Federalist,* No. 39, James Madison rebuts this charge and asserts that the new government is "neither a national nor a federal Constitution, but a composition of both." Being a politician, Madison took great pains to point out that the national government's powers are strictly limited to those enumerated in the Constitution and that the residual sovereignty of the states is greater than that of the national government. The first part of this paper can also be regarded as an elegant statement of what Madison meant by the term *republic.*

*T*o the People of the State of New York: The first question that offers itself is, whether the general form and aspect of the government be strictly republican?* It is evident that no other form would be reconcilable with the genius of the people of America; with the fundamental principles of the revolution; or with that honorable determination, which animates every votary [devotee] of freedom, to rest all our political experiments on the capacity of mankind for self-government. If the plan of the Convention therefore be found to depart from the republican character, its advocates must abandon it as no longer defensible.

What then are the distinctive characters of the republican form? Were an answer to this question to be sought, not by recurring to principles, but in the

---

*A *republican* form of government is one in which power resides in the people but is formally exercised by their elected representatives.

application of the term by political writers, to the constitutions of different States, no satisfactory one would ever be found. Holland, in which no particle of the supreme authority is derived from the people, has passed almost universally under the denomination of a republic. The same title has been bestowed on Venice, where absolute power over the great body of the people, is exercised in the most absolute manner, by a small body of hereditary nobles. Poland, which is a mixture of aristocracy and of monarchy in their worst forms, has been dignified with the same appellation. The government of England, which has one republican branch only, combined with a hereditary aristocracy and monarchy, has with equal impropriety been frequently placed on the list of republics. These examples, which are nearly as dissimilar to each other as to a genuine republic, show the extreme inaccuracy with which the term has been used in political disquisitions.

If we resort for a criterion, to the different principles on which different forms of government are established, we may define a republic to be, or at least may bestow that name on, a government which derives all its powers directly or indirectly from the great body of the people; and is administered by persons holding their offices during pleasure, for a limited period, or during good behaviour. It is *essential* to such a government, that it be derived from the great body of the society, not from an inconsiderable proportion, or a favored class of it; otherwise a handful of tyrannical nobles, exercising their oppressions by a delegation of their powers, might aspire to the rank of republicans, and claim for their government the honorable title of republic. It is *sufficient* for such a government, that the persons administering it be appointed, either directly or indirectly, by the people; and that they hold their appointments by either of the tenures just specified; otherwise every government in the United States, as well as every other popular government that has been or can be well organized or well executed, would be degraded from the republican character. According to the Constitution of every State in the Union, some or other of the officers of government are appointed indirectly only by the people. According to most of them the chief magistrate himself is so appointed. And according to one, this mode of appointment is extended to one of the coordinate branches of the legislature. According to all the Constitutions also, the tenure of the highest offices is extended to a definite period, and in many instances, both within the legislative and executive departments, to a period of years. According to the provisions of most of the constitutions, again, as well as according to the most respectable and received opinions on the subject, the members of the judiciary department are to retain their offices by the firm tenure of good behaviour.

On comparing the Constitution planned by the Convention, with the standard here fixed, we perceive at once that it is in the most rigid sense conformable to it. The House of Representatives, like that of one branch at least of all the State Legislatures, is elected immediately by the great body of the people. The Senate, like the present Congress, and the Senate of Maryland, derives its appointment indirectly from the people.* The President is indirectly derived from the choice of the people, according to the example in most of the States. Even the judges, with all other officers of the Union, will, as in the several States, be the choice, though a remote choice, of the people themselves. The duration of the appointments is equally conformable to the republican standard, and to the model of the State Constitutions. The House of Representatives is periodically elective as in all the States: and for the period of two years as in the State of South-Carolina. The Senate is elective for the period of six years; which is but one year more than the period of the Senate of Maryland; and but two more than that of the Senates of New-York and Virginia. The President is to continue in office for the period of four years; as in New-York and Delaware, the chief magistrate is elected for three years, and in South-Carolina for two years. In the other States the election is annual. In several of the States, however, no constitutional provision is made for the impeachment of the Chief Magistrate. And in Delaware and Virginia, he is not impeachable till out of office. The President of the United States is impeachable at any time during his continuance in office. The tenure by which the Judges are to hold their places, is, as it unquestionably ought to be, that of good behaviour. The tenure of the ministerial offices generally will be a subject of legal regulation, conformably to the reason of the case, and the example of the State Constitutions.

Could any further proof be required of the republican complexion of this system, the most decisive one might be found in its absolute prohibition of titles of nobility, both under the Federal and the State Governments; and in its express guarantee of the republican form to each of the latter.

But it was not sufficient, say the adversaries of the proposed Constitution, for the Convention to adhere to the republican form. They ought, with equal care, to have preserved the *federal* form, which regards the union as a *confederacy* of sovereign States; instead of which, they have framed a *national* government, which regards the union as a *consolidation* of the States. And it is asked by what authority this bold and radical innovation was undertaken. The handle which has been made of this objection requires, that it should be examined with some precision.

Without enquiring into the accuracy of the distinction on which the objection is founded, it will be necessary to a just estimate of its force, first to ascertain the real character of the government in question; secondly, to enquire how far the Convention were authorised to propose such a government; and thirdly, how far the duty they owed to their country, could supply any defect of regular authority.

First. In order to ascertain the real character of the government it may be considered in relation to the foundation on which it is to be established; to the

---

*The Seventeenth Amendment, adopted in 1913, changed the election procedure for U.S. senators from indirect election by state legislatures to direct election by the people of each state.

sources from which its ordinary powers are to be drawn; to the operation of those powers; to the extent of them; and to the authority by which future changes in the government are to be introduced.

On examining the first relation, it appears on one hand that the Constitution is to be founded on the assent and ratification of the people of America, given by deputies elected for the special purpose; but on the other, that this assent and ratification is to be given by the people, not as individuals composing one entire nation; but as composing the distinct and independent States to which they respectively belong. It is to be the assent and ratification of the several States, derived from the supreme authority in each State, the authority of the people themselves. The act therefore establishing the Constitution, will not be a *national* but a *federal* act.

That it will be a federal and not a national act, as these terms are understood by the objectors, the act of the people as forming so many independent States, not as forming one aggregate nation, is obvious from this single consideration that it is to result neither from the decision of a *majority* of the people of the Union, nor from that of a *majority* of the States. It must result from the *unanimous* assent of the several States that are parties to it, differing no other wise from their ordinary assent than in its being expressed, not by the legislative authority, but by that of the people themselves. Were the people regarded in this transaction as forming one nation, the will of the majority of the whole people of the United States would bind the minority; in the same manner as the majority in each State must bind the minority; and the will of the majority must be determined either by a comparison of the individual votes; or by considering the will of a majority of the States, as evidence of the will of a majority of the people of the United States. Neither of these rules has been adopted. Each State in ratifying the Constitution, is considered as a sovereign body independent of all others, and only to be bound by its own voluntary act. In this relation then the new Constitution will, if established, be a *federal* and not a *national* Constitution.

The next relation is to the sources from which the ordinary powers of government are to be derived. The house of representatives will derive its powers from the people of America, and the people will be represented in the same proportion, and on the same principle, as they are in the Legislature of a particular State. So far the Government is *national* not *federal*. The Senate on the other hand will derive its powers from the States, as political and co-equal societies; and these will be represented on the principle of equality in the Senate, as they now are in the existing Congress. So far the government is *federal*, not *national*. The executive power will be derived from a very compound source. The immediate election of the President is to be made by the States in their political characters. The votes allotted to them are in a compound ratio, which considers them partly as distinct and co-equal societies; partly as unequal members of the same society. The eventual election again is to be made by that branch of the Legislature which consists of the national representatives; but in this particular act, they are to be thrown into the form of individual delegations from so many distinct and co-equal bodies politic. From this aspect of the Government, it appears to be of a mixed character presenting at least as many *federal* as *national* features.

The difference between a federal and national Government as it relates to the *operation of the Government* is supposed to consist in this, that in the former, the powers operate on the political bodies composing the confederacy, in their political capacities: In the latter, on the individual citizens, composing the nation, in their individual capacities. On trying the Constitution by this criterion, it falls under the *national*, not the *federal* character; though perhaps not so compleatly, as has been understood. In several cases and particularly in the trial of controversies to which States may be parties, they must be viewed and proceeded against in their collective and political capacities only. So far the national countenance of the Government on this side seems to be disfigured by a few federal features. But this blemish is perhaps unavoidable in any plan; and the operation of the Government on the people in their individual capacities, in its ordinary and most essential proceedings, may on the whole designate it in this relation a *national* Government.

But if the Government be national with regard to the *operation* of its powers, it changes its aspect again when we contemplate it in relation to the *extent* of its powers. The idea of a national Government involves in it, not only an authority over the individual citizens; but an indefinite supremacy over all persons and things, so far as they are objects of lawful Government. Among a people consolidated into one nation, this supremacy is compleatly vested in the national Legislature. Among communities united for particular purposes, it is vested partly in the general, and partly in the municipal Legislatures. In the former case, all local authorities are subordinate to the supreme; and may be controuled, directed or abolished by it at pleasure. In the latter the local or municipal authorities form distinct and independent portions of the supremacy, no more subject within their respective spheres to the general authority, than the general authority is subject to them, within its own sphere. In this relation then the proposed Government cannot be deemed a *national* one; since its jurisdiction extends to certain enumerated objects only, and leaves to the several States a residuary and inviolable sovereignty over all other objects. It is true that in controversies relating to the boundary between the two jurisdictions, the tribunal which is ultimately to decide is to be established under the general Government.* But this does not change the principle of the case. The decision is to be impartially made, according to the rules of the Constitution; and all the usual and most effectual precautions are taken to secure this impartiality. Some such tribunal is clearly essential to prevent an appeal to the sword, and a dissolution of the compact; and that it ought to be established under the general

---

*The tribunal to resolve boundary disputes became the Supreme Court (see *McCulloch* v. *Maryland,* which follows this selection).

rather than under the local Governments; or to speak more properly, that it could be safely established under the first alone, is a position not likely to be combated.

If we try the Constitution by its last relation, to the authority by which amendments are to be made, we find it neither wholly *national*, nor wholly *federal*. Were it wholly national, the supreme and ultimate authority would reside in the *majority* of the people of the Union; and this authority would be competent at all times, like that of a majority of every national society, to alter or abolish its established Government. Were it wholly federal on the other hand, the concurrence of each State in the Union would be essential to every alteration that would be binding on all. The mode provided by the plan of the Convention is not founded on either of these principles. In requiring more than a majority, and particularly, in computing the proportion by *States*, not by *citizens*, it departs from the *national*, and advances towards the *federal* character: In rendering the concurrence of less than the whole number of States sufficient, it loses again the *federal*, and partakes of the *national* character.

The proposed Constitution therefore is in strictness neither a national nor a federal constitution; but a composition of both. In its foundation, it is federal, not national; in the sources from which the ordinary powers of the Government are drawn, it is partly federal, and partly national; in the operation of these powers, it is national, not federal; in the extent of them again, it is federal, not national. And finally, in the authoritative mode of introducing amendments, it is neither wholly federal, nor wholly national.

Questions for Discussion

1. According to Madison, why was the new U.S. Constitution neither a "national" nor a "federal" document? Which of its features were designed to curb the national government's domination of the states?
2. Madison believed the Constitution set up a republican rather than a democratic form of government. What features of the document were designed to give the people an indirect rather than a direct influence on public policy?

McCulloch v. Maryland (1819)

In many areas, the framers of the Constitution were explicit about the powers granted to the national government and to the states. In other areas, however, such as the power to tax, the two were given many of the same responsibilities. The Constitution leaves open the relationship of state and national authority when their policies conflict. In 1819, *McCulloch* v. *Maryland* settled the issue in favor of the national government.

In 1791 Congress created a national bank to print money, make loans, and engage in a variety of banking activities. The bank was deeply resented by a number of state legislatures, which held that Congress did not have the authority to charter a bank, and in 1818 Maryland passed a law that taxed its Baltimore branch $15,000. James McCulloch, a cashier at the bank, refused to pay and was sued in state court. The state's tax was upheld, and the bank appealed to the U.S. Supreme Court.

Chief Justice John Marshall delivered a landmark opinion for the Court with a decision that markedly expanded the powers of the national government over those explicitly stated in the Constitution and affirmed the supremacy of the national government over the states. According to the Court, Congress had the power to charter a national bank because it had been granted the power "to make all laws which shall be necessary and proper for carrying into execution" the expressed powers. In short, Congress has a number of implied powers in addition to its enumerated powers. Further, because the power to tax could be used to destroy an institution that is necessary for the operations of the national government, Maryland's attempt to levy a tax on the national bank was unconstitutional. The Court upheld the supremacy of the national government when policies collide.

M r. Chief Justice Marshall* delivered the opinion of the Court.
In the case now to be determined, the defendant, a sovereign State, denies the obligation of a law enacted by the legislature of the Union, and the plaintiff, on his part, contests the validity of an act which has been

---

*John Marshall became chief justice of the United States in 1801. He is probably most famous for his opinion in *Marbury* v. *Madison* (see selection 13.2), which established the principle of judicial review—the power of the Court to declare laws unconstitutional.

passed by the legislature of that State. The constitution of our country, in its most interesting and vital parts, is to be considered; the conflicting powers of the government of the Union and of its members, as marked in that constitution, are to be discussed; and an opinion given, which may essentially influence the great operations of the government. . . .

The first question made in the case is, has Congress power to incorporate a bank? . . .

The power now contested was exercised by the first Congress elected under the present constitution. The bill for incorporating the bank of the United States did not steal upon an unsuspecting legislature, and pass unobserved. Its principle was completely understood, and was opposed with equal zeal and ability. After being resisted, first in the fair and open field of debate, and afterward in the executive cabinet, with as much persevering talent as any measure has ever experienced, and being supported by arguments which convinced minds as pure and as intelligent as this country can boast, it became a law. The original act was permitted to expire; but a short experience of the embarrassments to which the refusal to revive it exposed the government, convinced those who were most prejudiced against the measure of its necessity, and induced the passage of the present law. It would require no ordinary share of intrepidity to assert that a measure adopted under these circumstances was a bold and plain usurpation, to which the constitution gave no countenance. . . .

In discussing this question, the counsel for the State of Maryland have deemed it of some importance, in the construction of the constitution, to consider that instrument not as emanating from the people, but as the act of sovereign and independent States. The powers of the general government, it has been said, are delegated by the States, who alone are truly sovereign; and must be exercised in subordination to the States, who alone possess supreme dominion.

It would be difficult to sustain this proposition. The Convention which framed the constitution was indeed elected by the State legislatures. But the instrument, when it came from their hands, was a mere proposal, without obligation, or pretensions to it. It was reported to the then existing Congress of the United States, with a request that it might "be submitted to a Convention of Delegates, chosen in each State by the people thereof, under the recommendation of its Legislature, for their assent and ratification." This mode of proceeding was adopted; and by the Convention, by Congress, and by the State Legislatures, the instrument was submitted to the people. They acted upon it in the only manner in which they can act safely, effectively, and wisely, on such a subject, by assembling in Convention. It is true, they assembled in their several States—and where else should they have assembled? No political dreamer was ever wild enough to think of breaking down the lines which separate the States, and of compounding the American people into one common mass. Of consequence, when they act, they act in their States. But the measures they adopt do not, on that account, cease to be the measures of the people themselves, or become the measures of the State governments.

From these Conventions the constitution derives its whole authority. The government proceeds directly from the people; is "ordained and established" in the name of the people; and is declared to be ordained, "in order to form a more perfect union, establish justice, ensure domestic tranquillity, and secure the blessings of liberty to themselves and to their posterity." The assent of the States, in their sovereign capacity, is implied in calling a Convention, and thus submitting that instrument to the people. But the people were at perfect liberty to accept or reject it; and their act was final. It required not the affirmance, and could not be negatived, by the State governments. The constitution, when thus adopted, was of complete obligation, and bound the State sovereignties.

It has been said, that the people had already surrendered all their powers to the State sovereignties, and had nothing more to give. But, surely, the question whether they may resume and modify the powers granted to government does not remain to be settled in this country. Much more might the legitimacy of the general government be doubted, had it been created by the States. The powers delegated to the State sovereignties were to be exercised by themselves, not by a distinct and independent sovereignty, created by themselves. To the formation of a league, such as was the confederation, the State sovereignties were certainly competent. But when, "in order to form a more perfect union," it was deemed necessary to change this alliance into an effective government, possessing great and sovereign powers, and acting directly on the people, the necessity of referring it to the people, and of deriving its powers directly from them, was felt and acknowledged by all.

The government of the Union, then (whatever may be the influence of this fact on the case) is, emphatically, and truly, a government of the people. In form and in substance it emanates from them. Its powers are granted by them, and are to be exercised directly on them, and for their benefit.

This government is acknowledged by all to be one of enumerated powers. The principle, that it can exercise only the powers granted to it, would seem too apparent to have required to be enforced by all those arguments which its enlightened friends, while it was depending before the people, found it necessary to urge. That principle is now universally admitted. But the question respecting the extent of the powers actually granted, is perpetually arising, and will probably continue to arise, as long as our system shall exist. . . .

If any one proposition could command the universal assent of mankind, we might expect it would be this—that the government of the Union, though limited in its powers, is supreme within its sphere of action. This would seem to result necessarily from its nature. It is the government of all; its powers are delegated by all; it represents all, and acts for all. Though any one State may be willing to control its operations, no State is willing to allow others to control them. The nation, on those subjects on which it can act, must necessarily bind its component parts. But this question is not left to mere reason: the people have, in express terms, decided it, by saying, "this constitution, and the laws of the United States, which shall be made in pursuance thereof, . . . shall be the supreme law of the land," and by requiring that the members of the State legislatures, and the officers of the executive and judicial departments of the States, shall take the oath of fidelity to it.

The government of the United States, then, though limited in its powers, is supreme; and its laws, when made in pursuance of the constitution, form the supreme law of the land, "any thing in the constitution or laws of any State to the contrary notwithstanding."

Among the enumerated powers, we do not find that of establishing a bank or creating a corporation. But there is no phrase in the instrument which, like the articles of confederation, excludes incidental or implied powers; and which requires that every thing granted shall be expressly and minutely described. Even the 10th amendment, which was framed for the purpose of quieting the excessive jealousies which had been excited, omits the word "expressly," and declares only that the powers "not delegated to the United States, nor prohibited to the States, are reserved to the States or to the people"; thus leaving the question, whether the particular power which may become the subject of contest has been delegated to the one government, or prohibited to the other, to depend on a fair construction of the whole instrument. The men who drew and adopted this amendment had experienced the embarrassments resulting from the insertion of this word in the articles of confederation, and probably omitted it to avoid those embarrassments. A constitution, to contain an accurate detail of all the subdivisions of which its great powers will admit, and of all the means by which they may be carried into execution, would partake of the prolixity of a legal code, and could scarcely be embraced by the human mind. It would probably never be understood by the public. Its nature, therefore, requires, that only its great outlines should be marked, its important objects designated, and the minor ingredients which compose those objects be deduced from the nature of the objects themselves. That this idea was entertained by the framers of the American constitution, is not only to be inferred from the nature of the instrument, but from the language. Why else were some of the limitations, found in the ninth section of the 1st article, introduced?* It is also, in some degree, warranted by their having omitted to use any restrictive term which might prevent its receiving a fair and just interpretation. In consideration of this question, then, we must never forget, that it is a *constitution* we are expounding.

Although, among the enumerated powers of government, we do not find the word "bank" or "incorporation," we find the great powers to lay and collect taxes; to borrow money; to regulate commerce; to declare and conduct a war; and to raise and support armies and navies. The sword and the purse, all the external relations, and no inconsiderable portion of the industry of the nation,

---

*Article I, Section 9, follows the provision enumerating the national government's powers and is a broad list of specific prohibitions that restrain the national government, including the inability to levy taxes or duties on articles from any state or to give preferential treatment to the ports of one state at the expense of another.

are entrusted to its government. It can never be pretended that these vast powers draw after them others of inferior importance, merely because they are inferior. Such an idea can never be advanced. But it may with great reason be contended, that a government, entrusted with such ample powers, on the due execution of which the happiness and prosperity of the nation so vitally depends, must also be entrusted with ample means for their execution. The power being given, it is the interest of the nation to facilitate its execution. It can never be their interest, and cannot be presumed to have been their intention, to clog and embarrass its execution by withholding the most appropriate means. Throughout this vast republic, from the St. Croix to the Gulf of Mexico, from the Atlantic to the Pacific, revenue is to be collected and expended, armies are to be marched and supported. The exigencies of the nation may require that the treasure raised in the north should be transported to the south, *that* raised in the east conveyed to the west, or that this order should be reversed. Is that construction of the constitution to be preferred which would render these operations difficult, hazardous, and expensive? Can we adopt that construction, (unless the words imperiously require it), which would impute to the framers of that instrument, when granting these powers for the public good, the intention of impeding their exercise by withholding a choice of means? If, indeed, such be the mandate of the constitution, we have only to obey; but that instrument does not profess to enumerate the means by which the powers it confers may be executed; nor does it prohibit the creation of a corporation, if the existence of such a being be essential to the beneficial exercise of those powers. It is, then, the subject of fair inquiry, how far such means may be employed. . . .

But the constitution of the United States has not left the right of Congress to employ the necessary means, for the execution of the powers conferred on the government, to general reasoning. To its enumeration of powers is added that of making "all laws which shall be necessary and proper, for carrying into execution the foregoing powers, and all other powers vested by this constitution, in the government of the United States, or in any department thereof." . . .

We admit, as all must admit, that the powers of the government are limited, and that its limits are not to be transcended. But we think the sound construction of the constitution must allow to the national legislature that discretion, with respect to the means by which the powers it confers are to be carried into execution, which will enable that body to perform the high duties assigned to it, in the manner most beneficial to the people. Let the end be legitimate, let it be within the scope of the constitution, and all means which are appropriate, which are plainly adapted to that end, which are not prohibited, but consist with the letter and spirit of the constitution, are constitutional. . . .

It being the opinion of the Court, that the act incorporating the bank is constitutional; and that the power of establishing a branch in the State of Maryland might be properly exercised by the bank itself, we proceed to inquire—

Whether the State of Maryland may, without violating the constitution, tax that branch?

That the power of taxation is one of vital importance; that it is retained by the States; that it is not abridged by the grant of a similar power to the government of the Union; that it is to be concurrently exercised by the two governments: are truths which have never been denied. But, such is the paramount character of the constitution, that its capacity to withdraw any subject from the action of even this power, is admitted. The States are expressly forbidden to lay any duties on imports or exports, except what may be absolutely necessary for executing their inspection laws. If the obligation of this prohibition must be conceded—if it may restrain a State from the exercise of its taxing power on imports and exports; the same paramount character would seem to restrain, as it certainly may restrain, a State from such other exercise of this power, as is in its nature incompatible with, and repugnant to, the constitutional laws of the Union. A law, absolutely repugnant to another, as entirely repeals that other as if express terms of repeal were used.

On this ground the counsel for the bank place its claim to be exempted from the power of a State to tax its operations. There is no express provision for the case, but the claim has been sustained on a principle which so entirely pervades the constitution, is so intermixed with the materials which compose it, so interwoven with its web, so blended with its texture, as to be incapable of being separated from it, without rending it into shreds.

This great principle is, that the constitution and the laws made in pursuance thereof are supreme; that they control the constitution and laws of the respective States, and cannot be controlled by them. From this, which may be almost termed an axiom, other propositions are deduced as corollaries, on the truth or error of which, and on their application to this case, the cause has been supposed to depend. These are, 1st. that a power to create implies a power to preserve. 2nd. That a power to destroy, if wielded by a different hand, is hostile to, and incompatible with these powers to create and to preserve. 3d. That where this repugnancy exists, that authority which is supreme must control, not yield to that over which it is supreme.

These propositions, as abstract truths, would, perhaps, never be controverted. Their application to this case, however, has been denied; and, both in maintaining the affirmative and the negative, a splendor of eloquence, and strength of argument, seldom, if ever, surpassed, have been displayed.

The power of Congress to create, and of course to continue, the bank, was the subject of the preceding part of this opinion; and is no longer to be considered as questionable.

That the power of taxing it by the States may be exercised so as to destroy it, is too obvious to be denied. . . .

The Court has bestowed on this subject its most deliberate consideration. The result is a conviction that the States have no power, by taxation or otherwise, to retard, impede, burden, or in any manner control, the operations of the constitutional laws enacted by Congress to carry into execution the powers vested in the general government. This is, we think, the unavoidable consequence of that supremacy which the constitution has declared.

We are unanimously of opinion, that the law passed by the legislature of Maryland, imposing a tax on the Bank of the United States, is unconstitutional and void. . . .

Questions for Discussion

1. Why did the Court believe that the national government possessed powers beyond those enumerated in the Constitution?
2. Does Marshall's view in this case seem consistent with the view of national-state relations expressed by James Madison in *The Federalist*, No. 39?

 2.3

The Devil in Devolution

John D. Donahue

In the contemporary era, public support for transferring power from the government in Washington to the states is nearly at consensus levels. Polls regularly show that respondents overwhelmingly trust their state government to do a better job of "running things" than the federal government. Both major political parties and their leading candidates for office have strongly endorsed the concept of "devolution," the return of power and responsibility to state and local governments by the federal government. In the 1990s a number of federally dominated programs, welfare being the most prominent example, underwent major changes in the direction of increasing the role of the states in priority setting, funding discretion, and administration.

John D. Donahue is a professor at Harvard University's John F. Kennedy School of Government.

From *Disunited States* by John D. Donahue. Copyright © 1997 by John D. Donahue. Reprinted by permission of Basic Books, a member of Perseus Books, L.L.C.

In this selection, John Donahue raises a number of concerns about devolutionary trends. He argues that "state borders are becoming more, not less, permeable," and that devolution eventually leads to destructive state rivalries. In Donahue's view, the collective good of the nation suffers a "tragedy of the commons" as interstate rivalries create temptations for states to pursue their narrow interests by passing on significant policy costs to other states. From Donahue's perspective, devolution leads to the fragmentation of authority and makes success in addressing such issues less likely.

The shift in government's center of gravity away from Washington and toward the states—a transition propelled by both popular sentiment and budget imperatives, and blessed by leaders in both major parties—reflects an uncommon pause in an endless American argument over the balance between nation and state. That argument got underway when the Framers gathered in Philadelphia to launch a second attempt at nationhood, after less than a decade's dismal experience under the feeble Articles of Confederation. The Constitution they crafted was a compromise between those who wanted to strengthen the ties among essentially autonomous states, and those who sought to establish a new nation to supersede the states as the locus of the commonwealth. While anchoring the broad contours of state and federal roles, the Framers left it to their successors to adjust the balance to fit the circumstances of the world to come and the priorities of future generations.

This moment of consensus in favor of letting Washington fade while the states take the lead is badly timed. The public sector's current trajectory—the devolution of welfare and other programs, legislative and judicial action circumscribing Washington's authority, and the federal government's retreat to a domestic role largely defined by writing checks to entitlement claimants, creditors, and state and local governments—would make sense if economic and cultural ties reaching across state lines were *weakening* over time. But state borders are becoming more, not less, permeable.

From a vantage point three-fifths of the way between James Madison's day and our own, Woodrow Wilson wrote that the "common interests of a nation brought together in thought and interest and action by the telegraph and the telephone, as well as by the rushing mails which every express train carries, have a scope and variety, an infinite multiplication and intricate interlacing, of which a simpler day can have had no conception." Issues in which other states' citizens have no stakes, and hence no valid claim to a voice, are becoming rarer still in an age of air freight, interlinked computers, nonstop currency trading, and site-shopping global corporations. . . .

The concept of "the commons" can help to cast in a sharper light the perils of fragmented decision-making on issues of national consequence. In a much-noted 1968 article in *Science,* biologist Garrett Hardin invoked the parable of a herdsman pondering how many cattle to graze on the village commons. Self-interest will lead the herdsman to increase the size of his herd even if the commons is already overburdened, since he alone benefits from raising an extra animal, but shares the consequent damage to the common pasture. As each farmer follows the same logic, overgrazing wrecks the commons.

Where the nation as a whole is a commons, whether as an economic reality or as a political ideal, and states take action that ignores or narrowly exploits that fact, the frequent result is the kind of "tragedy" that Hardin's metaphor predicts: Collective value is squandered in the name of a constricted definition of gain. States win advantages that seem worthwhile only because other states bear much of the costs. America's most urgent public challenges—shoring up the economic underpinnings of an imperiled middle-class culture; developing and deploying productive workplace skills; orchestrating Americans' engagement with increasingly global capital—involve the stewardship of common interests. The fragmentation of authority makes success less likely. The phenomenon is by no means limited to contemporary economic issues, and a smattering of examples from other times and other policy agendas illustrate the theme.

Faith and Credit

In the late 1700s, states reluctant to raise taxes instead paid public debt with paper money, with progressively little gold or silver behind it. Even states like Georgia, Delaware, and New Jersey that exercised some restraint in issuing paper money saw merchants lose confidence in their currencies, as the flood of bad money debased the reputation of American money in general. Half a century later defaults and debt repudiations by Pennsylvania, Arkansas, Florida, Illinois, and a few other states—which for the states concerned were unfortunate, but apparently preferable to the alternative of paying what they owed—polluted the common American resource of creditworthiness, and for a time froze even solvent states and the federal government out of international credit markets.

Presidential primaries, which are run state by state, provide another example. Each state prefers to be first in line to hold its primary (or at least early in the queue). In recent presidential election seasons—and especially the 1996 Republican primaries—states have wrecked the common resource of a deliberative primary process in a rational (but nonetheless tragic) pursuit of parochial advantage. California's primary in June 1992 had come too late to matter; anxious to avoid another episode of irrelevance four years later, it staked out March 26 for its vote. But several other states, whose *own* votes would be rendered superfluous once California's crowd of delegates was selected, rescheduled their primaries in response. A spiral of competitive rescheduling led to ugly squabbles as Delaware and Louisiana crowded New Hampshire's traditional first-in-the-nation franchise; a mass of state primaries ended up bunched right behind New Hampshire, and a grotesquely compressed primary season ensued. The outcome was clear by the first days of March, and California's primary—although held two months earlier than it had been in 1992—was just as irrelevant. Most voters perceived the 1996 primary season as a brief spasm of televised name-calling. Even supporters of the eventual nominee felt that Senator Dole, and the voters, had been ill served by the process. . . .

The Constitution's "full faith and credit" clause, a court case in Hawaii, and the quadrennial uptick in political tawdriness brought an unusual sort of commons problem to center stage in 1996. The issue was whether the definition of "marriage" should be broadened to include same-sex unions. A handful of Hawaiian same-sex couples had asserted the right to have their relationships reckoned under state law as no different from heterosexual marriages, invoking provisions in the state constitution that bar sex discrimination in almost any form (including, the plaintiffs argued, restrictions on the gender of one's spouse). When a shift in the composition of Hawaii's supreme court made a seemingly lost cause suddenly viable, it dawned on advocates and opponents alike that if Hawaii legitimated same-sex marriage, those unions would have to be recognized nationwide. If any homosexual couple—at least those able to afford two tickets to Hawaii—could bypass more restrictive laws in their home states, the rapid result could be a national redefinition of what marriage means, without anyone outside Hawaii having any voice in the outcome.

National opponents of gay marriage staged a preemptive strike in the form of the Defense of Marriage Act, requiring the federal government to counter heterodoxy in Hawaii or anywhere else by declaring a *national* definition of marriage—one man, one woman, and that's that. Beyond excluding same-sex spouses from receiving benefits under any federal program, the act gave states the right to refuse recognition to other states' marriages. The Defense of Marriage Act raced through Congress and President Clinton quickly signed it (albeit without ceremony and literally in the middle of the night). Annoyed at being forced to alienate his gay supporters in order to stay wrapped in the family-values mantle, Clinton charged, no doubt correctly, that the bill's authors were driven by the partisan spirit of the election year. But whatever their motivations—and however one feels about same-sex marriage—they had a point: The definition of marriage in the United States should be settled by national deliberation.

There is an interesting historical irony here, however. Not so long ago, divorce was only a little more common, and only a little less out of the mainstream, than homosexual unions seem today. While the causes for its increase are many and complex, the pace was set in part by states' calculations of parochial advantage. Around the turn of the century legislators in several Western states—notably Nevada—passed liberal divorce legislation in part to encourage economic development. Unhappy couples facing onerous divorce laws in their home state could head West for a few weeks or months. There they could dissolve their union, while solidifying the local economy, in some striving desert town. Other states might have resisted the trend to more lenient divorce laws. But any couple—at least any able to afford a ticket to Reno— could bypass their home-state restrictions. If a legislature held the line it would only be subjecting its citizens to extra expense while sending money out of state.

The wholesale liberalization of American divorce laws is often seen as a mistake—if not from the perspective of men who can cast off unwanted obligations with minimal bother, at least from the perspective of women and, especially, young children who all too often are left economically stranded. Which raises a question: If states should be free to refuse recognition to marriages made elsewhere, on the grounds that another state's definition of marriage offends local morals, should they also be able to refuse to recognize out-of-state divorces? Suppose that Vermont, say, passed legislation toughening divorce laws and declaring Vermont marriages immune to dissolution by another state's laws. If the legislation survived constitutional challenge (which is doubtful, as it is for the Defense of Marriage Act's comparable provisions) there would be some definite advantages: More traditional states could wall themselves off as enclaves against unwelcome national trends; a potential spouse could signal the depth of his or her commitment by proposing a Vermont wedding. On the other hand, the United States would become a little bit less of a nation.

In one of the less glorious episodes in American history, this country attempted to define human slavery as an issue each state could settle on its own, according to its own economic and ethical lights. Northern states, however, eventually proved unwilling to accept the proposition that the moral commons could be so neatly subdivided. The Fugitive Slave Act required antislavery states to make room in their moral world for slaveholders to transport their "property" for use anywhere in the nation. The repercussions ultimately led to attempted secession, and then to the national abolition of slavery. The meaning of marriage may be another moral issue so basic that it must be dealt with through a national debate, protracted and painful as that will doubtless turn out to be.

Environmental Regulation

Antipollution law is perhaps the most obvious application of the "commons" metaphor to policymaking in a federal system. If a state maintains a lax regime of environmental laws it spares its own citizens, businesses, and government agencies from economic burdens. The "benefits" of environmental recklessness, in other words, are collected in-state. Part of the pollution consequently dumped into the air or water, however, drifts away to do its damage elsewhere in the nation. If states held all authority over environmental rule-making, the predictable result would be feeble regulations against any kinds of pollution where in-state costs and benefits of control are seriously out of balance. Even in states whose citizens valued the environment—even if the citizens of *all* states were willing to accept substantial economic costs in the name of cleaner air and water—constituents and representatives would calculate that their sacrifice could not on its own stem the tide and reluctantly settle for weaker rules than they would otherwise prefer.

A state contemplating tough antipollution rules might calculate that its citizens will pay for environmental improvements that will be enjoyed, in part, by others. Even worse, by imposing higher costs on business than do other states, it risks repelling investment, and thus losing jobs and tax revenues to states with weak environmental laws. Congress explicitly invoked the specter of a "race for the bottom"—competitive loosening of environmental laws in order to lure business—to justify federal standards that would "preclude efforts on the part of states to compete with each other in trying to attract new plants." In a series of legislative changes starting in the early 1970s, the major choices about how aggressively to act against pollution were moved to the federal government. While aspects of enforcement remained state responsibilities—introducing another level of complications that continues to plague environmental policy—the trade-off between environmental and economic values moved much closer to a single national standard.

National regulation in a diverse economy does have a downside. States differ in their environmental problems, and in the priorities of their citizens. Requiring all states to accept the same balance between environmental and economic values imposes some real costs and generates real political friction. Yet even if the tilt toward national authority is, on balance, the correct approach to environmental regulation, there is reason to doubt we got all the details right. Moreover, logic suggests that the federal role should be stronger for forms of pollution that readily cross state borders, and weaker for pollution that stays put. But federal authority is actually weaker under the Clean Air Act and the Clean Water Act than under the "Superfund" law covering hazardous waste. Toxic waste sites are undeniably nasty things. But most of them are situated within a single state, and stay there. . . .

Legalized Gambling

There has never been a time in America when a person determined to gamble could not find some action. Nor is *legal* gambling, for that matter, anything new. The Continental Congress fed and armed Washington's army, in part, with revenues from a lottery, and state-sanctioned games of chance financed the early growth of Harvard and other colleges. For much of this century, however, gambling has operated in the economic shadows. Except for the exotic enclave of Nevada, government's stance toward gambling ranged, until recently, from vigilant hostility to narrowly circumscribed tolerance.

This has changed with an astonishing speed and completeness. In 1988 Nevada and New Jersey were alone in allowing casino gambling. Eight years later there were around 500 casinos operating in 27 states, and some form of gambling was legal in all but two states. The total annual amount wagered legally in the United States is about $500 billion. (For a sense of scale, consider that America's entire annual output is in the range of $7,000 billion.)

Gambling brings some obvious benefits to the state that runs the lottery or hosts the casinos. It can generate relatively high-paying jobs even for workers without much training. It yields welcome revenues for the state treasury. (States took in $27 billion from lotteries in 1994, and had $9.8 billion in revenues left over after paying off winners and covering administrative costs. In 1994, taxes paid by casinos alone yielded $1.4 billion for states and localities.) Legalized gambling can also produce political benefits, most directly the rich lodes of campaign contributions available from a highly profitable industry that is so intensely dependent on political favor.

Yet there are costs as well. Some people will always gamble whether it is legal or not, but many more do so only when the law allows. Access to legal opportunities for gambling has been found to increase the number of people who develop a gambling problem. The consequences range from mild economic inconvenience to bankruptcy, embezzlement, divorce, and suicide. In 1995— ten years after their state launched a lottery, and four years after the first legal riverboat casino opened—nine out of ten Iowans indulged in gambling. One in twenty reported having a gambling problem, and Iowa social-service agencies were coping with a surge of collateral family and financial damage.

But shouldn't we leave it to officials in each state to tally up the expected costs and benefits and make decisions that sum to the right national policy? The logic of the commons makes this less than likely. If a state loosens its own restrictions on gambling, it gains the benefits in jobs, tax revenues, and political favor. It also suffers cost—but not *all* the costs. When citizens of *other* states buy the lottery tickets and visit the casinos, they leave their money behind when they return home, but take their gambling-related problems back with them. States that still ban gambling suffer much of the damage from the national trend toward legalization, but without sharing in the benefits.

Iowa, in fact, had maintained stringent antigambling laws until the mid-1980s. But as a growing number of Iowans played lotteries in neighboring states it became harder to resist proposals to revitalize a battered economy through riverboat casinos aimed at attracting out-of-state gamblers, especially from the prosperous, casino-free Chicago area. At first, Chicagoans did come, by the busload. But Illinois legislators, seeing gambling dollars heading down the interstate to Iowa, opted to allow riverboat gambling in their state, too. Iowa's initial liberalization law had tried to lower the risk of problem gambling by limiting the size of any one bet and the amount any person could gamble away in a single day. But when Illinois, Mississippi, and Louisiana introduced riverboats *without* any limits, Iowa lifted its own restrictions. In a similar way, after Montana allowed slot machines in taverns in 1985 neighboring South Dakota called and raised, allowing slot machines in bars *and* convenience stores.

By 1996 the only two states with no legal gambling at all were Utah, whose Mormon culture was uniquely resistant to the national trend, and Hawaii, where it is a good deal harder than in most other states for citizens to escape local restrictions by doing their gambling in the state next door. The federal government's absolute deference to the separate states began to bend that same year with legislation establishing a commission to examine the broader national impacts of gambling. A Nevada congresswoman denounced the bill as "the nose under the tent of Federal interference with the right of states to regulate gambling." She was entirely correct. But it is questionable whether exclusive state control over so massive a change in the legal economy's scope, with such sweeping implications for our culture, ever made much sense.

Not every issue, to be sure, can be cast as a commons problem. And even where state officials *are* tempted to pursue narrow agendas at the expense of national interests, it is not automatically true that the shared loss exceeds the advantages of state autonomy, or that an acceptable way can be found of safeguarding common interests without straining the framework of our federal system. There are two basic strategies for overcoming the confusion of incentives that trigger the tragedy of the commons. One is to fragment the commons into private holdings where property rights are unambiguous. The other is to maintain a polity that commands both the capacity and the legitimacy to give force to common interests. The debate over the future of America's federal-state balance can be seen, in a sense, as pivoting on this strategic choice. Devolution seeks to simplify incentives by subdividing the commons into separate plots. Federal reform requires accepting the challenge of balancing multiple interests within the national commonwealth. . . .

Questions for Discussion

1. What is the "tragedy of the commons"? Give some examples of how the concept is relevant to federal/state relations.
2. How would defenders of states' rights refute the arguments that Donahue puts forth? Are there any negative consequences to regulating at the national level a diverse economy and culture?

2.4

Health and Welfare: Contagious Confusion

Sydney J. Freedberg, Jr., and Marilyn Werber Serafini

American federalism has constantly changed over the past two centuries; in fact, many important changes have occurred as the result of the nation's experience in dealing with unsettling events such as military conflicts and economic depressions. The terrorist attacks of September 11, 2001, provided a new challenge for the federal structure; protection from terrorist threats within the nation's borders called for a coordinated, unified response to keep the homeland secure.

In this article, the authors explore the difficulties that federal, state, and local officials faced in the aftermath of 9/11 when dealing with a potential public health crisis that appeared to be the result of bioterrorism. A number of government workers, members of Congress, and media personalities reported receiving envelopes in the mail containing a powdery substance holding anthrax, an infectious agent that is usually fatal. While only a few people actually received anthrax-laced envelopes, these discoveries provided a test of the readiness of the public health system. Coping with the threat proved difficult. Although the federal government appears to be dominant, American government remains remarkably decentralized among its various levels. Even within levels, division and rivalry among bureaucratic agencies often pose problems when mobilizing resources for unified action. The situation was compounded in the public health arena, where medical care is largely delivered by the private sector.

The authors suggest the pieces are in place for the federal system to deal effectively with public health challenges in the future. From their perspective, the federal government must provide the incentives, standards, and framework for the public health system, but other units of government and private groups must be able to tailor their own approaches to their unique needs within the overall setting.

Sydney J. Freedberg, Jr., is a reporter for *National Journal* covering homeland security and interagency cooordination issues. Marilyn Werber Serafini is a reporter for *National Journal* covering public health issues.

I n a way that the far bloodier September 11 attacks did not, the anthrax assault has required unprecedented collaboration: among law enforcement,
emergency management, and public health officials; among federal, state,
and local government; and between government at all levels and the medical
community. If the attacks-by-mail did America any kind of favor, it was to
highlight how many weak links there are in the chains that bind these agencies
to each other in a crisis—links that must be strengthened before a far heavier
blow breaks them apart completely.

The American public health system is decentralized and uncoordinated, and
its response to anthrax wasn't pretty. But some lessons are being learned.

Consider Clifford Ong, Indiana's new statewide counter-terrorism coordinator, appointed two weeks into the crisis as the Hoosier version of national
Homeland Security chief Tom Ridge. Ong's office, intended to be the state's
central clearinghouse for anthrax information, first learned about Indiana's
most serious anthrax scare, not through official channels, but from the media.
Although about 600 miles from any confirmed case of anthrax, Indianapolis
happens to have one of the only two facilities nationwide that repair and recy-
cle post office sorting machines—including a tainted printer from Trenton,
N.J. State authorities did not even know the repair plant was there until a sub-
contractor called asking for advice about how to handle machinery possibly exposed to anthrax. The state then tested for anthrax at the repair plant, and the
report came back negative. Ong relaxed. But he didn't know that the main
contractor at the plant had asked the U.S. Postal Service to come and do its
own test. This second test, performed by an out-of-state lab, came back positive. Suddenly, there was anthrax in Indiana, and yet state authorities weren't
told. Reporters in Washington were. Ong had to field the frantic calls.

"Our problem isn't locally," said Ong, who has long worked with the local
U.S. district attorney and the FBI field office. "Washington seems to respond
within the Beltway to national media without any concern that we have local
media. . . . It puts us in somewhat of a defensive position."

This snafu—just one of many—shows how vital information can fall into the
cracks between organizations, into blind spots where fear can flourish like mold
inside a wall. Considering that just four people died of anthrax in one month, the
average American was far more likely to be struck by lightning, which kills 80 to
100 people every year, than to contract the disease. The point is that anthrax is
not contagious—but fear is. "The medical problem was actually pretty small," said
Jack Harrald, the director of the Institute for Crisis, Disaster, and Risk Management at George Washington University in Washington. "The terror problem, in
terms of managing people's fear, was pretty huge—and not very well managed."

The failure of government, medicine, and media to respond to fears and ignorance about anthrax with real understanding led to millions of dollars in
losses—to businesses that had to find substitute mail carriers or evacuate their
workplaces for testing, as well as to local governments that had to respond to
every emergency anthrax scare. In Los Angeles, where hazardous-materials

responses increased 300 percent in mid-October, "we received a call from an employee at a doughnut shop that there's a white, powdery substance on the floor," said Deputy Chief Darrell Higuchi, of the Los Angeles County Fire Department. The shop, of course, sold doughnuts with powdered sugar. "Yet," said Higuchi, "you feel for the callers, because they are scared."

Fear thrives on ignorance. But there is no effective, authoritative, nationwide system to communicate information about bioterror. Nor is there a single national spokesperson for the public's health. Indeed, some have criticized the Bush Administration for failing to designate someone as the voice of the anthrax crisis, even acknowledging White House reluctance to call on Surgeon General David Satcher, a leftover Clinton Administration appointee. Instead, information has moved through dozens of parallel and poorly coordinated channels of communication: The Centers for Disease Control and Prevention talks to state health officers, the FBI to local sheriffs, the Federal Emergency Management Agency to disaster officials, medical associations to their members. But when people in different fields, such as police and physicians, must work together, or when there simply is no state or local counterpart to a federal agency, the channels are less clear—as Ong found out in dealing with the Postal Service. The system simply isn't set up to share information.

In fact, civil liberties laws often forbid necessary communication. Said Lawrence Gostin, the director of the Center for Law and the Public's Health, a joint project of Georgetown University and Johns Hopkins University: "The law thwarts vital information-sharing vertically from federal to state, and horizontally between law enforcement, emergency management, and public health."

The biggest gap is between government and the medical community. A CDC alert on bioterrorism, sent to state health officials just after September 11, had still not reached many local emergency rooms a week later. And the crucial linchpins between doctors and officials—local public health offices—are notoriously overworked and short of funds. As many as one in five public health offices do not even have e-mail, said Sen. Bill Frist, R-Tenn., a physician. Many localities still collect epidemiological data on disease outbreaks only by asking doctors to send postcards through the mail—hardly an ideal approach in any fast-moving outbreak, let alone one that strikes at the postal system.

Anthrax has finally kick-started efforts to revive public health systems, after decades of neglect. In North Carolina, for example, the Legislature is about to allocate millions of dollars to replace reporting by postcard with high-speed, highly secure electronic links. Ultimately, the network will connect not only local officials, but also every hospital, pharmacy, and doctor's office in the state.

New funding and new networks are essential first steps. But in a country where almost all health care is provided by the private sector—indeed, where most critical terrorist targets, from Internet servers to nuclear plants to sports arenas, are privately owned—defense against terrorism probably cannot be achieved by a new agency, a new program, or a new technology. True "homeland security," most experts say, will require an overarching system that links not just every level and agency of government, but also the private sector, nonprofit groups, and the general public. Computers and the Internet will be vital in helping to set up this new national network, but it will be the intangible connections between people working together in a common cause that will really make the new system work.

The Broken Linchpin

If it sometimes seems as if the world has turned upside down since September 11, that's because it has. Terrorism has upset the traditional pyramid of who protects whom. No longer do the Pentagon's armed troops bear the brunt of foreign blows. Whether the danger comes from airliners-as-bombs or from anthrax envelopes, local firefighters, medics, and police respond long before Washington can act. But even the local emergency teams come second to the scene. In a terrorist attack, the first responder is the ordinary citizen—the airline passenger who decides to rush the hijackers, the mailroom clerk who notices a suspicious package, or anyone who wonders whether these flu-like symptoms they're feeling might be anthrax. It is their decisions, prudent or paranoid, that trigger the government response. Said Peter Probst, a former Pentagon and CIA official, "The first line of defense is an educated, engaged public."

That word, "educated," signals where things start breaking down. Even those officials who should be best equipped to inform have stumbled over their own statements, and each other's—and that includes Surgeon General Satcher and Health and Human Services Secretary Tommy G. Thompson.

"You've got Satcher saying one thing, Tommy Thompson saying another, and the CDC saying a third," fumed one local official who spoke with *National Journal*. One day the word is to put everyone on Cipro, the next day not, the third day it's another antibiotic altogether. "There isn't a consistent message."

With that confusion at the top, many officials, never mind ordinary citizens, admit turning to the news media as their first source of knowledge. But as reporters themselves grope in the dark for information, and constantly face the pressure for round-the-clock, up-to-the-minute coverage, they may magnify inconclusive clues, or even outright rumors, into major scare stories. There was so much misinformation about anthrax early on, said one congressional staffer well versed in bioterror, "the first few days, I was kicking the television a lot."

Many confused citizens dialed 911, just to be sure. Far more fell back on the second line of defense: their doctors. Physicians are still trusted more than most other professionals. And even though only a handful of American doctors have ever seen a case of inhalation anthrax (the last U.S. case was in 1978), most rushed to learn what they could. Until recently, medical education on bioweapons has been minimal. But after September 11, well before the first anthrax case in Florida, sensitivity to terror of all kinds was so high that the major medical associations quickly rallied to upload data to their Web sites and downlink teleconferences to their members.

That information probably saved lives. Had Florida photo editor Bob Stevens died in August, said Randall Larsen, director of the Anser Institute for Homeland Security, a consulting group in Northern Virginia, "it's highly unlikely he would have been diagnosed as dying with anthrax, because they weren't looking for it." Before September 11, when authorities sent anthrax samples to four medical laboratories as a test of their bioterrorism alertness, three of the labs just threw the samples out, mistaking the anthrax bacteria for contamination on the slides. In another test, out of a roomful of doctors at Johns Hopkins medical center, just one recognized an X-ray of a strange chest inflammation as characteristic of anthrax. Even after the September 11 attacks, HHS Secretary Thompson initially suggested that Stevens's death was due to a freak natural cause. But doctors were on high enough alert by then to spot the symptoms.

Although the professional medical associations could deluge their members with basic references on anthrax, they lacked the quick communications systems to collect and broadcast up-to-date data on the ever-changing outbreak. In fact, since most associations serve only a single medical specialty—and even the mighty American Medical Association serves fewer than half of all doctors—they could not even help share information among different types of doctors in a given community.

The painstaking, county-by-county collation of data gathered from individual physicians has always fallen to local public health offices—the traditional American defensive line against disease. But emergency officials, medical associations, and independent experts alike all agree that the public health infrastructure has long been, to quote one congressional staffer, "the forgotten stepchild." These local offices are perpetually short on funds, technology, and—above all—personnel. They are burdened with laws written to guard against 19th-century scourges such as syphilis and tuberculosis, and few of these laws even require doctors to report outbreaks of likely bioweapons such as anthrax, much less the subtler indications of spreading disease.

"Suppose there's a run on anti-diarrhea medication. How would we know that? If there are a lot of absences from school or work, how would we know that?" said Georgetown University's Gostin. "We need a public health agency to be able to get information from the private sector."

New York City, considered a national model, does keep hourly tabs on such things as sales of the anti-diarrheal Kaopectate. Los Angeles hospitals are linked by computer to share diagnosis data. But most areas lack such sophisticated "disease surveillance" systems, even in states that have really tried. Virginia, for example, connects its local health offices across the state by computer, said George Foresman, a Virginia emergency management official, but the state's effort to bring private practices into the network stalled because "we just had not been able to secure the funding."

The problems are not only fiscal. Even with a $1.4 million federal grant, Michigan found the private sector deeply reluctant to share information.

"We've asked pharmacies if we could monitor what antibiotics are going out," said Dr. Sandro Cinti, of the University of Michigan medical center, "but they didn't want to give away that information."

In the absence of even such imperfect electronic systems, most public health officials collect data the old-fashioned way: slowly. In some places, doctors' offices fill out and mail in forms to health agencies; in other places, they call in, and local officials must laboriously enter the information by hand, and then in turn mail another piece of paper to the state health office. Conversely, when Illinois authorities, who have invested heavily in linking public health offices to local hospitals, wanted to send every physician in the state advice on anthrax, they had to take the licensing board's master list of addresses and mail every one of them a letter. There was no comprehensive e-mail or electronic system.

"The information-gathering and decision-making loop isn't fast enough," said Clark Staten, the executive director of the Emergency Response & Research Institute in Chicago. "The bad guys can move faster than the good guys—at the present time." And during that lag, fear can spread, and people can die.

More Than Medical

Even in a better-than-average flu season, doctors may run out of vaccine and hospitals out of beds. In some cities last year, said Sen. Edward Kennedy, D-Mass., "they had sick patients that couldn't even be treated in the emergency rooms—they were out in cars."

Any major natural disease outbreak overtaxes American medicine. But biological terrorism takes the complexity an octave higher. Each scattering of spores is obviously a public health problem. But it is also evidence of a crime— and of a hazardous material in the environment. Anthrax not only requires close "vertical" cooperation among federal, state, local, and private medical organizations, it also cuts horizontally across functional lines. Ordinary disease can be dropped neatly into an organizational box marked "medical." Bioterrorism requires out-of-the-box cooperation among public health professionals, private doctors, law enforcement agencies, firefighters, emergency management systems, and even foreign intelligence agencies.

This kind of jurisdiction-crossing is so alien to American government that it is often outright illegal. If the Central Intelligence Agency had somehow found out beforehand about the anthrax-laced letter addressed to Senate Majority Leader Thomas A. Daschle, for example, it may not have been allowed to warn health officials until after it was sent, according to James Hodge, the project director of the Center for Law and Public's Health. To protect civil liberties, said Hodge, "there's a firewall between intelligence agencies and public health."

Even when there's no legal obstacle to collaboration, many of the various agencies lack the experience, the contacts, or the procedures to work together. Both the U.S. Postal Inspection Service and the Centers for Disease Control are trying to track the anthrax letters to their source. The two agencies share information, but they don't share people: Instead of combining forces, detectives and doctors are on two separate teams following different methods to reach the same goal.

Sometimes, the lack of coordination could have even worse consequences. "When I was the health commissioner of New York, I had no clue who was the head of the FBI office, and he had no clue who I was," said Margaret Hamburg, who went on to become HHS's top bioterror official under President Clinton. "The last thing they want to be doing is exchanging business cards in the middle of a crisis." Yet, that is just what often happened with the anthrax scare.

In the District of Columbia, for instance, where traditional federal-local complications compounded all the other problems, the initial confusion and inconsistencies in testing and treatment for Capitol Hill staff versus postal workers boiled over into racially tinged fury. One community forum turned, unfairly, into a pillorying of D.C. public health chief Ivan Walks. Soon Dr. Walks and Mayor Anthony Williams were holding joint press conferences with Postal Service officials and the CDC. But those relationships had to be set up on the spot—and the public health office still does not have a full-time representative in the District's interagency Emergency Operations Center.

D.C.'s problem is not uncommon. "We somehow managed to leave the public health system . . . outside the emergency system," said Harrald, at D.C.'s George Washington University. Emergency managers, firefighters, and police have largely overcome past problems of coordination by planning and training together before disasters, and by jointly staffing command posts during times of crisis. Such a combined system cranked into action in New York City on September 11. "The federal government had thousands of people moving in the right direction 20 minutes after the second tower was hit," Harrald said. "We know how to do this. That's the good news."

The bad news is that, in most places, no one told public health officials the good news. In D.C., "it took a long time before the emergency room at [George Washington University] hospital and the emergency room at Children's Hospital and the attending physician of the Capitol and the CDC had the same picture of what they were dealing with," Harrald said. "I'm not throwing stones at individuals. The problem is that we didn't set the systems up before the event."

The American Answer

In the first month of anthrax attacks, the country's system of defenses against bioterror often seemed to be no system at all, only chaos. Fortunately, reality is more nuanced, and more heartening, than that. True, there is no one coherent national system. But there are systems—all partial, all imperfect, but needing mainly to be strengthened and brought into an overarching structure. Senate Health, Education, Labor, and Pensions Committee Chairman Kennedy and panel member Frist last year [2000] co-sponsored the Public Health Threats and Emergencies Act of 2000, which authorized $540 million a year to strengthen the public health infrastructure and to better recognize and respond to bioterrorism attacks. Congress has not yet funded the new law, but already the two Senators have upped their request to $1.4 billion a year.

The final sum needed for homeland security will surely be much higher. But "we're not going to create a whole new Department of Defense," with a $350 billion budget and staff of 3 million, said David McIntyre of the Anser Institute. "We're going to play with the chips that are on the table."

"The pieces are there," said Frist. The task is taking the pieces that exist—federal, state, local, and private—"and coordinating them in a seamless way. It can be done." In Frist's own field, transplant surgery, moving precious organs quickly across the country and then ensuring that patients' bodies do not reject the new tissue require far-flung hospitals and diverse disciplines to work closely together—and they do it, every day.

High on Capitol Hill's agenda is a massive reinvestment in the nation's long-neglected public health system. Top priority is a secure, high-speed electronic data-link for doctors and public health officials who are now scrawling disease reports on postcards. The CDC already has an electronic Epidemic Information Exchange system to share outbreak alerts among federal, state, and local public health officials, as well as the military. And long before September 11, the CDC had given all 50 states seed money to start work on a National Electronic Disease Surveillance System to link all 2,000-plus local health offices around the country. This network could automatically and swiftly share, for example, the results of a crucial diagnostic test. Ultimately, it could also tap into hospitals and even private practices. But for now, the surveillance network does not actually exist. A bare-bones "base system" is scheduled to begin in 20 states in 2002. That seemed plenty fast—before September 11. Now, lawmakers are likely to hit the gas.

But strengthening public health is only half the battle, because public health officials will still get their information from the private sector. The real challenge is to track—from every hospital, every doctor's office, and every pharmacy around the country—the telltale upticks in certain symptoms, or prescriptions, that although seemingly innocuous in isolation, could signal an impending crisis. It is a daunting task.

Yet it is also mostly done already. Insurance companies routinely require doctors to code each diagnosis and report it electronically for reimbursement, keeping electronic tabs on everything from pharmaceutical sales to major surgeries. The Health Insurance Portability and Accountability Act of 1996 (HIPAA) made such reporting systems mandatory nationwide, though a significant 43 percent of doctors are not yet hooked up. In its patient-privacy rules, the act also has a little-known exception that requires doctors to share data on threats to public health.

Medical information companies are already on the Hill touting software solutions. A properly designed system could tap into the existing streams of data, strip off names and other individual identifiers, and crunch the numbers into trends. To be sure, such an early-warning system might well find false patterns.

An upsurge in sales of certain drugs might indicate an outbreak of disease, or it could simply reflect effective advertising. Conversely, the system might miss a real outbreak if doctors consistently misdiagnosed as flu the ambiguous early symptoms of, say, anthrax—the reason why D.C.'s Walks is currently working on a system that codes not just final diagnoses but actual symptoms as well.

Still, the most sophisticated computer is only a tool. The most important linkages are among people. And in small ways, that linking process has already begun, too. Tom Ridge has held teleconferences with all 50 state governors. Local officials and medical associations are reaching out to one another, often through e-mail. And a FEMA program called "Project Impact" gives local governments grants and training to bring together different agencies, businesses, and community groups for disaster planning. Mayor Susan Savage of tornado-prone Tulsa, Okla., says that Project Impact simply but systematically asks, "What does the private sector bring to the table that can complement public resources?" On September 11, for example, when 800 airline passengers were stranded at the Tulsa airport, the city mobilized everything from public buses for transportation to local preachers for counseling, pulling resources freely from the public, private, and nonprofit sectors.

Officials, legislators, and experts increasingly agree that such bottom-up approaches are the model for homeland security. Imposing a single national system from the top down is not only impractical, it is probably unwise. What makes more sense is a "network of networks," an overarching system that lets each local government or private group tailor its approach to its own unique needs—within the overall framework.

A prototype nationwide network of networks has actually already been built. Unfortunately, it was promptly taken apart soon after. Late in 1999, when the public and private sectors alike were fretting that their computers might crash once the year hit "oo," then-Secretary of State Madeleine K. Albright visited the national Y2K crisis center and exclaimed, "You could really run the world from here."*

Like a terrorist, the Y2K bug threatened to strike unpredictably at any target: federal, state, local, or, in the vast majority of cases, private. Imposing a top-down structure to address the potential threat was impossible, recalled John Koskinen, Clinton's Y2K coordinator: "You need to build off existing struc-

---

*Y2K—When computers were first built starting in the 1950s—and continuing until the early 1990s in some cases—program designers used only two numbers to designate a year, to save space and money. The year 1980 became 80, for example. Many in business and government believed that when the year 2000 was reached, many of the older microprocessors in computers would read the year 2000 as 00, causing computers to crash and creating havoc with everything from business billing, to government records, to running elevators, to providing electricity and water. The national government first became aware of the problem as early as 1989 and in the ensuing years a national government crisis center was developed to find ways to deal with the Y2K threat. When 2000 finally arrived, damage from the Y2K threat was minimal.

tures, and not create new ones." So Koskinen pulled together existing net-works—government agencies, corporations, trade associations, and industry groups—in a loose but comprehensive confederation that reached into every threatened sector, with himself as the lead spokesman.

"The year-2000 preparations were a pretty good dress rehearsal" for the kind of coordination required since September 11, said David Vaughan, a Texas public health official. JoAnne Moreau, the emergency preparedness director of Baton Rouge, La., agreed: "We developed relationships with agencies and companies and factions that we never knew would have some kind of role."

The lesson that Y2K holds for homeland defense is that the federal government cannot, need not, and probably should not, do everything. Of course, without strong guidance from Washington, the thousands of private and local-government responses could create an irrational tangle, like an ill-tended garden. The federal role is to fertilize the growth and, when necessary, prune it back. "There are 1,800 separate legal jurisdictions in the United States, and the American people and the Constitution like it that way," said David Siegrist of the Potomac Institute for Policy Studies think tank. "The federal government needs to offer incentives . . . and set standards."

In a shadow war with an amorphous foe, America can prevail only by empowering individuals and small groups to innovate—because it is they, and not any federal official, who will be on the front lines. Thirty years ago, noted McIntyre, if a child showed up at school beaten black and blue, teachers might think, "Tough parents," and move on. Today, they would report the possible abuse—and thereby set various responses in motion. A public similarly well-educated to watch for something genuinely wrong in their world would go a long way, not just toward calming panic, but toward stopping terrorists before they strike.

"We don't want to be people who watch each other. We want to be people who watch out for each other," said McIntyre. "It's the distinction between a controlled society and a civil society. A civil society requires citizens. And in good times, maybe we forgot that."

We have certainly been reminded now.

Questions for Discussion

1. Why was it so difficult for the government to deal with the threat of biological terrorism in the case of the anthrax attacks by mail?
2. The authors suggest that the "pieces are in place" to greatly improve the public health sector's response to crisis situations. What suggestions do they offer? What kinds of political considerations might make implementation of their suggestions difficult?

Chapter 3

Civil Liberties and Civil Rights

Abortion. Prayer in public schools. Libel and slander. School integration and vouchers. Affirmative action and racial quotas. The right to legal counsel. These often-emotional issues strike at the core of the relationship between the citizen and the state. The framers understood the central position of individual rights, seeing them as inalienable—that is, as God-given, neither handed down nor taken away by rulers or the government as a whole. Still, the government serves as the chief agency for protecting individual rights, even though it can effectively deny them as well (for example, through the long history of legal segregation). The framers and subsequent generations of policymakers have thus performed a pair of balancing acts with civil liberties and civil rights issues.

First, they have strived to balance the rights of individuals with the needs of the community at large. On many occasions, the individual and the community are best served by the same policy. For example, the court decision in *Gideon* v. *Wainwright* that guarantees indigents the right to counsel was a victory both for individual poor people and for society as a whole. Frequently, however, the interests of the community and the individual are, or appear to be, at odds. Does the right to freedom of speech and assembly extend to Nazis who wish to march through a predominantly Jewish community like Skokie, Illinois? The list of troubling and important questions in this area is endless and has produced a river of cases for the Supreme Court to wade through.

The second balance policymakers must maintain lies in the relative amounts of power accorded the government and its citizens. The government stands as the ultimate protector of individual liberties, such as the Constitution's enumerated rights of speech, religion, petition, and so forth. At the same time, the government can adopt policies and procedures that deny rights. The actions of an overzealous FBI or CIA have infringed on privacy rights, and many legislative initiatives have overstepped the bounds of propriety in seeking to regulate political organizations and speech. The Supreme Court's willingness to curb the government's assertion of power has varied. The Supreme Court of the 1990s was probably more likely to decide in favor of the government—whether national, state, or local—than it had been at any time since Earl Warren became chief justice in 1953.

More recently, the terrorist attacks of 2001 have prompted a broad re-evaluation of the balance between security and liberty. The hastily written and passed Patriot Act provided the federal government with many more tools to address terrorism within domestic settings. Civil libertarians have predictably objected to many federal initiatives, including more freedom to gather personal information and to hold those suspected of terror-related activities. Stuart Taylor (see selection 3.6) argues that this rebalancing of security and liberty has not eroded fundamental freedoms while addressing legitimate concerns for national security.

What makes the study of civil rights and civil liberties so fascinating is the simultaneous timelessness and immediacy of the issues. For example, the notion of freedom of speech is as important today as it was in the eighteenth century, and contemporary controversies place basic issues, such as the potential defamation of a public figure, in new contexts. Likewise, civil rights and civil liberties issues hold our interest because their implications are extensive. Millions of individuals are directly affected by the Supreme Court's ruling in abortion or desegregation cases.

Although the legislative and executive branches play important roles in making and implementing rights policies, it is the judiciary that stands at center stage in this arena. At first such a responsibility may seem incongruous, since the courts are insulated from the influence of most citizens. In the end, however, this very independence from the popular will and the daily intrigues of politics is what renders the judicial branch, especially in its upper reaches, well suited to consider questions of rights. Protecting rights is frequently an unpopular business. In the 1940s and 1950s, for instance, Congress shied away from legislation that challenged racial separation, and the Supreme Court ruled on a series of desegregation cases, culminating in *Brown* v. *Board of Education*.

The direction of the Court is influenced by precedent and societal context as well as by individual justices. Although the membership of the Court during the last twenty-five years has become more conservative, its decisions have not dramatically turned away from the expansive civil liberties positions under Chief Justice Earl Warren (1953–1969). For example, the Burger (1969–1986) and Rehnquist (from 1986) Courts have gradually expanded the flexibility of the police in carrying out searches and seizures. But their decisions have not overturned any of the key Warren Court precedents, such as *Mapp* v. *Ohio* (1961), which limited the use of evidence from an illegal search, or *Miranda* v. *Arizona* (1966), which guaranteed that the accused be made aware of their right to counsel and protection from self-incrimination. Still, the increasing willingness of the Rehnquist Court of the 1990s to limit or overturn previous decisions may indicate that some fundamental changes (such as overturning *Roe* v. *Wade*) remain possible, though unlikely. Indeed, as Ramesh Ponnuru notes in Chapter 13, Sandra Day O'Connor has become the fulcrum of many evenly divided court decisions. A single change in the Court's personnel might shift the balance of power and the content of important rulings.

The following selections show the variety of civil rights and civil liberties issues. The first two address the conflict over the possibility of limiting free speech. In *Near* v. *Minnesota* (1931), the Supreme Court refused to bar the publication of an irresponsible newspaper that had mounted vicious anti-Semitic attacks on Minneapolis public officials. This decision reflects the Court's great reluctance to order the prior restraint of any publication, even the most despicable. The *Near* decision was notable not for its immediate impact, which was next to nothing, but for the precedent it set. In 1971, the Court ruled in *New York Times* v. *United States* that the government could not suppress the publication of the Pentagon Papers, a highly critical history of U.S. involvement in Vietnam. The Defense Department had commissioned the extensive study and distributed it internally (though not widely). As Fred Friendly notes (see selection 3.2), the justices relied heavily on *Near* in their reasoning. That obscure Minnesota case thus had a major impact on an issue of great national importance.

One contested area of civil liberties is the so-called right to privacy. Unlike enumerated rights, which protect speech, religion, assembly, and so on, the right to privacy is not acknowledged in the Constitution. Such a right has evolved, however, becoming explicit in *Griswold* v. *Connecticut* (1965). The *Griswold* ruling was a focal point in the 1987 confirmation hearings of Robert Bork, President Reagan's unsuccessful nominee for a Supreme Court seat. Moreover, the 1973 *Roe* v. *Wade* abortion decision relied heavily on the "right of privacy" that Griswold began to establish. More recently, the Court ruled in *Lawrence and Gardner* v. *Texas* (see selection 3.5) that privacy rights extend to consenting adults who were convicted of a crime (sodomy) under a Texas statute that made "it a crime for two persons of the same sex to engage in certain intimate sexual conduct."

Much as the right of privacy has evolved, so too has antidiscrimination policy. Although many civil rights cases preceded *Brown* v. *Board of Education,* this 1954 decision proved a watershed in our willingness to address past discrimination. Although *Brown* eventually put an end to *de jure* (in law) segregation, it did relatively little to address *de facto* separation.

In the wake of *Brown,* affirmative action policies have sought to address inequities in both opportunity and outcome on racial, gender, and ethnic grounds. The Court has ruled numerical quotas to be unconstitutional, but has allowed some consideration of race as a criterion for admission to law school (see selection 3.9, "Reaffirming Diversity").

Still, as Peter Schuck argues in "Affirmative Action: Don't Mend It or End It— Bend It" (see selection 3.8), an active affirmative action plan in the public sector may produce unintended negative consequences, with preferences producing skepticism about the merit of those who receive them. At present, the Court has laid out narrow guidelines under which race may be considered in providing opportunities. Sandra Day O'Connor, in the Michigan affirmative action cases (see selection 3.9), has expressed the hope that preferences will not be needed in twenty-five years. But given the fifty-year record of *Brown* and continuing segregation in many school systems, one can scarcely be too optimistic.

3.1

Near v. Minnesota (1931)

Among the rights guaranteed in the Constitution, perhaps the most fundamental is the freedom of expression. Without unfettered speech and a free press, the idea of democracy loses its meaning. Freedom of expression issues emerge in many forms, including controversies over libel, obscenity, and political speech. Even a very large number of articles could not capture the range of questions that courts regularly face in deciding freedom of expression cases.

In *Near* v. *Minnesota,* the central question revolves around prior restraint of the press. In 1931, the Supreme Court ruled 5 to 4 that Minnesota could not muzzle the publisher of a newspaper that was attacking various Minneapolis public officials. Although any public official who is the subject of a "malicious, scandalous, and defamatory" article can sue for libel, the state could not halt publication of a newspaper merely because it expected that paper to defame public officials.

M r. Chief Justice Hughes delivered the opinion of the Court. . . .
Under this statute, [section one, clause (b)], the County Attorney of Hennepin County brought this action to enjoin the publication of what was described as a "malicious, scandalous and defamatory newspaper, magazine and periodical," known as "The Saturday Press," published by the defendants in the city of Minneapolis. The complaint alleged that the defendants, on September 24, 1927, and on eight subsequent dates in October and November, 1927, published and circulated editions of that periodical which were "largely devoted to malicious, scandalous and defamatory articles" concerning Charles G. Davis, Frank W. Brunskill, the *Minneapolis Tribune,* the *Minneapolis Journal,* Melvin C. Passolt, George E. Leach, the Jewish Race, the members of the Grand Jury of Hennepin County impaneled in November 1927, and then holding office, and other persons, as more fully appeared in exhibits annexed to the complaint, consisting of copies of the articles described and constituting 327 pages of the record. While the complaint did not so allege, it appears from the briefs of both parties that Charles G. Davis was a special law enforcement officer employed by a civic organization, that George E. Leach was Mayor of Minneapolis, that Frank W. Brunskill was its Chief of Police, and that Floyd B. Olson (the relator in this action) was County Attorney.

Without attempting to summarize the contents of the voluminous exhibits attached to the complaint, we deem it sufficient to say that the articles charged in substance that a Jewish gangster was in control of gambling, bootlegging and racketeering in Minneapolis, and that law enforcing officers and agencies were not energetically performing their duties. Most of the charges were directed against the Chief of Police; he was charged with gross neglect of duty, illicit relations with gangsters, and with participation in graft. The County Attorney was charged with knowing the existing conditions and with failure to take adequate measures to remedy them. The Mayor was accused of inefficiency and dereliction. One member of the grand jury was stated to be in sympathy with the gangsters. A special grand jury and a special prosecutor were demanded to deal with the situation in general, and, in particular, to investigate an attempt to assassinate one Guilford, one of the original defendants, who, it appears from the articles, was shot by gangsters after the first issue of the periodical had been published. There is no question but that the articles made serious accusations against the public officers named and others in connection with the prevalence of crimes and the failure to expose and punish them. . . .

If we cut through mere details of procedure, the operation and effect of the statute in substance is that public authorities may bring the owner or publisher of a newspaper or periodical before a judge upon a charge of conducting a business of publishing scandalous and defamatory matter—in particular that the matter consists of charges against public officers of official dereliction—and unless the owner or publisher is able and disposed to bring competent evidence to satisfy the judge that the charges are true and are published with good motives and for justifiable ends, his newspaper or periodical is suppressed and further publication is made punishable as a contempt. This is of the essence of censorship.

The question is whether a statute authorizing such proceedings in restraint of publication is consistent with the conception of the liberty of the press as historically conceived and guaranteed. In determining the extent of the constitutional protection, it has been generally, if not universally, considered that it is the chief purpose of the guaranty to prevent previous restraints upon publication. The struggle in England, directed against the legislative power of the licenser, resulted in renunciation of the censorship of the press. The liberty deemed to be established was thus described by Blackstone.* "The liberty of the press is indeed essential to the nature of a free state; but this consists in laying no *previous* restraints upon publications, and not in freedom from censure for criminal matter when published. Every freeman has an undoubted right to lay what sentiments he pleases before the public; to forbid this, is to destroy the freedom of the press; but if he publishes what is improper, mischievous or illegal, he must take the consequence of his own temerity." . . . The distinction

_____

*Sir William Blackstone (1723–1780) was an English jurist and legal scholar whose writings served as the core of legal education in the United States during the nineteenth century.

was early pointed out between the extent of the freedom with respect to censorship under our constitutional system and that enjoyed in England. Here, as Madison said, "the great and essential rights of the people are secured against legislative as well as against executive ambition. They are secured, not by laws paramount to prerogative, but by constitutions paramount to laws. This security of the freedom of the press requires that it should be exempt not only from previous restraint by the Executive, as in Great Britain, but from legislative restraint also." . . .

The objection has . . . been made that the principle as to immunity from previous restraint is stated too broadly, if every such restraint is deemed to be prohibited. That is undoubtedly true; the protection even as to previous restraint is not absolutely unlimited. But the limitation has been recognized only in exceptional cases: "When a nation is at war many things that might be said in time of peace are such a hindrance to its effort that their utterance will not be endured so long as men fight and that no Court could regard them as protected by any constitutional right." . . . No one would question but that a government might prevent actual obstruction to its recruiting service or the publication of the sailing dates of transports or the number and location of troops. On similar grounds, the primary requirements of decency may be enforced against obscene publications. The security of the community life may be protected against incitements to acts of violence and the overthrow by force of orderly government. The constitutional guaranty of free speech does not "protect a man from an injunction against uttering words that may have all the effect of force. . . ." These limitations are not applicable here. Nor are we now concerned with questions as to the extent of authority to prevent publications in order to protect private rights according to the principles governing the exercise of the jurisdiction of courts of equity.

The exceptional nature of its limitations places in a strong light the general conception that liberty of the press, historically considered and taken up by the Federal Constitution, has meant, principally although not exclusively, immunity from previous restraints or censorship. The conception of the liberty of the press in this country had broadened with the exigencies of the colonial period and with the efforts to secure freedom from oppressive administration. That liberty was especially cherished for the immunity it afforded from previous restraint of the publication of censure of public officers and charges of official misconduct. . . . Madison, who was the leading spirit in the preparation of the First Amendment of the Federal Constitution, thus described the practice and sentiment which led to the guaranties of liberty of the press in state constitutions.[1]

"In every State, probably, in the Union, the press has exerted a freedom in canvassing the merits and measures of public men of every description which has not been confined to the strict limits of the common law. On this footing the freedom of the press has stood; on this footing it yet stands. . . . Some degree of abuse is inseparable from the proper use of everything, and in no instance is this more true than in that of the press. It has accordingly been de-cided by the practice of the States, that it is better to leave a few of its noxious branches to their luxuriant growth, than, by pruning them away, to injure the vigour of those yielding the proper fruits. And can the wisdom of this policy be doubted by any who reflect that to the press alone, chequered as it is with abuses, the world is indebted for all the triumphs which have been gained by reason and humanity over error and oppression; who reflect that to the same beneficent source the United States owe much of the lights which conducted them to the ranks of a free and independent nation, and which have improved their political system into a shape so auspicious to their happiness? Had 'Sedi-tion Acts,' forbidding every publication that might bring the constituted agents into contempt or disrepute, or that might excite the hatred of the people against the authors of unjust or pernicious measures, been uniformly enforced against the press, might not the United States have been languishing at this day under the infirmities of a sickly Confederation?* Might they not, possibly, be miserable colonies, groaning under a foreign yoke?"

The fact that for approximately one hundred and fifty years there has been almost an entire absence of attempts to impose previous restraints upon publi-cations relating to the malfeasance of public officers is significant of the deep-seated conviction that such restraints would violate constitutional right. Public officers, whose character and conduct remain open to debate and free discus-sion in the press, find their remedies for false accusations in actions under libel laws providing for redress and punishment, and not in proceedings to restrain the publication of newspapers and periodicals. The general principle that the constitutional guaranty of the liberty of the press gives immunity from previous restraints has been approved in many decisions under the provisions of state constitutions.

The importance of this immunity has not lessened. While reckless assaults upon public men . . . exert a baleful influence and deserve the severest condem-nation in public opinion, it cannot be said that this abuse is greater, and it is believed to be less, than that which characterized the period in which our insti-tutions took shape. Meanwhile, the administration of government has become more complex, the opportunities for malfeasance and corruption have multi-plied, crime has grown to most serious proportions, and the danger of its pro-tection by unfaithful officials and of the impairment of the fundamental security of life and property by criminal alliances and official neglect, empha-sizes the primary need of a vigilant and courageous press, especially in great cities. The fact that the liberty of the press may be abused by miscreant purvey-ors of scandal does not make any the less necessary the immunity of the press

---

*The fear of such legislation was scarcely idle. In 1798 Congress passed the Alien and Sedition Acts, which provided for indicting those who conspired against the administration or who spoke or wrote "with intent to defame" the government. The Sedition Act was enforced against a few individuals before being repealed during the Jefferson administration.

from previous restraint in dealing with official misconduct. Subsequent punishment for such abuses as may exist is the appropriate remedy, consistent with constitutional privilege.

In attempted justification of the statute, it is said that it deals not with publication *per se*, but with the "business" of publishing defamation. If, however, the publisher has a constitutional right to publish, without previous restraint, an edition of his newspaper charging official derelictions, it cannot be denied that he may publish subsequent editions for the same purpose. He does not lose his right by exercising it. If his right exists, it may be exercised in publishing nine editions, as in this case, as well as in one edition. If previous restraint is permissible, it may be imposed at once; indeed, the wrong may be as serious in one publication as in several. Characterizing the publication as a business, and the business as a nuisance, does not permit an invasion of the constitutional immunity against restraint. Similarly, it does not matter that the newspaper or periodical is found to be "largely" or "chiefly" devoted to the publication of such derelictions. If the publisher has a right, without previous restraint, to publish them, his right cannot be deemed to be dependent upon his publishing something else, more or less, with the matter to which objection is made.

Nor can it be said that the constitutional freedom from previous restraint is lost because charges are made of derelictions which constitute crimes. With the multiplying provisions of penal codes, and of municipal charters and ordinances carrying penal sanctions, the conduct of public officers is very largely within the purview of criminal statutes. The freedom of the press from previous restraint has never been regarded as limited to such animadversions as lay outside the range of penal enactments. Historically, there is no such limitation; it is inconsistent with the reason which underlies the privilege, as the privilege so limited would be of slight value for the purposes for which it came to be established.

The statute in question cannot be justified by reason of the fact that the publisher is permitted to show, before injunction issues, that the matter published is true and is published with good motives and for justifiable ends. If such a statute, authorizing suppression and injunction on such a basis, is constitutionally valid, it would be equally permissible for the legislature to provide that at any time the publisher of any newspaper could be brought before a court, or even an administrative officer (as the constitutional protection may not be regarded as resting on mere procedural details) and required to produce proof of the truth of his publication, or of what he intended to publish, and of his motives, or stand enjoined. If this can be done, the legislature may provide machinery for determining in the complete exercise of its discretion what are justifiable ends and restrain publication accordingly. And it would be but a step to a complete system of censorship. The recognition of authority to impose previous restraint upon publication in order to protect the community against the circulation of charges of misconduct, and especially of official misconduct, necessarily would carry with it the admission of the authority of the censor against which the constitutional barrier was erected. The preliminary freedom, by virtue of the very reason for its existence, does not depend, as this Court has said, on proof of truth. . . .

Equally unavailing is the insistence that the statute is designed to prevent the circulation of scandal which tends to disturb the public peace and to provoke assaults and the commission of crime. Charges of reprehensible conduct, and in particular of official malfeasance, unquestionably create a public scandal, but the theory of the constitutional guaranty is that even a more serious public evil would be caused by authority to prevent publication. "To prohibit the intent to excite those unfavorable sentiments against those who administer the Government, is equivalent to a prohibition of the actual excitement of them; and to prohibit the actual excitement of them is equivalent to a prohibition of discussions having that tendency and effect; which, again, is equivalent to a protection of those who administer the Government, if they should at any time deserve the contempt or hatred of the people, against being exposed to it by free animadversions on their characters and conduct."[2] There is nothing new in the fact that charges of reprehensible conduct may create resentment and the disposition to resort to violent means of redress, but this well-understood tendency did not alter the determination to protect the press against censorship and restraint upon publication. As was said in *New Yorker Staats-Zeitung* v. *Nolan* . . . : "If the township may prevent the circulation of a newspaper for no reason other than that some of its inhabitants may violently disagree with it, and resent its circulation by resorting to physical violence, there is no limit to what may be prohibited." The danger of violent reactions becomes greater with effective organization of defiant groups resenting exposure, and if this consideration warranted legislative interference with the initial freedom of publication, the constitutional protection would be reduced to a mere form of words.

For these reasons we hold the statute, so far as it authorized the proceedings in this action under clause (b) of section one, to be an infringement of the liberty of the press guaranteed by the Fourteenth Amendment. We should add that this decision rests upon the operation and effect of the statute, without regard to the question of the truth of the charges contained in the particular periodical.* The fact that the public officers named in this case, and those associated with the charges of official dereliction, may be deemed to be impeccable, cannot affect the conclusion that the statute imposes an unconstitutional restraint upon publication.

Notes

1. Report on the Virginia Resolutions, Madison's Works, vol. iv, p. 544.
2. Madison, *op. cit.*, p. 549.

------

*Note the strength of this declaration. The falsity of a statement does not constitute adequate grounds for imposing prior restraint.

Questions for Discussion

1. Why should public figures be treated differently when libel or slander is alleged? Is it possible to libel someone as public as the president?
2. In what instances might prior restraint of a publication be appropriate? In wartime? In the case of a consistently obscene magazine?

 3.2

From the *Saturday Press* to the *New York Times*

Fred Friendly

Fred Friendly notes the importance of the *Near* decision in the Pentagon Papers case of 1971. In this instance the publisher was not a purveyor of sensational accusations but the *New York Times* and the *Washington Post,* which were printing long extracts of the Pentagon's classified history of American involvement in Vietnam. The only common thread between the Pentagon Papers case (*New York Times Co. v. United States*) and *Near* was the issue of prior restraint. But that thread held fast, demonstrating the importance of maintaining freedom of speech both in distasteful circumstances (*Near*) and when the national interest is at stake.

Although his name is hardly a household word, the ghost of Jay M. Near still stalks most U.S. courtrooms. There exists no plaque that bears his name, and even Colonel McCormick's marble memorial to Chief Justice Hughes's opinion omits the name of the case.* Near is truly the unknown

The late Fred Friendly, formerly president of CBS News (1964–1966), was the Edward R. Murrow Professor of Journalism at Columbia University.

From *Minnesota Rag* by Fred W. Friendly, copyright © 1981 by Fred W. Friendly and Ruth Friendly. Used by permission of Random House, Inc.

*Robert R. McCormick was an owner and publisher of the *Chicago Tribune* who attacked a host of public officials and took on various crusades.

soldier in the continuing struggle between the powers of government and the power of the press to publish the news.

Near v. *Minnesota* placed freedom of the press "in the least favorable light"; as Minnesota and New York newspapers and lawyers viewed the litigation, it was the worst possible case. But perhaps it is just because Near's cause did not at first appear to be significant, except to Colonel McCormick and Roger Baldwin,* that it created such sturdy law. So indestructible has it proved that its storied progeny, the Pentagon Papers case, was able to survive the political firestorms of 1971. If "great cases like hard cases make bad law," as the [Justice Oliver Wendell] Holmes proverb warns, it may follow that since few knew or cared about Near's cause, freedom of the press was transformed successfully from an eighteenth- and nineteenth-century ideal into a twentieth-century constitutional bulwark.

By his admonition, Holmes meant that volatile national confrontations which appeal to prejudices and distort judgment can be counterproductive in shaping the law of the future. Such emotional conflicts as slavery, as in the Dred Scott decision, and minimum-wage laws, as in *Adkins*, Holmes suggested seventy-seven years ago, "exercise a kind of hydraulic pressure which makes what previously was clear seem doubtful, and before which even well-settled principles of law will bend." In 1931 an American public plagued by economic panic, unemployment, Prohibition and the likes of Al Capone cared little about the civil rights of a scandalmonger from Minnesota. To paraphrase Holmes, Near's case embodied all the underwhelming interests required to shape the grand law of the future. His success was based not in frenzied national debate, but in quirks-of-fate delays in the Minnesota courts, the deaths of two conservative Justices, and Hoover's subsequent appointments.† It was the new Chief Justice who made the difference, not simply because he added one more vote to Near's side, but because of his unexpected passion for the First Amendment and his intellectual capacity to lead others, especially Justice Roberts.

The precedent of *Near* v. *Minnesota* has withstood onslaughts from Presidents, legislatures and even the judiciary itself in its attempts to enforce basic rights which seemed to clash with the First Amendment. It demonstrated the latent strengths for an amendment which had gone untested for 150 years. That five-to-four decision achieved far more than simply asserting Near's rights. . . . It marked the beginning of a concerted process "to plug the holes punched in the Bill of Rights," and what [Baltimore *Sun* writer George] Mencken had called in 1926 "the most noble opportunity that the Supreme Court, in all its history, ever faced." . . .

There have been hundreds of other press cases before the Court since 1931—some won, some lost. Perhaps the seminal judgment was the 1964 decision in *New York Times Co.* v. *Sullivan*, which prevented Southern courts from

---

*Roger Baldwin founded the American Civil Liberties Union.

†Justices William H. Taft and Edward T. Sanford died. President Herbert Hoover appointed Charles E. Hughes and Owen J. Roberts to replace them.

using the law of libel to thwart national news coverage of the civil rights battle. Although not a prior-restraint case, *Sullivan* freed the press from the threat of chilling damages in reporting the conduct of public officials in Alabama in the explosive sixties. Associate Justice William Brennan's majority opinion established that officials, and later public figures, could not recover libel damages for reports concerning their official actions without proving "malice," that is, deliberate lying or "reckless disregard for the truth."

But *Near*'s ultimate legacy was finally realized forty years later, almost to the day, in the clash between the power of the presidency of the United States and two powerful newspapers, the *New York Times* and the *Washington Post*. Its official name was *New York Times Co. v. United States*, but it is remembered as the Pentagon Papers case. It began when the *New York Times* obtained a forty-seven-volume secret history of the Vietnam war from Daniel Ellsberg, a former analyst of the Rand Corporation; it ended with a major victory for the press in the Supreme Court. On June 13, 1971, the *New York Times* began publishing its synopsis and analysis of the secret documents, and two days later the Nixon Administration began legal efforts to restrain it. Later that week the government also sought to enjoin the *Washington Post* from publishing the same classified material. In a "frenzied train of events," as one Justice described it, the cases bobbed back and forth between district and appeals courts until, eleven days later, the Supreme Court agreed to try to untangle the conflicting and confusing opinions.

What dominated all the arguments in all briefs and opinions, from district court to Supreme Court, was the theory of no previous restraint, codified by Blackstone and incorporated by Madison, but made concrete in *Near*.

The Court met hastily on Saturday morning, June 25, and five days later announced its six-to-three decision. Leaning heavily on *Near v. Minnesota*, the Court held that the heavy burden of justifying the imposition of prior restraint had not been met by the government. It required nine opinions for the Supreme Court to explain its votes, and *Near* was cited ten times.

Justice William O. Douglas, in an opinion joined by Justice Hugo Black, quoted long passages from Chief Justice Hughes's majority opinion in *Near*. Believing that the government had no power to punish or restrain "material that is embarrassing to the powers-that-be," Douglas and Black reiterated Hughes's opinion: "The fact that liberty of the press may be abused . . . does not make any less necessary the immunity of the press." But it was Douglas' concluding statement that emphasized the tremendous strength of *Near*: "The stays in these cases that have been in effect for more than a week constitute a flouting of the principles of the First Amendment as interpreted in *Near v. Minnesota*."

Justice Black's language, in an opinion joined by Justice Douglas, also echoed some of the discussion during oral arguments in *Near*:

> Both the history and language of the First Amendment support the view that the press must be left free to publish news, whatever the source, without censorship, injunctions or prior restraints. . . . Only a free and unrestrained press can effectively

expose deception in government. . . . [T]he *New York Times*, the *Washington Post*, and other newspapers should be commended for serving the purpose that the Founding Fathers saw so clearly. In revealing the workings of government that led to the Vietnam War, the newspapers did precisely what the founders hoped and trusted they would do.

Even in the dissents in the Pentagon Papers case, *Near* was ubiquitous. Chief Justice Warren Burger, Justice John Harlan and Justice Harry Blackmun in their dissenting opinions also cited Hughes's exceptions to the prohibitions against prior restraint such as interfering with recruiting during wartime and publishing troopship sailing dates. As in *Near*, the Court's judgment in the Pentagon Papers case did not establish the absolutism of the First Amendment (as some journalists still contend) against *all* prior restraints. Justice Byron White wrote: "I do not say that in no circumstances would the First Amendment permit an injunction against publishing information about government plans and operations."

Although it was the judgment of the divided Court that lifted the prior restraint on the *New York Times*, the *Washington Post* and twenty other newspapers, which were prepared to publish sections of the Pentagon Papers, five sentences by District Court Judge Murray Gurfein endure. It is the kind of quotation Colonel McCormick might have had chiseled in his hall:

> The security of the Nation is not at the ramparts alone. Security also lies in the value of our free institutions. A cantankerous press, an obstinate press, a ubiquitous press must be suffered by those in authority in order to preserve the even greater values of freedom of expression and the right of the people to know. . . . These are troubled times. There is no greater safety valve for discontent and cynicism about the affairs of Government than freedom of expression in any form.

. . . *Near* was a perilously close case, but "a morsel of genuine history," as Jefferson described such events, "a thing so rare as to be always valuable." . . .

Questions for Discussion

1. In light of the ruling in *New York Times Co. v. United States*, can you imagine any circumstances that would justify prior restraint of the press?
2. Does libel law adequately guard against an irresponsible and overaggressive press, or should there be other safeguards, such as an independent review board?

3.3

Gideon v. Wainwright (1963)

Clarence Gideon, an indigent, was accused of breaking and entering a poolroom, a felony under Florida law. He proclaimed his innocence and requested that he be provided with a lawyer. The trial judge refused this request, Gideon was found guilty, and he was sentenced to a five-year term in the state penitentiary. In a handwritten statement Gideon appealed his case to the Supreme Court, which took the case and appointed Abe Fortas, a prominent Washington attorney and later Supreme Court justice, to represent him.

The Supreme Court had frequently ruled in specific circumstances that the Sixth Amendment guaranteed a right to counsel and that this right was incorporated by the Fourteenth Amendment and was thus applicable to the states. Still, before *Gideon* v. *Wainwright* (1963), the Court had not ruled that there was any general right to counsel. Indeed, the governing rule was that of *Betts* v. *Brady,* a 1942 decision that the right to counsel was not a "fundamental" right. The Court's reconsideration of the *Betts* rule after only twenty-one years was unusual.

After the decision in this case, Gideon was retried in Florida, with counsel, and found innocent. Subsequently, thousands of prisoners in Florida and elsewhere won their release on the grounds that they had not been represented by counsel at their trials.

M r. Justice Black delivered the opinion of the Court. . . .
. . . Since 1942, when *Betts* v. *Brady* . . . was decided by a divided Court, the problem of a defendant's federal constitutional right to counsel in a state court has been a continuing source of controversy and litigation in both state and federal courts. To give this problem another review here, we granted certiorari. Since Gideon was proceeding *in forma pauperis,* we appointed counsel to represent him and requested both sides to discuss in their briefs and oral arguments the following: "Should this Court's holding in *Betts* v. *Brady* be reconsidered?" . . .

We think the Court in *Betts* had ample precedent for acknowledging that those guarantees of the Bill of Rights which are fundamental safeguards of liberty immune from federal abridgment are equally protected against state invasion by the Due Process Clause of the Fourteenth Amendment. This same principle was recognized, explained, and applied in *Powell* v. *Alabama* . . . , a case upholding the right of counsel, where the Court held that despite sweeping language to the contrary in *Hurtado* v. *California* . . . , the Fourteenth Amendment "embraced" those " 'fundamental principles of liberty and justice which lie at the base of all our civil and political institutions,' " even though they had been "specifically dealt with in another part of the federal Constitution." . . . In many cases other than *Powell* and *Betts*, this Court has looked to the fundamental nature of original Bill of Rights guarantees to decide whether the Fourteenth Amendment makes them obligatory on the States. . . .

We accept *Betts* v. *Brady's* assumption, based as it was on our prior cases, that a provision of the Bill of Rights which is "fundamental and essential to a fair trial" is made obligatory upon the States by the Fourteenth Amendment. We think the Court in *Betts* was wrong, however, in concluding that the Sixth Amendment's guarantee of counsel is not one of these fundamental rights. Ten years before *Betts* v. *Brady*, this Court, after full consideration of all the historical data examined in *Betts*, had unequivocally declared that "the right to the aid of counsel is of this fundamental character." *Powell* v. *Alabama*. . . . While the Court at the close of its *Powell* opinion did by its language, as this Court frequently does, limit its holding to the particular facts and circumstances of that case, its conclusions about the fundamental nature of the right to counsel are unmistakable. . . .

In light of . . . many other prior decisions of this Court, it is not surprising that the *Betts* Court, when faced with the contention that "one charged with crime, who is unable to obtain counsel, must be furnished counsel by the State," conceded that "[e]xpressions in the opinions of this court lend color to the argument. . . ." The fact is that in deciding as it did—that "appointment of counsel is not a fundamental right, essential to a fair trial"—the Court in *Betts* v. *Brady* made an abrupt break with its own well-considered precedents. In returning to these old precedents, sounder we believe than the new, we but restore constitutional principles established to achieve a fair system of justice. Not only these precedents but also reason and reflection require us to recognize that in our adversary system of criminal justice, any person haled into court, who is too poor to hire a lawyer, cannot be assured a fair trial unless counsel is provided for him. This seems to us to be an obvious truth. Governments, both state and federal, quite properly spend vast sums of money to establish machinery to try defendants accused of crime. Lawyers to prosecute are everywhere deemed essential to protect the public's interest in an orderly society. Similarly, there are few defendants charged with crime, few indeed, who fail to hire the best lawyers they can get to prepare and present their defenses. That government hires lawyers to prosecute and defendants who have the money hire lawyers to defend are the strongest indications of the widespread belief that lawyers in criminal courts are necessities, not luxuries. The right of one charged with crime to counsel may not be deemed fundamental and essential to fair trials in some countries, but it is in ours. From the very beginning, our state and national constitutions and laws have laid great emphasis on procedural and substantive safeguards designed to assure fair trials before impartial tribunals in which every defendant stands equal before the law. This noble ideal cannot be realized if the poor man charged with crime has to face his accusers without a lawyer to assist him. . . . The Court in *Betts* v. *Brady* departed from the sound wisdom upon which the Court's holding in *Powell* v. *Alabama* rested. Florida, supported by two other states, has asked that *Betts* v. *Brady* be left intact. Twenty-two States, as friends of the Court,* argue that *Betts* was "an anachronism when handed down" and that it should now be overruled. We agree.

The judgment is reversed and the cause is remanded to the Supreme Court of Florida for further action not inconsistent with this opinion.

Mr. Justice Harlan, concurring:

I agree that *Betts* v. *Brady* should be overruled, but consider it entitled to a more respectful burial than has been accorded, at least on the part of those of us who were not on the Court when that case was decided.

I cannot subscribe to the view that *Betts* v. *Brady* represented "an abrupt break with its own well-considered precedents." In 1932, in *Powell* v. *Alabama* . . . , a capital case, this Court declared that under the particular facts there presented—"the ignorance and illiteracy of the defendants, their youth, the circumstances of public hostility . . . and above all that they stood in deadly peril of their lives"—the state court had a duty to assign counsel for the trial as a necessary requisite of due process of law. It is evident that these limiting facts were not added to the opinion as an afterthought; they were repeatedly emphasized, and were clearly regarded as important to the result.

Thus when this Court, a decade later, decided *Betts* v. *Brady*, it did no more than to admit of the possible existence of special circumstances in noncapital as well as capital trials, while at the same time insisting that such circumstances be shown in order to establish a denial of due process. The right to appointed counsel had been recognized as being considerably broader in federal prosecutions, see *Johnson* v. *Zerbst* . . . , but to have imposed these requirements on the States would indeed have been "an abrupt break" with the almost immediate past. The declaration that the right to appointed counsel in state prosecutions, as established in *Powell* v. *Alabama*, was not limited to capital cases was in truth not a departure from, but an extension of, existing precedent.

The principles declared in *Powell* and in *Betts*, however, have had a troubled journey throughout the years that have followed first the one case and then the other. Even by the time of the *Betts* decision, dictum in at least one of the Court's opinions had indicated that there was an absolute right to the services

---

*Various organizations and individuals, such as interest groups or state attorneys general, offer *amicus curiae* (friend of the court) briefs on major cases. Since the 1950s, *amicus* briefs as practiced by groups such as the National Association for the Advancement of Colored People (NAACP) and the American Civil Liberties Union (ACLU) have become a major tool for promoting social change.

of counsel in the trial of state capital cases. Such dicta continued to appear in subsequent decisions and any lingering doubts were finally eliminated by the holding of *Hamilton* v. *Alabama*. . . .

In noncapital cases, the "special circumstances" rule has continued to exist in form while its substance has been substantially and steadily eroded. In the first decade after *Betts*, there were cases in which the Court found special circumstances to be lacking, but usually by a sharply divided vote. However, no such decision has been cited to us, and I have found none, after *Quicksall* v. *Michigan* . . . , decided in 1950. At the same time, there have been not a few cases in which special circumstances were found in little or nothing more than the "complexity" of the legal questions presented, although those questions were often of only routine difficulty. The Court has come to recognize, in other words, that the mere existence of serious criminal charge constituted in itself special circumstances requiring the services of counsel at trial. In truth the *Betts* v. *Brady* rule is no longer a reality.

This evolution, however, appears not to have been fully recognized by many state courts, in this instance charged with the front-line responsibility for the enforcement of constitutional rights. To continue a rule which is honored by this Court only with lip service is not a healthy thing and in the long run will do disservice to the federal system.

The special circumstances rule has been formally abandoned in capital cases, and the time has now come when it should be similarly abandoned in noncapital cases, at least as to offenses which, as the one involved here, carry the possibility of a substantial prison sentence. (Whether the rule should extend to *all* criminal cases need not now be decided.) This indeed does no more than to make explicit something that has long since been foreshadowed in our decisions. . . .

Questions for Discussion

1. At what point does having access to counsel become a constitutional right? Is it a right for any felony? What about for a serious misdemeanor?
2. *Gideon* paved the way for the *Miranda* case, which required the police to inform a suspect of his or her constitutional rights, including the right to counsel. Should the police be able to question a suspect without counsel present?
3. Has *Gideon* completely closed the gap between the wealthy and the poor when it comes to obtaining adequate counsel?

3.4

Griswold v. Connecticut (1965)

Since the 1960s, one of the most interesting and controversial fields of constitutional law has involved the alleged right of privacy. The Constitution nowhere explicitly spells out any such right, yet preserving privacy is of paramount concern in an increasingly intrusive society.

One key case (not presented here) is *Roe* v. *Wade* (1973), which declared abortion laws in almost all states unconstitutional. Justice Harry A. Blackmun held that the constitutional right to privacy allowed women to determine whether to go ahead with an abortion, although the rights of the mother were to be balanced against the potential right to life of the fetus (which was not a person in a constitutional sense). *Roe* v. *Wade* set off almost ceaseless attempts by prolife activists to ban abortions. It also became a turning point in the Senate's defeat of Ronald Reagan's Supreme Court nominee, Appeals Court Judge Robert Bork, in 1987.

Griswold v. *Connecticut* (1965) laid the groundwork for *Roe* by giving the right of privacy formal constitutional protection. The decision grew from a challenge to Connecticut's restrictive but rarely enforced birth control laws. Estelle Griswold, executive director of the Planned Parenthood League of Connecticut, was convicted of dispensing birth control information to married people. The Supreme Court overturned the lower court's decision.

M r. Justice Douglas delivered the opinion of the Court. . . .
Coming to the merits, we are met with a wide range of questions that implicate the Due Process Clause of the Fourteenth Amendment. Overtones of some arguments suggest that *Lockner* v. *State of New York . . .* should be our guide. But we decline that invitation. . . . We do not sit as superlegislature to determine the wisdom, need, and propriety of laws that touch economic problems, business affairs, or social conditions. This law, however, operates directly on an intimate relation of husband and wife and their physician's role in one aspect of that relation.

The association of people is not mentioned in the Constitution nor in the Bill of Rights. The right to educate a child in a school of the parents' choice—whether public or private or parochial—is also not mentioned. Nor is the right to study any particular subject or any foreign language. Yet the First Amendment has been construed to include certain of those rights.

By *Pierce* v. *Society of Sisters* . . . , the right to educate one's children as one chooses is made applicable to the States by the force of the First and Fourteenth Amendments. By *Meyer* v. *State of Nebraska* . . . , the same dignity is given the right to study the German language in a private school. In other words, the State may not, consistently with the spirit of the First Amendment, contract the spectrum of available knowledge. The right of freedom of speech and press includes not only the right to utter or to print, but the right to distribute, the right to receive, the right to read (*Martin* v. *City of Struthers* . . .) and freedom of inquiry, freedom of thought, and freedom to teach (see *Wieman* v. *Updegraff* . . .)—indeed the freedom of the entire university community. . . . Without those peripheral rights the specific rights would be less secure. And so we reaffirm the principle of the *Pierce* and the *Meyer* cases.

In *NAACP* v. *State of Alabama* . . . we protected the "freedom to associate and privacy in one's associations," noting that freedom of association was a peripheral First Amendment right. Disclosure of membership lists of a constitutionally valid association, we held, was invalid "as entailing the likelihood of a substantial restraint upon the exercise by petitioner's members of their right to freedom of association." In other words, the First Amendment has a penumbra where privacy is protected from governmental intrusion.* In like context, we have protected forms of "association" that are not political in the customary sense but pertain to the social, legal, and economic benefit of the members. In *Schware* v. *Board of Bar Examiners*, . . . we held it not permissible to bar a lawyer from practice, because he had once been a member of the Communist Party. The man's "association with that Party" was not shown to be "anything more than a political faith in a political party" and was not action of a kind proving bad moral character.

Those cases involved more than the "right of assembly"—a right that extends to all irrespective of their race or ideology. The right of "association," like the right of belief is more than the right to attend a meeting; it includes the right to express one's attitudes or philosophies by membership in a group or by affiliation with it or by other lawful means. Association in that context is a form of expression of opinion; and while it is not expressly included in the First Amendment its existence is necessary in making the express guarantees fully meaningful.

The foregoing cases suggest that specific guarantees in the Bill of Rights have penumbras, formed by emanations from those guarantees that help give them life and substance. Various guarantees create zones of privacy. The right of association contained in the penumbra of the First Amendment is one, as we have seen. The Third Amendment in its prohibition against the quartering of sol-

---

*Justice William O. Douglas developed the analogy to a penumbra, "the partial shadow surrounding a complete shadow (as in an eclipse)." Douglas found a right to privacy in the "penumbras" of the First, Third, Fourth, Fifth, and Ninth Amendments. Most scholars of the Constitution agree that some right to privacy does exist, but the extension of that right is open to debate.

diers "in any house" in time of peace without the consent of the owner is another facet of that privacy. The Fourth Amendment explicitly affirms the "right of the people to be secure in their persons, houses, papers, and effects, against unreasonable searches and seizures." The Fifth Amendment in its Self-Incrimination Clause enables the citizen to create a zone of privacy which government may not force him to surrender to his detriment. The Ninth Amendment provides: "The enumeration in the Constitution, of certain rights, shall not be construed to deny or disparage others retained by the people."

The Fourth and Fifth Amendments were described in *Boyd v. United States* . . . as protection against all governmental invasions "of the sanctity of a man's home and the privacies of life." We recently referred in *Mapp v. Ohio* . . . to the Fourth Amendment as creating a "right to privacy, no less important than any other right carefully and particularly reserved to the people." . . .

The present case, then, concerns a relationship lying within the zone of privacy created by several fundamental constitutional guarantees. And it concerns a law which, in forbidding the use of contraceptives rather than regulating their manufacture or sale, seeks to achieve its goals by means having a maximum destructive impact upon that relationship. Such a law cannot stand in light of the familiar principle, so often applied by this Court, that a "governmental purpose to control or prevent activities constitutionally subject to state regulation may not be achieved by means which sweep unnecessarily broadly and thereby invade the area of protected freedoms." *NAACP v. Alabama.* . . . Would we allow the police to search the sacred precincts of marital bedrooms for telltale signs of the use of contraceptives? The very idea is repulsive to the notions of privacy surrounding the marriage relationship.

We deal with a right to privacy older than the Bill of Rights—older than our political parties, older than our school system. Marriage is a coming together for better or for worse, hopefully enduring, and intimate to the degree of being sacred. It is an association that promotes a way of life, not causes; a harmony in living, not political faiths; a bilateral loyalty, not commercial or social projects. Yet it is an association for as noble a purpose as any involved in our prior decisions.

Mr. Justice Goldberg, whom the Chief Justice and Mr. Justice Brennan join, concurring:

I agree with the Court that Connecticut's birth-control law unconstitutionally intrudes upon the right of marital privacy, and I join in its opinion and judgment. Although I have not accepted the view that "due process" as used in the Fourteenth Amendment includes all of the first eight Amendments . . . I do agree that the concept of liberty protects those personal rights that are fundamental, and is not confined to the specific terms of the Bill of Rights. My conclusion that the concept of liberty is not so restricted and that it embraces the right of marital privacy though that right is not mentioned explicitly in the Constitution is supported both by numerous decisions of this Court, referred to in the Court's opinion, and by the language and history of the Ninth Amendment. In reaching the conclusion that the right of marital privacy is protected, as being within the protected penumbra of specific guarantees of the Bill of Rights, the Court refers to the Ninth Amendment. I add these words to emphasize the relevance of that Amendment to the Court's holding. . . . The Framers did not intend that the first eight amendments be construed to exhaust the basic and fundamental rights which the Constitution guaranteed to the people.

While this Court has had little occasion to interpret the Ninth Amendment "[i]t cannot be presumed that any clause in the constitution is intended to be without effect." *Marbury* v. *Madison.* . . . In interpreting the Constitution, "real effect should be given to all the words it uses." *Myers* v. *United States.* . . . The Ninth Amendment to the Constitution may be regarded by some as a recent discovery but since 1791 it has been a basic part of the Constitution which we are sworn to uphold. To hold that a right so basic and fundamental and so deep-rooted in our society as the right of privacy in marriage may be infringed because that right is not guaranteed in so many words by the first eight amendments to the Constitution is to ignore the Ninth Amendment and to give it no effect whatsoever. Moreover, a judicial construction that this fundamental right is not protected by the Constitution because it is not mentioned in explicit terms by one of the first eight amendments or elsewhere in the Constitution would violate the Ninth Amendment, which specifically states that "[t]he enumeration in the Constitution, of certain rights shall not be *construed* to deny or disparage others retained by the people." (Emphasis added.) . . . [T]he Ninth Amendment simply lends strong support to the view that the "liberty" protected by the Fifth and Fourteenth Amendments from infringement by the Federal Government or the States is not restricted to rights specifically mentioned in the first eight amendments. . . .

In sum, I believe that the right of privacy in the marital relation is fundamental and basic—a personal right "retained by the people" within the meaning of the Ninth Amendment. Connecticut cannot constitutionally abridge this fundamental right, which is protected by the Fourteenth Amendment from infringement by the States. I agree with the Court that petitioners' convictions must therefore be reversed.

Mr. Justice Black, with whom Mr. Justice Stewart joins, dissenting: . . .

The Court talks about a constitutional "right of privacy" as though there is some constitutional provision or provisions forbidding any law ever to be passed which might abridge the "privacy" of individuals. But there is not. . . .

One of the most effective ways of diluting or expanding a constitutionally guaranteed right is to substitute for the crucial word or words of a constitutional guarantee another word or words, more or less flexible and more or less restricted in meaning. This fact is well illustrated by the use of the term "right of privacy" as a comprehensive substitute for the Fourth Amendment's guarantee against "unreasonable searches and seizures." "Privacy" is a broad, abstract and ambiguous concept which can easily be shrunken in meaning but which can also, on the other hand, easily be interpreted as a constitutional ban against many things other than searches and seizures. I have expressed the view many times that First Amendment freedoms, for example, have suffered from a failure of the courts to stick to the simple language of the First Amendment in construing it, instead of invoking multitudes of words substituted for those the Framers used. For these reasons I get nowhere in this case by talk about a constitutional "right of privacy" as an emanation from one or more constitutional provisions. I like my privacy as well as the next one, but I am nevertheless compelled to admit that government has a right to invade it unless prohibited by some specific constitutional provision. For these reasons I cannot agree with the Court's judgment and the reasons it gives for holding this Connecticut law unconstitutional. . . .

My Brother Goldberg has adopted the recent discovery that the Ninth Amendment as well as the Due Process Clause can be used by this Court as authority to strike down all state legislation which this Court thinks violates "fundamental principles of liberty and justice," or is contrary to the "traditions and [collective] conscience of our people." He also states, without proof satisfactory to me, that in making decisions on this basis judges will not consider "their personal and private notions." One may ask how they can avoid considering them. Our Court certainly has no machinery with which to take a Gallup Poll. And the scientific miracles of this age have not yet produced a gadget which the Court can use to determine what traditions are rooted in the "[collective] conscience of our people." Moreover, one would certainly have to look far beyond the language of the Ninth Amendment to find that the Framers vested in this Court any such awesome veto powers over lawmaking, either by the States or by the Congress. Nor does anything in the history of the Amendment offer any support for such a shocking doctrine. The whole history of the adoption of the Constitution and Bill of Rights points the other way, and the very material quoted by my Brother Goldberg shows that the Ninth Amendment was intended to protect against the idea that "by enumerating particular exceptions to the grant of power" to the Federal Government, "those rights which were not singled out, were intended to be assigned into the hands of the General Government [the United States], and were consequently insecure." That Amendment was passed, not to broaden the powers of this Court or any other department of "the General Government," but, as every student of history knows, to assure the people that the Constitution in all its provisions was intended to limit the Federal Government to the powers granted expressly or by necessary implication. If any broad, unlimited power to hold laws unconstitutional because they offend what this Court conceives to be the "[collective] conscience of our people" is vested in this Court by the Ninth Amendment, the Fourteenth Amendment, or any other provision of the Constitution, it was not given by the Framers, but rather has been bestowed on the Court by the Court. This fact is perhaps responsible for the peculiar phenomenon that for a period of a century and a half no serious suggestion was ever made that the Ninth Amendment, enacted to protect state powers against federal invasion, could be used as a weapon of federal power to prevent state legislatures from passing laws they consider appropriate to govern local affairs. Use of any such broad, unbounded judicial authority would make of this Court's members a day-to-day constitutional convention. . . .

Questions for Discussion

1. Can a right be fundamental yet not enumerated in the Constitution?
2. Should the state ever have an interest in the relationships and actions between consenting adults? In what instances?

 3.5

Lawrence and Garner v. Texas (2003)

Although the 1965 *Griswold* decision provided a basis for claiming a constitutional right to privacy, and the 1973 *Roe* v. *Wade* holding built on that foundation, such a "right" remains a matter of contention. In 1986, the Supreme Court ruled, in *Bowers* v. *Hardwick,* that the "Federal Constitution confers [no] fundamental right upon homosexuals to engage in sodomy." Bowing to precedent, the Court rarely reverses itself after only seventeen years, but societal changes and the widespread (though scarcely unanimous) opinion that *Bowers* had been wrongfully decided led the justices to reconsider this decision in 2003. In the decision excerpted here, Justice Anthony Kennedy concludes that the Court failed to "appreciate the extent of the liberty at stake." In other words, it was the privacy to act within a personal relationship that was at stake, not the more limited question of sexual relations. He continues, "When sexuality finds overt expression in intimate conduct with another person, the conduct can be but one element in a personal bond that is more enduring. The liberty provided by the Constitution allows homosexual persons the right to make this choice."

At least three justices, various interests, and many other people disagree with the conclusion reached here. Justice Antonin Scalia's dissent is also excerpted below. In 2004 a movement was undertaken to revisit not only *Roe* and this case, but also to overturn the long-standing decision of *Griswold,* which remains the underpinning of the Court's interpretation of a core right of privacy.

J
ustice Kennedy delivered the opinion of the Court.

Liberty protects the person from unwarranted government intrusions into a dwelling or other private places. In our tradition the State is not omnipresent in the home. And there are other spheres of our lives and existence, outside the home, where the State should not be a dominant presence. Freedom extends beyond spatial bounds. Liberty presumes an autonomy of self that includes freedom of thought, belief, expression, and certain intimate conduct. The instant case involves liberty of the person both in its spatial and more transcendent dimensions.

I

The question before the Court is the validity of a Texas statute making it a crime for two persons of the same sex to engage in certain intimate sexual conduct.

In Houston, Texas, officers of the Harris County Police Department were dispatched to a private residence in response to a reported weapons disturbance. They entered an apartment where one of the petitioners, John Geddes Lawrence, resided. The right of the police to enter does not seem to have been questioned. The officers observed Lawrence and another man, Tyron Garner, engaging in a sexual act. The two petitioners were arrested, held in custody over night, and charged and convicted before a Justice of the Peace.

The complaints described their crime as "deviate sexual intercourse, namely anal sex, with a member of the same sex (man)." The applicable state law is Tex. Penal Code Ann. §21.06(a) (2003). It provides: "A person commits an offense if he engages in deviate sexual intercourse with another individual of the same sex." The statute defines "[d]eviate sexual intercourse" as follows:

> (A) any contact between any part of the genitals of one person and the mouth or anus of another person; or
> (B) the penetration of the genitals or the anus of another person with an object.

§21.01 (1).

The petitioners exercised their right to a trial *de novo* in Harris County Criminal Court. They challenged the statute as a violation of the Equal Protection Clause of the Fourteenth Amendment and of a like provision of the Texas Constitution. Tex. Const., Art. 1, §3a. Those contentions were rejected. The petitioners, having entered a plea of *nolo contendere*, were each fined $200 and assessed court costs of $141.25.

The Court of Appeals for the Texas Fourteenth District considered the petitioners' federal constitutional arguments under both the Equal Protection and Due Process Clauses of the Fourteenth Amendment. After hearing the case en banc the court, in a divided opinion, rejected the constitutional arguments and affirmed the convictions. The majority opinion indicates that the Court of Appeals considered our decision in *Bowers* v. *Hardwick* to be controlling on the federal due process aspect of the case. *Bowers* then being authoritative this was proper. . . .

II

We conclude the case should be resolved by determining whether the petitioners were free as adults to engage in the private conduct in the exercise of their liberty under the Due Process Clause of the Fourteenth Amendment to the Constitution. For this inquiry we deem it necessary to reconsider the Court's holding in *Bowers*. . . .

In *Griswold* the Court invalidated a state law prohibiting the use of drugs or devices of contraception and counseling or aiding and abetting the use of contraceptives. The Court described the protected interest as a right to privacy and placed emphasis on the marriage relation and the protected space of the marital bedroom.

After *Griswold* it was established that the right to make certain decisions regarding sexual conduct extends beyond the marital relationship. In *Eisenstadt* v. *Baird*, the Court invalidated a law prohibiting the distribution of contraceptives to unmarried persons. . . .

> It is true that in *Griswold* the right of privacy in question inhered in the marital relationship. . . . If the right of privacy means anything, it is the right of the *individual*, married or single, to be free from unwarranted governmental intrusion into matters so fundamentally affecting a person as the decision whether to bear or beget a child.

The opinions in *Griswold* and *Eisenstadt* were part of the background for the decision in *Roe* v. *Wade*. As is well known, the case involved a challenge to the Texas law prohibiting abortions, but the laws of other States were affected as well. Although the Court held the woman's rights were not absolute, her right to elect an abortion did have real and substantial protection as an exercise of her liberty under the Due Process Clause. . . .

In *Carey* v. *Population Services Int'l*, the Court confronted a New York law forbidding sale or distribution of contraceptive devices to persons under 16 years of age. Although there was no single opinion for the Court, the law was invalidated. Both *Eisenstadt* and *Carey*, as well as the holding and rationale in *Roe*, confirmed that the reasoning of *Griswold* could not be confined to the protection of rights of married adults. This was the state of the law with respect to some of the most relevant cases when the Court considered *Bowers* v. *Hardwick*. . . .

The Court began its substantive discussion in *Bowers* as follows: "The issue presented is whether the Federal Constitution confers a fundamental right upon homosexuals to engage in sodomy and hence invalidates the laws of the many States that still make such conduct illegal and have done so for a very long time." That statement, we now conclude, discloses the Court's own failure to appreciate the extent of the liberty at stake. To say that the issue in *Bowers* was simply the right to engage in certain sexual conduct demeans the claim the individual put forward, just as it would demean a married couple were it to be said marriage is simply about the right to have sexual intercourse. The laws involved in *Bowers* and here are, to be sure, statutes that purport to do no more than prohibit a particular sexual act. Their penalties and purposes, though, have more far-reaching consequences, touching upon the most private human conduct, sexual behavior, and in the most private of places, the home. The statutes do seek to control a personal relationship that, whether or not entitled to formal recognition in the law, is within the liberty of persons to choose without being punished as criminals. . . .

The policy of punishing consenting adults for private acts was not much discussed in the early legal literature. We can infer that one reason for this was the very private nature of the conduct. Despite the absence of prosecutions, there may have been periods in which there was public criticism of homosexuals as such and an insistence that the criminal laws be enforced to discourage their practices. But far from possessing "ancient roots," American laws targeting same-sex couples did not develop until the last third of the 20th century. The reported decisions concerning the prosecution of consensual, homosexual sodomy between adults for the years 1880–1995 are not always clear in the details, but a significant number involved conduct in a public place.

It was not until the 1970's that any State singled out same-sex relations for criminal prosecution, and only nine States have done so. . . .

In summary, the historical grounds relied upon in *Bowers* are more complex than the majority opinion and the concurring opinion by Chief Justice Burger indicate. Their historical premises are not without doubt and, at the very least, are overstated.

It must be acknowledged, of course, that the Court in *Bowers* was making the broader point that for centuries there have been powerful voices to condemn homosexual conduct as immoral. The condemnation has been shaped by religious beliefs, conceptions of right and acceptable behavior, and respect for the traditional family. For many persons these are not trivial concerns but profound and deep convictions accepted as ethical and moral principles to which they aspire and which thus determine the course of their lives. These considerations do not answer the question before us, however. The issue is whether the majority may use the power of the State to enforce these views on the whole society through operation of the criminal law. "Our obligation is to define the liberty of all, not to mandate our own moral code." *Planned Parenthood of Southeastern Pa. v. Casey.* . . .

In our own constitutional system the deficiencies in *Bowers* became even more apparent in the years following its announcement. The 25 States with laws prohibiting the relevant conduct referenced in the *Bowers* decision are reduced now to 13, of which 4 enforce their laws only against homosexual conduct. In those States where sodomy is still proscribed, whether for same-sex or heterosexual conduct, there is a pattern of nonenforcement with respect to consenting adults acting in private. The State of Texas admitted in 1994 that as of that date it had not prosecuted anyone under those circumstances. . . .

The rationale of *Bowers* does not withstand careful analysis. In his dissenting opinion in *Bowers* Justice Stevens came to these conclusions:

> Our prior cases make two propositions abundantly clear. First, the fact that the governing majority in a State has traditionally viewed a particular practice as immoral is not a sufficient reason for upholding a law prohibiting the practice; neither history nor tradition could save a law prohibiting miscegenation from constitutional attack. Second, individual decisions by married persons, concerning the intimacies of their physical relationship, even when not intended to produce offspring, are a form of "liberty" protected by the Due Process Clause of the Fourteenth Amendment. Moreover, this protection extends to intimate choices by unmarried as well as married persons.

Justice Stevens' analysis, in our view, should have been controlling in *Bowers* and should control here.

Bowers was not correct when it was decided, and it is not correct today. It ought not to remain binding precedent. *Bowers* v. *Hardwick* should be and now is overruled.

The present case does not involve minors. It does not involve persons who might be injured or coerced or who are situated in relationships where consent might not easily be refused. It does not involve public conduct or prostitution. It does not involve whether the government must give formal recognition to any relationship that homosexual persons seek to enter. The case does involve two adults who, with full and mutual consent from each other, engaged in sexual practices common to a homosexual lifestyle. The petitioners are entitled to respect for their private lives. The State cannot demean their existence or control their destiny by making their private sexual conduct a crime. Their right to liberty under the Due Process Clause gives them the full right to engage in their conduct without intervention of the government. "It is a promise of the Constitution that there is a realm of personal liberty which the government may not enter." *Casey.* The Texas statute furthers no legitimate state interest which can justify its intrusion into the personal and private life of the individual.

Had those who drew and ratified the Due Process Clauses of the Fifth Amendment or the Fourteenth Amendment known the components of liberty in its manifold possibilities, they might have been more specific. They did not presume to have this insight. They knew times can blind us to certain truths and later generations can see that laws once thought necessary and proper in fact serve only to oppress. As the Constitution endures, persons in every generation can invoke its principles in their own search for greater freedom.

The judgment of the Court of Appeals for the Texas Fourteenth District is reversed, and the case is remanded for further proceedings not inconsistent with this opinion.

It is so ordered.

Justice Scalia, with whom The Chief Justice and Justice Thomas join, dissenting.

. . . Texas Penal Code Ann. §21.06(a) (2003) undoubtedly imposes constraints on liberty. So do laws prohibiting prostitution, recreational use of heroin, and, for that matter, working more than 60 hours per week in a bakery. But there is no right to "liberty" under the Due Process Clause, though today's opinion repeatedly makes that claim. ("The liberty protected by the Constitution allows homosexual persons the right to make this choice"); ("'These matters . . . are central to the liberty protected by the Fourteenth Amendment'"); ("Their right to liberty under the Due Process Clause gives them the full right to engage in their conduct without intervention of the government"). The Fourteenth Amendment expressly *allows* States to deprive their citizens of "liberty," so long as "*due process of law*" is provided:

> No state shall . . . deprive any person of life, liberty, or property, *without due process of law*." Amdt. 14 (emphasis added).

Our opinions applying the doctrine known as "substantive due process" hold that the Due Process Clause prohibits States from infringing *fundamental* liberty interests, unless the infringement is narrowly tailored to serve a compelling state interest. We have held repeatedly, in cases the Court today does not overrule, that *only* fundamental rights qualify for this so-called "heightened scrutiny" protection—that is, rights which are "'deeply rooted in this Nation's history and tradition.'" All other liberty interests may be abridged or abrogated pursuant to a validly enacted state law if that law is rationally related to a legitimate state interest.

Bowers held, first, that criminal prohibitions of homosexual sodomy are not subject to heightened scrutiny because they do not implicate a "fundamental right" under the Due Process Clause. Noting that "[p]roscriptions against that conduct have ancient roots," that "[s]odomy was a criminal offense at common law and was forbidden by the laws of the original 13 States when they ratified the Bill of Rights," and that many States had retained their bans on sodomy, *Bowers* concluded that a right to engage in homosexual sodomy was not "'deeply rooted in this Nation's history and tradition.'"

The Court today does not overrule this holding. Not once does it describe homosexual sodomy as a "fundamental right" or a "fundamental liberty interest," nor does it subject the Texas statute to strict scrutiny. Instead, having failed to establish that the right to homosexual sodomy is "'deeply rooted in this Nation's history and tradition,'" the Court concludes that the application of Texas's statute to petitioners' conduct fails the rational-basis test, and overrules *Bowers*' holding to the contrary. "The Texas statute furthers no legitimate state interest which can justify its intrusion into the personal and private life of the individual." . . .

Today's opinion is the product of a Court, which is the product of a law-profession culture, that has largely signed on to the so-called homosexual agenda, by which I mean the agenda promoted by some homosexual activists directed at eliminating the moral opprobrium that has traditionally attached to homosexual conduct. I noted in an earlier opinion the fact that the American Association of Law Schools (to which any reputable law school *must* seek to belong) excludes from membership any school that refuses to ban from its job-interview facilities a law firm (no matter how small) that does not wish to hire as a prospective partner a person who openly engages in homosexual conduct.

One of the most revealing statements in today's opinion is the Court's grim warning that the criminalization of homosexual conduct is "an invitation to subject homosexual persons to discrimination both in the public and in the private spheres." It is clear from this that the Court has taken sides in the culture war, departing from its role of assuring, as neutral observer, that the democratic rules of engagement are observed. Many Americans do not want persons who openly engage in homosexual conduct as partners in their business, as scout-masters for their children, as teachers in their children's schools, or as boarders in their home. They view this as protecting themselves and their families from a lifestyle that they believe to be immoral and destructive. The Court views it as "discrimination" which it is the function of our judgments to deter. So imbued is the Court with the law profession's anti-anti-homosexual culture, that it is seemingly unaware that the attitudes of that culture are not obviously "mainstream"; that in most States what the Court calls "discrimination" against those who engage in homosexual acts is perfectly legal; that proposals to ban such "discrimination" under Title VII have repeatedly been rejected by Congress; that in some cases such "discrimination" is *mandated* by federal statute, see 10 U. S. C. §654(b)(1) (mandating discharge from the armed forces of any service member who engages in or intends to engage in homosexual acts); and that in some cases such "discrimination" is a constitutional right.

Let me be clear that I have nothing against homosexuals, or any other group, promoting their agenda through normal democratic means. Social perceptions of sexual and other morality change over time, and every group has the right to persuade its fellow citizens that its view of such matters is the best. That homosexuals have achieved some success in that enterprise is attested to by the fact that Texas is one of the few remaining States that criminalize private, consensual homosexual acts. But persuading one's fellow citizens is one thing, and imposing one's views in absence of democratic majority will is something else. I would no more *require* a State to criminalize homosexual acts—or, for that matter, display *any* moral disapprobation of them—than I would *forbid* it to do so.

What Texas has chosen to do is well within the range of traditional democratic action, and its hand should not be stayed through the invention of a brand-new "constitutional right" by a Court that is impatient of democratic change. It is indeed true that "later generations can see that laws once thought necessary and proper in fact serve only to oppress"; and when that happens, later generations can repeal those laws. But it is the premise of our system that those judgments are to be made by the people, and not imposed by a governing caste that knows best.

One of the benefits of leaving regulation of this matter to the people rather than to the courts is that the people, unlike judges, need not carry things to their logical conclusion. The people may feel that their disapprobation of homosexual conduct is strong enough to disallow homosexual marriage, but not strong enough to criminalize private homosexual acts—and may legislate accordingly. The Court today pretends that it possesses a similar freedom of action, so that that we need not fear judicial imposition of homosexual marriage, as has recently occurred in Canada (in a decision that the Canadian Government has chosen not to appeal). At the end of its opinion—after having laid waste the foundations of our rational-basis jurisprudence—the Court says that the present case "does not involve whether the government must give formal recognition to any relationship that homosexual persons seek to enter." Do not believe it. More illuminating than this bald, unreasoned disclaimer is the progression of thought displayed by an earlier passage in the Court's opinion, which notes the constitutional protections afforded to "personal decisions relating to *marriage*, procreation, contraception, family relationships, child rearing, and education," and then declares that "[p]ersons in a homosexual relationship may seek autonomy for these purposes, just as heterosexual persons do." Today's opinion dismantles the structure of constitutional law that has permitted a distinction to be made between heterosexual and homosexual unions, insofar as formal recognition in marriage is concerned. If moral disapproval of homosexual conduct is "no legitimate state interest" for purposes of proscribing that conduct; and if, as the Court coos (casting aside all pretense of neutrality), "[w]hen sexuality finds overt expression in intimate conduct with another person, the conduct can be but one element in a personal bond that is more enduring"; what justification could there possibly be for denying the benefits of marriage to homosexual couples exercising "[t]he liberty protected by the Constitution"? Surely not the encouragement of procreation, since the sterile and the elderly are allowed to marry. This case "does not involve" the issue of homosexual marriage only if one entertains the belief that principle and logic have nothing to do with the decisions of this Court. Many will hope that, as the Court comfortingly assures us, this is so.

The matters appropriate for this Court's resolution are only three: Texas's prohibition of sodomy neither infringes a "fundamental right" (which the Court does not dispute), nor is unsupported by a rational relation to what the Constitution considers a legitimate state interest, nor denies the equal protection of the laws. I dissent.

Questions for Discussion

1. Conservatives often desire that government not expand its powers to affect the lives of ordinary citizens. Why would they not embrace a "right of privacy" that had achieved constitutional status?
2. How does the decision in this case flow from *Griswold*? Some legislators have suggested that *Griswold* should be overturned. What implications would such a ruling have for this case?

⭐ 3.6

Rights, Liberties, and Security: Recalibrating the Balance after September 11

Stuart Taylor, Jr.

Since the 9/11 terrorist attacks, both governmental officials and the public at large have had to reassess the proper balancing point between two core values—security and liberty. Americans prize freedom and individual liberty, to be sure, but they also understand that, in Harvard Law professor Lawrence Tribe's words, "the Constitution is not a suicide pact." That is, when faced with real dangers to society, the government must restrike the balance between liberty and security. To some extent, this is unexceptionable. We all put up with more inconvenience at airports, and few object when security is tightened at ports or nuclear plants.

At the same time, civil libertarians have grown increasingly uneasy over various data-collecting provisions in the Patriot Act, which contains few limits on federal investigations of "national security" matters, and which would open up various records (such as library checkouts) to scrutiny.

In this article, Stuart Taylor, Jr., calmly assesses the tradeoffs between enhancing security and protecting individual liberties. He rejects alarmism over the loss of rights, relative to the government's need to protect its citizens. Taylor argues that civil libertarians will be better off by welcoming more stringent security measures, which may well prevent another major attack—an event that might produce far more aggressive restraints on Americans' freedoms. No alarmist, Taylor addresses central issues of how a nation can protect itself, while retaining as many liberties as possible.

When dangers increase, liberties shrink. That has been our history, especially in wartime. And today we face dangers without precedent: a mass movement of militant Islamic terrorists who crave martyrdom, hide in shadows, are fanatically bent on slaughtering as many of us as possible and—if they can—using nuclear truck bombs to obliterate New York or Washington or both, without leaving a clue as to the source of the attack.

How can we avert catastrophe and hold down the number of lesser mass murders? Our best hope is to prevent al-Qaida from getting nuclear, biological, or chemical weapons and [smuggling] them into this country. But we need be unlucky only once to fail in that. Ultimately we can hold down our casualties only by finding and locking up (or killing) as many as possible of the hundreds or thousands of possible al-Qaida terrorists whose strategy is to infiltrate our society and avoid attention until they strike.

The urgency of penetrating secret terrorist cells makes it imperative for Congress—and the nation—to undertake a candid, searching, and systematic reassessment of the civil liberties rules that restrict the government's core investigative and detention powers. Robust national debate and deliberate congressional action should replace what has so far been largely ad hoc presidential improvisation. While the USA-PATRIOT Act—no model of careful deliberation—changed many rules for the better (and some for the worse), it did not touch some others that should be changed.*

Carefully crafted new legislation would be good not only for security but also for liberty. Stubborn adherence to the civil liberties status quo would probably damage our most fundamental freedoms far more in the long run than would judicious modifications of rules that are less fundamental. Considered congressional action based on open national debate is more likely to be sensitive to civil liberties and to the Constitution's checks and balances than unilateral expansion of executive power. Courts are more likely to check executive excesses if Congress sets limits for them to enforce. Government agents are more likely to respect civil liberties if freed from rules that create unwarranted obstacles to doing their jobs. And preventing terrorist mass murders is the best way of avoiding a panicky stampede into truly oppressive police statism, in which measures now unthinkable could suddenly become unstoppable. . . .

Stuart Taylor writes a regular column on public affairs, often focusing on legal issues, for *National Journal*.

Stuart Taylor, Jr. "Rights, Liberties, and Security: Recalibrating the Balance after September 11, 2001," *The Brookings Review* 21, no. 1 (Winter 2003): 25–31. Reprinted by permission of The Brookings Institution.

*The Patriot Act was signed into law on October 26, 2001, 45 days after the 9/11 terrorist attacks.

Recalibrating the Liberty-Security Balance

The courts, Congress, the president, and the public have from the beginning of this nation's history demarcated the scope of protected rights "by a weighing of competing interests . . . the public-safety interest and the liberty interest," in the words of Judge Richard A. Posner of the U.S. Court of Appeals for the Seventh Circuit. "The safer the nation feels, the more weight judges will be willing to give to the liberty interest."

During the 1960s and 1970s, the weight on the public safety side of the scales seemed relatively modest. The isolated acts of violence by groups like the Weather Underground and Black Panthers—which had largely run their course by the mid-1970s—were a minor threat compared with our enemies today. Suicide bombers were virtually unheard of. By contrast, the threat to civil liberties posed by broad governmental investigative and detention powers and an imperial presidency had been dramatized by Watergate and by disclosures of such ugly abuses of power as FBI Director J. Edgar Hoover's spying on politicians, his wiretapping and harassment of the Rev. Martin Luther King, Jr., and the government's disruption and harassment of antiwar and radical groups.

To curb such abuses, the Supreme Court, Congress, and the Ford and Carter administrations placed tight limits on law enforcement and intelligence agencies. . . . Congress barred warrantless wiretaps and searches of suspected foreign spies and terrorists—a previously untrammeled presidential power—in the 1978 Foreign Intelligence Surveillance Act. And Edward Levi, President Ford's attorney general, clamped down on domestic surveillance by the FBI.

As a result, today many of the investigative powers that government could use to penetrate al-Qaida cells—surveillance, informants, searches, seizures, wiretaps, arrests, interrogations, detentions—are tightly restricted by a web of laws, judicial precedents, and administrative rules. Stalked in our homeland by the deadliest terrorists in history, we are armed with investigative powers calibrated largely for dealing with drug dealers, bank robbers, burglars, and ordinary murderers. We are also stuck in habits of mind that have not yet fully processed how dangerous our world has become or how ill-prepared our legal regime is to meet the new dangers.

Rethinking Government's Powers

Only a handful of the standard law-enforcement investigative techniques have much chance of penetrating and defanging groups like al-Qaida. The four most promising are: infiltrating them through informants and undercover agents; finding them and learning their plans through surveillance, searches, and wiretapping; detaining them before they can launch terrorist attacks; and interrogating those detained. All but the first (infiltration) are now so tightly restricted by Supreme Court precedents (sometimes by mistaken or debatable readings of them), statutes, and administrative rules as to seriously impede terrorism investigators. Careful new legislation could make these powers more flexible and useful while simultaneously setting boundaries to minimize overuse and abuse.

Searches and Surveillance

The Supreme Court's caselaw involving the Fourth Amendment's ban on "unreasonable searches and seizures" does not distinguish clearly between a routine search for stolen goods or marijuana and a preventive search for a bomb or a vial of anthrax. . . .

Federal agents and local police alike need more specific guidance than the Supreme Court can quickly supply. Congress should provide it, in the form of legislation relaxing for terrorism investigations the restrictions on searching, seizing, and wiretapping, including the undue stringency of the burden of proof to obtain a search warrant in a terrorism investigation.

Search and seizure restrictions were the main (if widely unrecognized) cause of the FBI's famous failure to seek a warrant during the weeks before September 11 to search the computer and other possessions of Zacarias Moussaoui, the alleged "20th hijacker." He had been locked up since August 16, technically for overstaying his visa, based on a tip about his strange behavior at a Minnesota flight school. The FBI had ample reason to suspect that Moussaoui—who has since admitted to being a member of al-Qaida—was a dangerous Islamic militant plotting airline terrorism.

Congressional and journalistic investigations of the Moussaoui episode have focused on the intelligence agencies' failure to put together the Moussaoui evidence with other intelligence reports that should have alerted them that a broad plot to hijack airliners might be afoot. Investigators have virtually ignored the undue stringency of the legal restraints on the government's powers to investigate suspected terrorists. Until these are fixed, they will seriously hobble our intelligence agencies no matter how smart they are.

From the time of FDR until 1978, the government could have searched Moussaoui's possessions without judicial permission, by invoking the president's inherent power to collect intelligence about foreign enemies. But the 1978 Foreign Intelligence Security Act (FISA) barred searches of suspected foreign spies and terrorists unless the attorney general could obtain a warrant from a special national security court (the FISA court). The warrant application has to show not only that the target is a foreign terrorist, but also that he is a member of some international terrorist "group." . . .

[I]t is clear that FISA—even as amended by the USA-PATRIOT Act— would not authorize a warrant in any case in which the FBI cannot tie a suspected foreign terrorist to one or more confederates, whether because his confederates have escaped detection or cannot be identified or because the suspect is a lone wolf.

Congress could strengthen the hand of FBI terrorism investigators by amending FISA to include the commonsense presumption that any foreign terrorist who comes to the United States is probably acting for (or at least inspired by) some international terrorist group. Another option would be to lower the burden of proof from "probable cause" to "reasonable suspicion." A third option—which could be extended to domestic as well as international terrorism investigations—would be to authorize a warrantless "preventive" search or wiretap of anyone the government has reasonable grounds to suspect of preparing or helping others prepare for a terrorist attack. To minimize any temptation for government agents to use this new power in pursuit of ordinary criminal suspects, Congress could prohibit the use in any prosecution unrelated to terrorism of any evidence obtained by such a preventive search or wiretap. . . .

Exaggerated Fear of Big Brother

Proposals to increase the government's wiretapping powers awaken fears of unleashing Orwellian thought police to spy on, harass, blackmail, and smear political dissenters and others. Libertarians point out that most conversations overheard and e-mails intercepted in the war on terrorism will be innocent and that the tappers and buggers will overhear intimacies and embarrassing disclosures that are none of the government's business.

Such concerns argue for taking care to broaden wiretapping and surveillance powers only as much as seems reasonable to prevent terrorist acts. But broader wiretapping authority is not all bad for civil liberties. It is a more accurate and benign method of penetrating terrorist cells than the main alternative, which is planting and recruiting informers—a dangerous, ugly, and unreliable business in which the government is already free to engage without limit. The narrower the government's surveillance powers, the more it will rely on informants. . . .

To keep the specter of Big Brother in perspective, it's worth recalling that the president had unlimited power to wiretap suspected foreign spies and terrorists until 1978 (when FISA was adopted); if this devastated privacy or liberty, hardly anyone noticed. It's also worth noting that despite the government's already-vast power to comb through computerized records of our banking and commercial transactions and much else that we do in the computer age, the vast majority of the people who have seen their privacy or reputations shredded have not been wronged by rogue officials. They have been wronged by media organizations, which do far greater damage to far more people with far less accountability.

Nineteen years ago, in *The Rise of the Computer State*, David Burnham wrote: "The question looms before us: Can the United States continue to flourish and grow in an age when the physical movements, individual purchases, conversations and meetings of every citizen are constantly under surveillance by private companies and government agencies?" It can. It has. And now that the computer state has risen indeed, the threat of being watched by Big Brother or smeared by the FBI seems a lot smaller than the threat of being blown to bits or poisoned by terrorists.

The Case for Coercive Interrogation

. . . We all know the drill. Before asking any questions, FBI agents (and police) must warn the suspect: "You have a right to remain silent." And if the suspect asks for a lawyer, all interrogation must cease until the lawyer arrives (and tells the suspect to keep quiet). This seems impossible to justify when dealing with people suspected of planning mass murder. But it's the law, isn't it?

Actually, it's not the law, though many judges think it is, along with most lawyers, federal agents, police, and cop-show mavens. You do *not* have a right to remain silent. The most persuasive interpretation of the Constitution and the Supreme Court's precedents is that agents and police are free to interrogate any suspect without *Miranda** warnings; to spurn requests for a lawyer; to press hard for answers; and—at least in a terrorism investigation—perhaps even to use hours of interrogation, verbal abuse, isolation, blindfolds, polygraph tests, death-penalty threats, and other forms of psychological coercion short of torture or physical brutality. Maybe even truth serum.

The Fifth Amendment self-incrimination clause says only that no person "shall be compelled in any criminal case to be a witness against himself." The clause prohibits forcing a defendant to testify at his trial and also making him a witness against himself indirectly by using compelled pretrial statements. It does not prohibit compelling a suspect to talk. *Miranda* held only that in determining whether a defendant's statements (and information derived from them) may be used against him at his trial, courts must treat all interrogations of arrested suspects as inherently coercive unless the warnings are given. . . .

Fortunately for terrorism investigators, the Supreme Court said in 1990 that "a constitutional violation [of the Fifth Amendment's self-incrimination clause] occurs only at trial." It cited an earlier ruling that the government can obtain court orders compelling reluctant witnesses to talk and can imprison them for contempt of court if they refuse, if it first guarantees them immunity from prosecution on the basis of their statements or any derivative evidence. These decisions support the conclusion that the self-incrimination clause "does not forbid the forcible extraction of information but only the use of informa-

---

*In 1963, Ernesto Miranda was accused of kidnapping and rape. He subsequently confessed, but was not informed of his right to counsel. The Supreme Court ruled his conviction unconstitutional in 1966, but the circumstances of receiving a *Miranda* warning remain under scrutiny by the Supreme Court in the post-2000 era.

tion so extracted as evidence in a criminal case," as a federal appeals court ruled in 1992.

Of course, even when the primary reason for questioning a suspected terrorist is prevention, the government could pay a heavy cost for ignoring *Miranda* and using coercive interrogation techniques, because it would sometimes find it difficult or impossible to prosecute extremely dangerous terrorists. But terrorism investigators may be able to get their evidence and use it too, if the Court—or Congress, which unlike the Court would not have to wait for a proper case to come along—extends a 1984 precedent creating what the justices called a "public safety" exception to *Miranda*. That decision allowed use at trial of a defendant's incriminating answer to a policeman's demand (before any *Miranda* warnings) to know where his gun was hidden. . . .

Congress should neither wait for the justices to clarify the law nor assume that they will reach the right conclusions without prodding. It should make the rules as clear as possible as soon as possible. Officials . . . need to know that they are free to interrogate suspected terrorists more aggressively than they suppose. While a law expanding the public safety exception to *Miranda* would be challenged as unconstitutional, it would contradict no existing Supreme Court precedent and—if carefully calibrated to apply only when the immediate purpose is to save lives—would probably be upheld. . . .

Bringing Preventive Detention Inside the Law

Of all the erosions of civil liberties that must be considered after September 11, preventive detention—incarcerating people because of their perceived dangerousness even when they are neither convicted nor charged with any crime—would represent the sharpest departure from centuries of Anglo-American jurisprudence and come closest to police statism.

But the case for some kind of preventive detention has never been as strong. Al-Qaida's capacity to inflict catastrophic carnage dwarfs any previous domestic security threat. Its "sleeper" agents are trained to avoid criminal activities that might arouse suspicion. So the careful ones cannot be arrested on criminal charges until it is too late. And their lust for martyrdom renders criminal punishment ineffective as a deterrent. . . .

What should the government do when it is convinced of a suspect's terrorist intent but lacks admissible evidence of any crime? Or when a criminal trial would blow vital intelligence secrets? Or when ambiguous evidence makes it a tossup whether a suspect is harmless or an al-Qaidan? What should it do with suspects like Jose Padilla, who was arrested in Chicago and is now in military detention because he is suspected of (but not charged with) plotting a radioactive "dirty-bomb" attack on Washington, D.C.? Or with a (hypothetical) Pakistani graduate student in chemistry, otherwise unremarkable, who has downloaded articles about how terrorists might use small planes to start an anthrax epidemic and shown an intense but unexplained interest in cropdusters?

Only four options exist. Let such suspects go about their business unmonitored until (perhaps) they commit mass murders; assign agents to tail them until (perhaps) they give the agents the slip; bring prosecutions without solid evidence and risk acquittals; and preventive detention. The latter could theoretically include not only incarceration but milder restraints such as house arrest or restriction to certain areas combined with agreement to carry (or to be implanted with) a device enabling the government to track the suspect's movements at all times. . . .

As Alan Dershowitz notes, "[N]o civilized nation confronting serious danger has ever relied exclusively on criminal convictions for past offenses. Every country has introduced, by one means or another, a system of preventive or administrative detention for persons who are thought to be dangerous but who might not be convictable under the conventional criminal law." . . .

[T]he dangers of punishing dissident speech, guilt by association, and overuse of preventive detention could be controlled by careful legislation. This would not be the first exception to the general rule against preventive detention. The others have worked fairly well. They include pretrial detention without bail of criminal defendants found to be dangerous, civil commitment of people found dangerous by reason of mental illness, and medical quarantines, a practice that may once again be necessary in the event of bioterrorism. All in all, the danger that a preventive detention regime for suspected terrorists would take us too far down the slippery slope toward police statism is simply not as bad as the danger of letting would-be mass murderers roam the country.

In any event, we already have a preventive detention regime for suspected international terrorists—three regimes, in fact, all created and controlled by the Bush administration without congressional input. First, two U.S. citizens—Jose Padilla, the suspected would-be dirty bomber arrested in Chicago, and Yaser Esam Hamdi, a Louisiana-born Saudi Arabian captured in Afghanistan and taken first to Guantanamo—have been in military brigs in this country for many months without being charged with any crime or allowed to see any lawyer or any judge. The administration claims that it never has to prove anything to anyone. It says that even U.S. citizens arrested in this country—who may have far stronger grounds than battlefield detainees for denying that they are enemy combatants—are entitled to no due process whatever once the government puts that label on them. This argument is virtually unprecedented, wrong as a matter of law, and indefensible as a matter of policy.

Second, Attorney General John Ashcroft rounded up more than 1,100 mostly Muslim noncitizens in the fall of 2001, which involved preventive detention in many cases although they were charged with immigration violations or crimes (mostly minor) or held under the material witness statute. This when-in-doubt-detain approach effectively reversed the presumption of innocence in the hope of disrupting any planned followup attacks. We may never know whether it succeeded in this vital objective. But the legal and moral bases for holding hundreds of apparently harmless detainees, sometimes without access to legal counsel, in conditions of unprecedented secrecy, seemed less and less plausible as weeks and months went by. Worse, the administration treated many (if not most) of the detainees shabbily and some abusively. (By mid-2002, the vast majority had been deported or released.)

Third, the Pentagon has incarcerated hundreds of Arab and other prisoners captured in Afghanistan at Guantanamo, apparently to avoid the jurisdiction of all courts—and has refused to create a fair, credible process for determining which are in fact enemy combatants and which of those are "unlawful."

These three regimes have been implemented with little regard for the law, for the rights of the many (mostly former) detainees who are probably innocent, or for international opinion. It is time for Congress to step in—to authorize a regime of temporary preventive detention for suspected international terrorists, while circumscribing that regime and specifying strong safeguards against abuse.

Civil Liberties for a New Era

It is senseless to adhere to overly broad restrictions imposed by decades-old civil-liberties rules when confronting the threat of unprecedented carnage at the hands of modern terrorists. In the words of Harvard Law School's Laurence H. Tribe, "The old adage that it is better to free 100 guilty men than to imprison one innocent describes a calculus that our Constitution—which is no suicide pact—does not impose on government when the 100 who are freed belong to terrorist cells that slaughter innocent civilians, and may well have access to chemical, biological, or nuclear weapons." The question is not whether we should increase governmental power to meet such dangers. The question is how much.

Questions for Discussion

1. Should the rules for pursuing terrorists be different from those for pursuing drug dealers or bank robbers? Why or why not? What are the dangers in taking a more aggressive approach, even when it may be essential?
2. Taylor advocates the limited use of "preventive detention" for suspected international terrorists. Can this extreme measure be squared with the ordinary constitutional guarantees of a speedy trial, due process, and protection against self-incrimination?

3.7

Brown v. Board of Education (1954; 1955)

No single contemporary court case has had more widespread impact than *Brown* v. *Board of Education* (1954; 1955). The 1954 case consolidated four suits, from Kansas, South Carolina, Virginia, and Delaware; each state mandated the separate schooling of children by race. The lead case was brought by Oliver Brown, whose daughter Linda attended an all-black school twenty-one blocks from her Topeka home, each day passing by an all-white school five blocks away. In *Brown,* the Court unanimously ruled that such legalized practices were unconstitutional.

The 1954 decision promised so much social change that the justice reheard the case a year later to consider how it should be implemented. In the process, Chief Justice Earl Warren coined the ambiguous phrase "with all deliberate speed" to describe how desegregation should be ended. Warren was sensitive to the fact that the Court cannot easily enforce its decisions, especially when they are controversial and require substantial changes in both laws and patterns of behavior.

1954

Mr. Chief Justice Warren delivered the opinion of the Court.

These cases come to us from the States of Kansas, South Carolina, Virginia, and Delaware. They are premised on different facts and different local conditions, but a common legal question justifies their consideration together in this consolidated opinion.

In each of the cases, minors of the Negro race, through their legal representatives, seek the aid of the courts in obtaining admission to the public schools of their community on a nonsegregated basis. In each instance, they had been denied admission to schools attended by white children under laws requiring or permitting segregation according to race. This segregation was alleged to deprive the plaintiffs of the equal protection of the laws under the Fourteenth Amendment. In each of the cases other than the Delaware case, a three-judge federal district court denied relief to the plaintiffs on the so-called "separate but equal" doctrine announced by this Court in *Plessy* v. *Ferguson*. . . . Under that

doctrine, equality of treatment is accorded when the races are provided substantially equal facilities even though these facilities be separate. In the
Delaware case, the Supreme Court of Delaware adhered to that doctrine, but
ordered that the plaintiffs be admitted to the white schools because of their superiority to the Negro schools.

The plaintiffs contend that segregated public schools are not "equal" and
cannot be made "equal," and that hence they are deprived of the equal protection of the laws. Because of the obvious importance of the question presented,
the Court took jurisdiction. Argument was heard in the 1952 Term, and reargument was heard this Term on certain questions propounded by the Court.

Reargument was largely devoted to the circumstances surrounding the adoption of the Fourteenth Amendment in 1868. It covered exhaustively consideration of the Amendment in Congress, ratification by the states, then existing
practices in racial segregation, and the views of proponents and opponents of
the Amendment. This discussion and our own investigation convince us that,
although these sources cast some light, it is not enough to resolve the problem
with which we are faced. At best, they are inconclusive. The most avid proponents of the post-War Amendments undoubtedly intended them to remove all
legal distinctions among "all persons born or naturalized in the United States."
Their opponents, just as certainly were antagonistic to both the letter and the
spirit of the Amendments and wished them to have the most limited effect.
What others in Congress and the state legislatures had in mind cannot be determined with any degree of certainty.

An additional reason for the inconclusive nature of the Amendment's history, with respect to segregated schools, is the status of public education at that
time. In the South, the movement toward free common schools, supported by
general taxation, had not yet taken hold. Education of white children was
largely in the hands of private groups. Education of Negroes was almost nonex-
istent, and practically all of the race were illiterate. In fact, any education of
Negroes was forbidden by law in some states. Today, in contrast, many Negroes
have achieved outstanding success in the arts and sciences as well as in the
business and professional world. It is true that public education had already advanced further in the North, but the effect of the Amendment on Northern
States was generally ignored in the congressional debates. Even in the North,
the conditions of public education did not approximate those existing today.
The curriculum was usually rudimentary; ungraded schools were common in
rural areas; the school term was but three months a year in many states; and
compulsory school attendance was virtually unknown. As a consequence, it is
not surprising that there should be so little in the history of the Fourteenth
Amendment relating to its intended effect on public education.

In the first cases in this Court construing the Fourteenth Amendment, decided shortly after its adoption, the Court interpreted it as proscribing all state-
imposed discriminations against the Negro race. The doctrine of "separate but
equal" did not make its appearance in this court until 1896 in the case of *Plessy*

v. Ferguson, supra, involving not education but transportation. American courts have since labored with the doctrine for over half a century. In this Court, there have been six cases involving the "separate but equal" doctrine in the field of public education. In *Cumming v. County Board of Education* . . . and *Gong Lum v. Rice* . . . , the validity of the doctrine itself was not challenged. In more recent cases, all on the graduate school level, inequality was found in that specific benefits enjoyed by white students were denied to Negro students of the same educational qualifications. *Missouri* ex rel. *Gaines v. Canada; Sipuel v. Oklahoma; Sweatt v. Painter; McLaurin v. Oklahoma State Regents.* In none of these cases was it necessary to reexamine the doctrine to grant relief to the Negro plaintiff. And in *Sweatt v. Painter, supra,* the Court expressly reserved decision on the question whether *Plessy v. Ferguson* should be held inapplicable to public education.

In the instant cases, that question is directly presented. Here, unlike *Sweatt v. Painter,* there are findings below that the Negro and white schools involved have been equalized, or are being equalized, with respect to buildings, curricula, qualifications and salaries of teachers, and other "tangible" factors. Our decision, therefore, cannot turn on merely a comparison of these tangible factors in the Negro and white schools involved in each of the cases. We must look instead to the effect of segregation itself on public education.

In approaching this problem, we cannot turn the clock back to 1868 when the Amendment was adopted, or even to 1896 when *Plessy v. Ferguson* was written. We must consider public education in the light of its full development and its present place in American life throughout the Nation. Only in this way can it be determined if segregation in public schools deprives these plaintiffs of the equal protection of the laws.

Today, education is perhaps the most important function of state and local governments. Compulsory school attendance laws and the great expenditures for education both demonstrate our recognition of the importance of education to our democratic society. It is required in the performance of our most basic public responsibilities, even service in the armed forces. It is the very foundation of good citizenship. Today it is a principal instrument in awakening the child to cultural values, in preparing him for later professional training, and in helping him to adjust normally to his environment. In these days, it is doubtful that any child may reasonably be expected to succeed in life if he is denied the opportunity of an education. Such an opportunity, where the state has undertaken to provide it, is a right which must be made available to all on equal terms.

We come then to the question presented: Does segregation of children in public schools solely on the basis of race, even though the physical facilities and other "tangible" factors may be equal, deprive the children of the minority group of equal educational opportunities? We believe that it does.

In *Sweatt v. Painter, supra,* in finding that a segregated law school for Negroes could not provide them equal educational opportunities, this Court relied in large part on "those qualities which are incapable of objective measurement but which make for greatness in a law school." In *McLaurin v. Oklahoma State*

Regents, supra, the Court, in requiring that a Negro admitted to a white graduate school be treated like all other students, again resorted to intangible considerations: ". . . his ability to study, to engage in discussions and exchange views with other students, and, in general, to learn his profession." Such considerations apply with added force to children in grade and high schools. To separate them from others of similar age and qualifications solely because of their race generates a feeling of inferiority as to their status in the community that may affect their hearts and minds in a way unlikely ever to be undone. The effect of this separation on their educational opportunities was well stated by a finding in the Kansas case by a court which nevertheless felt compelled to rule against the Negro plaintiffs:

> Segregation of white and colored children in public schools has a detrimental effect upon the colored children. The impact is greater when it has the sanction of the law; for the policy of separating the races is usually interpreted as denoting the inferiority of the Negro group. A sense of inferiority affects the motivation of a child to learn. Segregation with the sanction of law, therefore, has a tendency to retard the educational and mental development of Negro children and to deprive them of some of the benefits they would receive in a racially integrated school system.

Whatever may have been the extent of psychological knowledge* at the time of *Plessy* v. *Ferguson,* this finding is amply supported by modern authority. Any language in *Plessy* v. *Ferguson* contrary to this finding is rejected.

We conclude that in the field of public education the doctrine of "separate but equal" has no place. Separate educational facilities are inherently unequal. Therefore, we hold that the plaintiffs and others similarly situated for whom the actions have been brought are, by reason of the segregation complained of, deprived of the equal protection of the laws guaranteed by the Fourteenth Amendment. This disposition makes unnecessary any discussion whether such segregation also violates the Due Process Clause of the Fourteenth Amendment.

Because these are class actions, because of the wide applicability of this decision, and because of the great variety of local conditions, the formulation of decrees in these cases presents problems of considerable complexity. On reargument, the consideration of appropriate relief was necessarily subordinated to the primary question—the constitutionality of segregation in public education. We have now announced that such segregation is a denial of the equal protection of the laws. In order that we may have the full assistance of the parties in formulating decrees, the cases will be restored to the docket, and the parties are requested to present further argument. . . .

---

*The decision in *Brown* v. *Board of Education* was justified in part on psychological and sociological grounds. This line of argument helped Chief Justice Warren obtain a unanimous decision, but it did not provide the strongest legal foundation for attacking desegregation.

1955

Mr. Chief Justice Warren delivered the opinion of the Court.

These cases were decided on May 17, 1954. The opinions of that date, declaring the fundamental principle that racial discrimination in public education is unconstitutional, are incorporated herein by reference. All provisions of federal, state, or local law requiring or permitting such discrimination must yield to this principle. There remains for consideration the manner in which relief is to be accorded.

Because these cases arose under different local conditions and their disposition will involve a variety of local problems, we requested further argument on the question of relief. In view of the nationwide importance of the decision, we invited the Attorney General of the United States and the Attorneys General of all states requiring or permitting racial discrimination in public education to present their views on that question. The parties, the United States, and the States of Florida, North Carolina, Arkansas, Oklahoma, Maryland, and Texas filed briefs and participated in the oral argument.

These presentations were informative and helpful to the Court in its consideration of the complexities arising from the transition to a system of public education freed of racial discrimination. The presentations also demonstrated that substantial steps to eliminate racial discrimination in public schools have already been taken, not only in some of the communities in which these cases arose but in some of the states appearing as *amici curiae*, and in other states as well. Substantial progress has been made in the District of Columbia and in the communities in Kansas and Delaware involved in this litigation. The defendants in the cases coming to us from South Carolina and Virginia are awaiting the decision of this Court concerning relief.

Full implementation of these constitutional principles may require solution of varied local school problems. School authorities have the primary responsibility for elucidating, assessing, and solving these problems; courts will have to consider whether the action of school authorities constitutes good faith implementation of the governing constitutional principles. Because of their proximity to local conditions and the possible need for further hearings, the courts which originally heard these cases can best perform this judicial appraisal.* Accordingly, we believe it appropriate to remand the cases to those courts.

In fashioning and effectuating the decrees, the courts will be guided by equitable principles. Traditionally, equity has been characterized by a practical flexibility in shaping its remedies and by a facility for adjusting and reconciling public and private needs. These cases call for the exercise of these traditional attributes of equity power. At stake is the personal interest of the plaintiffs in admission to public schools as soon as practicable on a non-discriminatory basis. To effectuate this interest may call for elimination of a variety of obstacles

---

*The emphasis on local interpretation of the Court's decision makes sense, but it allowed for great variation in implementation well into the 1970s.

in making the transition to school systems operated in accordance with the constitutional principles set forth in our May 17, 1954, decision. Courts of equity may properly take into account the public interest in the elimination of such obstacles in a systematic and effective manner. But it should go without saying that the vitality of these constitutional principles cannot be allowed to yield simply because of disagreement with them.

While giving weight to these public and private considerations, the courts will require that the defendants make a prompt and reasonable start toward full compliance with our May 17, 1954, ruling. Once such a start has been made, the courts may find that additional time is necessary to carry out the ruling in an effective manner. The burden rests upon the defendants to establish that such time is necessary in the public interest and is consistent with good faith compliance at the earliest practicable date. To that end, the courts may consider problems related to administration, arising from the physical condition of the school plant, the school transportation system, personnel, revision of school districts and attendance areas into compact units to achieve a system of determining admission to the public schools on a nonracial basis, and revision of local laws and regulations which may be necessary in solving the foregoing problems. They will also consider the adequacy of any plans the defendants may propose to meet these problems and to effectuate a transition to a racially nondiscriminatory school system. During this period of transition, the courts will retain jurisdiction of these cases.

The judgments below, except that in the Delaware case, are accordingly reversed and the cases are remanded to the District Courts to take such proceedings and enter such orders and decrees consistent with this opinion as are necessary and proper to admit to public schools on a racially nondiscriminatory basis with all deliberate speed the parties to these cases. The judgment in the Delaware case—ordering the immediate admission of the plaintiffs to schools previously attended only by white children—is affirmed on the basis of the principles stated in our May 17, 1954, opinion, but the case is remanded to the Supreme Court of Delaware for such further proceedings as that Court may deem necessary in light of this opinion.

Questions for Discussion

1. What is wrong with the idea of "separate but equal" facilities? Could this notion ever have some merit?
2. Could the Court have speeded the process of desegregation by handing down a more detailed ruling on how the *Brown* decision was to be implemented? What kinds of problems would such a ruling have faced?
3. *Brown* v. *Board of Education* concerned legal (*de jure*) desegregation. Have the courts been as capable of dealing with segregation in practice (*de facto*), such as that produced by housing patterns? Why or why not?

Affirmative Action: Don't Mend It or End It—Bend It

Peter H. Schuck

Since the mid-1970s, no civil rights issue has generated more heat and light within the American public than that of "affirmative action." In the wake of *Brown v. Board of Education* and the civil rights legislation of the 1960s, many activists came to believe that racial equality could result only from some "affirmative" assistance that would help minorities climb the educational and vocational ladders of opportunity in the United States. Conversely, opponents of affirmative action argued that such a policy explicitly violated the vision of a color-blind, nondiscriminatory society that stood at the heart of the civil rights movement of the 1950s and 1960s.

Peter Schuck's article comes to the affirmative action debate at a very mature stage. That is, the Supreme Court limited affirmative action with its 1978 *Bakke* decision that ruled numerical quotas (for medical school admission) unconstitutional. Subsequently, the Court has walked a fine line in limiting affirmative action in some employment cases, but allowing it as a consideration in admissions to some university programs (see the interpretation of the 2003 University of Michigan cases in selection 3.9).

Schuck argues that there may be a place for affirmative action, but that place is not embedded in laws and regulations. Indeed, he embraces the principle of "nondiscrimination" for all public institutions, although he does not tease out all of its implications (for instance, should a large university care only about academic records, and not about one's ability to shoot a basketball, play the flute, or write for a newspaper?). At the same time, he would encourage private entities, such as Notre Dame or Stanford, to engage in affirmative action practices, as long as they clearly stated their intent. Given that most universities accept federal funds (and thus fall under federal rules on discrimination), this solution is problematic. Still, Schuck provides a thoughtful approach to a thorny problem.

Peter H. Schuck is professor of law at Yale University and New York University.

Peter H. Schuck, "Affirmative Action: Don't Mend It or End It—Bend It," *The Brookings Review* 20, no. 1 (Winter 2002): 24–27. Reprinted by permission of The Brookings Institution.

Affirmative action policy—by which I mean ethno-racial preferences in the allocation of socially valuable resources—is even more divisive and unsettled today than at its inception more than 30 years ago.

Affirmative action's policy context has changed dramatically since 1970. One change is legal. Since the Supreme Court's 1978 *Bakke* decision, when Justice Lewis Powell's pivotal fifth vote endorsed certain "diversity"-based preferences in higher education, the Court has made it increasingly difficult for affirmative action plans to pass constitutional muster unless they are carefully designed to remedy specific past acts of discrimination. Four other changes— the triumph of the nondiscrimination principle; blacks' large social gains; evidence on the size, beneficiaries, and consequences of preferences; and new demographic realities—persuade me that affirmative action as we know it should be abandoned even if it is held to be constitutional.

"As we know it" is the essential qualifier in that sentence. I propose neither a wholesale ban on affirmative action ("ending" it) nor tweaks in its administration ("mending" it). Rather, I would make two structural changes to curtail existing preferences while strengthening the remaining ones' claim to justice. First, affirmative action would be banned in the public sector but allowed in the private sector. Second, private-sector institutions that use preferences would be required to disclose how and why they do so. These reforms would allow the use of preferences by private institutions that believe in them enough to disclose and defend them, while doing away with the obfuscation, duplicity, and lack of accountability that too often accompany preferences. Affirmative action could thus be localized and customized to suit the varying requirements of particular contexts and sponsors.

Triumph of the Nondiscrimination Principle

Why is change necessary? To explain, one must at the outset distinguish affirmative action entailing preferences from nondiscrimination, a principle that simply requires one to refrain from treating people differently because of their race, ethnicity, or other protected characteristics. Although this distinction can blur at the edges, it is clear and vital both in politics and in principle.

When affirmative action became federal policy in the late 1960s, the nondiscrimination principle, though fragile, was gaining strength. Preferences, by contrast, were flatly rejected by civil rights leaders like Hubert Humphrey, Ted Kennedy, and Martin Luther King, Jr. In the three decades that followed, more and more Americans came to embrace nondiscrimination and to oppose affirmative action, yet . . . federal bureaucrats extended affirmative action with little public notice or debate. Today, nondiscrimination, or equal opportunity, is a principle questioned by only a few bigots and extreme libertarians, and civil rights law is far-reaching and remedially robust. In contrast, affirmative action is widely seen as a demand for favoritism or even equal outcomes.

Social Gains by Blacks

Blacks, the intended beneficiaries of affirmative action, are no longer the insular minority they were in the 1960s. Harvard sociologist Orlando Patterson shows their "astonishing" progress on almost every front. "A mere 13% of the population," he notes, "Afro-Americans dominate the nation's popular culture. . . . [A]t least 35 percent of Afro-American adult, male workers are solidly middle class." The income of young, intact black families approaches that of demographically similar whites. On almost every other social index (residential integration is a laggard), the black-white gap is narrowing significantly; indeed, the income gap for young black women has disappeared.

Even these comparisons understate black progress. Much of racism's cruel legacy is permanently impounded in the low education and income levels of older blacks who grew up under Jim Crow; their economic disadvantages pull down the averages, obscuring the gains of their far better-educated children and grandchildren. These gains, moreover, have coincided with the arrival of record numbers of immigrants who are competing with blacks. To ignore this factor, economist Robert Lerner says, is like analyzing inequality trends in Germany since 1990 without noting that it had absorbed an entire impoverished country, East Germany. In addition, comparisons that fail to age-adjust social statistics obscure the fact that blacks, whose average age is much lower than that of whites, are less likely to have reached their peak earning years.

My point, emphatically, is not that blacks have achieved social equality—far from it—but that the situation facing them today is altogether different than it was when affirmative action was adopted. . . .

Size, Beneficiaries, and Consequences of Preferences

When we weigh competing claims for scarce resources—jobs, admission to higher education, public and private contracts, broadcast or other spectrum licenses, credit, housing, and the like—how heavy is the thumb that affirmative action places on the scales? This is a crucial question. The larger the preference, the more it conflicts with competing interests and values, especially the ideal of merit—almost regardless of how one defines merit.

The best data concern higher education admissions where (for better or for worse) schools commonly use standardized test scores as a proxy for aptitude, preparation, and achievement. William Bowen and Derek Bok, the former presidents of Princeton and Harvard, published a study in 1999 based largely on the academic records of more than 80,000 students who entered 28 highly selective institutions in three different years. Affirmative action, they claimed, only applies to these institutions, although a more recent study suggests that the practice now extends to some second- and even third-tier schools.

Selective institutions, of course, take other factors into account besides race. Indeed, some whites who are admitted have worse academic credentials than the blacks admitted under preferences. Still, Bowen and Bok find a difference of almost 200 points in the average SAT scores of the black and white applicants, and even this understates the group difference. First, the deficit for black applicants' high school grade point average (GPA), the other main admission criterion, is even larger. Thomas Kane finds that black applicants to selective schools "enjoy an advantage equivalent to an increase of two-thirds of a point in [GPA]—on a four-point scale—or [the equivalent of] 400 points on the SAT." Second, although the SAT is often criticized as culturally biased against blacks, SAT (and GPA) scores at every level actually overpredict their college performance. Third, the odds were approximately even that black applicants with scores between 1100 and 1199 would be admitted, whereas the odds for whites did not reach that level until they had scores in the 1450–1499 range. With a score of 1500 or above, more than a third of whites were rejected while every single black gained admission. The University of Michigan . . . weighs race even more heavily than the average school in the Bowen and Bok sample.* At Michigan, being black, Hispanic, or Native American gives one the equivalent of a full point of GPA; minority status can override any SAT score deficit. And a recent study of 47 public institutions found that the odds of a black student being admitted compared to a white student with the same SAT and GPA were 173 to 1 at Michigan and 177 to 1 at North-Carolina State.

These preferences, then, are not merely tie-breakers; they are huge. . . .

How much of blacks' impressive gains is due to reduced discrimination resulting from changing white attitudes and civil rights enforcement, as distinct from preferences? How would they have fared had they attended the somewhat less prestigious schools they could have attended without preferences? What would the demographics of higher education be without those preferences? We cannot answer these vital questions conclusively. We know that black gains were substantial even before preferences were adopted, that preference beneficiaries are overwhelmingly from middle- and upper-class families, and that most black leaders in all walks of life did not go to elite universities. We also know that many institutions are so committed to affirmative action that they will find ways to prefer favored groups—, legacies, athletes, and others—no matter what the formal rules say. . . .

New Demographic Realities

The moral case for affirmative action rests on the bitter legacy of black slavery, Jim Crow, and the violent dispossession of Native Americans. Yet the descendants of slaves and Native Americans constitute a shrinking share of affirma-

---

*The Supreme Court ruled these standards unconstitutional. (See Selection 3.9.)

tive action's beneficiaries. Political logrolling has extended preferential treatment to the largest immigrant group, Hispanics, as well as to blacks from
Africa, the Caribbean, and elsewhere, Asians and Pacific Islanders, and in
some programs to women, a majority group.

Some affirmative action advocates acknowledge this problem and want to fix
it. Orlando Patterson, for example, would exclude "first-generation persons of
African ancestry" but not "their children and later generations—in light of the
persistence of racist discrimination in America." He would also exclude all Hispanics except for Puerto Ricans and Mexican Americans of second or later
generations and would exclude "all Asians except Chinese-Americans descended from pre-1923 immigrants. . . ." With due respect for Patterson's path-
breaking work on race, his formula resembles a tax code provision governing
depreciation expenses more than a workable formula for promoting social
justice.

Centuries of immigration and intermarriage have rendered the conventional
racial categories ever more meaningless. The number of Americans who consider themselves multiracial and who wish to be identified as such (if they must
be racially identified at all) was 7 million in the 2000 census, including nearly
2 million blacks (5 percent of the black population) and 37 percent of all Native Americans. This is why advocacy groups who are desperate to retain the
demographic status quo lobbied furiously to preempt a multiracial category.

In perhaps the most grimly ironic aspect of the new demographic dispensa-
tion, the government adopted something like the one-drop rule that helped en-
slave mulattos and self-identifying whites before Emancipation. Under OMB's
rules, any response combining one minority race and the white race must be allocated to the minority race. This, although 25 percent of those in the United
States who describe themselves as both black and white consider themselves
white, as do almost half of Asian-white people and more than 80 percent of In-
dian-white people. The lesson is clear: making our social policy pivot on the
standard racial categories is both illogical and politically unsustainable.

Alternatives

Even a remote possibility that eliminating affirmative action would resegregate
our society deeply distresses almost all Americans. Nothing else can explain
the persistence of a policy that, contrary to basic American values, distributes
valuable social resources according to skin color and surname. But to say that
we must choose between perpetuating affirmative action and eliminating it entirely is false. To be sure, most suggested reforms—using social class or economic disadvantage rather than race, choosing among minimally qualified
students by lottery, and making preferences temporary—are impracticable or
would make matters worse. Limiting affirmative action to the descendants of
slaves and Native Americans would minimize some objections to the policy

but, as Patterson's proposal suggests, would be tricky to implement and would still violate the nondiscrimination and merit principles.

Most Americans who favor affirmative action would probably concede that it fails to treat the underlying problem. Black applicants will continue to have worse academic credentials until they can attend better primary and secondary schools and receive the remediation they need. A root cause of their disadvantage is inferior schooling, and affirmative action is simply a poultice. We must often deal with symptoms rather than root causes because we do not know how to eliminate them, or consider it too costly to do so, or cannot muster the necessary political will. If we know which social or educational reforms can substantially improve low-income children's academic performance, then we should by all [means] adopt them. But this does not mean that we should preserve affirmative action until we can eliminate the root causes of inequality.

I propose instead that we treat governmental, legally mandated preferences differently than private, voluntary ones. While prohibiting the former (except in the narrow remedial context approved by the Supreme Court), I would permit the latter—but only under certain conditions discussed below. A liberal society committed to freedom and private autonomy has good reasons to maintain this difference; racial preferences imposed by law are pernicious in ways that private ones are not. [T]o most Americans (including many minorities), affirmative action is not benign. [R]ace is perhaps the worst imaginable category around which to organize political and social relations. The social changes I have described only reinforce this lesson. A public law that affirms our common values should renounce the distributive use of race, not perpetuate it.

There are other differences between public and private affirmative action. A private preference speaks for and binds only those who adopt it and only for as long as they retain it. It does not serve, as public law should, as a social ideal. [L]egal rules tend to be cruder, more simplistic, slower to develop, and less contextualized than voluntary ones, which are tailored to more specific needs and situations. Legal rules reflect interest group politics or the vagaries of judicial decision; voluntary ones reflect the chooser's own assessment of private benefits and costs. Legal rules are more difficult to reform, abandon, or escape. Voluntary ones can assume more diverse forms than mandated ones, a diversity that facilitates social learning and problem solving.

Still, many who believe in nondiscrimination and merit and who conscientiously weigh the competing values still support affirmative action. If a private university chooses to sacrifice some level of academic performance to gain greater racial diversity and whatever educational or other values it thinks diversity will bring, I cannot say—nor should the law say—that its choice is impermissible. Because even private affirmative action violates the nondiscrimination principle, however, I would permit it only on two conditions: transparency and protection of minorities. First, the preference—its criteria, weights, and reasons—must be fully disclosed. If it cannot withstand public criticism, it should be scrapped. The goal is to discipline preferences by forcing institutions to reveal their value choices. This will trigger market, reputational, and other informal mechanisms that make them bear more of the policy's costs rather than just shifting them surreptitiously to nonpreferred applicants, as they do now. Second, private affirmative action must not disadvantage a group to which the Constitution affords heightened protection. A preference favoring whites, for example, would violate this condition.

The Commitment to Legal Equality

For better *and* for worse, American culture remains highly individualistic in its values and premises, even at some sacrifice (where sacrifice is necessary) to its goal of substantive equality. The illiberal strands in our tangled history that enslaved, excluded, and subordinated individuals as members of racial groups should chasten our efforts to use race as a distributive criterion. Affirmative action in its current form, however well-intended, violates the distinctive, deeply engrained cultural and moral commitments to legal equality, private autonomy, and enhanced opportunity that have served Americans well—even though they have not yet served all of us equally well.

Questions for Discussion

1. In this piece, Peter Schuck differentiates between public institutions, such as Indiana University, and private ones, such as Notre Dame. Is this a legitimate distinction when it comes to permitting affirmative action to affect decisions (in admissions or hiring)?
2. The notion of "colorblind" admissions and advancement sounds more than reasonable. Why might universities, corporations, and other organizations desire *not* to be colorblind? Is the society at large colorblind?

3.9

Reaffirming Diversity: A Legal Analysis of the University of Michigan Affirmative Action Cases

Joint Statement of Constitutional Law Scholars

The 2003 Supreme Court decisions in two related affirmative action cases provided some clarity on how far public institutions can go in weighing diversity in their admissions decisions. The Court adopted a relatively expansive view of affirmative action in promoting diversity for the University of Michigan Law School (*Grutter*), while opting for substantial limitations on affirmative action in undergraduate admissions (*Gratz*); still, the justices did rule that race could continue to be a consideration in admissions policies, a line of reasoning that was expressed in 1978 by Justice Lewis Powell, even as he ruled against a quota system for minorities in *Bakke* v. *California.*

Affirmative action remains a hot-button issue in many quarters because it juxtaposes two different ways of addressing the broad value of equality—a value that Americans frequently see through different lenses. Those who oppose affirmative action view equality through the lens of nondiscrimination at any given point where advantage might occur, such as admission to college, or to law school, or in obtaining a job. Equality here means simply that the process does not discriminate against any individual. Advocates of affirmative action, in whatever form, argue that a lack of discrimination does not equate to real equality of opportunity. Life situations create all kinds of inequalities that affect actual opportunity. Affirmative action advocates have relied less and less on such arguments, however, in large part because Americans find equality a less compelling value than those of freedom and merit. Rather, as "Reaffirming Diversity" demonstrates, the idea of diversity within an institution has become the foundation for contemporary support for affirmative action policies.

"Reaffirming Diversity: A Legal Analysis of the University of Michigan Affirmative Action Cases," from The Joint Statement of Constitutional Law Scholars, 2003, pp. 1–27. Reprinted by permission of The Civil Rights Project at Harvard University. Released July 6, 2003; accessed at http://www.civilrightsproject.harvard.edu/policy/legal_docs/MIReaffirming.php.

Effective participation by members of all racial and ethnic groups in the civic life of our Nation is essential if the dream of one Nation, indivisible, is to be realized.

—GRUTTER V. BOLLINGER

Introduction

On June 23, 2003, the United States Supreme Court upheld the constitutionality of race-conscious admissions policies designed to promote diversity in higher education. In a 5-to-4 decision in *Grutter v. Bollinger,* the Supreme Court, drawing on Justice Powell's opinion in the 1978 case of *Regents of the University of California v. Bakke,* held that student body diversity is a compelling governmental interest that can justify the use of race as a "plus" factor in a competitive admissions process. Applying its "strict scrutiny" standard of review within the context of higher education, the Supreme Court upheld the University of Michigan Law School admissions policy as constitutional. However, in a 6-to-3 decision in *Gratz v. Bollinger,* the Supreme Court held that the University's current undergraduate admissions policy was not narrowly tailored to advance an interest in diversity because it was not sufficiently flexible and did not provide enough individualized consideration of applicants to the University.

In ruling that the promotion of student body diversity is a compelling interest, the Supreme Court's decisions resolve a disagreement among the lower federal courts and allow selective colleges and universities throughout the country to employ race in admissions. The decisions reject the absolute race-blind approach to higher education admissions advanced by the *Grutter* and *Gratz* plaintiffs and by the U.S. government and others as *amici curiae.* The Court's decisions also effectively overrule major portions of the 1996 ruling of the U.S. Court of Appeals for the Fifth Circuit in *Hopwood v. Texas,* and will allow colleges and universities in the states of Texas, Louisiana, and Mississippi to use race-conscious admissions policies designed to advance diversity. State universities in California, Washington, and Florida are still prohibited under their state laws from employing race-conscious admissions policies; however, private universities in those states can employ properly designed race-conscious policies consistent with their obligations under Title VI of the Civil Rights Act of 1964 and other federal laws.

Taken together, the Court's opinions in the *Grutter* and *Gratz* cases reinforce the importance of flexible and holistic admissions policies that employ a limited use of race. The Court's opinion in the law school case, *Grutter v. Bollinger,* confirms that admissions programs which consider race as one of many factors in the context of an individualized consideration of all applicants can pass constitutional muster. The Court's decision to strike down the undergraduate admissions policy in *Gratz* as unconstitutional also makes clear that policies which automatically and inflexibly assign benefits on the basis of race, such as the

University's undergraduate point system that allocated a fixed number of points for underrepresented minority group members, are constitutionally suspect. Universities that employ systems which lack sufficient individualized review will need to re-examine their current admissions policies to determine whether their policies require adjustment or revision in light of the Court's decision in *Gratz*. Institutions that have adopted more restrictive policies than the Court's decisions allow may wish to re-examine their policies to ensure that they are not "overcorrecting" out of a misplaced fear of being held legally liable. . . .

Although the Supreme Court has yet to address the constitutionality of diversity-based affirmative action programs outside of higher education admissions, language in the *Grutter* decision acknowledges the importance of diversity in other contexts, including K-12 education, government, and private employment and business. For instance, the Court states expressly that the benefits of affirmative action "are not theoretical but real, as major American businesses have made clear that the skills needed in today's increasingly global marketplace can only be developed through exposure to widely diverse people, cultures, ideas, and viewpoints." This and other statements by the Court imply that diversity may be a constitutional predicate for race-conscious affirmative action programs in areas outside of higher education. . . .

I. *Grutter, Gratz,* and the Constitutional Boundaries of Race-Conscious Admissions

The University of Michigan cases reaffirm the Supreme Court's fundamental requirement that race-conscious policy making—even if designed to benefit racial minority groups—is subject to "strict scrutiny," the highest standard of review used by the courts to evaluate the constitutionality of policies under the Equal Protection Clause of the Fourteenth Amendment. Under strict scrutiny, the courts ask two questions to assess the ends and the means that underlie race-conscious policy making: (1) Is the goal of a race-conscious policy sufficiently important to constitute a "compelling governmental interest"? and (2) If so, is the policy "narrowly tailored" to advance that interest?

Strict scrutiny is exacting but it is not rigid. As the Supreme Court made clear in *Grutter v. Bollinger*, "[c]ontext matters when reviewing race-based governmental action under the Equal Protection Clause" and "strict scrutiny must take 'relevant differences' into account." Applying strict scrutiny within the context of evaluating an inclusive higher education policy, the Supreme Court ruled in *Grutter v. Bollinger* that colleges and universities do have a compelling interest in obtaining a diverse student body. Employing a multi-factor test of narrow tailoring, the Court upheld the University of Michigan Law School's admissions policy in *Grutter*, but struck down the University's undergraduate policy in *Gratz* for lacking the necessary flexibility and individualized consideration required under narrow tailoring.

A. The Compelling Interest in Diversity

Like hundreds of selective colleges and universities throughout the country, the University of Michigan relied on Justice Powell's opinion in *Regents of the University of California* v. *Bakke* as the legal underpinning for its diversity-based admissions policies. In *Bakke*, a fragmented Supreme Court struck down the race-conscious special admissions policy at the medical school of the University of California, Davis, but reversed a lower court's ruling that race could never be considered a factor in admissions. Justice Powell provided the fifth vote for a majority of the Court which found that the medical school's special admissions policy—a plan that set aside 16 out of 100 seats in the entering class for disadvantaged minority applicants—was illegal because it precluded white applicants from competing for those special admissions seats. But Justice Powell, as part of a different five-member majority, also held that the use of race as one of many factors in a competitive admissions process would be constitutionally permissible.

Justice Powell's pivotal opinion stated that a university's interest in promoting broad diversity—and not just racial diversity—within its student body is grounded partly in the academic freedoms historically accorded to institutions of higher education and constitutes a compelling governmental interest that can justify the limited use of race in admissions. Relying on the undergraduate admissions policy at Harvard College as a case in point, Justice Powell went on to distinguish an illegal policy such as the Davis medical school plan, in which white applicants could not compete for specified seats in an entering class, from a legal policy such as the Harvard plan, in which race is employed as a "plus" factor in a competitive process in which all applicants are eligible to compete for the same seats in the entering class. Under a plus-factor admissions policy, an applicant's race could "tip the balance" in an admissions decision, but race would be only one of many factors under consideration. . . .

The *Grutter* opinion offers a ringing endorsement of the value of student body diversity in promoting numerous benefits, including:

♦ concrete educational benefits;
♦ assisting in the breakdown of racial and ethnic stereotypes; and
♦ the development of a diverse, racially integrated leadership class

Citing expert reports in the trial record and research studies documenting the educational benefits of diversity, the *Grutter* opinion recognizes that student body diversity leads to substantial educational benefits for *all* students, including the promotion of cross-racial understanding, improved classroom discussions and other positive learning outcomes, and enhanced preparation for an increasingly diverse workforce and society. Moreover, according to the Court, student body diversity "helps to break down racial stereotypes" and "diminishing the force of such stereotypes is both a crucial part of [an institution's] mission, and one that it cannot accomplish with only token numbers of minority students. Just as growing up in a particular region or having particular professional experiences is likely to affect an individual's views, so too is one's own, unique experience of being a racial minority in a society, like our own, in which race unfortunately still matters."

Citing *Sweatt v. Painter*,* the *Grutter* Court also recognized that institutions of higher learning, and law schools in particular, provide the training ground for many of our Nation's leaders. Individuals with law degrees, for instance, occupy large numbers of the nation's state governorships, seats in both houses of Congress, and federal judgeships. According to the Court, "[i]n order to cultivate a set of leaders with legitimacy in the eyes of the citizenry, it is necessary that the path to leadership be visibly open to talented and qualified individuals of every race and ethnicity." Access to higher education "must be inclusive of talented and qualified individuals of every race and ethnicity, so that all members of our heterogeneous society may participate in the educational institutions that provide the training and education necessary to succeed in America." . . .

One of the Court's most powerful statements thus underscores the compelling interest in promoting diversity in higher education and the importance of racial integration and diversity in civic life more generally: "'[E]nsuring that public institutions are open and available to all segments of American society, including people of all race and ethnicities, represents a paramount government objective.' . . . And, '[n]owhere is the importance of such openness more acute than in the context of higher education.' . . . Effective participation by members of all racial and ethnic groups in the civic life of our Nation is essential if the dream of one Nation, indivisible, is to be realized."

B. Narrow Tailoring: A Bakke+ Test

Under the narrow tailoring prong of strict scrutiny, the courts evaluate the "fit" between a compelling interest and the policy adopted to advance that interest. The Supreme Court has not developed a uniform test of narrow tailoring in equal protection cases, but the Court has offered various guidelines in its earlier cases addressing race-conscious policies; the analyses employed in *Grutter* and *Gratz* draw on several of these guidelines. In *Bakke*, Justice Powell discussed two elements of narrow tailoring specific to admissions policies designed to promote diversity in higher education: First, an admissions policy must not rely on separate tracks or quotas that insulate racial minorities from competitive review. Second, race must be employed as a "plus"

---

*In 1950, the Supreme Court overturned a state supreme court decision and ordered the integration of the University of Texas School of Law.

factor that serves as only one of many factors being weighed in a competitive process that evaluates the particular qualifications of each individual applicant. . . .

Stating that the narrow tailoring test "must be calibrated to fit the distinct issues raised by the use of race to achieve student body diversity in public higher education," the Supreme Court's articulation of the narrow tailoring test in *Grutter* combines elements from *Bakke* and the Court's remedial cases into five basic inquiries:

♦ Does the program offer a competitive review of all applications (i.e., no quotas or separate tracks to insulate minorities)?
♦ Does the program provide flexible, individualized consideration of applicants so that race is only one of several factors being considered?
♦ Has the institution considered workable race-neutral alternatives to its program?
♦ Does the program unduly burden non-minority applicants?
♦ Is the program limited in time, so that it has a logical end point?

The *Grutter* Court applied all five of these inquiries in upholding the University of Michigan Law School's admissions policy. The *Gratz* Court focused on the second inquiry and found that the University's undergraduate admissions policy lacked the necessary flexibility and individualized review to satisfy narrow tailoring.

The *Grutter* Court stressed that context is critical in strict scrutiny analysis, and the Court may be more inclined to uphold race-conscious policies in employment contexts that closely parallel the higher education context, where the benefits of diversity in the workplace are well documented and race is used as a "plus" factor in a non-mechanical hiring or promotion process that also considers non-racial factors and allows applicants to compete for jobs on an equal footing.

Conclusion

The *Grutter* and *Gratz* decisions have affirmed the underlying values of diversity in higher education and of racial integration in American society, and the cases provide clear guidelines for institutions to use in designing inclusive admissions policies. Yet, as the Court stated in *Grutter*, "race unfortunately still matters," and affirmative action will continue to be an issue that divides much of our country, notwithstanding our nation's broad commitment to equal educational opportunity. The University of Michigan decisions have settled one set of legal questions, but we can expect many more to arise in our courts and legislatures with the passage of time.

In *Brown* v. *Board of Education*, the Supreme Court observed that education is "the very foundation of good citizenship." Those words ring as true today as they did nearly fifty years ago. Considerable progress has been made in the past fifty years, but the University of Michigan cases remind us that progress has been slow and much remains to be done. The Court's more recent words, echoing *Brown*, are thus worth repeating: "Effective participation by members of all racial and ethnic groups in the civic life of our Nation is essential if the dream of one Nation, indivisible, is to be realized."

Questions for Discussion

1. Why did the U.S. Supreme Court broadly accept the idea of affirmative action for the University of Michigan Law School while rejecting any such interpretation for undergraduates at the same institution?
2. Does a university have a "compelling interest" in diversity? If so, should race be one of the categories that make up the working definition of "diversity"? Why?

 # Chapter 4

PUBLIC OPINION

At base, politics is the relationship between those who govern and those who are governed. Public opinion plays a crucial role in this relationship. Governments—even totalitarian states—must take into account the attitudes and perspectives of the public, because without the people's support no government can endure.

In modern democracies, the idea that governments should consider the wishes of the governed can be traced to the late seventeenth and eighteenth centuries, particularly to the egalitarian and majoritarian ideas of John Locke and Thomas Jefferson. Governing authority had previously been based on an aristocratic ideology that defended social and legal inequality as a proper and permanent fact of life. The various classes had fixed places in society, and the ruling class devised elaborate justifications for the exclusion of others from politics. But the dissemination of radically different social ideas, plus changes in economic circumstances, broadened the base of political participation. What the growing middle class thought became important, and in the early 1800s the term *public opinion* became commonplace.

In countries that boast democratic forms of government, like the United States, it appears virtually mandatory that the "will of the people" prevail. The difficulty is in determining what the will of the people is—or indeed, whether it exists. "To speak with precision of public opinion," wrote political scientist V. O. Key, "is a task not unlike coming to grips with the Holy Ghost," partly because the distinction between "public" and "private" opinion is not easy to make and is constantly changing. For example, thirty-five years ago cigarette smoking was a private matter, unregulated by government and absent from the agenda of political debate. By the 1970s, however, when smoking had been identified as a major public health hazard, advertising by tobacco companies was severely curtailed and movements to ban smoking in all public places were afoot. Today smoking is a public matter, and interest groups on both sides of the issue are involved in legislative deliberations. Questions about smoking now are a routine component of national public opinion polls.

The meaning of *opinion* is similarly vague. Opinions, beliefs, and attitudes are often treated as if they were the same, but scholars increasingly make distinctions among these terms. One social scientist, Bernard Hennessy, defines opinions as "immediate orientations toward contemporary controversial political objects," whereas attitudes are "more diffused and enduring orientations toward political objects not necessarily controversial at the moment."

For most purposes, however, it is preferable to think of public opinion in the broadest sense—in Key's definition, as "those opinions held by private persons which governments find it prudent to heed." Public opinion may be expressed in a letter (or many letters) to an elected official or to the editor of a newspaper, turnout at a protest march, the statements of a special interest group, the results of an election, or the findings of survey research. Often public opinion is gathered by impressions—legislators' sense of their districts, what their political intimates tell them, or the number of interest group representatives they see or hear. More and more often, however, public opinion is being derived scientifically from efforts to poll citizens.

Survey research is now a major element of political life, and citizens are constantly bombarded with poll results. Besides independent polling concerns such as the Gallup Organization, which periodically release information concerning public attitudes, the three television networks have joined with major newspapers to create polling groups. Other efforts abound, and it seems fair to say that polling has become a major way of interpreting public opinion at the state and local as well as national level. Virtually all issues on the public agenda have generated public opinion data.

As opinion-gathering devices, polls are powerful vehicles for those who believe in majoritarian democracy. Unlike other methods of discovering public opinion, polls can represent the entire public, not just those elements with political resources or well-organized interest groups. Polls can be superior even to elections, because they report what everyone thinks rather than only what those who bother to vote think. Since poll results can make politicians aware of citizens' wishes, polls have the capacity to make government more responsible.

But not everyone believes poll-measured public opinion serves democratic ideals well. Often polls solicit opinions (and get them) on subjects on which little or no real opinion exists, such as on foreign policy. Not all polls are accurate, but their scientific aura lends them some credibility. Because all opinions count equally, polls tend to underrepresent intense opinion and give extra influence to the apathetic. Critics tend to believe that polls actually inhibit responsible government by forcing politicians to respond to public wishes that may be ill informed. Political leaders, in their quest for office, may follow poll results even when the long-term interests of the public are not well served.

Overall, both defenders and critics of opinion polls can point to convincing evidence for their views. Politicians are probably somewhat constrained by poll data and are restrained from taking action of which the public would disapprove. Programs such as Social Security, for example, are retained in their current form largely because the public strongly supports them. But it is also true that consistent, overwhelming majorities in the polls do not necessarily dictate public policy. This can be seen in the case of gun control; as early as 1938 the national polls showed that over 80 percent of the public favored hand-gun registration, but the organized efforts of the National Rifle Association have thwarted the passage of such a law.

The selections in this chapter were chosen to explain public opinion through the instrument of political polling. In the first selection, Benjamin Ginsberg criticizes polling as an instrument for assessing public opinion and suggests that the character of public opinion has changed because of its widespread use. In the second selection, Larry Bartels argues that survey questions on policy matters typically are so prone to "framing effects" that it is virtually impossible to discern public preferences. He questions whether the idealized notion of "popular rule," where decision makers translate citizen wishes into government policy, is possible, given the current state of opinion polling. Finally, Michael Traugott raises a number of issues concerning the survey design quality of many polling efforts. Technological advances have increased the numbers of those in the polling business, particularly at the local level, but it has become more difficult to separate "good" polls from "bad" ones. Response rates are down as well, raising issues about the representative nature of many polls.

4.1

Polling and the Transformation of Public Opinion

Benjamin Ginsberg

Public opinion is usually seen as flowing from citizens to public officials. Polling represents an important way for the public to make its wishes and preferences known to decision makers. The increasing use of polls to assess public opinion seems to enhance citizen influence, giving elected officials more to go on as they attempt to respond to their constituents' demands and concerns.

But polls are more than neutral indicators of the public's preferences. According to Benjamin Ginsberg, polling has fundamentally altered the character of public opinion and the relationship between citizens and their government. In his view, polling has made contemporary public opinion less likely to constrain authorities and possibly more subject to government manipulation and control. Rather than responding to public opinion, government may create, distort, or modify it. Ginsberg also believes that public opinion polling has weakened the impact of certain groups and their leaders in politics, particularly organized labor and working-class interests. In the past, these groups were closely linked with mass public opinion.

Much of the prominence of opinion polling as a civic institution derives from the significance that present-day political ideologies ascribe to the will of the people. Polls purport to provide reliable, scientifically derived information about the public's desires, fears, and beliefs, and so to give concrete expression to the conception of a popular will. The availability of accurate information certainly is no guarantee that governments will actually pay heed to popular opinions. Yet many students and practitioners of survey research have always believed that an accurate picture of the public's views might at least increase the chance that governments' actions would be informed by and responsive to popular sentiment.

Benjamin Ginsberg is a professor of political science at Johns Hopkins University.

Unfortunately, however, polls do more than simply measure and record the natural or spontaneous manifestation of popular belief. The data reported by opinion polls are actually the product of an interplay between opinion and the survey instrument. As they measure, the polls interact with opinion, producing changes in the character and identity of the views receiving public expression. The changes induced by polling, in turn, have the most profound implications for the relationship between public opinion and government. In essence, polling has contributed to the domestication of opinion by helping to transform it from a politically potent, often disruptive force into a more docile, plebiscitary phenomenon.

Publicizing Opinion

Poll results and public opinion are terms that are used almost synonymously. As one indication of the extent to which public opinion is now identified with the polls, a sophisticated new national magazine entitled *Public Opinion* matter-of-factly devotes virtually all its attention to the presentation and discussion of survey data.

Yet, in spite of this general tendency to equate public opinion with survey results, polling is obviously not the only possible source of knowledge about the public's attitudes. Means of ascertaining public opinion certainly existed prior to the development of modern survey techniques. Statements from local notables and interest group spokespersons, letters to the press and to public officials, and sometimes demonstrations, protests, and riots provided indications of the populace's views long before the invention of the sample survey. Governments certainly took note of all these symptoms of the public's mood. As corporate executive and political commentator Chester Barnard once noted, prior to the availability of polling, legislators "read the local newspapers, toured their districts and talked with voters, received letters from the home state, and entertained delegations which claimed to speak for large and important blocks of voters."[1]

Obviously, these alternative modes of assessing public sentiment continue to be available. But it is significant that whenever poll results differ from the interpretation of public opinion offered by some other source, almost invariably the polls are presumed to be correct. The labor leader whose account of the views of the rank and file differs from the findings of a poll is automatically assumed to have misrepresented or misperceived membership opinion. Politicians who dare to quarrel with polls' negative assessments of their popularity or that of their programs are immediately derided by the press.

This presumption in favor of opinion polls stems from both their scientific and their representative character. Survey research is modeled after the methodology of the natural sciences and at least conveys an impression of technical sophistication and scientific objectivity. . . .

At the same time, polls can also claim to offer a more representative view of popular sentiment than any alternative source of information. Group spokesmen sometimes speak only for themselves. The distribution of opinion reflected by letters to newspapers and public officials is notoriously biased. Demonstrators and rioters, however sincere, are seldom more than a tiny and unrepresentative segment of the populace. Polls, by contrast, at least attempt to take equal account of all relevant individuals. And, indeed, by offering a representative view of public opinion, polls have often served as antidotes for false spokesmen and as guides to popular concerns that might never have been mentioned by individuals writing letters to legislators or newspaper editors.

Nevertheless, polling does more than just offer a scientifically derived and representative account of popular sentiment. The substitution of polling for other means of gauging the public's views also has the effect of changing several of the key characteristics of public opinion. Critics of survey research have often noted that polling can affect both the beliefs of individuals asked to respond to survey questions and the attitudes of those who subsequently read a survey's results. However, the most important aspect of polls is not their capacity to change individuals' beliefs. Rather the major impact of polling is the way polls cumulate and translate individuals' private beliefs into collective public opinions. . . .

Four fundamental changes in the character of public opinion can be traced directly to the introduction of survey research. First, polling alters both what is expressed and what is perceived as the opinion of the mass public by transforming public opinion from a voluntary to an externally subsidized matter. Second, polling modifies the manner in which opinion is publicly presented by transforming public opinion from a behavioral to an attitudinal phenomenon. Third, polling changes the origin of information about public beliefs by transforming public opinion from a property of groups to an attribute of individuals. Finally, polling partially removes individuals' control over their own public expressions of opinion by transforming public opinion from a spontaneous assertion to a constrained response.

. . . These four transformations have contributed markedly to the domestication or pacification of public opinion. Polling has rendered public opinion less dangerous, less disruptive, more permissive, and, perhaps, more amenable to governmental control.

From Voluntarism to Subsidy

In the absence of polling, the cost and effort required to organize and publicly communicate an opinion are normally borne by one or more of the individuals holding the opinion. Someone wishing to express a view about civil rights, for example, might write a letter, deliver a speech, contribute to an organization, or join a protest march. A wealthy individual might employ a public relations expert; a politically astute individual might assert that he or she represented the views of many others. But whatever the means, the organization and public communication of opinion would entail a voluntary expenditure of funds, effort, or time by the opinion holder. Polls, by contrast, organize and publicize opinion without requiring initiative or action on the part of individuals. With the exception of the small sample asked to submit to an interview, the individuals whose opinions are expressed through polls need take no action whatsoever. Polls underwrite or subsidize the costs of eliciting, organizing, and publicly expressing opinion.

This displacement of costs from the opinion holder to the polling agency has important consequences for the character of the opinions likely to receive public expression. In general, the willingness of individuals to bear the cost of publicly asserting their views is closely tied to the intensity with which they hold those views. Other things being equal, individuals with strong feelings about any given matter are more likely to invest whatever time and effort are needed to make their feelings known than are persons with less intense views. One seldom hears, for example, of a march on Washington by groups professing not to care much about abortion. As this example suggests, moreover, individuals with strongly held views are also more likely than their less zealous fellow citizens to be found at the extremes of opinion on any given question. Thus as long as the costs of asserting opinions are borne by opinion holders themselves, those with relatively extreme viewpoints are also disproportionately likely to bring their views to the public forum.

Polls weaken this relationship between the public expression of opinion and the intensity or extremity of opinion. The assertion of an opinion through a poll requires little effort. As a result, the beliefs of those who care relatively little or even hardly at all are as likely to be publicized as the opinions of those who care a great deal about the matter in question. The upshot is that the distribution of public opinion reported by polls generally differs considerably from the distribution that emerges from forms of public communication initiated by citizens. Political scientists Aage Clausen, Philip E. Converse, Warren E. Miller, and others have shown that the public opinion reported by surveys is, on the aggregate, both less intense and less extreme than the public opinion that would be defined by voluntary modes of popular expression. Similarly, poll respondents typically include a much larger proportion of individuals who "don't know," "don't care," or exhibit some other form of relative detachment from the debate on major public issues than the population of activists willing to express their views through voluntary or spontaneous means.

. . . Polls, in effect, submerge individuals with strongly held views in a more apathetic mass public. The data reported by polls are likely to suggest to public officials that they are working in a more permissive climate of opinion than might have been thought on the basis of alternative indicators of the popular mood. A government wishing to maintain some semblance of responsiveness to public opinion would typically find it less difficult to comply with the preferences reported by polls than to obey the opinion that might be inferred from letters, strikes, or protests. Indeed, relative to these other modes of public expression, polled opinion could be characterized as a collective statement of permission.

Certainly, even in the era of polling, voluntary expressions of public opinion can still count heavily. In recent years, for example, members of Congress were impressed by calls, letters, and telegrams from constituents—and threats from contributors—regarding President Reagan's various tax reform proposals. Groups like the National Rifle Association are masters in the use of this type of campaign. Nevertheless, contradiction by polls tends to reduce the weight and credibility of other sources of public opinion, an effect that can actually help governments to resist the pressure of constituent opinion. Constituency polls, for example, are often used by legislators as a basis for resisting the demands of political activists and pressure groups in their districts. . . .

The relatively permissive character of polled opinion can provide a government faced with demonstrations, protests, and other manifestations of public hostility a basis for claiming that its policies are compatible with true public opinion and opposed only by an unrepresentative group of activist malcontents.

A good illustration of how polls can play this role is the case of the "silent majority" on whose behalf Richard Nixon claimed to govern.* The silent majority was the Nixon administration's answer to the protestors, demonstrators, rioters, and other critics who demanded major changes in American foreign and domestic policies. Administration spokespersons frequently cited poll data, often drawing on Richard Scammon and Ben Wattenberg's influential treatise, *The Real Majority,* to question the popular standing of the activist opposition. According to the administration's interpretation, its activist opponents did not represent the views of the vast majority of "silent" Americans who could be found in the polls but not on picket lines or marches, or in civil disturbances.

Undoubtedly a majority of Americans were less than sympathetic to the protestors. But from the administration's perspective, the real virtue of the silent majority was precisely its silence. Many of those Americans who remained silent did so because they lacked strong opinions on the political issues of the day. The use of polls to identify a "silent majority" was a means of diluting the political weight and undermining the credibility of those members of the public with the strongest views while constructing a permissive majority of "silent" Americans. . . .

Another illustration of the permissive character of polled opinion is Lyndon Johnson's reaction to public opinion surveys about the Vietnam War. Johnson constantly referred to the polls in his attempt to convince friends, visitors, col-

---

*Members of the "silent majority" were those respondents in the national public opinion polls who disapproved of the protests and demonstrations against the Vietnam War. They made up an overwhelming majority of the electorate, but their disapproval of the protesters deflected attention from the fact that many of them did not approve of government policy on the war.

leagues, and most of all himself that the public supported his war policies. Indeed, Johnson's eventual realization that public opinion had turned against his administration weighed heavily in his decision not to seek another term in office. The significance of this case is that polls permitted a president who was apparently actually concerned with his administration's responsiveness to public opinion to believe that he was doing what the people wanted. The polls appeared to indicate that despite the contrary assertions of protesters, demonstrators, and rioters, public opinion did not really demand an end to the war. After all, it was not until late in Johnson's term that a majority of those polled disapproved of his policies. In effect, the polls permitted a public official who had some actual desire to be responsive to public opinion to more easily convince himself that he had been.

From Behavior to Attitude

Prior to the advent of polling, public opinion could often only be inferred from political behavior. Before the availability of voter survey data, for example, analysts typically sought to deduce electoral opinion from voting patterns, attributing candidates' electoral fortunes to whatever characteristics of the public mood could be derived from election returns. Often population movements served as the bases for conclusions about public preferences. Even in recent years the movement of white urbanites to the metropolitan fringe, dubbed "white flight," has been seen as a key indicator of white attitudes toward racial integration. Especially in the case of the least articulate segments of the population, governments before the advent of polls often had little or no knowledge of the public mood until opinion manifested itself in some form of behavior. Generally this meant violent or disruptive activity.

In the modern era public opinion is synonymous with polls. But certainly through the nineteenth century, public opinion was usually equated with riots, strikes, demonstrations, and boycotts. Nineteenth-century public sentiment could sometimes reveal itself through the most curious forms of behavior. In London during the 1830s, for example, a favorite mechanism for the expression of popular opinion was the "illumination." In an "illumination" those espousing a particular point of view placed lanterns or candles in their windows. Often mobs went from house to house demanding that the occupants "illuminate." Householders who declined might have their windows smashed and dwelling sacked. On April 27, 1831, a large mob formed to demand electoral reform. According to a contemporary account:

> On that evening, the illumination was pretty general. . . . The mobs did a great deal of mischief. A numerous rabble proceeded along the Strand, destroying all windows that were not lighted. . . . In St. James' Square they broke the windows in the houses of the Bishop of London, the Marquis of Cleveland and Lord Grantham. The Bishop of

Winchester and Mr. W.W. Wynn, seeing the mob approach, placed candles in their windows, which thus escaped. The mob then proceeded to St. James Street where they broke the windows of Crockford's, Jordon's, the Guards, and other Club houses. They next went to the Duke of Wellington's residence in Piccadilly, and discharged a shower of stones which broke several windows. The Duke's servants fired out of the windows over their heads to frighten them, but without effect. The policemen then informed the mob that the corpse of the Duchess of Wellington was on the premises, which arrested further violence against Apsley House.[2]

. . . The advent of polling transformed public opinion from a behavioral to an attitudinal phenomenon. Polls elicit, organize, and publicize opinion without requiring any action on the part of the opinion holder. Of course, public presentation of an opinion via polls by no means precludes its subsequent expression through behavior. Nevertheless, polling does permit any interested party an opportunity to assess the state of the public's mood without having to wait for some behavioral manifestation. From the perspective of political elites, the obvious virtue of polls is that they make it possible to recognize and deal with popular attitudes—even the attitudes of the most inarticulate segments of the populace—before they materialize in some unpleasant, disruptive, or threatening form of political action. In democracies, of course, the most routine behavioral threat posed by public opinion is hostile action in the voting booth, and polling has become one of the chief means of democratic political elites to attempt to anticipate and avert the electorate's displeasure. But in both democratic and dictatorial contexts, governments have also employed polling extensively to help forestall the possibility of popular disobedience and unrest.

In recent years, for example, many Eastern European regimes have instituted survey programs. Polling has been used, in part, to forewarn the leadership of potential sources of popular disaffection, hostility, or antigovernment activities. As sociologist Bogdan Osolnik observed, in Eastern Europe opinion research provides "a warning that some attitudes which political actors consider to be generally accepted . . . have not yet been adopted by public opinion." Such "misunderstandings," says Osolnik, "can be extremely harmful—and dangerous."[3] Polling allows the regime an opportunity to resolve these potential "misunderstandings" before they pose a serious threat.

As early as the 1950s, to cite one concrete case, the Polish government obtained extensive survey data indicating that strong religious sentiment was widespread among the young. The regime became quite concerned with the implications of the continuing hold of "unorthodox ritualistic attitudes" on the generation that was expected to possess the strongest commitment to socialism. In response to its survey findings, the government embarked on a major program of antireligious and ideological indoctrination aimed at young people. . . .

Gestapo chief Heinrich Himmler is reputed to have carefully studied polls of German attitudes toward the Nazi regime and its policies. Apparently, when-

ever he noted that some of those surveyed failed to respond with the appropriate opinions, he demanded to know their names.

In the United States, polling has typically been used as an adjunct to policy
implementation. Polling can provide administrators with some idea of what
citizens are and are not likely to tolerate and, thus, help them to avoid popular
disobedience and resistance. As early as the 1930s, federal agencies began to
poll extensively. During that decade the United States Department of Agriculture established a Division of Program Surveys to undertake studies of attitudes
toward federal farm programs. At the same time, extensive use was made of surveys by the Works Progress Administration, the Social Security Administration, and the Public Health Service. . . .

Nor is polling by U.S. governmental agencies confined to the domestic policy
arena. Various units of the State Department and other foreign policy agencies
have engaged in extensive polling abroad to assess the likely response of citizens
of other nations to American foreign policy initiatives aimed at them. During the
era of American involvement in Vietnam, both the Defense Department and the
Agency for International Development sponsored extensive polling in that country to examine the effects of existing and proposed American programs. Similarly,
polling was conducted in Cuba and the Dominican Republic to assess likely popular reaction to contemplated American intervention. A good deal of polling has
also been sponsored in Europe by American governmental agencies concerned
with European reactions to American propaganda appeals. . . .

Let me emphasize again that even the most extensive and skillful use of
polling does not ensure that public opinion will manifest itself only attitudi-
nally. Behavioral expressions of opinion in the form of protests, riots, strikes,
and so on are common enough even in the era of survey research. . . .

In some instances, of course, the knowledge of popular attitudes gleaned
from polls may convince those in power simply to bow to the popular will before it is too late. Such a response would certainly be consistent with the hopes
expressed by polling advocates. Yet often enough the effect of polling is to
lessen the threat or pressure that public opinion is likely to impose on administrators and policy makers. By converting opinion from a behavioral to an attitudinal phenomenon, polling is, in effect, also transforming public opinion into
a less immediately threatening and dangerous phenomenon.

Polls can, however, also give a government a better opportunity to manipulate and modify public opinion and thus to avoid accommodation to citizens'
preferences. One interesting recent example of this process is the activity of the
1965 American "Riot Commission." Charged with the task of preventing repe-
titions of the riots that rocked American cities during the 1960s, the National
Advisory Commission on Civil Disorders sponsored and reviewed a large number of surveys of black attitudes on a variety of political, social, and economic
questions. These surveys allowed the commission to identify a number of attitudes held by blacks that were said to have contributed to their disruptive behavior. As a result of its surveys, the commission was able to suggest several

programs that might modify these attitudes and thus prevent further disorder. Significantly enough, the Riot Commission's report did not call for changes in the institutions and policies about which blacks had been violently expressing their views. The effect of polling was, in essence, to help the government find a way to *not* accommodate the opinions blacks had expressed in the streets of the urban ghettos of the United States.

From Group to Individual

Mass behavior was not the sole source of information about popular opinion prior to the advent of polling. Reports on the public's mood could usually also be obtained from the activists, leaders, or notables of the nation's organized and communal groups. Public officials or others interested in the views of working people, for example, would typically consult trade union officers. Similarly, anyone concerned with the attitudes of, say, farmers would turn to the heads of farm organizations. Of course, interest-group leaders, party leaders, and social notables seldom waited to be asked. These worthies would—and still do—voluntarily step forward to offer their impressions of membership opinion. While such impressions might not always be fully accurate, certainly group, party, and communal leaders often do have better opportunities to meet with and listen to their adherents than would be available to outsiders. Before the invention of polling these leaders quite probably possessed the most reliable data available on their followers' views. In the absence of contradictory evidence, at least, the claims of these leaders to have special knowledge of some portion of public opinion were strong enough to help give them a good deal of influence in national affairs. . . .

The advent of polling transformed public opinion from a property of groups to an attribute of individuals. Opinion surveys can elicit the views of individual citizens directly, allowing governments to bypass putative spokespersons for public opinion. Polls have never fully supplanted communal and interest-group leaders as sources of information about popular attitudes. Yet they do lessen the need for such intermediaries by permitting whatever agencies or organizations interested in learning the public's views to establish their own links with opinion holders. At the same time, polling often undermines the claims of group leaders and activists to speak for membership opinion. Frequently enough, polls seem to uncover discrepancies between the claims of leaders or self-appointed spokespersons on the one hand, and the opinions of the mass publics whose views these activists claim to reflect on the other. For example, during the 1960s and 1970s opponents of the American antiwar movement often took heart from poll data apparently indicating that youthful antiwar protesters who claimed to speak for "young people" really did not. Some poll data, at least, suggested that on the average individuals under thirty years of age were even more "hawkish" than respondents over the age of fifty.

This conversion of public opinion from a property of groups and their leaders to a more direct presentation of popular preferences has several consequences. On the one hand, polls undoubtedly provide a somewhat more representative picture of the public's views than would usually be obtained from group leaders and notables, who sometimes carelessly or deliberately misrepresent their adherents' opinions. Even with the best of intentions, the leaders of a group may be insufficiently sensitive to the inevitable disparity of viewpoints between activists and ordinary citizens and simply assume that their followers' views are merely echoes of their own. Polling can be a useful antidote to inaccuracy as well as to mendacity.

At the same time, however, by undermining the capacity of groups, interests, parties, and the like to speak for public opinion, polling can also diminish the effectiveness of public opinion as a force in political affairs. In essence, polling intervenes between opinion and its organized or collective expression. Though they may sometimes distort member opinion, organized groups, interests, and parties remain the most effective mechanisms through which opinion can be made to have an impact on government and politics. Polls' transformation of public opinion into an attribute of individuals increases the accuracy but very likely reduces the general efficacy with which mass opinion is publicly asserted.

Consider the role of labor unions during the Nixon era. Many of the Nixon administration's policies—wage and price controls in particular—were strongly opposed by organized labor. Yet polls constantly undercut the capacity of labor leaders to oppose the programs or to threaten electoral reprisals against legislators who supported it. Poll data seemed generally to suggest that Nixon was personally popular with union members and that most of the rank and file had no strong views on the programs that troubled the unions' leadership. As a result, the administration came to feel that it was reasonably safe to ignore the importunities of organized labor on a host of public issues. By enhancing the visibility of the opinions of ordinary workers, the polls surely drew a more representative picture of working-class opinion than had been offered by union officials. Yet the real cost of this more fully representative account of workers' views was, in a sense, a diminution of organized labor's influence over policy. . . .

Historically, the introduction of polling was, in fact, most damaging to the political fortunes of the groups that represented the interests and aspirations of the working classes. Polling erodes one of the major competitive advantages that has traditionally been available to lower-class groups and parties—a knowledge of mass public opinion superior to that of their middle- and upper-class opponents. The inability of bourgeois politicians to understand or sympathize with the needs of ordinary people is, of course, the point of one of the favorite morality tales of American political folklore, the misadventures of the "silk-stocking" candidate. To cite just one example, during the New York City mayoral race of 1894, the Committee of Seventy, a group that included the city's socially most prominent citizens, argued vehemently for improvements in the city's baths and lavatories, "to promote cleanliness and increased public comfort." The committee's members seemed undisturbed by the fact that the city and nation in 1894 were in the grip of a severe economic downturn accompanied by unusually high unemployment and considerable distress and misery among the working classes. The Committee of Seventy did not receive the thanks of many working-class New Yorkers for its firm stand on the lavatory issue.

Simply as a matter of social proximity, working-class parties or associations may have better access to mass opinion than is readily available to their rivals from the upper end of the social spectrum. As one Chicago precinct captain told University of Chicago political scientist Harold Gosnell during the 1930s, ". . . you think you can come in here and help the poor. You can't even talk to them on their own level, because you're better, you're from the University. I never graduated from high school, and I'm one of them."

Even more important than social proximity, however, is the matter of organization. In general, groups and parties that appeal mainly to working-class constituencies rely more heavily than their middle- and upper-class rivals on organizational strength and coherence. Organization has typically been the strategy of groups that must cumulate the collective energies of large numbers of individuals to counter their opponents' superior material means or institutional standing. In the course of both American and European political history, for example, disciplined and coherent party organizations were generally developed first by groups representing the working classes. . . .

What is important here is that their relatively coherent and disciplined mass organizations gave parties of the left a more accurate and extensive view of the public's mood than could normally be acquired by their less well organized opponents. . . . In the United States, the urban political machines that mobilized working-class constituencies employed armies of precinct workers and canvassers who were responsible for learning the preferences, wants, and needs of each and every voter living within an assigned precinct or election district. A Chicago machine precinct captain interviewed by Gosnell, for example, "thought that the main thing was to meet and talk to the voters on a man-to-man basis. . . . It did not matter where the voters were met—in the ball park, on the rinks, at dances, or at the bar. The main thing was to meet them." Through its extensive precinct organization, the urban machine developed a capacity to understand the moods and thus to anticipate and influence the actions of hundreds of thousands of voters.

The advent of polling eroded the advantage that social proximity and organization had given working-class parties in the competition for mass electoral support. Of course, any sort of political group can use an opinion survey. Polls are especially useful to carpetbaggers of all political stripes as a means of scouting what may be new and foreign territory. . . .*

---

*The term *carpetbagger* originally was applied to northerners who moved to the South to make money during Reconstruction, after the Civil War. Hostile southerners believed these individuals stuffed everything they owned into a suitcase, or carpetbag. Today the term is used to describe any opportunistic people who try to exert power or influence in places where they do not belong.

In the United States, where systematic political polling was initiated during the second half of the nineteenth century, most of the early polls were sponsored by newspapers and magazines affiliated with conservative causes and middle- and upper-class political factions. Thus the conservative *Chicago Tribune* was a major promoter of the polls during this period. Prior to the critical election of 1896, the *Tribune* polled some 14,000 factory workers and purported to show that 80 percent favored McKinley over William Jennings Bryan. Many of the newspapers and periodicals that made extensive use of political polling at that time were linked with either the Mugwumps or the Prohibitionists— precisely the two political groupings whose members might be least expected to have much firsthand knowledge of the preferences of common folk.* During the 1896 campaign the Mugwump *Chicago Record* spent more than $60,000 to mail postcard ballots to a random sample of one voter in eight in twelve midwestern states. An additional 328,000 ballots went to all registered voters in Chicago. The Democrats feared that the *Record* poll was a Republican trick and urged their supporters not to participate. . . .

This affiliation of many of the major polls with groups on the political right continued through the early years of the twentieth century. The Hearst newspapers, for example, polled extensively. *Fortune* magazine published widely read polls. The *Literary Digest*, which sponsored a famous presidential poll, was affiliated with the Prohibitionists. The clientele of most of the major pre–World War II pollsters—George Gallup, Elmo Roper, and Claude Robinson, for example—was heavily Republican, reflecting both the personal predilections of the pollsters and relative capacities of Democrats and Republicans of the period to understand public opinion without the aid of complex statistical analysis. In recent years the use of political polling has become virtually universal. Nevertheless, the polling efforts and uses of other forms of modern political technology by groups on the political right have been far more elaborate and extensive than those of other political factions. . . .

At the present time, polling is used by parties and candidates of every political stripe in the United States and all the European democracies. Opinion surveys are hardly a monopoly of the political right. Yet the fact remains that in the absence of polling, parties and groups representing the working classes would normally reap the political advantage of a superior knowledge of public opinion. The irony of polling is that the development of scientific means of

---

Mugwump, an Indian word meaning "chief," was used to label Republicans who refused to support James Blaine, the Republican presidential nominee in 1884, because they believed him to be opposed to many governmental reforms. Many came from wealthy, elitist backgrounds and were critical of patronage politics and political machines. Because the Mugwumps voted for Democrat Grover Cleveland, the term is sometimes used to describe individuals who leave their party when they are not pleased with a nominee. Prohibitionists were interested in banning the legal sale and consumption of alcohol. Because drinking was often associated with urban ethnic groups, Prohibitionists were considered to be hostile to lower- and working-class interests.

measuring public opinion had its most negative effect on precisely those groups whose political fortunes were historically most closely linked with mass public opinion.

From Assertion to Response

In the absence of polling, individuals typically choose for themselves the subjects of any public assertions they might care to make. Those persons or groups willing to expend the funds, effort, or time needed to acquire a public platform normally also select the agenda or topics on which their views will be aired. The individual writing an angry letter to a newspaper or legislator generally singles out the object of his or her scorn. The organizers of a protest march typically define the aim of their own wrath. . . .

The introduction of opinion surveys certainly did not foreclose opportunities for individuals to proffer opinions on topics of their own choosing. Indeed, in the United States a multitude of organizations, groups, and individuals are continually stepping forward to present the most extraordinary notions. Nevertheless, polls elicit subjects' views on questions that have been selected by an external agency—the survey's sponsors—rather than by the respondents themselves. Polling thus erodes individuals' control over the agenda of their own expressions of opinion. . . .

The most obvious consequence of this change is that polling can create a misleading picture of the agenda of public concerns, for what appears significant to the agencies sponsoring polls may be quite different from the concerns of the general public. Discrepancies between the polls' agenda and the general public's interests were especially acute during the political and social turmoil of the late 1960s and early 1970s. Though, as we saw, polling was used by the government during this period to help curb disorder, the major commercial polls took little interest in the issues that aroused so much public concern. The year 1970, for example, was marked by racial strife and antiwar protest in the United States. At least fifty-four major antiwar protests and some forty major instances of racial violence occurred. Yet the 1970 national Gallup Poll devoted only 5 percent of its questions to American policy in Vietnam and only two of 162 questions to domestic race relations. Similarly, in 1971, despite the occurrence of some thirty-five major cases of racial unrest and twenty-six major episodes of student violence or protest, the national Gallup Poll that year devoted only two of its 194 questions to race relations and asked no questions at all about student protest. By contrast, that year's poll asked forty-two political "horse race" questions, concerning citizens' candidate preferences and electoral expectations, as well as eleven questions relating to presidential popularity. An observer attempting to gauge the public's interests from poll data might have concluded that Americans cared only about election forecasts and official popularity and were blithely unconcerned with the matters that were actually rending the social fabric of the era. . . .

Given the commercial character of the polling industry, differences between the polls' concerns and those of the general public are probably inevitable. Polls generally raise questions that are of interest to clients and purchasers of poll data—newspapers, political candidates, governmental agencies, business corporations, and so on. Questions of no immediate relevance to government, business, or politicians will not easily find their way into the surveys. This is particularly true of issues such as the validity of the capitalist economic system or the legitimacy of governmental authority, issues that business and govern-ment usually prefer not to see raised at all, much less at their own expense. Be-cause they seldom pose questions about the foundations of the existing order, while constantly asking respondents to choose from among the alternatives de-fined by that order—candidates and consumer products, for example—polls may help to narrow the focus of public discussion and to reinforce the limits on what the public perceives to be realistic political and social possibilities.

But whatever the particular changes polling may help to produce in the focus of public discourse, the broader problem is that polling fundamentally alters the character of the public agenda of opinion. So long as groups and individuals typically present their opinions on topics of their own choosing, the agenda of opinion is likely to consist of citizens' own needs, hopes, and aspirations. Opin-ions elicited by polls, on the other hand, mainly concern matters of interest to government, business, or other poll sponsors. Typically, poll questions have as their ultimate purpose some form of exhortation. Businesses poll to help per-suade customers to purchase their wares. Candidates poll as part of the process of convincing voters to support them. Governments poll as part of the process of inducing citizens to obey. . . .

In essence, rather than offer governments the opinions that citizens want them to learn, polls tell governments—or other sponsors—what they would like to learn about citizens' opinions. The end result is to change the public expression of opinion from an assertion of demand to a step in the process of persuasion.

Making Opinion Safer for Government

Taken together, the changes produced by polling contribute to the transforma-tion of public opinion from an unpredictable, extreme, and often dangerous force into a more docile expression of public sentiment. Opinion stated through polls imposes less pressure and makes fewer demands on government than would more spontaneous or natural assertions of popular sentiment. Though opinion may be expressed more democratically via polls than through alternative means, polling can give public opinion a plebiscitary character—robbing opinion of precisely those features that might maximize its impact on government and policy.

Notes

1. Chester F. Barnard, "Public Opinion in a Democracy" (Herbert L. Baker Foundation, Princeton University, Princeton, N.J., 1939, pamphlet), 13.
2. Allan Silver, "The Demand for Order in Civil Society," in *The Police*, ed. David Bordua (New York: Wiley, 1967), 17–18.
3. Bogdan Osolnik, "Socialist Public Opinion," *Socialist Thought and Practice* 20 (October 1955): 120.

Questions for Discussion

1. How have the widespread use and acceptability of polls changed the character of public opinion? What are the consequences of such changes for democratic government?
2. Why might governments engage in polling?
3. How has the rise of polling affected interest-group politics? Which groups and elements in society have gained or lost?

 4.2

Is "Popular Rule" Possible?

Larry M. Bartels

Many believe an essential component of modern democracy is the ability of elected representatives to convert public preferences into public policy. An assumption underlying this premise is that such preferences exist and that tools such as public opinion polls can help discover such information.

In this provocative piece, Larry Bartels argues that the notion of "popular rule" is at odds with what researchers have found concerning the electorate's attitudes and preferences. Evidence suggests that although citizens may have meaningful beliefs and values, survey-gathered information often identifies vague and fluid attitudes rather than clear, meaningful public preferences on issues of public policy. A major problem is that survey questions are susceptible to "framing effects"—situations in which different ways of posing a policy issue produce distinctly different public responses. The way a question is worded, the order of the question in the survey, and the context in which the survey is administered may all cause great variation in citizen responses on policy matters. As a consequence, inferences from polls claiming to discern the policy preferences of the public must be viewed with extreme caution.

The celebrated political philosopher H. L. Mencken once characterized democracy as "the theory that the common people know what they want, and deserve to get it good and hard." Democratic theorists have mostly focused on the latter issue, without taking seriously the complexities lurking beneath the notion that "the common people know what they want." The ubiquity of opinion polls probing every conceivable aspect of modern politics and government both reflects and reinforces the notion that the primary problem of modern democracy is to translate definite public preferences into policy. Leaders may ignore the dictates of public opinion, but they are assumed to do so only with good reason—and at their electoral peril.

My aim here is to suggest that this conventional view of democracy is fundamentally unrealistic. Whether it would be desirable to have a democracy based on public opinion is beside the point, because public opinion of the sort necessary to make it possible simply does not exist. The very idea of "popular rule" is starkly inconsistent with the understanding of political psychology provided by the past half-century of research by psychologists and political scientists. That research offers no reason to doubt that citizens have meaningful values and beliefs, but ample reason to doubt that those values and beliefs are sufficiently complete and coherent to serve as a satisfactory starting point for democratic theory. In other words, citizens have attitudes but not preferences—a distinction directly inspired by the work of psychologists Daniel Kahneman and Amos Tversky. My argument extends [certain research,] which challenges the behavioral assumptions underlying conventional economic theory, to the realm of politics and emphasizes particularly the challenge it poses to the most fundamental assumptions of democratic theory.

"Framing Effects"

Kahneman and Tversky have called attention to "framing effects"—situations in which different ways of posing, or "framing," a policy issue produce distinctly different public responses. Framing effects are hard to accommodate within a

Larry M. Bartels is the Donald Stokes Professor of Public and International Affairs and the Director of the Center for the Study of Democratic Politics, Woodrow Wilson School of Public and International Affairs, Princeton University

Larry M. Bartels, "Is 'Popular Rule' Possible? Polls, Political Psychology, and Democracy," *The Brookings Review* 21, no. 3 (Summer 2003): 12–15. Reprinted by permission of The Brookings Institution. Online at www.brook.edu/press/review/summer2003/bartels.htm.

theory built on the assumption that citizens have definite preferences to be elicited; but they are easy to reconcile with the view that any given question may tap a variety of more or less relevant attitudes. The problem for democratic theory is that the fluidity and contingency of attitudes make it impossible to discern meaningful public preferences on issues of public policy, because seemingly arbitrary variations in choice format or context may produce contradictory expressions of popular will.

Survey researchers have been generating examples of framing effects for several decades in experimental work on question wording and question ordering. But only recently have they begun to think of them as manifestations of more general psychological phenomena—especially of the fundamental context-dependency of attitudes. The normative implications of question-wording and question-ordering effects for our understanding of democracy remain virtually unexplored.

Framing effects can be demonstrated most simply by noting the impact on survey responses of prompting respondents to consider some particular aspect of an issue that might otherwise have been overlooked. In a classic 1950 study by Herbert Hyman and Paul Sheatsley, half of a national sample was asked, "Do you think the United States should let Communist newspaper reporters from other countries come in here and send back to their papers the news as they see it?" To that question, 36 percent said yes. The other half of the sample was asked the same question, but only after being asked whether "a Communist country like Russia should let American newspaper reporters come in and send back to America the news as they see it." In this second group, 90 percent agreed that American reporters should be allowed in Russia, and 73 percent—twice the share in the first half-sample—said that communist reporters should be allowed to work in the United States. Clearly, asking first about American reporters in Russia prompted respondents in the second group to apply a norm of reciprocity that blunted (though it did not entirely supplant) strong anti-communist attitudes. . . .

What's in a Name?

Even more perplexing issues arise when the original question is not merely elaborated but altered. Some of the most striking framing effects on record come from question-wording experiments conducted as part of the 1984, 1985, and 1986 General Social Surveys. Respondents were asked whether "we" are spending "too much, too little, or about the right amount" on each of a variety of government programs. Separate random subsamples evaluated essentially similar sets of programs, but with more or less subtle differences in how each was denoted. Some of these subtle differences produced large differences in apparent public opinion. Most spectacularly, while only 20–25 percent of the respondents each year said that too little was being spent on "welfare," 63–65 percent said that too little was being spent on "assistance to the poor."

"Welfare" clearly has deeply unpopular connotations for significant segments of the American public and evokes rather different mental images than does "assistance to the poor." But these different images are attached to the same set of programs and policies; any effort to make subtle distinctions of substance between "welfare" and "assistance to the poor" seems fruitlessly tendentious. Nevertheless, one frame suggests that a substantial majority of the public supports spending more on those programs, while the other—equally legitimate on its face—suggests that the same programs are deeply unpopular. What should a democratic theorist make of this perplexing situation? How might either question—or either outcome—be judged more appropriate than the other?

Sometimes even more arbitrary choices of question wording can produce large differences in opinion. Most people, for example, would presumably acknowledge that "forbidding" an action is substantively equivalent to "not allowing" it. But as Howard Schuman and Stanley Presser have noted, in three separate split-sample experiments in the mid-1970s, between 44 percent and 48 percent of the American public would "not allow" a communist to give a speech, while only about half that share would "forbid" him or her to do so. Substantively identical questions produce markedly different results. Which result reflects the public's "true" opinion? I can suggest no sensible way to answer that question.

I interpret these framing effects as evidence for the thesis that citizens have attitudes rather than preferences. The contrasting patterns of responses documented in a variety of opinion surveys and experiments reflect real attitudes. The attitudes are neither meaningless nor whimsical nor—at least in any common-language sense—irrational. But neither are they the solid bedrock of comprehensive, logically consistent preferences that most liberal political theorists have taken as a starting point for democratic theory.

No Issue Is Immune

How ubiquitous are these framing effects? Are the examples cited here simply carefully selected anomalies, or are they the tips of icebergs? There is good reason to be wary of overgeneralization, given the wide variety of political issues and choice contexts in any functioning democracy, as well as the striking variation in information, motivation, and cognitive capacity in any mass public. But if these framing effects reflect fundamental aspects of the psychology of attitudes, they should appear with some frequency even in situations that seem ripe for the assumption that citizens have complete and consistent preferences over policy outcomes. This point may be dramatized by drawing examples from two issue areas often seen as prime exceptions to the generally disorganized and fluid character of American public opinion—abortion and affirmative action. The vagaries of survey responses evident even in these realms of unusual salience and concreteness reinforce the notion that public opinion is inherently sensitive to arbitrary aspects of how political issues are framed and political objects denoted.

Some of the complexities running beneath the surface of public opinion even on abortion are suggested by Paul Freedman and Ken Goldstein's analysis of responses to two questions on the topic in American National Election Study surveys. In response to a general question about abortion in the 1996 survey, about 40 percent of respondents said that "by law, a woman should always be able to obtain an abortion as a matter of personal choice." However, in response to a different abortion question posed in 1997, 39 percent of these same 1996 pro-choice respondents favored "a proposed law to ban certain types of late-term abortions, sometimes called partial birth abortions." (Of the remaining pro-choice respondents, 49 percent opposed a ban on partial birth abortions; 12 percent were undecided.) That is, a substantial fraction of those who believed that abortions should "always" be permitted "as a matter of personal choice" also believed that "partial birth abortions" should be banned. While it might be possible to render these two positions logically consistent (for example, by stipulating the availability of some practical alternative to partial birth abortions in situations where they are now being chosen), it seems more straightforward simply to acknowledge that when it comes to public opinion, "always" never means always. . . .

Nor is it obvious how one could clarify public preferences regarding abortion policy through more careful question writing. Some of the ambiguities inherent in any such attempt at clarification are suggested by another analysis of data from the 1997 National Election Study survey, this one by Virginia Sapiro. Half the respondents were asked to rate "opponents of abortion" and "supporters of abortion" on a 100-point "feeling thermometer"; the other half were asked to rate "pro-life people" and "pro-choice people."* It seems fruitless to deny that these are, in essence, alternative ways of tapping exactly the same substantive attitudes. Nevertheless, Sapiro found that they produced significantly different results, with both "pro-life" and "pro-choice" people being rated much more favorably than abortion "opponents" or "supporters," respectively. The differences appeared consistently among men and women, among more and less politically informed respondents, and among those who were themselves opponents and supporters of abortion. While these differences testify to the success of the rhetorical strategies adopted by abortion partisans in labeling themselves as "pro-choice" and "pro-life," they do nothing to justify one's faith in the reality of public attitudes toward them independent of the particular words by which they are denoted.

---

*A "feeling thermometer" is a device used to access a respondent's feelings (affective orientation) toward groups, political figures, countries, etc. Respondents are given a ratings scale ranging from 0 to 100 degrees in the form of a thermometer, where a rating of 0 degrees represents maximum "coldness" toward the object being assessed, 50 degrees represents a neutral point, and 100 degrees represents maximum "warmth" toward the object.

From Opinion Polls to Referenda

One might still object that questions in opinion surveys are a far cry from real political decisions and that peculiar responses to survey questions even about an issue as salient and fundamental as abortion have little genuine relevance for democratic theory. That objection seems to me misguided in both its aspects. Although most consequential decisions in democracies are made by representatives, and not directly by citizens in policy referenda, theories of representation are almost invariably grounded in analogous choices of policies by representatives, or of representatives by citizens, or both. As long as we continue to evaluate democracy in terms of the correspondence between citizens' preferences and policy outcomes, all the same theoretical problems will reappear when we attempt to specify what kind of representation is most democratic. . . .

The practical reality of these conceptual problems is illustrated by a 1997 referendum on affirmative action programs in Houston. As reported on November 6 in the *New York Times* by Sam Howe Verhovek, "the future of affirmative action may depend more than anything else on the language in which it is framed."

> The vote Tuesday came only after a tumultuous debate in the City Council over the wording of the measure. Rather than being asked whether they wanted to ban discrimination and "preferential treatment," to which voters said a clear "yes" in California last year and to which polls showed Houston voters would also say "yes," residents were instead asked whether they wished specifically to ban affirmative action in city contracting and hiring.
>
> The legal effect was the same under either wording, but to this revised question they answered "no" by 55 percent to 45 percent. . . .
>
> Affirmative-action proponents around the nation hailed not just the result of Houston's vote, but the phrasing of the referendum as a straight up-or-down call on affirmative action, and they said that is the way the question should be put to voters elsewhere.
>
> Its opponents, meanwhile, who are already in court challenging the City Council's broad rewording as illegal, denounced it as a heavy-handed way of obscuring the principles that were really at stake.

Who is to decide what principles are "really at stake" in such a policy choice? If we accept, for the sake of argument, that a referendum using the original wording "taken almost directly from the Civil Rights Act of 1964" would have passed, as most observers seem to have believed, would that result have been more or less legitimate than the actual result? These questions are of a piece with those raised by the research of psychologists and public opinion researchers. Political elites who pose referendum questions must frame complex, difficult political issues in specific, concrete language. If citizens had definite, preexisting preferences regarding the underlying issues, any reasonable choice of language might elicit those preferences equally well. But democracy with attitudes requires some more detailed, normatively compelling account of what makes one frame more appropriate than another as a basis for democratic choice. In the absence of such an account, political debate and policy choice become a rhetorical free-for-all—a practical art in which, at best, the ends justify the means. . . .

Popular Rule—Or Popular Veto?

The realization that attitude expressions are powerfully (and, in my view, intrinsically and unavoidably) context-dependent should spur democratic theorists to specify more clearly how political issues ought to be framed. Theoretical work along these lines may be inspired and informed by relevant empirical research, but first and foremost it will require a more subtle specification of the moral grounds on which one political context or institution might be deemed superior to another. It will not be sufficient to evaluate contexts or institutions by reference to their success or failure in reflecting citizens' preferences, since that is merely to beg the question.

The most obvious alternative to theoretical progress along these lines is a much-diluted version of democratic theory in which the ideal of "popular rule" is replaced by what William Riker once characterized as "an intermittent, sometimes random, even perverse, popular veto" on the machinations of political elites. If that sort of democracy is the best we can hope for, we had better reconcile ourselves to the fact. On the other hand, if we insist on believing that democracy can provide some attractive and consistent normative basis for evaluating policy outcomes, we had better figure out more clearly what we are talking about.

Questions for Discussion

1. In his conclusion, Bartels questions whether or not it would ever be possible to achieve the idealized notion of "popular rule" that some believe is essential for democracy. What do you think?
2. How might questions on a public opinion survey on the recent Iraq War be "framed" to show broad public support for the efforts of the Bush administration? To show opposition to the Bush administration's efforts?

4.3

Can We Trust the Polls?

Michael W. Traugott

Public opinion polls—frequently conducted, and with results that are widely dis-seminated—are considered to be an essential feature of modern American democracy. But how much confidence should we place in the polls? In this se-lection, Michael Traugott suggests that poll consumers should be very cautious in assigning meaning to many of the surveys that are reported; extra attention should be placed on how individual polls are conducted. In his view, although there has been an increase in the availability of polls, in some respects their quality may have declined.

Traugott identifies a number of serious problems. Thanks to technology and the falling costs of computers, phone service, and statistical software, it is inex-pensive for almost anyone to get into the polling business. One consequence is that there has been a huge proliferation of polls being conducted at the local level. Such polls, in particular, may not be well administered and it is often diffi-cult to determine if they meet the rigorous standards of the polling profession. "The problem is exacerbated because journalists and others who report on pub-lic opinion are not generally well trained in assessing poll results and thus can-not always weed out 'bad' poll results before they enter the news stream and become 'fact.'"

Even the national-level polling industry faces challenges in designing surveys representative of the population under study. Response rates have been declin-ing and new technologies (such as the increasing use of cell phones and caller ID) make it difficult for all members of the population to be included in the frame from which a sample is drawn. Pre-election pollsters must now contend with the fact that many Americans vote well before election day (early voting, absentee voting, vote-by-mail, etc.), and in some states citizens can decide at the last minute that they want to vote, even if they were not registered previously. Predic-tions on turnout and preferences may be muddled as a result. Such problems can be managed, but it takes a major commitment of resources and much more sophisticated survey designs.

Can we trust the polls? Under the best of circumstances, the answer is "Not necessarily without a fair amount of detailed information about how they were conducted." This general note of caution applies at any time to any poll consumer. But today, with polls proliferating in the media and with methodological concerns increasing within the polling industry, caution is even more warranted. This is not to suggest that the general quality of polling data is declining or that the problems facing pollsters have no answers. Still, consumers of polling data need to be more careful than ever.

Proliferating Polls

In a period of rapidly advancing technology and falling costs for computers, long-distance telephone service, and statistical software, it is easier than ever for start-up companies to get into the polling business. Because most polling now takes place on the telephone, it is cheap and easy for someone who wants to get into the polling business to buy a sample, write a short questionnaire for a Computer Assisted Telephone Interviewing (CATI) application, buy interviewing services from a field house, and receive a report based on the marginals for each question and a limited set of cross-tabulations.

As a consequence, the opportunity to see the results of a poorly conducted poll has become more frequent, even if we can't assess exactly whether the probability of seeing one has changed. The problem is exacerbated because journalists and others who report on public opinion are not generally well trained in assessing poll results and thus cannot always weed out "bad" poll results before they enter the news stream and become "fact." So the risk is growing that local polls on national or local issues may be less well conducted or less well reported than those conducted by major national organizations.

Neither poll consumers nor journalists who write about polls have access to quality-control criteria or certification processes by which to assess specific firms or individuals. As a result, all must rely on news organizations to evaluate polls on the basis of the standards of disclosure of poll results adopted by organizations like the American Association for Public Opinion Research (AAPOR) and the National Council of Public Polls (NCPP). And they should report any concerns they have about such items. Information thus made available on details such as sampling, question wording, field dates, and response rates is useful for the few informed poll consumers who can interpret it.

Michael W. Traugott is a professor of communications studies and political science at the University of Michigan and senior research scientist at the Institute for Social Research.

Michael W. Traugott, "Can We Trust the Polls? It All Depends," *The Brookings Review* 21, no. 3 (Summer 2003): 8–11. Reprinted by permission of The Brookings Institution. Online at www.brook.edu/press/review/summer2003/traugott.htm.

Declining Response Rates

Falling response rates are a concern for the entire survey research industry, whether academic researchers, political consultants who work for candidates, or news organizations. Recent compilations of response rates in telephone surveys by the Council for Marketing and Opinion Research suggest that studies with short field periods are now averaging about 10 percent, although most media polls have response rates in the 30–45 percent range. Although analysts have identified many factors behind this long-term trend—such as the negative impacts of tele-marketers posing as pollsters and the increased use of various call-screening devices—we don't yet understand well how much each contributes to the overall decline. Researchers are also beginning to understand that declining participation rates probably affect different kinds of political polls in different ways.

For preelection polls that project the outcome of a race, preliminary research suggests that the same factors that may lower participation in surveys may also lower participation in elections. Declining response rates thus do not seem to pose dangers to the accuracy of estimates of the outcome of recent presidential elections. More research will help clarify whether declining participation will affect preelection estimates in lower-turnout elections held in nonpresidential years or whether over time it will have different effects on future preelection estimates.

Preelection polls are unusual in that their accuracy can be checked against the outcome of the election itself. (That characteristic may create a misplaced confidence in polling generally, since similar external validations do not apply in many other polling situations.) When it comes to polling on issues of general government policy, we do not know the potential impact of declining survey participation rates because we have no way to check the accuracy of the polls. For example, when polls assess the public's response to or appraisal of policies such as military action in Iraq or a proposed tax cut, there is no equivalent independent way to measure the validity of the measurements. There is, however, some suggestion that policy polling results may reflect more conservative or Republican views than are present in the population as a whole—a bias that would not be surprising because Republicans have long been known to be more likely to vote than Democrats (a fact accounted for in the likelihood estimators used by most polling firms).

Emerging Technology

Many polling organizations embrace new technology as a way to cut costs and speed data collection. Some new technologies also make it possible to collect more types of data. Web-based surveys, for example, can employ visual or audio stimuli that are not possible with other questionnaire designs, making them an excellent way to evaluate political commercials, especially when applied in a full experimental design. Many organizations have also turned to Web-based surveys to reduce the turnaround time between the design of a questionnaire and the start of data analysis and production of a first report of results.

Applied inappropriately, however, this technology offers several potential pitfalls for data quality. First and foremost are sampling issues related to respondent selection. Pollsters obtain respondents in three ways. They take "volunteers" who self-select themselves to answer generally available questionnaires on a Web site. They recruit volunteers, sometimes for a single survey and sometimes for a panel from which subsequent samples will be drawn. And they use a probability sample to select respondents on the telephone and supply Internet access to those who need it.

Because the availability of Web connections is not uniformly or randomly distributed in society, the existence of a "digital divide" can introduce one source of bias in volunteer samples.* This technique, for example, tends to produce samples that are more Republican and with more conservative leanings, as we have seen in such varied circumstances as post-debate polls in 2000 and more general public policy assessments since. The resulting bias tends to favor the current Bush administration and could work against a Democratic administration. Other possible problems include fatigue from the requirement to respond to periodic and frequent surveys to maintain panel status—a requirement that could even lead, in some circumstances, to "professional" respondents. More research needs to be done on these issues, but at a minimum a poll consumer ought to know about respondent recruitment and selection for Web-based surveys.

Pollsters must also contend with the rise of cell phones. Despite the increasing penetration of these devices in the United States (approaching 75 percent), fewer than 5 percent of Americans rely solely on a cell phone. But that share is growing—and presenting pollsters with a new set of problems. First, cell phone exchanges have no general directory, and they are excluded from samples that most public polling firms can buy. Second, people who rely on cell phones are more mobile than the rest of the population, and many use phones provided by their business. If, as is likely, the geographical correspondence between the phones' assigned area codes and their owners' place of residence is poor, it may or may not be an issue for firms conducting surveys with national samples, but it could be for those conducting state or local surveys and effectively dialing out of their target area.

One further problem linked to new technology is telephone caller ID. This screening device, which alerts households to who is calling, makes it possible to avoid calls from "out of their area" or from unfamiliar numbers. In response to citizens' pleas for protection from telemarketers, the federal government is moving to develop a "do not call" list. Pollsters need not honor such list membership now, but future abuses by pollsters or telemarketers could change that. This technology too is exerting downward pressure on response rates.

---

*As a group, individuals with access to computers and the Internet tend to be of higher socioeconomic and educational status and reflect a different racial and ethnic profile from those without such access, creating what is known as the "digital divide." One consequence is that samples based on Web users tend to be unrepresentative of the population at large, typically undersampling those with liberal attitudes and Democratic preferences.

New Voting Methods and Preelection Pollsters

Preelection pollsters face two relatively new problems, both of which they can manage by devoting more financial resources to their work. Whether firms will be willing to pay more to collect data with less error or bias remains to be seen.

For almost 10 years, new administrative procedures have been allowing Americans to change the way they cast their ballots. Increasingly, citizens are voting before election day—or rather, as it is coming to mean, "Vote Counting Day."

Through procedures such as "early voting" (where machines are set up in convenient locations such as malls or shopping centers as early as three weeks before election day), voting by mail (where every registered voter is sent a ballot up to 20 days before election day), and permanent absentee registration (where voters can ask to be mailed a ballot in advance of election day without indicating that they will be out of town), more and more voters are casting ballots early. In the 2000 election, about one-sixth of the national electorate voted early, and the share is growing. In selected states, the proportion can be much greater. This trend is also facilitated by other administrative changes, such as election day registration, whereby citizens can decide at the last minute that they want to vote, even if they have not previously registered.

These developments do not mean that preelection telephone polls are outmoded or will fade away. They do suggest that telephone pollsters will have to use hybrid designs that include different screening questions (Have you voted yet? Are you registered to vote in the upcoming election?). Voter News Service used such techniques in past elections, as did firms in large states—such as California, Texas, and Florida—with many early voters. Eventually telephone polls may be supplemented by exit polls of voters leaving early voting sites. Such problems are not insurmountable, but they imply added expense as well as the need for more sophisticated designs, which will likely complicate modeling the outcome of elections based on more and more disparate data sources.

A second issue for preelection pollsters—one that cropped up in the 2002 election—is the development by the Republican Party of 24-Hour Task Forces to counter union-based get-out-the-vote campaigns. Volunteer recruits were solicited on the Internet to make at least three calls in the final 72 hours of the campaign to encourage likely Republican voters to get to the polls. The effectiveness of these efforts has not been analyzed systematically, but they may have been of use in at least some states, especially in the South. The difficulty is that preelection pollsters, especially those linked to newspapers, traditionally poll up through Friday or Saturday to produce a story for Sunday's paper. Because their polling typically ends just as these mobilization efforts get under way, their polls could underestimate the Republican share of the vote. Pollsters could counter the problem by extending the period for preelection polling, even through Monday evening, but that would defy a set of news-making norms about the best time to publish stories about the campaign to reach the largest audience. And it also would increase data collection costs. . . .

The Internationalization of Polling

The recent military action in Iraq has increased news organizations' interest in what foreign publics, especially those in the Middle East or in states such as Afghanistan and Pakistan, think about the United States and its policies. But the polling industry in these regions is not yet well developed and typically relies on samples drawn from a few major urban areas rather than countrywide. The National Council of Public Polls has recently suggested that the issue may often be a pragmatic one for the data collection firm. In addition to cutting travel costs, these simpler designs may also reduce translation and language problems. But the resulting data also require journalists wishing to report about what others think of Americans to be careful about the level and type of generalizations they draw.

More Polls, More Problems

Public opinion polls, frequently conducted and with results that are widely disseminated, are one distinguishing feature of a healthy democracy. They provide a means for citizens to communicate with their elected representatives, and vice versa. But their value in this regard depends on the collection of high-quality data, well analyzed and appropriately interpreted.

Of late there has been a step-function increase in the availability of polls, accompanied by issues of potential reductions in quality. Such developments are not unprecedented: new technologies have before, and will again, become available to produce data faster and cheaper, while the resulting savings are not devoted to reducing various kinds of error. No one yet fully understands what the consequences might be of the various problems outlined above. Poll consumers, as ever, have no recourse but to pay as much attention as they can to where the data came from and how they were analyzed.

Questions for Discussion

1. What factors underlie the proliferation of polling efforts, on one hand, and the potential for the decreased quality of polling results on the other? Why is the problem most pronounced at the local level?
2. Technological changes, from the Web to cell phones, appear to have the potential to bias many poll results. What political perspectives might be overrepresented? Underrepresented?

# Chapter 5

Participation and Civic Engagement

In a democracy, political participation may take many forms, ranging from efforts by citizens merely to inform themselves about politics to running for and holding public office. Some citizens may even attempt to bypass more conventional modes of participation altogether by engaging in political protest marches or acts of civil disobedience—the nonviolent violation of laws that they believe to be unjust. For most citizens, however, political participation centers around the act of voting in an election.

Participation in free elections provides citizens with many benefits. When people believe they can communicate their needs and wants to those who govern, government becomes both stable and legitimate. Elections teach civic virtues and give citizens a sense of responsibility and personal satisfaction.

The key role of elections, however, is to provide a check on power. As James Madison wrote in *The Federalist,* No. 51, "If Angels were to govern men, neither external nor internal controls on the government would be necessary," but in the absence of heavenly guidance government must be restrained, and "a dependence on the people is, no doubt, the primary control." The ballot box offers the public a way to control those who govern, since people seeking election must further citizens' interests to achieve public office. The public does not rule, but it influences those who do.

Although most Americans probably would be hard-pressed to give a sophisticated answer to the question "Why vote?" most firmly believe that democracy is "rule by the people" and that the cornerstone of popular democracy is free elections. Students are taught that everyone "ought to vote," and voting for the first time is a political rite of passage that serves as a powerful symbol of adulthood and allegiance to the American system. Many Americans hold the view that anyone who doesn't vote has forfeited the right to criticize the government.

In spite of these beliefs and feelings, however, many citizens do not participate in contemporary elections, a fact that could challenge the validity of popular democracy. The United States ranks near the bottom of Western democracies in voter turnout. Furthermore, current turnout rates do not compare favorably with those of past elections. For example, in presidential elections in the last half of the 1800s, about 75 percent of eligible voters turned out (nearly 82 percent in the election of 1876), whereas in recent elections only slightly more than 50 percent voted. Turnout rates in off-year state and local elections are often less than 30 percent. President Reagan, who beat President Carter by an overwhelming margin in 1980, was elected by just a little more than 27 percent of the eligible voters in that year.

Comparisons of our own past with that of other nations are fraught with difficulties. A century ago, the electorate included neither women nor blacks. Ballots were not secret, and there were few registration barriers to restrict participation by white males. This created a strong incentive for political parties to mobilize voters, sometimes by herding citizens to the polls and giving them ballots containing only one party's candidates. The eastern cities in particular were dominated by political machines. Consequently, some of the high turnout figures undoubtedly resulted from political corruption.

Some countries impose a fine for not voting—a policy that would raise turnout rates in the United States but would be interpreted as undemocratic by most Americans. Many Western democracies calculate turnout as the percentage of those on the electoral rolls who actually participate in an election, whereas in the United States turnout is calculated by dividing the number who vote by the total potential electorate—all persons of voting age, as determined by the U.S. Bureau of the Census. If this method were applied by other countries, U.S. voting rates would differ little from those of Canada, Great Britain, and Japan.

Surprisingly, voter turnout in the United States has constantly declined since the 1960 presidential election. This period has been marked by rising educational levels, increasingly prominent issues, and the removal of many voting barriers, such as poll taxes and registration and residency requirements. In addition, tremendous amounts of political information have been provided by the mass media, and campaigns have grown enormously in terms of cost and candidate exposure. Newspapers often chastise citizens for being lazy and uninterested in exercising their right to vote, but explanations for the turnout decline are much more complex.

One widely held belief is that, beginning in the mid-1960s, citizens developed mistrust of government officials and a diminished sense that their participation would make a difference. In 1966, about a quarter of the public believed the "people running the country don't care what happens to people like me." By 1977, 60 percent felt this way. By 1978, only 30 percent of Americans believed they could trust the government in Washington "to do what's right." In 1958, a similar poll revealed that 55 percent trusted the government.

Such disillusionment grew from the social disruptions of the 1960s, the assassinations of John F. Kennedy, Robert Kennedy, and Martin Luther King, Jr., the unpopular Vietnam War, the Watergate scandal, and the subsequent resignation of President Nixon. Huge increases in consumer prices in the 1970s and the perceived ineffectiveness of the Carter administration in dealing with the energy crisis and with the Iranian hostage situation also contributed to citizens' perception that leaders were neither trustworthy nor competent. Some scholars suggest that television played a role, too. According to the theory of "video malaise,"

TV tends to overwhelm viewers with the complexities of political controversies, which convinces the public that individuals are politically ineffective and that problems may be too difficult to solve. Further, the tone of the TV medium has been generally critical of authorities, highlighting the human weaknesses and mistakes of political leaders. Many voters thus question the value of political participation.

A second widely accepted explanation for decreasing turnout relies on demographic factors. The arrival of the baby boomers at voting age during the mid-1960s, and constitutional changes that enfranchised eighteen- to twenty-year-olds, dramatically expanded the potential electorate between 1960 and 1972. Young voters made up an increasingly high proportion of the total electorate in the 1960s, 1970s, and early 1980s, yet this group participated less than older Americans did. Few saw politics as relevant to their lives. First-time eligible voters have had the lowest participation rates of any age group, perhaps because politics has to compete with schooling, social events, and courtship.

The articles in this chapter have been chosen to encourage students to think about political involvement from a broad perspective, not just voting. In the first selection, Micah L. Sifry challenges the notion that apathy is largely responsible for low voter turnout. He argues that party candidates with a populist or progressive message have the potential to greatly enlarge the active electorate. The second selection deals with the role of the citizen in contemporary politics. Michael Schudson argues that our current concept of citizenship, based on the Progressive model, needs revision. He asserts that we need a new concept of citizenship, one that makes demands on us but is not burdened with impossible expectations. The third selection, by Robert D. Putnam, posits a linkage between the broad involvement of citizens in the associational life of their community and the health of American democracy. Putnam is dismayed by the decline of "social capital" that seems to characterize American politics over the past quarter of a century. In the final selection, Putnam examines the impact of 9/11 on American civic attitudes. He finds that the trend toward civic disengagement has been interrupted. He believes a "window of opportunity" now exists for civic renewal.

5.1

Finding the Lost Voters

Micah L. Sifry

Few subjects engender more heated discussion during and after an election than the nation's low voter-turnout rate. For those who believe that citizen participation in elections is fundamental to American democracy, the 2000 presidential election was especially frustrating. Although voter registration barriers had been virtually eliminated and party and candidate expenditures set records in an effort to reach voters in one of the closest presidential contests in recent memory, barely half of the age-eligible voters went to the polls.

In this selection, Micah L. Sifry suggests that growing alienation from the major parties lies at the heart of why many people choose not to participate in elections. Besides the rise in the number of registered independents, who tend to vote less than partisans, poll data indicates that roughly a third of nonvoters aren't apathetic about voting, but are unhappy with the choices typically offered by Republicans and Democrats. Sifry believes the best way to enlarge the active electoral would be for parties to choose candidates committed to running progressive and populist campaigns, appealing to "potential voters" rather than solely concentrating on turning out "likely voters."

A l Garcia is one frustrated Democratic campaign manager. A criminal defense lawyer by trade and a 20-year veteran of Minnesota politics, he ran two candidates for the state assembly in 1998. Both were in Anoka County, ground zero of the Jesse Ventura vote.* One candidate, Jerry Newton, a decorated Vietnam veteran and small-business owner, fiscally conservative but very supportive of public schools and the environment, lost badly to a far-right pro-lifer as the voters who turned out for Ventura voted for Republican state representatives down the ballot. Garcia's other candidate, Luanne Kos-

Micah L. Sifry is a senior analyst for Public Campaign, a public-interest group focusing upon campaign finance.

"Finding the Lost Voters" by Micah L. Sifry. Reprinted with permission from *The American Prospect*, Volume 11, Number 6: January 21, 2000. The American Prospect, 11 Beacon Street, Suite 1120, Boston, MA 02108. All rights reserved.

*Jesse Ventura, a former professional wrestler, was elected in 1998 as governor of Minnesota running on the Reform Party ticket.

kinen, an incumbent with strong labor backing, barely held onto her office. Garcia's problems were hardly unique: Ventura voters across the state ended up costing Democrats control of the state assembly.

Over lunch last winter at Billie's, a popular Anoka County restaurant, Garcia delivered his postmortem: Democrats had gotten whipped because they hadn't reached out to new voters—and there had been a lot of them. . . .

And why had his candidates fared so poorly? "We were too focused on the regular voters," Garcia said. "If you hadn't voted in two out of the last four elections, you didn't get anything from Luanne or Jerry." Targeting likely voters, of course, is standard practice in most campaigns these days. But Garcia said he'd known that strategy wouldn't be enough.

"I could sense it coming," he said. "My wife told me early on that she would support Ventura, and she hates politics. All my legal clients were supporting Jesse, from the first-time DWI offenders to the major dope dealers! And he was pulling at me, in my gut. I'm a blue-collar guy who grew up in north Minneapolis. My dad's a dockworker, my mother's a waitress. Like the folks in Anoka. And he was saying things that average people could connect with."

Garcia said he'd wanted his candidates to do the same thing. "The number-one issues in Anoka are taxes, wages, and traffic. That's what we wanted to focus on." But he'd been hamstrung by a centralized campaign effort run out of the House Democratic Caucus. "They had a $15,000 mail program—half of our budget—that we were forced to buy into or lose our field worker and party funds. Six out of the nine pieces they mailed were on education, even though we said that wasn't our top concern. And they mailed to too small a target group, and they wouldn't let us change it."

Campaigns at all levels of American politics these days are focused narrowly on "likely voters," people who vote regularly. Eric Johnson, campaign manager to Hubert "Skip" Humphrey, the losing Democratic candidate for governor, admitted as much after the election. "We didn't see Ventura coming because our polling screened out unlikely voters," he told *The Wall Street Journal*. All four of Minnesota's major polling organizations also failed to predict Ventura's victory because they factored out these voters.

The assumption governing the typical political campaign is that the American electorate is a stable, predictable mass—or, worse, that they're apathetic and easily manipulated. Ventura's victory is just the latest and loudest explosion of that piece of conventional wisdom.

Indeed, politicians are making a huge mistake when they focus only on "likely voters." A large subset of the "unlikely voters" filtered out by pollsters and left out of campaign targeting efforts might be better described as *discouraged* voters—potential participants who have been turned off or pushed out by an increasingly money-driven and manipulative electoral process.

Many of these citizens, people who are disproportionately downscale and correspondingly attracted to working-class issues and symbols, can be remotivated to turn out. A central question is whether more Democrats will take their

campaigns to these voters or, by failing to do so, will continue to create opportunities for outsiders ranging from Jesse Ventura to Bernie Sanders to Patrick
Buchanan.

Apathy or Independence?

Public trust in government has been declining steadily over the past four
decades. The authoritative surveys conducted biennially since the 1950s by the
University of Michigan's National Election Studies (NES) have found that
large majorities of Americans, across all demographic groups, don't believe
"you can trust the government in Washington to do what is right just about always [or] most of the time." Similarly, most people think "the government is
pretty much run by a few big interests looking out for themselves." According
to the NES, the percentage agreeing that "people like me don't have any say
about what the government does" rose from 31 percent in 1952 to 53 percent
in 1996. This is a strong statement of disaffection.

But some Americans still feel better represented than others. People are
more likely to believe that they "don't have any say" if they are black rather
than white, are poor rather than well-off, have a limited education compared
to a college diploma or postgraduate degree, or work in blue-collar jobs rather
than white-collar or professional fields. For example, 62 percent of people with
a high school diploma said they don't have any say in what government does,
compared to 40 percent of those with more education. And about 56 percent of
those in the bottom two-thirds of the national income distribution felt left out,
compared to 38 percent in the top twentieth.

A similar pattern applies to how Americans think about the major political
parties. In general, polls find that between 50 and 60 percent of the population
believes there are "important differences in what the Republicans and Democrats stand for." But in 1996, while most people in the top income brackets believed that there were significant differences between the parties, 50 percent of
people in the bottom sixth of income distribution thought there was no difference. Similarly, 59 percent of those with less than a high school education and
40 percent of those with a high school diploma said there was no difference between the parties, compared to just 25 percent of those with at least some college education. Overall, blue-collar workers were almost twice as likely as
professionals to believe party distinctions were meaningless.

Among active voters, the trend is away from the major parties and toward independence. From 1990 to 1998, while the number of voters registered as independent or third-party increased approximately 57 percent, the number of
registered Republicans dropped by almost 5 percent and the number of Democrats by almost 14 percent, according to data collected from state agencies by
the Committee for the Study of the American Electorate. Voters' political preferences—a looser definition than party registration—showed the same trend.

The proportion of people identifying themselves as independents increased from 23 percent in 1952 to an average of 35 percent in the 1990s, according to the NES. Independent voters are somewhat more likely to be of lower income, education, age, and occupational status than hard-core party partisans (though this variation is tempered by the strong Democratic loyalties of many blacks). And 41 percent of people under the age of 29 self-identify as independents, according to a 1999 Gallup poll.

Independents are the most volatile of active voters, with a marked tendency to support candidates who come from "outside the box." All the exit polls going back to George Wallace's 1968 presidential candidacy show that voters who identify themselves as independents are about twice as likely as other voters to support third-party candidates. In Minnesota in 1998, Ventura won with 37 percent overall, but got 52 percent of independents.

As the National Voter Registration Act of 1993 (known as the motor-voter law) brings more voters onto the registration rolls, this trend toward electoral volatility seems likely to strengthen. In Florida, the numbers of registered Republicans, Democrats, and nonaffiliates/third-party registrants each rose by about 500,000 in the first two years of the law's implementation. Since 1996, however, the number of major party registrants has declined slightly, while the number of non-major party registrants has risen another 250,000. The same thing has happened in California, where the number of major party registrants has held steady since 1996, while the number of non-major party registrants has risen about 300,000.

Of course, rising voter alienation and disaffection from the two major parties does not prove that a different kind of political engagement is possible. After all, as measures of political alienation have risen, turnout in national and state elections has declined. But are citizens really just signaling their apathy when they fail to vote? Or are they more specifically alienated from the Democratic and Republican establishments and their candidates? In fact, a significant number of nonvoters look a lot like politically active independent voters.

It is difficult to find data that distinguishes those abstainers who are principled or angry and those who are merely indifferent, but it does exist. In May of 1996, the League of Women Voters released a poll that showed nonvoters were no more distrustful of the federal government than regular voters. Active voters were, however, far more likely to see significant differences between the parties on major issues, to believe that elections mattered and that their votes made a difference. The poll also suggested that efforts to mobilize voters were highly important: About three-quarters of voters said they had been contacted by a candidate or party, compared with less than half of the nonvoters.

But this says little about the actual political preferences of nonvoters. More answers can be found in two little-noticed surveys, one conducted in the summer of 1983 by ABC News, and the second done after the election of 1996 by Republican pollster Kellyanne Fitzpatrick. ABC News polled more than 2,500 voting-age Americans and then compared highly likely voters (people who were registered to vote who said they always vote) with very unlikely voters (people who were not registered to vote and gave little inclination that they were planning to vote in the next election). The Fitzpatrick poll compared a sample of 800 voters with one of 400 nonvoters. Together, the two surveys reveal some telling points.

First, about a third of nonvoters aren't apathetic. Rather, they're angry and feel shut out by the choices offered. When asked by ABC why they didn't vote in the 1980 presidential election, 36 percent of the nonvoters gave a political reason such as "None of the candidates appealed to me." Thirty-eight percent of the nonvoters in the Fitzpatrick poll didn't vote in 1996 because they "did not care for any of the candidates" or were "fed up with the political system" or "did not feel like candidates were interested in people like me."

Second, nonvoters tilt toward liberalism. In the ABC News poll, 60 percent of the nonvoters who said they had voted in 1980 recalled choosing either Jimmy Carter or John Anderson;* only 30 percent said they had voted for Ronald Reagan. Considering that after an election, voters tend to "recall" voting for the winner, this is a striking finding. Sixty-seven percent of nonvoters said they had voted for the Democratic candidate for the House of Representatives, compared to 52 percent of regular voters. In the Fitzpatrick poll, just 38 percent of nonvoters identified as conservatives, compared to 48 percent of the voting public. And while 17 percent of voters called themselves liberals, 22 percent of nonvoters chose that label. (A *New York Times*/CBS News poll found that those who were not planning to vote in the 1998 election preferred Democrats for Congress by 49 percent to 27 percent; likely voters, on the other hand, were evenly split between Republicans and Democrats.)

How to Reach Discouraged Voters

"Low turnout is the compound consequence of legal and procedural barriers intertwined with the parties' reluctance to mobilize many voters, especially working-class and minority voters," says Frances Fox Piven, who along with her husband Richard Cloward wrote *Why Americans Don't Vote* and built the movement that passed the motor-voter law. "I've come to the conclusion that party competition takes the form of demobilizing, not mobilizing, voters, because new voters threaten incumbents, raise new issues, or create the incentive to raise new issues," she adds. "You need mavericks, outsiders to try to mobilize new voters—nobody else wants to take the risk."

"Nonvoters matter a lot," agrees pollster Stanley Greenberg, "though most candidates act as if they don't. . . . There's no question that you can change the

---

*John Anderson, a Republican congressman who failed to receive his party's nomination for president, ran in the 1980 general election as an Independent. He received 6.7 percent of the votes cast.

shape and size of the electorate, though that is more true for presidential elections than for individual, even statewide, campaigns." For example, turnout increased by 5.5 percent in the three-way presidential race of 1992. "There's reason to believe that the populist economic issues that Clinton was raising and the independent-libertarian issues that Perot was raising were at work there," Greenberg argues. "By comparison, in 1994, conservative definitions of the issues brought in more rural, conservative portions of the electorate while the health care reform failure led many noncollege women to drop out." Pollster John Zogby agrees: "If there's a strong independent candidate in the race, you begin to see the numbers of undecided voters in those groups who often don't vote—younger voters, registered independents—start to decline in our surveys, a sign they are planning to vote."

Representative Jesse Jackson, Jr., points to his father's 1984 and 1988 campaigns as proof that discouraged voters can be effectively mobilized. Indeed, the number of Democratic primary voters rose from 18 million in 1984 to nearly 23 million in 1988, with Reverend Jackson's total share rising by 3.4 million. "If you're able to tap into the people who aren't consciously involved in politics or following it," the younger Jackson says, "and show how everything they do has something to do with politics—that shirt they wear, the stop sign, the taxes they pay, the schools they attend, the police officer on their street . . . you can inspire them and give them reason to participate."

It takes a certain kind of candidate, message, and campaign to reach these voters. "You're not going to be able to cater to traditional economic forces that have significant influence," says Jackson. "You have to have some relationship to them, but you can't be seen as beholden to them. You have to be seen as a real American; you have to be someone who can look the press right in the face and tell them exactly how it is. You have to be Beattyite, almost Bulworthian."

Not many American politicians are trying to run this kind of campaign or can convincingly pull it off. However, there are a number of successful examples that predate Jesse Ventura. What seems to matter most is that the candidate have a populist message and style—someone who wants to empower ordinary people versus the establishment, who is blue collar as opposed to buttoned-down, who favors effective government on behalf of the interests of average working people, and who supports sweeping efforts to clean up politics and reform the electoral process itself.

Those were Paul Wellstone's attributes in 1990, when he came from nowhere—he had been a college professor and progressive activist—to win the Minnesota Senate race. Not only did Wellstone draw more votes than the Democratic candidate in the previous Senate contest; more voters came out in 1990 than did in 1988, a presidential election year. (According to Francis Fox Piven, Wellstone attributed his victory in part to the increased number of poorer voters on the rolls, thanks to the earlier passage of a state-level, agency-based voter registration system.) Something similar happened in 1998 with Iowan Tom Vilsack, who waged a successful underdog run for governor and

raised the Democratic vote total nearly 20 percent over the previous gubernatorial race. And activists in Washington State argue that their 1998 ballot initiative to raise the state minimum wage to the highest level in the country had
a similar effect—drawing more votes than any other item or candidate on the
ballot and bringing in enough new voters to swing control of both houses of the
state legislature back to the Democratic column.

In 1990, Bernie Sanders, the former socialist mayor of Burlington, won Vermont's lone seat in Congress as an independent. He ran on issues like national
health care, tax fairness, environmental activism, addressing the needs of the
poor, and involving working people in the political process. In his first try for
Congress in 1988, he came close, drawing 37.5 percent of the vote. Two years
later, he won a solid victory with 56 percent of the vote. In both races, the total
vote was way up—13 percent higher—compared to the previous election cycle.

And while Sanders did well in his breakthrough victory in 1990 with the
college-educated, alternative life-style types who have moved up to Vermont in
the past generation, his strongest support actually came from the poor conservative hill towns and farm communities of the state's "Northeast Kingdom." For
example, Sanders's strongest showing statewide came in the county of Orleans,
where he pulled 62 percent of the vote. A rural county on the border of
Canada that voted solidly for George Bush in 1988, Orleans had a median
household income in 1990 of $22,800, about $7,000 less than the state average.
Only 14.2 percent of Orleans's residents were college graduates. The standard
of living was low, with homes worth on average just $66,500, compared to
$95,600 statewide. Nearly 15 percent of Orleans's residents were living under
the official poverty line, 4 percent more than in the rest of the state.

And then there is Jesse Ventura, a socially liberal, fiscally conservative, pro-
campaign finance reform, anti-establishment candidate with a working-class
style, who hit discouraged voters—as well as disaffected Democrats and Republicans—on the bull's-eye. His campaign deliberately targeted "unlikely voters"
by focusing his public appearances in an "Independent Belt" of bedroom communities to the north and west of Minnesota's Twin Cities, and by placing his
offbeat TV ads not on the nightly news shows but on FOX programs like *The
Simpsons* and *The X-Files*, and on cable TV wrestling programs. Helped by
same-day voter registration, his candidacy drastically boosted turnout, and
most of those new voters pulled his lever. He won a near-majority of 18- to
44-year-olds, the heart of political independents.

In several other ways, Ventura's vote corresponded with those groups least
satisfied with the existing political choices. Far more self-identified liberals
than conservatives voted for him. Women voted for him almost as much as
men. In the high-income professional suburbs, Ventura did poorly. In the less
affluent suburbs, he did very well. Turnout in many of these blue-collar districts
was over 70 percent, with as many as 20 percent of the total registering on
Election Day. Many rank-and-file union members swung to Ventura as well. "I
could tell going into the election," said Doug Williams, head of an electrical

workers' union. "I was getting requests for information on him from my members. People were wearing his T-shirts and bumper stickers—people who hadn't really participated before."

People think Ventura won because he was a celebrity. But his early name recognition in Minnesota, while high for a third-party candidate, only gave him a chance to get the voters' attention. It's what he said and how he said it that made him a contender. "The voters saw Jesse as someone who's an outsider who's going to change things," says Ed Gross, who worked on voter targeting for the Ventura campaign. "Watching the TV debates, they saw two 'suits' and one 'nonsuit'—and most of them don't wear suits. Not only that, one of the 'suits' had worked for the other, and they both were owned by big money."

Gross recognized the dynamic from the 1990 and 1996 Wellstone campaigns for Senate, on which he had also worked. "I told Ventura, in a lot of ways, to the voters, you are a Wellstone. And voters went for Wellstone because they want to have a connection. They've felt disconnected for a long time. They want to feel like the guy up there knows how they live." In the end, they latched onto Ventura with enthusiasm. And the strength of his campaign—which succeeded in a state with one of the lowest unemployment rates in the country—stands as a warning to both of the major parties: This could happen to you.

Raising Turnout, Reviving Politics

As the barriers to voter registration have fallen with the gradual implementation of motor-voter, the pool of potential voters has grown. According to the Federal Election Commission, the total number of registered voters rose from 129 million in 1994 to 151 million in 1998, an increase of 8 percent of the total voting-age population. But politicians haven't caught on. "Candidates aren't yet campaigning to those voters," says Linda Davidoff, the former executive director of Human SERVE, the nonprofit organization set up by Piven and Cloward to spearhead the motor-voter drive. "[But] motor-voter is laying the groundwork for poorer people to participate differently. There's an enormous opportunity here for candidates who get the picture and campaign to the potential voter," she says.

Jesse Jackson, Jr., is one politician who understands very well the new potential of reaching out to discouraged voters. One of the keys to his first race, in which he beat a veteran Democratic legislator backed by the Daley political machine in a special election to fill Mel Reynolds's seat, was his energetic campaign to register young voters. "He set up voter registration tables during local college registration," says Frank Watkins, his press secretary, "and we kept a record of those people and sent them a personal letter just before the election." Jackson registered about 6,500 new voters—5,000 of whom lived in his district. It's likely that many of them made up his winning margin of 6,000 votes.

Despite Jackson's evident success and personal energy (even though he's in a safe district, he's continued to work to turn out more voters, winning more votes than almost any other member of Congress), there's been little interest from the Democratic Party establishment in helping him spread his message of increasing political participation. "We went to the DNC and showed them how we did it," Watkins says, "and they sat there and looked at us like we were crazy. They'd rather focus on raising more and more money to spend on advertising to fewer and fewer people."

Obviously, going after the discouraged voters involves taking some risks, and it may be especially hard to do so in states that close their registration rolls weeks before Election Day. And there is a deeper challenge: convincing these citizens that voting really can matter again. Noting that outward expressions of populist anger seem to have declined in recent years, pollster John Zogby points to despair about politics as the explanation. "In one of my focus groups, a guy in Cleveland said, 'I'm now in the third of a series of lousy jobs. I lost my good job in '85. I was angry before. But now it's not going to happen. Government can't do anything. And my vote doesn't matter at all.' He had downsized his expectations," Zogby concludes. Piven agrees: "The sense that politics is so corrupt, combined with neoliberal rhetoric that argues that government can't do anything, tends to demobilize people."

The ultimate challenge then for anyone seeking to connect with discouraged voters is to restore their hope while not denying that they have good reason to be cynical. What is fascinating and exciting about each of the handful of populist victories of the last decade—by Jackson, Sanders, Wellstone, and Ventura—is that in every case, their success raised expectations about politics across the country. Hope, it seems, can be contagious; we need to keep it alive.

Questions for Discussion

1. Why does Micah L. Sifry believe so few people choose to vote in American elections, despite massive campaign efforts by competing candidates? What other factors do you believe play a role in the nation's poor record for voter turnout?

2. Sifry argues that voter turnout would increase if party candidates ran progressive and populist campaigns. Is it likely that parties in the future will take his advice? Do you have any additional suggestions that might help to increase voter participation?

5.2

Voting Rites: Why We Need a New Concept of Citizenship

Michael Schudson

In the face of voting turnout far less than that found in other countries or even in our own country's early history, a common response of political observers such as the mass media is to chastise the electorate for its failure to exercise the most basic of all citizen responsibilities. According to the common wisdom, well supported by public opinion surveys, many American voters are uninformed, are disengaged from politics, and participate at a level that, in the eyes of many, is an embarrassment to a country that prides itself on "rule by the people."

In this provocative essay, Michael Schudson suggests that the lack of electoral participation "may not be individual failure so much as our contemporary conception of how democratic citizenship ought to work." He finds that the Progressive ideal of citizenship, with its expectations that each citizen possess a high level of political information and pay constant attention to public affairs, sets an unrealistic standard in the contemporary political world.

In Schudson's view, citizens flourish in an environment that encourages worthwhile citizenship activities in the broadest sense, and we should be intent on creating such an environment, not on turning every voter into an expert.

If recent trends hold up, only about one of every three eligible voters will show up at the polls this fall. Inevitably, many will conclude that Americans have once again failed as citizens. The problem, however, may not be individual failure so much as our contemporary conception of how democratic citizenship ought to work. Nothing puts that conception into clearer perspective than changes in the act of voting over the past 200 years.

Imagine yourself a voter in the world of colonial Virginia where George Washington, Patrick Henry, and Thomas Jefferson learned their politics. As a

Michael Schudson is professor of communication and sociology at the University of California, San Diego.

matter of law, you must be a white male owning at least a modest amount of property. Your journey to vote may take several hours since there is probably only one polling place in the county. As you approach the courthouse, you see the sheriff supervising the election. Two candidates for office stand before you, both of them members of prominent local families. You watch the most promi- nent members of the community, the leading landowner and clergyman, cast their votes, and you know whom they have supported because they announce their votes in loud, clear voices. You do the same and then step over to the can- didate for whom you have voted, and he treats you to a glass of rum punch. Your vote has been an act of restating and reaffirming the social hierarchy of a community where no one but a local notable would think of standing for office.

Now imagine you are in eighteenth century Massachusetts rather than Vir- ginia. The model of voting is different, as you elect town selectmen and repre- sentatives at a town meeting. But, like Virginia, the New England model reflects an organic view that the polity has a single common good and that the leaders of locally prominent, wealthy, and well established families can be trusted to represent it. Dissent and conflict are no more acceptable in New England than in Virginia.

Move the clock ahead to the nineteenth century, as mass political parties cultivate a new democratic order. Now there is much more bustle around the polling place. The area is crowded with the banners and torches of rival parties. Election day is not set off from other days but is the culmination of a campaign of several months. You must still be a white male but not necessarily of prop- erty. During the campaign, you have marched in torchlight processions in mili- tary uniform with a club of like-minded men from your party. They may accompany you to the polls. If you were not active in the campaign, you may be roused on election day by a party worker to escort you on foot or by carriage. On the road, you may encounter clubs or groups from rival parties, and it would not be unusual if fisticuffs or even guns were to dissuade you from casting a bal- lot after all.

If you do proceed to the ballot box, you may step more lively with the en- couragement of a dollar or two from the party—less a bribe than an acknowl- edgment that voting is a service to your party. A party worker hands you a colored ballot with the printed names of the party's candidates. You may also receive a slightly smaller ballot with the same names on it that can be surrepti- tiously placed inside the other so that you can cast two ballots rather than one. You are willing to do so not out of a strong sense that your party offers better public policies but because your party is your party, just as, in our own day, your high school is your high school. In any event, parties tend to be more devoted to distributing offices than to advocating policies.

Now turn to the early twentieth century as Progressive era reforms cleanse voting of what made it both compelling and, by our standards, corrupt. Reform- ers find the emphasis in campaigns on spectacle rather than substance much too emotional. They pioneer what they term an "educational campaign" that

stresses the distribution of pamphlets on the issues rather than parades of solidarity. They pass legislation to ensure a secret ballot. They enact voter registration statutes. They help create an atmosphere in which it becomes more
common for traditionally loyal party newspapers to "bolt" from party-endorsed
candidates. They insist on official state ballots rather than party ballots and in
some states develop state-approved voter information booklets rather than
leaving education up to the parties themselves. At the same time, civil service
reform limits the rewards parties can distribute to loyal partisans.

The world we experience today at the polls has been handed down to us from
these reforms. What does voting look like and feel like today?

I asked my students at the University of California, San Diego to write about
their experience of voting in 1992. Many of them had never voted before;
hardly any had voted in a presidential election. It is something they looked forward to doing, especially those who supported Clinton. Still, some students felt
a let-down in the act of voting:

> As I punched in the holes on my voting card, a slight sense of disappointment
> clouded my otherwise cheerful mood. First of all, the building behind Revelle Bargain
> Books was not what I had always imagined as a polling place. How could a location
> this close to the all-you-can-eat cafeteria be the site of a vote to choose the leader of
> our nation? Second, I could not understand why there were no curtains around my
> booth. As a child I can always remember crawling under curtains in voting booths to
> spy on my parents. Why couldn't I have those curtains to hide all of my important,
> private decisions?

Or listen to this student, a Filipino-American who voted for Bush:

> The more I tried to be aware of the political goings-on, through television mainly, the
> more I became aggravated with the whole situation. Perot represented the evil of a
> one man monopoly, while Clinton was a man who knew how to manipulate an audi-
> ence and use the media. In addition, Hillary reminded me of the stories and com-
> ments my parents made about Imelda Marcos. Taxes came to mind every time I
> considered Bush, but I decided he might be the best qualified candidate.
>
> My Dad was an influential part of my decision to go; not because he urged me to do
> so, but so that after the election I would finally be able to tell him that I voted.
>
> Needless to say, no one at the polling site seemed to talk politics, at least not when
> I was there. The silence did not bother me, though, since I am definitely not confi-
> dent enough to talk politics to anyone outside of my family!

Or this immigrant Russian:

> My Mom went to vote with me that day (at the polling place in a neighbor's garage).
> The night before, I had marked my mother's sample ballot with circles around "yes"
> and "no" on particular propositions and checked the boxes next to "Feinstein" and
> "Boxer" so she would not forget. The sample ballot is very convenient. The propositions

are especially grueling to read. They disguise themselves in legal/state jargon and refuse to give way to meaning.

I felt distantly connected to other voters in other garages who would be making the same vote for change as I would. Nevertheless, I went through my ballot, standing in that cardboard cubicle, in a very ordinary way, feeling that I was, most likely, insignificant and that my views would find no representation. I remember guessing on some local offices, like county supervisor, and trying not to pick a "Christian right" candidate.

The individuality and jealously guarded privacy of voting today contrasts dramatically with the *viva voce* process of eighteenth century Virginia or the colorful party ticket voting of the nineteenth century. So do the indecision and uncertainty. The students felt inadequate to the election—and why not? The list of propositions and complex voter information pamphlets in California were overwhelming. My voter information pamphlet for the June 1994 primary ran forty-eight pages—and that was just for city and county offices and referenda. For state offices and ballot measures, a separate publication ran sixty-four pages. The obscurity of many candidates and issues encouraged mass pre-election mailings of leaflet slates of candidates produced by profit-making organizations with no connection to political parties. I received, for instance, "Voter Information Guide for Democrats" and "Crime Fighters '94" produced by "Democratic Choice '94." The weary voter had to read the fine print to learn that neither slate was endorsed by the Democratic party.

Whatever else we learn from elections, we are tutored in a sense of helplessness and fundamental inadequacy to the task of citizenship. We are told to be informed but discover that the information required to cast an informed vote is beyond our capacities. We are reminded that the United States has the lowest voter turnout of any democracy but rarely told that we have more elections for more levels of government with more elective offices at each level than any other country in the world. . . .

The Burden of Progressivism

We need a new concept of citizenship, one that asks something from us but is not burdened with the impossible expectations of the Progressive model. Contrast what we implicitly expect of ourselves today and what Thomas Jefferson hoped for citizens 200 years ago. In the preamble of Bill 79 to establish universal elementary instruction in Virginia, Jefferson observed that the people normally elect men of standing in the community. The community needs especially to educate these leaders. As for the citizenry at large, Jefferson sought to inculcate through the study of history knowledge that "they may be enabled to know ambition under all its shapes, and prompt to exert their natural powers to defeat its purposes." That was the whole of the citizen's job—watchfulness to defeat ambition.

Citizens were decidedly not to undertake their own evaluation of issues before the legislature. That was the job of representatives. The Founding Fathers
assumed that voters would and should choose representatives on the basis of
character, not issues. Representatives would have enough in common with the
people they represented to keep their "interests" in mind. For the Founding Fathers, elected representatives—not parties, not interest groups, not newspapers,
not citizens in the streets—were to make policy.

We have come to ask more of citizens. Today's dominant views about citizenship come from the Progressives' rationalist and ardently individualist worldview. The Progressive impulse was educational—to bring science to politics
and professional management to cities, to substitute pamphlets for parades and
parlors for streets. The practice of citizenship, at least in campaigning and voting, became privatized, more effortful, more cognitive, and a lot less fun.

In the eighteenth and nineteenth centuries, there was no concern about the
people who did not vote. Political science and public discourse began to worry
about nonvoters only after World War I when voting rates had declined to a
low not reached again until the 1970s. . . .

The Progressive ideal requires citizens to possess a huge fund of political information and a ceaseless attentiveness to public issues. This could never be.
Even at the Constitutional convention of 1787 a delegate observed that people
grew "listless" with frequent elections. Fifty years later Tocqueville lamented,
"Even when one has won the confidence of a democratic nation, it is a hard
matter to attract its attention." . . .

. . . Perhaps television or party decline exacerbates it. But public inattention
has been a fact of political life, with only momentary escapes, through our history. If this is so, what is a reasonable expectation for citizens, a reasonable
standard of citizen competence?

A Practical Citizenship

Under democratic government, as the Founding Fathers constituted it, the representatives of the people could carry on the business of governing without individual citizens becoming experts on the questions of policy placed before the
Congress. . . .

Citizens are not to be created one by one, pouring into each of them enough
newspapers, information, or virtuous resolve for them to judge each issue and
each candidate rationally. That is where the Progressive vision went wrong.
Citizens flourish in an environment that supports worthwhile citizenship activities. We should be intent on creating such an environment, not on turning
every voter into an expert.

If, like the Progressives, we take citizenship to be a function of the individual, we are bound to be discouraged. A classical model of citizenship asks that
people seek the good of the general, the public. But this is either utopian—

people just do not pay that kind of attention—or else undesirable because it honors public life to the exclusion of work-a-day labor or inner spiritual pursuits. A more Lockean, modern, realistic version is that citizens should be moved in public life by self-interest and so should acquire a fair understanding of their own interests and which public policies best serve them. But people's knowledge of public affairs fails even by this standard. Even self-interest in politics is a surprisingly weak reed since the gratifications of private life—getting home on time rather than stopping at the polls to vote, spending seven or eight dollars for a movie rather than for a campaign contribution—are more visible and immediate than the marginal contribution one might make to determining policy by voting, signing a petition, or writing a letter.

How low can we go? We can seek to build a political system where individuals will perform the right actions for their own or the public's interest without knowing much at all. People will do the right thing in general ignorance. User-friendly technology works this way; almost anyone can drive a car while knowing scarcely anything about what makes it run.

In *The Reasoning Voter*, Samuel Popkin suggests we are pretty close to this user-friendly politics already. Relatively little of what voters know, Popkin argues, comes to them as abstract political intelligence. They make intelligent voting decisions based only in small measure on their attending to campaign issues. People have little of the propositional knowledge that models of citizenship demand, but they have more background knowledge than they may realize. They know about economic issues because they have savings accounts, home mortgages, or mutual funds. They have views about health care reform because they know someone personally who has been denied health insurance because of a pre-existing condition. They have enough "by-product information" from daily life to make the broad, either-or choice of a presidential candidate in ways consistent with their own interests and views. . . .

In elections for school boards and other local contests, however, where public information about candidates is more limited and there are often no party labels (again, thanks to Progressive reforms), voters may find themselves in the polling booth without a clue about whom to support. . . .

The Citizens' Trustees

Citizens have to find trustees for their citizenship. Identifying adequate trustees and holding them responsible, I submit, is where we should focus attention. There are three main sets of trustees: politicians, lobbyists, and journalists. Elected officials are our primary trustees. Their obligation is to act with the public in view. They act not so much in response to deliberative public opinion—which rarely exists—but in anticipation of future reward or punishment at the polls. The politicians may not always perceive public opinion accurately. They may not judge well just how much they can lead and shape and how much they must follow and bow to public sentiment. But the motivational structure of elective office demands that they must always be sensitive on this point.

Lobbyists are a second set of trustees. If you believe in the individual's right to bear arms unrestrained by federal legislation, send your annual dues to the National Rifle Association. If you believe that the environment needs aggressive protection, send your dues to an environmental action group. If you do not know what you believe—and this is the common condition for most people on most issues before the nation—you will do better at expressing your will if you at least know that you tend to favor one party over another. Partisanship is a still useful cue. . . .

Two mechanisms keep politician-trustees responsible. The first is the election, fallible as it is. If the representative does not satisfy the citizens, they have a regularly scheduled opportunity to throw the bum out. The second constraint on the politician is the party system. Of course, the party is a more effective discipline on wayward politicians in strong parliamentary systems than in the United States. Here parties are relatively weak, and entrepreneurial politicians relatively independent of them. Still, a politician's party affiliation is a check on his or her policy views and a useful piece of information for voters.

The demands citizens make on lobbyists are much narrower than those placed on politicians—lobbyists are expected to be advocates rather than judges, suppliers of information and resources to sympathetic politicians rather than builders of politically viable solutions to public problems. They are the instructed agents of their organizations rather than Burkean independent-minded representatives. As individuals, they are easy to hold responsible. The question of responsibility with lobbyists is how to hold the whole system responsible since the balance of lobbying power tilts heavily toward the richest and most powerful groups in society. If the system works, it facilitates expression for intensely felt interests from the far corners of the country; if it works badly, it twists and clogs up the primary system of political representation.

The usual answer is to seek to limit the influence of lobbies through campaign finance reform and other restrictions on lobbying activities. An alternative approach seeks to grant lobbyists more authority rather than less influence. Instead of closing down access where the rich and powerful have the resources to guarantee their over-representation, can entree be opened in settings where a broad array of interest groups are assured a voice? In decision making in some federal administrative agencies, interest groups have been granted quasi-public standing. The Negotiated Rulemaking Act of 1990 enables agencies like the Environmental Protection Agency and the Occupational Safety and Health Administration to create committees of private organizations to write regulatory rules.

For instance, EPA arranged for the Sierra Club and the Natural Resources Defense Council to sit down with the American Petroleum Institute and the National Petroleum Refiners Association to work out rules to carry out the

Clean Air Act. Millions of Americans belong to organizations that employ paid lobbyists; the lobbies are not about to disappear nor should they. But controlling them may be a delicate balance of restraining some kinds of influence while orchestrating other public opportunities for special interests to take on responsibility for governing.

The third set of trustees—the media—is the most difficult to hold accountable. The market mechanism does not serve well here. People buy a newspaper or watch a television network for many purposes besides gathering political information. The quality or quantity of political intelligence does not correlate well with the rise and fall of newspaper circulations or television news ratings.

There are, as the French press critic Claude-Jean Bertrand suggests, a variety of "media accountability systems"—nongovernmental mechanisms to keep the news media responsible to public interests and opinions. These include codes of ethics, in-house critics, media reporters, and ombudsmen, as well as liaison committees that news institutions have sometimes established with social groups they may report on or clash with. There are also letters to the editor, journalism reviews, journalism schools, awards for good news coverage, and libel suits or the threat of libel. . . .

The Overworked Citizen

William James said nearly a century ago that our moral destiny turns on "the power of voluntarily attending." But, he added, though crucial to our individual and collective destinies, attention tends to be "brief and fitful." This is the substantial underlying reality of political life that any efforts at enlarging citizenship must confront. Can we have a democracy if most people are not paying attention most of the time? The answer is that this is the only kind of democracy we will ever have. Our ways of organizing and evoking that brief and fitful attention are different but not necessarily any worse from those in our past.

One response could be to harness the rare moments of attentiveness. Social movements and the occasional closely fought, morally urgent election have sometimes done that. When political scientists have looked at intensively fought senatorial campaigns, for instance, and compared them to run-of-the-mill campaigns, they find much more information in the news media about candidates' policy positions, increased knowledge among voters about those positions, and apparently increased inclination of voters to make decisions on the issues. At the level of presidential politics and occasionally in senatorial or gubernatorial politics, there is enough information available for voter rationality to have a chance; but for other offices, . . . our elections say much more about the supply of candidates than the demands of voters.

An alternate response would be to build a society that makes more of situations that build citizenship without taxing attentiveness. In an environment that supports worthwhile citizenship activity, there is intrinsic reward for doing the right thing. If we interpret citizenship activity to mean taking unpaid and uncoerced responsibility for the welfare of strangers or the community at large, examples of good citizenship abound. I think of the people who serve as "room parents" in the schools or coach Little League. Why do they do it? Their own children would do just as well if someone else took on the job. Coaching Little League or serving in the Parent-Teachers Association are activities or practices rather than cognitive efforts; they are social and integrated into community life. They make citizenship itself into a "by-product" effect. Their success suggests that citizenship may be harder to instill when it involves burdens beyond daily life than to engineer it as an everyday social activity. The volunteers may not enjoy every minute, but they find intrinsic social reward in having friends, neighbors, and strangers praise and admire them.

Our common language for a better public life seems impoverished. We think of politicians with distrust rather than thinking of ways to enforce their trustworthiness. We think of lobbyists with disdain instead of thinking of ways to recognize and harness their virtues. We think of journalists alternately as heroes or scoundrels. And we think of our own citizenship too often with either guilt at our ignorance and lack of participation or with a moral pat on the back for having sacrificed more than our neighbors. We must think more about building a democratic environment that will make us smarter as a people than we are as individuals.

Questions for Discussion

1. What does Schudson mean by "the burden of Progressivism"? Does the Progressive model of citizenship seem unrealistic when applied to today's voters? Have you personally experienced the "burden of Progressivism"?
2. What components does Schudson believe should underlie a new concept of citizenship? In your view, how practical is Schudson's viewpoint?

5.3

Bowling Alone: America's Declining Social Capital

Robert D. Putnam

Political behavior is learned behavior. Although individual freedoms and rights provide the fundamental underpinnings of the nation, citizens learning by experience to act collectively in pursuit of shared goals has long been thought crucial to the success of American democracy. Over 150 years ago, Alexis de Tocqueville in *Democracy in America* acknowledged the critical role played by associational life in supporting democratic values.

In this selection, Robert D. Putnam questions whether the United States has retained the characteristics of civil society. He suggests that there is an important linkage between "citizen engagement" in community affairs and government performance. Civic engagement refers to people's associational connections to the life of their communities in the broadest sense, from going to church to participating in a bowling league to becoming involved in a political group. Experience in a wide array of such activities develops what Putnam calls "social capital": "features of social organization such as networks, norms, and social trust that facilitate coordination and cooperation for mutual benefit."

M any students of the new democracies that have emerged over the past decade and a half have emphasized the importance of a strong and active civil society to the consolidation of democracy. Especially with regard to the postcommunist countries, scholars and democratic activists alike have lamented the absence or obliteration of traditions of independent civic engagement and a widespread tendency toward passive reliance on the state. To those concerned with the weakness of civil societies in the developing or postcommunist world, the advanced Western democracies and above all the United States have typically been taken as models to be emulated. There is

Robert D. Putnam is Malkin Professor of Public Policy at Harvard University.

From "Bowling Alone: America's Declining Social Capital" by Robert D. Putnam. From *Journal of Democracy,* January 1995, Vol. 6, No. 1, pp. 65–78. Reprinted by permission from The Sagalyn Literary Agency.

striking evidence, however, that the vibrancy of American civil society has notably declined over the past several decades.

Ever since the publication of Alexis de Tocqueville's *Democracy in America,*
the United States has played a central role in systematic studies of the links between democracy and civil society. Although this is in part because trends in
American life are often regarded as harbingers of social modernization, it is also
because America has traditionally been considered unusually "civic" (a reputation that, as we shall later see, has not been entirely unjustified).

When Tocqueville visited the United States in the 1830s, it was the Americans' propensity for civic association that most impressed him as the key to
their unprecedented ability to make democracy work. "Americans of all ages,
all stations in life, and all types of disposition," he observed, "are forever forming
associations. There are not only commercial and industrial associations in which
all take part, but others of a thousand different types—religious, moral, serious,
futile, very general and very limited, immensely large and very minute....
Nothing, in my view, deserves more attention than the intellectual and moral
associations in America."[1]

Recently, American social scientists of a neo-Tocquevillean bent have un-
earthed a wide range of empirical evidence that the quality of public life and
the performance of social institutions (and not only in America) are indeed
powerfully influenced by norms and networks of civic engagement. Researchers
in such fields as education, urban poverty, unemployment, the control of crime
and drug abuse, and even health have discovered that successful outcomes are
more likely in civically engaged communities. Similarly, research on the varying economic attainments of different ethnic groups in the United States has
demonstrated the importance of social bonds within each group. These results
are consistent with research in a wide range of settings that demonstrates the
vital importance of social networks for job placement and many other economic outcomes....

No doubt the mechanisms through which civic engagement and social connectedness produce such results—better schools, faster economic development,
lower crime, and more effective government—are multiple and complex....
Social scientists in several fields have recently suggested a common framework
for understanding these phenomena, a framework that rests on the concept of
social capital.[2] By analogy with notions of physical capital and human capital—
tools and training that enhance individual productivity—"social capital" refers
to features of social organization such as networks, norms, and social trust that
facilitate coordination and cooperation for mutual benefit.

For a variety of reasons, life is easier in a community blessed with a substantial stock of social capital. In the first place, networks of civic engagement foster sturdy norms of generalized reciprocity and encourage the emergence of
social trust. Such networks facilitate coordination and communication, amplify
reputations, and thus allow dilemmas of collective action to be resolved. When
economic and political negotiation is embedded in dense networks of social

interaction, incentives for opportunism are reduced. At the same time, networks of civic engagement embody past success at collaboration, which can serve as a cultural template for future collaboration. Finally, dense networks of interaction probably broaden the participants' sense of self, developing the "I" into the "we," or (in the language of rational-choice theorists) enhancing the participants' "taste" for collective benefits. . . .

Whatever Happened to Civic Engagement?

We begin with familiar evidence on changing patterns of political participation, not least because it is immediately relevant to issues of democracy in the narrow sense. Consider the well-known decline in turnout in national elections over the last three decades. From a relative high point in the early 1960s, voter turnout had by 1990 declined by nearly a quarter; tens of millions of Americans had forsaken their parents' habitual readiness to engage in the simplest act of citizenship. Broadly similar trends also characterize participation in state and local elections.

It is not just the voting booth that has been increasingly deserted by Americans. A series of identical questions posed by the Roper Organization to national samples ten times each year over the last two decades reveals that since 1973 the number of Americans who report that "in the past year" they have "attended a public meeting on town or school affairs" has fallen by more than a third (from 22 percent in 1973 to 13 percent in 1993). Similar (or even greater) relative declines are evident in responses to questions about attending a political rally or speech, serving on a committee of some local organization, and working for a political party. By almost every measure, Americans' direct engagement in politics and government has fallen steadily and sharply over the last generation, despite the fact that average levels of education—the best individual-level predictor of political participation—have risen sharply throughout this period. Every year over the last decade or two, millions more have withdrawn from the affairs of their communities.

Not coincidentally, Americans have also disengaged psychologically from politics and government over this era. The proportion of Americans who reply that they "trust the government in Washington" only "some of the time" or "almost never" has risen steadily from 30 percent in 1966 to 75 percent in 1992.

These trends are well known, of course, and taken by themselves would seem amenable to a strictly political explanation. Perhaps the long litany of political tragedies and scandals since the 1960s (assassinations, Vietnam, Watergate, Irangate, and so on) has triggered an understandable disgust for politics and government among Americans, and that in turn has motivated their withdrawal. I do not doubt that this common interpretation has some merit, but its limitations become plain when we examine trends in civic engagements of a wider sort.

Our survey of organizational membership among Americans can usefully begin with a glance at the aggregate results of the General Social Survey, a scientifically conducted, national-sample survey that has been repeated 14 times over the last two decades. Church-related groups constitute the most common type of organization joined by Americans; they are especially popular with women. Other types of organizations frequently joined by women include school-service groups (mostly parent-teacher associations), sports groups, professional societies, and literary societies. Among men, sports clubs, labor unions, professional societies, fraternal groups, veterans' groups, and service clubs are all relatively popular.

Religious affiliation is by far the most common associational membership among Americans. Indeed, by many measures America continues to be (even more than in Tocqueville's time) an astonishingly "churched" society. For example, the United States has more houses of worship per capita than any other nation on Earth. Yet religious sentiment in America seems to be becoming somewhat less tied to institutions and more self-defined.

How have these complex crosscurrents played out over the last three or four decades in terms of Americans' engagement with organized religion? The general pattern is clear: The 1960s witnessed a significant drop in reported weekly churchgoing—from roughly 48 percent in the late 1950s to roughly 41 percent in the early 1970s. Since then, it has stagnated or (according to some surveys) declined still further. Meanwhile, data from the General Social Survey show a modest decline in membership in all "church-related groups" over the last 20 years. It would seem, then, that net participation by Americans, both in religious services and in church-related groups, has declined modestly (by perhaps a sixth) since the 1960s.

For many years, labor unions provided one of the most common organizational affiliations among American workers. Yet union membership has been falling for nearly four decades, with the steepest decline occurring between 1975 and 1985. Since the mid-1950s, when union membership peaked, the unionized portion of the nonagricultural work force in America has dropped by more than half, falling from 32.5 percent in 1953 to 15.8 percent in 1992. By now, virtually all of the explosive growth in union membership that was associated with the New Deal has been erased. The solidarity of union halls is now mostly a fading memory of aging men.

The parent-teacher association (PTA) has been an especially important form of civic engagement in twentieth-century America because parental involvement in the educational process represents a particularly productive form of social capital. It is, therefore, dismaying to discover that participation in parent-teacher organizations has dropped drastically over the last generation, from more than 12 million in 1964 to barely 5 million in 1982 before recovering to approximately 7 million now.

Next, we turn to evidence on membership in (and volunteering for) civic and fraternal organizations. These data show some striking patterns. First, membership in traditional women's groups has declined more or less steadily since the mid-1960s. For example, membership in the national Federation of Women's Clubs is down by more than half (59 percent) since 1964, while membership in the League of Women Voters (LWV) is off 42 percent since 1969.[3]

Similar reductions are apparent in the numbers of volunteers for mainline civic organizations, such as the Boy Scouts (off by 26 percent since 1970) and the Red Cross (off by 61 percent since 1970). But what about the possibility that volunteers have simply switched their loyalties to other organizations? Evidence on "regular" (as opposed to occasional or "drop-by") volunteering is available from the Labor Department's Current Population Surveys of 1974 and 1989. These estimates suggest that serious volunteering declined by roughly one-sixth over these 15 years, from 24 percent of adults in 1974 to 20 percent in 1989. The multitudes of Red Cross aides and Boy Scout troop leaders now missing in action have apparently not been offset by equal numbers of new recruits elsewhere.

Fraternal organizations have also witnessed a substantial drop in membership during the 1980s and 1990s. Membership is down significantly in such groups as the Lions (off 12 percent since 1983), the Elks (off 18 percent since 1979), the Shriners (off 27 percent since 1979), the Jaycees (off 44 percent since 1979), and the Masons (down 39 percent since 1959). . . .

The most whimsical yet discomfiting bit of evidence of social disengagement in contemporary America that I have discovered is this: more Americans are bowling today than ever before, but bowling in organized leagues has plummeted in the last decade or so. Between 1980 and 1993 the total number of bowlers in America increased by 10 percent, while league bowling decreased by 40 percent. (Lest this be thought a wholly trivial example, I should note that nearly 80 million Americans went bowling at least once during 1993, *nearly a third more than voted in the 1994 congressional elections* and roughly the same number as claim to attend church regularly. Even after the 1980s' plunge in league bowling, nearly 3 percent of American adults regularly bowl in leagues.) The rise of solo bowling threatens the livelihood of bowling-lane proprietors because those who bowl as members of leagues consume three times as much beer and pizza as solo bowlers, and the money in bowling is in the beer and pizza, not the balls and shoes. The broader social significance, however, lies in the social interaction and even occasionally civic conversations over beer and pizza that solo bowlers forgo. Whether or not bowling beats balloting in the eyes of most Americans, bowling teams illustrate yet another vanishing form of social capital.

Countertrends

At this point, however, we must confront a serious counterargument. Perhaps the traditional forms of civic organization whose decay we have been tracing have been replaced by vibrant new organizations. For example, national environmental organizations (like the Sierra Club) and feminist groups (like the National Organization for Women) grew rapidly during the 1970s and 1980s and now count hundreds of thousands of dues-paying members. An even more dramatic example is the American Association of Retired Persons (AARP), which grew exponentially from 400,000 card-carrying members in 1960 to 33 million in 1993, becoming (after the Catholic Church) the largest private organization in the world. The national administrators of these organizations are among the most feared lobbyists in Washington, in large part because of their massive mailing lists of presumably loyal members.

These new mass-membership organizations are plainly of great political importance. From the point of view of social connectedness, however, they are sufficiently different from classic "secondary associations" that we need to invent a new label—perhaps "tertiary associations." For the vast majority of their members, the only act of membership consists in writing a check for dues or perhaps occasionally reading a newsletter. Few ever attend any meetings of such organizations, and most are unlikely ever (knowingly) to encounter any other member. The bond between any two members of the Sierra Club is less like the bond between any two members of a gardening club and more like the bond between any two Red Sox fans (or perhaps any two devoted Honda owners): they root for the same team and they share some of the same interests, but they are unaware of each other's existence. Their ties, in short, are to common symbols, common leaders, and perhaps common ideals, but not to one another. The theory of social capital argues that associational membership should, for example, increase social trust, but this prediction is much less straightforward with regard to membership in tertiary associations. From the point of view of social connectedness, the Environmental Defense Fund and a bowling league are just not in the same category.

If the growth of tertiary organizations represents one potential (but probably not real) counterexample to my thesis, a second countertrend is represented by the growing prominence of nonprofit organizations, especially nonprofit service agencies. This so-called third sector includes everything from Oxfam and the Metropolitan Museum of Art to the Ford Foundation and the Mayo Clinic. In other words, although most secondary associations are nonprofits, most nonprofit agencies are not secondary associations. To identify trends in the size of the nonprofit sector with trends in social connectedness would be another fundamental conceptual mistake.[4]

A third potential countertrend is much more relevant to an assessment of social capital and civic engagement. Some able researchers have argued that the last few decades have witnessed a rapid expansion in "support groups" of various sorts. Robert Wuthnow reports that fully 40 percent of all Americans claim to be "currently involved in [a] small group that meets regularly and provides support or caring for those who participate in it."[5] Many of these groups are religiously affiliated, but many others are not. For example, nearly 5 percent of Wuthnow's national sample claim to participate regularly in a "self-help" group, such as Alcoholics Anonymous, and nearly as many say they belong to book-discussion groups and hobby clubs.

The groups described by Wuthnow's respondents unquestionably represent an important form of social capital, and they need to be accounted for in any serious reckoning of trends in social connectedness. On the other hand, they do not typically play the same role as traditional civic associations. As Wuthnow emphasizes,

> Small groups may not be fostering community as effectively as many of their proponents would like. Some small groups merely provide occasions for individuals to focus on themselves in the presence of others. The social contract binding members together asserts only the weakest of obligations. Come if you have time. Talk if you feel like it. Respect everyone's opinion. Never criticize. Leave quietly if you become dissatisfied.... We can imagine that [these small groups] really substitute for families, neighborhoods, and broader community attachments that may demand lifelong commitments, when, in fact, they do not.[6]

All three of these potential countertrends—tertiary organizations, nonprofit organizations, and support groups—need somehow to be weighed against the erosion of conventional civic organizations. One way of doing so is to consult the General Social Survey.

Within all educational categories, total associational membership declined significantly between 1967 and 1993. Among the college-educated, the average number of group memberships per person fell from 2.8 to 2.0 (a 26-percent decline); among high-school graduates, the number fell from 1.8 to 1.2 (32 percent); and among those with fewer than 12 years of education, the number fell from 1.4 to 1.1 (25 percent). In other words, at *all* educational (and hence social) levels of American society, and counting *all* sorts of group memberships, *the average number of associational memberships has fallen by about a fourth over the last quarter-century.* Without controls for educational levels, the trend is not nearly so clear, but the central point is this: *more Americans than ever before are in social circumstances that foster associational involvement (higher education, middle age, and so on), but nevertheless aggregate associational membership appears to be stagnant or declining.*

Broken down by type of group, the downward trend is most marked for church-related groups, for labor unions, for fraternal and veterans' organizations, and for school-service groups. Conversely, membership in professional associations has risen over these years, although less than might have been predicted, given sharply rising educational and occupational levels. Essentially the same trends are evident for both men and women in the sample. In short, the available survey evidence confirms our earlier conclusion: American social capital in the form of civic associations has significantly eroded over the last generation.

Good Neighborliness and Social Trust

I noted earlier that most readily available quantitative evidence on trends in social connectedness involves formal settings, such as the voting booth, the union hall, or the PTA. One glaring exception is so widely discussed as to require little comment here: the most fundamental form of social capital is the family, and the massive evidence of the loosening of bonds within the family (both extended and nuclear) is well known. This trend, of course, is quite consistent with—and may help to explain—our theme of social decapitalization.

A second aspect of informal social capital on which we happen to have reasonably reliable time-series data involves neighborliness. In each General Social Survey since 1974 respondents have been asked, "How often do you spend a social evening with a neighbor?" The proportion of Americans who socialize with their neighbors more than once a year has slowly but steadily declined over the last two decades, from 72 percent in 1974 to 61 percent in 1993. (On the other hand, socializing with "friends who do not live in your neighborhood" appears to be on the increase, a trend that may reflect the growth of workplace-based social connections.)

Americans are also less trusting. The proportion of Americans saying that most people can be trusted fell by more than a third between 1960, when 58 percent chose that alternative, and 1993, when only 37 percent did. The same trend is apparent in all educational groups; indeed, because social trust is also correlated with education and because educational levels have risen sharply, the overall decrease in social trust is even more apparent if we control for education.

Our discussion of trends in social connectedness and civic engagement has tacitly assumed that all the forms of social capital that we have discussed are themselves coherently correlated across individuals. This is in fact true. Members of associations are much more likely than nonmembers to participate in politics, to spend time with neighbors, to express social trust, and so on. . . .

Why Is U.S. Social Capital Eroding?

As we have seen, something has happened in America in the last two or three decades to diminish civic engagement and social connectedness. What could that "something" be? Here are several possible explanations, along with some initial evidence on each.

The Movement of Women into the Labor Force

Over these same two or three decades, many millions of American women have moved out of the home into paid employment. This is the primary, though not the sole, reason why the weekly working hours of the average American have increased significantly during these years. It seems highly plausible that this social revolution should have reduced the time and energy available for building social capital. For certain organizations, such as the PTA, the League of Women Voters, the Federation of Women's Clubs, and the Red Cross, this is almost certainly an important part of the story. The sharpest decline in women's civic participation seems to have come in the 1970s; membership in such "women's" organizations as these has been virtually halved since the late 1960s. By contrast, most of the decline in participation in men's organizations occurred about ten years later; the total decline to date has been approximately 25 percent for the typical organization. On the other hand, the survey data imply that the aggregate declines for men are virtually as great as those for women. It is logically possible, of course, that the male declines might represent the knock-on effect of women's liberation, as dishwashing crowded out the lodge, but time-budget studies suggest that most husbands of working wives have assumed only a minor part of the housework. In short, something besides the women's revolution seems to lie behind the erosion of social capital.

Mobility: The "Re-potting" Hypothesis

Numerous studies of organizational involvement have shown that residential stability and such related phenomena as homeownership are clearly associated with greater civic engagement. Mobility, like frequent re-potting of plants, tends to disrupt root systems, and it takes time for an uprooted individual to put down new roots. It seems plausible that the automobile, suburbanization, and the movement to the Sun Belt have reduced the social rootedness of the average American, but one fundamental difficulty with this hypothesis is apparent: the best evidence shows that residential stability and homeownership in America have risen modestly since 1965, and are surely higher now than during the 1950s, when civic engagement and social connectedness by our measures was definitely higher.

Other Demographic Transformations

A range of additional changes have transformed the American family since the 1960s—fewer marriages, more divorces, fewer children, lower real wages, and so on. Each of these changes might account for some of the slackening of civic engagement, since married, middle-class parents are generally more socially involved than other people. Moreover, the changes in scale that have swept over the American economy in these years—illustrated by the replacement of the corner grocery by the supermarket and now perhaps of the supermarket by electronic shopping at home, or the replacement of community-based enterprises by outposts of distant multinational firms—may perhaps have undermined the material and even physical basis for civic engagement.

The Technological Transformation of Leisure

There is reason to believe that deep-seated technological trends are radically "privatizing" or "individualizing" our use of leisure time and thus disrupting many opportunities for social-capital formation. The most obvious and probably the most powerful instrument of this revolution is television. Time-budget studies in the 1960s showed that the growth in time spent watching television dwarfed all other changes in the way Americans passed their days and nights. Television has made our communities (or, rather, what we experience as our communities) wider and shallower. In the language of economics, electronic technology enables individual tastes to be satisfied more fully, but at the cost of the positive social externalities associated with more primitive forms of entertainment. The same logic applies to the replacement of vaudeville by the movies and now of movies by the VCR. The new "virtual reality" helmets that we will soon don to be entertained in total isolation are merely the latest extension of this trend. Is technology thus driving a wedge between our individual interests and our collective interests? It is a question that seems worth exploring more systematically.

What Is to Be Done?

The last refuge of a social-scientific scoundrel is to call for more research. Nevertheless, I cannot forbear from suggesting some further lines of inquiry.

♦ ... What types of organizations and networks most effectively embody—or generate—social capital, in the sense of mutual reciprocity, the resolution of dilemmas of collective action, and the broadening of social identities? ...

♦ Another set of important issues involves macrosociological crosscurrents that might intersect with the trends described here. What will be the impact, for example, of electronic networks on social capital? My hunch is that meeting in an electronic forum is not the equivalent of meeting in a bowling alley—or even in a saloon—but hard empirical research is needed. What about the development of social capital in the workplace? ...

♦ A rounded assessment of changes in American social capital over the last quarter-century needs to count the costs as well as the benefits of community engagement. We must not romanticize small-town, middle-class civic life in the America of the 1950s. In addition to the deleterious trends emphasized in this essay, recent decades have witnessed a substantial decline in intolerance and probably also in overt discrimination, and those beneficent trends may be related in complex ways to the erosion of traditional social capital. ...

♦ Finally, and perhaps most urgently, we need to explore creatively how public policy impinges on (or might impinge on) social-capital formation. In some well-known instances, public policy has destroyed highly effective social networks and norms. American slum-clearance policy of the 1950s and 1960s, for example, renovated physical capital, but at a very high cost to existing social capital. The consolidation of country post offices and small school districts has promised administrative and financial efficiencies, but full-cost accounting for the effects of these policies on social capital might produce a more negative verdict. On the other hand, such past initiatives as the county agricultural-agent system, community colleges, and tax deductions for charitable contributions illustrate that government can encourage social-capital formation. Even a recent proposal in San Luis Obispo, California, to require that all new houses have front porches illustrates the power of government to influence where and how networks are formed.

The concept of "civil society" has played a central role in the recent global debate about the preconditions for democracy and democratization. In the newer democracies this phrase has properly focused attention on the need to foster a vibrant civic life in soils traditionally inhospitable to self-government. In the established democracies, ironically, growing numbers of citizens are questioning the effectiveness of their public institutions at the very moment when liberal democracy has swept the battlefield, both ideologically and geopolitically. In America, at least, there is reason to suspect that this democratic disarray may be linked to a broad and continuing erosion of civic engagement that began a quarter-century ago. . . . High on America's agenda should be the question of how to reverse these adverse trends in social connectedness, thus restoring civic engagement and civic trust.

Notes

1. Alexis de Tocqueville, *Democracy in America*, ed. J. P. Maier, trans. George Lawrence (Garden City, N.Y.: Anchor Books, 1969), 513–17.
2. James S. Coleman deserves primary credit for developing the "social capital" theoretical framework. See his "Social Capital in the Creation of Human Capital," *American Journal of Sociology* (Supplement) 94 (1988): S95–S120, as well as his *The Foundations of Social Theory* (Cambridge: Harvard University Press, 1990), 300–21. See also Mark Granovetter, "Economic Action and Social Structure: The Problem of Embeddedness," *American Journal of Sociology* 91 (1985): 481–510; Glenn C. Loury, "Why Should We Care About Group Inequality?" *Social Philosophy and Policy* 5 (1987): 249–71; and Robert D. Putnam, "The Prosperous Community: Social Capital and Public Life," *American Prospect* 13 (1993): 35–42. To my knowledge, the first scholar to use the term "social capital" in its current sense was Jane Jacobs, in *The Death and Life of Great American Cities* (New York: Random House, 1961), 138.
3. Data for the LWV are available over a longer time span and show an interesting pattern: a sharp slump during the Depression, a strong and sustained rise after World War II that more than tripled membership between 1945 and 1969, and then the post-1969 decline, which has already erased virtually all the postwar gains and continues still. This same historical pattern applies to those men's fraternal organizations for which comparable data are available—steady increases for the first seven decades of the century, interrupted only by the Great Depression, followed by a collapse in the 1970s and 1980s that has already wiped out most of the postwar expansion and continues apace.

4. Cf. Lester M. Salamon, "The Rise of the Nonprofit Sector," *Foreign Affairs* 73 (July–August 1994): 109–22. See also Salamon, "Partners in Public Service: The Scope and Theory of Government-Nonprofit Relations," in Walter W. Powell, ed., *The Nonprofit Sector: A Research Handbook* (New Haven: Yale University Press, 1987), 99–117. Salamon's empirical evidence does not sustain his broad claims about a global "associational revolution" comparable in significance to the rise of the nation-state several centuries ago.
5. Robert Wuthnow, *Sharing the Journey: Support Groups and America's New Quest for Community* (New York: The Free Press, 1994), 45.
6. Ibid., 3–6.

Questions for Discussion

1. What is "social capital" and how is it linked to politics? What indicators suggest that social capital is in decline in the United States?
2. What explanations for the decline in social capital does Putnam put forth? Does he offer any suggestions for reversing this undesirable trend? Does the rise in the use of the Internet bode well for the growth of social capital?

⭐ 5.4

Bowling Together: The United State of America

Robert D. Putnam

In the previous selection (5.3), Robert D. Putnam explored what he believes to be a disturbing trend in American society in recent decades—the disengagement of citizens from the "civic life" of the communities where they live. In Putnam's view, the values and orientations that citizens develop through participation in a vibrant civic life, such as social trust and an appreciation of working together, translate into all kinds of benefits for society at large and represent the underpinnings of a healthy democratic political system.

In this piece, Putnam examines the state of American civic attitudes shortly after the nation's experience in coping with the terrorist attacks of 9/11/2001. He finds that the trend toward civic disengagement has been interrupted. Survey

results suggested that "Americans were more united, readier for collective sacrifice, and more attuned to public purpose than we have been for several
decades." Trust in other citizens and trust in government rose immediately after
9/11, as did interest in public affairs, particularly among the younger generation.

Putnam believes 9/11 created a "window of opportunity for a sort of civic renewal that occurs only once or twice a century." Although changes in civic attitudes are promising, more permanent changes in the civic behavior of citizens
will not come automatically. In Putnam's view, the crucial question to be answered is whether or not public leaders will have the foresight to be proactive in
helping create a civic-minded younger generation.

T he closing decades of the twentieth century found Americans growing
ever less connected with one another and with collective life. We voted
less, joined less, gave less, trusted less, invested less time in public affairs,
and engaged less with our friends, our neighbors, and even our families. Our
"we" steadily shriveled.

The unspeakable tragedy of September 11 dramatically interrupted that trend.
Almost instantly, we rediscovered our friends, our neighbors, our public institutions, and our shared fate. Nearly two years ago, I wrote in my book *Bowling
Alone* that restoring civic engagement in America "would be eased by a palpable
national crisis, like war or depression or natural disaster, but for better *and* for
worse, America at the dawn of the new century faces no such galvanizing crisis."

Now we do.

But is September 11 a period that puts a full stop to one era and opens a new,
more community-minded chapter in our history? Or is it merely a comma, a
brief pause during which we looked up for a moment and then returned to our
solitary pursuits? In short, how thoroughly and how enduringly have American
values and civic habits been transformed by the terrorist attacks of last fall?

During the summer and fall of 2000, my colleagues and I conducted a nationwide survey of civic attitudes and behaviors, asking about everything from voting to choral singing, newspaper readership to interracial marriage. Recently,
we returned to many of the same people and posed the same questions. Our survey period extended from mid-October to mid-November 2001, encompassing
the anthrax crisis and the start of the Afghan war. Emerging from the immediate trauma of unspeakable death and destruction, these 500 Americans were
adjusting to a changed world and a changed nation.

Though the immediate effect of the attacks was clearly devastating, most
Americans' personal lives returned to normal relatively quickly. For example,

---

Robert D. Putnam is the Malkin Professor of Public Policy at Harvard University.

Robert D. Putnam, "Bowling Together: The United State of America," *The American Prospect* (February 11,
2002), pp. 20–22. Reprinted with permission from *The American Prospect,* Volume 13, Number 3: February
11, 2002. The American Prospect, 11 Beacon Street, Suite 1120, Boston, MA 02108. All rights reserved.

despite anecdotal reports of increased religious observance in the immediate aftermath of the tragedy, we found no evidence of any change in religiosity or in reported church attendance. Our primary concern, however, was not with change in the private lives of Americans but with the implications of the attacks and their aftermath for American civic life. And in those domains, we found unmistakable evidence of change.

The levels of political consciousness and engagement are substantially higher than they were a year ago in the United States. In fact, they are probably higher now than they have been in at least three decades. Trust in government, trust in the police, and interest in politics are all up. Compared with a year ago, Americans are somewhat more likely to have attended a political meeting or to have worked on a community project. Conversely, we are less likely to agree that "the people running my community do not really care what I think." This is no doubt partly the result of a spurt of patriotism and "rally round the flag" sentiment, but it also reflects a sharper appreciation of public institutions' role in addressing not just terrorism but other urgent national issues. The result? A dramatic and probably unprecedented burst of enthusiasm for the federal government.

Using a standard question ("How much can you trust the government in Washington to do what is right—all of the time, most of the time, some of the time, or none of the time?"), we found that 51 percent of our respondents expressed greater confidence in the federal government in 2001 than they had a year earlier. No doubt the identity of the commander in chief has something to do with the somewhat greater increase in confidence among Republicans, southerners, and whites; even before September 11, the advent of a Republican administration probably changed the partisan polarity of this question. Nevertheless, the bipartisan, nationwide effect of the terrorist attacks and their aftermath is clear.

Although we found most of the changes in civic attitudes to be relatively uniform across ethnic groups, social classes, and regions, some registered more sharply among younger Americans (those aged 35 and under) than among their elders. Interest in public affairs, for example, grew by 27 percent among younger people, as compared with 8 percent among older respondents. Trust in "the people running your community" grew by 19 percent among younger people, as compared with 4 percent among older ones.

Nonetheless, Americans from all walks of life expressed greater interest in public affairs than they had during the national political campaign of 2000. This spike in political awareness has not, however, led most Americans to run out and join community organizations or to show up for club meetings that they used to shun. Generally speaking, attitudes (such as trust and concern) have shifted more than behavior has. Will behavior follow attitudes? It's an important question. And if the answer is no, then the blossom of civic-mindedness after September 11 may be short-lived.

Americans don't only trust political institutions more: We also trust one another more, from neighbors and co-workers to shop clerks and perfect strangers. More Americans now express confidence that people in their community would cooperate, for example, with voluntary conservation measures in an energy or water shortage. In fact, in the wake of the terrorist attacks, more Americans reported having cooperated with their neighbors to resolve common problems. Fewer of us feel completely isolated socially, in the sense of having no one to turn to in a personal crisis. At the same time, we are now less likely to have friends over to visit. Television viewing increased from about 2.9 hours to 3.4 hours a day. In that sense, whether because of fear or because of the recession, Americans are cocooning more now than a year ago.

We were especially surprised and pleased to find evidence of enhanced trust across ethnic and other social divisions. Whites trust blacks more, Asians trust Latinos more, and so on, than these very same people did a year ago. An identical pattern appears in response to classic questions measuring social distance: Americans in the fall of 2001 expressed greater open-mindedness toward intermarriage across ethnic and racial lines, even within their own families, than they did a year earlier.

To be sure, trust toward Arab Americans is now about 10 percent below the level expressed toward other ethnic minorities. We had not had the foresight to ask about trust in Arab Americans a year ago, so we cannot be certain that it has declined, but it seems likely that it has. Similarly, we find that Americans are somewhat more hostile to immigrant rights. Other surveys have shown that public skepticism about immigration increased during 2001, but that trend may reflect the recession as much as it does the terrorist attacks. Yet despite signs of public support for antiterrorist law-enforcement techniques that may intrude on civil liberties, our survey found that Americans are in some respects *more* tolerant of cultural diversity now than they were a year ago. Opposition to the exclusion of "unpopular" books from public libraries actually rose from 64 percent to 71 percent. In short—with the important but partial and delimited exception of attitudes toward immigrants and Arab Americans—our results suggest that Americans feel both more united and more comfortable with the nation's diversity.

We also found that Americans have become somewhat more generous, though the changes in this domain are more limited than anecdotal reports have suggested. More people in 2001 than in 2000 reported working on a community project or donating money or blood. Occasional volunteering is up slightly, but regular volunteering (at least twice a month) remains unchanged at one in every seven Americans. Compared with figures from immediately after the tragedy, our data suggest that much of the measurable increase in generosity spent itself within a few weeks.

As 2001 ended, Americans were more united, readier for collective sacrifice, and more attuned to public purpose than we have been for several decades. Indeed, we have a more capacious sense of "we" than we have had in the adult

Change in Selected Civic Attitudes and Behavior, 2000–2001

	Increased	Decreased	Net Change
Trust national government	51%	7%	44%
Trust local government	32%	13%	19%
Watch TV (hours)	40%	24%	16%
Express interest in politics	29%	15%	14%
Trust local police	26%	12%	14%
Trust people of other races	31%	20%	11%
Trust shop clerks	28%	17%	11%
Support keeping unpopular books in library	28%	18%	10%
Trust neighbors	23%	13%	10%
Contributed to religious charity	29%	20%	9%
Expect crisis support from friends	22%	14%	8%
Trust "people running my community"	32%	24%	8%
Worked with neighbors	15%	8%	7%
Trust local news media	30%	23%	7%
Gave blood	11%	4%	7%
Volunteered	36%	29%	7%
Expect local cooperation in crisis	23%	17%	6%
Worked on community project	17%	11%	6%
Attended political meeting	11%	6%	5%
Read the newspaper	27%	24%	3%
Visit relatives	43%	40%	3%
Attended club meeting	29%	26%	3%
Attended public meeting	27%	26%	1%
Contributed to secular charity	28%	27%	1%
Attend church	20%	19%	1%
Belong to organizations (number)	39%	39%	0%
Had friends visit your home	39%	45%	−6%
Support immigrant rights	21%	32%	−11%

experience of most Americans now alive. The images of shared suffering that followed the terrorist attacks on New York and Washington suggested a powerful idea of cross-class, cross-ethnic solidarity. Americans also confronted a clear foreign enemy, an experience that both drew us closer to one another and provided an obvious rationale for public action.

In the aftermath of September's tragedy, a window of opportunity has opened for a sort of civic renewal that occurs only once or twice a century. And yet, though the crisis revealed and replenished the wells of solidarity in American communities, those wells so far remain untapped. At least, this is what that gap between attitudes and behavior suggests. Civic solidarity is what Albert Hirschman called a "moral resource"—distinctive in that, unlike a material resource, it increases with use and diminishes with disuse. Changes in attitude alone, no matter how promising, do not constitute civic renewal.

Americans who came of age just before and during World War II were enduringly molded by that crisis. All their lives, these Americans have voted more, joined more, given more. But the so-called Greatest Generation forged not merely moods and symbols, as important as those were; it also produced great national policies and institutions (such as the GI Bill) and community-minded personal practices (such as scrap drives and victory gardens). So far, however, America's new mood has expressed itself largely through images—of the attacks themselves, for instance, or the Ad Council's "I am an American" campaign, which powerfully depicts our multicultural society—and gestures, such as the president's visit to a mosque.

Images matter. . . . But images alone do not create turning points in a nation's history. That requires institutionalized change. To help foster a new "greatest generation," the Bush administration should endorse the bill offered by Senators John McCain and Evan Bayh to quintuple funds for the AmeriCorps program of national youth service. And given that young Americans are more open to political participation than they have been in many years, educational and political leaders should seize this moment to encourage youths' engagement in political and social movements. The grass-roots movement to restore the Pledge of Allegiance in American classrooms advocates fine symbolism; but the time is right to introduce a new, more activist civics education in our schools as well.

Finally, activists should recognize that wartime mobilization can also spark progress toward social justice and racial integration, much as the experiences of World War II helped to generate the civil-rights movement of the 1950s. Americans today, our surveys suggest, are more open than ever to the idea that people of all backgrounds should be full members of our national community. Progressives should work to translate that national mood into concrete policy initiatives that bridge the ethnic and class cleavages in our increasingly multicultural society.

Questions for Discussion

1. Why did the experience of 9/11 appear to have such an impact on Americans' civic attitudes? Why did social trust and political tolerance seem to increase after such an event, particularly among the younger generation?
2. Do you believe the short-run changes in civic attitudes as the result of 9/11 will translate into positive changes in civic behavior, or is the long-term trend toward social disengagement likely to resume?

 # Chapter 6

POLITICAL PARTIES

The word *party* does not appear in the U.S. Constitution. The nation's founders, suspicious of special interests, viewed parties as devices to organize factions—"to put in the place of the delegated will of the nation the will of party," as George Washington put it. Yet within a generation of the nation's founding, parties had emerged as instruments for structuring political conflict and encouraging mass participation.

In retrospect, the development of political parties seems almost inevitable. The United States has always harbored a diverse political culture, and the practical necessity of governing demands that majorities be forged among contending interests. Political parties evolved as the only solution to the problem of reconciling individual diversity with majority rule.

The American political party functions as an intermediary between the public and the government. A party can combine citizens' demands into a manageable number of issues, thus enabling the system to focus on society's most crucial problems. The party performs its mediating function primarily through coalition building—in the words of journalist David Broder, "the process of constructing majorities from the broad sentiments and interests that can be found to bridge the narrower needs and hopes of separate individuals and communities."

For example, Franklin Roosevelt's New Deal, forged in the 1930s in the face of deep economic depression, brought about a Democratic coalition that essentially dominated national policymaking for thirty years. Generally speaking, socioeconomic divisions shaped politics in the 1930s. Less affluent citizens tended to support the Roosevelt administration's provisions for social and economic security and government regulation of private enterprise. Those who were better off usually took the opposite position. By and large, the New Deal coalition came to represent northern urban workers, immigrants and ethnic minorities, blacks, Catholics, Jews, and many southerners.

Such coalition building has contributed greatly to the stability of American political life, but the parties also serve as the major vehicle for political change. Political coalitions are never permanent. Old issues are dealt with or decrease in importance, while new issues move onto the agenda. New voters enter the electorate, older ones die, and the economic and social circumstances of groups and regions change.

Confronted with a new political environment, parties may realign—rearrange the bases of their coalitions to reflect new issues and public concerns. Critical realignments usually occur in the midst of an economic crisis such as a depression. Such an event causes sharp and durable changes in voter perceptions and identities because of the parties' differing positions on how to handle the situation. Scholars have concluded that party realignment has taken place a number of times since the early 1800s as the party system has adjusted to the changing issues in politics.

There is a general consensus among political observers that the American party system today is again in the midst of change, but there is little consensus as to its direction. Throughout the system's first 150 years, political realignment took place roughly every thirty-two to thirty-six years, but after the transforming election of 1932, the "expected" rearrangement did not occur by the early 1970s. New Deal political issues had faded in importance by the late 1960s, yet neither party appeared able or willing to build stable coalitions around the new issues.

Civil rights and the Vietnam War deeply divided the dominant Democrats in the 1960s, and divisions among constituent elements intensified in the 1970s as the governing system addressed such questions as women's rights, affirmative action, and consumer and environmental protection. As the party's agenda moved from guaranteeing equality of opportunity to pushing for equality of circumstance, the old coalition became impossible to sustain. Similarly, the Republican party, though experiencing a variety of successes (especially at the presidential level), did not develop a stable electoral and governing coalition. During the Nixon years, the Watergate scandal stopped what many viewed as a long-term shift in the balance of power toward the Republican party. Ronald Reagan's popularity caused some voters to shift party allegiance and may have enticed increasing numbers of young voters to identify with the Republican party, but economic, cultural, and social divisions among Republicans remained a barrier to coalition unity.

The lack of a critical realignment by the party system has caused some political analysts to claim that the system is undergoing "dealignment"—the movement of voters away from both parties. This viewpoint holds that "candidate politics" is more prevalent than "party politics." Some observers even suggest that party politics is not possible in the age of high technology, mass media dominance, and a highly educated electorate that engages in split-ticket voting. Those who believe in dealignment point to the decline of the importance of party identification in voting, to the growth of independence among older voters, and to the nonalignment of young voters entering the electorate. They also note the great stress on the American political system over the past forty years. The Vietnam War, the energy crisis, the hyperinflation of the 1970s, and scandals in the highest places in government during the Reagan and Clinton administrations have heightened citizen awareness of political affairs and increased mistrust of public officials and political institutions, including parties.

Much of the decline in the importance of parties has been blamed on their in-ability to perform their traditional functions in the electoral process. For example, post-1968 reforms in both parties (but particularly in the Democratic party) mean that delegates to presidential nomination conventions are selected largely in primaries rather than in caucuses and state conventions, thus increasing the number of narrow-issue activists and decreasing the number of elected officials and party professionals. Some believe the parties have lost their ability to set the political agenda in the nomination process as well. Candidates no longer have to spend years working within the party hierarchy to become contenders; today fresh faces quickly emerge, thanks to the role played by the media, particularly television, in determining who is or is not a "serious" candidate.

Changes in campaigning and finances have also reduced the parties' tradi-tional role in campaign organization. Campaigns are now largely run by candi-date organizations rather than by the parties. The ever-increasing importance of money and the growth of political action committees (PACs) since the Campaign Reform Acts of 1971 and 1974 (which mandated financial reporting by candi-date committees) have enabled individuals to rely less on traditional party sources of funds and more on funds made available by special interests. Not surprisingly, those interests play a major role in recruiting candidates, setting issue agendas, and, in some cases, actually mobilizing voters.

Campaigns have also become more oriented toward the media than toward personal contact with voters in recent decades, and independent political con-sultants are now more likely than party professionals to run campaigns. Candi-dates for most national or statewide offices routinely place their campaigns in the hands of a comprehensive political consulting firm, which is charged with raising funds, polling, advertising, and designing campaign strategy. One conse-quence is that officeholders now owe little allegiance either to party organiza-tions or to party leaders; they are elected by their own efforts and are accountable to no one but themselves.

In spite of these trends, some political scientists assert that the two major par-ties are adjusting to the challenge of PAC politics, high technology, and mass media and are staging a resurgence, especially at the national level. Both have taken advantage of the PAC phenomenon by forming loose alliances with some prominent groups. In their emerging role as brokers, the national parties assist PACs in directing contributions to particular campaigns. Likewise, they aid candi-dates by soliciting contributions from PACs. In addition, the national parties pro-vide professional assistance to candidates in the form of direct mail and polling services.

During the 1990s the national parties clearly renewed their ability to influence campaign politics. Taking advantage of a loophole in the campaign finance laws, both national parties raised and spent large amounts of so-called soft money, funds collected from individuals and organized interests outside the contribution limits of federal election law. The money was originally intended to be used for "party-building" purposes, especially at the state and local level; some contributors gave over $1 million. However, beginning in the mid-1990s the parties typically used such funds for campaign advertising on behalf of party candidates. In the 2000 federal elections, party spending on campaign advertising outstripped that spent by candidate campaign committees or interest groups.

In 2002, however, Congress passed and President Bush signed a new campaign finance law, the Bipartisan Campaign Reform Act (BCRA). A major provision banned soft money contributions to national party committees. Most observers believe that the influence of parties in elections will again decline as the parties, particularly the Democrats, are strapped for funds.

The readings that follow were chosen to give readers insight into the sometimes misunderstood role of parties in the American political system. John H. Aldrich discusses why parties were created by "ambitious politicians" after the nation's founding, and the influence they have both inside and outside government in making democracy function. Jeffrey Toobin examines some recent efforts at partisan gerrymandering, where congressional district lines are deliberately drawn in such a manner as to advantage one party over the other. Toobin worries that excessive partisanship in redistricting makes elections less democratic. Finally, Paul Allen Beck looks at the party in the electorate, particularly efforts by each of the major parties to build a majority coalition of partisans in the years since the collapse of the New Deal party system. He finds the contemporary party system to be highly polarized, though neither party can depend upon the loyalty of a majority of the voters. Indeed, a large group of dedicated nonpartisan voters hold the balance of power in contemporary elections.

6.1

The Case for the Importance of Political Parties

John H. Aldrich

Political parties, as they have been for over a century and a half, are prominent features of U.S. politics both inside and outside government. Parties are most conspicuous when they are nominating candidates and contesting elections or are organizing and managing political conflict in the policy process.

In this selection, John H. Aldrich offers a theory of political parties based upon the central actors in the party—those who seek or hold public office. Political parties did not exist at the nation's founding, but they soon emerged when ambitious politicians came to realize that certain fundamental problems had to be solved if leaders were to achieve their goals. For politicians, parties reduce uncertainty and offer valuable resources. They regulate access to public office by their control of the nomination process, and they help mobilize the electorate on behalf of their candidates. Parties help manage the career advancement of officials once they are elected by providing leadership opportunities within institutions such as legislatures. Further, the party in government helps structure decision making in the government itself; it is important in proposing alternatives, shaping the agenda, passing (or rejecting) legislation, and implementing what is enacted.

In Aldrich's view, parties are essential to democracy. They help both public officials and the mass public make sense of a political system that is fragmented, multilayered, and complex.

The path to office for nearly every major politician begins today, as it has for over 150 years, with the party. Many candidates emerge initially from the ranks of party activists, all serious candidates seek their party's nomination, and they become serious candidates in the general

---

John H. Aldrich is the Pfizer-Pratt University Professor of political science at Duke University.

John H. Aldrich, *Why Parties? The Origin and Transformation of Political Parties in America* (Chicago: University of Chicago Press, 1995), pp. 14–27. Reprinted by permission of the publisher, The University of Chicago Press and the author.

election only because they have won their party's endorsement. Today most partisan nominations are decided in primary elections—that is, based on votes cast by self-designated partisans in the mass electorate. Successful nominees count on the continued support of these partisans in the general election, and for good reason. At least since surveys have provided firm evidence, all presidential nominees have won the support of no less than a majority of their party in the electorate, no matter how overwhelming their defeat may have been.

This is an age of so-called partisan dealignment in the electorate.* Even so, a substantial majority today consider themselves partisans. The lowest percentage of self-professed (i.e., "strong" and "weak") partisans yet recorded in National Election Studies (NES) surveys was 61 percent in 1974, and another 22 percent expressed partisan leanings that year. Evidence from panel surveys demonstrates that partisanship has remained as stable and enduring for most adults after dealignment as it did before it, and it is often the single strongest predictor of candidate choice in the public.

If parties have declined recently, the decline has not occurred in their formal organizations. Party organizations are if anything stronger, better financed, and more professional at all levels now. Although its importance to candidates may be less than in the past, the party provides more support—more money, workers, and resources of all kinds—than any other organization for all but a very few candidates for national and state offices.

Once elected, officeholders remain partisans. Congress is organized by parties. Party-line votes elect its leadership, determine what its committees will be, assign members to them, and select their chairs. Party caucuses remain a staple of congressional life, and they and other forms of party organizations in Congress have become stronger in recent years. Party voting in committee and on the floor of both houses, though far less common in the United States than in many democracies, nonetheless remains the first and most important standard for understanding congressional voting behavior, and it too has grown stronger, in this case much stronger, in recent years.

Relationships among the elected branches of government are also heavily partisan. Conference committees to resolve discrepancies between House and Senate versions of legislation reflect partisan as well as interchamber rivalries. The president is the party's leader, and his agenda is introduced, fought for, and supported on the floor by his congressional party. His agenda becomes his party's congressional agenda, and much of it [sic] finds its way into law.

---

*Partisan dealignment describes the movement of voters away from identity with either of the parties. This may involve voters leaving one party and not affiliating with the other or entering the electorate without any party identification and never acquiring it. Issues and candidate attractiveness, rather than party identification, dominate such voters' decisions.

The Case for Weak and Weakening Parties

As impressive as the scenario above may be, not all agree that parties lie at the heart of American politics, at least not anymore. The literature on parties over the past two decades is replete with accounts of the decline of the political party. Even the choice of titles clearly reflects the arguments. David Broder perhaps began this stream of literature with *The Party's Over* (1972). Since then, political scientists have written extensively on this theme: for example, Crotty's *American Political Parties in Decline* (1984), Kirkpatrick's *Dismantling the Parties* (1978), Polsby's *Consequences of Party Reform* (1983 . . .), Ranney's thoughtful *Curing the Mischiefs of Faction* (1975), and Wattenberg's *The Decline of American Political Parties* (1990).

Those who see larger ills in the contemporary political scene often attribute them to the failure of parties to be stronger and more effective. In "The Decline of Collective Responsibility" (1980), Fiorina argued that such responsibility was possible only through the agency of the political party. Jacobson concluded his study of congressional elections (1992) by arguing that contemporary elections induce "responsiveness" of individual incumbents to their districts but do so "without [inducing] responsibility" in incumbents for what Congress does. As a result, the electorate can find no one to hold accountable for congressional failings. He too looked to a revitalized party for redress. These themes reflect the responsible party thesis, if not in being a call for such parties, at least in using that as the standard for measuring how short the contemporary party falls.

The literature on the presidency is not immune to this concern for decaying parties. Kernell's account of the strategy of "going public" (1986)—that is, generating power by marshaling public opinion—is that it became more common as the older strategy of striking bargains with a small set of congressional (and partisan) power brokers grew increasingly futile. The earlier use of the president's power to persuade (Neustadt 1960, 1990) failed as power centers became more diverse and fragmented and brokers could no longer deliver. Lowi argued this case even more strongly in *The Personal President* (1985). America, he claimed, has come to invest too much power in the office of the president, with the result that the promise of the presidency and the promises of individual presidents go unfulfilled. Why? Because the rest of government has become too unwieldy, complicated, and fragmented for the president to use that power effectively. His solution? Revitalize political parties.

Divided partisan control over government, once an occasional aberration, has become the ordinary course of affairs. Many of the same themes in this literature are those sounded above—fragmented, decentralized power, lack of coordination and control over what the government does, and absence of collective responsibility. Strong political parties are, among other things, those that can deliver the vote for most or all of their candidates. Thus another symptom of weakened parties is regularized divided government, in the states as well as in the nation.

If divided government is due to weakened parties, that condition must be due in turn to weakened partisan loyalties in the electorate. Here the evidence is clear. The proportions and strength of party attachments in the electorate declined in the mid-1960s. There was a resurgence in affiliation twenty years later, but to a lower level than before 1966. The behavioral consequences of these changes are if anything even clearer. Defection from party lines and split-ticket voting are far more common for all major offices at national, state, and local levels today than before the mid-1960s. Elections are more candidate centered and less party centered, and those who come to office have played a greater role in shaping their own more highly personalized electoral coalitions. Incumbents, less dependent on the party for winning office, are less disposed to vote the party line in Congress or to follow the wishes of their party's president. Power becomes decentralized toward the individual incumbent and, as Jacobson argues, individual incumbents respond to their constituents. If that means defecting from the party, so be it.

Is the Debate Genuine?

Some believe that parties have actually grown stronger over the past few decades. This position has been put most starkly by Schlesinger: "It should be clear by now that the grab bag of assumptions, inferences, and half-truths that have fed the decline-of-parties thesis is simply wrong" (1985, p. 1152). Rather, he maintains, "Thanks to increasing levels of competition between the parties, then, American political parties are stronger than before" (p. 1168). More common is the claim that parties were weakened in the 1960s but have been revitalized since then. Rohde pointed out that "in the last decade, however, the decline of partisanship in the House has been reversed. Party voting, which had been as low as 27 percent in 1972, peaked at 64 percent in 1987" (1989, p. 1). Changes in party voting in the Senate have been only slightly less dramatic, and Rohde has also demonstrated that party institutions in the House strengthened substantially in the same period (1991). If, as Rohde says, parties in the government are stronger, [and if] . . . the others are correct that party organizations are stronger, a thesis of decline with resurgence must be taken seriously. The electorate's partisan affiliations may be a lagging rather than a leading indicator, and even they have rebounded slightly.

A Theory of Political Parties

. . . How is it that such astute observers of American politics and parties, writing at virtually the same time and looking at much the same evidence, come to such diametrically opposed conclusions about the strength of parties? Eldersveld provided an obvious answer. He wrote that "political parties are complex

institutions and processes, and as such they are difficult to understand and evaluate" (1982, p. 407). As proof, he went on to consider the decline of parties
thesis. At one point he wrote, "The decline in our parties, therefore, is difficult
to demonstrate, empirically or in terms of historical perspective" (p. 417). And
yet he then turned to signs of party decline and concluded his book with the
statement: "Despite their defects they continue today to be the major instruments for democratic government in this nation. With necessary reforms we
can make them even more central to the governmental process and to the lives
of American citizens. Eighty years ago, Lord James Bryce, after studying our
party system, said, 'In America the great moving forces are the parties. The
government counts for less than in Europe, the parties count for more. . . .' If
our citizens and their leaders wish it, American parties will still be the 'great
moving forces' of our system" (1982, pp. 432–33).

The "Fundamental Equation" of the New Institutionalism*
Applied to Parties

That parties are complex does not mean they are incomprehensible. Indeed
complexity is, if not an intentional outcome, at least an anticipated result of
those who shape the political parties. Moreover, they are so deeply woven into
the fabric of American politics that they cannot be understood apart from either their own historical context and dynamics or those of the political system
as a whole. Parties, that is, can be understood only in relation to the polity, to
the government and its institutions, and to the historical context of the times.

The study of political parties, second, is necessarily a study of a major pair of political *institutions*. Indeed, the institutions that define the political party are
unique, and as it happens they are unique in ways that make an institutional account especially useful. Their establishment and nature are fundamentally extralegal; they are nongovernmental political institutions. Instead of statute, their basis
lies in the actions of ambitious politicians that created and maintain them. . . .

. . . I mean it was the actions of political actors that created political parties in
the first place, and it is the actions of political actors that have shaped and altered them over time. And political actors have chosen to alter their parties dramatically at several times in our history, reformed them often, and tinkered with
them constantly. Of all major political bodies in the United States, the political
party is the most variable in its rules, regulations, and procedures—that is to say,
in its formal organization—and in its informal methods and traditions. It is
often the same set of actors who write the party's rules and then choose the

---

New institutionalism is a broad term used to describe a movement beginning in the early
1980s to refocus the attention of political scientists on the role played by informal and formal institutions in the political process. Within this approach, a political party would be considered an
extralegal institution rather than an "official" government institution like a legislature.

party's outcomes, sometimes at nearly the same time and by the same method. Thus, for example, one night national party conventions debate, consider any proposed amendments, and then adopt their rules by a majority vote of credentialed delegates. The next night these same delegates debate, consider any proposed amendments, and then adopt their platform by majority vote, and they choose their presidential nominee by majority vote the following night.

Who, then, are these critical political actors? Many see the party-in-the-electorate as comprising major actors. To be sure, mobilizing the electorate to capture office is a central task of the political party. But America is a republican democracy. All power flows directly or indirectly from the great body of the people, to paraphrase Madison's definition. The public elects its political leaders, but it is that leadership that legislates, executes, and adjudicates policy. The parties are defined in relation to this republican democracy. Thus it is political leaders, those Schlesinger (1975) has called "office-seekers"—*those who seek and those who hold elective office*—who are the central actors in the party.

Ambitious office seekers and holders are thus the first and most important actors in the political party. A second set of important figures in party politics comprises those who hold, or have access to, critical resources that office seekers need to realize their ambitions. It is expensive to build and maintain the party and campaign organizations necessary to compete effectively in the electoral arena. Thomas Ferguson, for example, has made an extended argument for the "primary and constitutive role large investors play in American politics" (1983, p. 3 . . .). Much of his research emphasizes this primary and constitutive role in party politics in particular, such as in partisan realignments. The study of the role of money in congressional elections has also focused in part on concentrations of such sources of funding, such as from political action committees which political parties are coming to take advantage of. Elections are also fought over the flow of information to the public. The electoral arm of political parties in the eighteenth century was made up of "committees of correspondence," which were primarily lines of communication among political elites and between them and potential voters, and one of the first signs of organizing of the Jeffersonian Republican party was the hiring of a newspaper editor. The press was first a partisan press, and editors and publishers from Thomas Ritchie to Horace Greeley long were critical players in party politics. Today those with specialized knowledge relevant to communication, such as pollsters, media and advertising experts, and computerized fund-raising specialists, enjoy influence in party, campaign, and even government councils that greatly exceeds their mere technical expertise.

In more theoretical terms, this second set of party actors include those Schlesinger (1975) has called "benefit seekers," those for whom realization of their goals depends on the party's success in capturing office. Party activists shade from those powerful figures with concentrations of, or access to, money and information described above to the legions of volunteer campaign activists who ring doorbells and stuff envelopes and are, individually and collectively, critical to the first level of the party—its office seekers. All are critical because they command the resources, whether money, expertise, and information or merely time and labor, that office seekers need to realize their ambitions. As a result, activists' motivations shape and constrain the behavior of office seekers, as their own roles are, in turn, shaped and constrained by the office seekers. . . . I argue that the changed incentives of party activists have played a significant role in the fundamentally altered nature of the contemporary party, but the impact of benefit seekers will be seen scattered throughout this account.

Voters, however, are neither office seekers nor benefit seekers and thus are not a part of the political party at all, even if they identify strongly with a party and consistently support its candidates. Voters are indeed critical, but they are critical as the targets of party activities. Parties "produce" candidates, platforms, and policies. Voters "consume" by exchanging their votes for the party's product (see Popkin et al. 1976). Some voters, of course, become partisans by becoming activists, whether as occasional volunteers, as sustained contributors, or even as candidates. But until they do so, they may be faithful consumers, "brand name" loyalists [as] it were, but they are still only the targets of partisans' efforts to sell their wares in the political marketplace.

Why, then, do politicians create and recreate the party, exploit its features, or ignore its dictates? The simple answer is that it has been in their interests to do so. That is, this is a *rational choice* account of the party, an account that presumes that rational, elective office seekers and holders use the party to achieve their ends.

I do not assume that politicians are invariably self-interested in a narrow sense. This is not a theory in which elective office seekers simply maximize their chances of election or reelection, at least not for its own sake. They may well have fundamental values and principles, and they may have preferences over policies as means to those ends. They also care about office, both for its own sake and for the opportunities to achieve other ends that election and reelection make possible. . . . Just as winning elections is a means to other ends for politicians (whether career or policy ends), so too is the political party a means to these other ends.

Why, then, do politicians turn to create or reform, to use or abuse, partisan institutions? The answer is that parties are designed as attempts to solve problems that current institutional arrangements do not solve and that politicians have come to believe they cannot solve. These problems fall into three general and recurring categories.

The Problem of Ambition and Elective Office Seeking

Elective office seekers, as that label says, want to win election to office. Parties regulate access to those offices. If elective office is indeed valuable, there will be more aspirants than offices, and the political party and the two-party system are means of regulating that competition and channeling those ambitions. Major party nomination is necessary for election, and partisan institutions have been developed—and have been reformed and re-reformed—for regulating competition. Intra-institutional leadership positions are also highly valued and therefore potentially competitive. There is, for example, a fairly well institutionalized path to the office of Speaker of the House. It is, however, a Democratic party institution. Elective politicians, of course, ordinarily desire election more than once. They are typically careerists who want a long and productive career in politics. Schlesinger's ambition theory (1966) . . . is precisely about this general problem. Underlying this theory, though typically not fully developed, is a problem. The problem is that if office is desirable, there will be more, usually many more, aspirants than there are offices to go around. . . . And it is a problem that can adversely affect the fortunes of a party. In 1912 the Republican vote was split between William Howard Taft and Theodore Roosevelt. This split enabled Woodrow Wilson to win with 42 percent of the popular vote. Not only was Wilson the only break in Republican hegemony of the White House in this period, but in that year Democrats increased their House majority by sixty-five additional seats and captured majority control of the Senate. Thus failure to regulate intraparty competition cost Republicans dearly.

For elective office seekers, regulating conflict over who holds those offices is clearly of major concern. It is ever present. And it is not just a problem of access to government offices but is also a problem internal to each party as soon as the party becomes an important gateway to office.

The Problem of Making Decisions for the Party and for the Polity

Once in office, partisans determine outcomes for the polity. They propose alternatives, shape the agenda, pass (or reject) legislation, and implement what they enact. The policy formation and execution process, that is, is highly partisan. The parties-in-government are more than mere coalitions of like-minded individuals, however; they are enduring institutions. Very few incumbents change their partisan affiliations. Most retain their partisanship throughout their career, even though they often disagree (i.e., are not uniformly like-minded) with some of their partisan peers. When the rare incumbent does change parties, it is invariably to join the party more consonant with that switcher's policy interests. This implies that there are differences between the two parties at some fundamental and enduring level on policy positions, values, and beliefs. Thus, parties are institutions designed to promote the achievement of collective choices—choices on which the parties differ and choices reached by majority rule. As with access to office and ambition theory, there is a well-developed theory for this problem: *social choice theory*.* Underlying this theory is the well-known problem that no method of choice can solve the elective of-

---

*Social choice theory is a formal theory, typically abstract and mathematical, concerned with how a group of voters or public officials with varying opinions and faced with a range of choices makes decisions.

ficeholders' problem of combining the interests, concerns, or values of a polity that remains faithful to democratic values, as shown by the consequences flowing from Arrow's theorem (Arrow 1951).* Thus, in a republican democracy politicians may turn to partisan institutions to solve the problem of collective choice. In the language of politics, parties may help achieve the goal of attaining policy majorities in the first place, as well as the often more difficult goal of maintaining such majorities.

The Problem of Collective Action

The third problem is the most pervasive and thus the furthest-ranging in substantive content. The clearest example, however, is also the most important. To win office, candidates need more than a party's nomination. Election requires persuading members of the public to support that candidacy and mobilizing as many of those supporters as possible. This is a problem of collective action. How do candidates get supporters to vote for them—at least in greater numbers than vote for the opposition—as well as get them to provide the cadre of workers and contribute the resources needed to win election? The political party has long been the solution.

As important as wooing and mobilizing supporters are, collective action problems arise in a wide range of circumstances facing elective office seekers. Party action invariably requires the concerted action of many partisans to achieve collectively desirable outcomes. Jimmy Carter was the only president in the 1970s and 1980s to enjoy unified party control of government. Democrats in Congress, it might well be argued, shared an interest in achieving policy outcomes. And yet Carter was all too often unable to get them to act in their shared collective interests. In 1980 not only he but the Democratic congressional parties paid a heavy price for failed cooperation. . . .

The Elective Office Seekers' and Holders' Interests Arc to Win

Why should this crucial set of actors, the elective office seekers and officeholders, care about these three classes of problems? The short answer is that these concerns become practical problems to politicians when they adversely affect their chances of winning. Put differently, politicians turn to their political party—that is, use its powers, resources, and institutional forms—when they believe doing so increases their prospects for winning desired outcomes, and they turn from it if it does not.

---

*Kenneth Arrow was an economist who gained fame for his mathematical proof demonstrating that the "ideal" voting system does not exist.

Ambition theory is about winning per se. The breakdown of orderly access to office risks unfettered and unregulated competition. The inability of a party to develop effective means of nomination and support for election therefore directly influences the chances of victory for the candidates and thus for their parties. The standard example of the problem of social choice theory, the "paradox of voting,"* is paradoxical precisely because all are voting to win desired outcomes, and yet there is no majority-preferred outcome. Even if there happens to be a majority-preferred policy, the conditions under which it is truly a stable equilibrium are extremely fragile and thus all too amenable to defeat. In other words, majorities in Congress are hard to attain and at least as hard to maintain. And the only reason to employ scarce campaign resources to mobilize supporters is that such mobilization increases the odds of victory. Its opposite, the failure to act when there are broadly shared interests—the problem of collective action—reduces the prospects of victory, whether at the ballot box or in government. . . .

So why have politicians so often turned to political parties for solutions to these problems? Their existence creates incentives for their use. It is, for example, incredibly difficult to win election to major office without the backing of a major party. It is only a little less certain that legislators who seek to lead a policy proposal through the congressional labyrinth will first turn to their party for assistance. But such incentives tell us only that an ongoing political institution is used when it is useful. Why form political parties in the first place? . . .

First, parties are institutions. This means, among other things, that they have some durability. They may be endogenous institutions, yet party reforms are meant not as short-term fixes but as alterations to last for years, even decades. Thus, for example, legislators might create a party rather than a temporary majority coalition to increase their chances of winning not just today but into the future. Similarly, a long and successful political career means winning office today, but it also requires winning elections throughout that career. A standing, enduring organization makes that goal more likely.

Second, American democracy chooses by plurality or majority rule. Election to office therefore requires broad-based support wherever and from whomever it can be found. So strong are the resulting incentives for a two-party system to emerge that the effect is called Duverger's law (Duverger 1954). It is in part the need to win vast and diverse support that has led politicians to create political parties.

---

*"The paradox of voting" refers to the possibility that simple majority rule voting may fail to give an unambiguous choice between alternatives. Consider the situation where, when choosing among at least three alternatives, a majority of voters may prefer each alternative over the others in head-to-head competition. In essence, the voter's paradox is that each alternative is the majority winner in head-to-head competition. This is not because the voters change their individual preferences, but because aggregating all their preferences does not always lead to a stable group preference ordering.

Third, parties may help officeholders win more, and more often, than alternatives. Consider the usual stylized model of pork barrel politics. All winners get a piece of the pork for their districts. All funded projects are paid for by tax revenues, so each district pays an equal share of the costs of each project adopted, whether or not that district receives a project. Several writers have argued that this kind of legislation leads to "universalism," that is, adoption of a "norm" that every such bill yields a project to every district and thus passes with a "universal" or unanimous coalition. Thus everyone "wins." . . . As a result, expecting to win only a bit more than half the time and lose the rest of the time, all legislators prefer consistent use of the norm of universalism. But consider an alternative. Suppose some majority agree to form a more permanent coalition, to control outcomes now and into the future, and develop institutional means to encourage fealty to this agreement. If they successfully accomplish this, they will win regularly. Members of this institutionalized coalition would prefer it to universalism, since they always win a project in either case, but they get their projects at lower cost under the institutionalized majority coalition, which passes fewer projects. Thus, even in this case with no shared substantive interests at all, there are nonetheless incentives to form an enduring voting coalition—to form a political party. And those in the excluded minority have incentives to counterorganize. United, they may be more able to woo defectors to their side. If not, they can campaign to throw those rascals in the majority party out of office.

In sum, these theoretical problems affect elective office seekers and officeholders by reducing their chances of winning. Politicians therefore may turn to political parties as institutions designed to ameliorate them. In solving these theoretical problems, however, from the politicians' perspective parties are affecting who wins and loses and what is won or lost. And it is to parties that politicians often turn, because of their durability as institutionalized solutions, because of the need to orchestrate large and diverse groups of people to form winning majorities, and because often more can be won through parties. Note that this argument rests on the implicit assumption that winning and losing hang in the balance. Politicians may be expected to give up some of their personal autonomy only when they face an imminent threat of defeat without doing so or only when doing so can block opponents' ability to build the strength necessary to win. . . .

The political party has regularly proved useful. Their permanence suggests that the appropriate question is not When parties? but How much parties and how much other means? . . . [P]arties are but a (major) part of the institutional context in which current historical conditions—the problems—are set, and solutions are sought with permanence only by changing that web of institutional arrangements. Of these the political party is by design the most malleable, and thus it is intended to change in important ways and with relatively great frequency. But it changes in ways that have, for most of American history, retained major political parties and, indeed, retained two major parties.

References

Arrow, Kenneth J. 1951. *Social choice and individual values*. New York: Wiley.

Broder, David S. 1972. *The party's over: The failure of politics in America*. New York: Harper and Row.

Crotty, William. 1984. *American political parties in decline*. 2d ed. Boston: Little, Brown.

Duverger, Maurice. 1954. *Political parties: Their organization and activities in the modern state*. New York: Wiley.

Eldersveld, Samuel J. 1982. *Political parties in American society*. New York: Basic Books.

Ferguson, Thomas. 1983. Party realignment and American industrial structures: The investment theory of political parties in historical perspective. In *Research in political economy*, vol. 6, ed. Paul Zarembka, pp. 1–82. Greenwich, Conn.: JAI Press.

Fiorina, Morris P. 1980. The decline of collective responsibility in American politics. *Daedalus* 109 (summer): 25–45.

Kernell, Samuel. 1986. *Going public: New strategies of presidential leadership*. Washington D.C.: CQ Press.

Kirkpatrick, Jeane J. 1978. *Dismantling the parties: Reflections on party reform and party decomposition*. Washington, D.C.: American Enterprise Institute of Public Policy Research.

Lowi, Theodore. 1985. *The personal president: Power invested, promise unfulfilled*. Ithaca, N.Y.: Cornell University Press.

Neustadt, Richard E. 1960. *Presidential power: The politics of leadership*. New York: Wiley.

Polsby, Nelson W. 1983. *Consequences of party reform*. Oxford: Oxford University Press.

Popkin, Samuel, John W. Gorman, Charles Phillips, and Jeffrey A. Smith. 1976. Comment: What have you done for me lately? Toward an investment theory of voting. *American Political Science Review* 70 (September): 779–805.

Ranney, Austin. 1975. *Curing the mischiefs of faction: Party reform in America*. Berkeley and Los Angeles: University of California Press.

Rohde, David W. 1989. "Something's happening here: What it is ain't exactly clear": Southern Democrats in the House of Representatives. In *Home style and Washington work: Studies of congressional politics*, ed. Morris P. Fiorina and David W. Rohde, pp. 137–163. Ann Arbor: University of Michigan Press.

Schlesinger, Joseph A. 1966. *Ambition and politics: Political careers in the United States*. Chicago: Rand McNally.

———. 1975. The primary goals of political parties: A clarification of positive theory. *American Political Science Review* 69 (September): 840–49.

———. 1985. The new American political party. *American Political Science Review* 79 (December): 1152–69.

Wattenberg, Martin P. 1990. *The decline of American political parties: 1952–1988*. Cambridge: Harvard University Press.

Questions for Discussion

1. What factors necessitated the rise of political parties in the United States? What problems do parties solve for those who seek to serve in public office?
2. What role do voters play in Aldrich's theory of political parties? If voters move away from the political parties, how will "ambitious politicians" respond? What alternatives to the parties exist for office seekers and holders in contemporary American politics?

6.2

The Great Election Grab

Jeffrey Toobin

Party politicians are always looking for ways to extend their political advantage. One tactic with a long history of creating a party advantage in Congress is the process of gerrymandering by state legislatures, which are in charge of redistricting on the basis of the decennial federal census. Policy makers in states where one party controls the legislature and governor's office may be able to draw congressional district lines in such a manner that the dominant party is able to gain additional seats. Gerrymandering typically involves designing congressional districts that heavily concentrate the opposing party's voters in a small number of districts where that party wins by overwhelming margins, basically "wasting" votes, while simultaneously maximizing the number of districts where the advantaged party candidates are safe electorally, but do not waste votes.

In this selection, Jeffrey Toobin describes recent efforts by Republican leaders to increase their numbers in Congress after release of the 2000 census by encouraging various Republican-controlled state legislatures to engage aggressively in partisan gerrymandering. In one state, Texas, the state legislature has attempted to redraw the lines a second time in mid-decade in order to increase the number of Republicans in the congressional delegation.

Toobin worries that aggressive partisan gerrymandering undermines the democratic process by diminishing the number of competitive elections. Further, those elected in safe districts tend to be more ideologically extreme than those from competitive districts, making compromise and collaboration between the parties in the policy process in the House less likely and debates more polarized.

With his West Texas twang, loping swagger, and ever-present cowboy boots, Charlie Stenholm doesn't much look like or sound like anybody's idea of a victim. Since 1979, he has been the congressman for a sprawling district west of Dallas, and his votes have reflected the conservative values of the cattle, cotton, and oil country back home. He opposes abortion,

Jeffrey Toobin is a CNN legal analyst for the CNN News Group and a staff writer at *The New Yorker*.

Jeffrey Toobin, "The Great Election Grab," *The New Yorker* (December 8, 2003): 63–66, 75–80. Reprinted by permission of the author.

fights for balanced budgets, and voted for the impeachment of President Clinton. His Web site features photographs of him carrying or firing guns. Through it all, though, Stenholm has remained a member of the Democratic Party, and for that offense he appears likely to lose his job after the next election.

Stenholm was a principal target in one of the more bizarre political dramas of recent years—the Texas redistricting struggle of 2003. Following the 2000 census, all states were obligated to redraw the boundaries of their congressional districts in line with the new population figures. In 2001, that process produced a standoff in Texas, with the Republican state senate and the Democratic state house of representatives unable to reach an agreement. As a result, a panel of federal judges formulated a compromise plan, which more or less replicated the current partisan balance in the state's congressional delegation: seventeen Democrats and thirteen Republicans. Then, in the 2002 elections, Republicans took control of the state house, and Tom DeLay, the Houston-area congressman who serves as House Majority Leader in Washington, decided to reopen the redistricting question. DeLay said that the current makeup of the congressional delegation did not reflect the state's true political orientation, so he set out to insure that it did.

"This was a fundamental change in the rules of the game," Heather Gerken, a professor at Harvard Law School, said. "The rules were, Fight it out once a decade but then let it lie for ten years. The norm was very useful, because they couldn't afford to fight this much about redistricting. Given the opportunity, that is all they will do, because it's their survival at stake. DeLay's tactic was so shocking because it got rid of this old, informal agreement." But Texas law contained no explicit prohibition on mid-decade redistricting, so the leadership of the state government, now unified in Republican hands, tried during the summer of 2003 to push through a new plan. Democrats attempted novel forms of resistance. In May, fifty-one House members fled to Oklahoma, to deprive the new leadership of a quorum; in July, a dozen senators decamped to New Mexico, for the same purpose. But defections and the passage of time weakened Democratic resolve, and, on October 13th, the plan sponsored by DeLay was passed.

"They did everything they could to bust up my political base," Stenholm told me. "They drew my farm and where I grew up into the Amarillo district, and they drew Abilene, where I live now, into the Lubbock district." As a result, Stenholm will be forced to run in one of these districts if he wants to remain in the House. The new map creates similar problems for half a dozen other incumbent Texas Democrats, so the reapportionment may add as many as seven new Republicans to the G.O.P. majority in the House of Representatives and shift the state's delegation to 22-10 in favor of the Republicans. "Politics is a contact sport," Stenholm said. "I've been in this business twenty-five years. I will play the hand I was dealt."

In Texas and elsewhere, redistricting has transformed American politics. The framers of the Constitution created the House of Representatives to be the branch of government most responsive to changes in the public mood, but gerrymandered districts mean that most of the four hundred and thirty-five members of Congress never face seriously contested general elections. In 2002, eighty-one incumbents ran unopposed by a major party candidate. "There are now about four hundred safe seats in Congress," Richard Pildes, a professor of law at New York University, said. "The level of competitiveness has plummeted to the point where it is hard to describe the House as involving competitive elections at all these days." The House isn't just ossified; it's polarized, too. Members of the House now effectively answer only to primary voters, who represent the extreme partisan edge of both parties. As a result, collaboration and compromise between the parties have almost disappeared. The Republican advantage in the House is modest—just two hundred and twenty-nine seats to two hundred and six—but gerrymandering has made the lead close to insurmountable for the foreseeable future.

There is, it appears, just one chance to change the cycle. On December 10th, the United States Supreme Court will hear arguments in a case that could alter the nature of redistricting—and, with it, modern American electoral politics. The court has long held that legislators may not discriminate on the basis of race in redistricting, but the question now before the court is whether, or to what extent, they may consider politics in defining congressional boundaries. . . .

The off-cycle timing of the Texas redistricting fight, as well as the farcical drama of the fleeing Democratic legislators, made the saga look like a colorful aberration. But the results of that altercation merely replicated what happened, after the 2000 census, in several other states where Republicans controlled the governorship and the legislature. Even in states where voters were evenly divided, the Republicans used their advantage in the state capitals to transform their congressional delegations. In Florida, the paradigmatically deadlocked state, the new district lines sent eighteen Republicans and seven Democrats to the House. In the Gore state of Michigan, which lost a seat in redistricting, the delegation went from 9-7 in favor of the Democrats to 9-6 in favor of the Republicans—even though Democratic congressional candidates received thirty-five thousand more votes than their Republican opponents in 2002. (The Michigan plan was approved on September 11, 2001, so it received little publicity.) Pennsylvania, which also went to Gore, had one of the most ruthless Republican gerrymanders, and it is the one being challenged before the Supreme Court.

After 2000, Pennsylvania lost two seats in Congress, and its legislature had to establish new district lines. Republican legislative leaders there engaged in no subterfuge; they candidly admitted that they intended to draw the lines to favor their party as much as possible. In the midst of the battle over the Pennsylvania plan, DeLay and Dennis Hastert, the Speaker of the House, sent a letter to the Pennsylvania legislators, saying, "We wish to encourage you in these efforts, as they play a crucial role in maintaining a Republican majority in the

United States House of Representatives." The Republicans in Harrisburg used venerable techniques in redistricting, like "packing," "cracking," and "kidnapping." Packing concentrates one group's voters in the fewest possible districts, so they cannot influence the outcome of races in others; cracking divides a group's voters into other districts, where they will be ineffective minorities; and kidnapping places two incumbents from the same party in the same district. . . .

The Republicans carved up Pennsylvania into many strangely shaped districts, which won monikers like the "supine seahorse" and the "upside-down Chinese dragon." Such nicknames for gerrymandered districts go back to the origin of the term, which was coined as an epithet to mock Massachusetts Governor Elbridge Gerry, who in 1811 approved an election district that was said to resemble a salamander. Like most gerrymanders throughout history, the Republicans' creation in Pennsylvania produced the desired results. Even though a Democrat, Ed Rendell, won the governorship in 2002, Republicans in that election took control of twelve of the nineteen House seats.

Democrats accomplished less in the 2000 redistricting cycle only because they controlled fewer states and thus could do less to protect their interests. DeLay's mid-cycle reapportionment may be without precedent, but Democrats have their own inglorious history of gerrymandering. Before the Texas coup this year, the most notorious redistricting operation in recent years was the one run by Representative Philip Burton, following the 1980 census in California, which transformed the Democrats' advantage in House seats there from 22-21 to 27-18. In 2002, a Democratic plan in Maryland turned that delegation from being evenly divided to a 6-2 Democratic advantage, and Georgia Democrats gained two seats in the House even though in the same election voters rejected a Democratic governor and a Democratic United States senator. In California, where Democrats also controlled the process, they settled for protecting incumbents of both parties. There, in 2002, not one of fifty general-election House challengers won even forty per cent of the total vote.

There is no doubt, though, that on balance the 2000 redistricting cycle amounted to a major victory for Republicans. Even though Al Gore and George W. Bush split the combined vote in Florida, Pennsylvania, Ohio, and Michigan, Republican control of the process meant that, after redistricting, the G.O.P. now holds fifty-one of those states' seventy-seven House seats. "The important thing to realize was in 1991 the Republicans had control of line-drawing in a total of five congressional districts," one G.O.P. redistricting expert told me. "In 2001, it was almost a hundred seats. Both parties made the most of it."

The transformation of congressional redistricting began long before the 2000 census, and the crucial issue was race. In the early nineteen-sixties, the Supreme Court, under Chief Justice Earl Warren, transformed American politics by enforcing the principle of one man, one vote, and requiring that all legislative districts contain the same number of people. Before these decisions, which started with the famous case of *Baker* v. *Carr,* in 1962, Southern (and some Northern) states had designed districts so that black voters had no mean-ingful say in Congress. Later in the decade, the Voting Rights Act established the principle that not only did blacks have the right to vote but they had to be placed in districts where black candidates stood a good chance of winning. The act, which was one of Lyndon B. Johnson's most important civil-rights initia-tives, led to the election of many more black members of Congress—and was a classic demonstration of the law of unintended consequences.

"When the civil-rights movement started, you had a lot of white Democrats in power in the South," Bobby Scott, a congressman from Virginia who was first elected in 1992, said. "And, when these white Democrats started redis-tricting, they wanted to keep African-American percentages at around thirty-five or forty per cent. That was enough for the white Democrats to keep winning in these districts, but not enough to elect any black Democrats. The white Democrats called these 'influence' districts, where we could have a say in who won." But Republicans sensed an opportunity. "They came to us and said, We want these districts to be sixty per cent black," Scott, who is African-American, said. "And blacks liked that idea, because it meant we elected some of our own for the first time. That's where the 'unholy alliance' came in."

The unholy alliance—between black Democrats and white Republicans—shaped redistricting during the eighties and nineties. Republicans recognized the value of concentrating black voters, who are reliable Democrats, in single districts, which are known in voting-rights parlance as "majority-minority." As Gerald Hebert, a Democratic redistricting operative and former Justice Depart-ment lawyer, puts it, "What you had was the Republicans who were in charge for every redistricting cycle at the Justice Department—'81, '91, '01. And there was a kind of thinking in the eighties and in the early nineties that if you could create a majority-minority district anywhere in the state, regardless of how it looked and what its impact was on surrounding districts, then you simply had to do it. What ended up happening was that they went out of their way to divide and conquer the Democrats." The real story of the Republican congres-sional landslide of 1994, many redistricting experts believe, is the disappear-ance of white Democratic congressmen, whose black constituents were largely absorbed into majority-minority districts.

It was a version of the unholy alliance which may doom Charlie Stenholm and his fellow Texas Democrats. All the congressmen who are likely to lose their jobs in the new DeLay plan are white. Many of their black constituents have been transferred to safe Democratic seats, where they can't harm Republi-cans. The unholy alliance has had the additional side effect, especially in the South, of making the Democrats the party of blacks and the Republicans the party of whites—which presents daunting long-term political problems for the Democratic Party. Many Democrats can't help but express a perverse admi-ration for the cleverness of the strategy. . . .

Since the 2000 cycle, these Republican gains have locked in and even ex-panded. To see how this was done, I asked Nathaniel Persily, a genial assistant professor of law and political science at the University of Pennsylvania, to visit my office and bring his laptop. Persily, who is thirty-three, has built a reputation as a nonpartisan expert and occasional practitioner in the field of redistricting.

Before 1990, most state legislators did their redistricting by taking off their shoes and tiptoeing with Magic Markers around large maps on the floor, marking the boundaries on overlaid acetate sheets. Use of computers in redistricting began in the nineties, and, as Persily demonstrated, it has now become a science. When Persily opened his computer, he showed me a map of Houston, detailed to the last census block. (The population of each block usually ranges from fewer than a dozen to about a thousand.) "This is the same map that DeLay's people used to redistrict," Persily said. Indeed, DeLay's political operation purchased ten copies of the software, which is called Caliper's Maptitude for Redistricting and costs about four thousand dollars per copy. The software permits map-makers to analyze an enormous amount of data—party registration, voting patterns, ethnic makeup from census data, property-tax records, roads, railways, old district lines. "There's only one limit to the kind of information you can use in redistricting—its availability," Persily said. (In Pennsylvania, Republicans used Carnegie-Mellon University's mainframe computer, which would have allowed them to add even more data, such as real-estate transactions.)

With a few clicks, Persily changed the map from one that showed party registration in each census block to one that revealed voting results in each block. The colors ranged from dark red, for heavily Democratic votes, to dark blue, for strongly Republican. He showed voting results in about two dozen races, from President to governor and from congressman to local offices. "The whole process has got much more sophisticated," Persily went on. "Party-registration data are not the only kind of data you want to use. You want to use real election results. That's a big change from ten years ago. We have become very good at predicting how people are going to vote. People's partisanship is at a thirty-year high. If I know you voted for Gore, I am better able to predict that you are going to vote for any given Democrat in a future election."

I asked Persily to give me a demonstration of how to draw district lines. He moved his mouse to the border between two congressional districts. A ledger on the top half of the screen showed that one of the districts, as currently configured, had about forty thousand more people than the other one. "The Supreme Court has said that the requirement of one man, one vote means that each district must have exactly—exactly— the same number of people," Persily explained. An early version of the Pennsylvania plan was rejected by the courts because the districts were just nineteen voters apart, in districts of about a half million people. Requirements for that sort of precision virtually mandate the use of computers for redistricting.

Persily zeroed in even more closely, and a little donkey popped up inside one of the census blocks. "That's where the local congressman lives, a Democrat," he explained. "We have little elephants for the Republican incumbents." The program seemed easy to use, justifying the boast, on the software company's Web site, that you could "start building plans thirty minutes after opening the box." Persily chuckled. "At a certain point, you admire the video-game appeal of all this.

"There used to be a theory that gerrymandering was self-regulating," Persily explained. "The idea was that the more greedy you are in maximizing the number of districts your party can control, the more likely it is that a small shift of votes will lead you to lose a lot of districts. But it's not self-regulating anymore. The software is too good, and the partisanship is too strong."

The effects of partisan gerrymandering go well beyond the protection of incumbents and the guarantee of continued Republican control. It has also changed the kind of people who win seats in Congress and the way they behave once they arrive. Jim Leach, a moderate Republican and fourteen-term congressman from Iowa, has watched the transformation. Leach agrees with Richard Pildes on the numbers: "A little less than four hundred seats are totally safe, which means that there is competition between Democrats and Republicans only in about ten or fifteen per cent of the seats.

"So the important question is who controls the safe seats," Leach said. "Currently, about a third of the over-all population is Democrat, a third is Republican, and a third is no party. If you ask yourself some mathematical questions, what is half of a third?—one-sixth. That's who decides the nominee in each district. But only a fourth participates in primaries. What is a fourth of a sixth? A twenty-fourth. So it's one twenty-fourth of the population that controls the seat in each party.

"Then you have to ask who are those people who vote in primaries," Leach went on. "They are the real partisans, the activists, on both sides. A district that is solidly Republican is a district that is more likely to go to the more conservative side of the Republican part of the Party for candidates and platforms. Presidential candidates go to the left or the right in the primaries and then try to get back in the center. In House politics, if your district is solidly one party, your only challenge is from within that party, so you have every incentive for staying to the more extreme side of your party. If you are Republican in an all-Republican district, there is no reason to move to the center. You want to protect your base. You hear that in Congress all the time, in both parties—'We've got to appeal to our base.' It's much more likely that an incumbent will lose a primary than he will a general election. So redistricting has made Congress a more partisan, more polarized place. The American political system today is structurally geared against the center, which means that the great majority of Americans feel left out of the decision-making process."

Scholarly research gives some support to Leach's impressions. "Partisan gerrymandering skews not only the positions congressmen take but also who the candidates are in the first place," Issacharoff, of Columbia, said. "You get more ideological candidates, the people who can arouse the base of the party, because they don't have to worry about electability. It's becoming harder to get things done, whether in Congress or in state legislatures, because partisan redistricting goes on at the state level, too." Among members of the House, partisan redistricting has also bred an almost comic sense of entitlement to landslides. In a hearing on the post-2000 reapportionment in New York, Representative Benjamin Gilman, an upstate Republican, said that during the 1982 redistricting he was promised by the majority leader of the state senate that "if I accepted that challenge of a fair-fight district, I would never again be asked or forced by the state to face that prospect of a fair fight once again. . . . I think it would be unfair not only to myself and my district to face that divisive prospect once again."

With partisan gerrymandering, House members in effect pay a penalty if they reach out too much to members of the other party. "What is laughable is the basic premise of what is going on," Charlie Stenholm, the endangered Texan, said. "The great sin I committed is that I won the last election 51-47 in a district that went 71-28 for President Bush. But I am a conservative Democrat, and that's why these people vote for me. There shouldn't be a penalty for reaching out across party lines." If Stenholm and his ilk disappear, they will be replaced by reliable Republicans—who won't have to worry about their own chances for reelection.

The question before the Supreme Court later this month is not whether partisan gerrymandering is wise but whether it is constitutional. The issues are strikingly similar to those faced by the Warren Court in the early sixties—and the stakes may be as large as well. The framers of the Constitution designed the House of Representatives to reflect the popular will. James Madison, in the Federalist Papers, said the House was meant to be a "numerous and changeable body," where the members would have "an habitual recollection of their dependence on the people." While the House was supposed to be impetuous, the Senate was intended to be stable. Madison said that senators would serve six-year terms as a defense against "the impulse of sudden and violent passions" of the House, and the members of the Senate were to be elected by state legislators, providing a further level of insulation from the popular will. (The Constitution was amended to require direct election of senators in 1913.) The Senate had to remain stable, Madison wrote, because "every new election in the states is found to change one half of the representatives."

Today, the House and the Senate have precisely flipped roles. Senate races, which are not subject to redistricting, are decided by actual voters, who do indeed change their minds with some regularity. Control of the Senate has shifted five times since the nineteen-eighties. The House, by contrast, has changed hands just once in the same period, in the Republican takeover of 1994. In 2002, only one out of twelve House elections was decided by ten or fewer percentage points, while half of the governors' and Senate races were that close. In 2002, only four House challengers defeated incumbents in the general election—a record low in the modern era. In a real sense, the voters no longer select the members of the House of Representatives; the state legislators who design the districts do.

The question, then, is what, if anything, is unlawful about that? The legal debate on that question is especially stark. In the case now before the Supreme Court, Pennsylvania Democrats argued that the Republican gerrymander denied them equal protection of the laws, asserting in their brief that it is "unconstitutional to give a State's million Republicans control over ten seats while leaving a million Democrats with control over five." The Republican response is to say, in effect, "Welcome to the big leagues. State legislatures have always played this kind of hardball, the courts ought to stay out of the game altogether, and there's no such thing as a nonpartisan solution." Justice Sandra Day O'Connor, a former Arizona state senator herself, may have put the argument best when, in the mid-eighties, the Supreme Court last considered a political-gerrymandering case. According to Justice William Brennan's notes of the court's internal debate, O'Connor said that any legislative leader who failed to protect his party's interest in redistricting "ought to be impeached." . . .

The best argument for Republicans in the Pennsylvania case, it seems, is that it's simply not the court's business to scrutinize legislative maps for partisan gerrymandering. "Redistricting deals with inherently political questions," J. Bart DeLone, the senior deputy state attorney general who will argue for the case for Pennsylvania, said, "and those questions should be left to the political branches of government, where they belong, not to the courts. Then you are trying to measure things that have no standards unless you are making political judgments." Still, this is a Supreme Court that has not hesitated to tell politicians what to do. . . .

In any case, the situation appears to be getting worse, even as the Pennsylvania case has been pending. While Texas was shifting its districts, the governing Republicans in Colorado did their own mid-cycle reapportionment, to solidify their hold on the one House seat in the state that produced a close election in 2002. (Legal challenges to the new Texas and Colorado districts are now pending.) At one point, the Democrats who control Oklahoma and New Mexico threatened retaliation, but the Party lacks a DeLay-like figure to press the issue. One state that has gone its own way is Iowa, which turned redistricting over to a nonpartisan civil-service commission after the 2000 census. Consequently, four of Iowa's five House races in 2002 were competitive, so a state with one per cent of the seats in the House produced ten per cent of the nation's close elections. The rest of the country will follow only, it seems, if the Supreme Court requires it.

When it comes to drawing political boundaries, there never was a golden age of statesmanship. "When we Democrats controlled the legislature, sure we protected Democrats," Charlie Stenholm said. "But we didn't do harm to the Republicans who were in office. This thing today is a whole different order of magnitude." . . .

Questions for Discussion

1. According to the author, how does the process of partisan gerrymandering undercut the democratic process in elections? How might partisan gerrymandering affect the representative relationship between members of Congress and their constituents?
2. How has the racial gerrymandering in the 1980s, which was designed to increase the number of minority members of Congress, affected the fortunes of the two major parties? Which party has been advantaged as a result? All things considered, was racial gerrymandering a good idea from the standpoint of representation?

⭐ 6.3

A Tale of Two Electorates: The Changing American Party Coalitions, 1952–2000

Paul Allen Beck

Those interested in the long-term fortunes of American parties typically focus their attention upon how the loyalties of components of the party coalitions change. In this article, Paul Allen Beck examines how the partisan identities and voting behavior of categories of voters have been altered over the past half century. He finds that although there have been some distinct shifts in partisan loyalties between the parties since the 1950s (when the Democrats were the majority party), neither party can currently claim majority status.

Today's electorate, according to Beck, has two distinct components that are at odds. In the 2000 election, roughly 60 percent of the electorate was highly partisan and ideologically oriented. The followers of the two major parties represented more polar opposites in terms of political values and orientations than they did in the 1950s; the Democrats have become a more homogeneous party

Paul Allen Beck is professor of political science and department chair at Ohio State University.

Paul Allen Beck, "A Tale of Two Electorates: The Changing American Party Coalitions, 1952–2000," in *The State of the Parties: The Changing Role of Contemporary American Parties,* 4/e, edited by John C. Green and Rick Farmer (Lanham, MD: Rowman and Littlefield, 2003): 38–53. Copyright © 2003. Reprinted by permission of Rowman & Littlefield.

of the left, the Republicans of the right. But the other 40 percent of the electorate are nonpartisan in orientation and resistant to any long-term commitment to a political party. According to Beck, these nonpartisan voters "are moved by the candidates and issues of the moment" and are disgusted by the divisive partisan politics they often observe.

With virtual parity between the two major parties, nonpartisan voters now hold the balance of power in contemporary American politics. "The dilemma for the major parties and their candidates is that what mobilizes their partisan core voters repels the nonpartisan electorate, potentially costing them the election or, if victorious, a mandate to govern."

For several decades, the party loyalties of the American electorate have been undergoing contrasting changes. On the one hand, there has been a slow but steady change in the composition of the Democratic and Republican Party coalitions—what V. O. Key (1959) originally referred to as a "secular realignment."* Some see the realignment as beginning as early as the 1960s. . . . On the other hand, fewer Americans now claim party loyalties than did prior to the mid-1960s (Wattenberg 1998). Even though this partisan "dealignment" appears to have been concentrated in the late 1960s and early 1970s, and an overwhelming majority of Americans remain identified with a party, it has left a larger portion of the electorate as nonpartisans than at any time since the development of the American two-party system.[†] The story of recent American electoral politics revolves around this confluence of realignment and dealignment. It is a tale of two electorates.

One electorate is partisan and ideologically polarized. It has been shaped since the 1950s, which is a convenient benchmark for comparison, by a steady erosion of Democratic loyalists and recent gains in Republican identifiers that have recovered the Republican Party's 1950s share of the electorate. By 2000, these two party electorates were essentially equal in electoral influence, with the smaller GOP group attaining parity through its somewhat higher rates of turnout. The two parties' coalitions also have been reshuffled to a significant degree since the 1950s. By the beginning of the twenty-first century, Democratic loyalists were more dominant among blacks, women

---

*"Secular realignment" involves the shift in a population category of voters from one party to the other over an extended period of time. An example would be the change in the partisan identities and voting behavior of white voters in the American South, a core component of the Democratic New Deal coalition first formed in the 1930s, to become a key element of the Republican Party base by the latter half of the twentieth century.

[†]"Dealignment" describes the movement of voters away from identity with either of the parties. This may involve voters leaving one party and not affiliating with the other or entering the electorate without any party identification and never acquiring it. Issues and candidate attractiveness, rather than party identification, dominate such voters' decisions.

were more Democratic than men, and Catholics were less Democratic than they had been fifty years before. By contrast, Republican identifiers now outnumber Democrats among the overlapping groups of white Southerners and white fundamentalist Protestants. These changes have transformed the nature of the two parties and have made them more ideological opposites than they were in the 1950s.

The other electorate is independent and nonpartisan, sometimes even fiercely antipartisan. More inclined to respond to short-term factors involving the candidates and their campaigns, it is available for temporary mobilization on behalf of either a major party candidate or a third-party or independent candidate—or for demobilization into nonvoting. . . . In 2000 this pool of nonpartisan potential voters was more numerous than either self-identified Democrats or Republicans. With parity in party strength within the partisan electorate, this nonpartisan electorate now holds the balance of power between the parties, and election outcomes depend even more than before on short-term factors.

Theoretical Considerations

Detailing the story of the development of these two contrasting electorates and their effect on American politics is the task of this [selection]. Before providing the details of this story, though, the ideas on which it depends need to be made more explicit. The vote outcome of any election is best seen as the joint product of long-term predispositions of the electorate toward the parties and short-term orientations toward the issues and candidates of the day. Long-term predispositions are embodied in enduring party loyalties. Most voters possess these loyalties, even amidst today's largely unprecedented dealignment. Voters holding these loyalties seem to be readily aware of them, because they report them more reliably than any other political orientations in responding to survey questions.

When the distribution of these enduring party loyalties changes in a significant way, so that the coalitions of party loyalists are transformed or the balance between the parties is altered . . . , we speak of the electorate as having "realigned." Analyses of aggregate vote patterns suggest that the American electorate has realigned at regular thirty- to forty-year intervals throughout much of American history. When the share of the electorate professing party loyalties declines and more voters are basing electoral decisions necessarily on election-specific factors, the process is described as a "dealignment." . . .

This theoretical perspective focuses attention on the distribution of party loyalties, including their presence or absence, as the fundamental characteristic of an electorate at any particular time and on changes in these distributions as the principal dynamic in electoral politics. It relegates actual votes to the background—as consequences of enduring partisanship and immediate, and temporary, candidate or issue-specific forces. . . .

Changing American Partisanship: Realignment Amidst Dealignment

Since the mid-1960s, two important changes have taken place in the party loyalties of the American electorate. First came a decay or dealignment of partisan loyalties, especially within the Democratic Party coalition that had dominated American electoral politics since the 1930s. It was followed, most noticeably in the early 1980s but foreshadowed somewhat earlier, by the reshuffling of the major party coalitions and a slight growth of Republican Party loyalists after their dealignment-era decline. Together these two changes have altered the social composition of the American parties in significant ways.

Figure 1 reports the party identifications of the electorate from 1952 to 2000. From relatively stable levels during the 1950s and early 1960s, with Democrats outnumbering Republicans by a five to three margin, the partisan strength of both parties eroded, starting after 1962 for the Republicans and 1964 for the Democrats. The GOP had recovered its 1950s level of party loyalty in 1994, only to fall slightly from that apex for the rest of the decade. In 2000, even after winning both houses of Congress and the presidency, albeit by razor-thin margins in the most controversial election since 1876, the Republicans still were unable to attract more loyalists than either their Democratic opposition or nonpartisan independents. Indeed, they began the twenty-first century with no more loyalists as a percentage of the American electorate than they had in 1952.

That Republican identifiers are no larger a portion of the electorate today than they were in the 1950s is ignored by those who have seen the recent years as a time of pro-GOP realignment. The Republicans are better positioned

Figure 1
Party Loyalties of Americans, 1952–2000

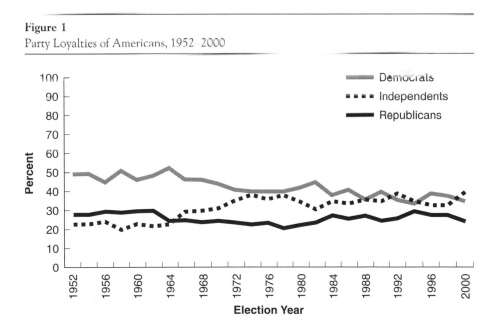

electorally than in the 1950s and early 1960s. But the reasons are Democratic decay, Republicans' higher turnout rates at the polls, and the disappearance of the solid South as a dependably Democratic voting block—rather than any nationwide realignment to Republicanism. The current GOP hold on the House and the presidency, as well as on many of the state governments, consequently rests on shaky foundations.

It has been the Democratic Party that has borne the major brunt of the changes since the early 1960s. Erosion in its loyalist base first became visible in 1966 and, despite a few temporary surges, typically in midterm elections, has continued through 2000. The beneficiary of these declines in partisanship has been the amorphous category called "independents." After being outnumbered by both Democrats and Republicans through 1964, independents have become more numerous than Republican loyalists ever since. They came close to comprising a plurality of the electorate in the mid-1970s and again in the mid-1980s, and, beginning in 1992, they attracted a plurality of the electorate in three of the following six election years. Within the range of sampling error these changes can be said to have produced an electorate almost evenly balanced among Democrats, Republicans, and independents by the turn of the century.

Partisan Changes in Key Groups Within the Electorate

To gain a better appreciation for how changes in partisan loyalties have transformed the American party system, it is necessary to disaggregate the movements of the entire electorate into the behavior of particular groups. Table 1 contains the divisions among Democrats, Republicans, and independents of seven groups that were divided noticeably along partisan lines either in the New Deal party system in place in the 1950s or in the system that replaced it.

As it is with many dominant coalitions, the roots of the post-1964 Democratic decay are found to a considerable degree within the political tensions of its original formulation. At its core, the New Deal Democratic majority was based on an alliance of white Southerners and liberal Northerners. Such an alliance could remain intact only so long as economic issues dominated the political agenda and the South was left alone to pursue its traditional segregation of blacks and whites. Once Southern autonomy was challenged over civil rights, the loyalties of both white Southerners and African Americans were put in motion. New Deal politics were largely organized around economic policy and social class issues. As the agenda of American politics shifted to embrace new social and moral issues, the partisanship of other key groups in the American population was challenged. The success of the New Deal welfare state in overcoming the problems of the Great Depression in the 1930s and lifting ethnic minorities and workers into the middle class undermined the subsequent attraction of the Democratic Party to many of its beneficiaries, especially their children and grandchildren. Moreover, the new issue agenda that emerged, like newly electrified poles of an electromagnet, yielded different party coalition clusters than before.

The Countermovements of White Southerners and African Americans

By the 1950s, the Democratic alliance between white Southerners and liberal Northerners was beginning to fray. Southern autonomy on matters of racial policy had become untenable to many Northern Democrats, and a movement to secure equal rights for blacks was emerging in the South. Once the national Democratic Party moved to champion civil rights for Southern blacks in the early 1960s and the GOP took the opposite position in 1964, the die was cast. White Southerners began to desert their traditional party's candidates as early as the 1950s. This desertion was manifested first in voting Republican for president. As long as Democratic candidates for state and local offices continued to reflect their region's mores, they retained the support of its white voters. Over the years, however, Republicanism steadily penetrated down the ballot as old-time Democratic officeholders retired and new, more mainstream party candidates replaced them.

It was not too long before the civil rights revolution in the South and the opposing postures of the parties toward it began to affect party loyalties. As the first columns of table 1 show, Democratic loyalties already were declining within the white Southern electorate in the 1950s; the reasons at first had little to do with race. As race became the most salient regional issue, though, this erosion of the solidly Democratic South continued with only occasional and partial reversals through the early 1990s. By 2000, Democratic loyalists among white Southerners had fallen to what undoubtedly is their lowest point in the history of the party. The Democratic share of this group is less than one-third of what it was fifty years before. The days of a solid South, built upon the Democratic commitments of its white electorate, are gone.

The GOP has been able to capitalize upon this Democratic decay to a considerable degree. Steadily, with only occasional slight reversals in the mid-1960s, 1990, and 1996, it gained a stronger base of party loyalists among white Southerners. By the 1990s, there were roughly equal numbers of Republicans and Democrats within this group. By 2000, with another surge in GOP loyalists and decline in Democratic loyalists, white Southerners had become significantly more Republican than Democratic. Republican advances have been especially pronounced within the new generations of white Southerners, many of whom have rejected inherited Democratic loyalties. . . .

It took several decades for the Republicans to outnumber Democrats among white Southerners, and they remain far short of dominance. At first, in the 1960s, the breakup of the solid South featured a surge of independents, reaching levels that were to be more or less sustained over the next twenty years. In

Table 1

Changing Partisan Loyalties of Key Groups, 1952–2000

Year	White Southerners			African Americans			Catholics			Union Households			Men			Women			White Fundamentalists		
	Dems	Inds	Reps	Dems	Inds	Reps	Dems	Inds	Reps	Dems	Inds	Reps	Dems	Inds	Reps	Dems	Inds	Reps	Dems	Inds	Reps
1952	77	12	11	64	21	16	56	26	18	55	23	22	48	26	26	49	21	30			
1954				62	20	19	53	27	21	59	20	21	51	24	25	48	22	30			
1956	68	16	16	61	16	23	52	27	21	52	27	21	46	28	26	44	22	34			
1958	68	17	15	62	18	21	58	25	17	63	20	17	49	23	28	52	18	30			
1960	60	18	21	50	31	18	61	23	16	57	28	15	43	29	28	49	19	32	48	22	30
1962	57	22	21	70	14	16							50	24	26	47	20	32			
1964	66	20	15	77	15	7	58	25	17	64	23	13	50	26	24	54	21	26	55	18	27
1966	55	29	16	62	28	9	55	29	17	56	25	18	46	24	24	47	26	26	46	28	26
1968	50	37	13	88	10	2	53	32	15	51	30	19	43	32	25	48	28	24	42	31	27
1970	43	38	19	78	18	4	52	31	17	54	31	15	42	34	23	45	29	26	42	33	26
1972	47	34	19	69	23	8	51	35	14	46	39	15	37	39	23	44	32	24	38	36	26
1974	47	34	19	68	29	3	48	36	16	45	42	13	35	43	22	43	34	23	40	36	24
1976	45	34	21	71	24	4	50	35	15	47	40	12	37	42	20	42	32	26	36	36	28
1978	41	38	20	68	27	5	50	36	14	50	36	14	38	44	18	42	34	23	37	39	24
1980	43	34	23	75	20	5	43	38	19	46	39	14	38	40	22	44	32	24	42	34	24
1982	49	29	22	79	19	2	55	29	16	50	32	18	39	35	26	50	27	23	40	32	28
1984	37	38	24	65	31	4	43	36	21	46	35	19	34	39	28	41	32	28	33	34	32
1986	40	34	26	74	22	4	45	33	22	47	34	20	37	38	25	44	30	26	37	32	32
1988	34	40	26	64	30	6	38	36	26	43	37	20	30	42	29	40	32	28	32	37	30
1990	37	42	20	64	31	5	45	33	23	50	31	20	36	36	27	43	34	23	35	36	29
1992	32	42	26	66	29	4	41	39	20	45	38	17	32	40	28	40	37	23	28	39	33
1994	32	33	35	62	33	6	40	36	24	44	36	20	30	38	33	39	32	29	30	32	39
1996	36	34	30	66	31	3	43	33	24	43	39	18	34	34	32	44	32	24	37	29	34
1998	33	34	33	73	23	4	40	33	27	43	37	20	35	37	28	41	34	25	28	36	36
2000	24	40	36	68	29	3	35	40	25	46	36	18	30	41	29	39	38	23	23	38	39

Note: Entries are percentages of the group members who identify as Democrats; independents (pure + leaners), and Republicans, respectively. Within each group, these percentages sum to within rounding error of 100 percent across the (three) columns.

their flight from Democratic loyalties, many white Southerners seemed to take refuge in nonpartisanship. Perhaps this shift is a phase in the natural journey of partisan realignment for a group. Older members first defect in their voting, as many white Southern Democrats did in presidential contests in the 1950s. Next they desert their traditional party identifications, but cannot bring themselves to convert to the other party, even if they are consistently voting for its candidates, as easily as newer members of the electorate can. Over time as the inexorable process of population replacement works it way, the group's partisan loyalties are brought into line with their votes.

The undeniable consequence of the changes in partisanship among white Southerners through 2000 is a realigned Southern party system—more Republican than ever before yet still competitive. . . . Many Southern whites have changed partisan loyalties due to racial issues, yet many others are drawn to the Republican Party for reasons that have little to do with race. Large numbers of Northerners moved to the South, bringing their traditional GOP loyalties with them. With the modernization of the Southern economy has come an expanding middle class, which as early as the 1950s was drawn to the GOP for many of the same reasons that middle-class Northerners were. The return of religious fundamentalism to the political arena, with its focus on moral and social conservatism, also has been a part of the Southern equation in recent years. More than elsewhere in the nation, it has further eroded the white working-class base of the Democratic Party in the South.

The changes in the South have had enormous consequences for party politics at the national level. Without a solid South, which had comprised the most loyal share of its vote since the 1870s and given it a regional "lock" in the Electoral College, the Democratic Party is no longer dominant in American politics. Important changes have occurred in the party coalitions outside of the South to be sure, but they pale in comparison to the changes wrought in the South.

The movement away from the Democratic Party by white Southerners is paralleled, and has been inextricably linked, to a consolidation of African American support for the Democrats, as shown in the next three columns of Table 1. Since 1952, African Americans inside and outside of the South have become the most dependable Democratic loyalists. . . . They began the era with widespread Democratic loyalties, although they were not nearly as devoted to the party as white Southerners. Moreover, the early figures are somewhat illusory, for more than one-half of all African Americans lived in the South in the 1950s, and few of them were permitted to participate in elections because of the state registration laws and practices of that era (Matthews and Prothro 1966). Not only were Southern blacks mobilized into politics in the 1960s, so that their Democratic loyalties became more consequential, but the positioning of the parties on opposite sides of the civil rights divide by the mid-1960s pushed most of the remaining black Republicans out of the GOP.

Discussions of possible growth in black Republicanism in recent years ignore the fact that the "party of Lincoln" enjoyed much more support in the African American community a generation ago than it does today. . . . No group within the modern American electorate contains proportionately fewer GOP adherents. . . .

Democratic Decay Among Catholics and Labor and Their Contrasting Consequences

Like Southern whites, Catholics and labor unions were core constituencies of the Democratic majority established in the 1930s. Catholics had long been attracted to the Democratic Party in the nation's cities, where they were heavily concentrated, but it took the events of the 1920s—the party's choice of a Catholic as its presidential nominee in 1928, the Great Depression, and Roosevelt's policies of the 1930s—to consolidate their loyalties. Labor unions were empowered by New Deal legislation in the 1930s, which secured the Democratic loyalties of their members. As the next two sets of columns in table 1 show, the legacy of these partisan commitments was present in the 1950s and 1960s, when Catholics and people in households containing a union member favored the Democrats over the Republicans by margins of about three to one.

From these parallel baselines, the partisan loyalties of Catholics and union families followed a familiar spiral for a while, and then diverged. Beginning in the late 1960s, the two groups joined in the general dealignment of the American electorate. They contributed to the declines in Democratic and Republican loyalists and the increases in independents through the 1970s. The dealignment of these two groups seems to have halted by 1980—a bit later than it had ended for the electorate as a whole. For union families, the ensuing period was a time of little net change in partisanship. By contrast, Catholics turned in a Republican direction beginning in 1980, and their movement came at the expense of Democratic loyalties. The net exchange of Democratic for Republican loyalties among Catholics is not large, but it is noticeable.

These changes in partisan loyalties leave Catholics and union families still more Democratic than Republican by the beginning of the twenty-first century. Union households now are over two to one Democratic, down from what they were in the 1950s and 1960s, but nonetheless decisively unbalanced. It is dealignment, rather than realignment, that best characterizes their movement. By contrast, Catholics underwent elements of first dealignment, then realignment, to the point that they show an almost equal balance between Democrats and independents, and a Republican minority that has grown to almost rival them. Union families are no more Republican, on net, at the end of the period than they were at the beginning, but more Catholics are supportive of the GOP than was the case a half-century ago. The emergence of religious issues as powerful shapers of partisan loyalties, it seems fair to surmise, has affected many Catholics just as it has affected many Protestant fundamentalists.

An Emerging Gender Gap in Partisan Loyalties

After years of no differences between men and women in partisan preferences, scholars and commentators have identified a consistent gender gap in recent decades in both partisanship and voting. The next six columns in table 1 show the extent of the gender gap in partisanship. The partisan loyalties of men and women began to diverge in the 1970s and had become significantly different by the 1980s and 1990s, especially where Democratic loyalties were concerned.

Comparison of the party loyalties of men and women over time yields insight into what has happened, although exactly why it has happened defies simple explanation. Both groups joined in the post-1964 dealignment. Republican loyalties eroded to about the same extent between both groups. Democratic loyalties declined between both as well, albeit at different rates, with the decline coming earlier and reaching deeper among men. This shift left women somewhat more Democratic than men by the mid-1970s. Beginning in the 1980s, Democratic loyalties among women stabilized, with no further losses or Republican gains for the most part; but the decline in Democratic loyalties and growth of Republicanism continued among men. By the turn of the twenty-first century, men were equally likely to be Republican or Democrat, while almost twice as many women were Democrats as were Republicans.

The gender gap, then, is the work of a substantial pro-GOP shift in the partisan orientations of men in the 1980s and 1990s at the same time most women were resisting the movement away from the Democrats. Scholars have been unable to attribute these changes to so-called women's issues and now consider them a result of different expectations about the role of government as well as myriad other forces. The gender changes are modest compared to those of Southern whites and even African Americans, but what makes them important is the size of the groups involved.

The Delayed Realignment of White Fundamentalist Protestants

Another important change in group party loyalties since the 1950s is a result of the growing importance of religion in American politics. Rather than the Protestant versus Catholic conflict of earlier times, contemporary religious politics has revolved more around the importance of religion in one's life. The GOP has been the traditional home for Protestants, especially in the North before the 1960s, but the party in earlier times represented middle-class "high church" Protestants better than their more fundamentalist and lower-status brethren. Recent years have witnessed the ascendancy of white Protestant fundamentalists in Republican nomination politics and its party organizations and policy-making circles. This new influence of fundamentalists is typically attributed to the group's growing Republicanism.

The changes in party loyalties of white Protestant fundamentalists, presented in the last columns of table 1, however, do not quite fit these first impressions. The group has become more Republican than Democratic, but only *after* it became more influential in GOP circles. Early on, white fundamentalists joined in the dealignment of the broader electorate, with its deeper erosion of Democratic than Republican loyalties. As the axis of American politics turned to religious and social questions, though, the Democratic loyalties of fundamentalists continued to decline—reaching their lowest point in the series (slightly more than 20 percent of the electorate) in 2000. The decline was not as steady or as sharp as that of Southern whites, particularly Southern white fundamentalists, but it has been persistent. During the time of dealignment, Republican loyalties among white fundamentalists fell off as well. They did not regain their 1960 high point (occasioned because the 1960 Democratic nominee was a Catholic) until 1984. The sharpest growth in Republican loyalties in this group, though, came recently—in the last decade of the twentieth century. By 2000, it had left Republicans tied with independents as the identification of choice for white Protestant fundamentalists.

What is surprising, given their considerable weight in the inner circles of Republican politics for some years, is the delay of a Republican surge in partisan loyalties among white fundamentalists. Strongly courted by GOP candidates since Richard Nixon in 1968, for two decades white fundamentalists seemed to resist becoming Republicans. Only in the early 1990s, then again in 1998 and 2000, have they been significantly more Republican than Democratic in professed party identifications. By 2000, this gap had widened considerably, with continued decline in Democratic identifications, but its significance is challenged by a recent surge of independents. What began as a story of Democratic dealignment seems only of late to have become a story of pro-Republican realignment among white Protestant fundamentalists.

Putting Everything Together

An important part of the story of partisan change in the American electorate during the past half-century can be told by the overall trends in party identification and the patterns for the seven groups discussed above. Overall the electorate has dealigned, becoming less partisan and more independent since the 1950s and early 1960s. The dealignment occurred during the ten-year period between Lyndon Johnson's reelection in 1964 and the immediate aftermath of the departure of Richard Nixon from the White House in 1974 under the threat of impeachment. The percentage of independents in the American electorate at the turn of the century is little different than it was in 1974, but they now may be more numerous than either Democrats or Republicans.

The seven groups I analyze . . . present a more variegated picture. White Southerners and white Protestant fundamentalists (and many Americans are both) have realigned from being overwhelmingly Democratic to marginally more Republican by century's end. At the same time, African Americans have become even more attached to the Democratic Party. Two other key groups within the Democratic coalition that emerged from the 1930s, Catholics and labor union households, remain more Democratic than Republican, but their loyalties to the party of Franklin Roosevelt and John Kennedy have eroded, contributing to the dealignment. Democratic (and Republican) loyalties among women have eroded as well, while those of men were realigning to the point that they are now as Republican as they are Democratic.

In describing these changes, I addressed in passing the question of why they took place. In a nutshell, changes in the political world—chief among them the Democrats' support for integration in the South, the traumas of Vietnam and urban riots, the replacement of class-based economic conflict by divisions over civil rights, social policy, and religion—tore the majority Democratic coalition apart. . . .

Although some scholars resist calling the result in this case a realignment, when seen in all of its complexity it certainly possesses key realignment charac-teristics—changes in the nature of the party coalitions, new issues dominating the political agenda, and differences in who exercises governmental power. It also exhibits signs of realignment in yet another way. The hallmark of a newly aligned party system, one may logically surmise, is that ideology and partisan-ship are more strongly linked than they have been before. As measured straightforwardly by the correlation (r) between respondents' self-locations on seven-point ideology and party identification scales, the connection between ideology and party loyalty has strengthened between 1960 and 2000. What we used to describe in 1960 as a remarkably nonideological party system now ap-pears to have been only a snapshot of an electorate at the end of one party sys-tem and the beginning of another. Today's highly polarized parties in Washington and the state capitals are now paralleled by more ideologically po-larized party electorates than we have experienced in decades.

What we miss here to complete a realignment scenario are two important in-gredients. First, this "realignment" is not as broadly encompassing as past re-alignments have been. More than one-third of the electorate, virtually 40 percent in 2000, is unwilling to join the new two-party arrangement by choos-ing a major party as the object of their loyalty. Second, for all of its successes since 1968 at the presidential level and from 1994 to 2000 with the Congress, the Republican Party has not been able to become the party choice of a major-ity of Americans. Through 2000 at least, the GOP has fallen far short of achieving the gains expected for the ascendant party in realignment. Nor have more voters been mobilized into politics by the realignment, as they were in past realignments. Rather, with the exception of the Perot-induced boost in 1992, turnout has declined to where only half of the American electorate casts a presidential ballot and far fewer participate below the presidential level.

Instead of a decisive realignment, then, partisan changes in recent years have yielded a Democratic Party no longer in command of the loyalties of the dominant share of the electorate, and an enlarged group of political independents who are not dependable supporters of either party. There has been some recent Republican growth to be sure, but it has not been sufficient to recapture the levels of Republicanism of the 1950s, hardly a halcyon era for the GOP in terms of party loyalties.

Conclusion

The result of the 2000 presidential election—with George W. Bush's Electoral College victory turning on a U.S. Supreme Court decision about how to count votes in Florida's "dead heat" contest amid Bush's popular vote defeat nationwide—reflects the state of Americans' partisan loyalties as they entered the new century. It is indeed a tale of two electorates—the one partisan, the other nonpartisan.

By 2000, about 60 percent of the electorate was composed of Democratic and Republican partisans, somewhat below the mid-60s average percentage from 1992 to 2000. Like the 2000 results in Florida, the partisan battle comes close to being a "dead heat." With the realignment of the party coalitions, these partisans also have become more ideologically polarized than in earlier times. Such polarization was evident in the 2000 presidential contest and especially its contentious aftermath, from the partisan warfare over the Florida vote through the first eight months of the Bush presidency. The tragic events of September 11 and the "rally around the flag" politics of a nation under attack temporarily muted partisan divisions, but the political battle between two parties with opposing policy dispositions and ideologically polarized partisans has reappeared.

The other electorate, about 35 percent of eligible voters from 1992 to 2000 and up to 40 percent in 2000, is nonpartisan. It opts out of Democratic or Republican identification when asked and, even where it may vote rather consistently for one party's candidates, it is unwilling to commit to that party for the long term. Not only is this electorate less involved in politics than its partisan counterpart, it also seems inclined to withdraw from the political fray as the major parties become more polarized—unless an attractive non–major party alternative is on the ballot. These nonpartisan voters are moved by the candidates and issues of the moment, not by the long-term positioning of the parties, and they add a considerable element of volatility to the electoral arena.

It is a combination of realignment and dealignment that most aptly characterizes contemporary electoral politics in the United States. The realignment has changed the major parties, reshuffling their loyalists along more ideological lines. But the dealignment has prevented either of these more ideological parties from dominating the political world—as is evidenced by persistent divided government, fluctuations in presidential voting from election to election, and slender margins of party control over governmental institutions. Nonpartisans hold the balance of power in the contemporary electorate between equally balanced major parties and provide fertile ground for non–major party candidates. The dilemma for the major parties and their candidates is that what mobilizes their partisan core voters repels the nonpartisan electorate, potentially either costing them the election or, if victorious, a mandate to govern. . . .

. . . The story of our current party system can best be told in terms of the relative sizes, compositions, and electoral tendencies of its two electorates—one partisan and about evenly divided, the other estranged from party politics. They shape the prime characteristics of party politics and American politics in our time.

References

Key, V. O., Jr. "Secular Realignment and the Party System." *Journal of Politics* 21: 198–210.
Wattenberg, Martin P. 1998. *The Decline of American Political Parties, 1952–1996.* Cambridge, Mass.: Harvard University Press.

Questions for Discussion

1. What factors have contributed to the realignment of key components of the Democratic and Republican party coalitions since the 1950s? What categories of voters have been most affected? Why does Beck believe that realignment, in the classic sense, is still "incomplete"?
2. Do you consider yourself a partisan voter or a nonpartisan voter? Is there anything that might change your orientation?
3. Are third-party and independent candidacies likely to become more common in the contemporary electoral environment? What kinds of partisan presidential candidates are most likely to fare well in the current environment?

Chapter 7

Campaigns and Elections

Few aspects of American politics have changed as much in recent decades as the ways in which candidates campaign for national office. A half century ago, electioneering was dominated by political parties, which were the main means of communication between candidates and voters. Party parades, mailings, rallies, and door-to-door canvassing were the essential ingredients of campaigns. Party affiliation, based on strong bonds of ethnic, class, regional, or religious identity, was the key factor in determining how voters cast their ballots. Ticket splitters who voted for a president from one party and Senate or House members from another were a small minority.

Today's campaigns are candidate centered. An individual politician's campaign organization raises funds, mobilizes activists, advertises on television, conducts sophisticated direct-mail operations, and polls voters, all largely independent of party organization. Political consultants, pollsters, and outside strategists have replaced the party bosses as central figures in campaigns. Candidates' issue positions and personal attractiveness have challenged party loyalties as key factors in voters' decisions. Split-ticket voting is now quite common.

The new style of campaigning is especially apparent in presidential elections. Prior to the 1970s, candidates were nominated by party professionals who were usually chosen through state conventions or caucuses tightly controlled by the party organization. The eventual nominee typically had worked his way up the party hierarchy over a long period, had served in a number of elected positions in government, and was able to put together a coalition of state party delegations to win the nomination. Once such a person was nominated, the presidential campaign was usually run by the national party organization. Between 1952 and 1968, for example, at least one of the party campaigns was run by the national committee staff in each election; in 1956 and 1964, both campaigns were run by the national party organizations.

The contemporary route to the presidency is quite different. Nominations are often won or lost on the basis of the personal appeal of candidates on television and their ability to put together effective campaign organizations. Traditional party factors are far less influential, as candidates with commanding media presence can gain recognition and stature almost overnight. Having held elected political office is now no longer a prerequisite to becoming a serious candidate, as demonstrated by the campaigns of television evangelist Pat Robertson and preacher/activist Jesse Jackson in 1988. Moreover, the nominating delegates are often amateurs in politics, motivated more by issues than by party loyalty. After the nomination, the presidential campaign is run by the candidate's organization rather than by the national party. (Since 1972, no general election campaign has been run by either the Republican or the Democratic national committee staffs.)

A number of factors have contributed to the new style of campaign politics. Some reflect social changes, such as rising levels of education, which have created an electorate far more independent and unwilling to follow party labels blindly. Others have resulted from reforms in the political parties, especially the Democratic party, which are now far more open and democratic. New people have the opportunity to enter politics despite little partisan background. Perhaps most important has been the emergence of television as the primary political communications medium and of technological improvements in direct-mail techniques, polling, and other practices.

In general, there has been a shift in the nature of key campaign resources. The skill and labor of party functionaries, who are often volunteers, are less important; financial resources, so necessary in purchasing the services and skills of the new campaign operatives, consultants, pollsters, and media specialists, have become crucial. Expensive campaign travel by jet is now the norm, and the cost of network television advertising is exorbitant.

Not surprisingly, the costs of running national campaigns have risen tremendously. The 2000 presidential election campaign was by far the most expensive in history. According to Federal Election Commission data, George W. Bush raised more than $191 million in private funds for his campaign, and his Democratic counterpart Al Gore was the recipient of more than $132 million of such funds. In addition, each of the major party candidates received more than $67 million in federal funds. Even third party efforts can be expensive. Reform party candidate Pat Buchanan, who received less than 1 percent of the vote on Election Day, spent more than $44 million on his campaign.

Senate and House races have been affected by the new style of campaigning as well. Senate contests are often highly competitive, typically attracting wealthy, prominent challengers and inspiring huge expenditures of funds, particularly for television advertising. Senate races that cost between $10 million and $20 million are common. In a 1996 U.S. Senate race in California, the two candidates together spent more than $45 million. Four years later, the New York U.S. Senate contest between Democrat Hillary Clinton and Republican Rick Lazio cost nearly $93 million all told. In the 2000 U.S. Senate race in New Jersey, Democrat John Corzine spent more than $60 million of his own money to win the seat!

House races are far less competitive than their Senate counterparts. Challengers are often relatively unknown, and they find it difficult to get funding and free media attention. Incumbents, in contrast, stay in the public eye through their work in Congress and their actions to help constituents. Also, their large victory margins in elections attract contributions for future campaigns. Despite the fact that incumbent safety in the House appears to be greater than at any time in history, House elections have not escaped huge campaign expenditures. According to Federal Election Commission figures, in 1974 the average House incumbent spent about $56,000, the average challenger $40,000. By 1992 incumbents were outspending challengers on the average of three and a half to one, with the average incumbent spending over $560,000. In 2000, Democratic incumbents averaged $673,000 in their races; Republican incumbents, $775,000. Open-seat congressional contests are especially expensive. In 2000, Democrats spent on average just under $1 million contesting such seats; Republicans spent more than $1.25 million.

For the first time in over a quarter of a century, the 2004 federal elections will be conducted under the rules of a new campaign law, the 2002 Bipartisan Campaign Reform Act (BCRA). The act was primarily directed at two loopholes that had emerged under the then-existing campaign finance regulations, the use of "soft money" raised and spent by the national parties and "issue advocacy electioneering" by organized interests. Throughout the 1990s, ever larger amounts of money were spent in federal elections outside the constraints of the Federal Election Commission (FEC), which was charged with enforcing the campaign finance laws. Most expenditures were unlimited, and contributors were often undisclosed.

Soft money, which was originally intended to be money contributed to the national parties for nonfederal election purposes, such as strengthening local parties, had become a tool for influencing federal elections as well. Most bothersome to reformers was that contributions to the national parties were unlimited in size (and until the 1992 election contributors were undisclosed); businesses, unions, and wealthy individuals in some cases contributed over $1 million per donation to the national parties.

Much of the money was used by the national parties for "issue advocacy electioneering," spending large amounts of soft money to influence federal elections by circumventing campaign laws that drastically limited the amounts parties could directly use to support their candidates. As long as the party advertisers avoided "express advocacy," or used words like "vote for" or "elect" or "cast a ballot for," which were spelled out in a 1976 Supreme Court Decision, large amounts could be spent. Interest groups had even greater flexibility, with no limits at all on how much they could spend to influence elections with their broadcast messages, as long as they avoided direct "express advocacy" terminology such as "vote for" or "vote against." With such broadcast advertising by organized interests, the sources of funds used to pay for the ads did not even have to be disclosed. The ads were often negative in tone, and it was sometimes difficult to identify the sponsor of the ad.

The new BCRA prohibits party soft money. National party committees may now spend only "hard money," funds subject to the contribution and source limits of federal law. Some observers believe the influence of parties on campaigns will diminish as a consequence of the law. The Democrats, who had relied heavily on soft money, may be the party most hurt.

The new law also bans broadcast advertising by organized interests, such as corporations and unions, in support of or in opposition to a candidate close to a federal election. Future elections may see groups spending less time on "air wars" and more time on "ground wars," especially grassroot get-out-the-vote (GOTV) efforts.

The selections in this chapter examine campaigns and elections from a variety of perspectives. In the first selection, Thomas E. Patterson raises questions about the value of the lengthy American presidential campaign, which typically begins a least a year in advance of Election Day. He makes a strong case that a more informed and engaged electorate would result if the campaign were more focused and shorter. The second selection examines the Supreme Court's decision in *McConnell* v. *The Federal Election Commission* (2003), a 5-to-4 decision that upheld the Bipartisan Campaign Reform Act of 2002. Starting in 2004, the act is likely to greatly affect the role of political parties and interest groups in federal campaigns. The third piece, by James E. Campbell, deals with the serious problem of the lack of meaningful competition in House elections. Campbell suggests that the new campaign law may actually make matters worse despite the good intentions of the reformers. Finally, Dan Hellinger examines how ex-Vermont governor Howard Dean emerged as a serious candidate for the Democratic nomination for president in 2003. While Dean eventually failed in his quest for the nomination, his campaign's skillful use of the Internet in creating a grassroots organization was crucial to the candidate's early success.

7.1

The Long Campaign: The Politics of Tedium

Thomas E. Patterson

Unlike European national elections, which usually last no more than a few weeks, the U.S. presidential election campaign typically lasts for a year or more and seems to be getting longer. Defenders of a long campaign argue that it has the potential for helping voters make an informed choice on the issues and provides insight into the character and leadership abilities of those who seek the nation's highest office. Candidates can be seen and heard in a variety of contexts, including debates and news conferences during the primary/caucus season, the party conventions, and the October debates, which are usually held a few weeks before the general election. Reporting on campaign developments by the printed press and the broadcast media is usually an everyday affair, once the nomination process formally begins in early January or February of a presidential year.

As Thomas E. Patterson argues, however, "Time itself does not create an informed electorate." Using the 2000 presidential race as the basis for his contention, he finds that too much time can actually be detrimental if the aim is a knowledgeable electorate with positive feelings about the electoral process. The long campaign dulls the senses of the electorate, taxes its attention, and discourages rather than fosters public involvement; it frustrates learning and diminishes the inclination to vote.

Patterson makes a strong case that American presidential campaigns should be shorter and more focused because people would actually learn more about the candidates and feel better about the democratic process.

It seems like it goes on for umpteen months.

—SIXTY-NINE-YEAR-OLD WYOMING RESIDENT

There's too much attention to people whose primaries go first.

—THIRTY-SIX-YEAR-OLD WASHINGTON STATE RESIDENT

Thomas E. Patterson is the Bradlee Professor of Government and the Press at Harvard University's John F. Kennedy School of Government.

The convention is all staged for the TV. It is no fun anymore. I don't want to watch celebrities introducing one another. It's a big joke now.

—FORTY-SIX-YEAR-OLD TEXAS RESIDENT

Sixty-year-old Pennsylvania resident Bill Pelligrini[1] seemed almost surprised to be asked during the Christmas season how much attention he'd been paying to the presidential campaign. "Not much," he told the interviewer. "The election's too far away."

Two months later, Bill was drawn to the campaign by John McCain's candidacy. "McCain seems willing," said Bill, "to say what needs to be said even if it hurts his chances." Bill made a point of watching the election returns on Super Tuesday* and was disappointed that Bush and Gore won nearly every state, effectively bringing the nominating races to an end. When the Pennsylvania primary was held a month later, Bill shrugged it off. "Didn't vote," he said. "The choice was already made. No competition anymore."

During the next several months Bill took almost no notice of the campaign, although a June news story did catch his attention. "Gore wants to create a new type of retirement account," said Bill, who is nearing retirement and found Gore's plan intriguing. In August, Bill turned on his television set to watch Bush's acceptance speech at the Republican National Convention. "I thought Bush's speech was positive," he observed. He also saw part of the Democratic convention two weeks later. "I think Al Gore presented himself well," Bill said. "I also liked Lieberman's moral character."

As he has done in every presidential election, Bill watched the October debates. "Bush sounded better than I thought he would," he said. "Gore has a better understanding of the policies, though." As Election Day neared, Bill began for the first time in the campaign to follow the news closely. He had a mixed reaction to the story about Bush's drunken driving arrest in 1976, saying it was "kind of interesting" but "not important."

Bill voted on Election Day. He liked Bush and Gore well enough, saying he was "fairly satisfied" with the candidates. However, he described the campaign itself as "depressing, not nearly as good as it should be." He added: "The campaign is too damn long."

The long presidential campaign has been criticized for disrupting the policy process—every four years, Washington slows to a crawl awaiting the election of the next president. But the long campaign has been praised for its capacity to

---

*"Super Tuesday" is the name the media has given a designated Tuesday, usually in early March, when a large number of states conduct their primary or caucus contests in order to select delegates to the presidential nominating conventions. The 2004 "Super Tuesday" contests were held on March 2; ten states chose more than 1,151 delegates to go to the Democratic national convention, held in August. The number of delegates represented more than half the total needed to claim the nomination and the right to challenge President Bush in November.

inform the voters' judgment. "That year-long test of endurance . . . reduces the risk that voters will make a rash decision they will come to regret not too much later," says the journalist Robert Friedman.

The long campaign would seem to offer everything that a citizen would need to cast an informed vote. Unlike European national elections, which are crammed into a few weeks, the U.S. presidential contest spans a full year and includes a score of televised events, including the primary debates, the October debates, and the national party conventions. Moreover, unlike Europeans, Americans get two chances—once in the primaries and again in the general election—to cast a vote.

But time by itself does not create an informed electorate. Having the time and taking the time are two different things, as students who put off their homework until the last minute know only too well. This point may seem so obvious that it hardly requires emphasis. What makes the point relevant, however, is that too much time can actually work to the detriment of an informed electorate. That's one of the problems with today's campaign. It is not delightfully long. It is numbingly long.

The long campaign dulls citizens' interest and taxes their attention. Although the campaign is filled with events, many of them are so devoid of meaning or so remote from Election Day that they get little attention. Rather than stimulating interest, the long campaign blunts it. The campaign chugs along at the start, accelerates during the early primaries, idles when they are over, revs up for the conventions, creeps along in September, and races to the finish in late October and early November. If, after each stage, people simply took off from where they had stopped, not much would be lost. But that is not how citizens behave. They tend to forget where they were heading and need a push to get going again.

How early is too early? Most Americans think that a campaign that includes Halloween, Thanksgiving, and Christmas is one that starts too early. Yet the holiday season is now part of the campaign. By Christmas 1999, the candidates had been on the hustings every day for three months. Nine televised debates had been held. Several candidates, including Elizabeth Dole, Dan Quayle, and Lamar Alexander, had already quit the race. More than $50 million had been spent, and hundreds of news stories had been filed.

Few cared. During the average week only one in seven was following the election with any degree of regularity. The average citizen didn't say anything at all about the campaign to anyone more than once a week. When Elizabeth Dole withdrew from the GOP race in the fall, it made news without making a splash. A lot of people were unaware she had dropped out because they did not know she was running. When asked in our Vanishing Voter survey in late 1999 why they were not following the campaign more closely, more than half the respondents indicated "it's simply too early in the campaign."

Before the first primaries are held, candidate debates are the main attraction. They do not get as much fanfare as the October election debates, but they are the biggest challenge that the candidates face until actual votes are cast, and they get reporters' attention. "George W. Bush [is] being put to the test tonight, alongside his five rivals for the GOP presidential nomination. Bush is heading into his first debate of the 2000 campaign, mindful of what he has to prove, and what his opponents hope to gain," chimed CNN anchor Bernard Shaw.

However, the Republican debate drew only 1.6 million viewers—a fifth of the audience of the average prime-time broadcast. The first Democratic debate a few days later fared no better. The two dozen primary debates in 2000 drew 36 million viewers, less than the number who watch a single October debate.

Even for the interested few, the primary debates gradually lost their appeal. Cable networks carried fourteen prior to the Iowa caucuses. The first seven attracted 1.7 million viewers on average. The last seven averaged only 675,000. Only 200,000 saw a January debate in Iowa that was carried on MSNBC and C-SPAN. "I'm tired of hearing the same answers over and over again," said one citizen in explaining why she quit watching after only a few minutes. . . .

. . . [A] lack of interest more than anything else explains the small debate audiences. Half who came across a primary debate while watching television quickly switched to another channel. "I had little interest, so I turned it off," said one such viewer.

Robert Dole once compared the U.S. Senate to a wet noodle: "If it doesn't want to move, it's not going to move." The same can be said of the American electorate. Not much can be done to persuade people to take an interest in a presidential campaign before they are ready to do so. Citizens care about the election of the president, but they have other demands on their time.

Why are the candidates and the voters on such completely different timetables? What compels candidates to be on the campaign trail months before most citizens are willing to pay attention? . . .

Active campaigning far in advance of the first primary is attributable to a change three decades ago in the nominating process. Before then, primary elections were held in a third of the states, but most of the national convention delegates were selected through party caucuses controlled by party leaders. In 1952, for example, Senator Estes Kefauver of Tennessee defeated President Harry S Truman by a 55–45 margin in New Hampshire's opening primary. Kefauver then won all but one of the other twelve primaries he entered and was the favorite of rank-and-file Democrats in the final Gallup poll before the party's national convention. Yet Democratic leaders rejected the maverick Kefauver and chose instead Illinois governor Adlai Stevenson, a traditional New Dealer, who was not even a declared presidential candidate. When asked about the significance of the primaries, Stevenson replied: "All [they do] is destroy some candidates."

The bitter 1968 presidential election shattered the party-centered nominating system. The country was mired in Vietnam, and Robert Kennedy and Eugene McCarthy challenged Lyndon Johnson's bid for a second term. Their strong showing led Johnson to make a surprise announcement on national television: "I shall not seek, and I will not accept, the nomination of my party for another term as your president." Kennedy's assassination in Los Angeles on the night of the California primary left the field to McCarthy. But McCarthy had lost a string of primaries to Kennedy and had infuriated party leaders. On the first ballot, they nominated Johnson's vice president, Hubert Humphrey, who had not contested a single primary. Insurgent Democrats were outraged, and after Humphrey narrowly lost the general election, they engineered a change in the nominating process.

Through its McGovern-Fraser Commission,* the Democratic Party adopted rules designed to put the voters in charge of the nominating process. State parties were directed to choose their convention delegates through either a primary election or a caucus open to all registered party voters. The commission anticipated that the caucus states would reform their traditional method, but several switched immediately to the primary system and more followed thereafter. The state legislatures that authorized these primaries applied them also to the GOP, thus binding the Republicans to the change.

By placing nominations in voters' hands, the reform system dictated how candidates would campaign. To gain nomination, they would have to aggressively court the public. . . .

Candidates must begin early, but citizens are not forced to do so. Their natural impulse is to ignore the early phase of the campaign, unless they revel in election politics, which only a few now do.

As a result, Americans do not learn all that much about the candidates and issues in the months before the Iowa caucuses. In 2000, some of them were blithely misinformed. When asked in a December survey what first came to mind when they thought about the Republican candidate George W. Bush, 11 percent of the respondents said he was the former president. Only 1 percent referred to a Bush policy proposal. Respondents' comments about Bill Bradley were also sparse. Half said they had never heard of him and, of those who had, many described him as a former basketball player. Fewer than 1 percent made reference to a Bradley policy proposal, despite the emphasis he was placing on his health-care plan.

---

*The McGovern-Fraser Commission was set up by the Democratic party after the 1968 election and charged with examining party rules relating to the presidential nomination process. The eventual rule changes made by the commission were designed to make the selection of delegates to the convention more representative of previously underrepresented elements such as woman and racial minorities, and had the effect of diminishing the role played by party professionals in the nominating process. Beginning in 1972, delegates to the Democratic national convention had to be chosen in open primaries or caucuses.

Information is fleeting unless people are interested enough to try to pin it down. Within an hour of a newscast, most have difficulty recalling anything they saw, unless a story was on a subject of keen interest. Candidate stories a year in advance of Election Day are not of that order. When asked in December whether George Bush "favors or opposes the registration of all guns," 73 percent said they had no idea where he stood. Only 16 percent said he opposed the policy and 11 percent wrongly said (a sure sign that many of the correct responses were also mere guesses) that he favored universal gun registration.

Most Americans had given so little thought to the 2000 campaign that they didn't even have a candidate in mind, despite media polls that suggested otherwise. The media's trial heats force respondents into a choice by reading them a list of candidates and asking them which one they like best. Our Vanishing Voter surveys posed the question differently: "Which candidate do you support at this time, or haven't you picked a candidate yet?"* Shortly before the Iowa caucuses, the landslide winner with 66 percent was "no candidate yet." Lagging far behind were Bush (15 percent), Gore (10 percent), and McCain and Bradley (3 percent each).

The New Hampshire primary accomplished in 2000 what months of campaigning had failed to do. It got people interested in the election. In academic studies, scholars often treat the campaign as a seamless flow of messages and decisions. But campaigns are not seamless. They are punctuated by key moments when citizens sit up, take notice, and more actively listen and learn.

Interest rose sharply at the time of the New Hampshire February 1 primary. John McCain's surprising victory over George W. Bush was a major reason, but so, too, was the fact that votes were now being cast and counted.[2] Respondents in our surveys had been saying for weeks that the campaign was "discouraging" and "uninformative." Now they were calling it "encouraging" and "informative."

Interest continued upward as the March 7 Super Tuesday primaries neared. At peak, shortly after Super Tuesday, more than a third said they were paying quite a bit of attention to the campaign. Nearly half could recall an election story they had seen, read, or heard in the past day, and two-fifths said they had engaged in campaign-related conversation within the past day. Not everyone, of course, was caught up in the excitement of the primaries. At least half of the public had no real interest in the nominating races even during this intensely competitive period. Nevertheless, interest had increased sharply from its pre-primary level and was still on the rise when the Super Tuesday primaries were held.

---

*The bulk of the poll data reported in this selection are based on data from the Vanishing Voter Project, which Professor Patterson headed. National samples of 1,000 Americans were interviewed weekly to determine how much attention potential voters were paying to the campaigns and what they were learning. The Vanishing Voter Project was funded by a grant from The Pew Charitable Trusts.

After Super Tuesday, however, interest had nowhere to go but down. Americans could hardly have thought at the time of the Iowa and New Hampshire contests that they would have only a month or so to engage the campaign and make a choice. But that is all the time they would get. Super Tuesday brought the nominating races to a screeching halt, just as it had in 1996.

The time that voters had was inadequate to their task. Nominating elections provide the most difficult choice that voters face. They can't rely on party labels to make their choice: the candidates are all Democrats or all Republicans. Nominating races also typically attract a half dozen or so contenders, most of them relative newcomers to presidential politics. Of the eight Republican contenders in 1996, for example, only Dole and Pat Buchanan had national reputations. In 1988, the Democratic contenders had such low recognition levels they were dubbed "the seven dwarfs." In 1976, the six active contenders for the Democratic nomination were also relative unknowns. Carter's recognition level before the New Hampshire primary was similar to that of his opponents. Most said they knew him only by name. Of the 20 percent who claimed to know more, about the best many of them could muster was that he was a peanut farmer or was from Georgia.

The 2000 campaign fit the pattern. By Super Tuesday, only one in five could say, even by guessing, where the candidates stood on specific issues. Of course, primary voters were not completely in the dark on Super Tuesday when they chose Bush and Gore as the party nominees. They recognized that Bush and Gore were the established candidates and that McCain and Bradley were the upstarts. Bush's support, for example, came mainly from registered Republicans, while McCain's was disproportionately from independents and crossover Democrats. Nevertheless, Bush, like Gore, was nominated as much by ascription as by informed judgment. . . .

Today's nominating contests end abruptly because of "front-loading"—the bunching of state contests early in the nominating process. In 2000, fifteen states held their primaries on Super Tuesday. In that kind of contest, opponents did not stand a chance against Bush's and Gore's superior name recognition, financing, and organization. Bradley quit the race the next day. McCain retreated to his Arizona home and, two days later, announced he was dropping out. The 1996 nominating campaign also ended abruptly. When Robert Dole dominated the six Junior Tuesday contests on March 5 and the seven Super Tuesday contests a week later, his chief rivals—Lamar Alexander, Richard Lugar, and Steve Forbes—quit the race. . . .

In theory, the McGovern-Fraser reform created a system in which the states are unequal only in that larger states select proportionately more delegates than smaller states. Theory and practice, however, have been quite different. The reformed system loaded the dice in favor of states with early contests. As the journalist Jules Witcover said in 1977: "The fact is that the reality in the early going of a presidential campaign is not the delegate count at all. The reality at the beginning stage is the psychological impact of the results—the perception by press, public, and contending politicians of what has happened."

The smart folks in Iowa were the first ones to figure out the new system. They placed their caucuses just ahead of the New Hampshire primary and, by 1976, were basking in the national limelight. "With 88 percent of Iowa's caucuses in, no amount of bad-mouthing by the others can lessen the importance of Jimmy Carter's finish," said CBS correspondent Roger Mudd. "He was the clear winner in this psychologically crucial test." CBS then singled Carter out for extra coverage. "So the candidate with the highly prized political momentum tonight is Jimmy Carter, covered now by Ed Rabel in New Hampshire." . . .

After Carter's unexpected victory, however, the new dynamic was apparent to all. The initial contests winnowed the field of candidates and bestowed momentum on the top finishers. To prevent an all-out fight over the opening positions, the Democratic Party reserved the initial spots for Iowa and New Hampshire and created "a window" for the other states. They would be allowed to hold their contests anytime between the second Tuesday in March (later changed to the first Tuesday) and the second Tuesday in June. The GOP followed a similar policy.

The stage was set for front-loading. Although Iowa and New Hampshire had a lock on the starting positions, there was nothing to prevent other states from moving to the front of the window. By 1988, two dozen had elbowed their way into March. All southern states except South Carolina, along with seven others, staged their primaries and caucuses on the same March day. It was the first bona fide "Super Tuesday."

Some states stayed away from the front of the schedule to avoid the expense of a second primary later in the year to select their statewide, congressional, and local nominees. But the action was clearly at the front end of the process. Traditionally, California's primary was on the final day of the nominating calendar. Until 1976 it was often a decisive encounter. McGovern's victory in 1972 enabled him to secure the Democratic nomination, just as Goldwater's in 1964 gave him the Republican nod. After 1976, however, the race in *every* case was over by the time it reached California. In 1996, the state moved its primary to March 26, three weeks after the first allowable date. Even that position was too far back to enable delegate-rich California to exert its muscle. For 2000, the state moved its primary to the first Tuesday in March, the earliest allowable date. "California voters are finally going to have some clout in deciding who the major parties nominate for president," said Governor Pete Wilson at the bill-signing ceremony.

California joined a crowded field. In 2000, twenty-nine states held contests in March—half of them on Super Tuesday. Sixty-three percent of the delegates were chosen by mid-March. In 1980, only 21 percent had been selected by then.

In effect, the nominees are now picked in a de facto national primary that takes place on Super Tuesday. No rule says the nominations must be decided then, and in some circumstances they might not. But the odds are they will. Whichever candidate has the most money, strongest organization, and deepest party support—like Bush and Gore in 2000, and Dole and Clinton in 1996—is likely to win big on Super Tuesday and bring the race to a sudden halt.

Although front-loading has advantages for the victorious candidates, it has no commensurate benefits for citizens. An abbreviated campaign discounts their involvement, learning, and even votes. The thousands of Florida voters disenfranchised on Election Day 2000 were for a time the most talked-about people in the nation. Almost no one commented, however, on the millions of voters in the roughly thirty states who, six months earlier, were effectively disenfranchised when Bush's and Gore's victories on March 7 completely devalued their yet-to-be-held presidential primaries and caucuses.

Front-loading explains why the overall turnout rate in presidential primaries has fallen from nearly 30 to 17 percent since the 1970s. Turnout has become schizophrenic—respectable in states with early contests and embarrassing in those with later contests. In 2000, the voting rate averaged 21 percent in primaries held on or before Super Tuesday and only 14 percent thereafter. Since the advent of front-loading, turnout has been half again as high in contested primaries as in those held after the races were decided. Were it not for the primaries for other offices also being held in the late-scheduled states, almost no one would bother to vote. . . .

Even in the contested states, the attention given to a state by the candidates and the media affected involvement levels. Residents of the states where the heaviest campaigning occurred or where the media's attention was concentrated followed the election more closely than did residents of the other contested states.

Information levels were also affected by the attention a state received. According to an Annenberg Center study of the 2000 campaign, residents of heavily contested primary states were 30 percent more likely to have particular knowledge of the candidates and issues. "What we are seeing," concluded Annenberg director Kathleen Hall Jamieson, "is a primary season of haves and have-nots—those states that have primaries with aggressive campaigning have more understanding of candidates and their positions."

The presidential nominating campaign is now only in principle a national system. The sequence of primaries affects one's ability to engage and influence the campaign. There are now two different nominating electorates, one formed by residents of early-contest states and one consisting of residents of late-contest states. The first electorate chooses the nominees and is the more heavily involved.

Front-loading produces a Silent Spring that affects all Americans, whatever their state of residence. Once the nominations are settled, the campaign loses its appeal. The conventions are still months away, but the races are over, and people retreat to the sidelines. . . .

Within a month of Super Tuesday in 2000, the number paying close attention to the campaign had been sliced in half. Bush and Gore kept on campaigning, but citizens were only slightly more attentive than they had been in
the period before the New Hampshire primary. This had also happened in
1996. Election interest declined sharply after Dole's win on Super Tuesday and
did not rise again until the national party conventions in August. . . .

As involvement declined, learning slowed to a crawl. A month after Super
Tuesday in 2000, Americans were actually less informed about some of Gore's
and Bush's issue positions than they had been earlier in the campaign. For example, only 13 percent in April could accurately identify Bush's stand on gun control compared with 24 percent in February. Issue awareness would rise slightly
during the next several months as the campaign worked its way toward the summer conventions. By and large, however, the post–Super Tuesday period was a
time when issue awareness languished. Candidate support also slipped. Fewer in
June said they had picked a candidate than had said so in March.

In the 1970s, when the nominating races ended later, citizens remained interested for a longer period. In 1976, for example, interest rose month by
month as the campaign moved toward the final early June contests in California, Ohio, and New Jersey. Today's front-loaded nominating system has a different dynamic. The nominating races end quickly, and the national party
conventions are still months away. What is a public to do? Americans do what
good sense dictates. They turn their attention elsewhere.

Reform Democrats could hardly have envisioned today's nominating system
when they attempted after the 1968 election to create a system that would empower rank-and-file voters. Instead, they constructed a system that has become
ever more responsive to other influences, including money.

Super Tuesday is tailor-made for well-funded candidates. Presidential hope-
fuls need to raise a lot of cash up front to compete in today's front-loaded system. Money does not guarantee success, as Steve Forbes discovered the hard
way, twice. But money is to a candidacy what gas is to a car. It can go a lot farther if it is running on full. An underfunded candidate can sometimes survive
Iowa and New Hampshire, but, after that, person-to-person campaigning gives
way to a multi-state effort based on televised political ads, which cost huge
sums. McGovern and Carter were the last poorly funded candidates to win
nomination.

In 2000, John McCain looked for a time as if he might beat the odds. Outspent two to one, McCain still managed to stun Bush in New Hampshire and
Michigan. Nevertheless, even if he had not been a party maverick, McCain
had little chance of victory on Super Tuesday with its dozen or so primaries.
After New Hampshire he had only five weeks to build enough voter and financial support to stop Bush's juggernaut. Iowa and New Hampshire still bestow
momentum, but front-loading tips the balance toward candidates who have
deep pockets and start high in the polls.

Since 1984 the candidate who has raised the most money in advance of the opening contests has won *every* nominating race. Of course, money flows to candidates, like Bush and Gore, who already have substantial support. The frontrunners in pre-election national polls have won three-fourths of the contested nominating races. But whatever the exact influence of money, factors firmly in place before the first contests—that is, before a single vote is cast— now go a long way toward determining the winners.

The public has taken notice. When asked at the end of the 2000 primaries whether the current method of nominating presidential candidates gives more say to "the voters" or to "the party leaders and the people who contribute money to the candidates," only 15 percent said the voters have the larger voice. . . .

In the process, Americans have grown dissatisfied with the way presidential nominees are chosen. . . . Five times during the 2000 campaign, our Vanishing Voter weekly survey asked respondents whether they liked "the long presidential campaign because it gives [you] a better chance to get to know the candidates" or whether they disliked it because it is "so long that [you] don't have time to pay attention except now and then." Each time, a majority complained about the campaign's length. In November 1999, 64 percent expressed displeasure with the long campaign. A year later, as the campaign was finally drawing to a close, 61 percent objected to the timetable.

Respondents also said they would prefer any of the major alternatives to the current nominating system. In our Vanishing Voter survey, a national primary was at the top of their list (64–36 percent), but a narrow plurality (44–42 percent) even claimed they would prefer the old convention system where party activists select the nominees. . . .

Some of the excitement went out of convention politics when the Democrats dropped the two-thirds rule in 1936 in favor of a simple-majority rule, which the GOP had always used. That change was of small consequence, however, compared with the McGovern-Fraser reform, which stripped the conventions of their nominating power.* The formal authority is still there, but the real power resides in the primary and caucus process.

Some observers say the conventions were in irreversible decline before the change in 1972. No convention in the previous two decades had gone past the first ballot, and primaries had grown increasingly important. In 1960, John F. Kennedy had to show Democratic leaders that his youth and Roman Catholicism would not ruin the party's chances in the fall election, and he did so with victories in the Wisconsin and West Virginia primaries.

---

*Since delegates are selected in the spring and early summer of a presidential election year and are "bound" to support their choice at the convention, as soon as any candidate reaches a majority in the delegate count the party's nominee is known. Prior to the McGovern-Fraser reforms, large numbers of delegates were officially "unbound" or not officially committed to any particular candidate. Bargaining and compromise were possible as a consequence, and the convention had the potential to select the nominee.

Nevertheless, conventions were open and tumultuous affairs. Frontrunners always worried that a riveting speech, late revelation, new face, or strategic maneuver might derail their nomination. Even if they held on, there were platform fights to settle, when they could be settled. Supporters of Barry Goldwater shouted down his chief rival, Nelson Rockefeller, when he appeared on the podium at the 1964 Republican convention. Humphrey and McCarthy were each booed lustily, but from different quarters, at the 1968 Democratic convention. The delegates controlled the conventions, and every four years the electorate had the chance to see them in action.

Today, the nominees control the conventions. No viewer has witnessed anything even remotely resembling an open convention since 1984, when Gary Hart carried the delegate fight to the floor—the last candidate to do so. Jesse Jackson in 1988 and Pat Buchanan in 1992 took policy disputes into the convention, but even that form of dissent might be a thing of the past. Both parties in 1996 and 2000 presented tightly choreographed gatherings that kept any sign of division off the convention floor. "Boring is good," said the Democratic consultant James Carville as the Democrats gathered for their 1996 convention. . . .

The first nominations decided under the new rules were, indeed, tightly contested. Although none of the conventions from 1972 to 1984 went past the first ballot, the delegates were often at odds, as in the 1972 McGovern-Humphrey race, the 1976 Ford-Reagan race, the 1980 Carter-Kennedy race, and the 1984 Mondale-Hart race. Front-loading eliminated such conventions because it produces an early and conclusive end to the contests. The convention has become a four-day testimonial designed to cast the winner in the strongest possible light. A recent Republican convention was so expertly choreographed that one wag described it as "GOP-TV."

Today's conventions are akin to coronation events, a fact that riles the press to no end. Midway through the 1996 GOP convention in San Diego, Ted Koppel of ABC's *Nightline* left in a huff, saying that he was returning to New York in search of real news. Koppel's departure prompted one commentator to remark: "The smoke-filled rooms are gone, but the spectacle that remains is as barren as a pond hit by acid rain: crystal clear, utterly beautiful, and utterly dead." . . .

Convention audiences have fallen sharply. Even as late as 1976, 28 percent of American households at the average moment had their TV sets on and tuned to the convention. By 1988, convention ratings had slipped to 19 percent. In 2000, only 13 percent of TV households were tuned in during the average prime-time minute, which was below even that of 1996, when the race was one-sided and the nominees better known.

When our survey respondents were asked in 2000 why the conventions were getting so little of their attention, the leading response—aside from the customary ones, "I'm too busy" or "I don't care for politics"—was that the nominees had already been selected.

Cutbacks in broadcast coverage have also contributed to the declining convention audience. In 1976, each of the major networks—ABC, CBS, and NBC—broadcast 25 hours of coverage of each convention. By 1984, that average had fallen to 12 hours. It was a mere 5 hours in 2000. . . . Fully half the audience for the 2000 conventions consisted of inadvertent viewers—those who sat down in front of their television sets, discovered the convention was on, and decided to watch some of it. . . .

The eclipse of the convention as a deliberative forum and television sensation has reduced campaign involvement. In the heyday of the televised conventions—the 1950s through the 1970s—the average American household watched ten to twenty hours of coverage. Voters learned more about the candidates and issues during the conventions than at any other single period in the campaign. The convention was quite an education, even for children and adolescents. Just as the World Series served to awaken them to major league baseball, the summer conventions introduced them to party politics.

Conventions still do all this, only on a smaller scale. They remain a key moment in terms of their ability to draw people into the campaign. Their audience, though diminished, is not minuscule. In our Vanishing Voter surveys, roughly a fourth of the respondents said they had watched "all" or "most" of the previous night's coverage. Nearly 15 million were tuned in during the average prime-time minute. Four of five who watched said they liked what they saw.

Conventions also stimulate interest in the campaign. In 2000, interest rose by 50 percent during the convention period, nearly reaching the level of the contested primary period. On the average day, one in three claimed to have talked about the campaign and one in two followed news about it. With increased interest came accelerated learning. Above all, the conventions afforded citizens a chance to find out more about the candidates. "People want to know more about Bush and Gore—what they are really like," said Republican consultant Bob Teeter. "Conventions are still important [in helping] people get that information." In fact, awareness of Bush's and Gore's issue positions rose by 17 percent during this period.

Many Americans also picked their candidate during the 2000 conventions. The number who said they had not yet decided on a candidate fell from 55 to 41 percent, the sharpest drop of the campaign. Although the October debates are usually portrayed as the major showdown of the campaign, far more votes are decided during the conventions. More voters are undecided about their candidate choice at this stage of the campaign, and the conventions give the nominees a nearly unobstructed opportunity to make their pitch. In an era of ten-second sound bites and thirty-second political ads, conventions are a throwback to the time when lengthy speeches were the main form of address. Even with fewer viewers, the conventions provide by far the largest audiences the candidates have to themselves during the entire campaign. . . .

The audience for the nominees' acceptance speeches is a receptive one. If Americans' attention span, as some have claimed, can now be measured in seconds, the acceptance speeches are an exception. They are the most anticipated part of today's conventions, and the most favorably received.

Conventions have a final noteworthy effect: They lift the voters' spirits. They are upbeat events during which candidates get their most favorable news coverage. During the 2000 convention period, the public saw the campaign as positive, not negative (49–22 percent), and encouraging, not discouraging (41–27 percent). Both were election-year highs. . . .

Nearly a half million people turned out on Labor Day in Detroit in 1936 to see and hear presidential candidate Franklin D. Roosevelt. The crowd was so deep that it extended like fingers into the streets spreading out from Cadillac Square. It was the height of the Depression and Roosevelt was a hero to America's working class. By comparison, when Al Gore and Joseph Lieberman spoke at an outdoor rally in Pittsburgh on Labor Day 2000, only 10,000 showed up.

Labor Day speeches are the traditional kickoff to the fall campaign. They once served as coming-out parties for the newly chosen party nominees. The candidates were fresh news and so were their pronouncements. Today, the candidates are such old news by Labor Day that, as far as most people are concerned, it might as well be Groundhog Day. During Labor Day week in 2000, Americans were actually less attentive to the presidential campaign than in the preceding or the following week.

September was once a highlight of the campaign. As the candidates toured the nation, speaking in city squares, they packed in the crowds and laid out their positions. It was in September, for example, when Hubert Humphrey broke with Lyndon Johnson's Vietnam policy in a speech at Salt Lake City's Tabernacle on Temple Square. But September is now just another month on the long road to November. Because of front-loading, the general election campaign effectively begins in early March and has been under way for nearly half a year. The candidates are familiar faces and are running out of new things to say.

The voters, too, are worn out. In 2000, public involvement dropped during September. Unlike the post–Super Tuesday period, Americans did not flee the campaign. But they talked and thought about it less often and followed it less closely than they had during the convention period. As they pulled back, they forgot some of the information acquired earlier. Issue awareness dropped by 22 percent during the month after the convention period. The optimism of that period had also dissipated. A majority now claimed that the campaign was boring and uninformative.

Presidential elections might seem interminable if the October televised debates had not been resurrected in 1976. The first such debates had been held in 1960 and, for a time, they looked to be the last. After 1960 the candidate who was ahead in the polls refused each time to participate, shielded by a restriction on free broadcast time. Nixon had gone into the 1960 debates as the favorite to win the election. He emerged in second place and was narrowly defeated by Kennedy—a lesson not lost on subsequent frontrunners.

An administrative ruling and two public-minded nominees, Gerald Ford and Jimmy Carter, revived the debates. In 1960, Congress had temporarily suspended the federal law that prohibits broadcasters from giving free airtime without granting it to all candidates for the same office. In 1975, however, the Federal Communications Commission reinterpreted the federal statute to say that debates could be treated as bona fide news events rather than a free-time opportunity if sponsored by an independent organization. A year later, Carter, who was leading in the polls, accepted President Ford's challenge to meet in debates sponsored by the League of Women Voters. October debates have been held ever since. . . .

. . . [N]o development has done more to enliven the modern campaign than the October debates—the nearest things to national town meetings. That tens of millions gather at the same time to listen to presidential candidates is remarkable. More remarkable still is that a majority of viewers watch the bulk of the ninety-minute telecasts.

It is an audience that listens and learns. Although the press often complains that the debates raise no new issues (a "wind-festival" is how CBS's Dan Rather characterized the first Bush-Gore debate), much of what is said is new to the viewers. Studies indicate that the October debates, without exception, have increased the public's understanding of the candidates and issues. In 2000, Americans' ability to recognize Bush's and Gore's positions on key issues rose by 25 percent during the debate period.

Debates give the electorate an opportunity to view the candidates through something other than the negative lens of journalism, and, nearly always, they end up liking what they see. In a few cases—Kennedy in 1960, Reagan in 1980, and Perot in 1992—their image of a candidate improved substantially. Before the first 1992 debate, for example, 23 percent said they liked Perot and 45 percent said they disliked him. After the last debate, 47 percent said they liked him and 25 percent said they disliked him.

Few key moments spur public involvement as fully as the October debates. People do not just watch. They talk about what they have seen. On the day after the first Bush-Gore debate in 2000, 47 percent—twice the number on an average day—discussed the campaign. The second and third debates sparked nearly as much discussion. Debates also widen the circle of conversation. Most campaign-related discussions take place between family members, but friends and co-workers are frequently drawn into debate conversations. In 2000, half of debate-related conversations took place outside the family. . . .

. . . [C]itizen involvement—the extent to which Americans were following the campaign and thinking and talking about it—doubled during the two-and-a-half-week period when the debates were taking place. One in four said they were more interested in following the campaign in the news as a result of the debates. And the number who felt the campaign was exciting, informative, and encouraging rose significantly.

The debates are a springboard to the final days of the campaign, when the pace picks up and voters pay closer attention (Figure 1). Soon after the last debate in 2000, interest increased as the campaign moved toward Election Day. During the final week, involvement reached one of its highest levels of the entire campaign—34 percent said they were paying close attention. Citizens were more involved in other ways, too. On the average day, 49 percent reported having talked about the election—the highest level at any time during the campaign. Intense news coverage in the campaign's closing days contributed to the rise in interest. Although the news media have cut back on their election coverage in recent elections, the final days are still heavily reported. In the last week of the 2000 campaign, roughly half of Americans each day reported having read, seen, or heard an election story. This level, too, was a campaign high.

Figure 1
Key Moments and Involvement in the 2000 Presidential Campaign

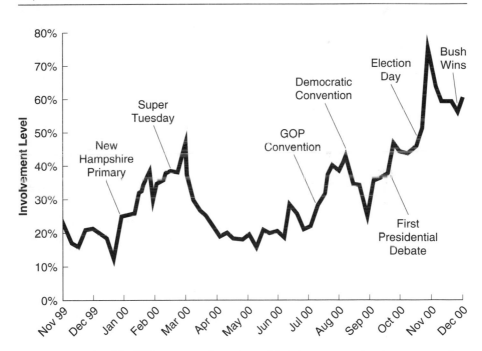

During most weeks of the 2000 campaign, the majority of Americans were paying almost no attention. Interest was high only around key moments—the contested primaries, the conventions, the October debates, and Election Day. Involvement rose dramatically during the post-election period when the election's outcome was at issue.

Although interest peaked at the end, its full potential had not been tapped, as the post-election period revealed. During the five weeks that the outcome of the 2000 election rested on the results of the Florida recount, citizen involvement—as measured by people's thoughts, conversations, and news exposure—averaged 61 percent, far higher than was registered at any time during the campaign. The Florida wrangling captured public attention in a way the campaign itself did not.

As voters went to the polls after having had twelve months to scrutinize Bush and Gore, some of them were still mulling over their decision. If a long campaign, as some have claimed, helps voters to understand their choices, they should have been flush with information. In fact, they were anything but highly informed. Our Vanishing Voter poll just before Election Day asked respondents to agree or disagree with twelve issue statements—six that addressed Gore's positions and six that concerned Bush's. On the average issue, 38 percent correctly identified the candidate's position, 16 percent incorrectly identified it (an indicator that a third or more of the correct responses were also mere guesses), and 46 percent said they did not know it.

On only one issue did a majority accurately identify Gore's position. Fifty-eight percent said he favored free prescription drugs for the elderly and only 8 percent said he did not. Awareness of Bush's positions was highest on his top issue, tax cuts. Fifty-two percent said he advocated "a large cut in personal income taxes" and 11 percent believed he opposed it.

On all other issues, less than half could correctly identify the candidates' positions, and many guessed wrong. The extreme case was Bush's stand on campaign finance reform. When asked whether he favored or opposed "a ban on very large contributions to political candidates," only one in ten said he opposed such a ban, which was his actual position. Two in ten believed he favored a ban and seven in ten said that they didn't know his position. Campaign finance reform had been a leading issue in the GOP nominating race eight months earlier, but as time passed, even most of those who had known Bush's position forgot it.

Issue awareness in 2000 may have been the lowest in modern times. Comparisons with past elections are risky because research methods have varied across the years. Nevertheless, no past election study found a level of issue awareness as low as what our Vanishing Voter surveys recorded. Even the 1948 and 1976 campaigns, which were conducted on issues of roughly the same salience as those of the 2000 campaign, did not produce electorates that knew so little about the issues. Using a generous estimate, only 25 percent of adults in 2000 could correctly identify three-fourths or more of the candidates' positions. In 1976, 33 percent identified at least three-fourths of the candidates' positions on major issues. In 1948, in a survey conducted two months before Election Day, 37 percent knew three-fourths or more of the candidates' positions on major issues. . . .

Of course, not every presidential campaign will spawn a well-informed electorate. A campaign's issues may be too bland or too numerous to stick in people's minds. The issues of the 2000 campaign might well have been of this nature. But no presidential campaign should be designed in a way that flattens learning. The long vacant stretches during the 2000 contest had this effect. Roughly 80 percent of what was learned about the issues during the year-long 2000 campaign was packed into the weeks of the contested primaries, the conventions, and the debates.

Moreover, no presidential campaign should leave citizens with a disheartened feeling. In the concluding week of the 2000 campaign, when asked whether the campaign had been "rather depressing, that it hasn't been nearly as good as a campaign should be" or whether it had been "uplifting, that it made [you] feel better about elections," respondents by more than two to one judged it "depressing."

Election structures have consequences. They can foster public involvement or discourage it. The long campaign of today runs in spurts, taxes people's attention, and dulls their sensibilities. It serves to frustrate learning, just as it dampens interest and, in the nominating period, the inclination to vote.

Major moments, such as the New Hampshire primary, Super Tuesday, the conventions, the October debates, and Election Day, have the capacity to engage and inform the public. They are the key to an involved electorate; they bring people into the campaign. But when these moments are widely spread out, their capacity is diminished. Time—in this case, too much time—invites the public to disengage.

The problems of the modern campaign, to abuse the title of an old Cole Porter song, "begin [at] the begin." A campaign that starts a full year before Election Day may seem to offer everything citizens could possibly want or need. Instead, it sends them forth on a mind-numbing trek. If the election system is to be made fit for the American people, a place to start is its length: shorten it.

Notes

1. Bill Pelligrini is a composite. For the Vanishing Voter surveys, a new national sample was chosen each week. Thus, no respondent was interviewed weekly throughout the campaign. However, the composite is based on actual interview responses and reflects what many Americans were doing and thinking at each stage of the 2000 campaign.
2. More so than the Iowa caucuses, the New Hampshire primary draws the public to the campaign, in part because of the enormous media buildup it receives. It typically garners a fourth or more of all primary coverage, which inflates public opinion of New Hampshire's role. Although the New Hampshire primary selects only about 1 percent of the national convention delegates, Americans think the total is much higher. When asked in our Vanishing Voter survey whether New Hampshire selects 25, 10, 5, or 1 percent of the delegates, only one in seven respondents picked 1 percent. One in seven also claimed that New Hampshire selects 25 percent.

Questions for Discussion

1. Why, overall, does the American presidential election process appear to fail in terms of informing the electorate about the stances of candidates on political issues? Do any events during the election appear to educate voters about their choices?
2. Patterson feels strongly that the presidential election campaign needs to be shortened. What kinds of political interests might be opposed to such a reform? Would shortening the campaign process potentially have any effect on the types of individuals who run for the presidency? What kinds of individuals would be advantaged or disadvantaged in a short campaign? A long campaign?

☆ 7.2

McConnell v. The Federal Election Commission (2003)

In 2002, Congress passed the Bipartisan Campaign Reform Act (BCRA) in an effort to lessen the role of big money in federal elections. By the late 1990s, it had become clear to most observers that the campaign finance regulation system put in place in the early 1970s now had little meaning; the intent of the law was being widely disregarded. With its emphasis on limiting direct contributions to parties and candidate committees ("hard money") and extensive public disclosure of contribution sources, existing federal campaign law was being overshadowed by both party and group fund raising and spending not regulated by federal law and often hidden from public scrutiny.

The new campaign law had a variety of provisions, but two were especially prominent. Soft-money contributions to national party committees by individuals and organized interests were now prohibited. The parties had been raising and spending virtually unlimited amounts of money to influence federal elections, thanks largely to the soft-money contributions raised from interested individuals and groups that sometimes approached seven figures. The parties now were restricted to raising and spending only hard money, which was subject to federal contribution limits and source restrictions.

The BCRA also put forth a new standard concerning the *content* of election-related political communications and *when* interest groups could engage in issue advocacy electioneering. An "electioneering communication" is a broadcast, cable, or satellite communication that refers to a clearly identified candidate sponsored by corporations (including nonprofit corporations) and unions within 30 days of a primary election or 60 days of a general election; such ads were prohibited by the new law. Essentially, interest groups were no longer allowed to broadcast advertisements supporting or opposing a candidate close to Election Day.

The BCRA was so controversial that one of its provisions provided for a quick review of its constitutionality, first by a three-judge panel of the U.S. District Court for the District of Columbia, with appeals then to go directly to the Supreme Court. Congressional reformers passionately believed that big money in politics so corrupted the process, or at least created the appearance of corruption, that drastic measures were needed to control it. Opponents saw the issue largely in First Amendment terms; banning campaign ads by groups so close to an election, for example, denied them their basic First Amendment right of political expression.

In December 2003, the U.S. Supreme Court surprised many by upholding virtually all of the new law's provisions in a very contentious five-to-four decision, including the banning of soft-money contributions to the national parties and restrictions on campaign advertising close to an election by groups. Corporations and unions were banned from making or financing electioneering communications except through their political action committees (PACs).

The majority opinion, written by Justices John Paul Stevens and Sandra Day O'Connor, reflected an overwhelming, practical concern with the corrosive effects of soft money and the destructive influence of campaign advertising by organized interests so close to Election Day. The four dissenters on the court argued from a more philosophical perspective; they believed there was simply little good, hard, overwhelming evidence of the corrupting influence of money on the political system, certainly not enough to warrant the drastic suppression of free expression in elections.

What follows are excerpts from the court decision.

For the Majority by Justices Stevens and O'Connor.
The question for present purposes is whether large soft-money contributions to national party committees have a corrupting influence or give rise to the appearance of corruption. Both common sense and the ample record in these cases confirm Congress's belief that they do. The F.E.C.'s allocation regime has invited widespread circumvention of F.E.C.A.'s [Federal Election Campaign Act of 1971] limits on contributions to parties for the purpose of influencing federal elections. Under this system, corporate, union and wealthy individual donors have been free to contribute substantial sums of soft money to the national parties, which the parties can spend for the specific purpose of influencing a particular candidate's federal election. It is not only plausible, but

likely, that candidates would feel grateful for such donations and that donors would seek to exploit that gratitude.

The evidence in the record shows that candidates and donors alike have in fact exploited the soft-money loophole, the former to increase their prospects of election and the latter to create debt on the part of officeholders, with the national parties serving as willing intermediaries. Thus, despite F.E.C.A.'s hard-money limits on direct contributions to candidates, federal officeholders have commonly asked donors to make soft-money donations to national and state committees "solely in order to assist federal campaigns," including the office-holder's own. Parties kept tallies of the amounts of soft money raised by each officeholder, and "the amount of money a member of Congress raised for the national political committees often affected the amount the committees gave to assist the member's campaign." . . .

Even when not participating directly in the fund-raising, federal officehold-ers were well aware of the identities of the donors: national party committees would distribute lists of potential or actual donors, or donors themselves would report their generosity to officeholders.

For their part, lobbyists, C.E.O.'s and wealthy individuals alike all have can-didly admitted donating substantial sums of soft money to national committees not on ideological grounds, but for the express purpose of securing influence over federal officials. For example, a former lobbyist and partner in a lobbying firm in Washington, D.C., stated in his declaration:

> You are doing a favor for somebody by making a large [soft money] donation and they appreciate it. Ordinarily, people feel inclined to reciprocate favors. Do a bigger favor for someone—that is, write a larger check—and they feel even more compelled to reciprocate. In my experience, overt words are rarely exchanged about contributions, but people do have understandings.

Particularly telling is the fact that in 1996 and 2000, more than half of the top 50 soft-money donors gave substantial sums to both major national parties, leaving room for no other conclusion but that these donors were seeking influ-ence, or avoiding retaliation, rather than promoting any particular ideology. . . .

Plaintiffs argue that without concrete evidence of an instance in which a federal officeholder has actually switched a vote (or, presumably, evidence of a specific instance where the public believes a vote was switched), Congress has not shown that there exists real or apparent corruption. But the record is to the contrary. The evidence connects soft money to manipulations of the legislative calendar, leading to Congress's failure to enact, among other things, generic drug legislation, tort reform, and tobacco legislation. More importantly, plain-tiffs conceive of corruption too narrowly. Our cases have firmly established that Congress's legitimate interest extends beyond preventing simple cash-for-votes corruption to curbing "undue influence on an officeholder's judgment, and the appearance of such influence." . . .

... To be sure, more political favoritism or opportunity for influence alone is insufficient to justify regulation. As the record demonstrates, it is the manner in which parties have sold access to federal candidates and officeholders that has given rise to the appearance of undue influence. Implicit (and, as the record shows, sometimes explicit) in the sale of access is the suggestion that money buys influence. It is no surprise then that purchasers of such access unabashedly admit that they are seeking to purchase just such influence. It was not unwarranted for Congress to conclude that the selling of access gives rise to the appearance of corruption.

In sum, there is substantial evidence to support Congress's determination that large soft-money contributions to national political parties give rise to corruption and the appearance of corruption.

Many years ago, we observed that "to say that Congress is without power to pass appropriate legislation to safeguard . . . an election from the improper use of money to influence the result is to deny to the nation in a vital particular the power of self-protection." We abide by that conviction in considering Congress's most recent effort to confine the ill effects of aggregated wealth on our political system. We are under no illusion that B.C.R.A. will be the last Congressional statement on the matter. Money, like water, will always find an outlet. What problems will arise, and how Congress will respond, are concerns for another day. In the main we uphold B.C.R.A.'s two principal, complementary features: the control of soft money and the regulation of electioneering communications.

From the dissent by Justice Scalia.

This is a sad day for the freedom of speech. Who could have imagined that the same court which, within the past four years, has sternly disapproved of restrictions upon such inconsequential forms of expression as virtual child pronography, tobacco advertising, dissemination of illegally intercepted communications, and sexually explicit cable programming would smile with favor upon a law that cuts to the heart of what the First Amendment is meant to protect: the right to criticize the government. For that is what the most offensive provisions of this legislation are all about. We are governed by Congress, and this legislation prohibits the criticism of members of Congress by those entities most capable of giving such criticism loud voice: national political parties and corporations, both of the commercial and the not-for-profit sort. It forbids preelection criticism of incumbents by corporations, even not-for-profit corporations, by use of their general funds; and forbids national-party use of "soft" money to fund "issue ads" that incumbents find so offensive.

But what about the danger to the political system posed by "amassed wealth"? The most direct threat from that source comes in the form of undisclosed favors and payoffs to elected officials which have already been criminalized, and will be rendered no more discoverable by the legislation at issue here. The use of corporate wealth (like individual wealth) to speak to the electorate is unlikely to "distort" elections—especially if disclosure requirements tell the people where the speech is coming from. The premise of the First Amendment is that the American people are neither sheep nor fools, and hence fully capable of considering both the substance of the speech presented to them and its proximate and ultimate source. If that premise is wrong, our democracy has a much greater problem to overcome than merely the influence of amassed wealth. Given the premises of democracy there is no such thing as too much speech.

But, it is argued, quite apart from its effect upon the electorate, corporate speech in the form of contributions to the candidate's campaign, or even in the form of independent expenditures supporting the candidate, engenders an obligation which is later paid in the form of greater access to the officeholder, or indeed in the form of votes on particular bills. Any quid-pro-quo agreement for votes would of course violate criminal law, and actual payoff votes have not even been claimed by those favoring the restrictions on corporate speech. It cannot be denied, however, that corporate (like noncorporate) allies will have greater access to the officeholder, and that he will tend to favor the same causes as those who support him (which is usually why they supported him). That is the nature of politics—if not indeed human nature—and how this can properly be considered "corruption" (or "the appearance of corruption") with regard to corporate allies and not with regard to other allies is beyond me. If the Bill of Rights had intended an exception to the freedom of speech in order to combat this malign proclivity of the officeholder to agree with those who agree with him, and to speak more with his supporters than his opponents, it would surely have said so. It did not do so, I think, because the juice is not worth the squeeze. . . .

The first instinct of power is the retention of power, and, under a Constitution that requires periodic elections, that is best achieved by the suppression of election-time speech. We have witnessed merely the second scene of Act I of what promises to be a lengthy tragedy.

From the dissent by Justice Kennedy.

Our precedents teach, above all, that government cannot be trusted to moderate its own rules for suppression of speech. The dangers posed by speech regulations have led the court to insist upon principled constitutional lines and a rigorous standard of review. The majority now abandons these distinctions and limitations.

Until today's consolidated cases, the court has accepted but two principles to use in determining the validity of campaign finance restrictions. First is the anticorruption rationale. The principal concern, of course, is the agreement for a quid pro quo between officeholders (or candidates) and those who would seek to influence them. The court has said the interest in preventing corruption allows limitations on receipt of the quid by a candidate or officeholder, regardless of who gives it or of the intent of the donor or officeholder. Second, the Court has analyzed laws that classify on the basis of the speaker's corporate or union identity under the corporate speech rationale. The court has said that the willing adoption of the entity form by corporations and unions justifies regulating them differently: their ability to give candidates quids may be subject not only to limits but also to outright bans; their electoral speech may likewise be curtailed. . . .

. . . The court . . . concludes that access, without more, proves influence is undue. Access, in the court's view, has the same legal ramifications as actual or apparent corruption of officeholders. This new definition of corruption sweeps away all protections for speech that lie in its path.

Access in itself, however, shows only that in a general sense an officeholder favors someone or that someone has influence on the officeholder. There is no basis, in law or in fact, to say favoritism or influence in general is the same as corrupt favoritism or influence in particular. By equating vague and generic claims of favoritism or influence with actual or apparent corruption, the court adopts a definition of corruption that dismantles basic First Amendment rules, permits Congress to suppress speech in the absence of a quid pro quo threat. . . . The generic favoritism or influence theory articulated by the court is at odds with standard First Amendment analyses because it is unbounded and susceptible to no limiting principle. . . .

The First Amendment underwrites the freedom to experiment and to create in the realm of thought and speech. Citizens must be free to use new forms, and new forums, for the expression of ideas. The civic discourse belongs to the people and Government may not prescribe the means used to conduct it. The First Amendment commands that Congress "shall make no law . . . abridging the freedom of speech." The command cannot be read to allow Congress to provide for the imprisonment of those who attempt to establish new political parties and alter the civic discourse. . . . The Court, upholding multiple laws that suppress both spontaneous and concerted speech, leaves us less free than before. Today's decision breaks faith with our tradition of robust and unfettered debate.

Questions for Discussion

1. Why, according to the majority of the Supreme Court in *McConnell v. The Federal Elections Commission*, does money corrupt politics even if there is no hard evidence of "buying" votes? Do you agree?
2. Some have called BCRA an "incumbent protection" act. On what basis might this charge be made? In your view, is it wise to limit free expression in elections to reduce corruption or the appearance of corruption in elections?

7.3

The Stagnation of Congressional Elections

James E. Campbell

The mere existence of elections does not guarantee a healthy democracy, in which citizens can hold public officials accountable in meaningful ways. When elections are not genuinely competitive, citizens are robbed of the opportunity to reward or punish candidates and parties for their performance in office, and political change is difficult to achieve.

In this selection, James E. Campbell explores why House incumbents are nearly invincible in running for public office; only a handful of districts change party hands during an election. He finds that the major reason is that congressional incumbents have a huge advantage over challengers in their abilities to raise and spend campaign funds. In recent House elections, incumbents typically spend six to twelve times what the challenger spends.

Campbell is skeptical of the newest campaign reform effort, the Bipartisan Campaign Reform Act of 2002 (BCRA), which proponents argued would help break the "stranglehold of money on the political process." In Campbell's view the elimination of soft money and restrictions on electioneering in the act are likely to only solidify incumbency advantage, as are provisions increasing contribution limits; meaningful competition may be even less likely in the future.

For the overwhelming majority of districts in 2002, there was never any real question that the election would leave the status quo intact. With a week to go, *Congressional Quarterly* rated only thirteen congressional districts as having no clear favorite (about 3 percent of the 435 districts). A total of 359 districts, about five out of every six districts, were rated as "safe," with no real uncertainty as to who would win. The results a week later confirmed that very few House races were competitive. The election produced a net change of only five seats, and 98 percent of incumbents were reelected. This was not unusual.

James E. Campbell is a professor of political science at the State University of New York at Buffalo.

Abridged version of James E. Campbell, "The Stagnation of Congressional Elections," in *Life After Reform: When the Bipartisan Campaign Reform Act Meets Politics*, edited by Michael J. Malbin (Lanham, MD: Rowman and Littlefield, 2003): 141–158. Copyright © 2003. Reprinted by permission of The Campaign Finance Institute, and James E. Campbell.

Congressional elections are stagnant. Because of the near invincibility of House incumbents, only a handful of districts are truly competitive, and elections shift very few seats from one party to the other. Perhaps the most important reason why incumbents are nearly unbeatable is that they normally have much better financed campaigns than their opponents. Though campaign finance reformers had as their principal goal reducing the potentially corrupting impact of large contributions, they also made claims that the reforms would diminish the financial advantage that incumbents had and that this would help restore competition and revitalize elections. Opponents of reform made the opposite claim, claiming that BCRA was an "incumbent protection act" that would further smother competition.* This [selection] examines how House elections have become stagnant and what the likely effects of BCRA will be for competition and change in House elections.

Electoral Stagnation

Competition in House elections has been on the decline for several decades. Nearly thirty years ago David Mayhew wrote of the "vanishing marginals," the decreasing number of congressional districts that were won by close vote margins and that could be considered competitive. In the typical election year between 1956 and 1964, about ninety-four districts were decided by a margin of fewer than 10 percentage points (55 percent to 45 percent of the vote or closer). From 1966 to 1972, the number of marginal districts dropped to about fifty-nine. Since Mayhew's observation, competition has eroded further and is now in very short supply.

One important indicator of competition is the partisan turnover of districts—the number of districts won by candidates of different parties in consecutive election years. Turnover is not essential for competition, but one would expect serious competition to result in a substantial amount of turnover. While some elections produced a great deal of turnover and others next to none, in general the amount of turnover in elections declined in the second half of the twentieth century and especially in the last few decades. As the first column in Table 1 indicates, elections in recent years have switched fewer and fewer districts from one party to the other. The typical election in the first half of the century resulted in a shift of about 55 seats between the parties. That declined

---

*In the spring of 2002 Congress passed and President Bush signed the Bipartisan Campaign Reform Act (BCRA), the first major piece of campaign reform legislation since the early 1970s. The law is discussed in some detail in the previous selection (selection 7.2). Among the law's many provisions was the banning of so-called soft-money contributions to the national parties, eliminating the solicitation and spending of soft money by federal candidates, and eliminating broadcast "electioneering communication" by interest groups within 30 days of a primary and 60 days of a general election.

to about 38 seats between 1952 and 1974 and to only 23 seats from 1976 to 2000. Competitiveness, at least as measured by the likelihood of an election changing the partisan outcome in a district, is now less than half of what it was throughout much of the twentieth century.

The decline in competition also affected the amount of change produced by elections. Elections as instruments of popular control of the government should permit citizens to redirect the government in significant ways, but this is becoming less the case for House elections. Elections used to shift large numbers of seats from one party to the other, signaling that voters wanted government set on a different course and providing the parties with enough support in Congress to have some real chance of moving government in a new direction. It was not uncommon in the first half of the twentieth century for the Democrats or the Republicans to register net seat swings of fifty seats or more. The parties gained or lost fifty seats or more in over a third of the twenty-five national elections for the House from 1902 to 1950 (nine of twenty-five). In stark contrast, setting aside the 1994 . . . election for the Republicans, neither party has gained or lost more than ten seats since 1984. As the right-hand column in table 1 indicates, the typical election in the first half of the century produced a shift of about thirty-one seats to a party. In the third quarter of the century the typical seat swing dropped to twenty seats, and in the last quarter it declined even further to only seven or eight seats. Seat changes are now only about a quarter of what they were. With fewer seats changing hands either way in our competition-poor electoral system, elections produce little change. The system is stagnant.

This is important. Competition is the lifeblood of elections. Without competition, elections become meaningless rituals. If few elections are truly competitive, and if elections overall produce little change in the composition of

Table 1

Median Seat Turnover and Absolute Seat Swings for Elections in the Twentieth Century

Elections	Median Seat Turnover (Gross Change)	Median Absolute Seat Swing (Net Change)
1900–1924	53.9	31.6
1926–1950	56.1	31.0
1952–1974	38.3	20.0
1976–2000	23.1	7.5

Note: "Gross change" indicates the total number of seats electing a representative from different parties in consecutive elections (D to R or R to D). The net change is the net seat shift toward either the Democrats or the Republicans. The data have been adjusted to a constant House size of 435. Third-party seats are halved for the major parties. Because of reapportionment, the gross amount of partisan seat turnover could not be calculated for years ending in 2.

Congress, it is only natural that a large number of citizens would come to regard the process as unresponsive and crooked, grow cynical, and stay home on Election Day.

The Increased Incumbency Advantage

The immediate cause of the stagnation in House elections is the increased electoral advantage that accrues to an incumbent by virtue of incumbency (as opposed, for example, to the advantage that comes from being a representative of the majority party in the district). There is no doubt that running as an incumbent rather than as a challenger or in an open seat race typically attracts some number of votes to a candidate. Over the years a number of different methods have been used to assess how many votes incumbency is worth. While estimates have varied, there is a broad consensus that incumbency per se did not make much of a difference prior to the mid-1960s. Most studies indicate that incumbency added perhaps only a couple of percentage points of the vote to the incumbent's column.

After the mid-1960s, the incumbency advantage became a larger factor. Again, while various methodologies produced different estimates, there is a consensus that the incumbency advantage grew significantly. Most estimates indicate that incumbency in recent decades has been worth between about 7 and 10 percentage points of the vote. My own estimates, based on an examination of a causal model of the district vote in elections from 1994 to 2000, are consistent with these. I estimate that incumbency was typically worth 7.9 percent of the vote in 1994 elections, 6.9 percent in 1996, 7.6 percent in 1998, and 10.0 percent in 2000.

The impact of incumbency quadrupled at the same time as competition and seat changes were plummeting. Districts were somehow made safer (less competitive) for incumbents and this buffered these districts from national political tides. The question is why this happened. What is the root cause of the increased incumbency advantage, the decline in district competition, and the constriction of seat swings?

The Cause of Electoral Stagnation

Several potential explanations for the increase in the incumbency advantage (and therefore electoral stagnation) have been proposed over the years. First, some have speculated that incumbents have increased their hold on their districts by manipulating the redistricting process to their advantage. In redrawing district lines after every census, there are choices to be made regarding the areas to be included or excluded from districts, and incumbents naturally attempt to have friendly areas added to their districts and areas inclined to the opposition appended to adjoining districts. Other scholars have speculated that the weakening of party identification, or party dealignment, caused voters to rely more on incumbency as a voting cue. Presumably, voters who lacked much information about the congressional candidates, their records, and their issue positions had relied on party identification to help them reach their vote choice. With their partisanship weakened, these voters gave greater weight to the low information cue of incumbency in reaching their vote decision. Still others have suggested that incumbents have won by larger margins because their challengers are weaker, less appealing candidates. Finally, the electoral advantage of incumbency may have grown because incumbents are doing a better job in serving their constituencies, in creating a "personal vote." Whether through casework, or position taking on issues important to the district, or bringing home "pork" for the district, or adapting their "home style" to their constituents' sensibilities, incumbents may have used their job to secure their job.

In general these explanations have fallen short of accounting for the increased incumbency advantage. There is little evidence, for example, that redistricting has strongly increased the advantage of incumbency. While some incumbents have had success in having district lines drawn to their liking, others have had just the opposite experience, and some incumbents are thrown into districts to run against each other. In general, given that they were all elected in the preredistricted districts, most incumbents would probably regard redistricting as more upsetting to their reelection chances than beneficial. Moreover, it is difficult to see why redistricting would have helped incumbents after the mid-1960s and not before.

The other explanations also fail to explain the increased incumbency advantage. Although partisanship weakened slightly in the 1970s, it did not weaken very much, and it rebounded in the mid-1980s. If dealignment had been the basis for the growth of the incumbency advantage, the effects of incumbency should have declined after the 1980s, as partisanship rebounded, but they did not. The timing of the increase in the incumbency advantage also undercuts the challenger and constituent service explanations. It is difficult to imagine that the quality of challengers should have inexplicably dropped off in the mid-1960s or that incumbents should have become much more proficient at doing their job at that time.

A Theory of Electoral Stagnation

If not redistricting, dealignment, weaker challengers, or improved constituency service, what accounts for the increase in the incumbency advantage and the decline in district competitiveness and changeability?

The answer is campaign spending. Figure 1 depicts the effects of the campaign financing system in increasing the incumbency advantage and bringing about electoral stagnation. Starting on the left, the model claims that the laws that have governed the financing of congressional campaigns have permitted huge campaign finance disparities between candidates. The laws are not the prime moving cause of these campaign finance disparities, but they allow the supply of contributions from those served by the incumbent to meet the incumbents' demand for these resources to pay for expensive campaign technologies. Together the laws and the contributions that they permit constitute a system in which incumbents have had many times the resources of their challengers. The campaign spending advantages of incumbents have funded first-rate campaigns using all of the available modern (and expensive) campaign techniques and technologies, from mass media to mass mailings to polling to whatever the candidate and his or her advisors think will help highlight the incumbent's record and appeal to the district. This spending has typically paid off in votes and generated a substantial electoral advantage for incumbents. This, in turn, depresses competition at the district level and insulates these seats from the national political forces that had previously generated substantial seat swings. Whether it is a good year for the Democrats or a good year for the Republicans, the party balance is pretty much what it was before the election. Combined with institutional arrangements that favor the status quo, electoral stagnation fosters gridlock and the public's reactions of cynicism, apathy, and low turnout rates.

Figure 1

A Causal Model of Electoral Stagnation

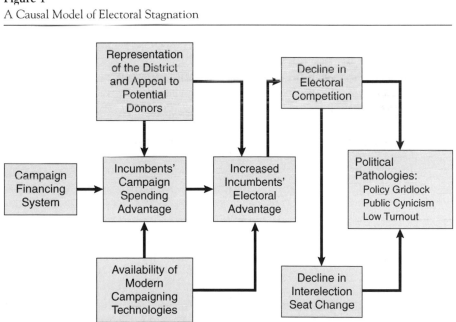

The Campaign Spending Advantage of Incumbents

There is substantial evidence for this theory of electoral stagnation. Much of the model has already been addressed. The national political pathologies of low turnout and political cynicism have been well documented elsewhere, and we have discussed the rise of the incumbency advantage and its accompanying decline in competition and electoral change. There is also no doubt that representatives do what they can to please their constituents and their potential donors outside the district and that expensive modern campaign technologies, from polling to mass media advertising, began to come into widespread use by candidates in the 1960s. The two links that remain to be established are the campaign financing advantage of incumbents over challengers (to pay for the technologies to communicate their district service to constituents) and the extent to which the incumbents' spending advantage affects their share of the district vote.

The typical incumbent is able to spend many times what his or her opponent is able to spend. Table 2 presents the disparity in campaign spending between incumbents and their challengers in contested House elections from 1992 to 2000. (A contested election is one with both a Democrat and a Republican candidate in the general election.) One might think that incumbents would have a significant advantage if they spent 50 percent more than their challengers, and that they would have a huge advantage if they spent twice what their challengers spent. However, in reality, the typical incumbent in every year examined spent more than five times what the challenger spent. In 1998, the typical incumbent spent more than eight times what the challenger spent, and in 2000, almost thirteen times more. . . .

The impact of the incumbent's campaign spending advantage on the election is also evident in the win-loss records of incumbents in contested elections from 1992 to 2000. In the rare cases in which challengers outspent incumbents (about 5 percent of contested elections in the 1990s), incumbents won about 61 percent

Table 2
Campaign Spending Disparities, Incumbents and Challengers in Contested
House Elections, 1992–2000

House Candidates	1992	1994	1996	1998	2000
Incumbent	86%	84%	83%	90%	93%
Challenger	14	16	17	10	7
Ratio	6.2 : 1	5.3 : 1	4.9 : 1	8.6 : 1	12.8 : 1

Note: The number of contested House elections with incumbents running was 316 in 1992, 330 in 1994, 358 in 1996, 303 in 1998, and 336 in 2000. The percentages are for the median contested district in the election.

of the time. When incumbents outspent their challengers by less than two-to-one—and only about 15 percent of contested elections fit this description—they won about 84 percent of the time. By far the most common situation was one in which the incumbent spent more than twice what his or her challenger spent. Four out of five contested races with an incumbent running in the 1990s involved this lopsided incumbent spending advantage. Incumbents won 98.5 percent of these elections. With a three-to-one spending advantage (which characterized about two-thirds of the elections), reelection is just about an absolute "lock."

The impact of the campaign spending advantage on the electoral fortunes of incumbents can perhaps be most graphically demonstrated by an "exception that proves the rule" case. Between 1992 and 2000 there were 1,643 contested House elections in which one of the candidates was an incumbent. In 905 of these (55 percent), the incumbent spent 84 percent or more of the total spending by the two major party candidates. These elections resulted in 904 incumbent victories and only one loss. The single exception, the exception that proves the rule, was the defeat of Democratic incumbent Dan Rostenkowski in the Fifth Congressional District of Illinois. Rostenkowski, serving in his eighteenth term, spent close to $2.5 million on the election to a mere $133,000 spent by his Republican opponent. The spending advantage of better than twenty-two to one for the incumbent was, however, not enough to save him from the fallout of a seventeen-count federal indictment on charges of "misuse of personal and congressional funds, extortion of gifts and cash, and obstruction of justice." This only goes to show that a lopsided campaign spending advantage does not buy an election, if you are under a seventeen-count federal indictment!

While some claim that money does not buy elections, there can be no doubt that at some point it does (at least if the incumbent is not on his or her way to federal prison). The typical election to the House is not one in which the incumbent spends twice or even three times what his or her opponent spends. It could not even be compared to an arms race in which both sides ratchet up spending to astronomical levels, though this happens in the few remaining competitive districts. In the typical election to the House in recent years the incumbent spends six to twelve times what the challenger spends. This is no arms race. . . . Incumbents are able to, and routinely do, drown out the opposition. The results are safe incumbents, very few competitive elections, very little electoral change in the composition of the House—in short, electoral stagnation. Some might argue that this reverses causes and effects, that the candidates who raise more money are better candidates, and that money has little independent effect. . . .

The Impact of Campaign Finance Reform

BCRA was enacted with the promise that it would break the stranglehold of money on the political process, that it would make money less important and reduce or eliminate the corrupting influence (real or perceived) of money that has tainted the democratic process. Will it live up to this billing with respect to opening up competition to incumbents and allowing for voters, when they feel the need, to register a real vote for change?

From one standpoint, one might expect that any reform would be an improvement on the current system. Competition in House elections has so seriously eroded that it would seem that there is no place to go but up. However, from another standpoint, it would be surprising if the campaign reform that was enacted had any beneficial effect in restoring competition. After all, the reforms were written with the intention of inhibiting the corrupting effects of big contributions and were not explicitly designed to make elections more competitive. Also, campaign finance reform was intended to eliminate soft money contributions to the political parties and restrict the impact of issue advocacy shadow campaigns funded by the independent expenditures of interest groups. The problems of an enlarged incumbency advantage and electoral stagnation are the results of a severe imbalance in *hard money* contributions to the candidates and not a consequence of either the huge influx of soft money into campaigns or the intrusion of issue advocacy ads funded by the independent expenditures of interest groups. Given the tremendous imbalance between incumbents and challengers in hard money, any other source of money in elections (including soft money and independent expenditures) would be welcomed as potentially helping challengers and increasing competition. It follows that any impediment to these alternative sources (such as BCRA) might not be helpful in revitalizing the process.

Whether intended to affect competition or not, four provisions of BCRA might have an impact on competitiveness: the elimination of soft money contributions to the political parties, the restrictions on issue advocacy ads in the weeks leading up to the election, the triggered increase in individual contribution limits for candidates facing high-spending, self-financed opponents (the "Millionaires' Amendment"), and the increased limits on hard money contributions by individuals to the candidates from $1,000 per election to $2,000 per election campaign.

Soft Money and Electioneering

While there is no doubt that political party soft money and nonparty expenditures on issue advocacy have grown enormously in recent election cycles, this "outside money" does not seem to have made much difference to competition levels. As we have seen, the district vote for a candidate can be quite fully explained without knowing how much soft money or independent expenditures were spent either for or against the candidate. Further, the rise in the incumbency advantage, the decline in competition, and the compression of seat change occurred well before the explosion in outside money. While it seems odd that the soft money and independent expenditure surges would not have had an effect on congressional competition (just because of their sheer magnitude), the distribution of the outside money spending may explain the absence of an effect. Both forms of outside money spending have been concentrated in the few remaining districts that are competitive rather than spread around to a larger set of races to make them competitive. This has the effect of producing a distorted and highly intense competition in a few districts. . . . [I]n most districts hard money disparities secure seats for incumbents and soft money spending apparently makes little difference. Thus, since the presence of party soft money and nonparty electioneering have had little to do with the rise of the incumbency advantage or the decline in competition, there is little reason to think that the elimination of soft money and restrictions on issue advocacy campaigning would appreciably reduce the advantage of incumbency or increase competition levels.

If anything, the elimination of soft money and the restrictions on electioneering might further solidify the incumbency advantage and maintain competition at anemic levels. . . .

Self-Financing Provisions

Another component of BCRA that might affect competition is the provision allowing for increased contribution limits once a self-financed candidate's spending exceeds a specified threshold.* . . . However, it should be noted here that self-financing works more to the advantage of challengers than incumbents. Incumbents are so well funded by others that they do not need to finance their own campaigns. Self-financing is thus an alternative source of campaign funds for some challengers that may offset the huge campaign financing advantage that incumbents otherwise enjoy. Any obstacle to self-financing or the effects of self-financing, such as those included in BCRA, would be to the detriment of competition in those few districts in which the challenger can afford to finance a viable campaign.

Raising Contribution Limits

The final provision of BCRA that might influence electoral competition is the increase in the limits on hard money contributions to candidates by individuals.[†] This change could work to the challengers' advantage (and restore some

*One provision in the new campaign finance law increases the ceiling for direct contributions to congressional candidates when they face "self-financed" candidates. Dubbed the "Millionaires' Amendment," the provision was pushed by incumbents worried about facing challengers with virtually unlimited funds at their disposal.

†Contributions by individuals to candidates was increased from $1,000 per election (primary, general election, or runoff) to $2,000 and indexed for inflation in the new campaign finance law.

competition) if those taking advantage of the liberalized limit are more evenly balanced in their contributions than the other sources of hard campaign monies (smaller contributors and PACs). On the other hand, this aspect of the reform would solidify the considerable advantage of incumbents if the big contributors are as biased in favor of incumbents as other contributors. To get an insight into the likely impact of the liberalization of the hard money contribution limits we can examine the extent to which incumbents and challengers have benefited in the past from individuals who contributed the maximum allowable under the old law. . . .

Have incumbents or challengers generally benefited more from the contributions of those who have given the maximum in the past? The figures are presented in Table 3 and are based on data provided to the Campaign Finance Institute by the Center for Responsive Politics. In examining individual contributions made in the 2000 election, it is clear that incumbents more than challengers have benefited from those who have made the maximum individual contribution. For our purposes, any contributor who gave a candidate at least $1,000 in the 2000 House elections is considered to have made the maximum contribution. In the 336 contested districts involving an incumbent in 2000, a total of 81,165 individuals gave at least $1,000 to a major party House candidate. Three-quarters of the candidates receiving these maxed-out contributions were incumbents (60,456 of the 81,165). The incumbent had more contributions from maxed-out contributors than the challenger in 304 (90.5 percent) of the 336 contested districts with an incumbent running.

This, in itself, is not surprising. Incumbents tend to receive more money from everyone. Even so, they fare particularly well among the big contributors. The median incumbent (in a contested election) received nearly $170,000

Table 3
House Incumbents' and Challengers' Receipts from Contributors of at Least $1,000 in the 2000 Election

Type of Candidates	Median in All Contested Elections (N = 336)		Median in Marginal Elections (N = 74)	
	Total from $1,000+ Contributors	Percentage of Total Receipts from $1,000+ Contributors	Total from $1,000+ Contributors	Percentage of Total Receipts from $1,000+ Contributors
Incumbents	$168,229	22.5	$340,013	25.7
Challengers	6,500	12.8	188,962	25.2

Note: Marginal elections are defined as those having two-party vote percentages within the 40 to 60 range.

from contributors who had maxed out, while the median challenger received $6,500—a ratio of almost twenty-six to one. From a different perspective, 22.5 percent of contributions to the typical incumbent were from these $1,000 plus contributors, while 12.8 percent of the typical challenger's contributions (a much lower base) were from these maximum contributors. Thus, with the big contributors allowed to give even more than in the past, incumbents should be the main beneficiaries. . . .

The bottom line assessment of the liberalized hard money contributions for individuals is that they will do virtually nothing to restore electoral competition in the overwhelming majority of districts. The most likely effect of liberalizing individual hard money contribution limits, instead, would be to entrench incumbents further by adding to their already considerable spending advantage.

Conclusion

At a November 7, 2002, meeting of the Commonwealth Club of California, in responding to a question about BCRA, campaign finance reform champion Senator John McCain said that "our reform threatens the political life of the incumbents." Although the focus of the reform was clearly directed at the issue of corruption rather than competition, McCain had made similar statements in the national media, prior to the law's passage, about BCRA being a threat to incumbency. This analysis indicates that Senator McCain's contention that BCRA poses a threat to incumbency is wrong. BCRA will probably leave incumbents unscathed and, if anything, will further reinforce their hold on their seats. . . .

Other defenders of BCRA admit that it is unlikely to restore competition, because it was never intended to have that effect. The purpose of campaign finance reform was only to reduce the corrupting impact, real or imagined, of contributions on the process—especially large contributions. It is too early to say how successful the reform will be in keeping large contributions out of the process, though it is quite likely that much of this money will find its way to the aid of its intended beneficiaries through one route or another.

It is not too early to say, however, that the promise of campaign finance reform to reduce the corrupting impact of money in the system will not be kept. It was a crucial mistake to see concerns about the corrupting influence of the campaign finance system and the anticompetitive effects of the campaign finance system as somehow separable. The issues are joined at the heart. Campaign contributions are potentially corrupting to the political process *because* campaign spending is so important to incumbents. Campaign spending is so important to incumbents because it allows incumbents effectively to buy their elections by outspending their opponents by huge margins. If money could not secure the election's result, it would lose much of its leverage over incumbents. Moreover, competitive elections are the linchpin in a defense against corruption. The real threat of a vengeful electorate is a valuable counter-weight to the temptations of corruption. The corruption issue of campaign finance is intrinsically intertwined with the competition issue. Since BCRA would appear to have failed or to have neglected the latter issue, it also risks failing on the former.

Questions for Discussion

1. Why is the lack of competition in congressional races so detrimental to democracy? What are some of the causes of it? What is the primary cause? Can you think of any ways campaign finance laws might be changed that would encourage genuine competition?
2. Campbell argues that "the corruption issue of campaign finance is intrinsically intertwined with the competition issue." Why is that so? Why is it difficult for Congress to address such a relationship?

7.4

Weaving the Tangled Web into Political Action

Dan Hellinger

In the spring of 2003, very few Americans had ever heard of ex-Vermont governor Howard Dean, a candidate for the Democratic nomination for president. His chances of success against far better known Democrats such as Senator John Kerry, ex-House Majority Leader Richard Gephardt, and Senator Joseph Lieberman, who had been the vice-presidential candidate in 2000, seemed remote. Yet by late fall 2003 Dean had emerged as the frontrunner among the contenders in the national polls, a position he held until right before the official primary/caucus season began in January of 2004. Although Dean did not eventually capture the nomination, his effort showed the potential of the Internet as an electioneering tool, especially during the early stages of a campaign.

As Dan Hellinger points out in this article, Dean utilized the Internet not so much in an effort to attract voters, but to build a well-funded, grassroots political organization characterized by energy and enthusiasm. The Dean campaign had the look of a spontaneous, insurgent operation that was appealing to activists, but central coordination behind the scenes characterized it as well. In Hellinger's view, Dean's approach has "revolutionized the way politicians will run for president in the future."

For more than a decade political communications specialists and computer geeks have predicted the Internet would became a major feature of campaigning, but for just as long, candidate websites have been little more than bells and whistles on campaign bandwagons.

Then came Howard Dean, Moveon.com, "meetups" and blogs. Today, no effective campaign can afford not to have a website.

Why this campaign? Why Dean?

The confluence of four factors is at work: the increased percentage of households with Internet access, the anti-war movement, the savvy of the Dean campaign staff and the synergetic way that the Internet can be linked to traditional campaign tactics.

Internet access in the United States has crossed a critical mass threshold. The 2000 census showed that 54 million households (51 percent) had one or more computers in the home. That was up from 42 percent in December 1998, and surely, the trend has continued.

Internet use continues to be skewed by class. Nearly 9-in-10 family households with annual incomes of $75,000 or more had at least one computer, and about 8-in-10 had at least one household member who used the Internet at home. Even among the less affluent, Internet use is growing. Among households below $25,000, nearly 3-in-10 had a computer and about 2-in-10 had Internet access.

The key, however, to effective electronic campaigning is not generating participation on the Internet but using the Internet to generate more traditional forms of political participation. Critical in this respect is that voting, working in campaigns, giving money to parties and candidates, especially in the primaries, is also heavily skewed toward the upper middle class and the wealthy, and grassroots activism is weighted toward the young. In other words, the demographics of Internet access and America's class-skewed culture of participation are synergistic.

Dan Hellinger is professor of political science at Webster University.

Dan Hellinger, "Weaving the Tangled Web into Political Action," *St. Louis Journalism Review* 33, no. 260 (October 2003): 22(2). Reprinted by permission.

In addition, as with other media, political communication via the Internet is a two-step process. Just as newspaper readers tend to influence less informed voters, those who seek public affairs information on the Internet tend to influence not only the less informed but the less connected. The importance of the Internet is not measured merely by census data.

Dean didn't invent Internet campaigning. His innovations have more to do with recognizing the potential of the anti-war movement's use of the Internet and its adaptability to national campaigning. Dean staffers were first and alone in recognizing the potential to capitalize on the work done by Moveon.com, a grassroots Internet organization formed originally to oppose President Clinton's impeachment. Move On used the Internet to gather signatures on an electronic petition urging Congress to censure Clinton for the Lewinsky scandal and then to "move on." Afterwards, Move On itself "moved on" to organize opposition to the war in Iraq. Dean campaigned to win (with a plurality, not a majority) a "primary" that Move On organized over the summer.

It was this campaigning and the existence of an already formidable campaign staff, backed by some early traditional fundraising, which helped Dean win the electronic primary.

Strictly on the issues, he might not have been the favorite. Carol Mosely Braun, Dennis Kucinich and Al Sharpton are all more closely aligned with the left tilt of Move On members on a number of issues, including gun control and social security. Like Dean, all vigorously opposed the Iraq War early-on. Only Dean, however, was ready to use the Internet to turn a symbolic vote with no impact on delegate counts into a launching point for a campaign with the appearance of a spontaneous movement. He not only had Internet innovators, but he had veterans of past Democratic presidential campaigns ready to raise funds and build a tangible campaign on the ground. The real genius of his campaign is the synergy between these two components.

Among the Democratic candidates, the Dean website (www.deanforamerica. com) is the most user-friendly and effectively linked to other elements of the campaign. It is the least cluttered, offering four immediate options. Part of the site is devoted to raising money, but the Dean pitch is unique in the way it links raising money to the candidate's campaign appearances. At rallies, Dean brandishes a baseball bat with which he intends to "bash" the Bush administration. Dean's site features a caricature of the candidate with a bar and a running tally of progress toward raising $5 million in contributions collected from visitors who click on the image. The idea is that collectively thousands of small contributions will empower the candidate to speak on behalf of average Americans.

"Dean for America" also features a graphic link for activists to participate in local "meetups." A "meetup" is a politician's version of "flash mobs." Flash mobs take place when a group of people in touch with one another on the Internet agree to meet at a certain time and place to carry out some silly, collective action. They constitute a form of guerrilla theater.

The page devoted to meetups on the Dean site allows visitors in each of hundreds of cities to nominate a place, usually a cafe or restaurant, to gather for a monthly session of "spontaneous" political talk. According to the Dean campaign, "Meetups are informal; it's peers talking to peers. Most meetups do have volunteer hosts that help make things go smoothly, but think of it as a casual get-together, not an official meeting." At these sessions, "chat, chew the fat, shoot the breeze, sling the bull, babble, cackle, chatter, gab, yak, yammer. No big whoop."

The reality is somewhat less spontaneous. The campaign is careful to post a suggested agenda (e.g., how to organize minorities more effectively). Anyone can nominate a place, but the Dean national campaign staff tallies votes and decides where gatherings are to take place. It is decentralized activism, but the registration process and coordination at the center make it more controlled than the idealized description.

If such participation in meetups is any gauge of grassroots enthusiasm and energy, Dean is way ahead in the cyberspace districts. Nationally, the Dean campaign had over 115,000 registered participants for October meetups. Local numbers were not posted, but seven different sites in the St. Louis area had been nominated as gathering points. Sen. John Kerry reported only 12,346 registered for his meetups. Richard Gephardt's website had 463 registrants.

However, it may not be only the early bird who gets the political worm on the net. Retired General Wesley Clark (www.clark04.com), only one week after announcing his candidacy, had 27,856 persons registered for his October meetups. Five St. Louis sites had been nominated. Dean may have been the first presidential candidate to use the Internet to become a national force, but Clark is showing how it can be used to catch up.

The Gephardt campaign has thrown its resources into more traditional political organizing in Iowa and now appears to be playing catch-up in cyberspace. In late September the campaign launched www.amiserablefailure.com, a site devoted to attacks on the Bush administration. Another link takes visitors to a page, www.DeanFacts.com, featuring "the governor in his own words." The intent is to diminish Dean's appeal to the left of the party by featuring conservative positions the governor has taken in the past on issues such as gun control and Social Security. The age of attack ads on the Internet has begun.

But "savvy" is hardly the word for Gephardt's web designers. For example, nothing annoys web surfers more than pop-up ads. Many computers now have programs to filter such ads out. However, every Gephardt page comes with a "pop-up" ad designed to guide surfers to the candidate's homepage.

The Gephardt site includes a link to a "virtual kitchen table." The candidate piously tells us, "I care about what you're saying around your kitchen table. I want to hear your thoughts, concerns and comments, and I am going to make sure that Bush, Cheney and the rest of Washington hear those concerns and act on them. I want your kitchen table conversations to once again focus on report cards and ballgames rather than on worries about money and health care."

All the major Democratic candidates feature "blogs," which are diaries featuring comments by the candidate or the campaign staff. Nothing better illustrates the Astroturf nature of Dean's Internet campaign than his blog, which features banal talk and banter among staffers. A truly spontaneous blog would include not only inspiring stories of the candidate's heroic efforts to "empower" the people, but also accounts of campaign snafus or spirited debates about the substantive issues.

Happy talk pervades the Dean blog. Consider this entry by Kate O'Connor, a Dean staffer, on Sept. 24: "Hi everyone! The Gov. and I are sitting in the green room at 'Good Morning America' in New York City (good muffins and pastries). Diane Sawyer just popped in to say hello! I just wanted you all to know that the Gov. will be on live at 7:10 a.m. So tune in!"

The Dean campaign is far from a spontaneous, insurgent operation, but it is hard to imagine that he could have surged into the lead in the race for the Democratic nomination without making effective use of the Internet. For this reason, while Dean is hardly a revolutionary politician, he has revolutionized the way politicians will run for president in the future.

Questions for Discussion

1. How did the Dean campaign link the Internet to more traditional campaign tactics?
2. Were the demographics of Internet access (where users tend to be primarily of higher socioeconomic-educational status) an asset or a liability to the Dean campaign?

Chapter 8

The Mass Media

Information is the lifeblood of a democratic system, and the communication of information is essential to democratic politics. Citizens need trustworthy, diverse, and objective information to perform their electoral role adequately. Decision makers need reliable information about the values, preferences, and opinions of citizens to respond intelligently to them. The mass media play a crucial role in the relationship between citizens and their government. Yet their potential impact on political life leaves many people feeling ambivalent.

On the one hand, the mass media have the potential to help the nation realize its democratic possibilities. They can expand the range of public debate and broaden the attentive audience, which creates an informed public. If they perform as a watchdog over elected officials, political accountability can be greatly improved.

On the other hand, the mass media's potential to propagandize and to manipulate the public could undermine the democratic process. In *Politics in the Media Age*, Ronald Berkman and Laura W. Kitch point out that even in the nineteenth century some people were worried that "by seeking the sensational and simplifying political matters," the mass media could "divert the attention of the masses, arouse irrational passions, and lower the level of political debate." In this century, government management of the news during both world wars exposed the danger that entire populations could be swayed. Government regulation of radio and television in our own period, as well as control over many of the sources of the news, raises concerns that the mass media are at best dependent on, and at worst captives of, the very institutions they scrutinize. The increasing concentration of media ownership, particularly in the last fifteen years, suggests that diverse political information is hard to come by.

It is not surprising that media critics are found at both ends of the political spectrum. Social conservatives claim that violence and sexually suggestive material on television have undermined the American family and contributed to a decline in morals. Social liberals assert that television's depiction of women and minorities perpetuates unflattering stereotypes and limits social progress. Economic conservatives worry that the media's focus on business abuses and tight-fisted bankers will undermine the capitalist system. Economic liberals bemoan the fact that the media can never be a force for economic justice and equality because they draw their revenue from commercial sources.

Of course, when our nation was founded there was no such thing as the mass media. The newspapers that existed were partisan forums, directed toward narrow groups of elite supporters. Not until the Jacksonian era of the late 1820s and 1830s did American politics develop its mass character and the first mass circulation newspapers came into being.

Today the mass media are a fact of life. Most of what we know about politics and government comes from the media. A. C. Nielsen reports that 98 percent of American families own at least one television set and that the nation has more radios than people. Few of us acquire political information from other people; instead, strangers decide what information most of us receive.

Television is particularly pervasive. By the time the average American reaches eighteen years of age, he or she has probably spent more time in front of a TV set than in a classroom (roughly 15,000 hours). Television is highly credible because it utilizes both sight and sound. Although television is primarily an entertainment medium, many programs have either explicit or implicit political content. News programs and documentaries are obviously political, and entertainment shows that deal with, say, the police or education have some underlying orientation toward the institution in question. Even a show such as "Sesame Street" reveals strong values about politically relevant subjects such as race relations. Advertisements too are full of politically relevant content, particularly in the stereotypes they convey.

Because there are so many potential influences on political behavior and values, it is difficult to assess what effect such factors have. The mass media's impact is often inferred from their content, but the relationship is difficult to pin down. The one apparent truism is that the media exert the least influence when they attempt to affect people's views and preferences directly, especially through such devices as political endorsements. In 1936, for example, Republican Alf Landon was endorsed by over 80 percent of the daily newspapers in the country, but Democrat Franklin Roosevelt achieved one of the biggest electoral landslides in U.S. history.

Media impact appears to be strongest in ambiguous, unstructured situations in which individuals have little prior information. Because most people know little about most political subjects, the media can set agendas, not so much by telling the public what to think as by telling it whom and what to think about. A good example is the presidential nomination process. By focusing citizens' attention on the actions of certain individuals and particular issues, the media can confer status (one candidate is "the strong frontrunner") and create disadvantage (another candidate "has little experience"). Audiences learn not only what the campaign issues are but how much importance to attach to them.

Research on the subject has yielded mixed results, suggesting the media are neither as benign as their supporters have argued nor as damaging as many critics have claimed. We need to distinguish among the various types of media and to specify the conditions under which they do influence political orientations and behavior. Their effect will remain controversial, as the selections in this chapter exemplify.

In the first selection, Joshua Meyrowitz makes a strong case that the electronic media have greatly affected our perceptions of political leadership, making it difficult for Americans to find leaders they respect and trust. The final two selections deal with media issues after the 9/11 terrorist attacks. Scott L. Althaus looks at where Americans got their news after 9/11, as he attempts to determine whether or not the crisis had a lasting impact on the public's news habits. He finds that within months Americans' attention to the news had returned to levels found before the devastating attacks and was again focused on domestic rather than foreign policy issues. Finally, Robert S. Pritchard examines media coverage in the Iraq War. The use of "embedded" journalists for the first time appeared to lessen the inherent tension between journalists and the military that typically occurs during wartime.

8.1

Lowering the Political Hero to Our Level

Joshua Meyrowitz

Image has always been important in politics. Whether an individual is viewed as honest or untrustworthy, hard-working or lazy, tough or mean has much to do with that person's political success. Moreover, the use of the electronic media, particularly television, has dramatically altered how the public views political figures and has especially affected the image of elected leadership.

According to Joshua Meyrowitz, before the invention of the electronic media, the public held political leaders in awe. Politicians' images were based on mystification and careful management of public impressions. Political figures operated at a great distance from the public, who had limited access to them.

Radio and television, however, "reveal too much and too often." Television in particular appears to make politicians available for public inspection. This clouds the distinction between politicians' "onstage" and "backstage" behavior. Their human frailties are highlighted, as TV cameras show them sweating or reacting with anger or tears. National politicians no longer have the opportunity to test their presentations. They appear to the whole nation at the same time, and so they are more likely to make mistakes. Ill-chosen words or the inevitable inconsistencies that arise during a campaign are exaggerated, and call into question a politician's honesty and competence.

In the end, "the familiarity fostered by electronic media all too easily breeds contempt." According to Meyrowitz, mystification is necessary for an image of strong leadership, yet disclosure eliminates mystery. As a result, few contemporary political leaders are universally revered in their own lifetime.

All our recent Presidents have been plagued with problems of "credibility." Lyndon Johnson abdicated his office; Richard Nixon left the presidency in disgrace; Gerald Ford's "appointment" to the presidency was later rejected by the electorate; Jimmy Carter suffered a landslide defeat after

Joshua Meyrowitz is a professor of communication at the University of New Hampshire.

being strongly challenged within his own party; and even the comparatively popular Ronald Reagan has followed his predecessors in the now familiar roller coaster ride in the polls.*

We seem to be having difficulty finding leaders who have charisma and style and who are also competent and trustworthy. In the wish to keep at least one recent leader in high esteem, many people have chosen to forget that in his thousand days in office, John Kennedy faced many crises of credibility and ac- cusations of "news management."

During the 1990 campaign, *Newsweek* analyzed recent political polls and con- cluded that "perhaps the most telling political finding of all is the high degree of disenchantment voters feel about most of the major candidates."[1] Of course, every horse race has its winner, and no matter how uninspiring the field of candi- dates, people will always have their favorites. The obsession with poll percentage points and the concern over who wins and who loses, however, tend to obscure the more fundamental issue of the decline in the image of leaders in general.

There are at least two ways to study the image and rhetoric of the presidency. One is to examine the content and form of speeches and actions; in other words, to look at specific strategies, choices, and decisions. Another method is to examine the situations within which Presidents perform their roles. This second method requires a shift in focus away from the specific rhetorical strate- gies of individual politicians and toward the general environment that sur- rounds the presidency and is therefore shared by all who seek that office.

This [selection] employs the latter method to reinterpret the causes of the political woes of some of our recent national politicians and to shed some light on our leadership problem in general. I suggest that the decline in presidential image may have surprisingly little to do with a simple lack of potentially great leaders, and much to do with a specific communication environment—a com- munication environment that undermines the politician's ability to behave like, and therefore be perceived as, the traditional "great leader."

The Merging of Political Arenas and Styles

Before the widespread use of electronic media, the towns and cities of the country served as backstage areas of rehearsal for national political figures. By the time William Jennings Bryan delivered his powerful "cross of gold" speech to win the nomination for President at the 1896 Democratic convention, for example, he had already practiced the speech many times in different parts of the country.

The legendary oratory of Bryan and the treasured images of many of our other political heroes were made possible by their ability to practice and modify

---

*Ronald Reagan, especially after 1982 and before 1987, enjoyed levels of public regard that were exceptional among recent presidents and presidential contenders.

their public performances. Early mistakes could be limited to small forums, minor changes could be tested, and speeches and presentations could be honed to perfection. Politicians could thrill many different crowds on different days with a single well-turned phrase. Bryan, for example, was very fond of his closing line in the 1896 speech ("You shall not press down upon the brow of labor this crown of thorns, you shall not crucify mankind upon a cross of gold")—so fond, in fact, that he had used it many times in other speeches and debates. In his memoirs, Bryan noted his early realization of the line's "fitness for the conclusion of a climax," and after using it in smaller public arenas, he "laid it away for a proper occasion."[2]

Today, through radio and television, the national politician often faces a single audience. Wherever the politician speaks, he or she addresses people all over the country. Major speeches, therefore, cannot be tested in advance. Because they can be presented only once, they tend to be relatively coarse and undramatic. Inspiring lines either are consumed quickly or they become impotent clichés.

Nineteenth century America provided multiple political arenas in which politicians could perfect the form and the substance of their main ideas. They could also buttress their central platforms with slightly different promises to different audiences. Today, because politicians address so many different types of people simultaneously, they have great difficulty speaking in specifics. And any slip of the tongue is amplified in significance because of the millions of people who have witnessed it. Those who analyze changing rhetorical styles without taking such situational changes into account overlook a major political variable.

Many Americans are still hoping for the emergence of an old-style, dynamic "great leader." Yet electronic media of communication are making it almost impossible to find one. There is no lack of potential leaders, but rather an overabundance of information about them. The great leader image depends on mystification and careful management of public impressions. Through television, we see too much of our politicians, and they are losing control over their images and performances. As a result, our political leaders are being stripped of their aura and are being brought closer to the level of the average person.

The impact of electronic media on the staging of politics can best be understood by analyzing it in relation to the staging requirements of *any* social role. . . . Regardless of competence, regardless of desire, there is a limit to how long any person can play out an idealized conception of a social role. All people must eat, sleep, and go to the bathroom. All people need time to think about their social behavior, prepare for social encounters, and rest from them. Further, we all play different roles in different situations. One man, for example, may be a father, a son, a husband, an old college roommate, and a boss. He may also be President of the United States. He needs to emphasize different aspects of his personality in order to function in each of these roles. The performance of social roles, therefore, is in many ways like a multistage drama. The strength and clarity of a particular onstage, or "front region," performance depend on isolating the audience from the backstage, or "back region." Rehearsals, relaxations, and behaviors from other onstage roles must be kept out of the limelight. The need to shield backstage behaviors is especially acute in the performance of roles that rely heavily on mystification and on an aura of greatness—roles such as those performed by national political leaders.

Yet electronic media of communication have been eroding barriers between the politician's traditional back and front regions. The camera eye and the microphone ear have been probing many aspects of the national politician's behavior and transmitting this information to 225 million Americans. By revealing to its audience both traditionally onstage and traditionally backstage activities, television could be said to provide a "sidestage," or "middle region," view of public figures. We watch politicians move from backstage to onstage to backstage. We see politicians address crowds of well-wishers, then greet their families "in private." We join candidates as they speak with their advisors, and we sit behind them as they watch conventions on television. We see candidates address many different types of audiences in many different settings.

By definition, the "private" behaviors now exposed are no longer true back region activities precisely because they are exposed to the public. But neither are they merely traditional front region performances. The traditional balance between rehearsal and performance has been upset. Through electronic coverage, politicians' freedom to isolate themselves from their audiences is being limited. In the process, politicians are not only losing aspects of their privacy—a complaint we often hear—but, more important, they are simultaneously losing their ability to play many facets of the high and mighty roles of traditional leaders. For when actors lose parts of their rehearsal time, their performances naturally move toward the extemporaneous.

The sidestage perspective offered by television makes normal differences in behavior appear to be evidence of inconsistency or dishonesty. We all behave differently in different situations, depending on who is there and who is not. Yet when television news programs edit together videotape sequences that show a politician saying and doing different things in different places and before different audiences, the politician may appear, at best, indecisive and, at worst, dishonest.

The reconfiguration of the stage of politics demands a drive toward consistency in all exposed spheres. To be carried off smoothly, the new political performance requires a new "middle region" role: behavior that lacks the extreme formality of former front region behavior and also lacks the extreme informality of traditional back region behavior. Wise politicians make the most of the new situation. They try to expose selected, positive aspects of their back regions in order to ingratiate themselves with the public. Yet there is a difference between *coping* with the new situation and truly *controlling* it. Regardless of how well individual politicians adjust to the new exposure, the overall image of leaders changes in the process. The new political performance remains a performance, but its style is markedly changed.

Mystification and awe are supported by distance and limited access. Our new media reveal too much and too often for traditional notions of political leadership to prevail. The television camera invades politicians' personal spheres like a spy in back regions. It watches them sweat, sees them grimace at their own ill-phrased remarks. It coolly records them as they succumb to emotions. The camera minimizes the distance between audience and performer. The speaker's platform once raised a politician up and away from the people—both literally and symbolically. The camera now brings the politician close for the people's inspection. And in this sense, it lowers politicians to the level of their audience. The camera brings a rich range of expressive information to the audience; it highlights politicians' mortality and mutes abstract and conceptual rhetoric. While verbal rhetoric can transcend humanity and reach for the divine, intimate expressive information often exposes human frailty. No wonder old style politicians, who continue to assume the grand postures of another era, now seem like clowns or crooks. The personal close-up view forces many politicians to pretend to be less than they would like to be (and, thereby, in a social sense, they actually become less).

Some people were privy to a sort of "middle region" for politicians before television. Through consistent physical proximity, for example, many reporters would see politicians in a multiplicity of front region roles and a smattering of back region activities. Yet, the relationship between politicians and some journalists was itself a personal back region interaction that was distinguished from press accounts to the public. Before television, most of the news stories released were not records of this personal back region relationship or even of a "middle region." The politician could always distinguish for the press what was "on" the record, what was "off" the record, what should be paraphrased, and what must be attributed to "a high government official." Thus, even when the journalists and the politicians were intimates, the news releases were usually impersonal social communications. Print media can "report on" what happens in one place and bring the report to another place. But the report is by no means a "presentation" of the actual place-bound experience. The print reporters who interviewed Theodore Roosevelt while he was being shaved, for example, did not have an experience "equivalent" to the resulting news reports. Because private interactions with reporters were once distinct from the public communications released in newspapers, much of a politician's "personality" was well hidden from the average citizen.

Private press-politician interactions continue to take place, but electronic media have created new political situations that change the overall "distance" between politician and voter. With electronic coverage, politicians lose a great deal of control over their messages and performances. When they ask that the television camera or tape recorder be turned off, the politicians appear to have something to hide. When the camera or microphone is on, politicians can no longer separate their interaction with the press from their interaction with the public. The camera unthinkingly records the flash of anger and the shiver in the cold; it determinedly shadows our leaders as they trip over words or down stairs. And, unlike the testimony of journalists or of other witnesses, words and actions recorded on electronic tape are impossible to deny. Thus, while politicians try hard to structure the *content* of the media coverage, the *form* of the coverage itself is changing the nature of political image. The revealing nature of television's presentational information cannot be fully counteracted by manipulation, practice, and high-paid consultants. Even a staged media event is often more personally revealing than a transcript of an informal speech or interview. When in 1977, President Carter allowed NBC cameras into the White House for a day, the result may not have been what he intended. As *The New York Times* reported:

> Mr. Carter is a master of controlled images, and he is obviously primed for the occasion. When he isn't flashing his warm smile, he is being soothingly cool under pressure. But the camera ferrets out that telltale tick, that comforting indication of ordinary humanity. It finds his fingers nervously caressing a paperclip or playing with a pen. It captures the almost imperceptible tightening of facial muscles when the President is given an unflattering newspaper story about one of his sons.[3]

Some politicians, of course, have better "media images" than others, but few can manipulate their images as easily as politicians could in a print era. The nature and the extent of this loss of control become even clearer when back and front regions are not viewed as mutually exclusive categories. Most actions encompass both types of behavior. In many situations, for example, an individual can play a front region role while simultaneously giving off covert back region cues to "teammates" (facial expressions, "code" remarks, fingers crossed behind the back, etc.). . . . Because expressions are constant and personal, an individual's exuding of expressions is a type of ongoing back region activity that was once accessible only to those in close physical proximity. Thus, the degree of control over access to back regions is not simply binary—access/no access—but infinitely variable. Any medium of communication can be analyzed in relation to those personal characteristics it transmits and those it restricts.

Print, for example, conveys words but no intonations or facial gestures; radio sends intonations along with the words but provides no visual information; television transmits the full audio/visual spectrum of verbal, vocal, and gestural. In this sense, the trend from print to radio to television represents a shrinking shield for back region activities and an increase in the energy required to manage impressions. Further, Albert Mehrabian's formula for relative message impact—7% verbal, 38% vocal, and 55% facial and postural—suggests that the trend in media development not only leads to revealing more, but to revealing more of more. From the portrait to the photograph to the movie to the video close-up, media have been providing a closer, more replicative, more immediate, and, therefore, less idealized image of the leader. "Greatness" is an abstraction, and it fades as the image of distant leaders comes to resemble an encounter with an intimate acquaintance.

As cameras continue to get lighter and smaller, and as microphones and lenses become more sensitive, the distinctions between public and private contexts continue to erode. It is no longer necessary for politicians to stop what they are doing in order to pose for a picture or to step up to a microphone. As a result, it is increasingly difficult for politicians to distinguish between the ways in which they behave in "real situations" and the ways in which they present themselves for the media. The new public image of politicians, therefore, has many of the characteristics of the former backstage of political life, and many once informal interactions among politicians and their families, staff, reporters, and constituents have become more stiff and formal as they are exposed to national audiences. . . .

Most politicians, even Presidents, continue to maintain a truly private backstage area, but that area is being pushed further and further into the background, and it continues to shrink both spatially and temporally.

Writing and print not only hide general back region actions and behaviors, they also conceal the act of producing "images" and messages. Presidents once had the time to prepare speeches carefully. Even seemingly "spontaneous" messages were prepared in advance, often with the help of advisors, counselors, and family members. Delays, indecision, and the pondering of alternative solutions in response to problems were hidden in the invisible backstage area created by the inherent slowness of older media. Before the invention of the telegraph, for example, a President never needed to be awakened in the middle of the night to respond to a crisis. A few hours' delay meant little.

Electronic media, however, leave little secret time for preparations and response. Because messages *can* be sent instantly across the nation and the world, any delay in hearing from a President is apparent. And in televised press conferences, even a few seconds of thought by a politician may be seen as a sign of indecisiveness, weakness, or senility. More and more, therefore, the public messages conveyed by officials are, in fact, spontaneous.

Politicians find it more difficult to hide their need for time and for advice in the preparation of public statements. They must either reveal the decision process (by turning to advisors or by saying that they need more time to study the issue) or they must present very informal, off-the-cuff comments that naturally lack the craftsmanship of prepared texts. The new media demand that the politician walk and talk steadily and unthinkingly along a performance tightrope. On either side is danger: A few seconds of silence or a slip of the tongue can lead to a fall in the polls.

The changing arenas of politics affect not only the perceptions of audiences but also the response of politicians to their own performances. In face-to-face behavior, we must get a sense of ourselves from the ongoing response of others. We can never see ourselves quite the way others see us. On videotape, however, politicians are able to see exactly the same image of themselves as is seen by the public. In live interactions, a speaker's nervousness and mistakes are usually politely ignored by audiences and therefore often soon forgotten by the speaker too. With television, politicians acquire permanent records of themselves sweating, stammering, or anxiously licking their lips. Television, therefore, has the power to increase a politician's self-doubt and lower self-esteem.

Highly replicative media are demystifying leaders not only for their own time, but for history as well. Few leaders are universally revered in their own lifetime. But less replicative media allowed, at least, for greater idealization of leaders after they died. Idiosyncrasies and physical flaws were interred with a President's bones, their good deeds and their accomplishments lived after them. Once a President died, all that remained were flattering painted portraits and the written texts of speeches. An unusual speaking style or an unattractive facial expression was soon forgotten.

If Lincoln had been passed down to us only through painted portraits, perhaps his homeliness would have faded further with time. The rest of the Lincoln legend, however, including Lincoln's image as a dynamic speaker, continues to be preserved by the *lack* of recordings of his unusually high, thin voice, which rose even higher when he was nervous. Similarly, Thomas Jefferson's slight speech impediment is rarely mentioned. Through new media, however, the idiosyncrasies of Presidents are preserved and passed down to the next generation. Instead of inheriting only summaries and recollections, future generations will judge the styles of former Presidents for themselves. They will see Gerald Ford lose his balance, Carter sweating under pressure, and Reagan dozing during an audience with the Pope. Presidential mispronunciations, hesitations, perspiration, and physical and verbal clumsiness are now being preserved for all time.

Expressions are part of the shared repertoire of all people. When under control and exposed briefly, expressive messages show the "humanity" of the "great leader." But when they are flowing freely and constantly, expressive messages suggest that those we look up to may, after all, be no different from ourselves. The more intense our search for evidence of greatness, the more it eludes us.

There is a demand today for two things: fully open, accessible administrations and strong, powerful leaders. Rarely do we consider that these two demands may, unfortunately, be incompatible. We want to spy on our leaders, yet we want them to inspire us. We cannot have both disclosure *and* the mystification necessary for an image of greatness. The post-Watergate fascination with uncovering cover-ups has not been accompanied by a sophisticated notion of what will inevitably be found in the closets of all leaders. The familiarity fostered by electronic media all too easily breeds contempt.

Notes

1. David M. Alpern, "A Newsweek Poll on the Issues," *Newsweek*, 3 March 1980, 29.
2. William Jennings Bryan and Mary Baird Bryan, *The Memoirs of William Jennings Bryan, Vol. I*, Reprint of 1925 edition (Port Washington, New York: Kennikat, 1971), 103.
3. John J. O'Connor, "TV: A Full Day at the White House," *The New York Times*, 14 April 1977.

Questions for Discussion

1. Why does the author believe that "old style" political heroes are no longer possible?
2. It has been said that American voters prefer a "candidate of the people but not like the people." What does this mean? Would Meyrowitz agree with this assertion?

★ 8.2

American News Consumption During Times of National Crisis

Scott L. Althaus

Although there is evidence that the events of 9/11 sparked changes in the civic attitudes of citizens (see selection 5.4), it is far less clear that the terrorist attacks have resulted in changes in the civic behavior of citizens. In this selection, Scott L. Althaus attempts to determine whether or not the attention Americans pay to news of national and international affairs has changed since the attacks. He compares the viewing habits of the news audience during and after the 1990–1991 Persian Gulf War with that of the most recent crisis to determine whether the respective crises altered the levels of attention paid to the news.

Althaus documents a number of changes in news consumption, including the decline of attention paid to network news broadcasts and the increasing reliance on cable news sources. He suggests Americans appear to increasingly gravitate toward media that specialize in the "latest" news while reducing their reliance on new sources that emphasize in-depth reporting and provide context.

Within months after 9/11, Americans' attention to the news had returned to levels found before the terrorist attacks. Concern with the economy had displaced the war on terrorism as the most important problem facing the country in

Scott L. Althaus is an Associate Professor of Political Science and an Associate Professor of Communications at the University of Illinois at Urbana-Champaign.

Scott L. Althaus, "American News Consumption During Times of National Crisis," *PS: Political Science and Politics* (September 2002): 517–521. Reprinted with permission of Cambridge University Press.

the polls. And many Americans had come to view the war on terrorism as a domestic rather than a foreign policy issue. Althaus believes that the impact of 9/11 "seems to have left Americans' collective appetite for news largely undisturbed."

Have 9/11 and the ensuing war on terrorism sparked a reinvigoration of civic life in the United States? Opinion surveys show dramatic changes in the political attitudes of American citizens. . . . However, it remains unclear whether these changed attitudes have resulted in higher levels of civic activity.

If Americans today are more engaged in civic life than they were a year ago, we should see evidence of this change in the amount of attention they pay to news of national and international affairs. Unlike many other civic behaviors, watching or reading the news is relatively low in opportunity costs. Because the choice between viewing a *Simpsons* rerun or a national news broadcast is made so easily, the size of the audience for national news should be fairly sensitive to shifts in the perceived importance of public affairs. And like the proverbial canary in the mine shaft, changing levels of civic-mindedness are likely to be seen first in lower-cost behaviors like paying attention to news before they are seen in higher-cost activities like volunteering or joining a group.

This article looks at changes in the size of American news audiences during the 1990–91 Persian Gulf Crisis and the more recent period surrounding the 9/11 attacks. Like the current situation, the Persian Gulf crisis started suddenly, when Iraq launched a surprise invasion of Kuwait on August 2, 1990. Since there are clear starting points for both national crises, comparing the percentage of adults watching television news broadcasts before and after each precipitating event should show whether the respective crises prompted changes in levels of popular attention to the news.

Audience Trends for Network News Broadcasts

Weekly television-ratings data collected by Nielsen Media Research are available for both cases. Since the television audience grows in winter months, the time of year in which a precipitating event occurs can influence the apparent impact of the crisis. For this reason, I collected weekly ratings data from each case over 16-month periods starting the first week of January in the year the crisis began and ending the last week of April in the following year. To measure the combined total audience for nightly national news programs, I combined ratings for ABC's *World News Tonight*, CBS's *Evening News*, and NBC's *Nightly News*. To ease interpretation across the two cases, I translated these ratings data into the percentage of American adults that were tuning in to the nightly news.

One striking feature of these trends (Figure 1) is that the evening news audience today is only about half as large as it was a decade before. During the 1990–91 period, between 23% and 33% of American adults watched nightly network news broadcasts, depending on the time of year. Since January 2001, Nielsen data put the total size of nightly news audiences at between 11% and 16% of American adults (not counting the week of 9/11). It is unclear whether today's total audience for all forms of public-affairs content is any smaller than it was a decade before, but if it is, the falloff is likely to be slight. Instead, the once-larger broadcast news audience of 1990–91 is today spread out across a wider range of news products, with cable, the Internet, primetime news magazines, and local television news each attracting sizable portions of a national news audience that once was shared mainly by the three evening news programs.

Because news audiences have become increasingly fragmented, absolute differences in the percentage of adults watching network news during each crisis period are less telling than the relative changes in audience size within each trend. If we begin our analysis immediately before each precipitating event and follow the trends over the next several months, the two cases appear to reveal different patterns of audience response. In the Persian Gulf crisis, the Iraqi invasion of Kuwait immediately produced a four-percentage-point spike in the

Figure 1
Weekly Percentage of American Adults Watching Nightly Network News Broadcasts

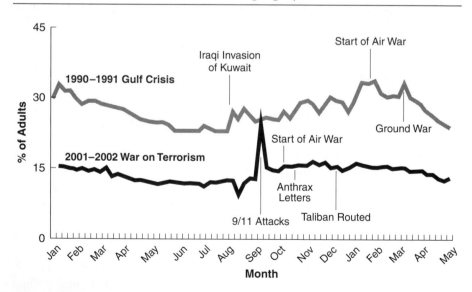

Source: Nielsen ratings data compiled from various media sources. These trends report the combined weekly audience for ABC's *World News Tonight*, CBS's *Evening News*, and NBC's *Nightly News*.

American news audience. The nightly news audience then grew steadily over the fall months as the American military buildup in Saudi Arabia signaled a looming confrontation with Iraq. Nearly a third of American adults were directly exposed to one of the three nightly news broadcasts in the weeks leading up to and immediately following the start of the air war, which began on January 17, as war against Iraq was vigorously debated in Congress and then witnessed live on television. The news audience shrank somewhat in early February before experiencing a three-percentage-point jump during the week of ground combat, which began on February 23. This rapid victory over Iraqi ground forces was followed by an abrupt turn away from the news, and the nightly audience dropped nearly 10 percentage points over the eight weeks following the close of the ground campaign.

Eleven years later, the tragedies of 9/11 had the immediate effect of more than doubling the size of the evening news audience, from 13% of American adults in the week of September 3–9 to more than 26% in the week of September 10–16. Nielsen Media Research later estimated that 79.5 million viewers were tuning into any of 11 broadcast or cable networks showing news coverage on the night of 9/11. As impressive as this level of attention seems, the January 2001 Super Bowl attracted about the same number of viewers. Moreover, the evening news audience just as swiftly contracted to 15% of American adults in the week of September 17–23 and never rose more than one-and-a-half percentage points above that level in the following seven months. In contrast to frequent event-driven surges in news attention throughout the Persian Gulf crisis, news attention in the post-9/11 U.S. held quite stable at about four percentage points above pre-9/11 levels for several months before declining steadily after the start of the new year in 2002. By the middle of April 2002, the size of the evening news audience had returned to the previous July's level of just 13% of adults.

When thus interpreting these postcrisis trends using the immediate precrisis period as a benchmark, it appears that the Persian Gulf crisis produced a gradual mobilization of adults into the television news audience, but that the present war on terrorism generated a smaller shock to the size of American news audiences that started decaying soon after it began. During the Persian Gulf crisis, the average size of the evening news audience grew by 13.8 million persons between the last week of July 1990, and the first week of January 1991. During the war on terrorism, the growth in the evening news audience between these two weeks was only half as large, amounting to 7.4 million more audience members in 2002.

However, this interpretation of postcrisis growth in the news audience requires us to ignore the left-hand side of Figure 1. The longer-term trends leading up to each precipitating event call into question whether either of these national crises fundamentally increased the size of the news audience. Once we take into account the cyclical shifts in the size of television news audiences, the apparent changes prompted by each crisis become harder to distinguish from normal seasonal movement. It seems impressive at first glance that 32.7% of American adults were following the evening news in a typical week during the critical month of January 1991, up from 23.2% for July 1990. However, this number loses some of its luster when we recognize that the evening news audience was nearly as large—31.4% of adults—in the previous January. Given the seasonal variation in the size of news audiences, a more appropriate way of measuring the impact of national crises is to calculate the size of the news audience after the precipitating event compared to its size from the same period in the previous year.

This comparison paints a very different picture. During the Gulf Crisis an average of approximately 2.4 million more adults per day were watching evening news broadcasts in the first four months of 1991 compared to the first four months of 1990. The same comparison for the war on terrorism produces a mean difference of just less than 900,000 more audience members per day in 2002 than in 2001. Seasonal-adjusted growth in the news audience was nearly three times as large during the Persian Gulf crisis as during the current war on terrorism, but in both cases the magnitude of growth was rather small, amounting to 0.4% of adults in 2001–2 and 1.3% in 1990–91. Seen from this perspective, the clearest impact of the Iraqi invasion of Kuwait was in increasing the amount of weekly variance around the seasonal mean rather than in shifting the mean itself. Similarly, 9/11 appears to have accelerated the seasonal growth curve for the evening news audience during the fall of 2001 without producing a substantive shift in its average size.

Where Else Are Americans Getting Their News?

The preceding analysis begs the question of whether Americans are still getting their news primarily from network news broadcasts. If people are turning instead to other sources for public affairs information, then an analysis of those sources might shed a more flattering light on levels of civic engagement in post-9/11 America.

According to surveys conducted by the Pew Center for the People and the Press (Figure 2), there have been some notable changes in the mix of news media used by Americans since 9/11. The questions from which I obtained these data allowed respondents to name up to three media as primary sources of news, so these survey data capture a potentially broad range of media involvement. In the first week of September 2001, newspapers were the most commonly mentioned source of information about public affairs. By the second week of January 2002, cable television news had become the most-cited news source, mentioned by over half of respondents.

All of the other pre- and post-9/11 differences are individually within the margins of sampling error for these surveys, but collectively they reveal some common patterns. First, there has been a decline in the percentage of Ameri-

Figure 2

Where Have People Been Getting Most of Their News About National and International Issues?

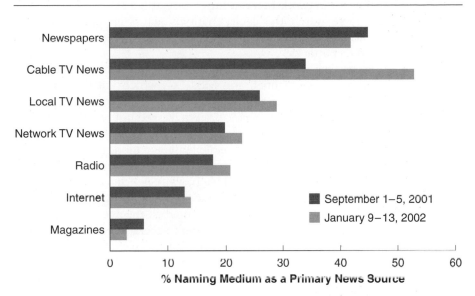

Source: Pew Center for the People and the Press surveys. Since up to three answers were accepted per respondent. . . , the sum for each survey adds up to well over 100%.

cans turning to print news since 9/11. . . . . Second, the declining reliance on newspapers and news magazines seems to be offset by a shift toward electronic news sources. Aside from the obvious jump for cable television news, slightly higher percentages of Americans reported in January 2002 that they turn to local television news, network television news, radio, and the Internet for public affairs information. Taken together, these two changes suggest that Americans now seem to be more attentive to media that specialize in delivering the "latest" news even as they reduce their reliance on sources of news that emphasize in-depth reporting and providing context for understanding the current crisis. But how many people are actually tuning in to cable?

Audience Trends for Cable News

The Pew surveys suggest that many more people now rely on cable news outlets than before 9/11, and Nielsen ratings data confirm that the cable news audience has experienced a sizeable gain. Since cable news outlets provide continuous public affairs programming, Nielsen measures cable news audiences differently than network news audiences. Instead of estimating the average number of viewers for a particular program, Nielsen estimates for each cable channel the average number of viewers per minute in an entire day. While not directly comparable to network news ratings, since these averages mask how many different people watch the cable channels across an entire day, the change in these ratings before and after 9/11 clarifies how cable audiences have responded to the terror attacks.

Figure 3 shows the combined average audience per minute for the Cable News Network, Fox News Channel, and MSNBC, which are the top three cable news channels. For the six months leading up to September 2001, the combined audience for the three cable channels averaged just less than 0.4% of American adults, or about 800,000 persons. For the period from September 2001, through March 2002, the average cable audience more than doubled to nearly 1% of American adults, or approximately two million people. Figure 3 shows that the changes in the size of the cable news audience followed a similar course as that for the broadcast news audience. After a fourfold increase from 800,000 persons in August to 2.7 million in September, the average cable news audience gradually declined in size over the next several months. By March 2002, the combined per-minute audience for the three cable channels averaged 1.5 million viewers. While this is just half the size of the peak audience in September, it is also twice the size of the combined cable audience from a year before, indicating that cable news has indeed retained an appreciable number of new viewers.

Although Figure 3 appears to suggest that the cable audience remains far smaller than the broadcast news audience (and media reporters frequently interpret these numbers in this way), it is possible that the cumulative cable news audience—that is, the total number of unique viewers—could include a fairly large proportion of American adults on a given day. For example, the average per-minute cable news audience for November 2001, was 905,000 persons for CNN and 747,000 for Fox News. But the number of different people who watched at least 15 minutes of programming at some point during that same month was 93.4 million for CNN (or about 46% of American adults) and 58.5 million for Fox (or about 29% of American adults).

However, it is unclear whether these cable viewers are getting a mix of news comparable to that received by network audiences. A recent content analysis of primetime news programming on CNN, Fox, and MSNBC during late January of this year (News Hour 2002) found that cable news shows focused on a small number of "headline" stories, and that much of the primetime programming took the form of personal interviews or panel discussions rather than traditional news reporting. If the past behavior of cable audiences is any guide to the present, it is also likely that these new viewers constitute an irregular audience for cable news, tuning in to catch up with developing stories or breaking news, but otherwise relying primarily on noncable sources for their daily diet of news.

Figure 3

Average Percentage of American Adults Watching Cable News, March 2001 to March 2002

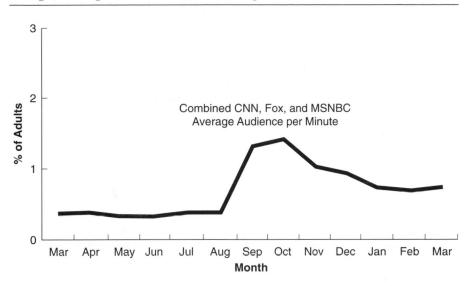

Source: Nielsen ratings data.

Consequences of Public Disengagement from the War on Terrorism

If 9/11 has founded a new era of civic-mindedness in the U.S., it seems to have left Americans' collective appetite for news largely undisturbed. The size of the network television news audience grew only slightly, and newspaper readership continued to decline after 9/11. While the average size of the cable news audience has doubled, it remains a small fraction of American adults, and the audiences for both network and cable news have diminished with each passing month.

It is too soon to identify any long-term implications for the public's limited attention to the early stages of this war, let alone to speculate whether the trends of the last year are likely to continue into even the near future. However, two consequences of the public's disengagement are already apparent.

First, many Americans consider the war on terrorism to be a domestic issue rather than a foreign-policy issue. The Pew Research Center for the People and the Press conducted a survey in January 2002, which asked two slightly different versions of the same question. The first read: "Right now, which is more important for President Bush to focus on: domestic policy or the war on terrorism?" A second version changed "the war on terrorism" to "foreign policy," but was otherwise identical. If Americans think about the war on terrorism as a foreign-policy issue, the percentages in both versions of the question should be nearly identical. Yet, the public's responses could hardly be more different. To the first version of the question, 33% of respondents answered domestic policy and 52% named the war on terrorism. These numbers were reversed in the second version, where 52% chose domestic policy and only 34% said foreign policy.

Question-wording effects of this magnitude—generating an 18-point shift in surveyed opinion—typically indicate that the mass public has insufficiently reasoned through its opinions. It is certainly understandable why many Americans see the war on terrorism as a domestic issue. Most paid close attention to news of the terrorist attacks in New York, Pennsylvania, and Washington, DC, but have been less attentive to the news during the Bush administration's subsequent military actions and diplomatic initiatives overseas. Further analysis of this wording effect by Pew researchers revealed that the tendency to think of the war on terrorism as a domestic policy issue was closely related to level of formal education: college graduates gave essentially the same mix of opinions in response to both versions of the question, while those with a high school education or less demonstrated the greatest sensitivity to these wording changes. Since people with higher levels of education also tend to be more attentive to the news, the tendency to see the war on terrorism as a matter of domestic policy may be a direct outgrowth of public disengagement from the news in the aftermath of 9/11.

A second consequence is that while opinion surveys reveal consistently high levels of support for American military action against countries and organizations suspected of sponsoring terrorism, the roots of this support may not run deep. This possibility is suggested in recent trends from Gallup polls that ask Americans to name "the most important problem facing the country today." Figure 4 shows how terrorism leaped onto the public's agenda following 9/11: nearly half of Americans named terrorism as the country's most important problem in an October Gallup poll (no data are available for the month of September). However, the ensuing months saw a rapid falloff in the percentage of the public concerned about terrorism, so that by January 2002, fewer than a quarter of Americans named terrorism as the country's most important problem. In contrast, unease with the state of the economy came to rival terrorism as the top issue of public concern in the first quarter of 2002. Given the impact of a shifting public agenda on evaluations of George Bush Sr.'s job performance in the aftermath of the Persian Gulf war, it is notable that the declining importance of terrorism and the increasing importance of economic concerns track George W. Bush's declining job-approval rating. Although President Bush has made it clear that the allied military campaign against terrorism is just beginning, fewer people today are likely to be evaluating him on the basis of his performance as commander in chief.

The rapid decline in public concern about terrorism is a sign that American support for U.S. military involvement abroad may be less firm than it seems. If

Figure 4

Percentages Naming Terrorism and the Economy as the "Most Important Problems,"
January 2001 to March 2002

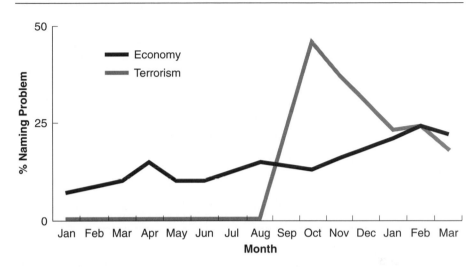

Source: Surveys by the Gallup Organization.

this American resolve is more closely tied to the dramatic events of 9/11 than
to a new appreciation for the complexities of the post-9/11 geopolitical landscape, it becomes increasingly difficult to predict how Americans will respond
to new developments or crises in the coming years of this war.

It remains to be seen whether this public disengagement has resulted from
the stunning successes of the U.S. military campaign in Afghanistan, or from the
secrecy in which the war on terrorism has necessarily been shrouded. But the
public's steady retreat from opportunities for news exposure should give pause
to military and political leaders pondering the next step in this solemn undertaking.

Questions for Discussion

1. What news sources do Americans use to learn about national and international issues? What sources are becoming more important? Less important?
   What factors underlie the increased importance of cable news sources in the
   aftermath of 9/11? What news sources do you use to learn about national
   and international issues?

2. Why have many Americans come to see the war on terrorism as a domestic rather than a foreign policy issue? What are the implications, if any, of this for public support for military involvement abroad?

 8.3

The Pentagon Is Fighting—and Winning—the Public Relations War

Robert S. Pritchard

Access to information about government activity is crucial in a democracy where the public relies upon the media watchdogs to aggressively uncover and transmit newsworthy material. The tendency of government, on the other hand, is to present itself in the best possible light and to obscure from public scrutiny anything that might create a negative image. This inherent tension between the media and the government is most pronounced regarding national security and military issues. Wars, in particular, severely test the relationship between government—especially the military—and the media; the recent Iraq War was no exception.

In this selection, Robert S. Pritchard surveys the history of media-military relations in the United States and how they have evolved. During some wars the press acted as vitual cheerleader for the military, often being forced by censors to suppress information that would cast the military in a bad light. At other times, the media was given so much free rein that it came to be seen by some as undermining the U.S. effort, such as in Vietnam, where a majority of military officers credited American journalists as the major factor for the U.S. defeat.

During the Iraq War, an imaginative effort was made to both accommodate the desire of journalists to cover the war with as little government restriction as possible and the desire of military commanders to pursue their objectives unimpeded and without risk to the safety of the troops. For the first time "embedded" journalists were assigned to and traveled with individual military units with only a minimum of prohibitions on what could be reported.

Robert S. Pritchard is Assistant Professor of Journalism at Ball State University.

Robert S. Pritchard, "The Pentagon Is Fighting—and Winning—the Public Relations War," *USA Today* Magazine, Vol. 132, No. 2698: 12(4). Reprinted by permission of Robert S. Pritchard, APR, Captain, U.S. Navy (Ret.).

After years of fighting with the media, the Pentagon can finally, and proudly, claim it has won the public relations war in Iraq. At least it has so far as its policy on how the media covers America's wars is concerned—for now.

Critics called it "the ultimate reality show," but what we witnessed was truly revolutionary coverage of armed conflict unprecedented in the annals of the military-media relationship. As Steve Bell, Ball State University telecommunications professor and veteran international news correspondent for ABC News, which included covering Vietnam, put it in April, 2003, "What we are living and watching is extraordinary. We have never fought wars like this."

Indeed, this news coverage was more closely akin to the way World War II was reported, although it was dramatically more radical a concept. Military censors were very much alive and well during World War II, and journalists' reports were still subjected to field press censorship. There was no censorship in Iraq. World War II correspondents were assigned to press camps, while the embedded journalists were assigned to individual units in Iraq. The manner of reporting on the individual soldier, sailor, airman, Marine, and Coast Guardsman in the Iraq war was similar to that of Ernie Pyle, who became famous with his endearing and perceptive reports on the average American serviceman.

As Pyle wrote in one of his columns, "I love the infantry because they are the underdogs. They are the mud-rain-frost-and-wind boys. They have no comforts, and they even learn to live without the necessities. And in the end they are the guys that wars can't be won without." We saw these modern-day "underdogs" up-close-and-personal, beamed from the desert sands of Iraq, 24 hours a day, seven days a week. . . . However, unlike World War II, we saw it all "live."

In another sense, there are similarities in the coverage of this conflict and how the Vietnam War was covered, except that reporters didn't just "hop a ride" to the war zone, cover the story, and head back to Saigon for a "cold one" at the end of the day. Film reports from Vietnam had to be flown out of the country before they could be shown a day or two later. Nonetheless, television brought the war into America's living room for the first time. Similarly, in the early days of the Iraqi conflict, we were glued to our TV screens, only now we were watching endless hours of desert rolling passively by, waiting for that instant of "breaking news." . . . "An awful lot of people have become addicted to this kind of 'Live from Baghdad' reporting." . . .

To place the scope of the Pentagon's—and the public's—victory in the proper context, a brief synopsis of the military-media relationship is in order. The road has been a rocky one.

Prior to the Mexican-American War in 1846, the press operated freely as long as their views corresponded to local views. Information gathering was haphazard and usually based on other publications, letters, and government proclamations. There were no reporters in the field. Military leaders were concerned, however, that some news undermined the war effort, although they were powerless to control it.

By 1846, technology and newsgathering had improved to the point where re-porters were competing daily for news. The telegraph and Pony Express offered quicker transmission of news, and correspondents routinely deployed with the military. George W. Kendall, founder of the New Orleans Picayune, was known to report from the front lines and spent time with generals. Newspaper ac-counts were still up to 10 days old, despite efforts like Kendall's and the arrival of the telegraph. "Camp newspapers" came into being to keep the troops in-formed (a prototype for later military public affairs efforts). Civilian newspapers were known to use these camp papers as a primary source.

Reporting on military conflict became quite problematic during the Civil War (1861–65). The telegraph made it possible for the first time to report mili-tary action in real time. Government and military leaders, both North and South, did all they could do to contain these reports. Pres. Abraham Lincoln, though, saw the press as a means to maintaining popular support and so did all he could to keep it unfettered. However, he, too, had to make difficult deci-sions with regard to press freedoms as he faced the venom of the Copperhead newspapers, which vehemently denounced the war and governmental and mili-tary leadership. "Must I shoot a simple-minded soldier boy who deserts, while I must not touch a hair of a wily agitator who induces him to desert . . . ?" he would write.

The Spanish-American War in 1898 was marked by two significant factors—substantial advances in technology and "yellow journalism." Printing presses were motorized; the transatlantic cable had been laid; and telegraph lines ran the width and breadth of the nation. Meanwhile, Joseph Pulitzer's New York World was locked in mortal combat with William Randolph Hearst's New York Journal. Some claim the war itself was the result of machinations the two en-terprises engaged in simply to drum up sales and publicity for their papers. In any event, the atmosphere lent itself to severe government restrictions, with the banning of reporters in combat zones and the closing of cable offices. Nonetheless, information continued to be "leaked" to the public, making gov-ernment retaliation largely ineffective.

20th-Century Wars

The most-restrictive period in the military-media relationship was World War I. Initially, this was not so. The Creel Committee created by Pres. Woodrow Wilson upon America's entry into the war in April, 1917, and headed by former newspaper editor George Creel, mounted an impressive program to mobilize public opinion in support of the war effort. Creel's agency was governed by a set of regulations drawn up by the State, War, and Navy departments that placed restrictions on publication of militarily sensi-tive information like troop movements, sailing schedules, anti-aircraft or harbor defenses, identification of units dispatched overseas, etc. The press voluntarily abided by these regulations.

Then Congress—prompted primarily by a national patriotic fervor reaching the level of wartime hysteria, and concern over internal hostile and disloyal activites as well as the effects of propaganda—enacted the most-onerous restrictions in history with passage of the Espionage Act in 1917 and the Sedition Act of 1918. The Espionage Act forbade publication of any information that might remotely be regarded as providing aid to the enemy. The Sedition Act prohibited any criticism of "the conductor actions of the United States government or its military forces, including disparaging remarks about the flag, military uniforms, [and] similar badges or symbols. . . ." Reporters had to be credentialed as either accredited or visiting correspondents, swear an oath to write the truth, put up a $10,000 bond, and sign an agreement to submit all correspondence, except personal letters (which were censored elsewhere in the system), to the press officer or his assistant.

The high point in military-media relations—until the present—was World War II. This was probably due to the nature of the conflict and the fact that patriotism was the order of the day. The Office of War Information and the Office of Censorship were created by Pres. Franklin D. Roosevelt in 1941. The latter issued detailed guidelines for what could not be published. Included in the list of restrictions were location, identification, and movement of units, ships, and aircraft; war production and supplies; weather forecasts and temperatures in major cities; casualties; and even locations of art treasures and archives.

Accreditation was used by the military to control access to the battlefield. Correspondents received a press pass from the War Department and a passport from the State Department and, once deployed, were assigned to "press camps" that were attached to regular military forces. All administration, communication, and briefings were handled by the press camps. Typically, these consisted of about 50 correspondents, and each moved with a field army through Western Europe.

Accredited correspondents wore officer's uniforms without rank insignia. Visitors could wear civilian garb, but had to receive special permission to travel in the war zone, were accompanied by an escort officer, and had to stick to a fixed itinerary.

Most of the engagements in the Pacific theater of operations were maritime, and Naval Chief of Operations Ernest J. King placed severe restrictions on military correspondents, frequently holding unfavorable reports until they could be paired with favorable ones. It was also far easier to control the media because correspondents were obliged to travel aboard U.S. naval vessels and relied on the ship's communications equipment to transmit reports. Eventually, the Navy got better at the release of information, but it was only after journalists, editors, and publishers complained enough about the Navy's performance that the Office of War Information stepped in to force changes.

Gen. Douglas McArthur was even more restrictive with the correspondents traveling with him. He required multiple layers of censorship and frequently pressured reporters to change the tone of their stories to show the troops—and especially him—in a more-favorable light.

Initially during the Korean War (1950–52), there were no restrictions on either media access to the war zone or content. The media covering this "police action" adopted their own guidelines and voluntarily censored themselves. Predictably, this led to security leaks and confusion. Critics were quick to point out that the negative reporting was eroding public opinion in the U.S. The Overseas Press Club eventually petitioned the Defense Department to impose censorship so the media would know what its limits were.

Thus, a system similar to that existing in World War II was instituted, with censors reviewing each story. Reports on inferior U.S. equipment, corruption in the South Korean government, and/or food shortages and panics were forbidden. McArthur once again took things even further by disallowing stories that he (or his censors by proxy) considered would be harmful to morale or cause embarrassment to the U.S., its allies, or the United Nations.

In Vietnam (1965–73), the media was free to move about the country, taking advantage of military transportation when it was available, and there was no censorship. Stories, photographs, and film were unimpeded by security review. For the media, this was the high-water mark in its relations with the military. Ultimately, though, a majority of military officers blamed the media for its "defeat" in that conflict, so Vietnam also provided the low-water mark in that relationship.

This opinion that the media lost the Vietnam War became deeply engrained in some of these officers and stayed with them as they rose through the ranks. The result was their ability to convince the Reagan Administration in 1983 to ban media access to operations in Grenada. The military was able to operate without regard to press scrutiny, which equated to success in the eyes of those senior commanders who distrusted the media. Criticism by the media was significant and vociferous, and rightly so. The good news is this tension drove both sides to find a better way to do things.

In 1984, Chairman of the Joint Chiefs of Staff John W. Vessey, Jr. appointed retired Major Gen. Winant Sidle to head a panel to study the issue. Vessey invited participation from the heads of major media organizations, such as the American Newspaper Publishers Association, American Society of Newspaper Editors, National Association of Broadcasters, and Radio-Television News Directors Association.

Their report, released in August, 1984, contained eight recommendations that were intended to ensure news media coverage of American military operations "to the maximum degree possible consistent with mission security and the safety of U.S. forces." One of the key recommendations of the Sidle Report, as it became known, endorsed media pools in combat zones when other methods of providing access were not feasible. A second notable recommendation was that access to military operations would be governed, as a basic tenet, by voluntary compliance with security guidelines or ground rules established by the Defense Department. Violation of them meant exclusion from further coverage of the operation.

The first test of these new roles was the invasion of Panama in 1989. Unfortunately for the media, the Pentagon's planning and response were poorly organized, much too slow, and did not involve the local military commanders upon whose support the public affairs effort was dependent. As a result, the media were not able to cover that operation until the key phases of the conflict were over.

Improving Relations

After a very critical self-evaluation, the Pentagon went back to the drawing board and, under the able and energetic guidance of Assistant Secretary of Defense Pete Williams, completely revamped its Defense Department (DOD) National Media Pool procedures. Williams got former Associated Press Pentagon reporter Fred Hoffman involved in analyzing the media aspects of Panama. Chairman of the Joint Chiefs of Staff Colin Powell also emphasized to his commanders the importance of including public affairs planners as part of the overall operations preparation, and this emphasis dramatically improved attitudes about the media within the military.

Against that backdrop, the Pentagon and the media worked hard for the six months prior to the liberation of Kuwait in 1991 (Operation Desert Storm) to organize the influx of nearly 1,600 journalists into the combat zone and keep them fed with information. The coverage of the Gulf War was the most comprehensive to date, but was not without its difficulties. The media complained of their treatment, particularly with two aspects of the operation the requirement that there be a public affairs escort with them wherever they went and the military's overreliance on pooling. Once again, representatives of media organizations and the Pentagon worked together to develop the DOD Principles for News Media Coverage of DOD Operations, which was published in 1992. This simply reiterated what had previously been published, but served to reinforce the importance of the military commanders' personal involvement in planning for media coverage of future conflicts.

During the operations in Somalia (1993–94) and Haiti (1995), the lessons learned were successfully applied. The level of cooperation between the military and the media was robust, and preparation for news coverage had the full attention of everyone in the planning process from the commander on down.

The relationship continued to improve as the military services sought to find innovative ways to accommodate the media. The Air Force went so far as to embark correspondents in B-52 bombers conducting combat missions during

the air war in Yugoslavia. For the first time, media deployed with special operations forces while on sensitive missions in Afghanistan.

Yet, there were still shortcomings to this inventiveness. Too few correspondents could take advantage of these opportunities, the media complained. The
solution often advanced by the news organizations was free and unfettered coverage of the war zone.

So, in a move as bold as any in the history of military-media relations, the
Assistant Secretary of Defense for Public Affairs, Torie Clarke, and her staff
prevailed on the Bush Administration, with the support of military commanders, to embed journalists with combat units, should it become necessary to
take action in Iraq. They would be able to report "real time" without censorship or security review. A handful of prohibitions had to be agreed to, all commonsense, such as not providing specific locations and movements of troops,
but reporters would be right in the thick of things, basically free and unfettered.

Preparation was intensive, and more than 600 journalists completed the required one-week course to familiarize them with military operations and equipment—a kind of miniboot camp. The media began to do some planning of its
own, which contrasted greatly with their response to preparations for the first
Gulf War.

When the first troops crossed the line of departure into Iraq, on their way to
Baghdad, correspondents went with them. Some of the most-enduring images
of those first hours and days were reporters . . . reporting live from HUMVEEs
as they rolled through the Iraqi desert. Reporters were getting shot at along
with their units. It wasn't just American journalists who crossed over with the
troops. Reporters from around the world traveled with them. Even al-Jazerra
had embedded with correspondents. Washington Post columnist Howard Kurtz
called it "old-fashioned war reporting, but with razzle-dazzle technology that
brings it into our living rooms in real time."

Allowing this kind of war coverage was a huge risk for the Pentagon, but it
has come with an equally large payoff. As independent observers, the media
have corroborated the U.S. and Allied military's adherence to the Geneva
Convention and the roles of war, as well as Saddam and his henchmen's lack
thereof. If and when the smoking gun of evidence of chemical and biological
weapons is found, the media will be there to convince the world the campaign
was justified.

Perhaps the biggest payoff is what this has done for the military in terms of
how it is now viewed by both the media and the public. Through the up-close-
and-personal view of America's fighting men and women provided by embedded
correspondents, the credibility of the individual soldier, sailor, airman, Marine,
and Coast Guardsman has dramatically improved. We have been witness to the
restraint they have exercised, sometimes with tragic consequences to themselves. We have seen the compassion and caring, as our troops have ignored
their own comfort by giving away food and clothing and sometimes ignoring
their own safety to pull an innocent victim out of the middle of the action.

Challenges

However, this news coverage significantly raises the ante as well as the challenges. Offered as evidence of the most-basic challenge this kind of coverage presents is the "poignant perspective" provided by Nancy Chamberlin, mother of Marine Jay Aubin, when she talked with NBC's Tom Brokaw about her son's death in a helicopter crash in the first week of the war.

"I truly admire what all of the network news and all the new technology is doing today to bring it into our homes," she said. "But for the mothers and the wives who are out there watching, it is murder. It's heartbreak. We can't leave the television. Every tank, every helicopter, 'Is that my son?' And I just need you to be aware that this technology is—it's great—but there are moms, there are dads, there are wives out there that are suffering because of this."

Brokaw's response was: "That is so eloquent, and it's so appropriate, and we will do whatever we can to reinforce that message repeatedly. . . . Behind those computer-generated graphics, there is a life at risk." Clearly, the media—and the public—need to stay focused on and be sensitive to the wideranging impacts this kind of coverage can have.

The real-time nature of embedded coverage and journalistic reports and images from the battlefield occasionally outpaced the Pentagon's reporting and confirmation process, especially with regard to next of kin in the event of a death or serious injury. Reporters in the thick of things and the attendant risk of someone being injured or killed "live" raise the stakes for both the media and the military. This has the potential for devastating consequences on families and loved ones and tends to erode the Pentagon's credibility.

On March 23, 2003, Secretary of Defense Donald H. Rumsfeld found himself face-to-face with this challenge as Bob Schieffer, host for CBS's "Face the Nation," decided to air breaking video made available by al-Jazeera showing American POWs as well as Iraqis displaying dead U.S. soldiers. In other cases, the military lagged behind the power curve in confirming incidents and answering questions based on those instant images. Clearly, we need to come to grips with what this immediacy means, especially in terms of impact on families of dead, injured, and captured U.S. soldiers. Further, both the military and the media need to analyze their respective reporting procedures and priorities more thoughtfully to find greater balance.

Inexperienced correspondents or those caught up in the emotion of the moment risk unwittingly divulging classified information. This is perhaps the most-serious challenge this new style of reporting creates for the media and the military. While the annals of the military-media relationship record a very small number of actual serious breaches of operational security, this risk is far too important to gloss over and must continue to be addressed.

Real-time reporting by embedded journalists risks presenting a false impression of the conflict. The ongoing phases of the war may be interpreted and presented by those without training in military strategy and planning as too lengthy, irrational, disjointed, [or] haphazard when, in fact, there is a clear military objective and plan for the sequencing and timing of actions.

Indeed, we only need look back at some of the early reporting to gather evidence of this concern. A Wall Street Journal editorial in March, 2003, pointed out that "the camera does lie, even unintentionally. The depressing weekend news—a firefight that caught our troops here, the American POWs there, the fragging of U.S. troops apparently by one of their own—are all real things that happened. But while the camera can record them accurately, the one thing it cannot do is provide the larger perspective. So a single ugly battle can mislead about the pace of the broader war."

Howard Kurtz commented in his March 27, 2003, online column Media Notes that, "If anything, the reports about individual units under attack may create the mistaken impression that the war effort is going to hell in a handbasket, rather than rolling inexorably toward Baghdad." On March 25, after just five days of conflict, the Los Angeles Times said, "The abrupt surge in bad news has given rise to questions: Has the U.S. battle plan come unraveled? Was it misconceived from the start?"

Columnist Charles Krauthammer put a fine edge on this point when he exclaimed, "Good grief. If there had been TV cameras not just at Normandy, but after Normandy, giving live coverage of firefights at every French village on the Allies' march to Berlin, the operation would have been judged a strategic miscalculation, if not a disaster."

The impact of embedded reporting on public opinion needs to be carefully studied. It has been said that images of Somalis dragging the bodies of dead American servicemen through the streets of Mogadishu hastened our departure from that country. ABC's Ted Koppel, in a report a few days before the Iraqi war, said, "What's totally unpredictable, of course, is the impact that all this coverage will have back at home and around the world." One pundit opined that this experiment in war coverage has the capacity to turn public opinion against the war, [à] la Vietnam, on "fast forward." This is more of a concern for the Pentagon and the Administration, however, for, as we've seen before, a flawed policy will not withstand much scrutiny, although it certainly demands further investigation.

A lesser, but equally destructive, consequence of this type of coverage is the potential for it to become an unintended distraction. Much of military training is based on habit patterns, and when they are broken, mistakes are made. Journalists represent potential, unintended "habit-breakers" unless they are quick to grasp the cultural imperatives of the military and its method of training.

Perhaps not a direct result of embedded correspondence as much as a shift in cultural expectations, another aspect of our national "fast forward" thinking is the concept of "victory on fast forward." The euphoria over the liberation of Baghdad lasted eight hours—literally a standard nine-to-five workday. Instant technology and instant reporting bring an expectation of instant gratification. This isn't just a problem for the Pentagon. The media have tended to largely ignore the phenomenon, claiming it is out of their hands. Now, it's time for them to be part of the solution.

Finally, a serious deficiency demonstrated in covering the Iraqi conflict with embedded journalists is the lack of "strategic" reporting that came out of the war. Almost all of the reporting was tactical, which is not surprising since the embedded correspondents had only the local unit perspective to share. The media recognize this shortcoming. The Philadelphia Inquirer noted a week into the war that, "For the last week, we have had the unprecedented experience of watching a war unfold in real time. But analysts maintain that television's ride-along reporters are too close to the story they are covering. And the unfiltered torrent of images they are sending back—NBC anchor Tom Brokaw has likened it to 'drinking from a fire hydrant'—had been overwhelming, leaving viewers confused about the course of the conflict." This leaves an opportunity for the Pentagon to add value to embedded reports, but there needs to be a fundamental shift in thinking from providing perspective (some would say "spin") to providing strategic context and being aggressive from the outset in doing so. Rumsfeld was mostly reactive in his attempts to place military actions in context.

The experiment has been largely and historically successful. The Pentagon certainly should be proud of its achievements, but this isn't a time to gloat. Much needs to be done to refine the current concept of embedding journalists. . . .

Questions for Discussion

1. What are some of the advantages of having "embedded" journalists report on a military conflict? What are some of the disadvantages?
2. Pritchard contends that real-time reporting by embedded journalists in wartime may give a false impression of the conflict. Why? Is it possible to avoid this problem?

Chapter 9

INTEREST GROUPS

The United States has always been a nation of joiners, and more interest groups are active in our governmental affairs than in any other nation. Still, Americans have never been comfortable with special-interest politics. Ever since James Madison first warned of the "mischiefs of faction" in *The Federalist,* No. 10 (the first selection in this chapter), citizens, politicians, and scholars have debated the role of special interests in policymaking.

The conflict between special interests and the public interest has been especially evident when the government has seemed to be functioning ineffectively. During the Progressive era, for example, the influence of railroads, oil companies, and insurance firms drew the attention of scholars and the popular press; consequently, regulation of lobbyists became a major aim of the reformers. During the New Deal, in contrast, relatively little attention was paid to special interests. The dominant view of scholars during and after that period was pluralism—the belief that competition among groups is healthy for democracy.

By the 1960s, however, it had become obvious that such competition was highly distorted; some special interests almost always lost in the political process, and others—especially those with money, access, or inside information—usually won. The interest group universe had a blatant representational bias, as well; some interests, such as business, were well represented in the process, whereas others (minorities, the poor, and consumers) were seriously underrepresented.

Renewed attention to the role of interest groups grew stronger in the 1970s and 1980s. The tremendous expansion in the number of interest groups, the decline of political parties, and the heightened visibility of interest groups in the electoral and policymaking processes appeared to parallel government's inability to deal with economic and social problems. From the inability of Congress and the president to work together during the Carter years to the $200 billion deficits and influence-peddling scandals of the Reagan presidency, interest groups have been accused of being at the heart of the problem of contemporary government.

Depending on one's perspective, the United States is either blessed or cursed with many special interests. The constitutional guarantees of free speech, free association, and petition are basic to group formation. Because political organizations often parallel government structure, federalism and the separation of powers have encouraged a multiplicity of groups as interests organize around various local, state, and national access points. Societal cleavages also help foster interest group development. Differences in economics, climate, culture, and tradition, and in racial, ethnic, and religious backgrounds, create ready-made interests within American life. Finally, our cultural values may well play a role. As Alexis de Tocqueville observed more than 150 years ago, values such as individuality and personal achievement underlie the propensity of citizens to join groups.

There is a difference, however, between the existence of special interests and the emergence of special interest groups—associations of individuals who share attitudes or goals and attempt to influence public policy. In a simple society there is little need for interest groups, because people have no political or economic reason to organize when they work only for their families. Not until the mid- to late-nineteenth century did interest groups start to appear regularly on the American political scene. As the nation became economically and socially complex, new interests were created and old ones redefined. Farming, for example, became specialized, commercialized, and dependent on other economic sectors. U.S. trade policies appeared to affect southern cotton farmers and midwestern grain producers, and it soon made sense for such people to organize.

Many political scientists argue that new interest groups are a natural consequence of a growing society. Groups develop both to improve individuals' positions or to protect existing advantages. For example, mobilization of business interests in the 1960s and 1970s often resulted from threats posed by consumer groups and environmentalists. The post–World War II era, especially since 1960, has witnessed a dramatic increase in the number of special interests that have organized for political purposes. New groups have crowded into areas such as business and agriculture, which already were well organized, but the most rapid expansion has taken place in areas that were poorly organized or not organized at all. Women, blacks, environmentalists, consumers, and other nonoccupational interests are now actively represented by groups.

Such changes have been so extensive that even the term *interest group* no longer seems appropriate. Much of the business lobbying in Washington, for example, is now done by representatives of individual companies as well as by "peak" associations, such as the National Association of Manufacturers, which represent groups of companies. Many institutions, even colleges and universities, have their own lobbyists. Some of the so-called groups operating in Washington are not mass membership organizations governed by a board of elected directors; one study of public interest groups discovered that 40 percent of the groups had fewer than one thousand members and 30 percent had no members at all. A large number of active groups are staff organizations, composed of a handful of individuals who are funded by foundation resources. Some are totally private concerns, like Ralph Nader's organization Public Citizen, which claims to lobby for all consumers.

Lobbying has become a growth industry. From 1975 to 1985, the number of registered lobbyists in Washington doubled; the number of attorneys more than tripled between 1973 and 1983, rising to more than 37,000. Washington now abounds with lobbying firms, which contract with companies and groups to represent their interests. Some have more than fifty clients, ranging from individual companies to entire nations. Some plan and manage political campaigns, as well as advise specialized interests.

New techniques of influence have also appeared as lobbyists have embraced technology. Orchestrated mass mailings to legislators or the president can be put in motion within minutes by some of the more sophisticated lobbies. The Campaign Finance Acts of 1971 and 1974 have made it possible for almost all groups to create political action committees (PACs) to coordinate financial contributions to candidates for public office. In 2000, over 4,500 PACs were registered.

To provide a sense of the controversy over interest groups and a flavor of today's environment, this chapter includes a diverse range of selections. *The Federalist,* No. 10, is a classic statement of the dilemma special interests posed to the framers, who sought to control the detrimental effects of factions, especially "majority factions." Jeffrey H. Birnbaum surveys the history of lobbying in America, focusing on some of the scandals that have given lobbyists an unsavory reputation. He suggests there is much improvement in how lobbyists conduct themselves today.

The final two selections look at the contemporary interest group universe and the influence of organized interests in both the electoral and policy processes. Theda Skocpol examines the factors underlying the decline of membership federations over the past half century and the recent proliferation of "associations without members" and attempts to assess the meaning of such trends for American democracy. In the final selection, Allan J. Cigler and Burdett A. Loomis argue that the scope of interest group activity at the beginning of the twenty-first century is much broader than in the past, as groups have come to dominate political communication in the nation. Politics, in the authors' view, has come to resemble marketing, in that well-funded organized interests have the advantage in this age of information.

9.1

The Federalist, No. 10

James Madison

There is an inherent tension in any democratic society. Liberty demands that citizens be allowed to pursue their special interests, even if those interests are offensive and selfish; yet the pursuit of special interests may conflict with the public interest. The nation's founders were well aware of this dilemma and directed many of their efforts toward constructing a government that respected personal freedom but was capable of acting for the collective good.

This paper is perhaps the best statement of what the founders thought about special interests or factions. At base they feared all special interests, especially "majority factions," which had the potential to tyrannize the system. Madison realized, however, that special interests "are sown In the nature of man" and any attempt to eliminate them would involve the destruction of liberty, a remedy "worse than the disease." Madison's solution was to limit the effects of factions by promoting competition among them and designing a government with an elaborate system of checks and balances to reduce the power of any single, strong group, whether made up of a majority or a minority of citizens.

Among the numerous advantages promised by a well constructed Union, none deserves to be more accurately developed than its tendency to break and control the violence of faction.* The friend of popular governments, never finds himself so much alarmed for their character and fate, as when he contemplates their propensity to this dangerous vice. He will not fail therefore to set a due value on any plan which, without violating the principles to which he is attached, provides a proper cure for it. The instability, injustice and confusion introduced into the public councils, have in truth been the mortal diseases under which popular governments have every where perished; as they continue to be the favorite and fruitful topics from which the adversaries to liberty derive their most specious declamations. The valuable improvements made by the American Constitutions on the popular models, both ancient and

---

*Madison used the term *faction* to denote any special interest, including parties. Although interest groups did exist, they were not organized in the sense in which we think of them today. Interest "groups" representing special interests were not common until after the Civil War.

modern, cannot certainly be too much admired; but it would be an unwarrantable partiality, to contend that they have as effectually obviated the danger on this side as was wished and expected. Complaints are every where heard from our most considerate and virtuous citizens, equally the friends of public and private faith, and of public and personal liberty; that our governments are too unstable; that the public good is disregarded in the conflicts of rival parties; and that measures are too often decided, not according to the rules of justice, and the rights of the minor party; but by the superior force of an interested and over-bearing majority. However anxiously we may wish that these complaints had no foundation, the evidence of known facts will not permit us to deny that they are in some degree true. It will be found indeed, on a candid review of our situation, that some of the distresses under which we labor, have been erroneously charged on the operation of our governments; but it will be found, at the same time, that other causes will not alone account for many of our heaviest misfortunes; and particularly for that prevailing and increasing distrust of public engagements, and alarm for private rights, which are echoed from one end of the continent to the other. These must be chiefly, if not wholly, effects of the unsteadiness and injustice, with which a factious spirit has tainted our public administrations.

By a faction I understand a number of citizens, whether amounting to a majority or minority of the whole, who are united and actuated by some common impulse of passion, or of interest, adverse to the rights of other citizens, or to the permanent and aggregate interests of the community.

There are two methods of curing the mischiefs of faction: the one, by removing its causes; the other, by controlling its effects.

There are again two methods of removing the causes of faction: the one by destroying the liberty which is essential to its existence; the other, by giving to every citizen the same opinions, the same passions, and the same interests.

It could never be more truly said than of the first remedy, that it is worse than the disease. Liberty is to faction, what air is to fire, an aliment without which it instantly expires. But it could not be a less folly to abolish liberty, which is essential to political life, because it nourishes faction, than it would be to wish the annihilation of air, which is essential to animal life, because it imparts to fire its destructive agency.

The second expedient is as impracticable, as the first would be unwise. As long as the reason of man continues fallible, and he is at liberty to exercise it, different opinions will be formed. As long as the connection subsists between his reason and his self-love, his opinions and his passions will have a reciprocal influence on each other; and the former will be objects to which the latter will attach themselves. The diversity in the faculties of men from which the rights of property originate, is not less an insuperable obstacle to a uniformity of interests. The protection of these faculties is the first object of Government. From the protection of different and unequal faculties of acquiring property, the possession of different degrees and kinds of property immediately results: and from

the influence of these on the sentiments and views of the respective proprietors, ensues a division of the society into different interests and parties.

The latent causes of faction are thus sown in the nature of man; and we see
them every where brought into different degrees of activity, according to the different circumstances of civil society. A zeal for different opinions concerning religion, concerning Government and many other points, as well of speculation as
of practice; an attachment to different leaders ambitiously contending for pre-
eminence and power; or to persons of other descriptions whose fortunes have
been interesting to the human passions, have in turn divided mankind into parties, inflamed them with mutual animosity, and rendered them much more disposed to vex and oppress each other, than to co-operate for their common good.
So strong is this propensity of mankind to fall into mutual animosities, that
where no substantial occasion presents itself, the most frivolous and fanciful distinctions have been sufficient to kindle their unfriendly passions, and excite
their most violent conflicts. But the most common and durable source of factions, have been the various and unequal distribution of property. Those who
hold, and those who are without property, have ever formed distinct interests in
society. Those who are creditors, and those who are debtors, fall under a like discrimination. A landed interest, a manufacturing interest, a mercantile interest, a
monied interest, with many lesser interests, grow up of necessity in civilized nations, and divide them into different classes, actuated by different sentiments
and views. The regulation of these various and interfering interests forms the
principal task of modern Legislation, and involves the spirit of party and faction
in the necessary and ordinary operations of Government.

No man is allowed to be a judge in his own cause; because his interest would
certainly bias his judgment, and, not improbably, corrupt his integrity. With
equal, nay with greater reason, a body of men, are unfit to be both judges and
parties, at the same time; yet, what are many of the most important acts of legislation, but so many judicial determinations, not indeed concerning the rights
of single persons, but concerning the rights of large bodies of citizens; and what
are the different classes of legislators, but advocates and parties to the causes
which they determine? Is a law proposed concerning private debts? It is a question to which the creditors are parties on one side, and the debtors on the
other. Justice ought to hold the balance between them. Yet the parties are and
must be themselves the judges; and the most numerous party, or, in other
words, the most powerful faction must be expected to prevail. Shall domestic
manufactures be encouraged, and in what degree, by restrictions on foreign
manufactures? are questions which would be differently decided by the landed
and the manufacturing classes; and probably by neither, with a sole regard to
justice and the public good. . . .

It is in vain to say, that enlightened statesmen will be able to adjust these
clashing interests, and render them all subservient to the public good. Enlightened statesmen will not always be at the helm: Nor, in many cases, can such an
adjustment be made at all, without taking into view indirect and remote

considerations, which will rarely prevail over the immediate interest which one party may find in disregarding the rights of another, or the good of the whole.

The inference to which we are brought, is, that the causes of faction cannot be removed; and that relief is only to be sought in the means of controlling its *effects*.

If a faction consists of less than a majority, relief is supplied by the republican principle, which enables the majority to defeat its sinister views by regular vote: It may clog the administration, it may convulse the society; but it will be unable to execute and mask its violence under the forms of the Constitution. When a majority is included in a faction, the form of popular government on the other hand enables it to sacrifice to its ruling passion or interest, both the public good and the rights of other citizens. To secure the public good, and private rights, against the danger of such a faction, and at the same time to preserve the spirit and the form of popular government, is then the great object to which our enquiries are directed: Let me add that it is the great desideratum, by which alone this form of government can be rescued from the opprobrium under which it has so long labored, and be recommended to the esteem and adoption of mankind.

By what means is this object attainable? Evidently by one of two only. Either the existence of the same passion or interest in a majority at the same time, must be prevented; or the majority, having such co-existent passion or interest, must be rendered, by their number and local situation, unable to concert and carry into effect schemes of oppression. If the impulse and the opportunity be suffered to coincide, we well know that neither moral nor religious motives can be relied on as an adequate control. They are not found to be such on the injustice and violence of individuals, and lose their efficacy in proportion to the number combined together; that is, in proportion as their efficacy becomes needful.

From this view of the subject, it may be concluded, that a pure Democracy, by which I mean, a Society, consisting of a small number of citizens, who assemble and administer the Government in person, can admit of no cure for the mischiefs of faction. A common passion or interest will, in almost every case, be felt by a majority of the whole; a communication and concert results from the form of Government itself; and there is nothing to check the inducements to sacrifice the weaker party, or an obnoxious individual. Hence it is, that such Democracies have ever been spectacles of turbulence and contention; have ever been found incompatible with personal security, or the rights of property; and have in general been as short in their lives, as they have been violent in their deaths. Theoretic politicians, who have patronized this species of Government, have erroneously supposed, that by reducing mankind to a perfect equality in their political rights, they would, at the same time, be perfectly equalized and assimilated in their possessions, their opinions, and their passions.

A Republic, by which I mean a Government in which the scheme of representation takes place, opens a different prospect, and promises the cure for which we are seeking. Let us examine the points in which it varies from pure Democracy, and we shall comprehend both the nature of the cure, and the efficacy which it must derive from the Union.

The two great points of difference between a Democracy and a Republic are, first, the delegation of the Government, in the latter, to a small number of citizens elected by the rest: secondly, the greater number of citizens, and greater sphere of country, over which the latter may be extended.

The effect of the first difference is, on the one hand to refine and enlarge the public views, by passing them through the medium of a chosen body of citizens, whose wisdom may best discern the true interest of their country, and whose patriotism and love of justice, will be least likely to sacrifice it to temporary or partial considerations. Under such a regulation, it may well happen that the public voice pronounced by the representatives of the people, will be more consonant to the public good, than if pronounced by the people themselves convened for the purpose. On the other hand, the effect may be inverted. Men of factious tempers, of local prejudices, or of sinister designs, may by intrigue, by corruption or by other means, first obtain the suffrages, and then betray the interests of the people. The question resulting is, whether small or extensive Republics are most favorable to the election of proper guardians of the public weal: and it is clearly decided in favor of the latter by two obvious considerations.

In the first place it is to be remarked that however small the Republic may be, the Representatives must be raised to a certain number, in order to guard against the cabals of a few; and that however large it may be, they must be limited to a certain number, in order to guard against the confusion of a multitude. Hence the number of Representatives in the two cases, not being in proportion to that of the Constituents, and being proportionally greatest in the small Republic, it follows, that if the proportion of fit characters, be not less, in the large than in the small Republic, the former will present a greater option, and consequently a greater probability of a fit choice.

In the next place, as each Representative will be chosen by a greater number of citizens in the large than in the small Republic, it will be more difficult for unworthy candidates to practise with success the vicious arts, by which elections are too often carried; and the suffrages of the people being more free, will be more likely to centre on men who possess the most attractive merit, and the most diffusive and established characters.

It must be confessed, that in this, as in most other cases, there is a mean, on both sides of which inconveniencies will be found to lie. By enlarging too much the number of electors, you render the representative too little acquainted with all their local circumstances and lesser interests; and by reducing it too much, you render him unduly attached to these, and too little fit to comprehend and pursue great and national objects. The Federal Constitution forms a happy combination in this respect; the great and aggregate interests being referred to the national, the local and particular, to the state legislatures.

The other point of difference is, the greater number of citizens and extent of territory which may be brought within the compass of Republican, than of Democratic Government; and it is this circumstance principally which renders factious combinations less to be dreaded in the former, than in the latter. The smaller the society, the fewer probably will be the distinct parties and interests composing it; the fewer the distinct parties and interests, the more frequently will a majority be found of the same party; and the smaller the number of individuals composing a majority, and the smaller the compass within which they are placed, the more easily will they concert and execute their plans of oppression. Extend the sphere, and you take in a greater variety of parties and interests; you make it less probable that a majority of the whole will have a common motive to invade the rights of other citizens; or if such a common motive exists, it will be more difficult for all who feel it to discover their own strength, and to act in unison with each other. . . .

Hence it clearly appears, that the same advantage, which a Republic has over a Democracy, in controlling the effects of faction, is enjoyed by a large over a small Republic—is enjoyed by the Union over the States composing it. Does this advantage consist in the substitution of Representatives, whose enlightened views and virtuous sentiments render them superior to local prejudices, and to schemes of injustice? It will not be denied, that the Representation of the Union will be most likely to possess these requisite endowments. Does it consist in the greater security afforded by a greater variety of parties, against the event of any one party being able to outnumber and oppress the rest? In an equal degree does the encreased variety of parties, comprised within the Union, encrease this security? Does it, in fine, consist in the greater obstacles opposed to the concern and accomplishment of the secret wishes of an unjust and interested majority? Here, again, the extent of the Union gives it the most palpable advantage.

The influence of factious leaders may kindle a flame within their particular States, but will be unable to spread a general conflagration through the other States: a religious sect, may degenerate into a political faction in a part of the Confederacy; but the variety of sects dispersed over the entire face of it, must secure the national Councils against any danger from that source: a rage for paper money, for an abolition of debts, for an equal division of property, or for any other improper or wicked project, will be less apt to pervade the whole body of the Union, than a particular member of it; in the same proportion as such a malady is more likely to taint a particular county or district, than an entire State.

In the extent and proper structure of the Union, therefore, we behold a Republican remedy for the diseases most incident to Republican Government. And according to the degree of pleasure and pride, we feel in being Republicans, ought to be our zeal in cherishing the spirit, and supporting the character of Federalists.

Questions for Discussion

1. What is Madison's view of human nature? What factors led him to this conclusion?
2. According to Madison, what are the differences between a democracy and a republic? Would Madison's view on the subject be "popular" today?

⭐ 9.2

Lobbyists—Why the Bad Rap?

Jeffrey H. Birnbaum

Lobbying activity has a long history in the United States, protected by constitutional provisions that give citizens "the right to petition the government for a redress of grievances." At the dawn of the republic this right was often expressed literally, as citizens signed and formally presented to elected representatives written petitions describing their problems. The petitioning process was all but forgotten shortly thereafter: Individuals quickly learned that traveling to Washington and dealing directly with public officials was a much more effective way to influence the new government on a range of concerns, from procuring jobs to policy. Today, it is estimated that roughly 80,000 lobbyists operate in Washington.

In this selection, Jeffrey H. Birnbaum surveys the colorful history of lobbying in the nation's capital. He finds that many incidents of unethical, if not illegal, behavior by special-interest representatives in D.C. have contributed to the unsavory stereotype of the Washington lobbyist. According to Birnbaum, well-financed American business and manufacturing interests have long used their resources to dictate public policy, their activities largely unregulated and undisclosed.

Jeffrey H. Birnbaum is a senior correspondent for *Time* magazine. This selection is adapted from his book *The Lobbyists* (Times Books, 1992).

Birnbaum, Jeffrey H. Reprinted from *The American Enterprise,* a Washington-based magazine of politics, business, and culture.

Birnbaum believes that the relationship between lobbyists and public officials has changed in recent decades, "representing a complex symbiosis of lobbyists and politicians." Lobbyists still seek influence, and money is still important, but blatant bribery by those seeking favors is now uncommon. More common are attempts to influence legislators through devices such as campaign contributions. And often it is the legislators rather than the lobbyists who initiate contact in attempts to raise money for their re-election campaigns. Lobbying techniques have changed as well. Grassroots lobbying, which involves mobilizing a legislator's home constituents, has emerged as one of the most effective ways for special interests to influence public policy.

I n the past 10 years, the number of lobbyists in Washington has, by some estimates, more than doubled. This modern army of 80,000 uses techniques that are as old as the republic, but its forces wield influence with a precision and sophistication that is purely high tech. Right behind the commanders are divisions of specialists: economists, lawyers, direct-mail producers and telephone salespeople, public relations experts, pollsters, and even accountants, all marching to the time-honored First Amendment–guaranteed beat of petitioning the government for redress of grievances. What follows is a look at the history of lobbying, which lobbyists themselves concede has not always been commendable. It explains in short why lobbying has a bad rap.

Booze, Broads, and Bribes

Lobbying in the early days of the republic was not performed with a great deal of finesse. The first attempt at mass pressure on the U.S. government—during a meeting of the First Continental Congress in Philadelphia in 1783—featured fixed bayonets. Several hundred soldiers from the local garrison felt they were due extra compensation and threatened the assembled legislators with their rifles. The Congress disagreed with them but boldly adjourned to meet again to consider the aggrieved soldiers' requests—at a safe distance, in Princeton, New Jersey. Business interests of the time used more subtle lobbying tactics. After the Continental Congress concluded its meetings each day, hogsheads of wine and port flowed without restraint at sumptuous meals. Wealthy merchants picked up the check.

Blatant bribery was swiftly added to the lobbyists' repertoire. One of the new Congress's major debates was whether to fund the national debt and to assume the debts of the states. Some historians believe that Rep. John Vining of Delaware sold his deciding vote to the money changers who stood to profit most from the action. Rumor had it that the bribe was 1,000 English guineas, but Sen. William Maclay of Pennsylvania wrote in his journal that Vining's vote was probably purchased for a "tenth part of the sum."

The word "lobbyist" comes from Britain, where the journalists who stood in lobbies of the House of Commons waiting to interview newsmakers were so dubbed. It was first used in America in 1829 during Andrew Jackson's presidency when privilege seekers in New York's capital, Albany, were referred to as lobby-agents. Three years later, the term was abbreviated to "lobbyist" and has been heard frequently ever since, mostly as an expression of reproach.

President Jackson was the first of many American presidents to rail against lobbyists and their business patrons. He sought to deflate financier Nicholas Biddle's power by withdrawing federal deposits from his Second Bank of the United States. But Biddle was not without supporters, notably the illustrious Daniel Webster, who would go on to become secretary of state. The ardency of Webster's convictions on the issue was bolstered not so much by principle as by cash. On December 21, 1833, Webster, then senator from Massachusetts, wrote to Biddle: "If it is wished that my relation to the bank should be continued, it may be well to send me the usual retainers." After an especially eloquent speech by Webster, Biddle paid him $10,000. Webster received in total $32,000 in what would be seen as bribes today but was then considered business as usual.

Lobbying flourished as America grew. Washington was swarming with so many big-business lobbyists by 1852 that future president James Buchanan wrote to his friend, future president Franklin Pierce, that "the host of contractors, speculators, stockjobbers, and lobby members which haunt the halls of Congress . . . are sufficient to alarm every friend of this country. Their progress must be arrested." The influence of business was so strong that at the close of one congressional session, Sen. J. S. Morrill sarcastically moved to appoint a committee to inquire if the president of the Pennsylvania Railroad, skulking in the outer lobby, wanted Congress to consider any further legislation before adjournment.

One of the most heavy-handed corporate lobbyists at the time was Samuel Colt, the famous gun manufacturer. Colt paid a "contingent fee" of $10,000 to one congressman and probably many others to refrain from attacking a patent-extension bill that would have helped his company's sales. To supplement the effort, Colt's high-living lobbyist, Alexander Hay, distributed beautifully decorated revolvers to lawmakers. Other more attractive gratuities were also dispensed: to wit, three young women known as Spiritualists, who, according to one account, were very active in "moving with the members" of Congress on Colt's behalf. Other women of less spiritual natures called "chicks" were also available upon request.

Washington was flooded with even more lobbyists in the wake of the financial panic of 1857. "Everywhere," wrote historian Roy Franklin Nichols, "there was importunity." The most underhanded lobbying battle raged between railroad and steamship companies as lobbyists for each side fought bitterly to reduce government subsidies to the other. Commodore Cornelius Vanderbilt himself led the steamship companies' campaign, often from the gaming tables of a night spot called Pendleton's Gambling House. Hapless lawmakers would fall into debt there and be forced to surrender their votes under threat of exposure or demand for payment. Other times, lawmakers would be allowed to win—as long as they agreed to vote the right way.

The 1850s' most powerful lobbyist was an imposing man named Thurlow Weed. His diverse background included working as a printer and newspaper editor, crusading against the perfidy of corporate power. But for the price of $5,000, Weed switched allegiances and began to lobby for lower duties on wool for the Bay State Mills of Lawrence, Massachusetts. His predecessor had come to Washington armed with facts and figures and was laughed out of town: Weed came armed with cold cash and stayed for years. Weed also has the distinction of being the first lobbyist to hire a journalist in a lobbying campaign, David M. Stone of New York's *Journal of Commerce*.

The Court Steps In

Washington got a new "King of the Lobby," Samuel Ward, after the Civil War. He reigned for 15 years as the undisputed master of dinner-table deceit. "The way to a man's 'Aye' is through his stomach," he said. Ward's pedigree was impeccable: he was the great-great-grandson of Richard Ward, a colonial governor; the great-grandson of Samuel Ward, one of the framers of the Constitution, and the great nephew of General Francis Marion, the famous "Swamp Fox" of the Revolutionary War. His father headed the New York banking firm of Prime, Ward and King, and his sister, Julia Ward Howe, wrote "The Battle Hymn of the Republic."

Washington suited Ward's penchant for living well, and he quickly proved he could charm the natives for profit. With his balding pate, sweeping mustache, and diamond-studded shirts, he was a striking figure, hosting dinners and breakfasts of ham boiled in champagne and seasoned with wisps of newly mown hay.

Ward's clients ran the gamut. He was hired for $12,000 plus dinner expenses by Hugh McCulloch, an Indiana banker who later became President Lincoln's treasury secretary, to "court, woo, and charm congressmen, especially Democrats prone to oppose the war." He was also associated with Joe Morrissey, the lottery boss. It seemed incongruous, but Morrissey retained Ward to promote a bill that would impose a tax on lotteries. Morrissey believed that he could afford the levy but that it would drive his less prosperous rivals out of business.

Ward could be quite conniving, despite his elegant manners. He once wrote to his friend, Henry Wadsworth Longfellow: "When I see you again I will tell you how a client, eager to prevent the arrival at a committee of a certain member before it should adjourn, offered me $5,000 to accomplish this purpose, which I did, by having [the congressman's] boots mislaid while I smoked a cigar and condoled with him until they could be found at 11:45. I had the satisfaction of a good laugh [and] a good fee in my pocket."

When a congressional committee questioned Ward about his activities, he deflected their inquiries with erudition and humor. "Talleyrand says that diplomacy is assisted by good dinners," he responded. "At good dinners people do not talk shop, but they give people a right, perhaps, to ask a gentleman a civil question and get a civil answer." Ward insisted that he refused to take on issues that were meritless, but he also conceded that "the profession of lobbying is not commendable," a characterization still echoing today.

Under the weak presidencies that followed the Civil War, lobbying reached new heights—and depths. Two of the most jarring events were the Crédit Mobilier scandal in 1872, in which millions of federal dollars earmarked for a transcontinental railroad were diverted into the pockets of representatives, senators, and even a future president, James Garfield; and Jay Gould and Jim Fisk's attempt to corner the gold market in 1869. This latter effort, which ultimately failed, implicated the president himself.

The Supreme Court heard a rare case in 1875 involving a lobbyist, *Trist v. Child*, during Ulysses Grant's troubled presidency. The High Court refused to uphold the lobbyist's claim for payment after he had fulfilled his part of a contract to influence legislation. The ruling denied the payment on the ground that such an undertaking was contrary to "sound policy and good morals." The opinion continued: "If any of the great corporations of the country were to hire adventurers who make market of themselves in this way, to propose passage of a general law with a view to promotion of their private interests, the moral sense of every right-minded man would instinctively denounce the employers and employed as steeped in corruption and employment as infamous. If the instances were numerous, open, and tolerated they would be regarded as a measure of decay of public morals and degeneracy of the time. No prophetic spirit would be needed to foretell the consequences near at hand." Notably absent from the learned decision was the simple, telling observation that lobbyists and lobbying had become so enmeshed in the fabric of the government that an aggrieved lobbyist did not hesitate to go to the highest court in the land for redress.

That same year, lobbying moved further into the modern age with the first recorded instance of grass-roots lobbying. Instead of simply relying on individual adventurers in Washington, business interests began to reach back to the states and districts of congressmen for constituents to support their causes. The bellowing of home-state voices became so loud that Rep. George Frisbie Hoar forced a resolution through his Judiciary Committee requiring for the first time public disclosure by lobbyists about their activities. Hoar said he offered the resolution because four people from different parts of the country representing an important corporation had accosted and tried to sway four of his committee members. The resolution went nowhere, but grass-roots lobbying became a standard tool of the lobbyists' trade.

The first president to seriously challenge the business lobby was Woodrow Wilson, who had prominently featured its villainy in his 1912 campaign. Wilson had studied lobbyists' impact in Washington as a Princeton professor and concluded that it was dangerous. In a scholarly paper, he noted that special interests could not buy an entire legislature but could purchase individual committees, which was where the real power resided anyway. Such observations became grist for his presidential campaign speeches: "The masters of the government of the United States are the combined capitalists and manufacturers. It is written over every intimate page of the records of Congress; it is written all through the history of conferences at the White House. . . . The government of the United States is a foster child of the special interests. It is not allowed to have a will of its own."

Wilson told the lobbyists to get out of town when he took office in 1913, and for the most part, they did. A few diehards stayed, but according to Cordell Hull, they "became less pestiferous when they discovered just what our policy was and saw they could not influence us."

A story printed in the *New York World* by Martin M. Mulhall, the top lobbyist for the National Association of Manufacturers, soon demonstrated exactly why Wilson was so eager to banish lobbyists. Mulhall held no public title, but, as a powerful lobbyist, he had his own private office in the Capitol. He wrote that he paid the chief page of the House $50 a month and maintained a close association with Rep. John Dwight, the House minority leader, and with Rep. James T. McDermott, a Democrat from Chicago, whom he paid $1,500 to $2,000. These well-placed lawmakers gave him advance information about legislation and helped him dictate appointments to key committees.

Finis J. Garrett, a Tennessee Democrat and the House's minority leader, chaired a four-month inquiry into Mulhall's revelations that eventually censured McDermott. Garrett later proposed legislation that would require lobbyists to register with the clerk of the House and to disclose their employers. The bill passed the House but died in the Senate, not to become law, despite many intervening scandals, for another 33 years.

Lobbyists, scandals, and the harried congressional committees investigating them had all roared back by the 1920s. The Caraway Committee, launched in 1927 by Sen. Thaddeus Caraway (D-Ark.), rocked the city with the contention that most lobbying was simply fraud. Fully 90 percent of the nearly 400 lobbying groups listed in the Washington telephone directory were "fakes" whose primary aim was not to affect legislation but to bilk clients, said the committee.

At the end of the investigation, Caraway recommended yet another bill to register lobbyists. He wanted lobbying defined as "any effort in influencing Congress upon any matter coming before it, whether it be by distributing literature, appearing before committees of Congress, or seeking to interview members of either the House or Senate" and a lobbyist as "one who shall engage, for pay, to attempt to influence legislation or to prevent legislation by the national Congress." The Senate passed the stringent measure without dissent, but it died in the House because of lobbyists' pressure.

Former government and party officials began running on the cash-paved track of lobbying in the late 1920s and 1930s, setting a precedent that continues today. Women started to become full-fledged lobbyists during this time period, too. Mabel Walker Williebrandt, once assistant attorney general in charge of enforcing Prohibition laws, traded in her experience for bananas, oranges, apples, and cherries as counsel to Fruit Industries, Ltd. Quite simply, lobbying power resided with people who had personal connections to government.

According to journalist and lobbying historian Kenneth Crawford: "In the Hoover days, one who wanted to put on the fix saw James Francis Burke, secretary of the Republican National Committee; C. Bascom Slemp, who had been secretary to President Coolidge; or Edward Everett Gann, husband of the redoubtable social warrior, Dolly Gann, sister of Vice President Charles Curtis. Early in the Roosevelt administration, the men to get things done were Bruce Kremer, a friend of the attorney general; Robert Jackson of New Hampshire, long-time treasurer of the Democratic National Committee; Arthur Mullen, National Committeeman from Nebraska; and Joe Davies, later ambassador to Russia and Belgium."

Senator Hugo L. Black (D-Ala.) who was later a Supreme Court justice, introduced a bill to register and regulate lobbyists after a particularly egregious display of lobbying power in a debate over regulation of public utilities. This time, it passed both chambers of Congress—but it died in a House-Senate conference committee, thanks to the efforts of hundreds of lobbyists. Lobbyists didn't escape unscathed, however, and for the first time, utility lobbyists were required to make limited disclosure of their activities under terms of the final Public Utilities Holding Company Act.

Congress finally got around to regulating the business of lobbying as a whole in the 1930s and 1940s, starting with the vast and influential shipping industry. The Merchant Marine Act of 1936 required shipping agents to file disclosures with the Commerce Department before working to influence marine legislation or administrative decisions. Two years later, amid reports of Fascist and Nazi propaganda circulating in the United States, the Foreign Agents Registration Act was passed, requiring anyone who represented a foreign government or individual to register with the Justice Department.

In 1946, Congress passed the Federal Regulation of Lobbying Act as part of the Congressional Reorganization Act, requiring all lobbyists to register in Congress and report the amount and sources of their income from lobbying. There was no attempt to limit lobbying; that would violate the First Amendment's right to petition the government. It defined a lobbyist as a person or organization whose job is to influence the passage or defeat of legislation and who receives money for that purpose.

Like all previous lobbying strictures, the law was ignored at first. In 1950, spurred by complaints from President Harry Truman, a committee headed by Rep. Frank M. Buchanan, Democrat from Pennsylvania, investigated a wide range of lobbying abuses. The Congress of the time, the president complained, was "the most thoroughly surrounded . . . with lobbies in the whole history of this great country of ours. . . . There were more lobbyists in Washington, there was more money spent by lobbyists in Washington, than ever before." The committee requested detailed information about lobbying from 200 corporations, labor unions, and farm groups. The 152 organizations that replied said they had spent $32 million on lobbying from January 1, 1948, through May 31, 1950, and fewer than 50 of them had disclosed a single dime of it as required by the new lobbying law.

The Buchanan report also noted that lobbying had changed over the years. In effect, it said, lobbying had become less blatant and, in this view, more insidious. In 1948, there were 1,016 registered lobbyists. Two years later, the number had more than doubled to 2,047. Buchanan said the figures "reflect a significant picture of tremendous amounts of time and money being expended by pressure groups and pressure interests through the country in seeking to influence actions by Congress."

In the 1870s and 1880s, he continued, "lobbying meant direct, individual solicitation of legislators, with a strong presumption of corruption attached . . . [but] modern pressure on legislative bodies is rarely corrupt. . . . It is increasingly indirect, and [it is] largely the product of group rather than individual effort. . . . The printed word is much more extensively used by organizations as a means of pursuing legislative aims than personal contact with legislators by individual lobbyists."

The Buchanan Committee recommended strengthening the lobbying law, but no action was taken. Instead, in 1954, the Supreme Court weakened the already porous lobbying statute by exempting many types of lobbyists from the law's disclosure requirements. The Court decided that only those who solicited and collected money specifically with lobbying in mind need comply and that organizations need register only if they had lobbying as their "principal purpose" when they collected the funds. What's more, only direct contacts with legislators were considered lobbying; indirect pressure, such as the growing practice of grass-roots lobbying, was excluded.

A Complex Relationship

In the late 1940s and 1950s, it was "often hard to tell where the legislator [left] off and the lobbyist begins," according to lobbying expert James Deakin. Entire pieces of legislation were drafted by lobbyists. According to Rep. Arthur Klein, a Democratic member of the House Labor Committee, the primary author of the Taft-Hartley Act of 1947,* which restricted labor union activities, was neither Taft nor Hartley but William G. Ingles, a $24,000-a-year lawyer and highly

---

*The Taft-Hartley Act of 1947 was technically a series of amendments to the National Labor Relations (Wagner) Act of 1935, which many members of the business community felt was too pro-union. A major provision of the Taft-Hartley Act allowed states to pass right-to-work laws, which in effect banned "closed shop" requirements (which had made it mandatory for employers to hire only members of unions). Taft-Hartley also delineated various unfair labor practices by unions (the 1935 act only listed unfair labor practices by employers).

labor-dependent lobbyist for Allis-Chalmers, Fruehauf Trailer, J. I. Case, and Inland Steel.

The unprecedented expansion of government after the war was accompanied by a rapid growth in the number of lobbyists. Sensing their advantage, lawmakers began to play one off against the other. "Everything in Washington is a two-way street," Deakin wrote: "The legislators use the lobbyists as much as the lobbyists use them. A cocktail party—like an office conversation—may give the congressman information he needs. Or it may give him something he needs even more: cash. The Washington party has become an increasingly utilitarian institution. Invited to a reception, the lobbyist may find that he is giving more than he gets. The pressure boy is pressured. As he leaves, pleasantly oiled, his attention is directed to a hat in which he is expected to drop $50 or $100 for the congressman's campaign. . . . Washington is a very practical town, and money and votes mean more than liquor. In the final analysis, this is why bribes, blondes, and booze don't rank as high as they once did in the lobbyist's scheme of things. They just aren't as important to the congressman (to his political survival, which is his first law) as votes and money with which to get votes. The legislator may accept the lobbyist's entertainment, and gladly, but he is far more likely to do what the lobbyist wants if votes are involved."

The 1940s and 1950s were also the heyday of the brilliant, brash Thomas "the Cork" Corcoran, former law clerk to Oliver Wendell Holmes and President Franklin Roosevelt's chief legislative operative. Corcoran helped write much of the New Deal legislation, including the Securities and Exchange Act. He also supplied Roosevelt with the phrase, "This generation has a rendezvous with destiny." He made enemies when he tried to help Roosevelt pack the Supreme Court,* and he was blocked from the job he most coveted, becoming the U.S. solicitor general. He became instead a high-priced lobbyist for corporate interests, cementing what has since become a well-established route from White House adviser to Washington lobbyist.

Top executives of corporations were increasingly enlisted as lobbyists during the 1960s, but always under the strict guidance of their Washington consultants. Lobbying had come far since the early days of the republic, representing a complex symbiosis of lobbyists and politicians—but traditional, big-money lobbyists still wooed, and occasionally brought crashing down, lawmakers. The most famous victim of lawmakers' penchant for fancy living was Robert G. (Bobby) Baker, whose route from Pickens, South Carolina, to riches on the banks of the Potomac River was eased by lobbyists. Baker was secretary to the Democratic majority in the Senate. With a salary of $19,600 a year, he managed to accumulate assets of $2,166,886 in less than nine years.

---

*President Franklin Roosevelt, frustrated with the Supreme Court's reluctance to uphold major pieces of New Deal legislation, proposed a plan in 1937 to expand the size of the Court by appointing a new member for each sitting justice who had reached seventy years of age. If the plan had been approved, Roosevelt could have immediately appointed six justices, making the Court a fifteen-member body. Congress and the nation's press were strongly against the measure, viewing it as a thinly veiled attempt to "pack" the Court to create a liberal majority.

Improper contacts with lobbyists also helped bring down Richard M. Nixon's presidency. Investigations revealed that a number of corporations violated the federal law that prohibits them from contributing to the campaigns of federal office seekers. Some of those funds found their way into the hands of the Republican operatives who broke into Democratic Party headquarters in Washington's Watergate complex on June 17, 1972.

Foreign interests have increasingly hired Washington lobbyists in recent years. This foreign money led to the 1976 Koreagate scandal. The *Washington Post* reported that South Korean agents gave between $500,000 and $1 million a year in cash and gifts to members of Congress to help maintain a "favorable legislative climate" for South Korea. The Koreans, led by businessman and socialite Tongsun Park, sought to bribe U.S. officials and buy influence among journalists, funneling illegal gifts to as many as 115 lawmakers. In 1978, the House voted to reprimand three California Democrats for their part in the scandal, and Richard T. Hanna, a former California congressman, was sentenced to prison.

Subtlety Wields Influence

During the 1980s, lobbying was rarely so heavyhanded, yet it became astonishingly effective. Communications techniques reached new heights of sophistication and complexity, and with them lobbyists were able to mobilize thousands of ordinary citizens for the first time. When Congress was considering increasing milk price supports in 1980, for example, lawmakers heard not just from lobbyists for the dairy farmers who wanted the subsidy hiked but also from thousands of worried managers of fast-food restaurants spurred on by an "action alert" newsletter distributed by the fast-food industry's trade association.

The break-up of American Telephone & Telegraph spurred one of the decade's biggest grass-roots lobbying efforts. Legislators heard from thousands of telephone company managers and employees; not only had AT&T put out an action alert but so had the Communications Workers of America, 90 percent of whose members were AT&T employees. At the same time, a coalition of AT&T competitors stirred up its own pressure in favor of the break-up, mailing 70,000 envelopes bearing an imitation of the Bell System logo and this attention-grabbing warning: "Notice of Telephone Rate Increase Enclosed." The letter inside warned the reader that unless the recipient helped lobby in favor of the break-up, telephone rates would double.

Individual corporations also began using their employees and suppliers as lobbyists, a method previously used with great success by labor unions. The National Association of Home Builders—the 125,000-member trade association of the housing industry—developed one of the most comprehensive electoral strategies ever devised in the corporate world. Its 250-page manual, "Blueprint for Victory: Homebuilder's Political Offensive," outlined all aspects of what it called its G. I.

(Get Involved) Program. The manual detailed telephone or house-to-house canvassing techniques, how to organize a "Victory Caravan" to transport campaign volunteers, and many other strategies previously reserved for political movements.

The Old and the New

In the postwar era, presidents continued to bash lobbyists. Harry Truman, whose presidency has been much discussed this campaign year, used these words: "There are a great many organizations with lots of money who maintain lobbyists in Washington. I'd say 15 million people in the United States are represented by lobbyists," he said. "The other 150 million have only one man who is elected at large to represent them—that is the president of the United States."

John F. Kennedy also attacked lobbyists, telling an audience at Ohio's Wittenberg College in 1960, "The consumer is the only man in our economy without a high-powered lobbyist in Washington. I intend to be that lobbyist." Yet throughout his presidency, he maintained a close friendship with one of Washington's prominent lawyer-lobbyists, Clark Clifford, remarking jovially at one point that Clifford was not like other consultants who wanted rewards for their assistance to him. "You don't hear Clark clamoring," Kennedy said. "All he asked in return was that we advertise his law firm on the back of the one-dollar bills." That lighthearted quip told much about the power of lobbyists and the personal relationships that nurture the business.

Lobbyists remain an integral part of the Washington establishment, but the scandals of the past continue to stigmatize their standing. One lobbyist captured the feeling: "My mother has never introduced me as 'my son, the lobbyist.' My son, the Washington representative, maybe, or the legislative consultant. But never as the lobbyist. I can't say I blame her." This explains a paradox of Washington life. While lobbyists are highly compensated and influential, they occupy a kind of underclass in the nation's capital. They are frequently left standing in hallways and reception areas for hours at a time. Theirs are the first appointments canceled or postponed when legislators are pressed by other business calls. Their activity suffuses the culture of the city, but their status suffers from a long history of lobbying scandals.

Questions for Discussion

1. How has Washington lobbying changed since the early days of the republic? What forces have brought about such changes? Is the negative image of lobbyists still warranted?
2. Why is it so difficult to regulate lobbying activity?

9.3

Associations Without Members

Theda Skocpol

Over the past half century, the interest group universe has experienced profound change. The number of organized interests in American politics has grown tremendously, as virtually every interest imaginable is now represented by a formally organized group. New voices have been heard, and the expansion of representation has had many positive consequences, including the expansion of rights for various categories of citizens.

In this selection, Theda Skocpol surveys the changes that have taken place in the style and substance of civic and association activities since the 1950s, and she speculates as to their consequences for a democratic polity. Particularly troublesome to Skocpol is the decline of "locally rooted and nationally active membership associations." Such groups have been replaced by "organizations without members," leadership-dominated advocacy groups with little democratic input. In Skocpol's view, the new groups are unable to mobilize mass support as well as the older membership organizations do, letting elites dominate policy-making and frustrating meaningful political reform.

In just a third of a century, Americans have dramatically changed their style of civic and political association. A civic world once centered in locally rooted and nationally active membership associations is a relic. Today, Americans volunteer for causes and projects, but only rarely as ongoing members. They send checks to service and advocacy groups run by professionals, often funded by foundations or professional fundraisers. Prime-time airways echo with debates among their spokespersons: the National Abortion Rights Action League debates the National Right to Life Committee; the Concord Coalition takes on the American Association of Retired Persons; and the Environmental Defense Fund counters business groups. Entertained or bemused, disengaged viewers watch as polarized advocates debate.

Theda Skocpol is professor of political science at Harvard University.

"Associations Without Members" by Theda Skocpol. Reprinted with permission from *The American Prospect*, Volume 10, Number 45: July 1, 1999. The American Prospect, 11 Beacon Street, Suite 1120, Boston, MA 02108. All rights reserved.

The largest membership groups of the 1950s were old-line and well-established, with founding dates ranging from 1733 for the Masons to 1939 for the Woman's Division of Christian Service (a Methodist women's association formed from "missionary" societies with nineteenth-century roots). Like most large membership associations throughout American history, most 1950s associations recruited members across class lines. They held regular local meetings and convened periodic assemblies of elected leaders and delegates at the state, regional, or national levels. Engaged in multiple rather than narrowly specialized pursuits, many associations combined social or ritual activities with community service, mutual aid, and involvement in national affairs. Patriotism was a leitmotif; during and after World War II, a passionate and victorious national endeavor, these associations sharply expanded their memberships and renewed the vigor of their local and national activities.

To be sure, very large associations were not the only membership federations that mattered in postwar America. Also prominent were somewhat smaller, elite-dominated civic groups—including male service groups like Rotary, Lions, and Kiwanis, and longstanding female groups like the American Association of University Women and the League of Women Voters. Dozens of ethnically based fraternal and cultural associations flourished, as did African-American fraternal groups like the Prince Hall Masons and the Improved Benevolent and Protective Order of Elks of the World.

For many membership federations, this was a golden era of national as well as community impact. Popularly rooted membership federations rivaled professional and business associations for influence in policy debates. The AFL-CIO was in the thick of struggles about economic and social policies; the American Legion and the Veterans of Foreign Wars advanced veterans' programs; the American Farm Bureau Federation (AFBF) joined other farmers' associations to influence national and state agricultural policies; and the National Congress of Parents and Teachers (PTA) and the General Federation of Women's Clubs were influential on educational, health, and family issues. The results could be decisive, as exemplified by the pivotal role of the American Legion in drafting and lobbying for the GI Bill of 1944.

Then, suddenly, old-line membership federations seemed passé. Upheavals shook America during "the long 1960s," stretching from the mid-1950s through the mid-1970s. The southern Civil Rights movement challenged white racial domination and spurred legislation to enforce legal equality and voting rights for African Americans. Inspired by Civil Rights achievements, additional "rights" movements exploded, promoting equality for women, dignity for homosexuals, the unionization of farm workers, and the mobilization of other nonwhite ethnic minorities. Movements arose to oppose U.S. involvement in the war in Vietnam, champion a new environmentalism, and further other public causes. At the forefront of these groundswells were younger Americans, especially from the growing ranks of college students and university graduates.

The great social movements of the long 1960s were propelled by combinations of grassroots protest, activist radicalism, and professionally led efforts to lobby government and educate the public. Some older membership associations ended up participating and expanding their bases of support, yet the groups that sparked movements were more agile and flexibly structured than preexisting membership federations.

The upheavals of the 1960s could have left behind a reconfigured civic world, in which some old-line membership associations had declined but others had reoriented and reenergized themselves. Within each great social movement, memberships could have consolidated and groups coalesced into new omnibus federations able to link the grass roots to state, regional, and national leaderships, allowing longstanding American civic traditions to continue in new ways.

But this is not what happened. Instead, the 1960s, 1970s, and 1980s brought extraordinary organizational proliferation and professionalization. At the national level alone, the *Encyclopedia of Associations* listed approximately 6,500 associations in 1958. This total grew by 1990 to almost 23,000. Within the expanding group universe, moreover, new kinds of associations came to the fore: relatively centralized and professionally led organizations focused on policy lobbying and public education.

Another wave of the advocacy explosion involved "public interest" or "citizens" groups seeking to shape public opinion and influence legislation. Citizens' advocacy groups espouse "causes" ranging from environmental protection (for example, the Sierra Club and the Environmental Defense Fund), to the well-being of poor children (the Children's Defense Fund), to reforming politics (Common Cause) and cutting public entitlements (the Concord Coalition).

The Fortunes of Membership Associations

As the associational explosions of 1960 to 1990 took off, America's once large and confident membership federations were not only bypassed in national politics; they also dwindled as locally rooted participant groups. To be sure, some membership associations have been founded or expanded in recent decades. By far the largest is the American Association of Retired Persons (AARP), which now boasts more than 33 million adherents, about one-half of all Americans aged 50 or older. But AARP is not a democratically controlled organization. Launched in 1958 with backing from a teachers' retirement group and an insurance company, the AARP grew rapidly in the 1970s and 1980s by offering commercial discounts to members and establishing a Washington headquarters to monitor and lobby about federal legislation affecting seniors. The AARP has a legislative and policy staff of 165 people, 28 registered lobbyists, and more than 1,200 staff members in the field. After recent efforts to expand its regional and local infrastructure, the AARP involves about 5 to 10 percent of its members in (undemocratic) membership chapters. But for the most part, the AARP national office—covering an entire city block with its own zip code—deals with masses of individual adherents through the mail.

Four additional recently expanded membership associations use modern mass recruitment methods, yet are also rooted in local and state units. Interestingly, these groups are heavily involved in partisan electoral politics. Two recently launched groups are the National Right to Life Committee (founded in 1973) and the Christian Coalition (founded in 1989). They bridge from church congregations, through which they recruit members and activists, to the conservative wing of the Republican Party, through which they exercise political influence. Two old-line membership federations—the National Education Association (founded in 1857) and the National Rifle Association (founded in 1871)—experienced explosive growth after reorienting themselves to take part in partisan politics. The NRA expanded in the 1970s, when right-wing activists opposed to gun control changed what had traditionally been a network of marksmen's clubs into a conservative, Republican-leaning advocacy group fiercely opposed to gun control legislation. During the same period, the NEA burgeoned from a relatively elitist association of public educators into a quasi-union for public school teachers and a stalwart in local, state, and national Democratic Party politics.

Although they fall short of enrolling 1 percent of the adult population, some additional chapter-based membership associations were fueled by the social movements of the 1960s and 1970s. From 1960 to 1990, the Sierra Club (originally created in 1892) ballooned from some 15,000 members to 565,000 members meeting in 378 "local groups." And the National Audubon Society (founded in 1905) went from 30,000 members and 330 chapters in 1958 to about 600,000 members and more than 500 chapters in the 1990s. The National Organization for Women (NOW) reached 1,122 members and 14 chapters within a year of its founding in 1966, and spread across all 50 states with some 125,000 members meeting in 700 chapters by 1978. But notice that these "1960s" movement associations do not match the organizational scope of old-line membership federations. At its post–World War II high point in 1955, for example, the General Federation of Women's Clubs boasted more than 826,000 members meeting in 15,168 local clubs, themselves divided into representative networks within each of the 50 states plus the District of Columbia. By contrast, at its high point in 1993, NOW reported some 280,000 members and 800 chapters, with no intermediate tier of representative governance between the national center and local chapters. These membership associations certainly matter, but mainly as counterexamples to dominant associational trends—of organizations without members.

After nearly a century of civic life rooted in nation-spanning membership federations, why was America's associational universe so transformed? A variety of factors have contributed, including racial and gender change; shifts in the political opportunity structure; new techniques and models for building organizations; and recent transformations in U.S. class relations. Taken together, I suggest, these account for civic America's abrupt and momentous transition from membership to advocacy.

Society Decompartmentalized

Until recent times, most American membership associations enrolled business and professional people together with white-collar folks, farmers, and craft or industrial workers. There was a degree of fellowship across class lines—yet at the price of other kinds of exclusions. With only a few exceptions, old-line associations enrolled either men or women, not both together (although male-only fraternal and veterans' groups often had ties to ladies' auxiliaries). Racial separation was also the rule. Although African Americans did manage to create and greatly expand fraternal associations of their own, they unquestionably resented exclusion by the parallel white fraternals.

Given the pervasiveness of gender and racial separation in classic civic America, established voluntary associations were bound to be shaken after the 1950s. Moreover, changing gender roles and identities blended with other changing values to undercut not just membership appeals but long-standing routes to associational leadership. For example, values of patriotism, brotherhood, and sacrifice had been celebrated by all fraternal groups. During and after each war, the Masons, Knights of Pythias, Elks, Knights of Columbus, Moose, Eagles, and scores of other fraternal groups celebrated and memorialized the contributions of their soldier-members. So did women's auxiliaries, not to mention men's service clubs and trade union "brotherhoods." But "manly" ideals of military service faded after the early 1960s as America's bitter experiences during the war in Vietnam disrupted the intergenerational continuity of male identification with martial brotherliness.

In the past third of a century, female civic leadership has changed as much or more than male leadership. Historically, U.S. women's associations—ranging from female auxiliaries of male groups to independent groups like the General Federation of Women's Clubs, the PTA, and church-connected associations—benefited from the activism of educated wives and mothers. Although a tiny fraction of all U.S. females, higher-educated women were a surprisingly substantial and widespread presence—because the United States was a pioneer in the schooling of girls and the higher education of women. By 1880, some 40,000 American women constituted a third of all students in U.S. institutions of higher learning; women's share rose to nearly half at the early twentieth-century peak in 1920, when some 283,000 women were enrolled in institutions of higher learning. Many higher-educated women of the late 1800s and early 1900s married immediately and stayed out of the paid labor force. Others taught for a time in primary and secondary schools, then got married and stopped teaching (either voluntarily or because school systems would not employ married women). Former teachers accumulated in every community. With skills to make connections within and across communities—and some time on their hands as their children grew older—former teachers and other educated women became mainstays of classic U.S. voluntary life.

Of course, more American women than ever before are now college-educated. But contemporary educated women face new opportunities and constraints. Paid work and family responsibilities are no longer separate spheres, and the occupational structure is less sex-segregated at all levels. Today, even married women with children are very likely to be employed, at least part-time. Despite new time pressures, educated and employed women have certainly not dropped out of civic life. Women employed part-time are more likely to be members of groups or volunteers than housewives; and fully employed women are often drawn into associations or civic projects through work. Yet styles of civic involvement have changed—much to the disadvantage of broad-gauged associations trying to hold regular meetings.

The Lure of Washington, D.C.

The centralization of political change in Washington, D.C. also affected the associational universe. Consider the odyssey of civil rights lawyer Marian Wright Edelman. Fresh from grassroots struggles in Mississippi, she arrived in Washington, D.C. in the late 1960s to lobby for Mississippi's Head Start program. She soon realized that arguing on behalf of children might be the best way to influence legislation and sway public sympathy in favor of the poor, including African Americans. So between 1968 and 1973 Edelman obtained funding from major foundations and developed a new advocacy and policy research association, the Children's Defense Fund (CDF). With a skillful staff, a small national network of individual supporters, ties to social service agencies and foundations, and excellent relationships with the national media, the CDF has been a determined proponent of federal antipoverty programs ever since. The CDF has also worked with Democrats and other liberal advocacy groups to expand such efforts; and during periods of conservative Republican ascendancy, the CDF has been a fierce (if not always successful) defender of federal social programs.

Activists, in short, have gone where the action is. In this same period, congressional committees and their staffs subdivided and multiplied. During the later 1970s and 1980s, the process of group formation became self-reinforcing—not only because groups arose to counter other groups, but also because groups begot more groups. Because businesses and citizens use advocacy groups to influence government outside of parties and between elections, it is not surprising that the contemporary group explosion coincides with waning voter loyalty to the two major political parties. As late as the 1950s, U.S. political parties were networks of local and state organizations through which party officials often brokered nominations, cooperated with locally rooted membership associations, and sometimes directly mobilized voters. The party structure and the associational structure were mutually reinforcing.

Then, demographic shifts, reapportionment struggles, and the social upheavals of the 1960s disrupted old party organizations; and changes in party rules led to nomination elections that favored activists and candidate-centered efforts over backroom brokering by party insiders. Such "reforms" were meant to enhance grassroots participation, but in practice have furthered oligarchical ways of running elections. No longer the preserve of party organizations, U.S. campaigns are now managed by coteries of media consultants, pollsters, direct mail specialists, and—above all—fundraisers. In this revamped electoral arena, advocacy groups have much to offer, hoping to get access to elected officials in return for helping candidates. In low-turnout battles to win party nominations, even groups with modest mail memberships may be able to field enough (paid or unpaid) activists to make a difference. At all stages of the electoral process, advocacy groups with or without members can provide endorsements that may be useful in media or direct mail efforts. And PACs pushing business interests or public interest causes can help candidates raise the huge amounts of money they need to compete.

A New Model of Association-Building

Classic American association-builders took it for granted that the best way to gain national influence, moral or political, was to knit together national, state, and local groups that met regularly and engaged in a degree of representative governance. Leaders who desired to speak on behalf of masses of Americans found it natural to proceed by recruiting self-renewing mass memberships and spreading a network of interactive groups. After the start-up phase, associational budgets usually depended heavily on membership dues and on sales of newsletters or supplies to members and local groups. Supporters had to be continuously recruited through social networks and person-to-person contacts. And if leverage over government was desired, an association had to be able to influence legislators, citizens, and newspapers across many districts. For all of these reasons, classic civic entrepreneurs with national ambitions moved quickly to recruit activists and members in every state and across as many towns and cities as possible within each state.

Today, nationally ambitious civic entrepreneurs proceed in quite different ways. When Marian Wright Edelman launched a new advocacy and research group to lobby for the needs of children and the poor, she turned to private foundations for funding and then recruited an expert staff of researchers and lobbyists. In the early 1970s, when John Gardner launched Common Cause as a "national citizens lobby" demanding governmental reforms, he arranged for start-up contributions from several wealthy friends, contacted reporters in the national media, and purchased mailing lists to solicit masses of members giving modest monetary contributions. Patron grants, direct mail techniques, and the capacity to convey images and messages through the mass media have changed the realities of organization building and maintenance.

The very model of civic effectiveness has been up-ended since the 1960s. No longer do civic entrepreneurs think of constructing vast federations and recruiting interactive citizen-members. When a new cause (or tactic) arises, activists envisage opening a national office and managing association-building as well as national projects from the center. Even a group aiming to speak for large numbers of Americans does not absolutely need members. And if mass adherents are recruited through the mail, why hold meetings? From a managerial point of view, interactions with groups of members may be downright inefficient. In the old-time membership federations, annual elections of leaders and a modicum of representative governance went hand in hand with membership dues and interactive meetings. But for the professional executives of today's advocacy organizations, direct mail members can be more appealing because, as Kenneth Godwin and Robert Cameron Mitchell explain, "they contribute without 'meddling'" and "do not take part in leadership selection or policy discussions." This does not mean the new advocacy groups are malevolent; they are just responding rationally to the environment in which they find themselves.

Associational Change and Democracy

This brings us, finally, to what may be the most civically consequential change in late-twentieth-century America: the rise of a very large, highly educated upper middle class in which "expert" professionals are prominent along with businesspeople and managers. When U.S. professionals were a tiny, geographically dispersed stratum, they understood themselves as "trustees of community," in the terminology of Stephen Brint. Working closely with and for nonprofessional fellow citizens in thousands of towns and cities, lawyers, doctors, ministers, and teachers once found it quite natural to join—and eventually help to lead—locally rooted, cross-class voluntary associations. But today's professionals are more likely to see themselves as expert individuals who can best contribute to national well-being by working with other specialists to tackle complex technical or social problems.

Cause-oriented advocacy groups offer busy, privileged Americans a rich menu of opportunities to, in effect, hire other professionals and managers to represent their values and interests in public life. Why should highly trained and economically well-off elites spend years working their way up the leadership ladders of traditional membership federations when they can take leading staff roles at the top, or express their preferences by writing a check?

If America has experienced a great civic transformation from membership to advocacy—so what? Most traditional associations were racially exclusive and gender segregated; and their policy efforts were not always broad-minded. More than a few observers suggest that recent civic reorganizations may be for the best. American public life has been rejuvenated, say the optimists, by social movements and advocacy groups fighting for social rights and an enlarged understanding of the public good.

Local community organizations, neighborhood groups, and grassroots protest movements nowadays tap popular energies and involve people otherwise left out of organized politics. And social interchanges live on in small support groups and occasional volunteering. According to the research of Robert Wuthnow, about 75 million men and women, a remarkable 40 percent of the adult population, report taking part in "a small group that meets regularly and provides caring and support for those who participate in it." Wuthnow estimates that there may be some 3 million such groups, including Bible study groups, 12-step self-help groups, book discussion clubs, singles groups, hobby groups, and disease support groups. Individuals find community, spiritual connection, introspection, and personal gratification in small support groups. Meanwhile, people reach out through volunteering. As many as half of all Americans give time to the community this way, their efforts often coordinated by paid social service professionals. Contemporary volunteering can be intermittent and flexibly structured, an intense one-shot effort or spending "an evening a week on an activity for a few months as time permits, rather than having to make a long-term commitment to an organization."

In the optimistic view, the good civic things Americans once did are still being done—in new ways and in new settings. But if we look at U.S. democracy in its entirety and bring issues of power and social leverage to the fore, then optimists are surely overlooking the downsides of our recently reorganized civic life. Too many valuable aspects of the old civic America are not being reproduced or reinvented in the new public world of memberless organizations.

Despite the multiplicity of voices raised within it, America's new civic universe is remarkably oligarchical. Because today's advocacy groups are staff-heavy and focused on lobbying, research, and media projects, they are managed from the top with few opportunities for member leverage from below. Even when they have hundreds of thousands of adherents, contemporary associations are heavily tilted toward upper-middle-class constituencies. Whether we are talking about memberless advocacy groups, advocacy groups with some chapters, mailing-list associations, or nonprofit institutions, it is hard to escape the conclusion that the wealthiest and best-educated Americans are much more privileged in the new civic world than their (less numerous) counterparts were in the pre-1960s civic world of cross-class membership federations.

Mostly, they involve people in "doing for" others—feeding the needy at a church soup kitchen; tutoring children at an after-school clinic; or guiding visitors at a museum exhibit—rather than in "doing with" fellow citizens. Important as such volunteering may be, it cannot substitute for the central citizenship functions that membership federations performed.

A top-heavy civic world not only encourages "doing for" rather than "doing with." It also distorts national politics and public policymaking. Imagine for a moment what might have happened if the GI Bill of 1944 had been debated and legislated in a civic world configured more like the one that prevailed during the 1993–1994 debates over the national health insurance proposal put forward by the first administration of President Bill Clinton. This is not an entirely fanciful comparison, because goals supported by the vast majority of Americans were at issue in both periods: in the 1940s, care and opportunity for millions of military veterans returning from World War II; in the 1990s, access for all Americans to a modicum of health insurance coverage. Back in the 1940s, moreover, there were elite actors—university presidents, liberal intellectuals, and conservative congressmen—who could have condemned the GI Bill to the same fate as the 1990s health security plan. University presidents and liberal New Dealers initially favored versions of the GI Bill that would have been bureaucratically complicated, niggardly with public expenditures, and extraordinarily limited in veterans' access to subsidized higher education.

But in the actual civic circumstances of the 1940s, elites did not retain control of public debates or legislative initiatives. Instead, a vast voluntary membership federation, the American Legion, stepped in and drafted a bill to guarantee every one of the returning veterans up to four years of post–high school education, along with family and employment benefits, business loans, and home mortgages. Not only did the Legion draft one of the most generous pieces of social legislation in American history, thousands of local Legion posts and dozens of state organizations mounted a massive public education and lobbying campaign to ensure that even conservative congressional representatives would vote for the new legislation.

Half a century later, the 1990s health security episode played out in a transformed civic universe dominated by advocacy groups, pollsters, and big-money media campaigns. Top-heavy advocacy groups did not mobilize mass support for a sensible reform plan. Hundreds of business and professional groups influenced the Clinton administration's complex policy schemes, and then used a combination of congressional lobbying and media campaigns to block new legislation. Both the artificial polarization and the elitism of today's organized civic universe may help to explain why increasing numbers of Americans are turned off by and pulling back from public life. Large majorities say that wealthy "special interests" dominate the federal government, and many Americans express cynicism about the chances for regular people to make a difference. People may be entertained by advocacy clashes on television, but they are also ignoring many public debates and withdrawing into privatism. Voting less and less, American citizens increasingly act—and claim to feel—like mere spectators in a polity where all the significant action seems to go on above their heads, with their views ignored by pundits and clashing partisans.

From the nineteenth through the mid-twentieth century, American democracy flourished within a unique matrix of state and society. Not only was America the world's first manhood democracy and the first nation in the world to establish mass public education. It also had a uniquely balanced civic life, in which markets expanded but could not subsume civil society, in which governments at multiple levels deliberately and indirectly encouraged federated voluntary associations. National elites had to pay attention to the values and interests of millions of ordinary Americans.

Over the past third of a century, the old civic America has been bypassed and shoved to the side by a gaggle of professionally dominated advocacy groups and nonprofit institutions rarely attached to memberships worthy of the name. Ideals of shared citizenship and possibilities for democratic leverage have been compromised in the process. Since the 1960s, many good things have happened in America. New voices are now heard, and there have been invaluable gains in equality and liberty. But vital links in the nation's associational life have frayed, and we may need to find creative ways to repair those links if America is to avoid becoming a country of detached spectators. There is no going back to the civic world we have lost. But we Americans can and should look for ways to recreate the best of our civic past in new forms suited to a renewed democratic future.

Questions for Discussion

1. What factors led to a decline in importance of membership federations in the nation's civic and political life? What kinds of organizations have taken their place?
2. Although Skocpol believes that the number of organized interests represented in the interest group universe over the past half century has grown, she also believes that the political system may be less democratic than it had previously been. How can such a paradox be explained?

9.4

From Big Bird to Bill Gates: Organized Interests and the Emergence of Hyperpolitics

Allan J. Cigler and Burdett A. Loomis

Not only have recent decades witnessed a proliferation of groups, but the scope of their political activity has increased as well. More groups than ever before are involved in more kinds of behaviors to influence policy and electoral outcomes. No longer are many groups satisfied to lobby just on issues of immediate concern or to play a secondary role in elections by contributing to candidates.

In this selection, Allan J. Cigler and Burdett A. Loomis argue that organized interests—especially moneyed interests—are involved in a permanent, ongoing campaign to influence political communication in the nation. According to the authors, politics has become an offshoot of marketing, where information is key. Most information is "interested," reflecting the underlying views of those who sponsor and disseminate it. In both the electoral and policymaking sides of American politics, information is shaped by organized interests that carry out expensive campaigns designed to dominate discourse on political matters. In the authors' view, we are in an era of "hyperpolitics," characterized by many voices being expressed, but with few guidelines to sort out their value.

I n 1995–1996, after gaining control of Congress, members of the new Republican majority set their sights on cutting all funds for television's Public Broadcasting Service (PBS), which they saw as representing both an inappropriate use of federal funds and a bastion of liberal thought. Given that federal spending on public broadcasting had been declining since the 1980s and that it could not lobby (at least formally) on its own behalf, PBS looked vulnerable, given the House Republicans' early success in 1995 in passing its Contract with America. But PBS did have an important, latent resource: the support of millions of individuals who watched public television, and

Allan J. Cigler is Chancellor's Club Teaching Professor of Political Science at the University of Kansas. Burdett A. Loomis is a professor of political science at the University of Kansas.

Cigler, Allan J., and Burdett A. Loomis. "From Big Bird to Bill Gates: Organized Interests and the Emergence of Hyperpolitics," from *Interest Group Politics,* Fifth Edition, by Allan J. Cigler and Burdett A. Loomis. Copyright © 1998 Congressional Quarterly Inc. Reprinted by permission of the publisher, CQ Press.

especially those whose children had grown up with *Sesame Street*'s endearing characters.

PBS and its member stations were prohibited from lobbying, yet they did find ways to mobilize their viewers and subscribers to communicate with their representatives in Congress. In that PBS supporters are widely distributed across the country and disproportionately well-educated, this group responded quickly and effectively to the congressional threats, as framed by PBS executives such as Paula Kerger of New York's WNET. Once the political conflict was defined in terms of increasingly unpopular Speaker Newt Gingrich (R-Ga.) against the always popular Big Bird, the battle was essentially over—and PBS survived, more or less intact. Indeed, in 1997 the Congress voted to appropriate $300 million for PBS in fiscal year 2000, an increase of $50 million above the 1999 spending level.

In 1988 Microsoft had no meaningful Washington presence, and Democrats controlled both houses of Congress. Ten years later Microsoft was discovered planning a huge (and surreptitious) public relations offensive to counter federal antitrust initiatives, to say nothing of burnishing the image of CEO Bill Gates. And Republicans were seeking to extend their four years of control on Capitol Hill, which might allow them to mount another attack on public broadcasting. Even more important than these major changes to the political landscape, however, has been the broad trend toward the politicization of almost all communication—ranging from television's *Ellen*'s conversion from a situation comedy to an advocacy program for gay rights to the exponential increase in Internet usage. . . .

In this [selection] we will broach the argument that interests—especially moneyed interests—increasingly have come to dominate political communication in the United States. Both on the electoral and policymaking sides of American politics, information is shaped by expensive campaigns that seek to dominate the discourse on the major issues of the day. This does not mean that traditional electoral politics is unimportant, nor that honored lobbying tactics of access and personal relationships are insignificant. Far from it. Still, in a post-Cold War–post-civil rights era, the absence of overarching societal issues (with abortion as something of an exception) means that interests will compete aggressively in selling their version of public policy problems and solutions— solutions that may, as with telecommunications reform, greatly enrich specific private groups.

Politics more than ever has become an offshoot of marketing. In such a context, most information is "interested." That is, the information reflects, sometimes subtley, sometimes not, the underlying views of the interests who sponsor and disseminate it. Even science becomes adversarial, because, it seems, every side on an issue can purchase a study to support its point of view. Indeed, the tobacco discourse of the late 1990s is noteworthy because the industry finally retreated from some of its most ludicrous "scientific" claims that denied the carcinogenic and addictive elements of smoking. Most lessons of the past thirty years have schooled interests to construct a coherent story line and stick to it, on policies ranging from teenage pregnancy to international trade.

We will examine the changing roles of organized interests in electoral politics and policymaking. . . .

Groups, Parties, and Campaigns: A Blurring of Roles

The long-standing relationship between political parties and interest groups in elections has changed in recent decades. Rather than aggregating various mass interests, parties have developed some of the policy-advocating characteristics typically associated with more narrow interests. At the same time parties have become less important to mobilizing voters and running campaigns. Although the vast majority of interest groups still refrain from direct electoral involvement, more and more of them have assumed some of the activities usually associated with parties, such as recruiting candidates, organizing campaigns, and running advertisements. In some tight races, interest group voices have even drowned out those of the candidates.

The decline of parties in elections represents a long-term trend that began around the turn of the century, but a series of party and campaign reforms in the early 1970s were responsible for drastically altering party interest group relations in the electoral process. The party reforms broke the state and local organizational control over party business, including the nomination process, and thus created opportunities for organized interest influence. The campaign finance changes of the early 1970s also offered advantages to interest groups. The growth of political action committees (PACs), the limitations on party spending, and the requirement that the individual campaign organization be the legal agent of the candidate all had the effect of decreasing an already diminished party role in providing campaign resources to candidates.

The parties did adapt to the interest group threat. By the mid-1980s the national parties were increasingly becoming service vendors to party candidates, successfully coping with the realities of modern, candidate-centered campaigns. PAC-party relations became less conflictual and more cooperative. Both parties embraced their emerging role as brokers by forming loose fund-raising alliances with many PACs and beginning to offer them regular assistance in directing contributions to particular campaigns, as well as aiding candidates in soliciting funds from potential donor PACs. The fear of some that organized interests (through PACs) would supplant parties in the electoral process never materialized.

The 1990s have witnessed another benchmark in relations between parties and organized interests, one that may presage an even more prominent role for *both* parties and organized interests in the electoral process, perhaps at the expense of candidate domination of campaign agendas. . . . [T]he candidate-centered system that has characterized electoral politics for more than half a century may face its most serious challenge to date.

There are a number of prominent features of the emerging system. Foremost is the huge escalation of organized interest money found in our most recent elections, much of it raised and spent outside of the controlling provisions of the Federal Election Campaign Act (FECA). Although some of the growth has been in PAC and independent spending . . . the most startling development has come in extensive soft money contributions by organized interests to the national political parties—money creatively spent by the parties beyond FECA restrictions.* These contributions, in some instances more than $1 million, do not typically come from interest groups per se but most notably from individual corporations. The rise in importance of soft money to the parties may increase organized interest leverage on individual campaigns, as well as on the parties. In 1996, for example, the major parties succeeded in raising $285 million in soft money, but this achievement rendered them highly dependent on large contributions from affluent interests.

The overall number of organized interests offering financial support has expanded as well, with many new groups entering the fray. For example, the American Cancer Society, a venerable nonprofit organization, recently contributed $30,000 to the Democratic and Republican parties in order to gain "the same access" as others, according to its national vice president for federal and state affairs, who said, "We wanted to look like players and be players."[1] Although this action is subject to a court challenge, the tax-exempt society sees such gifts as appropriate because the funds were targeted to party annual conferences and dinners, not campaign activity.

Beyond soft money contributions, the direct campaign efforts mustered by some organized interests in the mid-1990s were of historical proportions. Organized labor spent $35 million in 1996 to reverse the 1994 Democratic loss of Congress; some of these funds went to train union activists to organize targeted congressional districts and to increase voter registration, but the bulk of the funds went to buy air time for 27,000 television commercials in forty congressional districts—almost 800 spots per district. In 1996 the National Rifle Association became active in more than 10,000 political races at local, state, and national levels despite running a deficit and cutting its staff.

Another distinguishing feature of the emerging system is the blurring of traditional party and interest group roles in campaigns. In 1996, for example, both national parties became *group patrons*, as they used some of their soft money to

---

*The Bipartisan Campaign Reform Act of 2002 (BCRA), upheld by the Supreme Court in December 2003, prohibits national parties from raising and spending soft money; parties are now limited to raising and spending money subject to the contribution limits and source restrictions of federal election law (see selection 7.2). The effect of the new law at this writing is unclear, but it is likely to affect the way federal campaigns are funded, weakening the role of the national party but increasing the influence of state/local parties, political action committees (PACs), and nonprofit organizations. Previous party soft-money donors may now contribute to the increasing number of nonparty groups with a partisan orientation. Organized interest influence on campaigns is unlikely to diminish.

fund group electoral activity such as registration drives and telephone banks. Republicans contributed to a number of antitax and prolife groups, and Democrats channeled some of their funds to a variety of groups they believed would mobilize minority voters. In a very real sense, the parties were contracting out their voter mobilization function to various organized interests. Both parties, but the Republicans in particular, have also "created a dazzling galaxy of policy institutes, foundations and think tanks, each of which can raise money from private interests and which can aid the party and party candidates in a variety of ways."[2]

A number of organized interests have been increasing the level of their activities in what traditionally has [been] thought of as party arena. As James Guth and his associates put it, "In an era when party organizations have either atrophied or find it difficult to activate sympathetic voters, religious interest groups are an important new force. . . . Such groups have become significant electoral competitors (and often adjuncts) to party committees, candidate organizations, and other traditional interest groups." Thus, in 1996 religious grassroots contacts of potential voters compared "quite favorably" with voters' contacts by party organizations, political candidates, and business or labor groups. More than 54 million voter guides were distributed using church-based networks in 1996. In a number of states, Christian Right adherents have captured the formal Republican Party organization, and one estimate counted roughly 200,000 movement activists as involved in the 1996 elections at various levels.

Although many of the efforts of organized labor and the Christian Right have been coordinated with party or candidate efforts (most often unofficially, so campaign finance laws would not be violated), a lot of interest group electoral activity in the 1990s has been independent of candidate or party efforts. It is difficult at times to discern which organized interests were involved, because expenditures and disclosure are not regulated by current campaign finance laws. For example, at least $150 million was spent on issue advocacy campaigns in 1996.* As long as the ads did not advocate voting for or defeating a specific candidate, interests could express their issue-based concerns in a thinly veiled attempt to support or oppose a given candidate. Well-known groups such as the AFL-CIO, the Sierra Club, the National Education Association, the National Abortion Rights Action

---

*The 2002 campaign finance reform law banned any broadcast, cable, or satellite communication that refers to a specific candidate within 30 days of a primary or 60 days of a general election, essentially forbidding issue advocacy electioneering on public airways near an election. Corporations and unions are not allowed to engage in such activity at any time. As a consequence, broadcast electioneering by many groups is likely to begin earlier in the campaign process, outside the timing window of BCRA, while for others we are likely to witness a shift from an "air war" to a "ground war" strategy, with money concentrated on grassroots efforts rather than broadcast advertising. For example, one of the nation's wealthiest men, George Soros, has pledged $10 million to the liberal activist group America Coming Together (ACT) to be used for voter mobilization drives in 17 competitive states in an effort to defeat President George Bush in the 2004 election.

League, and the National Federation of Independent Businesses were especially prominent. Some entities operated in the shadows. Triad Management, a political consulting firm, apparently channeled at least $3 million from conservative donors to purchase television ads in support of competitive-seat Republican candidates. Approximately twenty-five groups sponsored $100 million in issue advocacy ads in 1996, and they concentrated their efforts in fifty-four competitive House and Senate races. In some cases the amount spent on issue advocacy in a race has exceeded that spent by the candidates, raising concerns that the candidates themselves had lost control over the discourse of the campaign. That is precisely the point for some interest group leaders. As Paul Jacob, executive director of U.S. Term Limits, observed, "If politicians get to control the campaign, these issues [such as term limits] won't be talked about."[3] . . .

The meaning of all this for American representative democracy is unclear. In many ways party-interest group relations have been functionally altered, especially in that the party now has an enhanced electoral role as a fund-raiser. But in the process of becoming a vendor engaged in modern candidate-centered elections, the party has surrendered some of its traditional functions of grassroots activism and voter mobilization, which have been largely left to those organized interests with adequate resources to perform them.

National parties look suspiciously like special interests themselves, with their primary concern being to raise campaign resources for their parties' officeholders seeking reelection (the party of the incumbents), with little advice from party activists. When incumbents are threatened, both national parties may even cooperate with each other, as they did in 1987 in the face of a public outcry over congressional pay raises (the party chairs agreed not to offer financial support to challengers of those incumbents who had made the pay raise a campaign issue).

An electoral system based largely on the ability of parties and their candidates to raise funds from organized interests, especially through large contributions, inevitably clashes with the dominant notion of parties as representatives of mass interests and potential counterweights to the excessive demands of particular interests. Rather, the parties may well have become, as political scientist Thomas Ferguson has theorized, not much more than investment vehicles for wealthy interests who can choose to invest directly in candidates, or broadly in parties, or specifically in issue advocacy advertisements.

Interests, Information, and Policies: Many Voices, Whose Tune?

If organized interests have changed their approaches to electoral politics, so too have they altered their strategies to affect governmental decisions. Although organized interests continue to lobby in time-honored ways within the corridors of Washington institutions, such as Congress and bureaucratic agencies, they have begun to spend more time shaping perceptions of problems and political agendas. In addition, they are devoting more and more attention to earlier stages of policy formulation, especially the fundamental defining and re-defining of issues. Indeed, successfully defining conditions as problems (such as smog, learning disabilities, or global warming) often represents the single most important step in changing policies.

In the politics of problem definition, everyone can play by calling a press conference, releasing a study, going on a talk show, commissioning a poll, or buying an advertisement. There is no shortage in Washington either of well-defined problems or potential solutions, as the capital is awash in arguments and evidence that seek to define problems and set agendas. What is more diffi-cult to understand very well is how certain definitions come to prevail within the context of political institutions that often, though not always, resist the consideration of new—or newly packaged—ideas.

As problem definition and agenda status become increasingly important ele-ments of policymaking, organized interests have stepped up their attempts to expand, restrict, or redirect conflict on given issues. The public interest and en-vironmental movements of the 1960s often led the way in understanding these elements of political life, leaving business to catch up in the 1970s and 1980s. Jeffrey Berry, a long-time student of public interest groups, has concluded that citizen groups have driven the policy agenda since the 1960s, thus forcing busi-ness interests to respond to sets of issues developed by groups such as Common Cause and environmental organizations.

Following on the heels of these agenda successes has been the institutional-ization of interests within the government, especially when broad public con-cerns are at stake. For instance, many of the 1995 battles over the Contract with America* placed legislators in sharp conflict with programs supported by members of government agencies, such as the Environmental Protection Agency. Moreover, many interests have found homes *within* the Congress in the form of caucuses composed of sitting legislators.

And there's the rub. As *more interests seek to define problems and push agenda items, more messages emanate from more sources.* For threatened interests, whether corporate, environmental, or professional, the decision to socialize a conflict (and to expand the attentive audience) has no meaning unless it can be accomplished. Even Ralph Nader, the past master of using the press to ex-pand the scope of conflict, has recently found it difficult to attract media atten-tion. Some interests can cut through the cacophony of voices; in particular, those in E. E. Schattschneider's "heavenly chorus" of affluent groups can—at a price—get their message across by spending lavishly on public relations

---

*In September 1994, in the midst of the congressional campaign, more than 300 Republican candidates signed a pledge on the Capitol steps, called the Contract with America, promising to act swiftly on a set of wide-sweeping proposals to address what they believed were major politi-cal concerns. Among the issues to be dealt with were constitutional amendments imposing term limits on members of Congress and requiring a balanced budget, making major income tax cuts, cutting back the number of government regulations, and reducing welfare spending.

campaigns or by buying advertising time and space. In addition, if such messages are directed toward legislators who have received substantial campaign contributions from these same interests, they typically reach an audience already inclined toward receptivity.

The emphasis on problem definition looms large when major public policy issues are on the table and tremendous uncertainty exists. Lots of substantive interests are in play, many competing scenarios are put forward, legislative decisions are always contingent, and public policy outcomes are often filled with unanticipated consequences. . . .

In policy battles, the capacity to obtain information and control its dissemination is the most important political power of all. Political scientist James Thurber echoes Schattschneider in arguing that if participants cannot resolve conflict on their own turf, "'outsiders' from other committees, agencies, bureaus, groups, the media, or the general public will take the issue away from them."[4] This scope-of-conflict perspective is extremely important to the dynamics of policy formulation, and it is also a source of the greatest type of uncertainty of all—conflict redefinition, as in changing a simple agricultural issue into a more complex environmental problem. . . .

Although some corporate interests (such as Microsoft, until the 1990s) have resisted involvement in Washington politics, there has been a surge of activity since the late 1970s. As Jeffrey Birnbaum has observed, the growth of corporate (and trade association) lobbying makes good economic sense: "[Even] in relatively small changes to larger pieces of legislation . . . big money is made and lost. Careful *investment* in a Washington lobbyist can yield enormous returns in the form of taxes avoided or regulations curbed— an odd negative sort of calculation, but one that forms the basis of the economics of lobbying."[5]

The nature of high-stakes decisions makes such investment almost mandatory, given the potential for tremendous gains and losses. In addition, the usual cost-benefit logic that applies to most managerial decisions—lobbying extensively versus building a new plant or embarking on an ambitious new research project—does not apply in high-stakes circumstances, because the potential benefits or costs are so great that virtually any expenditure can be justified, even if its chance to affect the outcome is minuscule. Indeed, spending on a host of tactics—from election contributions to insider access to public relations campaigns—may represent a strategy designed as much to protect lobbyists from criticism by their corporate or trade associations as to influence a given decision.

It may be a mistake to make too much of a distinction between an organized interest spending money in investing in candidates through contributions and providing information to elected officials with lobbying, advertising, or public relations campaigns. . . . Nevertheless, information exchanges between interest groups and legislators are distinct from the seeking of influence through contributions or favors. One scholar, Jack Wright, has noted that interests

> achieve influence in the legislative process not by applying electoral or financial pres-
> sure, but by developing expertise about politics and policy and by strategically sharing
> this expertise with legislators through normal lobbying activities. . . . [Organized in-
> terests] can and do exercise substantial influence even without making campaign con-
> tributions and . . . contributions and other material gifts or favors are not the primary
> sources of interest group influence in the legislative process.[6]

Even if information, and not favors or contributions, reflects the basis for interest group influence, does that mean that money is unimportant? Or that all
information is equal? Hardly. Inevitably, some interests have much greater resources to develop information that shapes policy debates. . . .

Interests, Hyperpolitics, and the Permanent Campaign

At the turn of the twenty-first century, the outward appearance of the Washington lobbying community remains true to its manifestations in 1975 or 1985;
the Gucci culture continues apace, with expensive suits and the constant buzz
of the telephone call (cellular these days). In many ways, this appearance of
stability is not deceptive at all. The big dogs of capital lobbying are still there—
a Tommy Boggs or a Tom Korologos*—trading on personal ties, political acu-
ity, and the ability to raise a quick $10,000 (maybe even $100,000) with a word
in the right ear at the right time. Favors are granted, favors are returned, and
the quality of their political intelligence remains top flight.

At the same time, things are not the same. Some of the changes are obvious:
the ability to create all varieties of grassroots pressure, a tactic raised to art form
by Jack Bonner's firm;[†] the promise and uncertainty of the Internet (a recent
survey reported that 97 percent of all legislative staff used the Internet to
gather information), and the rash of policy-oriented television advertisements
that have followed in the wake of the series of "Harry and Louise" commercials
used in the health care debate. Moreover, the assault of issue-advocacy advertising in the 1996 congressional campaigns (in the wake of liberating court decisions that weakened restrictions on spending for such ads) may have ushered
in an era of interest group–dominated electioneering. In addition, the entry of
highly sophisticated information industry players into the political process (for

---

*Thomas Hale Boggs is the well-connected son of Hale Boggs, former Democratic House
leader, and is the brother of ABC Commentator Cokie Roberts. Boggs has been a major presence in Washington politics since the 1970s, and his firm grosses more than $10 million a year
in lobbying fees. Korologos is similar to Boggs, except with a Republican spin; working as a
partner of Timmons and Company, he represents such powerful interests as Major League
Baseball, Anheuser-Busch, and the NRA.

†Jack Bonner and his firm represent the new breed of all-encompassing lobbying firms operating in Washington. They have been particularly innovative and very successful in orchestrating
grassroots campaigns that target key members of Congress for their clients.

example, Microsoft, a host of Silicon Valley firms, to say nothing of content providers such as Disney, which now owns ABC) may well lead to the politicization of many decisions over both the channels and the content of communication.

In general, we see three major trends taking shape and complementing each other. First, more interests are engaged in more kinds of behaviors to influence policy outcomes. Interests monitor more actions than they once did, and stand ready to swing into action more quickly when a red flag is raised (often by a lobbyist on retainer). Given the high stakes of governmental decisions, whether in a House committee or an EPA bureau, the monitoring-action combination is a worthwhile investment.

Second, there is little distinction, for most practical purposes, between "outside" and "inside" lobbying. Most effective influence relies on both. To be sure, a key provision can still find its way into an omnibus bill without a ripple, but battles over most major issues are fought simultaneously on multiple fronts. A call or fax from a House member's most important banker or editor or university president can be prompted by a lobbyist at the first sign of a problem in a committee hearing or, more likely, a casual conversation. Jack Bonner and a dozen other constituent-lobbying experts can construct a set of grassroots (or elite "grasstops") entreaties within a few days, if not a few hours. And a media buyer can target any sample of legislators for advertisements that run in their districts, thus ensuring that they know that their constituents and key Washington interests are watching their every action on an important bill.

Related to the diminished distinction between Washington and constituency-based lobbying is the increasing joint emphases on lobbying in state capitals and Washington. In particular, the tobacco settlement activity and the intensive campaigns of Microsoft to ward off antitrust actions in the states demonstrate how national and state politics are linked in an age of devolution.

Third, and perhaps most dramatic, is the declining distinction between the politics of elections and the politics of policymaking. Of course, in a democracy these are inextricably linked, and PACs may have solidified these ties since the 1970s. But these linkages have become much stronger—in many ways reflecting the "permanent campaign" of presidential elections—politics that emerged in the 1970s and 1980s. Blumenthal sees this as combining "image-making with strategic calculation. Under the permanent campaign government is turned into the perpetual campaign."[7] In the 1990s, many interests have come to see the combination of electoral and policy politics in much the same light, with the issue advocacy ads of 1996 serving as the initial demonstration of this new era. In addition, many interests are now viewing the "campaign" idea as one that defines their broader lobbying strategies and blurring the lines between electoral campaigns and public relations efforts.

All three of these trends—a move toward more activities, a lessened distinction between inside and outside lobbying, and the adoption of campaign-based strategies—come together in a 1998 business community initiative on international trade. Based on an initiative from the Commerce Department (and the tacit backing of a cautious White House), corporate advocates of free trade have embarked on a series of campaigns to argue publicly on behalf of free trade. As the *National Journal* reported, "The patrons of these pro-trade campaigns are typically multinational businesses, trade associations, lobbying groups and Washington think tanks, all called to action by Congress's declining support for . . . trade liberalization."[8] Responding to the growing strength of the much less well-funded loose coalition of labor, human rights, consumers, and environmental groups, the protrade interests, although not abandoning their insider initiatives, have reacted to their opponents' success in expanding the scope of the conflict over trade to issues such as domestic jobs, human rights, and environmental quality. Consider, for example, the actions of Cargill, the huge, privately held agriculture and financial services conglomerate. Historically, the firm has sought influence in the quiet ways, scarcely causing a ripple in public perceptions. But in 1998 the corporation sent 750 sets of videotapes, fact sheets, and sample speeches to its domestic plants and offices, so that its employees could make public pitches in community after community about the domestic impact of trade, especially in rural areas.[9]

At the same time, one thirty-year-old trade coalition (the less than aptly named Emergency Committee for American Trade) is sponsoring a campaign based on Cargill's efforts, while the Business Roundtable, another veteran group of top corporate leaders, "is spending a million dollars [in 1998] to shore up support of free trade in the districts of a dozen congressmen."[10] The Chamber of Commerce and the National Association of Manufacturers have initiated similar efforts to offer their members information and analyses to buttress free trade arguments beyond the Beltway.

In addition, a host of think tanks, from the moderate Brookings Institution to the libertarian Cato Institute, have developed initiatives to provide higher quality information on the benefits of trade. On a related tack, the Washington-based Center for Strategic and International Studies has embarked on a pilot project in Tennessee to educate public officials, corporate leaders, academics, and students on the strategic importance of enhanced international trade.

The combination of many business organizations, the Commerce Department, a variety of think tanks, and congressional supporters illustrates the "campaign" nature of large-scale lobbying. The direction of influence is not clear, as business leaders respond to administration entreaties, but also hope to pressure the White House to support free trade aggressively. The lobbying is directed at community leaders and the public at large, but there is little capacity to measure its effectiveness. It does not seek, at least in 1998, to influence a particular piece of legislation. Rather, the campaign emphasizes an entire set of narratives on free trade that can be used by the executive branch, legislators, lobbyists, or grassroots advocates. . . .

Given such cacophony, coupled to high-stakes decisions, it is no wonder that those cultural icons Bill Gates and Big Bird have entered the political fray.

Their respective interests, both economic and cultural, are great, and the costs of investing in lobbying, although substantial, pale before the potential benefits. But there is a cost to this extension of politics to much of our communication, what we choose to call *hyperpolitics*. If all information is seen as interested, as just one more story, then how do decision makers sort it all out? What voices cut through the "data smog" of a society that can cough up studies and stories at a moment's notice, and communicate them broadly or narrowly, as tactics suggest? Although some students of interest groups . . . see hopeful signs for a vigorous pluralism that accords major roles to consumers, public interest advocates, and environmentalists, we remain skeptical. The costs of lobbying in a hyperpolitics state are great, and the stakes are high. Money surely does not guarantee success, but the capacity to spend keeps well-heeled interests in the game, able to play the range of games that have come to define the politics of influence as we move further into the age of information.

Notes

1. Jonathan D. Salant, "Cancer Group Give to GOP, Democrats," *Kansas City Star*, March 30, 1998, A12.
2. Clyde Wilcox and Wesley Joe, "Dead Law: The Federal Election Finance Regulations, 1974–1996," *PS* 31 (March 1998): 15.
3. Donna Cassata, "Independent Groups' Ads Increasingly Steer Campaigns," *CQ Weekly*, May 2, 1998, 1114.
4. James Thurber, *Divided Democracy* (Washington, D.C.: CQ Press), 336.
5. Jeffrey Birnbaum, *The Lobbyists* (New York: Times Books, 1993), 4, emphasis added.
6. Wright, Interest Groups and Congress, 88.
7. Sidney Blumenthal, *The Permanent Campaign* (New York: Touchstone, 1982), 23.
8. Julie Kosterlitz, "Trade Crusade," *National Journal*, May 9, 1998, 1054. In addition to the specific citations noted here and later, the following paragraphs draw generally on this story.
9. Ibid., 1055.
10. Ibid.

Questions for Discussion

1. What do Cigler and Loomis mean by the term *hyperpolitics*? Why is it so difficult for public officials to make decisions in an environment characterized by hyperpolitics?
2. Cigler and Loomis argue that the traditional distinctions between political parties and interest groups no longer hold true in the contemporary political context. What factors have contributed to the "blurring of roles" between parties and interest groups? Is such a condition healthy for American democracy?

Chapter 10

Congress

Of the three branches of government, the legislature is invariably the most open to scrutiny and influence. Members of Congress are directly accountable to their constituents. Even in a security-conscious age of metal detectors and concrete barriers, the U.S. Congress remains easily accessible to citizens who seek to influence their representatives and senators or merely to observe them in action. Just as the growth of government has affected the presidency and, to a lesser extent, the Supreme Court (see Chapters 11 and 13), Congress has changed greatly in the post–World War II era, especially since the mid-1960s.

Some of these changes are straightforward. For example, in 1947 members of Congress employed 2,030 staff aides in their personal offices. In 2001 the total came to 7,209 and the overall cost of the legislative branch stood at $2 billion. Other developments have been more obscure, though no less important. The informal rules of legislative behavior have changed; today newcomers need not undergo a decade-long apprenticeship before wielding even a bit of power. Despite these and many other changes, however, contemporary legislators take on the same basic responsibilities as their predecessors: representing their constituents and making decisions about the major issues of the day.

Over the course of the American experience, Congress has received countless criticisms of its inefficiencies and its responsiveness to special interests. A bicameral (two-house) legislature is by nature difficult to control, even when a single political party holds majorities in both chambers. In addition, Congress often must face an executive branch whose interests run directly counter to its own. Differences in opinion between the two chambers or between Congress and the executive can and do produce deadlocks, especially when different parties control the different branches. In selection 10.2, Sarah Binder examines the extent of, and reasons for, stalemate in the legislative process. Although partisan differences between the branches do make a difference, disagreements between the House and Senate also contribute to deadlock within the policy-making process.

Similarly, the representative nature of Congress makes it an appropriate target for interest groups. Legislators run expensive reelection campaigns. These require substantial contributions, which frequently come from the growing number of political action committees that represent a wide range of groups. The structure of Congress allows interest groups easy access to a hundred

351

subcommittees that deal with very specific issues ranging from oil exploration to air traffic control to military construction. The small membership and narrow focus of most House and Senate subcommittees provide attractive opportunities for a seemingly limitless number of lobbyists to influence public policies.

The selections in this chapter emphasize both continuity and change in congressional politics. They illustrate the rise of individualism on Capitol Hill. The days are gone when autocratic committee chairs could control the legislative agenda. To exercise real power, a committee chair in the House has ordinarily required at least twenty years' consecutive service on a given panel. This fact encouraged long careers and promoted the image of Congress as a body of tottering graybeards who relied on seniority and the power of their committee positions, rather than the strength of their ideas or intellect, to dominate the process.

By the early 1970s, however, congressional structure and personnel had undergone a dramatic transformation, especially in the House. After the 1982 elections, more than two-thirds of the 535 members of Congress (100 senators, 435 representatives) had arrived on Capitol Hill since 1974. Accompanying this upheaval in personnel was a series of reforms that greatly dispersed power within the Congress. The changes of the 1969–1975 period profoundly affected the House of Representatives. Committee chairs lost much of their authority, and the big winners were the rank-and-file House members, especially the majority Democrats. These representatives demonstrated their new clout in 1975 by voting within the Democratic Caucus to oust three senior committee chairs.

Political scientist Kenneth A. Shepsle (selection 10.1) assesses these changes by first sketching the "textbook Congress" of the 1950s and then noting the various ways in which Congress has diverged from the conventional wisdom of that era. In particular, the decline of committees has led to more variability and uncertainty in congressional politics. The seeming equilibrium of the 1950s Congress gave way to a less predictable, less coherent legislative process within a fragmented House of Representatives by the 1980s. Changes in the way the House does business rest in large part on the replacement of veteran members with newcomers. Although this turnover slowed substantially during the 1980s as incumbents dominated electoral politics, 110 new representatives entered the House in the wake of the 1992 elections. Even more important was the group of 73 freshmen Republicans whose victories allowed the GOP to win control of the House in 1994.

Changes have affected the Senate less profoundly than they have the House, because the upper chamber has always relied on informal cooperation among its members. Nevertheless, some senators have become increasingly adept at tying the body into knots by relying on rules and traditions that evolved to protect minority rights. Senators have often acted to obstruct the regular flow of legislative business, acknowledging that in so doing they will win no popularity contests among their colleagues. Indeed, obstructionism has made leading the Senate a formidable—and perhaps impossible—task. Indeed, the greatest difficulty facing party leaders in the chamber derives from the profound individualism of the Senate. Given the power of a single senator to slow the legislative process, through filibusters and other means, each member must be accorded substantial respect, even deference, from the party leaders. When a senator comes to the chamber with an independent base of power, the leaders' task can grow even more difficult. Selection 10.4, by Elizabeth Kolbert, offers insights into the career development of the Senate's best-known recent entrant—Hillary Clinton (D-N.Y.). Senator Clinton has proven herself a patient and deferential new legislator—up to a point. Knowing that she can obtain attention with little effort, she has worked hard to win a reputation as a hard-working, cooperative, and state-oriented senator. By gaining the respect of her colleagues from both parties, Senator Clinton has established her own political profile, beyond that of First Lady. At the same time, she remains a major national figure, perhaps waiting her turn for the Democratic presidential nomination. Senators have a lot of latitude in establishing their political identities, and Hillary Clinton has succeeded in making herself into a well-respected, working senator—albeit the best-known, most-watched legislator on Capitol Hill.

Historically, congressional politics has reflected continuing tensions between forces of centralization and decentralization. In the late 1970s, for example, decentralizing trends prevailed as subcommittees proliferated and individual legislators gained substantial personal resources, such as staff. Electoral competition for House seats has also declined, and most representatives are well insulated from any pressures that party leaders may seek to employ. Speakers Tip O'Neill, Jim Wright, and Thomas Foley instituted a strategy of "inclusive" leadership that gave large numbers of the majority Democrats an increased stake in the process. In addition, the memberships of the Democratic and the Republican parties in the House have become more homogeneous. As Republicans have gained increasing numbers of seats in the South, moderate-to-conservative southern Democrats have lost much of their power. And fewer moderate Republicans have won election, as conservatives have come to dominate their party.

These trends came together in 1994–1995, when Republicans captured control of the House for the first time since 1955. The House Republicans, led by Speaker Newt Gingrich and bolstered by seventy-three first-term insurgents, had to learn how to govern as a majority. Using the ten-point Contract with America as their script, the House acted on a host of major legislative initiatives in the first 100 (actually 93) days of the 104th Congress in early 1995 and subsequently confronted President Clinton on budget issues to the point of shutting down parts of the federal government in late 1995 and early 1996. The Republicans did learn that they needed support in the Senate and the White House to accomplish much of their agenda, and they did, eventually, "learn to legislate," and they have maintained their majority status through the 108th Congress (2003–2004).

Indeed, the Republican majority in the House has demonstrated a cohesion that has given the lie to any idea that contemporary American politics cannot support strong legislative parties. Building on an increasingly partisan electoral base in the country, the Republican leadership has used ideology, fund-raising prowess, and a willingness to reach out to moderate GOP legislators to build consistent majorities in a chamber that can be run effectively by a disciplined majority. At the heart of this effort is Representative Tom DeLay (R-Tex.), who served as majority whip under Gingrich and moved up to majority leader when Dennis Hastert (R-Ill.) became speaker in 1999. Although he is renowned for his tough partisanship, DeLay understands that he must moderate his image (and his tactics) if he is to succeed Hastert. Veteran congressional reporter Richard E. Cohen paints a nuanced picture of a majority leader (selection 10.3) who increasingly seeks to balance his partisan tendencies with a more diplomatic, inclusive approach to politics. Cohen notes some real successes here, but the highly partisan DeLay surely remains, as witnessed by his aggressive and apparently successful 2003 attempt to push through a Texas redistricting map that may well gain five or six House seats for the Republicans. In the contemporary House, "politics ain't beanbag," to quote Peter Finley Dunne's fictional Mr. Dooley from a century ago.

Likewise, for all its individualism, the Senate has become more and more partisan since the mid-1980s. Although the smaller chamber provides greater opportunities for personal ties that cross party lines, Senate voting patterns have sometimes demonstrated even more partisanship than those of the House. When voters are thoroughly divided along partisan lines, it only makes sense that their representative institutions will follow suit.

10.1

The Changing Textbook Congress

Kenneth A. Shepsle

Ordinarily, it takes a while for political scientists to agree that a certain article is a "classic" piece of work. For Kenneth A. Shepsle's "The Changing Textbook Congress," however, the recognition came quickly and virtually universally. A most imaginative and provocative theorist, Shepsle places congressional developments of the 1960s through the 1980s in a context of an institution that has changed profoundly since scholars painted their definitive portrait of the Congress of the 1940s and 1950s.

One of Shepsle's chief interests is determining how institutional equilibrium, or balance among forces, is established. Committees dominated the earlier era's equilibrium, but since the 1960s, committees have come under pressure from individual members, with their considerable staff and technology resources, and from party leaders, who have gained substantial powers through a series of reform efforts. Moreover, most House members must represent increasingly large and diverse districts, which makes coalition building all the more difficult.

Writing in the late 1980s, Shepsle does not identify a clear contemporary equilibrium within Congress. With large numbers of power centers and stronger individual members, we may be entering an era marked more by uncertainty and fluidity than by a well-defined equilibrium. Still, given increasing partisanship in the 1990s and beyond, the Congress may well be governed more by a strong Republican majority, at least in the House, than by a balance among a number of powerful members.

When scholars talk about Congress to one another, their students, or the public, they often have a stylized version in mind, a textbook Congress characterized by a few main tendencies and described in broad terms. This is not to say that they are incapable of filling in fine-grained detail, making distinctions, or describing change. But at the core of their descriptions and distinctions are approximations, caricatures, and generalities.

Kenneth A. Shepsle is professor of government at Harvard University.

Shepsle, Kenneth A. Reprinted by permission from Kenneth A. Shepsle, "The Changing Textbook Congress," in *Can Government Govern?*

They are always incomplete and somewhat inaccurate, but still they consist of robust regularities. . . .

The textbook Congress I have in mind is the one that emerged from World War II and the Legislative Reorganization Act of 1946. Its main features persisted until the mid-1960s; its images remained in writings on Congress well into the 1970s. . . .

To illuminate the institutional dynamics of the past forty years, this [selection] describes some early signs of change in the textbook Congress in the 1950s, suggests how events of the 1960s and 1970s disrupted the equilibrium, and looks at some of the emerging features of a new textbook Congress, though I am not convinced that a new equilibrium has yet been established. The story I develop here is not a historical tour d'horizon [overview]. Rather it addresses theoretical issues of institutional development involving the capacity of Congress and its members to represent their constituencies, to make national policy, and to balance the intrinsic tensions between these tasks. . . .

The Textbook Congress: The Late 1940s to the Mid-1960s

Any portrait of Congress after World War II must begin with the member and, in a popular phrase of the time, "his work as he sees it." Then, as now, legislators divided their time between Washington and home, the relative proportions slowly changing in favor of Washington during the 1950s. In Washington they divided their time between chamber, committee, and personal office; all three demands grew from the 1940s to the 1960s as chamber work load, committee activity, and constituency demands increased.

In 1947, just after passage of the Legislative Reorganization Act, the average House member had three staff assistants and the average senator six. Because even these modest averages would be the envy of a contemporary member of the British Parliament or of most state legislatures, they indicate that by mid-century the American national legislature was a highly professional place. Nevertheless, by the mid-1960s congressional staffs had swelled even further: a typical House member now had twelve assistants and a typical senator eighteen. Committee staffs, too, grew dramatically from an average of ten to nearly thirty in the House and from fifteen to more than thirty in the Senate. These numbers do not include the substantial staffs of the nearly 400 offices of institutional leaders, informal groups, and legislative support agencies.

Since most committee staffers during these twenty years were in fact under the control of committee chairmen, some of the more senior legislators came to head sizable organizations. Indeed, if most legislators in the Eightieth Congress (1947–8) could be said to have headed mom 'n pop businesses with a handful of clerks and assistants, by the mid-1960s they had come to oversee major modern enterprises with secretaries, receptionists, interns, and a variety of legislative, administrative, and political professionals (typically lawyers). A committee chair or ranking minority member, who might also head a couple of sub-committees or party committees, might have a staff exceeding one hundred.

This growth transformed legislative life and work. In the 1940s the House had its norms and the Senate its folkways, perhaps even an inner club.* Hard work, long apprenticeship, restrained participation of younger members, specialization (particularly in the House), courtesy, reciprocity, and institutional loyalty characterized daily life in each chamber. Even if these norms of behavior were only suggestions, frequent contact among colleagues made them a reality. Undoubtedly, members who were neighbors in the same office building, who shared a committee assignment, or who traveled back and forth to Washington from the same state or region came to know each other exceedingly well. But even more distant relationships were based on familiarity and frequent formal or informal meeting.

By the mid-1960s this had all changed. The rubbing of elbows was replaced by liaisons between legislative corporate enterprises, typically at the staff level. Surrounded or protected by a bevy of clerks and assistants, members met other members only occasionally and briefly on the chamber floor or in committee meetings. And many of the norms supporting work and specialization eroded.

With limited time and resources, legislators of the 1940s and 1950s concentrated on only a few activities. They simply did not have the staffs or money to be able to involve themselves in a wide range of policy issues, manage a net-work of ombudsman activities back home, raise campaign finances, or intercede broadly and frequently in the executive branch's administration of programs. Rather, they picked their spots selectively and depended on jurisdictional decentralization and reciprocity among committees to divide the legislative labor, on the legislative party for voting cues inside the chamber, and on local party organizations for campaign resources and electioneering.

During the 1960s, as congressional offices gained staff and funding, members began to take on many new activities. Larger staffs in district offices, trips home, and franking privileges enabled them to develop a personal presence before their constituencies. This permitted them to orchestrate electioneering, polling, voter mobilization, and campaign finance activities themselves. They grew less dependent on organizations outside their own enterprises—local parties, for example—which previously performed such functions. The geographic constituency had, of course, always been important, but it had often been mediated by party, both local and national. By the mid-1960s the members' relationships with their constituencies were growing increasingly unmediated (just as the relationships between members were growing increasingly mediated). They were constant presences in their districts, had begun to develop personal followings, and consequently achieved a certain independence from their parties (and hence some insulation from party fortunes). As members made more

---

*The consensus view of the Senate of this era emphasized its dominance by a core of generally senior senators, who came disproportionately but not exclusively from the South.

trips home and allocated more staff to district offices and more Washington staff to constituency service and constituency-oriented legislation, calculations of how they would present themselves to the folks back home and explain their Washington activities took on added importance. Constituents' needs (the geographic imperative) began to compete with party as a guide to behavior.

Personal and institutional arrangements in Washington also changed. In the 1950s members, especially in the House, limited themselves to work on a few issues, determined to a considerable extent by their places in the committee system. Most members were able to land assignments to committees that were directly relevant to their constituencies. Much of their time, energy, and limited staff resources were devoted to work inside these little legislatures. By partitioning policy into committee jurisdictions, and matching member interests with those jurisdictions, legislative arrangements permitted members to get the most out of their limited resources. Aside from those with institutional ambitions, who hoped one day to be appointed to the Appropriations, Rules, or Ways and Means committees (Appropriations, Finance, Foreign Relations, or Armed Services in the Senate), most members had only limited incentives to become actively involved in policy areas outside their own assignments and were content to serve on legislative committees that had jurisdiction over the issues of central importance to their constituents. Thus, with limited means and incentives, members sustained a system of deference and reciprocity as part of the 1950s equilibrium, especially in the House.

Because of the growth of resources within their own enterprises in the 1960s, members began to acquire enhanced in-house capabilities. Deference to expert committee judgments on policy outside the jurisdiction of committees on which a member served was no longer so necessary. Members could now afford to assign some of their staff to track developments in other policy areas. The charge to the staffer became "Find something of interest for the boss, something that will help the district." Members were also no longer so dependent on party signals; with greater resources they were better able to determine their interests. In short, greater resources led to vertical integration—the absorption into the member enterprise of activities formerly conducted outside it—and with that, to member independence. Consequently, the relationship in which jurisdiction constrained both interest and activism began to fray as the 1960s came to an end.

Incentives for members to break away from the institutional niches in which they found themselves also multiplied. In both the 1960s and the 1970s, reapportionments,* along with economic and demographic changes, produced congressional districts that were neither so purely rural nor so purely urban as they

---

*The Constitution mandates reapportionment of House seats among the states every ten years. This requirement became especially significant in the 1960s and 1970s as the Supreme Court interpreted the Constitution to mean that districts should be drawn as equally in population as possible.

had been. Increasingly, the districts were mixed, often including a major city and a number of towns, as well as perhaps some rural areas. Member interests began to reflect this heterogeneity. Issues were also evolving in ways that cut across existing interest-group configurations and committee jurisdictions. Except in a few cases, one or two major committee jurisdictions could no longer encompass the interests of a district. Members thus had to diversify their portfolios of legislative activities. And this meant less specialization, less deference, less reciprocity.

Thus the limited resources and truncated policy interests characteristic of House members and to a lesser extent members of the Senate in the 1940s and 1950s began to give way in the 1960s and 1970s. Increased member resources and more diverse constituencies provided both the means and the incentives for members to break out of a now restrictive division and specialization of labor. Geographic imperatives were beginning to supersede considerations of party and seniority to become the principal basis on which members defined their responsibilities and work habits. Geography was also beginning to threaten jurisdiction as the principal basis on which the House organized its business.

These changes were less dramatic in the Senate only because it had traditionally been a much less specialized institution. Resources were more plentiful and constituencies more heterogeneous than in the House. And because the Senate was smaller, members had to have more diverse activities and interests. Yet even in the Senate the pressure toward less specialization was growing. Entire states were becoming more heterogeneous as a result of the industrialization of the South, the switch to a service economy in the North, and the nationalization of financial matters (so that even South Dakota could become a center for credit activities). And senators, like their House counterparts, were expanding their enterprises. By the end of the period the Senate, though less dramatically than the House, was also a less specialized place.

The argument I am making here is that geography, jurisdiction, and party hang together in a sort of equilibrium. The 1940s and 1950s represented one such equilibrium in which local parties helped the members get elected and legislative parties loosely coordinated committee activity. But the division of labor and committee dominance of jurisdiction were the central features of the textbook Congress. Committees both accommodated member needs and controlled agendas and decisionmaking. This arrangement "advantaged senior members, committees, and the majority party, with the chairmen of the standing committees sitting at the intersection of these groups." More heterogeneous constituencies and increased member resources upset this textbook equilibrium. Members have adapted by voting themselves even more resources and expanding their activities. By the 1970s parties both inside and outside the legislature had become considerably more submissive holding companies for member enterprises than had earlier been the case. Committees, too, had changed character. . . .

Beginning with the 1958 elections, however, and continuing throughout the 1960s, a new breed of legislator was coming to Washington, one more committed to legislative activism and policy entrepreneurship than in the past, one beginning to reflect demographic changes, and, most important, one that found ways to stay in office. By the early 1970s these legislators had accumulated considerable seniority. Thus the old equilibrium was disrupted and the stage set for institutional developments that would strike at the heart of the textbook Congress.

The Changing Textbook Congress: The 1970s and 1980s

An idiosyncratic historical factor had an important bearing on the institutional reforms of the 1970s that undermined the textbook Congress. For much of the twentieth century the Democratic party in Congress spoke with a heavy southern accent. In 1948, for example, more than 53 percent of the Democrats in the House and nearly 56 percent of those in the Senate came from the eleven Confederate states and five border states (Kentucky, Maryland, Missouri, Oklahoma, and West Virginia). These states accounted for only a third of all House and Senate seats. Beginning with the 1958 landslide, however, this distribution changed. In 1960 the same sixteen states accounted for just under 50 percent of Democratically held House seats and 43 percent of Democratically held Senate seats. By 1982 the numbers had fallen to 40 percent and 39 percent, respectively, and have held at that level. . . . Increasingly, Democrats were winning and holding seats in the North and West and, to a somewhat lesser extent, Republicans were becoming competitive in the South.

The nationalization of the Democratic coalition in Congress, however, was reflected far more slowly at the top of the seniority ladder.* Although between 1955 and 1967 the proportion of southern Democrats (border states excluded) in the House had dropped from 43 percent to 35 percent (46 percent to 28 percent in the Senate), the proportion of House committee chairs held by southerners fell from 63 percent to 50 percent, and rose from 53 percent to 56 percent in the Senate. Southerners held two of the three exclusive committee chairs in the House and two of the four in the Senate in 1955; in 1967 they held all of them.

The tension between liberal rank-and-file legislators and conservative southern committee chairs was important in the 1960s but had few institutional repercussions. True, Judge Howard Smith (Democrat of Virginia), the tyrannical chairman of the House Rules Committee, lost in a classic power struggle with Speaker Rayburn in 1961. But the defeat should not be exaggerated.

Seniority means the number of consecutive terms a legislator has served on a committee. The most senior majority-party member would automatically become chair of the committee. This practice was modified but not eliminated in the 1970s.

Committees and their chairs maintained both the power to propose legislation and the power to block it in their respective jurisdictions. In 1967 southern Democrats George H. Mahon of Texas, William M. Colmer of Mississippi, and Wilbur D. Mills of Arkansas chaired the Appropriations, Rules, and Ways and Means committees, respectively, in a manner not very different from that of the incumbents a decade earlier. Although the massive legislative productivity of the Eighty-ninth Congress (1965–66) did much to relieve this tension, it relieved it not so much by changing legislative institutions as by managing to mobilize very large liberal majorities. After the 1966 elections, and with the Vietnam War consuming more and more resources and attention, the Eighty-ninth Congress increasingly seemed like a brief interlude in the committee dominance that stretched back to World War II, if not earlier.

By the end of the 1960s a Democratic president had been chased from office, and the 1968 Democratic convention revealed the tensions created by the war in Vietnam and disagreements over a range of domestic issues. Despite a Democratic landslide in 1964, Republican gains for the decade amounted to thirty-eight seats in the House and eight in the Senate, further accentuating the liberal cast of the Democratic rank and file in Congress. As the 1970s opened, then, liberal Democratic majorities in each chamber confronted a conservative president [Richard Nixon], conservative Republican minorities in each chamber, and often conservative southern committee chairmen of their own party who together blocked many of their legislative initiatives. The liberals thus turned inward, using the Democratic Caucus to effect dramatic changes in institutional practices, especially in the House.

The Age of Reform

Despite the tensions it caused, the mature committee system had many advantages. The division of labor in the House not only allowed for decisions based on expertise, but perhaps more important, it sorted out and routinized congressional careers. Committees provided opportunities for political ambitions to be realized, and they did so in a manner that encouraged members to invest in committee careers. In an undifferentiated legislature, or in a committee-based legislature in which the durability of a committee career or the prospects for a committee leadership post depended on the wishes and whims of powerful party leaders (for example, the Speaker in the nineteenth century House), individual legislators have less incentive to invest effort in committee activities. Such investments are put at risk every time the political environment changes. Specialization and careerism are encouraged, however, when rewards depend primarily on individual effort (and luck), and not on the interventions and patronage of others. An important by-product is the encouragement given talented men and women to come to the legislature and to remain there. The slow predictability of career development under a seniority system may repel the impatient, but its inexorability places limits on risks by reducing a member's dependence on arbitrary power and unexpected events.

Even Voltaire's optimistic Dr. Pangloss, however, would recognize another side to this coin. When a committee system that links geography and jurisdiction through the assignment process is combined with an institutional bargain producing deference and reciprocity, it provides the foundation for the distributive politics of interest-group liberalism. But there are no guarantees of success. The legislative process is full of hurdles and veto groups, and occasionally they restrain legislative activism enough to stimulate a reaction. Thus in the 1950s, authorizing committees, frustrated by a stingy House Appropriations Committee, created entitlements as a means of circumventing the normal appropriations process. In the 1960s the Rules Committee became the major obstacle and it, too, was tamed. In the 1970s the Ways and Means Committee, which lacked an internal division of labor through subcommittees, bottled up many significant legislative proposals; it was dealt with by the Subcommittee Bill of Rights and the Committee Reform Amendments of 1974. The solution in the 1950s had no effect on legislative arrangements. The solution in the 1960s entailed modest structural reform that directly affected only one committee. In the 1970s, however, the committee system itself became the object of tinkering.

The decade of the 1970s was truly an age of legislative reform. In effect, it witnessed a representational revolt against a system that dramatically skewed rewards toward the old and senior who were often out of step with fellow partisans. It is a long story, admirably told in detail elsewhere. Here I shall focus on the way reforms enabled the rise of four power centers that competed, and continue to compete, with the standing committees for political influence.

First, full committees and their chairs steadily lost power to their subcommittees. At least since the Legislative Reorganization Act of 1946, subcommittees have been a significant structural element of the committee system in the House. However, until the 1970s they were principally a tool of senior committee members, especially committee chairmen, who typically determined subcommittee structure, named members, assigned bills, allocated staff resources, and orchestrated the timing and sequence in which the full committee would take up their proposals and forward them to the floor. Because the structures were determined idiosyncratically by individual chairmen, committees could be very different. Ways and Means had no subcommittees. Armed Services had numbered subcommittees with no fixed jurisdictions. Appropriations had rigidly arranged subcommittees. In almost all cases the chairman called the tune, despite an occasional committee revolt.

During the 1970s a series of reforms whittled away at the powers of the committee chairmen. In 1970 chairmen began to lose some control of their agendas. They could no longer refuse to call meetings; a committee majority could vote to meet anyway with the ranking majority member presiding. Once a rule had been granted for floor consideration of a bill, the chairman could not delay consideration for more than a week; after seven days, a committee majority could move floor consideration.

In 1973 the Democratic members of a House committee were designated as the committee caucus and empowered to choose subcommittee chairs and set subcommittee budgets. During the next two years, committees developed a procedure that allowed members, in order of committee seniority, to bid for subcommittee chairmanships. Also in 1973 the Democratic Caucus passed the Subcommittee Bill of Rights, which mandated that legislation be referred to subcommittees, that subcommittees have full control over their own agendas, and that they be provided with adequate staff and budget. In 1974 the Committee Reform Amendments required that full committees (Budget and Rules excepted) establish at least four subcommittees, an implicit strike against the undifferentiated structure of Ways and Means. In 1976 committee caucuses were given the authority to determine the number of subcommittees and their respective jurisdictions. Finally, in 1977 the selection procedure for committee chairs was changed, allowing the party caucus to elect them by secret ballot.

Full committees and their chairs thus had had their wings clipped. A chair was now beholden to the committee caucus, power had devolved upon subcommittees, and standing committees were rapidly becoming holding companies for their subunits.

Another center of power was created by the growth of member resources. Through House Resolution 5 and Senate Resolution 60, members were able to tap into committee and subcommittee budgets to hire staff to conduct their committee work. Additional resources were available for travel and office support. Budgets for congressional support agencies such as the General Accounting Office, the Congressional Research Service, and the Office of Technology Assessment, which individual members could employ for specific projects, also increased enormously. In short, member enterprises were becoming increasingly self-sufficient.

Committee power was also compromised by increased voting and amendment activity on the floor. The early 1970s marked the virtual end to anonymous floor votes. The secret ballot was never used in floor votes in the House, but voice votes, division votes, and unrecorded teller votes had allowed tallies to be detached from the identity of individual members. This changed as it became increasingly easy to demand a public roll call, a demand greatly facilitated by the advent of electronic voting in 1973. Roll call votes in turn stimulated amendment activity on the floor. In effect, full committees and their chairs, robbed of some of their control of agendas by subcommittees, were now robbed of more control by this change in floor procedure.

Floor activity was further stimulated by the declining frequency with which the Rules Committee was permitted to issue closed rules, which barred floor amendments to legislation. The specific occasion for this change was the debate on retaining the oil depletion allowance. Because this tax break was protected by the Ways and Means Committee, on which the oil-producing states were well represented, efforts to change the policy could only come about through floor amendments. But Ways and Means bills traditionally were protected by a closed rule. The Democratic Caucus devised a policy in which a caucus majority could instruct its members on the Rules Committee to vote specific amendments in order. Applying this strategy to the oil depletion allowance, the caucus in effect ended the tradition of closed-rule protection of committee bills. This encouraged floor amendments and at the same time reduced committee control over final legislation. It also encouraged committees to anticipate floor behavior more carefully when they marked up a bill.

Finally, committee dominance was challenged by the increased power of the Democratic Caucus and the Speaker. For all the delegation of committee operations to subcommittees and individual members, the changes in the congressional landscape were not all of one piece. In particular, before the 1970s the Democratic Caucus was a moribund organization primarily concerned with electing officers and attending to the final stages of committee assignments. After these activities were completed in the first few days of a new Congress, the caucus was rarely heard from. In the 1970s, however, as committees and chairmen were being undermined by subcommittees, there was a parallel movement to strengthen central party leadership and rank-and-file participation.

The first breach came in the seniority system. In 1971 the Democratic Caucus relieved its Committee on Committees—the Democratic members of the Ways and Means Committee—of having to rely on seniority in nominating committee chairs. This had the effect of putting sitting chairs on notice, although none was threatened at the time. In 1974 it became possible for a small number of caucus members to force individual votes on nominees for chairs and later to vote by secret ballot. In 1975 the caucus took upon itself the right to vote on subcommittee chairs of the Appropriations Committee. In that same year three incumbent chairmen were denied reelection to their posts (a fourth, Wilbur Mills, resigned under pressure).

Next came the democratizing reforms. Members were limited in the number of committee and subcommittee berths they could occupy and the number they could chair. As the constraints became more binding, it was necessary to move further down the ladder of seniority to fill positions. Power thus became more broadly distributed.

But perhaps the most significant reforms were those that strengthened the Speaker and made the position accountable to the caucus. In 1973 House party leaders (Speaker, majority leader, and whip) were included on the Committee on Committees, giving them an increased say in committee assignments. The caucus also established the Steering and Policy Committee with the Speaker as chair. In 1974 Democratic committee assignments were taken away from the party's complement on Ways and Means and given to the new committee. In addition, the Speaker was given the power to appoint and remove a majority of the members of the committee and the Democratic members of the Rules Committee. In 1974 the Speaker also was empowered to refer bills simultaneously or sequentially to several committees, to create ad hoc committees, and, in 1977, to set time limits for their deliberations. Finally, in 1977 Speaker Thomas P. O'Neill started employing task forces to develop and manage particular policy issues. These task forces overlapped but were not coincident with the committees of jurisdiction and, most significant, they were appointed by the Speaker.

The caucus itself became more powerful. As mentioned, caucus majorities could instruct the Rules Committee and elect committee chairs and Appropriations subcommittee chairs. Caucus meetings could be called easily, requiring only a small number of signatories to a request, so that party matters could be thoroughly aired. In effect, the caucus became a substitute arena for both the floor and the committee rooms in which issues could be joined and majorities mobilized.

The revolt of the 1970s thus strengthened four power centers. It liberated members and subcommittees, restored to the Speakership an authority it had not known since the days of Joe Cannon,* and invigorated the party caucus. Some of the reforms had a decentralizing effect, some a recentralizing effect. Standing committees and their chairs were caught in the middle. Geography and party benefited; the division-of-labor jurisdictions were its victims. . . .

A New Textbook Congress?

The textbook Congress of the 1940s and 1950s reflected an equilibrium of sorts among institutional structure, partisan alignments, and electoral forces. There was a "conspiracy" between jurisdiction and geography. Congressional institutions were organized around policy jurisdictions, and geographic forces were accommodated through an assignment process that ensured representatives would land berths on committees important to their constituents. Reciprocity and deference sealed the bargain. Committees controlled policy formation in their respective jurisdictions. Floor activity was generally dominated by members from the committee of jurisdiction. Members' resources were sufficiently modest that they were devoted chiefly to committee-related activities. Constituencies were sufficiently homogeneous that this limitation did not, for most members, impose much hardship. Coordination was accomplished by senior committee members, each minding his own store. This system was supported by a structure that rewarded specialization, hard work, and waiting one's turn in the queue. Parties hovered in the background as the institutional means for organizing each chamber and electing leaders. Occasionally they would serve to mobilize majorities for partisan objectives, but these occasions were rare. The parties, especially the Democrats, were heterogeneous holding companies, incapable of

---

*Representative Joseph Cannon (R-Ill.) served as Speaker from 1903 to 1911. His power in this office was successfully challenged by a coalition of Democrats and dissident Republicans in 1910.

cohering around specific policy directions except under unusual circumstances and therefore unwilling to empower their respective leaders or caucuses.

Something happened in the 1960s. The election of an executive and a congressional majority from the same party certainly was one important feature. Policy activism, restrained since the end of World War II, was encouraged. This exacerbated some divisions inside the Democratic coalition, leading to piecemeal institutional tinkering such as the expansion of the Rules Committee and the circumvention of the Appropriations Committee. At the same time the Voting Rights Act, occasioned by the temporarily oversized condition of the majority party in the Eighty-ninth Congress, set into motion political events that, together with demographic and economic trends, altered political alignments in the South. By the 1980s, Democrats from the North and the South were coming into greater agreement on matters of policy.

Thus the underlying conditions supporting the equilibrium among geographical, jurisdictional, and partisan imperatives were overwhelmed during the 1960s. The 1970s witnessed adjustments to these changed conditions that transformed the textbook Congress. Institutional reform was initiated by the Democratic Caucus. Demographic, generational, and political trends, frustrated by the inexorable workings of the seniority system, sought an alternative mode of expression. Majorities in the caucus remade the committee system. With this victimization came less emphasis on specialization, less deference toward committees as the floor became a genuine forum for policy formulation, and a general fraying of the division of labor.

One trend began with the Legislative Reorganization Act of 1946 itself. In the past forty years members have gradually acquired the resources to free themselves from other institutional players. The condition of the contemporary member of Congress has been described as "atomistic individualism" and the members themselves have been called "enterprises." The slow accretion of resources permitted members to respond to the changes in their home districts and encouraged them to cross the boundaries of specialization. These developments began to erode the reciprocity, deference, and division of labor that defined the textbook Congress.

The old equilibrium between geography and jurisdiction, with party hovering in the background, has changed. Geography (as represented by resource-rich member enterprises) has undermined the strictures of jurisdiction. But has the new order liberated party from its former holding-company status? In terms of political power the Democratic Caucus has reached new heights in the past decade. Party leaders have not had so many institutional tools and resources since the days of Boss Cannon. Committee leaders have never in the modern era been weaker or more beholden to party institutions. And, in terms of voting behavior, Democrats and Republicans have not exhibited as much internal cohesion in a good long while. Party, it would seem, is on the rise. But so, too, are the member enterprises.

What, then, has grown up in the vacuum created by the demise of the textbook Congress? I am not convinced that relationships have settled into a regular pattern in anything like the way they were institutionalized in the textbook Congress.

First, too many members of Congress remain too dissatisfied. The aggressive moves by Jim Wright* to redefine the Speaker's role are a partial response to this circumstance. Prospective changes in the Senate majority party leadership alignment in the 101st Congress convey a similar signal. The issue at stake is whether central party organs can credibly coordinate activities in Congress, thereby damping the centrifugal tendencies of resource-rich members, or whether leaders will remain, in one scholar's words, "janitors for an untidy chamber."

One possible equilibrium of a new textbook Congress, therefore, would have member enterprises balanced off against party leaders; committees and other manifestations of a specialized division of labor would be relegated to the background. Coordination, formerly achieved in a piecemeal, decentralized fashion by the committee system, would fall heavily on party leaders and their institutional allies, the Rules and Budget committees and the party caucuses. However, unless party leaders can construct a solution to the budgetary mess in Congress—a solution that will entail revising the budget process—the burden of coordination will be more than the leaders can bear. Government by continuing resolutions, reconciliation proposals, and other omnibus mechanisms forms an unstable fulcrum for institutional equilibrium.[†]

Second, any success from the continued strengthening of leadership resources and institutions is highly contingent on the support of the members. Strong leadership institutions have to be seen by the rank and file as solutions to institutional problems. This requires a consensus among majority party members both on the nature of the problems and the desirability of the solutions. A consensus of sorts has existed for several years: demographic and other trends have homogenized the priorities of Democrats; experience with the spate of reforms in the 1970s has convinced many that decentralized ways of doing things severely tax the capacity of Congress to act; and, since 1982, the Reagan presidency has provided a unifying target.

But what happens if the bases for consensus erode? A major issue—trade and currency problems, for instance, or war in Central America or the Middle East—could set region against region within the majority party and reverse the trend toward consensus. Alternatively, the election of a Democratic president could redefine the roles of legislative leaders, possibly pitting congressional and presidential factions against one another in a battle for partisan leadership.[‡]

---

*Jim Wright was Speaker from 1987 to 1989.

[†]Reconciliation proposals and continuing resolutions are budget-related bills that often combine many subjects in a catch-all (or omnibus) piece of legislation. Control by committees or other specialized groupings is rendered difficult by such practices.

[‡]As of 1994, that had not happened much in the Clinton administration, although House Democratic Whip David Bonior did lead the opposition to the Clinton-backed North American Free Trade Agreement in 1993.

The point here is that the equilibrium between strong leaders and strong members is vulnerable to perturbations in the circumstances supporting it.

. . . The member enterprises, however, will not go away. Members will never again be as specialized, as deferential, as willing "to go along to get along" as in the textbook Congress of the 1950s. For better or worse, we are stuck with full-service members of Congress. They are incredibly competent at representing the diverse interests that geographic representation has given them. But can they pass a bill or mobilize a coalition? Can they govern?

Questions for Discussion

1. How did the seniority system, which rewarded simple longevity rather than talent or political support, survive for so long? What are the advantages of promoting leaders based on seniority? The liabilities?
2. Why do you think legislators create strong "member enterprises"? Why might these undermine the committee system?

 10.2

Going Nowhere: A Gridlocked Congress?

Sarah A. Binder

Until the 1950s and 1960s, the same party usually controlled both the executive and legislative branches of the national government. When government was divided, it was likely part of a transition from one party's dominance to that of the other. Since 1969, however, divided control of the Congress and the presidency has been the rule rather than the exception. And in the 1981–2000 period, only in 1993–1994 did one party (the Democrats) win control of both branches. Most

Sarah A. Binder is a fellow in the Brookings Governmental Studies program and associate professor of political science at George Washington University. She is the author of *Stalemate* (Brookings, 2000).

scholars and journalists argue that divided government leads to gridlock and unresponsiveness. In 1990, however, David Mayhew published findings revealing that divided governments were just as productive as those controlled by a single party (he did not discuss the *contents* of the legislation in detail).

Subsequently, Sarah A. Binder examined the implications of divided control and found that it did make some differences in legislative productivity. Her careful research does not resolve the question of the ultimate impact of divided government, but in this brief *Brookings Review* article, she argues that divided government and other forces do contribute to so-called gridlock. Still, much of what we label gridlock is intrinsic to our system of extensive checks and balances.

G ridlock is not a modern legislative invention. Although the term is said to have entered the American political lexicon after the 1980 elections, Alexander Hamilton was complaining more than two centuries ago about the deadlock rooted in the design of the Continental Congress. In many ways, gridlock is endemic to our national politics, the natural consequence of separated institutions sharing and competing for power.

But even casual observers of Washington recognize tremendous variation in Congress's performance. At times, congressional prowess is stunning. The Great Society Congress under Lyndon Johnson, for example, enacted landmark health care, environment, civil rights, transportation, and education statutes (to name a few). At other times, gridlock prevails, as when, in 1992, congressional efforts to cut the capital gains tax and to reform lobbying, campaign finance, banking, parental leave, and voter registration laws (to name a few) ended in deadlock.

What accounts for such uneven performance? Why is Congress sometimes remarkably successful and other times mired in stalemate? For all our attention to the minutiae of Congress, we know little about the dimensions and causes of gridlock. How much do we have? How often do we get it? What drives it up and down? Such questions are particularly acute today, as Democrats and Republicans trade barbs over the do-nothing 106th Congress. Despite the first budget surplus in 30 years, Congress and the president remain deadlocked over numerous high-profile issues (including Social Security, Medicare, managed health care, and campaign finance reform), and they show few prospects of acting on these and other salient issues before the 2000 elections.*

---

*In fact, none of these issues were resolved in the 106th Congress (1999–2000).

An Elusive Concept

Some argue that gridlock is simply a constant of American political life. James Madison bequeathed us a political system designed not to work, a government of sharply limited powers. But surely the framers (dissatisfied with their governing experiment after the Revolution and fearful of rebellious debtors in the states) sought a strong national government that could govern—deliberately and efficiently, albeit insulated from the passions of popular majorities. Gridlock may be a frequent *consequence* of the Constitution, but that does not mean the framers *preferred* it.

Others might object to labeling legislative inaction as "gridlock." If a government that "governs least governs best," then policy stability should be applauded, not derided as gridlock. But views about gridlock tend to vary with one's political circumstance. Former Senate Majority Leader Bob Dole put it best: "If you're against something, you'd better hope there's a little gridlock." Legislative action, after all, can produce either liberal or conservative policy change. "Gridlock" might simply be an unfortunate choice of words, a clumsy term for Washington's inability to broach and secure policy compromise (whether liberal or conservative in design). If so, understanding the causes of gridlock should interest any keen observer or participant in national politics, regardless of party or ideology.

Evaluating Gridlock

Getting a handle on gridlock is tricky. Typically, scholars assess Congress's productivity, counting up the number of important laws enacted each Congress. When output is low, we say that gridlock is high, and vice versa. But measuring output without respect to the agenda of salient issues risks misstating the true level of gridlock. A Congress might produce little legislation because it is truly gridlocked. Or it might be unproductive because it faces a limited agenda. With little on its legislative plate, surely Congress should not be blamed for producing meager results. We can evaluate Congress's performance only if we have some idea of the size of the underlying policy agenda.

Gridlock is best viewed, then, as the share of salient issues on the nation's agenda left in limbo at the close of each Congress. Just what are the salient issues on the nation's agenda? The editorial page of the *New York Times* (the nation's paper of record) serves admirably as an indicator. Indeed, one can reconstruct the policy agenda for the past half-century of American politics by identifying all the legislative issues of each Congress discussed by the *Times* (whether in support or in opposition—to take into account the paper's often liberal political perspective). Salient issues are those addressed at least four times in a single Congress.

In terms of size, the agenda ranges as we might expect (table 1). It is smallest in the 1950s, in the quiescent years of the Eisenhower presidency. It jumps sharply under the activist administrations of JFK and LBJ in the 1960s and continues to rise steadily in the 1970s and 1980s. Only in recent years has the number of issues on the agenda declined, most likely reflecting the tightening of budgets and the associated dampening of legislative activism.

. . . Gridlock has led a rollercoaster existence over the past 50 years. Is Congress particularly gridlocked today? Critics who claim so are partially right. Gridlock has trended upward since 1947 and has been, on average, 25 points higher in the 1990s than it was in the 1940s. It peaked in the early 1990s, when George Bush faced a Democratic Congress. Fully 65 percent of the 23 most salient agenda issues remained unresolved when the 102nd Congress drew to a close in 1992. With the arrival of unified government under Bill Clinton and congressional Democrats after the 1992 elections, gridlock still remained at an historic high, with more than half of the 16 most visible issues left in limbo when the 103rd Congress adjourned.

But gridlock does not simply trend upward. From its unprecedented highs in the early 1990s, gridlock dropped 14 points in the 104th Congress (1995–96), reflecting election year compromises on reforming welfare, health care, immigration, and telecommunication laws, as well as increasing the minimum wage. Still, no recent Congress has matched the performance of the Kennedy–Johnson era, four years of legislative prowess in which the Democratic presidents and their Democratic Congresses stalemated on just roughly a quarter of

---

Table 1
Size of the Policy Agenda, 1947–96

Congress (Years)	Number of Issues on Agenda	Congress (Years)	Number of Issues on Agenda
80 (1947–48)	85	93 (1973–74)	133
81 (1949–50)	85	94 (1975–76)	138
82 (1951–52)	72	95 (1977–78)	150
83 (1953–54)	74	96 (1979–80)	144
84 (1955–56)	84	97 (1981–82)	127
85 (1957–58)	89	98 (1983–84)	138
86 (1959–60)	70	99 (1985–86)	160
87 (1961–62)	129	100 (1987–88)	140
88 (1963–64)	102	101 (1989–90)	147
89 (1965–66)	96	102 (1991–92)	126
90 (1967–68)	119	103 (1993–94)	94
91 (1969–70)	144	104 (1995–96)	118
92 (1971–72)	135		

the policy agenda (deadlocking on 14 of the 50 most salient issues across those four years).

The Usual Suspects

How do we account for such variation in Congress's performance? Pundits typically round up some usual suspects to explain unusually high levels of gridlock. Numerous explanations have been offered, for example, for the extreme gridlock that has stymied the current Congress. Among them are divided party control of government, the upcoming presidential election in 2000, the razor-thin majority in the House, and the meager safety cushion provided by a budget in the black for the first time in 30 years. All are plausible explanations for the current impasse in Washington. But how do these culprits stack up against the record of the past 50 years?

Arguments about the effects of divided government traditionally revolve around the importance of political parties for bridging our separated legislative and executive institutions. Unified party control is necessary, the argument goes, for ensuring that the two branches share common policy and electoral motivations. Under divided government, competing policy views and electoral incentives are said to make legislative compromise unlikely. Both parties seek policy outcomes that enhance their own electoral reputations, but neither side wants the other to reap electoral benefit from achieving its policy agenda.

If the traditional argument about divided government is correct, stalemate should be more prevalent in periods of split party control, less so under unified government. And, indeed, when control of Congress and the presidency has been divided between the parties, 43 percent of the agenda has ended in gridlock, whereas when party control is unified, only 38 percent of the agenda has been left undone. Still, given the pointed criticism perennially lodged against divided government, that mere 5 percentage point difference comes as something of a surprise—except to those who remember the "unified gridlock" of Clinton's first term, when Congress adjourned with much of the Democrats' agenda deadlocked.

What about the suggestion that stalemate is more likely in the run-up to a presidential election? At such times, the party out of power will have a strong incentive to block legislation in hopes of regaining the White House. Republican reluctance to negotiate over tax cuts in 1999 is a prime example of a party seeking to have an "issue" rather than a bill as a presidential election approaches. The logic is sound, the evidence mixed. Gridlock has increased, but only marginally, in the two-year periods leading up to presidential elections. After all, despite the fractious politics of 1995 and the approaching presidential election in 1996, Clinton and the Republican Congress managed to forge compromise on a number of salient issues—including welfare, telecommunications, immigration, health insurance, and lobbying reform. Similarly, the size of the

House majority party has not had any systematic effect on the level of gridlock in recent decades.

Conventional wisdom also holds that gridlock is a function of tough fiscal times. When the budget is in surplus, legislative compromise should be easier—because politicians are theoretically no longer caught in a zero-sum game. Whether a coalition seeks higher spending or lower taxes, ample federal coffers can cover the side-payments necessary to forge a successful coalition. The argument rings true at the extremes. The deficit relative to outlays stood at nearly 20 percent during the 102nd Congress (1991–92), when gridlock peaked at over 65 percent. When the surplus relative to outlays reached 20 percent during the 80th Congress (1947–48), gridlock was a mere 26 percent. Viewed more broadly over the past half-century, however, the relationship between the two is less direct, though sunnier fiscal times are generally associated with lower levels of deadlock. Excess resources by themselves cannot wipe out gridlock, a finding confirmed by Congress's current predicament despite the emergent budget surplus.

Other Causes of Deadlock

To accurately map the dynamics of gridlock, we need to recognize the electoral and institutional contexts in which Congress labors. Perhaps the most striking feature of today's electoral environment is the disappearing political center. If we think of political moderates as those legislators who are closer to the midpoint of the two parties than to their own party's center, we can size up the reach of the political center over the past five decades. By this score, more than 30 percent of the members of Congress in the 1960s and 1970s were centrists; today, moderates make up less than 10 percent of the House and Senate.

The number of moderates is important because it affects the ease with which policy compromise is reached. When the two major parties are polarized—with few centrist legislators bridging the gap—parties have little incentive to agree and every incentive to distinguish their records and positions. As Congressman Barney Frank (D-MA) observed this past fall, "Right now, the differences between the two parties are so great, it doesn't make sense for us to compromise. We'll show where we stand, and let the people decide." As a result, the relationship between partisan polarization and legislative gridlock is direct, with stalemate more frequent as the political center shrinks.

Similarly, if the two chambers are ideologically akin to one another—as boll weevil House Democrats* and the Senate's Republican median were in the early 1980s—bicameral agreements should be easier to reach. With the House and Senate quite distant, the prospects for bicameral agreement recede. The

---

*Boll weevils, named for a pernicious Southern insect, were conservative Southern Democrats, who exercised disproportionate power in Congress between the 1930s and the 1970s.

fate of Newt Gingrich's Contract with America is a good case in point, as many of the measures triumphantly passed by House Republicans in 1995 were killed or ignored by the Republican Senate. Over the past half-century, bicameral differences have strongly shaped the incidence of gridlock, leaving the two tightly entwined at century's end.

Institutional rules also shape the behavior of legislators and policy outcomes. They are particularly important in assessing the conduct of the Senate, where the filibuster makes simple majorities powerless in the face of a determined minority. "Tit-for-tat" filibustering has compounded the problem, as control of the Senate has passed back and forth between Democrats and Republicans over the past two decades. Republican filibusters stymied much of Clinton's agenda under unified Democratic control in 1993 and 1994. Then, when Republicans regained control of the chamber in 1995, Democrats returned the favor by filibustering conservative initiatives. Even a minority of one can take the Senate hostage by placing a "hold"* on bills or nominations headed for the Senate floor until the senator's (often unrelated) policy or political demands are met. By empowering supermajorities in a political system that moves primarily by majority rule, the Senate makes its own contribution to gridlock.

Forever Gridlocked?

In many ways, Washington's proclivity for deadlock is preordained—a fact of life given the electoral and institutional worlds of Congress (table 2). Using the past half-century as our guide, we can expect divided party control of government to increase the level of gridlock by roughly 8 percent. Given on average 25 salient issues on the agenda each Congress, the arrival of unified government should resolve on average only 2 additional issues. Incremental slips in the share of moderate legislators have similar effects, here increasing gridlock by roughly 10 percent or an additional 2 to 3 issues. When bicameral differences increase, gridlock also takes a marked step upward—here having the effect of stalemating 3 more legislative issues in the average Congress. In contrast, improved fiscal discipline only marginally affects the incidence of deadlock, with a large fall in the size of the deficit here reducing gridlock a mere 2 percent.

But neither institutional nor electoral features of Congress are immutable. True, we are likely stuck with a bicameral system, despite calls from Governor Jesse Ventura (Reform-MN) and others to consider the unicameral alternative. But the impact of the filibuster can be lessened by reforming Senate rules to make it easier to invoke cloture or by eliminating the noxious practice of anonymous holds. Elections, of course, are the ultimate recourse for voters dissatisfied by partisan polarization and the conduct of Congress. Nudging Con-

---

*An unofficial request to halt consideration of a proposal, at least temporarily.

Table 2
Contributors to Policy Gridlock, 1951–96

Independent Variable	Change in Independent Variable (From → To)	Simulated Change in Level of Gridlock
Divided government	unified → divided	+8%
Percentage of "centrists"	19% → 34%	−10%
Policy distance between House and Senate	.07 → .30	+13%
Filibuster threat	0 → 7.5	+6%
Budget situation (surplus/deficit as percentage of federal outlays)	−19% → −2%	−2%

Note: The simulated changes in gridlock are based on statistical estimates from a grouped logic model in which the level of gridlock is the dependent variable. Additional independent variables include a set of controls (not shown) for ideological diversity across members, time spent in the minority for each new majority party, and the public mood. Changes in gridlock are simulated by varying the values of each independent variable between the values in column 2 (i.e., one standard deviation below and above its mean value for continuous variables and between 0 and 1 for divided government). For parameter estimates and details on measurement, see Sarah A. Binder, "The Dynamics of Legislative Gridlock," *American Political Science Review*, vol. 93 (September 1999): 519–533.

gross back to the center by sending more centrist legislators to Washington would be one way to alleviate gridlock. Still, diagnosing the ills of a body politic is one thing; rousing the patient to seek treatment is another.

Questions for Discussion

1. Does a divided government necessarily guarantee "gridlock" in national policy making? Is George W. Bush, with narrow majorities in both House and Senate, any better off than Bill Clinton, who faced a Republican Congress?
2. Can you make an argument that the framers intentionally designed a governmental structure that was likely to produce gridlock?

10.3

The Evolution of Tom DeLay

Richard E. Cohen

Over the history of the Congress, the power of party leaders has waxed and waned. But even strong leaders, such as legendary Speaker of the House Sam Rayburn (D-Tex.), found themselves limited by the legislative context. In Rayburn's case, despite. Democratic control of the House in the 1950s, Southern Democrats often joined Republicans to form a "conservative coalition" that frequently prevailed on the House floor. Since the Rayburn era of the 1950s, Republicans made consistent inroads in Southern electoral politics, and by the 1990s, only a handful of conservative Southern Democrats remained. Among other changes for legislators, this has produced a House of Representatives that is highly partisan.

Although Representative Newt Gingrich (R-Ga.) was the original architect of the Republicans' 1994 victory that gave them control of the House after forty years of minority status, the person most responsible for organizing and maintaining the Republican majority has been Representative Tom DeLay (R-Tex.). First as GOP Whip (the third-ranking leader), and since 1999 as Majority Leader, DeLay has proved adept at keeping his Republican troops unified on most important votes. Although his nickname "the Hammer" indicates his toughness, DeLay has also worked with moderates to forge consistent majorities. In this selection, Richard E. Cohen paints a picture of a slightly mellowing DeLay, who sees a need to round off some of his edges if he is to one day become the Speaker of the House. Cohen captures both the tough-minded leader and the aspiring statesman, as he profiles a key member of Congress at the top of his game.

House Majority Leader Tom DeLay, R-Texas, and Rep. Jim Greenwood, R-Pa., are poles apart when it comes to federal policy on abortion. The moderate Greenwood is one of the few House Republicans who support abortion rights, a stance that DeLay and fellow conservatives traditionally haven't tolerated. So it may seem surprising that Greenwood sings DeLay's praises for his handling of this year's debate on the "partial-birth" abortion bill.

Richard E. Cohen is a long-time congressional correspondent for *National Journal*.

Richard E. Cohen, "The Evolution of Tom DeLay," *National Journal* (November 15, 2003): 3478–3486. Copyright 2003 by National Journal Group, Inc. All rights reserved. Reprinted by permission.

When the House had debated similar legislation in previous years, Republican leaders denied Greenwood and his allies the opportunity to offer an amendment on the floor permitting legal exceptions to an outright ban on the controversial abortion procedure. Early this year, Greenwood and moderate Rep. Nancy Johnson, R-Conn., took their plea to DeLay and reminded him of their party loyalty as senior members who have worked on other key issues. Recognizing that the request was vital to a small Republican cadre, DeLay acquiesced. He single-handedly overrode objections from other GOP conservatives and allowed House debate on the amendment.

"In rising through the leadership, Tom DeLay has recognized that he needs to keep the entire [House Republican] Conference on board," Greenwood said in an interview. "He has figured out how to be an outspoken leader of conservatives, and still represent all Republicans. I respect that."

True, DeLay's decision was made easier because he was confident—and correct—that the House would defeat the amendment, sponsored by Greenwood and House Minority Whip Steny Hoyer, D-Md. But the key point is that even though other Republicans had routinely rejected the moderates' request, DeLay took it seriously. "He respects that I have had to make some tough votes [on other bills], and that I expect to be treated as a member of the team," Greenwood added.

Not long ago, DeLay, too, would probably have dismissed Greenwood's request. During eight years as House majority whip, from 1995 through 2002, DeLay made himself famous as a snarling, highly partisan enforcer, with little stomach for those who didn't share his conservative fervor.

But now that DeLay has served as House majority leader for the past year, it is apparent that he has undergone something of an evolution. He has polished his public image and taken pains to portray himself as a disciplined, measured leader who is responsive to all types of House Republicans as he sets the agenda, hones strategy, and brokers deals.

"He has grown and reached out to members," said Rep. Jennifer Dunn, R-Wash. Likewise, Rep. Ray LaHood, R-Ill., said that in DeLay's new role, "Tom's strongest point has been his ability to reach out to members, one-on-one."

Of course, for DeLay, "reaching out" used to mean cracking his whip—using any means necessary to ensure that his party had sufficient votes to pass legislation on the House floor. But in the view of DeLay's chief of staff, Tim Berry, his boss's former whip duties helped to "increase his understanding of members' needs, and gave him credentials with conservatives, so that they take him at his word" now when he professes to protect their interests.

In a rare interview, DeLay acknowledged that he has changed to some degree since becoming majority leader. "I spend more time on planning, strategies, developing agendas, and making the trains run on time." . . . And DeLay said that because Republicans now control Congress and the White House, "I don't get up every day and put on my gloves to fight all day long. I get up every day to talk to this person and that person, and sooner or later, we'll work it out."

In the interview, DeLay made clear that he is keenly aware that Democrats are always ready to pounce on him. "I wear their attacks as a badge of honor," he said. "It's a concerted effort. They are trying to demonize me just like they did with Newt Gingrich." Yet, DeLay said, he has tried to minimize his lightning-rod status of late.

"The good thing that comes from [the Democratic attacks] is that I'm a lot more careful . . . in what I say, how I approach things, the battles that I pick to fight," he said. "When I was a new member, I shot from the hip a lot. . . . But it doesn't slow me down in doing what I think is the right thing. I'm just as aggressive as I have always been."

To be sure, suggesting that DeLay has undergone an evolution doesn't in any way mean that "The Hammer" has gone soft. He is still highly effective, steely, and determined. And he is fully capable of employing hardball, partisan tactics, particularly behind the scenes, to accomplish his party's conservative goals. But at 56, DeLay shows more savvy and maturity than before. Some insiders believe it is all part of DeLay's carefully calculated effort to groom himself for the speakership. . . .

Mellow the Leader

The post of House majority leader came open in December 2001, when then-Leader Dick Armey, R-Texas, announced he would retire after the 2002 elections. At the time, DeLay moved very quickly—within days—to privately shore up support among his Republican colleagues for his bid to succeed Armey, even though the actual election was almost a year away.

Democrats surely were licking their chops at the prospect of "Majority Leader DeLay" replacing former House Speaker Newt Gingrich, R-Ga., as their new national villain. But DeLay lay low during 2002. He deliberately avoided public comment on his plans and stayed behind the scenes, in remarkable contrast to some other high-profile congressional leadership contests of recent years. When House Republicans elected new leaders after last November's elections, DeLay faced no opposition and won the No. 2 job by acclamation.

Even then, it was apparent that DeLay was becoming more inclusive within the Republican Conference. Shortly after the elections, the moderate Johnson [said,] "I have confidence in Tom DeLay, because he listens to the moderates. When you're in the leadership, you cannot run your own agenda. You have to run an agenda that reflects the views of the caucus."

When DeLay assumed his new post in January, it was obvious that he had undergone a bit of a physical makeover as well. At his wife's encouragement, he had his dentist cap his two upper front teeth to fill the small gap between them. And he took Dunn's advice and visited her Capitol Hill hairstylist to switch from his dated, wet look to a more professional, styled cut. "I wanted him to look like a majority leader," Dunn said. . . .

While DeLay has raised his profile as a party spokesman on Capitol Hill, he has done it mostly on his own terms. He has carefully sought to avoid appearing on national TV or taking a prime legislative role that would open him up to Democratic attacks. In his weekly half-hour meetings with reporters in his office, DeLay bans television cameras, and his office does not issue a transcript afterward, as other congressional leaders usually do.

Meanwhile, the majority leader's staff has been publicizing another aspect of his "softer" side: DeLay has raised several million dollars in recent years for the construction of a huge facility in the Houston area for children in foster care programs. He and his wife, Christine, have fostered three kids in their home.

DeLay has also sought to round out his portfolio by increasing his focus on foreign-policy issues. He has given several high-profile foreign-policy speeches in recent years, including a well-publicized address at the Israeli parliament in August. In addition, he has continued his long-standing support for democracy in Taiwan and for anti-Castro Cubans.

A strong supporter of Israel in its conflict with the Palestinians, DeLay made waves when he pressed President Bush this summer not to force Israel to make difficult concessions as part of the internationally sanctioned "road map" to peace. The *Houston Chronicle* editorialized, "DeLay is in Israel trying to shove the Israeli-Palestinian peace process off the track." A front-page *New York Times* article about DeLay's trip noted that he had "emerged as a significant figure in Middle East policy, particularly since his ascension to the majority leader's post." The article added that DeLay, "by his presence, remind[s] the Bush administration to pay heed to its right flank as it seeks to make peace."

Up to His Elbows

. . . DeLay said he feels the pressure of increased public expectations from the all-Republican government.

"It is expected that you get things done," he said. "You can't go home and explain that there is only a one-vote margin in the Senate, and a filibuster, and we had to massage this bill a little bit, so that it's not as good as you would like, to get it through the Senate. You can't explain that to people. All they know is that there is a Republican Senate, a Republican House, and a Republican president, and you ought to be able to get something done."

By and large, DeLay has gotten things done this year, at least in the House. Those close to him say that his strength lies chiefly in his role as strategist. "He takes [members] where they don't necessarily want to go, but where they need to go," Rep. Kevin Brady, R-Texas, said.

DeLay has taken far more of a hands-on approach to legislation than Armey did. DeLay has held weekly meetings with committee chairmen, for example, a change from the more sporadic schedule that Armey maintained. DeLay's aides also hold a weekly session with committee chiefs of staff. These meetings have been "very effective in reaching out and informing members of leadership activities," LaHood said.

On many issues, DeLay's goal has been for the House to pass the most-conservative bill possible, sometimes even adding its own imprint to proposals from Bush. When the president used his State of the Union message to propose a $15 billion initiative to fight AIDS in Africa, for example, DeLay immediately praised the plan. But he moved to add a conservative flourish by requiring that one-third of the funds be allocated to sexual "abstinence" programs.

Despite opposition from some flanks, this provision increased enthusiasm among many conservative House Republicans who don't routinely support AIDS-fighting initiatives. The Senate made little change before approving the House-passed bill in May. Senate Foreign Relations Committee ranking member Joseph Biden, D-Del., even praised DeLay's support during the Senate debate.

DeLay has also been at the center of numerous crucial conference committee* negotiations this year between the House and the more-moderate Senate. During the springtime conference on the annual budget resolution, DeLay urged reluctant House Republicans to accept the Senate's insistence that the 10-year cost of this year's tax cut not exceed $350 billion; the original House budget called for more than twice that amount. As it turned out, however, DeLay had been privately consulting with House Ways and Means Committee Chairman Bill Thomas, R-Calif., who later unveiled a clever plan to "sunset" most of the tax cuts after several years to appear to keep the cost down. But the total tax cuts, if extended for the full decade, have been projected to exceed $1 trillion.

This fall, DeLay has played a prominent role in the conference on Medicare prescription drug benefit legislation. Even though DeLay has never served on a committee with jurisdiction over Medicare, House Speaker Dennis Hastert, R-Ill., named him as one of the five House Republicans on the conference committee. According to several sources, the primary reason was to reassure many dubious House conservatives that the final version of the legislation would not create escalating federal entitlement costs.

"He knows what conservatives need, and he's making sure that it happens," said Brady, a Ways and Means Committee member. At the same time, according to a DeLay aide, the majority leader has deliberately refrained from public meetings or statements about the issue that would permit Democrats to make him the "face" of Medicare reform.

On energy legislation, DeLay has participated more actively, in part because he has considerable experience with the energy issues that are vital to his Houston-area constituents. When Bush proposed energy legislation two years

---

*Conference committees are composed of both representatives and senators, who meet to reconcile differences between different versions of the same bill that has passed in each chamber.

ago, DeLay headed a task force that coordinated the several House committees that have jurisdiction over the measure.

"Tom deserves a lot of credit for the House's ability to produce a bill," said House Energy and Commerce Committee Chairman Billy Tauzin, R-La. "His expertise is not in the management of details, but in developing the strategic policy and message." . . .

Still Throwing 'Em Red Meat

At key moments this year, DeLay has pointedly sought to serve as the congressional Republican leader who is the quickest and harshest in defending Bush from Democratic attacks.

After Sen. Edward Kennedy, D-Mass., criticized the Iraq war as a "fraud . . . made up in Texas," for instance, DeLay called on Democratic leaders "to have the courage to tell their hero Ted Kennedy that he went too far." When Democratic presidential candidate Howard Dean told a rally that Attorney General John Ashcroft "is not a patriot," DeLay called Dean "a cruel and extremist demagogue." And DeLay declared before a Heritage Foundation audience, "The blame-America-first hate speech of the American Left has infected the Democratic Party's national leadership to a dangerous degree."

Talk like that sounds like the old Tom DeLay, and it delights the conservatives who make up the majority of the House Republican Conference. Although conservatives concede that they have not won everything they wanted this year—and that the verdict is still out on the success of the 108th Congress—they applaud DeLay's takeover as majority leader.

"Tom has represented conservative interests," said Rep. Sue Myrick, R-N.C., who chairs the House Republican Study Committee, a powerful 90-member bloc of conservatives. "He's toned down his rhetoric a bit because his job has changed. Now, he has to take the big picture into consideration. But it hasn't changed him. We work together closely with him and with Speaker Hastert."

Rep. Jeb Hensarling, R-Texas, said that despite the lack of a conservative working majority in the House, "we have done a good job in passing a conservative agenda. Tom DeLay has played the key role on that." Hensarling was a top aide to then-Sen. Phil Gramm, R-Texas, and has emerged as an outspoken GOP freshman. He said he has had reservations about voting for certain bills, such as the budget resolution and Medicare reform, but he has deferred to vigorous persuasion from senior Republicans, notably DeLay. "He's been here 20 years, and I've been here 10 months," Hensarling added.

As leader of the conservatives, DeLay has quietly pursued a broad agenda, and . . . he said that more is to come. "This is just the start," he said. "Hopefully, we come back after 2004 with a larger majority in the Senate and in the House. We will start talking next year about doubling the size of the economy in 15 years. . . . You start with Republican values: a major overhaul of the tax code, regulatory reform, redesigning the government, redesigning the Congress."

DeLay also continues to be a prolific fundraiser for his party, employing pioneering and often controversial techniques through his leadership political action committee, Americans for a Republican Majority, or ARMPAC. The organization contributed more money to congressional candidates in each of the past two cycles than did any other leadership PAC, said Jim Ellis, who has been its executive director since 1998. Although the 2002 campaign finance law has shut down some of ARMPAC's soft-money operations, pending the Supreme Court's decision, Ellis said that other programs are raising record sums.

While DeLay has won wide praise from across the GOP, he can still show a few rough edges in dealing with party members. Some Republicans who sit on the House Appropriations Committee, including LaHood, bristle that GOP leaders increasingly have adopted a top-down style. "The speaker, the majority leader, and their staffs really dictate a lot of what goes on in appropriations, especially when bills are in conference committees," LaHood said.

Moreover, sources close to both the White House and DeLay privately concede that he is not on close personal terms with the president, despite their mutual efforts to depict harmony. And while DeLay seems to have close, complementary relationships with Hastert and with the No. 3 in the GOP leadership, House Majority Whip Roy Blunt, R-Mo., even those relationships have been marked by occasional ambiguities and tensions this year.

Early on in his speakership, Hastert was sometimes depicted as DeLay's puppet, because it was DeLay who first tapped Hastert for the leadership track by selecting him as chief deputy majority whip in 1995 and then supported him for speaker in December 1998. That was a tumultuous time for House Republicans. In July 1997, DeLay confessed that he had actively encouraged the unsuccessful Republican coup against Gingrich; the two had a history of bitter clashes in past leadership races. Then House Republicans faced setbacks in the November 1998 election, and shortly afterward, Gingrich resigned under pressure. Amid President Clinton's impeachment in December 1998, Speaker-designate Bob Livingston, R-La., also stepped aside after revelations that he'd had extramarital affairs.

Through the turmoil, DeLay survived and prospered as whip. He pushed Hastert to the fore for speaker and tapped Blunt as chief deputy majority whip. DeLay himself held back, saying in the interview, "I did rule out being speaker when Newt Gingrich stepped down." In an interview, Blunt recalled that DeLay "decided because of impeachment and other matters that the House wasn't ready for him as speaker."

The DeLay-Hastert alliance has been a symbiotic relationship in which they serve as close partners. They have very different styles, however, with Hastert widely known as a "fair and good-hearted soul," in Hoyer's words, and the wily DeLay known as something else entirely.

As this year began and DeLay was set to become majority leader, even close allies noted that Hastert and DeLay, plus their chief aides, had some reservations. "There was an issue in Speaker Hastert's mind of how Tom's strong personality would fill that role," said Berry, DeLay's top aide. But Berry and Hastert's chief of staff, Scott Palmer, "discussed this at length," Berry said. "Tom is very deferential to the speaker. And he helps make the House run smoothly." Indeed, the two leaders seem to have benefited from their extensive collaboration and have managed to keep any differences largely under wraps. . . .

Dr. Jekyll or Mr. Hyde?

While DeLay's intense partisan drive draws plaudits from most Republicans, Democrats are still gnashing their teeth. Hoyer has blasted DeLay for "destroying the enemy outside the rules." Another veteran House Democrat contended, "DeLay has destroyed the House as a representative body."

Hoyer and Rep. Martin Frost, D-Texas, the ranking member on the House Rules Committee, have led the attack on DeLay for creating in the House a closed process that leaves virtually no room for bipartisanship or participation from the minority, and that punishes Democratic constituencies and programs. The Democrats' prime focus in recent weeks has been the effort by Republican appropriators to bar "earmarks"* for the Democrats who voted in July against the appropriations bill for the Labor, Health and Human Services, and Education departments.

Republican allies dismiss what they regard as the Democrats' obsession with DeLay. "[The Democrats] are the consummate generals fighting the last war. They are stuck in the 1980s," said Republican National Committee Chairman Ed Gillespie. "Personally, I feel badly for Tom. But, for the party, I can think of no one tougher" to take the Democrats' hits.

Whether the Democratic hits over DeLay's alleged bullying will resonate with the public and the media remains to be seen. But Democrats were able to shine a negative light on DeLay this year over his heavy involvement in Texas redistricting.

DeLay waged a highly controversial backroom effort to urge the GOP-controlled Texas Legislature to pass a new congressional redistricting map, even though Texas, like other states, had just completed redistricting following the 2000 census. If ratified by the Justice Department and federal courts, as Republicans fully expect, the final Texas congressional map could result in as many as seven new Republican seats, at the expense of incumbent Democrats. [See Chapter 6.]

Although state and national Republicans emphasize that DeLay did not write the actual details, there is widespread agreement that he placed redistricting

---

*Earmarks are appropriations for specific items that are not covered by broad spending initiatives. A $2 million allocation for a university building would be an example.

on the table in Austin and that he overcame numerous obstacles to win the enactment of a new map last month. In the final stages of negotiations among Republicans in the Texas House and Senate, DeLay engaged in shuttle diplomacy
between the two sides for three days.

Rep. Pete Sessions, R-Texas, called DeLay "the manager of the new map."
Rep. Thomas Reynolds, R-N.Y., who chairs the National Republican Congressional Committee, said, "If Tom DeLay hadn't been there, it wouldn't have
happened." Likewise, Brady, who was by DeLay's side during the final negotiations, echoed Reynolds's sentiment.

Democrats complained that the results blatantly violated civil-rights and
election law, and they griped about strong-arm tactics by federal and state
agencies during the lengthy battle in the state Legislature. "In Austin, senior
Republicans sent all kinds of signals that they didn't want to do redistricting,"
said Frost, the chief redistricting strategist for Texas Democrats. "DeLay's success shows a reckless kind of strength."

Most of the large Texas newspapers editorialized against DeLay's redistricting
efforts, as did other major papers across the country. "Texas wasn't just gerrymandered," *The New York Times* said in [a 2003] editorial. . . . "It was Hammer-
mandered." *The Times* added: "Black and Hispanic voters are complaining of
being electorally ghettoized into fewer districts. They have a strong case to
make. . . . The redistricting plan's zigzags, and nips and tucks, chart a partisan
willfulness that should come to haunt Mr. DeLay in the next elections."

Rep. Charles Stenholm, D-Texas, said that both Democrats and Republicans
in his region are angry about DeLay's maneuvers and that he already has determined his election plan. "I'm running against Tom DeLay and what he has
done," Stenholm said. "A legitimate issue for November 2004 is, Does West
Texas want Tom DeLay's version of conservatism, or Charlie Stenholm's? I
have great confidence."

Bring 'em on, replies DeLay. "To run against me is to run against the Republican record," he said. . . . "The polls in Texas show that I am very popular. . . . I
am very confident about the election."

What's Next for Tom DeLay?

For now, DeLay appears secure as the North Star of the House majority, its
most constant and influential presence. But the frequent chaos in the House
GOP's nearly decade-long rule suggests the unpredictability of his future.
DeLay's fate could hinge on various factors, including the outcomes of redistricting in Texas and of Bush's legislative programs in Congress, and the results
of the presidential election.

The next obvious step for DeLay is the speakership. But he won't need to
make that decision until the 61-year-old Hastert creates a vacancy. In January,
House Republicans abolished their eight-year limit on the speaker's term, and

Hastert has appeared intent on holding his post. "As long as I can achieve something," Hastert [has said], "I'll do this job." Some of those close to Hastert say he will not step down before Bush departs, given their close relationship.

But other House Republican insiders suggest that Hastert is "tired." They point to his announcement this summer that he will publish his memoirs early next year as a signal that he might step down within the year. Another camp contends that he might leave after one more term, possibly to take an ambassadorial post. . . .

"This is more about personality than ideology," contended one House Republican who has leadership ambitions and who is skeptical of DeLay's prospects. "They don't want another Gingrich." . . .

That sentiment suggests that DeLay has more work to do before his colleagues truly consider him speaker material. But many other Republican members . . . , from the party's moderate and conservative flanks alike, gushed about him.

For his part, [GOP Whip Roy] Blunt said he will defer to DeLay if Hastert steps down as speaker. As was the case when the speaker's job was last open, in 1998, "Tom will know before anyone else if it's the right time," Blunt said.

Indeed. . . . DeLay was largely unresponsive when asked about his ambitions and qualifications to be speaker. "I don't make that decision," he said. But he also suggested that he will move when the timing seems right. "All my life, I have been taught to do the best job in the job that you have, and that if you do that, opportunities always will present themselves," DeLay said. "Then, you make a decision whether you want to take those opportunities."

Questions for Discussion

1. Compare the House of Representatives under the Republican control of Speaker Dennis Hastert and Majority Leader Tom DeLay to that outlined by Shepsle in "The Changing Textbook Congress" (selection 10.1). How does the strength of the party relate to how the House operates? How does the role of the minority change when the majority can dominate?
2. Why wouldn't Tom DeLay in his "Hammer" role play well as the Speaker of the House? Can ambition change one's behavior in meaningful ways?

10.4

The Student: How Hillary Clinton Set Out to Master the Senate

Elizabeth Kolbert

If the House of Representatives is usually run through tight control of party majorities, the Senate remains a place where cooperation and compromise can often overcome partisanship. In part, this comes from the potential for filibusters, which require 60 voters to close off (invoking cloture is the technical term). If 60 votes cannot be found, either the bill dies or its sponsors must make some concessions. At least as important, however, is the long tradition of individualism that governs much Senate business. A single senator can often bring the chamber's business to a halt in that—unlike the rules-bound, majoritarian House—the Senate operates largely through "unanimous consent." That is, all senators must agree on how to proceed before major items will be taken up. Thus, even in an increasingly partisan era within the Senate, a single senator possesses substantial power.

Into this environment came newly elected Senator Hillary Clinton in 2001. Surely the best-known senator the moment she was sworn in, she had to win over her 99 colleagues, as well as her New York constituents. By all accounts, Senator Clinton succeeded in winning the admiration of fellow legislators from both sides of the aisle. In this 2003 article, Elizabeth Kolbert offers us a picture of a senator who has moved past her freshman tentativeness to become a real player within the institution. With future presidential possibilities hanging over her, as well as past memories of her husband's presidency, Hillary Clinton emerges as a skillful lawmaker on a number of fronts. Kolbert demonstrates how an individual senator must make her own way in this tradition-encrusted body, even as she may glance toward the brass ring of the presidency, gleaming in the distance.

Elizabeth Kolbert is a staff writer at *The New Yorker.*

Elizabeth Kolbert, "The Student: How Hillary Clinton Set Out to Master the Senate." *The New Yorker* (October 13, 2003), pp. 63–74. Reprinted by permission of the author.

S enator Hillary Clinton and her staff occupy the same L-shaped suite, on the fourth floor of the Russell Senate Office Building, that her predecessor, Daniel Patrick Moynihan, and his staff worked out of for twenty-two years. Clinton's office, which is at one end of the L, is spacious and airy, with a marble fireplace that holds four decoratively stacked logs. The room is painted a pale shade of daffodil, with drapes and upholstery to match, and projects what might best be described as reserved femininity. On the chairs, there are little needlepoint pillows, one stitched with a copy of the cover of Clinton's 1996 book, "It Takes a Village," another with the words "Senator Hillary." Like most politicians' offices, Clinton's is filled with photographs, but instead of the usual shots of the senator posing with luminaries, her collection includes a picture of Robert Kennedy, who also served as a senator from New York even though he wasn't from the state; a moody portrait of her husband, with his back to the camera, gazing out the windows of the Oval Office; and a composite picture of her sitting with Eleanor Roosevelt. The suite is not considered particularly desirable—Moynihan had many opportunities to upgrade, but chose not to—and Clinton ended up with it because, under the elaborate rules governing seniority, when she first entered the Senate she ranked below several other lawmakers who had entered on the same day. (Extra points go to those who have previously served as governors or congressmen, but the system gives no credit to former First Ladies.) After Moynihan retired, he came back to visit the office and pronounced the place a lot more yellow. . . .

Because she is so junior, Clinton usually speaks last at Senate press conferences, and at the conference on the defense bill, which dealt with an amendment to allow National Guard members and reservists to buy into the military's health-insurance system, she had to wait through remarks by the amendment's co-sponsors, Senator Patrick Leahy, of Vermont; Senator Tom Daschle, of South Dakota; and Senator Lindsey Graham, of South Carolina. Experienced politicians often seem to zone out while their colleagues rehearse the inevitable platitudes, in this case about doing right by the men and women risking their lives to serve their country; Clinton, in contrast, always seems to be paying rapt attention. She nodded vigorously as Daschle and Leahy and Graham emphasized and reemphasized the importance of assuring Guard members and reservists access to health care. When, finally, it was her turn to speak, she said, "What this bill basically says is that 'you're too valuable a resource for our country for us to treat you like this.' " Then she thanked her colleagues, especially Graham, the quartet's only Republican, who, she noted, had himself served in the National Guard. . . .

When Clinton was first elected, she was often asked how she thought she would fare in the Senate, given her and her husband's history with that body. Clinton professed herself unconcerned. "I think I will get a very positive reception," she asserted at her first post-election news conference, in Manhattan. "I have worked with a number of the Republican members in the past. I'm looking forward to working with them on a bipartisan basis on issues that affect their states, as well as New York, and of course our entire country." The same day, speaking in Mississippi, Senator Trent Lott, then the Majority Leader, declared, "I tell you one thing, when this Hillary gets to the Senate, if she does—maybe lightning will strike, and she won't—she will be one of a hundred, and we won't let her forget it."

To a large degree, Clinton's confidence now appears to have been justified. In addition to the amendment to the armed-services budget that she sponsored with Lindsey Graham, Clinton has co-sponsored measures with Gordon Smith, Republican of Oregon, to promote careers in nursing; with Don Nickles, Republican of Oklahoma, to extend unemployment benefits; and with John Warner, Republican of Virginia, to assist people caring for elderly or disabled relatives. (A measure that Clinton co-sponsored with Senator Kay Bailey Hutchison, a Republican from Texas, to establish a program to recruit professionals as teachers, was approved as part of the education bill that passed the Senate in 2001.) Some former Clinton detractors, like Senator James Inhofe, Republican of Oklahoma, now go so far as to refer to her as a friend. At the top of a voluminous pile of documents that Clinton's staff sent to me was a compilation of flattering quotes, including several from congressional and Senate colleagues, many of whom had wrangled with her in the past or voted in favor of throwing her husband out of office, or both.

"I think she's doing fine," Senator Lott was now quoted as saying. "I think she's trying to dig in and do her homework, trying to lower her profile a little bit."

As it happened, Clinton's next meeting of the day was with Asa Hutchinson, Under-Secretary for Border and Transportation Security at the Department of Homeland Security. Hutchinson, who is from Arkansas, is a former congressman and, with Graham, served as a manager in Bill Clinton's impeachment trial. Senator Clinton had requested the meeting, which took place in her office, to discuss topics like security at small airports. As it was breaking up, Hutchinson turned to her and said, with what seemed to be genuine admiration, "Congratulations. It's just an amazing feat what you have done."

"I'm having the time of my life," Clinton responded. "I pinch myself every morning." . . .

The Senate is a body governed by laws and by traditions, to the latter of which belongs the freshman visit to Senator Robert Byrd, the West Virginia Democrat. Byrd has served in the Senate for fifty years—longer, as he likes to point out, than all but two of the members who have passed through the chamber since it was created—and is widely acknowledged to be the world's reigning expert on its rules. By the time of Clinton's election, she and Senator Byrd were already well acquainted—too well, one might say. Their most consequential encounter occurred in 1993, during Clinton's disastrous tenure as head of the President's task force on health-care reform. The First Lady wanted the legislation that the task force had drafted, which ran to more than thirteen hundred pages, tacked onto the so-called budget-reconciliation bill. The justification for this was, substantively speaking, thin, but procedurally it offered a critical advantage. The budget-reconciliation bill practically has to pass—if it doesn't, the entire appropriations process gets bollixed up—and debate in the Senate is limited. Clinton needed Byrd, who was then the chairman of the Senate Appropriations Committee, to approve the move, something he refused to do. His decision had the effect—intentional or not—of killing off the legislation and, with it, Clinton's hopes of introducing universal health insurance.

"I had seen her a few times through a glass darkly, as the Scripture says," Byrd told me recently when I met with him in his office in the Capitol. "I would say she did not necessarily start out as one of my favorites, if I might use that term. But she is one of my favorites now, because I like her approach. I like her sincerity. I like her convictions." Byrd said that he was particularly impressed by Clinton's hard work and deference, which, he had advised her on the occasion of her freshman visit, in November, 2000, would be among the qualities her fellow-senators would judge her on. "I think she has been the perfect student," he said.

The first piece of legislation that Clinton introduced in the Senate was a package of seven bills designed, in her words, "to spur job growth in upstate New York and around the nation." The package, which fulfilled a campaign promise, called for, among other things, the creation of "technology bonds" to promote broadband access in rural communities. When Clinton introduced the package, on March 1, 2001, she handed her colleagues customized briefing packets with color-coded maps showing how each of their states would also benefit from her initiatives.

In general, Clinton has received high marks for her inaugural legislative efforts. This is not because they are particularly far-reaching, or even original on the contrary. Like most junior senators, Clinton has spent her first years in office largely trying to funnel federal dollars to her state. She has, for example, successfully worked to maneuver a new, hundred-million-dollar border-crossing station in Champlain, New York, through the Senate's Environment and Public Works Committee, of which she is a member.

"People thought, Well, gee, she's the First Lady, she's probably going to be very insulated," Garry Douglas, the president of the Plattsburgh-North Country Chamber of Commerce, who worked with her on the project, told me. "But not only does she take our phone calls—on occasion she calls us." Douglas also said that he was "remarkably impressed" with Clinton's staff, an assessment that I heard repeated from many sources. Other officials observed that there was almost no economic-development project too small-bore for Clinton to show an interest in. Last year, for instance, in an effort to promote local agriculture, she organized an event in the Capitol called New York farm day. At the event, which she repeated last month, she served only New York-grown products. "She is a true missionary for New York food and wine," Jim Trezise, president of the New York Wine & Grape Foundation, told me.

All the lawmakers who spoke to me on the record about Clinton—a self-selected group, to be sure—praised her in much the same terms as Senator Byrd. They noted her faithful attendance at committee hearings, her deference to more senior colleagues, her general willingness to fade into the background. "When she goes to meetings—you know, we have New York delegation meetings—she just sits there, the same as anybody else," Peter King, a Republican congressman from Long Island, told me. "She's not trying to jump out front and grab an issue from you, because she knows she's going to get the coverage anyway. Now, that may sound almost self-evident: of course Hillary Clinton can get her face in the paper. But the thing is, a lot of people, no matter how much publicity they get, they still don't have the confidence to know they can get it."

A few weeks after Clinton and Graham's amendment was passed, I went down to Washington again. The day was given over to the Homeland Security Appropriations bill for 2004. Ever since the September 11th attacks, Clinton has, for obvious reasons, devoted a great deal of time to homeland security and, in particular, to obtaining more funds for New York. Working with the state's senior senator, Charles Schumer, with whom she does not always enjoy the best relations—the pair have had at least two semi-public shouting matches—Clinton was instrumental in getting twenty billion dollars for New York in the days immediately following the disaster. This past winter, after months of lobbying, Clinton helped secure an additional ninety million dollars to track the health effects of the attacks on rescue workers.

"This was an issue where she might have said, 'Listen, this is bogged down someplace,' but she stayed with it," Peter Gorman, the president of the Uniformed Fire Officers' Association of New York City, which represents the F.D.N.Y.'s superior officers, told me. "That's the amazing thing about her. She's really a woman who is not afraid to get involved in any issue that's important to us."

The Homeland Security Appropriations Act finances the Department of Homeland Security. It also provides the states with security funds, using a formula based almost entirely on population. Clinton wanted to change this formula, by directing the Secretary of Homeland Security to take other factors into account, such as the risk of attack. To explain her proposal, she had had a series of charts made up. At one point, she went down to the floor of the Senate, propped the charts up on an easel, and was about to launch into her spiel when she was informed that a vote on two other amendments had been scheduled, and she would have to wait. She trekked back to her office to meet with members of the New York Farm Bureau, who were concerned about dairy prices and Canadian imports, then walked back to the Capitol to await her turn to speak. It came at about six in the evening. There were only two other senators on the floor, not an unusual number for a routine legislative matter.

"Now, this is obviously a bit confusing and arcane, because it has to do with formulas and percentages, but it is a very important issue," Clinton began, speaking to the mostly empty chamber. "There is an absolute clear consensus among security experts that a better formula must be devised," she went on. "I said the other day that if we were to determine our defense posture, our projection of force around the world, on some kind of per-capita basis, we would be placing soldiers in Canada and Sweden, because, after all, they are there. Well, obviously, it is nonsensical. We don't do that. We look at the threats. We try to design our weaponry and other responses to take account of all of the threats that military forces might encounter, and we should be doing the same here." Midway through Clinton's remarks, Susan Collins, the chairman of the Governmental Affairs Committee, rushed onto the floor; evidently, she had been advised that it would be unwise to let Clinton's comments go unanswered. After Clinton was done, Collins, a Maine Republican, stood to oppose her amendment, pointing out that the Governmental Affairs Committee had been trying to draft legislation to deal with precisely the same issue. She offered to work with the senator from New York on this legislation, because, as she put it, "I'm very sympathetic to what a high-risk, high-vulnerability state the Senator so ably represents"—at which point Clinton withdrew her proposal from consideration. Although it might have appeared that she had wasted the entire afternoon waiting around to offer her amendment, only to drop it at the crucial moment, Clinton was upbeat. By the unwritten rules of the Senate, she told me, the exchange with Collins had been filled with significance.

"Actually, it turned out better than I expected," she said as we walked back to her office. "When she said, 'You have a lot of good points, you have a special concern about New York that I want to work with you about,' that is a wonderful invitation to pull down your amendment and engage in a discussion based on that kind of comity. It's really the way things get done around here." . . .

On the Friday before Labor Day, Clinton had just wrapped up the last phase of her book tour and was midway through an upstate swing when a rumor about her began to circulate. According to this rumor, which surfaced online in the Drudge Report, Clinton had called a meeting with her top advisers, among them her husband, to discuss whether she should run for President. At a press conference in the Finger Lakes, Clinton denied that any such meeting was planned—she said that she was simply hosting a "thank-you dinner" for supporters—and insisted that, "for the nine-hundred-and-seventy-fifth time," she was ruling out the Presidential race. A few hours later, she denied the report again. This did not do much to dampen the speculation, which continued over the weekend and by Monday had made its way onto the front page of the *Post*. In a story headlined "My Girl" and labelled "exclusive," the *Post* quoted former Governor Mario Cuomo saying that if Clinton did decide to run he "would support her in a flash." The dinner, a week later, turned out to be as Clinton had described it; nevertheless, it set off a whole new round of rumors. Clinton told her supporters—jokingly, she later insisted—how important their help would be for her next campaign, "whatever that may be."

The recent surge of interest in Clinton's plans is in part a response to the weakness of the current Democratic field. Voicing a widely held view, Cuomo has referred to the candidates vying for the Party's nomination as a "babble," and Bill Clinton is reported to have told his wife's supporters that there were "two stars" in the Democratic Party—General Wesley Clark and Hillary. When Clark subsequently announced his candidacy, there were so many reports that the Clintons were backing him—perhaps as a "stalking-horse" for Hillary— that Bill reportedly felt compelled to call several of the other candidates to deny this. . . .

. . . Notwithstanding her sedulous attention to local issues, she has made several moves over the last year or so—including writing her memoir—which, if they do not conclusively demonstrate Presidential ambitions, are certainly open to that interpretation. (According to a Marist College poll taken just before the book was published, twenty-eight per cent of New York voters thought that Clinton's primary motivation for writing "Living History" was to set the stage for a national race, while twenty-seven per cent believed that she just wanted to tell her side of the story.) This past January, after only two years in office, Clinton assumed the chairmanship of the Senate's Democratic steering committee, a position that officially makes her part of the Senate's Democratic leadership and gives her a prominent role in shaping the Party's message. Clinton has emerged as one of the Democrats' most active—and successful—fundraisers, hosting events for fellow Democratic senators at her Washington residence, a fifty-five-hundred-square-foot house near Embassy Row, and also writing checks to Democratic officials around the country from her political-action committee, HILLPAC, which, in the first six months of 2003, raised more money than any other Democratic leadership PAC. Just recently, Clinton launched a Web site-cum-fund-raising operation (friendsofhillary.com), which chronicles how "Hillary is making a difference" in areas ranging from "agriculture" to "women" and has prominently featured letters importuning her to run for President. As Clinton likes to point out, she is the first New York senator ever to serve on the Senate Armed Services Committee, an appointment for which she had to give up her seat on the Senate Budget Committee. When I asked one longtime New York political operative whether he could think of an explanation for this choice aside from national aspirations, he claimed to be stumped: "You got me. For the Long Island defense contractors who all moved to Texas twenty years ago?"

Clinton has also been influential in setting up a new liberal think tank called the Center for American Progress, headed by Bill Clinton's former White House chief of staff John Podesta. The institute is not supposed to be explicitly partisan, but many Democrats are clearly hoping that it will come up with a more compelling agenda for the Party—if not by 2004, then at least by 2008. (One friend of the Clintons told me that Hillary would not run for President next year, although, as he noted, she has "very pointedly not ruled out" running in any other year.)

I asked Clinton about the state of Democratic politics one day when she was waiting to go onto the Senate floor. "I think it's been hard for our party to deal with both the loss of the White House and the loss of Congress," she told me. "That hasn't happened in the memory of anyone here." She went on, "I'm fundamentally optimistic, because I think that the policies of this Administration are distinctly wrongheaded, and that, after the photo ops are over, the facts and evidence actually count as to how people are experiencing their lives. And I believe that time and evidence are on our side."

Clinton voted in favor of authorizing the use of force against Iraq, and she has been careful not to question Bush's military judgment. On just about every other issue, though, including the handling of the aftermath of the war, she has been critical of the President. Referring to Bush's request for a supplemental appropriation to finance ongoing operations in Iraq, she said recently, "For me, the eighty-seven billion dollars is not just a bill for Iraq—it's a bill for failed leadership." . . . [I]n spite of her own experience with special prosecutors, she called for the appointment of one to investigate Administration leaks revealing the identity of the covert C.I.A. operative Valerie Plame. Clinton frequently faults Bush for his stewardship of the economy. "I'm absolutely convinced that the Administration's policy is the wrong medicine," she told me. "They have the same diagnosis and treatment for everything: it's tax cuts, tax cuts, tax cuts." Meanwhile, she argues, the Administration's shortsightedness on domestic security has left the country deeply vulnerable to another September 11th-like attack. "I alternate between frustration and outrage mixed with head-slapping amazement that we're not doing more," she told me. "Maybe we'll get really, really, really lucky and nothing bad will ever happen again. But I can't in good conscience operate from that assumption."

Clinton's criticism of the Bush Administration parallels that of most other Democrats, including most of the Democrats running for President. Occasionally, though, she veers off in a direction of her own.

One afternoon in the spring, I went to hear Clinton give a speech to a group of nurses at Roosevelt Hospital, in Manhattan. "You know, some of us need more help and guidance and support than others," Clinton told them. "Some of us are born healthy and others are not. Some of us have traumatic, terrible accidents or events or diseases that affect us. None of us know what will happen to any of us tomorrow, and therefore I think we are all bound together in a web of relationships where we do—not only for religious reasons or moral reasons but practical reasons—have an obligation and opportunity to support one another."

Clinton went on to say that she was worried that the nation's priorities were "getting misplaced." She emphasized the importance of sacrifice—"I think that's what makes a stronger country"—and introduced the concept of "future preference," under which tomorrow takes precedence over today. By the end of her speech, she was calling into question that most basic of American values—self-reliance. "I hope we don't forget that the idea of the rugged individual is a great idea for films, for books, but there are very few people who go through life without needing anyone, without having to make any sacrifice for anyone else," she said. "In fact, it's kind of an impoverished life, if that's the attitude."

At the same event, Clinton referred to the hospital's interim president. "I like the name 'interim president,' " she said. "I like the name 'president' even better." . . .

Ever since entering the Senate, Clinton has hosted an annual invitation-only lunch at the State Fair. Her guests include community leaders and elected officials from central New York, along with an assortment of people who somehow fit in with the lunch's annual theme. Last year's was agriculture, and the guests included several dairy farmers. This year's was the military. Clinton had a private meeting beforehand, so I went over to the lunch ahead of her. It was a steamy day, and many of the guests, especially those in uniform, had arrived early to escape the heat on the fairgrounds. Rhea Jezer, the former chairman of the state's Sierra Club, was sitting with her husband, Daniel, a rabbi. "When my mother died, when I had a foot operation that got infected, Hillary called," Jezer told me. "She really cares. Yet the press says that she's cold. I don't understand that."

Jezer introduced me to the Onondaga County executive, Nick Pirro, a Republican, who apparently had been invited out of a spirit of bipartisanship. He looked as if he were having second thoughts about his decision to show up. "There's no middle ground on Hillary," he told me. "People are either very for or very against her. There are a lot of people who believe she really is in this to run for President." . . .

By the time Clinton got to the lunch at the State Fair, there was not a single empty seat in the room, which had been set up for more than four hundred people. Clinton began her remarks by saying that it was a "great honor" for her to serve on the Senate Armed Services Committee, and she related how she had teamed up with Senator Graham to try to provide health insurance for members of the National Guard and reservists. "Some of you may recall Senator Graham and I have some significant differences," she said, prompting titters from the audience. "But on this we are absolutely united." Finally, to much cheering from the crowd, she vowed to fight the proposed closing of a V.A. hospital in nearby Canandaigua.

"That really raises an over-all issue, and that is: What are our priorities as a nation?" Clinton continued. "What is it we are going to focus on and value, and what is it we are willing to pay for? I am very disappointed that in just two and a half years we have gone from surplus back into huge and growing deficits. And I just have to respectfully disagree that the economic policies pursued by the Administration are working. I don't see the jobs being created; in fact, we have the worst job-creation record since Herbert Hoover, and that was not exactly a good time for our country."

After the lunch, Clinton made her way over to a neighboring building for a press conference. The place was packed with people, many of whom still seemed to be under the impression that they were going to see both Hillary and Bill. A microphone had been set up behind a display of apples and apple products, and a girl in an orange taffeta gown with a sash that said "Williamson Apple Blossom Queen" was waiting beside it. It was so hot that people began to help themselves to the apple-juice boxes. Clinton announced a program under which General Mills, in return for labels from New York apples, would donate money to the state's schools.

"We have the most delicious apples in the world, and we have the best students and kids in the world, so it's a perfect combination," she said. She took a few questions from the press, including one about her husband—"He just couldn't make it this year," she said curtly—and then began to work the crowd. People kept asking her to pose for pictures or to sign things—mostly copies of "Living History," but also baseballs, brochures from the fair, and scraps of used paper and envelopes. One man handed her an old copy of *Time* magazine with a menacing-looking picture of her on the cover and the headline "The Truth About Whitewater." Clinton looked nonplussed, but signed it anyway. "When am I going to get to vote for you for President?" one woman asked her. "You are such an inspiration," another one said.

Eventually, Clinton worked her way over to a building known as the Center of Progress, where her Senate office had a booth of its own, next to a booth for the state comptroller. It consisted of tables covered with pamphlets, including one for kids that asked, "Did You Know . . . New York has the longest Toll Expressway in the entire world? (Governor Thomas E. Dewey Thruway is 559 miles long.)" Hundreds more people had lined up to see her, and they grabbed the pamphlets and handed them to her to sign.

Unlike her husband, Clinton does not appear to draw energy from huge crowds of people. Such is her self-discipline, though, that, as she is beaming into the camera or scribbling her name for the umpteenth time, she is almost always able to convey the sense that there's nothing on earth she'd rather be doing. The effort she puts out doesn't resolve the contradictions of her career—ambition and self-sacrifice are never fully interchangeable—but it can make them blur together. One woman I met at the "Living History" reading in Chappaqua put the point this way: "Anyone who is willing to do what she's done to be in public service is a hero."

After about half an hour at her booth, it was time for Clinton to head over to a Friends of Hillary fund-raiser. On her way out of the building, she paused at the comptroller's booth, where she posed for a picture with the staff and signed more autographs. During her time at the fair, in addition to her Secret Service detail, Clinton had been guarded by a dozen or so state troopers, and they lined up to say goodbye to her at the door. She thanked them and, before getting into her car, shook hands with every single one.

Questions for Discussion

1. Both Senator Clinton and Representative DeLay seem to be taking a long-term approach to their political careers. Compare how they have laid out their courses to advance within (or past) their current institution (the Senate and House, respectively).
2. Why would Republicans like the conservative Lindsey Graham (R-S.C.) and the moderate Susan Collins (R-Maine) work with Senator Clinton? Why does Senator Clinton pay so much attention to her upstate constituents?
3. Think through how both Clinton and DeLay act as representatives in Washington. Both are national figures. Who is it exactly that they are representing?

Chapter 11

THE PRESIDENCY

On the surface, the public knows far more about the president than it does about any other political figure. What the president does—whether traveling to a summit of world leaders or going to church—is news. Presidents have become totally public figures, to the point that the public often holds unrealistically high expectations for their performance. Yet we usually know relatively little about how the president makes decisions and even less about how the institution of the presidency operates on a day-to-day basis.

A generation ago, Alexander Bickel called the Supreme Court "the least dangerous branch" because of its inability to implement decisions. Today, we might consider the presidency the most dangerous branch, because the possibility of exercising immense power, especially in military matters and foreign policy, resides there. From the Korean War to the Iraq invasion, presidents have demonstrated their dominance. Indeed, the 9/11 attacks and the resulting military actions have extended this predominance. In domestic policy, on the other hand, the president is far more constrained by Congress and, occasionally, by the courts. This continuing difference between the domestic and foreign/military policy arenas has been aptly labeled the "two presidencies" phenomenon by political scientist Aaron Wildavsky.

The power of the president has long attracted the attention of presidential scholars. Without question the presidency has become much more powerful since Franklin Roosevelt recast its very nature in the 1930s. Even those presidents who have been most reluctant to increase the reach of the federal government, such as Dwight Eisenhower and Ronald Reagan, have sought to take advantage of the prerogatives of executive authority. At the same time, presidential power has waxed and waned in the modern era. In large part it is dependent on the president's relationship with the legislative branch and capacity to retain substantial support from the public. And, as George W. Bush demonstrated, even the narrowest electoral victory can produce forceful presidential actions, given the right circumstances.

The presidencies of Lyndon Johnson, Richard Nixon, Gerald Ford, and Jimmy Carter all demonstrated that Congress and the American people can impose major limitations on any president, even those, like Johnson and Nixon, who are eager to extend the limits of executive authority. Each of these presidencies was judged a failure, to a greater or lesser extent, by the public. These presidents were held accountable for actions and policies they could not completely control. As the presidency became more visible in the 1960s and 1970s, its occupants confronted an unwieldy Congress and an increasingly skeptical citizenry. Scholars, politicians, and journalists wondered whether the job had become impossible.

Then came the Reagan presidency. Its record will be the subject of debate for decades to come, but one thing is abundantly clear from the Reagan years: The presidency is not an unmanageable job. Reagan demonstrated that, even without working congressional majorities in both houses, the president can act authoritatively and maintain relatively high popularity ratings well into a second term. George Bush, his successor, consistently received strong job approval ratings, especially in the wake of the 1991 Gulf War.

In the end, however, President Bush lost much of his support for taking a principled action—he endorsed a tax increase in order to help balance the budget, thus contradicting his 1988 campaign pledge ("Read my lips . . .") of no new taxes. Most economists conclude that the 1990 budget agreement eventually helped turn budget deficits into surpluses. But the economy's short-term performance, along with Bush's broken promise, led to his defeat in 1992 by Arkansas governor Bill Clinton.

As Clinton's presidency ended in January 2001, evaluating the state of the office was difficult. In many ways, Clinton had learned a great deal about serving effectively as president in an era of divided government and narrow partisan majorities. The public gave him considerable credit, and he departed the White House with a higher job-approval rating than the highly popular Reagan. At the same time, Clinton left only modest policy legacies, aside from the considerable accomplishment of serving during the great turnaround from huge deficits to large budget surpluses. Most analysts believe that Federal Reserve chairman Alan Greenspan was as much (if not more) responsible for the state of the economy as Clinton was. And in international relations, Clinton could genuinely claim credit for some major successes (expanded trade, intervention in Bosnia), but he created no general policy blueprint for how the United States might act as the sole remaining superpower. Finally, his moral failings led many Americans to distrust him and allowed his opponents to pursue him with an unrelenting vengeance throughout his presidency. At the beginning of the twenty-first century, the role of the president remained strangely undefined, in the realms of both domestic and foreign policymaking. Well into the presidency of George W. Bush, uncertainty remained over the proper presidential role.

The following selections examine the modern presidency from both institutional and psychological perspectives. Richard E. Neustadt offers his now classic formulation of presidential influence: Presidents must protect their reputations and popularity as they seek to persuade legislators and even their own administrative appointees to support their policy initiatives. Political scientist Robert A. Dahl dissects the notion of the presidential mandate as an element in the "pseudodemocratization" of the American presidency. Indeed, Dahl sees the contemporary presidency as representing exactly what the framers sought to avoid: an executive who obtains office by pandering to an ill-informed and malleable public that is incapable of producing a meaningful mandate for action. This has become all the more significant as presidents have adopted polling and other campaign strategies to frame and deliver their messages.

One staple of presidential analysis has been the rating—usually by historians, political scientists, and notable figures—of all the presidents. Begun by historian Arthur M. Schlesinger, Sr., and carried out by various successors, the ratings provide fodder for two useful discussions in selection 11.3. First, the raters can rank the entire lot of presidents, producing lists that generally begin with Lincoln and end with Harding. Second, and more usefully, these rankings allow scholars to think through what makes for great, good, and not-so-good presidents. Three notable scholars, including Arthur M. Schlesinger, Jr., reflect on the ratings and their limitations.

The last selection (11.4) offers an inside glimpse of the White House through the eyes of an energetic and smart political scientist, John J. Dilulio, Jr., who worked for President Bush during his first six months in office. Dilulio views the initial days of the Bush administration through a scholarly lens, which can focus upon the day-to-day activities of the White House. He provides confirmation of the agenda-setting importance of the president, even as the capacity to develop detailed initiatives has progressively weakened. The president tends to paint with a broad brush, while others provide details. Given the sweep of government, this seems inevitable, yet Dilulio pines for a simpler day when a policy wonk like him could have more control over the nuts and bolts of emerging policies.

The Power to Persuade

Richard E. Neustadt

The American president generally is regarded as the most powerful elected official in the world. Some of this power derives from the presidential power of command. The president can order a wide range of policies to be carried out, especially when dealing with foreign affairs or defense issues. At the same time, any chief executive must confront the numerous obstacles to exercising presidential authority. Some of these are constitutional, such as the independent power bases of the Congress and the Supreme Court. Others are less formal but no less restrictive; for example, the bureaucracy often serves as a brake on presidential initiatives (see Chapter 12).

In this selection, political scientist Richard E. Neustadt fleshes out the nature of presidential power as the power to persuade—a classic formulation on which a generation of scholars has built. Not only are presidents obliged to persuade Congress of the virtues of their proposals; they must also persuade their own administrations, and often their top aides, that their proposals have merit, even after they have won legislative approval. (Although Neustadt added three chapters to his book *Presidential Power* in 1980, this excerpt appeared in the original edition, published in 1960, and is replete with references to the Truman and Eisenhower administrations.)

T
he limits on command suggest the structure of our government. The constitutional convention of 1787 is supposed to have created a government of "separated powers." It did nothing of the sort. Rather, it created a government of separated institutions *sharing* powers. "I am part of the legislative process," Eisenhower often said in 1959 as a reminder of his veto. Congress, the dispenser of authority and funds, is no less part of the administrative process. Federalism adds another set of separated institutions. The Bill of Rights adds others. Many public purposes can only be achieved by voluntary acts of private institutions; the press, for one, in Douglass Cater's phrase, is a

Richard E. Neustadt is professor emeritus of government at Harvard University.

Excerpt from *Presidential Power* by Richard E. Neustadt, pp. 26–43. Copyright © 1986 by Macmillan Publishing Company. Reprinted by permission of Pearson Education, Inc.

"fourth branch of government." And with the coming of alliances abroad, the separate institutions of a London, or a Bonn, share in the making of American public policy.

What the Constitution separates our political parties do not combine. . . . The President and congressmen who bear one party's label are divided by dependence upon different sets of voters. The differences are sharpest at the stage of nomination. The White House has too small a share in nominating congressmen, and Congress has too little weight in nominating Presidents for party to erase their constitutional separation. Party links are stronger than is frequently supposed, but nominating processes assure the separation.

The separateness of institutions and the sharing of authority prescribe the terms on which a President persuades. When one man shares authority with another, but does not gain or lose his job upon the other's whim, his willingness to act upon the urging of the other turns on whether he conceives the action right for him.* The essence of a President's persuasive task is to convince such men that what the White House wants of them is what they ought to do for their sake and on their authority.

Persuasive power, thus defined, amounts to more than charm or reasoned argument. These have their uses for a President, but these are not the whole of his resources. . . . The status and authority inherent in his office reinforce his logic and his charm.

Status adds something to persuasiveness; authority adds still more. When Truman urged wage changes on his Secretary of Commerce while the latter was administering the steel mills, he and Secretary Sawyer were not just two men reasoning with one another.† Had they been so, Sawyer probably would never have agreed to act. Truman's status gave him special claims to Sawyer's loyalty, or at least attention. In [English political theorist] Walter Bagehot's charming phrase "no man can *argue* on his knees." Although there is no kneeling in this country, few men—and exceedingly few Cabinet officers—are immune to the impulse to say "yes" to the President of the United States. It grows harder to say "no" when they are seated in his oval office at the White House, or in his study on the second floor, where almost tangibly he partakes of the aura of his physical surroundings. . . .

A President's authority and status give him great advantages in dealing with the men he would persuade. Each "power" is a vantage point for him in the degree that other men have use for his authority. From the veto to appointments, from publicity to budgeting, and so down a long list, the White House now controls the most encompassing array of vantage points in the American

---

*From the vantage point of the 1990s, Neustadt's language seems insensitive to gender. Remember, he wrote in 1960 when (1) there was little such sensitivity and (2) virtually all top-level appointees were men.

†In 1952, President Truman seized control of the steel industry to prevent a strike during the Korean War. The Supreme Court ruled his action unconstitutional.

political system. With hardly an exception, the men who share in governing this country are aware that at some time, in some degree, the doing of *their* jobs, the furthering of *their* ambitions, may depend upon the President of the United States. Their need for presidential action, or their fear of it, is bound to be recurrent if not actually continuous. Their need or fear is his advantage.

A President's advantages are greater than mere listing of his "powers" might suggest. The men with whom he deals must deal with him until the last day of his term. Because they have continuing relationships with him, his future, while it lasts, supports his present influence. Even though there is no need or fear of him today, what he could do tomorrow may supply today's advantage. Continuing relationships may convert any "power," any aspect of his status, into vantage points in almost any case. When he induces other men to do what he wants done, a President can trade on their dependence now *and* later.

The President's advantages are checked by the advantages of others. Continuing relationships will pull in both directions. These are relationships of mutual dependence. A President depends upon the men he would persuade; he has to reckon with his need or fear of them. They too will possess status, or authority, or both, else they would be of little use to him. Their vantage points confront his own; their power tempers his.

Persuasion is a two-way street. Sawyer, it will be recalled, did not respond at once to Truman's plan for wage increases at the steel mills. On the contrary, the Secretary hesitated and delayed and only acquiesced when he was satisfied that publicly he would not bear the onus of decision. Sawyer had some points of vantage all his own from which to resist presidential pressure. If he had to reckon with coercive implications in the President's "situations of strength," so had Truman to be mindful of the implications underlying Sawyer's place as a department head, as steel administrator, and as a Cabinet spokesman for business. Loyalty is reciprocal. Having taken on a dirty job in the steel crisis, Sawyer had strong claims to loyal support. Besides, he had authority to do some things that the White House could ill afford. . . . He might have resigned in a huff (the removal power also works two ways). Or, . . . he might have declined to sign necessary orders. Or, he might have let it be known publicly that he deplored what he was told to do and protested its doing. By following any of these courses Sawyer almost surely would have strengthened the position of [steel] management, weakened the position of the White House, and embittered the union. But the whole purpose of a wage increase was to enhance White House persuasiveness in urging settlement upon union and companies alike. Although Sawyer's status and authority did not give him the power to prevent an increase outright, they gave him capability to undermine its purpose. . . .

The power to persuade is the power to bargain. Status and authority yield bargaining advantages. But in a government of "separated institutions sharing powers," they yield them to all sides. With the array of vantage points at his disposal, a President may be far more persuasive than his logic or his charm could make him. But outcomes are not guaranteed by his advantages. There remain the counter pressures those whom he would influence can bring to bear on him from vantage points at their disposal. Command has limited utility; persuasion becomes give-and-take. It is well that the White House holds the vantage points it does. In such a business any President may need them all— and more.

I

This view of power as akin to bargaining is one we commonly accept in the sphere of congressional relations. Every textbook states and every legislative session demonstrates that . . . a President will often be unable to obtain congressional action on his terms or even to halt action he opposes. The reverse is equally accepted: Congress often is frustrated by the President. Their formal powers are so intertwined that neither will accomplish very much, for very long, without the acquiescence of the other. By the same token, though, what one demands the other can resist. The stage is set for that great game, much like collective bargaining, in which each seeks to profit from the other's needs and fears. It is a game played catch-as-catch-can, case by case. And everybody knows the game, observers and participants alike. . . .

In only one sphere is the concept [of power as give-and-take] unfamiliar: the sphere of executive relations. Perhaps because of civics textbooks and teaching in our schools, Americans instinctively resist the view that power in this sphere resembles power in all others. Even Washington reporters, White House aides, and congressmen are not immune to the illusion that administrative agencies comprise a single structure, "the" Executive Branch, where presidential word is law, or ought to be. Yet . . . when a President seeks something from executive officials his persuasiveness is subject to the same sorts of limitations as in the case of congressmen, or governors, or national committeemen, or private citizens, or foreign governments. There are no generic differences, no differences in kind and only sometimes in degree. The incidents preceding the dismissal of [General Douglas] MacArthur* and the incidents surrounding seizure of the steel mills make it plain that here as elsewhere influence derives from bargaining advantages; power is a give-and-take.

Like our governmental structure as a whole, the executive establishment consists of separated institutions sharing powers. The President heads one of these; Cabinet officers, agency administrators, and military commanders head others. Below the departmental level, virtually independent bureau chiefs

---

*A strong-willed commander of U.N. and American forces in South Korea and a prospective Republican presidential nominee, General MacArthur repeatedly challenged President Truman over Korean War strategies. Truman ultimately removed him from his command. This action reinforced the president's role as commander-in-chief, although MacArthur received much popular and legislative support upon his return to the United States.

head many more. Under mid-century conditions, Federal operations spill across dividing lines on organization charts; almost every policy entangles many agencies; almost every program calls for interagency collaboration. Everything somehow involves the President. But operating agencies owe their existence least of all to one another—and only in some part to him. Each has a separate statutory base; each has its statutes to administer; each deals with a different set of subcommittees at the Capitol. Each has its own peculiar set of clients, friends, and enemies outside the formal government. Each has a different set of specialized careerists inside its own bailiwick. Our Constitution gives the President the "take-care" clause and the appointive power. Our statutes give him central budgeting and a degree of personnel control. All agency administrators are responsible to him. But they *also* are responsible to Congress, to their clients, to their staffs, and to themselves. In short, they have five masters. Only after all of those do they owe any loyalty to each other.

"The members of the Cabinet," Charles G. Dawes used to remark, "are a President's natural enemies." Dawes had been Harding's Budget Director, Coolidge's Vice-President, and Hoover's Ambassador to London; he also had been General Pershing's chief assistant for supply in the First World War. The words are highly colored, but Dawes knew whereof he spoke. The men who have to serve so many masters cannot help but be somewhat the "enemy" of any one of them. By the same token, any master wanting service is in some degree the "enemy" of such a servant. A President is likely to want loyal support but not to relish trouble on his doorstep. Yet the more his Cabinet members cleave to him, the more they may need help from him in fending off the wrath of rival masters. Help, though, is synonymous with trouble. Many a Cabinet officer, with loyalty ill-rewarded by his lights and help withheld, has come to view the White House as innately hostile to department heads. Dawes's dictum can be turned around.

A senior presidential aide remarked to me in Eisenhower's time: "If some of these Cabinet members would just take time out to stop and ask themselves, 'What would I want if I were President?', they wouldn't give him all the trouble he's been having." But even if they asked themselves the question, such officials often could not act upon the answer. Their personal attachment to the President is all too often overwhelmed by duty to their other masters. . . .

Some aides will have more vantage points than a selective memory. Sherman Adams, for example, as the Assistant to the President under Eisenhower, scarcely deserved the appelation "White House aide" in the meaning of the term before his time or as applied to other members of the Eisenhower entourage. Although Adams was by no means "chief of staff" in any sense so sweeping—or so simple—as press commentaries often took for granted, he apparently became no more dependent on the President than Eisenhower on him. "I need him," said the President when Adams turned out to have been remarkably imprudent in the Goldfine case, and delegated to him even the decision on his own departure.* This instance is extreme, but the tendency it illustrates is common enough. Any aide who demonstrates to others that he has the President's consistent confidence and a consistent part in presidential business will acquire so much business on his own account that he becomes in some sense independent of his chief. Nothing in the Constitution keeps a well-placed aide from converting status into power of his own, usable in some degree even against the President—an outcome not unknown in Truman's regime or, by all accounts, in Eisenhower's.

The more an officeholder's status and his "powers" stem from sources independent of the President, the stronger will be his potential pressure on the President. Department heads in general have more bargaining power than do most members of the White House staff; but bureau chiefs may have still more, and specialists at upper levels of established career services may have almost unlimited reserves of the enormous power which consists of sitting still. As Franklin Roosevelt once remarked:

> The Treasury is so large and far-flung and ingrained in its practices that I find it almost impossible to get the action and results I want—even with Henry [Morgenthau] there. But the Treasury is not to be compared with the State Department. You should go through the experience of trying to get any changes in the thinking, policy, and action of the career diplomats and then you'd know what a real problem was. But the Treasury and the State Department put together are nothing compared with the Na-a-vy. The admirals are really something to cope with—and I should know. To change anything in the Na-a-vy is like punching a feather bed. You punch it with your right and you punch it with your left until you are finally exhausted, and then you find the damn bed just as it was before you started punching.[1]

. . . Real power is reciprocal and varies markedly with organization, subject matter, personality, and situation. The mere fact that persuasion is directed at executive officials signifies no necessary easing of his [the President's] way. Any new congressman of the Administration's party, especially if narrowly elected, may turn out more amenable (though less useful) to the President than any seasoned bureau chief "downtown." *The probabilities of power do not derive from the literary theory of the Constitution.*

II

There is a widely held belief in the United States that were it not for folly or for knavery, a reasonable President would need no power other than the logic of his argument. No less a personage than Eisenhower has subscribed to that

---

*Businessman Bernard Goldfine gave Sherman Adams, Eisenhower's top aide, the gift of a vicuna coat. When it became public, Adams's acceptance of the gift caused substantial embarrassment to the president, and Adams subsequently resigned.

belief in many a campaign speech and press-conference remark. But faulty reasoning and bad intentions do not cause all quarrels with Presidents. The best of reasoning and of intent cannot compose them all. For in the first place, what the President wants will rarely seem a trifle to the men he wants it from. And in the second place, they will be bound to judge it by the standard of their own responsibilities, not his. However logical his argument according to his lights, their judgment may not bring them to his view. . . . An able Eisenhower aide with long congressional experience remarked to me in 1958: "The people on the Hill don't do what they might *like* to do, they do what they think they *have* to do in their own interest as *they* see it. . . ." This states the case precisely.

The essence of a President's persuasive task with congressmen and everybody else, is *to induce them to believe that what he wants of them is what their own appraisal of their own responsibilities requires them to do in their interest, not his.* Because men may differ in their views on public policy, because differences in outlook stem from differences in duty—duty to one's office, one's constituents, oneself—that task is bound to be more like collective bargaining than like a reasoned argument among philosopher kings. Overtly or implicitly, hard bargaining has characterized all illustrations offered up to now. This is the reason why: persuasion deals in the coin of self-interest with men who have some freedom to reject what they find counterfeit.

III

A President draws influence from bargaining advantages. But does he always need them? . . . Suppose most players of the governmental game see policy objectives much alike, then can he not rely on logic (or on charm) to get him what he wants? The answer is that even then most outcomes turn on bargaining. The reason for this answer is a simple one: most men who share in governing have interests of their own beyond the realm of policy *objectives.* The sponsorship of policy, the form it takes, the conduct of it, and the credit for it separate their interest from the President's, despite agreement on the end in view. In political government, the means can matter quite as much as ends; they often matter more. And there are always differences of interest in the means. . . .

Adequate or not, a President's own choices are the only means *in his own hands* of guarding his own prospects for effective influence. He can draw power from continuing relationships in the degree that he can capitalize upon the needs of others for the Presidency's status and authority. He helps himself to do so, though, by nothing save ability to recognize the preconditions and the chance advantages and to proceed accordingly in the course of the choice-making that comes his way. To ask how he can guard prospective influence is thus to raise a further question: what helps him guard his power stakes in his own acts of choice?

Note

1. Quoted in Marriner S. Eccles, *Beckoning Frontiers* (New York: Knopf, 1951), 336.

Questions for Discussion

1. Why must presidents be able to "persuade" their own administrative appointees?
2. Can presidents *increase* their ability to persuade? How? By making good choices?

 11.2

Myth of the Presidential Mandate

Robert A. Dahl

The term *mandate* appears frequently in discussions of presidential elections. Presidents claim mandates—often broadly defined—in the wake of their victories. The people, they say, have spoken. After all, among elected officials only the president has a national constituency. The problem comes in interpreting what the people have to say. Many potential voters do not cast their ballots; in recent presidential contests, these individuals constituted almost 50 percent of the potential electorate. Moreover, many reasons lie behind the millions of votes that support a given candidate.

Political scientist and democratic theorist Robert A. Dahl argues that not until Woodrow Wilson's presidency did chief executives begin to claim mandates for their policies and goals. Such claims have become commonplace, but Dahl casts substantial doubt on their validity. Even with sophisticated sample surveys, Dahl finds the complexities underlying mandates exceedingly difficult to fathom. In addition, presidents frequently win by less than a majority of the popular vote and often receive only a bit more than a quarter of the ballots of all those eligible

Robert A. Dahl is professor emeritus of political science at Yale University.

"Myth of the Presidential Mandate" by Robert A. Dahl. Reprinted by permission of *Political Science Quarterly,* 105 (1990): 355–372.

to vote. In sum, although presidents may be eager to claim mandates for their actions, in most instances these claims are self-serving rather than based on adequate criteria or clear relationships between the candidate and the electorate.

O n election night in 1980 the vice president-elect [George Bush] enthusiastically informed the country that Ronald Reagan's triumph was

> . . . not simply a mandate for a change but a mandate for peace and freedom; a mandate for prosperity; a mandate for opportunity for all Americans regardless of race, sex, or creed; a mandate for leadership that is both strong and compassionate . . . a mandate to make government the servant of the people in the way our founding fathers intended; a mandate for hope; a mandate for hope for the fulfillment of the great dream that President-elect Reagan has worked for all his life.

I suppose there are no limits to permissible exaggeration in the elation of victory, especially by a vice president elect. He may therefore be excused, I imagine, for failing to note, as did many others who made comments in a similar vein in the weeks and months that followed, that Reagan's lofty mandate was provided by 50.9 percent of the voters. A decade later it is much more evident, as it should have been then, that what was widely interpreted as Reagan's mandate, not only by supporters but by opponents, was more myth than reality.

In claiming that the outcome of the election provided a mandate to the president from the American people to bring about the policies, programs, emphases, and new directions uttered during the campaign by the winning candidate and his supporters, the vice president elect was like other commentators echoing a familiar theory.

Origin and Development

A history of the theory of the presidential mandate has not been written, and I have no intention of supplying one here. However, if anyone could be said to have created the myth of the presidential mandate, surely it would be Andrew Jackson. Although he never used the word mandate, so far as I know, he was the first American president to claim not only that the president is uniquely representative of all the people, but that his election confers on him a mandate from the people in support of his policy. Jackson's claim was a fateful step in the democratization of the constitutional system of the United States—or rather what I prefer to call the pseudodemocratization of the presidency.

As Leonard White observed, it was Jackson's "settled conviction" that "the President was an immediate and direct representative of the people." Presumably as a result of his defeat in 1824 in both the electoral college and the House of Representatives, in his first presidential message to Congress, in order that "as few impediments as possible should exist to the free operation of the public will," he proposed that the Constitution be amended to provide for the direct election of the president.

> "To the people," he said, "belongs the right of electing their Chief Magistrate: it was never designed that their choice should, in any case, be defeated, either by the intervention of electoral colleges or by . . . the House of Representatives."

His great issue of policy was the Bank of the United States, which he unwaveringly believed was harmful to the general good. Acting on this conviction, in 1832 he vetoed the bill to renew the bank's charter. Like his predecessors, he justified the veto as a protection against unconstitutional legislation; but unlike his predecessors in their comparatively infrequent use of the veto he also justified it as a defense of his or his party's policies.

Following his veto of the bank's charter, the bank became the main issue in the presidential election of 1832. As a consequence, Jackson's reelection was widely regarded, even among his opponents (in private, at least), as amounting to "something like a popular ratification" of his policy. When in order to speed the demise of the bank Jackson found it necessary to fire his treasury secretary, he justified his action on the ground, among others, that "The President is the direct representative of the American people, but the Secretaries are not."

Innovative though it was, Jackson's theory of the presidential mandate was less robust than it was to become in the hands of his successors. In 1848 James Polk explicitly formulated the claim in a defense of his use of the veto on matters of policy, that as a representative of the people the president was, if not more representative than the Congress, at any rate equally so.

> "The people, by the constitution, have commanded the President, as much as they have commanded the legislative branch of the Government, to execute their will. . . . The President represents in the executive department the whole people of the United States, as each member of the legislative department represents portions of them. . . ." The President is responsible "not only to an enlightened public opinion, but to the people of the whole Union, who elected him, as the representatives in the legislative branches are responsible to the people of particular States or districts. . . ."

Notice that in Jackson's and Polk's views, the president, both constitutionally and as representative of the people, is on a par with Congress. They did not claim that in either respect the president is superior to Congress. It was Woodrow Wilson who took the further step in the evolution of the theory by asserting that in representing the people the president is not merely equal to Congress but actually superior to it.

Earlier Views

Because the theory of the presidential mandate espoused by Jackson and Polk has become an integral part of our present-day conception of the presidency, it may be hard for us to grasp how sharply that notion veered off from the views of the earlier presidents.

As James Ceaser has shown, the Framers designed the presidential election process as a means of improving the chances of electing a *national* figure who would enjoy majority support. They hoped their contrivance would avoid not only the populistic competition among candidates dependent on "the popular arts," which they rightly believed would occur if the president were elected by the people, but also what they believed would necessarily be a factional choice if the president were chosen by the Congress, particularly by the House.

In adopting the solution of an electoral college, however, the Framers seriously underestimated the extent to which the strong impulse toward democratization that was already clearly evident among Americans—particularly among their opponents, the anti-Federalists—would subvert and alter their carefully contrived constitutional structure. Since this is a theme I shall pick up later, I want now to mention only two such failures that bear closely on the theory of the presidential mandate. First, the Founders did not foresee the development of political parties nor comprehend how a two-party system might achieve their goal of insuring the election of a figure of national rather than merely local renown. Second, as Ceaser remarks, although the Founders recognized "the need for a popular judgment of the performance of an incumbent" and designed a method for selecting the president that would, as they thought, provide that opportunity, they "did not see elections as performing the role of instituting decisive changes in policy in response to popular demands." In short, the theory of the presidential mandate not only cannot be found in the Framers' conception of the Constitution; almost certainly it violates that conception.

No president prior to Jackson challenged the view that Congress was the legitimate representative of the people. Even Thomas Jefferson, who adeptly employed the emerging role of party leader to gain congressional support for his policies and decisions,

> was more Whig than . . . the British Whigs themselves in subordinating [the executive power] to "the supreme legislative power." . . . The tone of his messages is uniformly deferential to Congress. His first one closes with these words: "Nothing shall be wanting on my part to inform, as far as in my power, the legislative judgment, nor to carry that judgment into faithful execution."

James Madison, demonstrating that a great constitutional theorist and an adept leader in Congress could be decidedly less than a great president, deferred so greatly to Congress that in his communications to that body his extreme caution rendered him "almost unintelligible"—a quality one would hardly expect from one who had been a master of lucid exposition at the Constitutional Convention. His successor, James Monroe, was so convinced that Congress should decide domestic issues without presidential influence that throughout the debates in Congress on "the greatest political issue of his day . . . the admission of Missouri and the status of slavery in Louisiana Territory," he remained utterly silent.

Madison and Monroe serve not as examples of how presidents should behave but as evidence of how early presidents thought they should behave. Considering the constitutional views and the behavior of Jackson's predecessors, it is not hard to see why his opponents called themselves Whigs in order to emphasize his dereliction from the earlier and presumably constitutionally correct view of the presidency.

Woodrow Wilson

The long and almost unbroken succession of mediocrities who succeeded to the presidency between Polk and Wilson for the most part subscribed to the Whig view of the office and seem to have laid no claim to a popular mandate for their policies—when they had any. Even Abraham Lincoln, in justifying the unprecedented scope of presidential power he believed he needed in order to meet secession and civil war, rested his case on constitutional grounds, and not as a mandate from the people. Indeed, since he distinctly failed to gain a majority of votes in the election of 1860, any claim to a popular mandate would have been dubious at best. Like Lincoln, Theodore Roosevelt also had a rather unrestricted view of presidential power; he expressed the view then emerging among Progressives that chief executives were also representatives of the people. Yet the stewardship he claimed for the presidency was ostensibly drawn—rather freely drawn, I must say—from the Constitution, not from the mystique of the mandate.

Woodrow Wilson, more as political scientist than as president, brought the mandate theory to what now appears to be its canonical form. His formulation was influenced by his admiration for the British system of cabinet government. In 1879, while still a senior at Princeton, he published an essay recommending the adoption of cabinet government in the United States. He provided little indication as to how this change was to be brought about, however, and soon abandoned the idea without yet having found an alternative solution. Nevertheless, he continued to contrast the American system of congressional government, in which Congress was all-powerful but lacked executive leadership, with British cabinet government, in which parliament, though all powerful, was firmly led by the prime minister and his cabinet. Since Americans were not likely to adopt the British cabinet system, however, he began to consider the alternative of more powerful presidential leadership. In his *Congressional*

Government, published in 1885, he acknowledged that "the representatives of the people are the proper ultimate authority in all matters of government, and that administration is merely the clerical part of government." Congress is "unquestionably, the predominant and controlling force, the center and source of all motive and of all regulative power." Yet a discussion of policy that goes beyond "special pleas for special privilege" is simply impossible in the House, "a disintegrate mass of jarring elements," while the Senate is no more than "a small, select, and leisurely House of Representatives."

By 1908, when *Constitutional Government in the United States* was published, Wilson had arrived at strong presidential leadership as a feasible solution. He faulted the earlier presidents who had adopted the Whig theory of the Constitution.

> . . . [T]he makers of the Constitution were not enacting Whig theory. . . . The President is at liberty, both in law and conscience, to be as big a man as he can. His capacity will set the limit; and if Congress be overborne by him, it will be no fault of the makers of the Constitution—it will be from no lack of constitutional powers on its part, but only because the President has the nation behind him, and Congress has not. He has no means of compelling Congress except through public opinion. . . . [T]he early Whig theory of political dynamics . . . is far from being a democratic theory. . . . It is particularly intended to prevent the will of the people as a whole from having at any moment an unobstructed sweep and ascendancy.

And he contrasted the president with Congress in terms that would become commonplace among later generations of commentators, including political scientists:

> Members of the House and Senate are representatives of localities, are voted for only by sections of voters, or by local bodies of electors like the members of the state legislatures. There is no national party choice except that of President. No one else represents the people as a whole, exercising a national choice. . . . The nation as a whole has chosen him, and is conscious that it has no other political spokesman. His is the only national voice in affairs. . . . He is the representative of no constituency, but of the whole people. When he speaks in his true character, he speaks for no special interest. . . . [T]here is but one national voice in the country, and that is the voice of the President.

Since Wilson, it has become commonplace for presidents and commentators alike to argue that by virtue of his election the president has received a mandate for his aims and policies from the people of the United States. The myth of the mandate is now a standard weapon in the arsenal of persuasive symbols all presidents exploit. For example, as the Watergate scandals emerged in mid-1973, Patrick Buchanan, then an aide in the Nixon White House, suggested that the president should accuse his accusers of "seeking to destroy the democratic mandate of 1972." Three weeks later in an address to the country Nixon said:

> Last November, the American people were given the clearest choice of this century. Your votes were a mandate, which I accepted, to complete the initiatives we began in my first term and to fulfill the promises I made for my second term.

If the spurious nature of Nixon's claim now seems self-evident, the dubious grounds for virtually all such pretensions are perhaps less obvious.

Critique of the Theory

What does a president's claim to a mandate amount to? The meaning of the term itself is not altogether clear. Fortunately, however, in his excellent book *Interpreting Elections*, Stanley Kelley has "piece[d] together a coherent statement of the theory."

> Its first element is the belief that elections carry messages about problems, policies, and programs—messages plain to all and specific enough to be directive. . . . Second, the theory holds that certain of these messages must be treated as authoritative commands . . . either to the victorious candidate or to the candidate and his party. . . . To qualify as mandates, messages about policies and programs must reflect the *stable* views both of individual voters and of the electorate. . . . In the electorate as a whole, the numbers of those for or against a policy or program matter. To suggest that a mandate exists for a particular policy is to suggest that more than a bare majority of those voting are agreed upon it. The common view holds that landslide victories are more likely to involve mandates than are narrow ones. . . . The final element of the theory is a negative imperative: Governments should not undertake major innovations in policy or procedure, except in emergencies, unless the electorate has had an opportunity to consider them in an election and thus to express its views.

To bring out the central problems more clearly, let me extract what might be called the primitive theory of the popular presidential mandate. According to this theory, a presidential election can accomplish four things. First, it confers constitutional and legal authority on the victor. Second, at the same time, it also conveys information. At a minimum it reveals the first preferences for president of a plurality of votes. Third, according to the primitive theory, the election, at least under the conditions Kelley describes, conveys further information: namely that a clear majority of voters prefer the winner because they prefer his policies and wish him to pursue his policies. Finally, because the president's policies reflect the wishes of a majority of voters, when conflicts over policy arise between president and Congress, the president's policies ought to prevail.

While we can readily accept the first two propositions, the third, which is pivotal to the theory, might be false. But if the third is false, then so is the fourth. So the question arises: Beyond revealing the first preferences of a plurality of voters, do presidential elections also reveal the additional information that a plurality (or a majority) of voters prefer the policies of the winner and wish the winner to pursue those policies?

In appraising the theory I want to distinguish between two different kinds of criticisms. First, some critics contend that even when the wishes of constituents can be known, they should not be regarded as in any way binding on a legislator. I have in mind, for example, Edmund Burke's famous argument that he would not sacrifice to public opinion his independent judgment of how well a policy would serve his constituents' interests, and the argument suggested by Hanna Pitkin that representatives bound by instructions would be prevented from entering into the compromises that legislation usually requires.

Second, some critics, on the other hand, may hold that when the wishes of constituents on matters of policy can be clearly discerned, they ought to be given great and perhaps even decisive weight. But, these critics contend, constituents' wishes usually cannot be known, at least when the constituency is large and diverse, as in presidential elections. In expressing his doubts on the matter in 1913, A. Lawrence Lowell quoted Sir Henry Maine: "The devotee of democracy is much in the same position as the Greeks with their oracles. All agreed that the voice of an oracle was the voice of god, but everybody allowed that when he spoke he was not as intelligible as might be desired."

It is exclusively the second kind of criticism that I want now to consider. Here again I am indebted to Stanley Kelley for his succinct summary of the main criticisms.

> Critics allege that 1) some particular claim of a mandate is unsupported by adequate evidence; 2) most claims of mandates are unsupported by adequate evidence; 3) most claims of mandates are politically self-serving; or 4) it is not possible in principle to make a valid claim of a mandate, since it is impossible to sort out voters' intentions.

Kelley goes on to say that while the first three criticisms may well be valid, the fourth has been outdated by the sample survey,* which "has again given us the ability to discover the grounds of voters' choices." In effect, then, Kelley rejects the primitive theory and advances the possibility of a more sophisticated mandate theory according to which the information about policies is conveyed not by the election outcome but instead by opinion surveys. Thus the two functions are cleanly split: presidential elections are for electing a president, opinion surveys provide information about the opinions, attitudes, and judgments that account for the outcome.

However, I would propose a fifth proposition, which I believe is also implicit in Kelley's analysis:

> 5) While it may not be strictly impossible in *principle* to make a reasoned and well-grounded claim to a presidential mandate, to do so *in practice* requires a complex analysis that in the end may not yield much support for presidential claims.

---

*Sampling techniques allow a relatively small number of respondents (1,500 for a national sample) to accurately reflect the views of a much larger population (150 million adults).

But if we reject the primitive theory of the mandate and adopt the more so-phisticated theory, then it follows that prior to the introduction of scientific sample surveys, no president could reasonably have defended his claim to a mandate. To put a precise date on the proposition, let me remind you that the first presidential election in which scientific surveys formed the basis of an ex-tended and systematic analysis was 1940.

I do not mean to say that no election before 1940 now permits us to draw the conclusion that a president's major policies were supported by a substantial ma-jority of the electorate. But I do mean that for most presidential elections be-fore 1940 a valid reconstruction of the policy views of the electorate is impossible or enormously difficult, even with the aid of aggregate data and other indirect indicators of voters' views. When we consider that presidents or-dinarily asserted their claims soon after their elections, well before historians and social scientists could have sifted through reams of indirect evidence, then we must conclude that before 1940 no contemporary claim to a presidential mandate could have been supported by the evidence available at the time.

While the absence of surveys undermines presidential claims to a mandate before 1940, the existence of surveys since then would not necessarily have supported such claims. Ignoring all other shortcomings of the early election studies, the analysis of the 1940 election I just mentioned was not published until 1948. While that interval between the election and the analysis may have set a record, the systematic analysis of survey evidence that is necessary (though perhaps not sufficient) to interpret what a presidential election means always comes well after presidents and commentators have already told the world, on wholly inadequate evidence, what the election means. Perhaps the most famous voting study to date, *The American Voter*, which drew primarily on interviews conducted in 1952 and 1956, appeared in 1960. The book by Stan-ley Kelley that I have drawn on so freely here, which interprets the elections of 1964, 1972, and 1980, appeared in 1983.

A backward glance quickly reveals how empty the claims to a presidential mandate have been in recent elections. Take 1960. If more than a bare major-ity is essential to a mandate, then surely Kennedy could have received no man-date, since he gained less than 50 percent of the total popular vote by the official count—just how much less by the unofficial count varies with the counter. Yet "on the day after election, and every day thereafter," Theodore Sorenson tells us, "he rejected the argument that the country had given him no mandate. Every election has a winner and a loser, he said in effect. There may be difficulties with the Congress, but a margin of only one vote would still be a mandate."

By contrast, 1964 was a landslide election, as was 1972. From his analysis, however, Kelley concludes that "Johnson's and Nixon's specific claims of mean-ingful mandates do not stand up well when confronted by evidence." To be sure, in both elections some of the major policies of the winners were supported by large majorities among those to whom these issues were salient. Yet "none of these policies was cited by more than 21% of respondents as a reason to like Johnson, Nixon, or their parties."

In 1968, Nixon gained office with only 43 percent of the popular vote. No mandate there. Likewise in 1976, Carter won with a bare 50.1 percent. Once again, no mandate there.

When Reagan won in 1980, thanks to the much higher quality of surveys undertaken by the media, a more sophisticated understanding of what that election meant no longer had to depend on the academic analyses that would only follow some years later. Nonetheless, many commentators, bemused as they so often are by the arithmetical peculiarities of the electoral college, immediately proclaimed both a landslide and a mandate for Reagan's policies. What they often failed to note was that Reagan gained just under 51 percent of the popular vote. Despite the claims of the vice president elect, surely we can find no mandate there. Our doubts are strengthened by the fact that in the elections to the House, Democratic candidates won just over 50 percent of the popular vote and a majority of seats. However, they lost control of the Senate. No Democratic mandate there, either.

These clear and immediate signs that the elections of 1980 failed to confer a mandate on the president or his Democratic opponents were, however, largely ignored. For it was so widely asserted as to be commonplace that Reagan's election reflected a profound shift of opinion away from New Deal programs and toward the new conservatism. However, from this analysis of the survey evidence, Kelley concludes that the commitment of voters to candidates was weak; a substantial proportion of Reagan voters were more interested in voting against Carter than for Reagan; and despite claims by journalists and others, the New Deal coalition did not really collapse. Nor was there any profound shift toward conservatism. "The evidence from press surveys . . . contradicts the claims that voters shifted toward conservatism and that this ideological shift elected Reagan." In any case, the relation between ideological location and policy preferences was "of a relatively modest magnitude."

In winning by a landslide of popular votes in 1984, Reagan achieved one prerequisite to a mandate. Yet in that same election, Democratic candidates for the House won 52 percent of the popular votes. Two years earlier, they had won 55 percent of the votes. On the face of it, surely the 1984 elections gave no mandate to Reagan.

Before the end of 1986, when the Democrats had once again won a majority of popular votes in elections to the House and had also regained a majority of seats in the Senate, it should have been clear and it should be even clearer now that the major social and economic policies for which Reagan and his supporters had claimed a mandate have persistently failed to gain majority support. Indeed, the major domestic policies and programs established during the thirty years preceding Reagan in the White House have not been overturned in the grand revolution of policy that his election was supposed to have ushered in. For eight years, what Reagan and his supporters claimed as a mandate to reverse those policies was regularly rejected by means of the only legitimate and constitutional processes we Americans have for determining what the policies of the United States government should be.

What are we to make of this long history of unsupported claims to a presidential mandate? The myth of the mandate would be less important if it were not one element in the larger process of the pseudodemocratization of the presidency—the creation of a type of chief executive that in my view should have no proper place in a democratic republic.

Yet even if we consider it in isolation from the larger development of the presidency, the myth is harmful to American political life. By portraying the president as the only representative of the whole people and Congress as merely representing narrow, special, and parochial interests, the myth of the mandate elevates the president to an exalted position in our constitutional system at the expense of Congress. The myth of the mandate fosters the belief that the particular interests of the diverse human beings who form the citizen body in a large, complex, and pluralistic country like ours constitute no legitimate element in the general good. The myth confers on the aims of the groups who benefit from presidential policies an aura of national interest and public good to which they are no more entitled than the groups whose interests are reflected in the policies that gain support by congressional majorities. Because the myth is almost always employed to support deceptive, misleading, and manipulative interpretations, it is harmful to the political understanding of citizens.

It is, I imagine, now too deeply rooted in American political life and too useful a part of the political arsenal of presidents to be abandoned. Perhaps the most we can hope for is that commentators on public affairs in the media and in academic pursuits will dismiss claims to a presidential mandate with the scorn they usually deserve.

But if a presidential election does not confer a mandate on the victor, what does a presidential election mean, if anything at all? While a presidential election does not confer a popular mandate on the president—nor, for that matter, on congressional majorities—it confers the legitimate authority, right, and opportunity on a president to try to gain the adoption by constitutional means of the policies the president supports. In the same way, elections to Congress confer on a member the authority, right, and opportunity to try to gain the adoption by constitutional means of the policies he or she supports. Each may reasonably contend that a particular policy is in the public good or public interest and, moreover, is supported by a majority of citizens.

I do not say that whatever policy is finally adopted following discussion, debate, and constitutional processes necessarily reflects what a majority of citizens would prefer, or what would be in their interests, or what would be in the public good in any other sense. What I do say is that no elected leader, including the president, is uniquely privileged to say what an election means—nor to claim that the election has conferred on the president a mandate to enact the particular policies the president supports. . . .

Questions for Discussion

1. What is a mandate? Why is it so important, or at least useful, for a president to make such a claim in establishing a set of policy priorities?
2. In what ways does the idea of a presidential mandate violate the assumptions of the Constitution's framers?
3. Did George W. Bush have any possible mandate after the 2000 election? Did he claim one?

 11.3

Rating the Presidents: Purpose, Criteria, Consequences

James MacGregor Burns, Arthur M. Schlesinger, Jr., and Fred I. Greenstein

Over the years, historians have played a kind of scholarly parlor game in which they rank all the presidents of the United States, from best to worst. Clustering at the top are the American deities, Lincoln and Washington, with the semideity Franklin Roosevelt not far behind. Bringing up the rear are Warren G. Harding, James Buchanan, and Ulysses S. Grant, though Grant has been moving up a bit recently. All in all, the ratings game does no real harm, and may do a little good. For one thing, over time, scholarly opinion may change, as with Truman's climb up the ranking ladder, along with Eisenhower's. In addition, the rating process gives serious historians and political scientists an opportunity to think through what they value in a president—what makes him (so far) great, good, or less than adequate. This is useful because the job itself both changes and remains constant over time, and presidents need to be considered within their own era. Who knows what FDR would have done in the 1920s, or Reagan after the fall of the Soviet Union?

James MacGregor Burns is professor emeritus at Williams College. Arthur M. Schlesinger, Jr., is the Albert Schweitzer Professor Emeritus in the Humanities at the Graduate School of the City University of New York; Fred I. Greenstein is professor emeritus at Princeton University.

James MacGregor Burns, Arthur M. Schlesinger, Jr., and Fred I. Greenstein, "Rating the Presidents: Purpose, Criteria, Consequences," *White House Studies 3.1* (Winter 2003): 73–80. Reprinted by permission.

In this selection, three veteran, highly respected presidential scholars reflect on the presidential ratings game. James MacGregor Burns, Arthur M. Schlesinger, Jr., and Fred I. Greenstein discuss the whys and hows of rating our presidents, along with the consequences of this exercise. In the end, the ratings can add only marginally to our understanding of presidential greatness, but both the public and the scholarly community like the game and both learn a bit in the process. And that's not a bad combination in our present-tense, ahistorical world.

James MacGregor Burns

The fact that so many of us are meeting here today attests to the attention that presidential evaluation receives, not only from the academy but from journalists and even many of the reading public. Ratings of presidents by presidential scholars have become a small industry. This makes it all the more important that we stand back and look critically at what we're doing. I'm not about to criticize comparative presidential ranking so much as to suggest four anomalies that raise serious questions about the endeavor.

The first is the sheer maleness of the rating game. It consists of mainly male scholars evaluating invariably male presidents. As a presidential scholar, a woman, said to me, "It's all so nineteenth century," to which I replied, "It's all so twentieth century." Women, she believes, have been socialized to be less hierarchical and more collaborative than men. Of course, we must not stereotype women politicians. The "Iron Lady," Margaret Thatcher, was one of Britain's strongest leaders since Churchill. But in America, note the criticism, for example, of both Elizabeth Dole and Hillary Clinton that they are too forthright and perhaps a bit assertive, while this is expected of male politicians. Our presidents, in short, are tested by so-called male qualities. Well, of course, we can't solve this problem until we elect a woman president, and I can hardly wait.

A second anomaly involves the presidency as an institution. To rate leaders, we must see them in their institutional settings, as we would leaders in the judiciary, or corporations, or universities. But we're not much agreed on what the presidency is as an institution. Presidential scholars and other analysts see the White House through highly dissimilar lenses. Unlike the blind men who touched different parts of the elephant, these analysts see the whole beast, but they're different beasts. This is reflected in the various titles, or emphases, in scholars' writings about the presidency, books called *The Rhetorical Presidency*, *The Imperial Presidency*, *The Unfinished Presidency*, etc. Naturally, since we disagree on how we see the presidency, we disagree on the key questions that should be asked of this institution. Is a presidency too strong or too weak? Should it fit comfortably into our fragmented checks-and-balances system, or be more independent, more autonomous? Should the presidency be a place of inspiring vision, a center of moral leadership, or should it be a seat of pragmatism, moving cautiously, incrementally, step by step, dealing in practical ways with problems as they come along?

This problem escalates when we evaluate individual presidents as leaders, my third anomaly. The presidential rating game, of course, does not evaluate presidents separately; it's a ranking. They're evaluated comparatively. And here, again, analysts disagree hugely on the qualities they want in a president.

Collectively, we want everything: a strong leader, a consensus builder, a good manager, a policy expert, a great communicator, an ethical model, a visionary, a negotiator. Fred Greenstein, in his excellent recent book, *The Presidential Difference*, has added two arresting qualities: cognitive style and emotional intelligence. Typically, though, we don't rank these qualities on the basis of priorities, in terms of what do we really want most in a presidency. And, of course, we disagree on those qualities and probably on the rankings. Hence, we rate different presidents by different standards. Then what happens to comparability, which lies at the heart of ranking?

One solution to this problem might be to judge presidents not by their behavior—how they act—but by their values—what they believe. The problem here is that this opens up another can of worms: What values do we test presidents by? Liberty, equality, justice, community, happiness? And how should we rank order such values? And how even to define values? There's a vast confusion here.

Some scholars, such as William Bennett, see values as virtues, like piety, or, for example, sobriety, chastity, frugality, and other such qualities. Others define values as ethical standards: honesty, accountability, responsibility, especially in dealing with one another in the business of politics. Still others see values as the kind of principles that define a great nation, such as Franklin Roosevelt's four freedoms.

But here, again, can we expect presidents to live up to all three of these definitions of values? If not, which are the most important? Thus, FDR violated values as virtues—he was unfaithful to his wife—and he sometimes violated values as ethics in his deceptive and even Machiavellian dealings with friend and foe. But for some of us, he was magnificent in articulating and carrying out his lofty moral values, like the four freedoms. So, as we study Roosevelt, we would play down the failings and play up the great achievements, which are the ones we feel would last in history. But others disagree with that, and that's the whole point.

So how do we compare presidents when our values are fuzzy and lack priorities, and when we mix up virtue, ethics, and values? My fourth anomaly poses the toughest problem of all. It stems from the old enigma or paradox in history in the social sciences, and particularly in leadership analysis—namely, . . . the interaction of would-be leaders and the situational opportunities and obstacles that confront them.

This problem often comes to presidential scholars as a question from a student or an audience. Can an American president be great without a huge crisis, such as war or depression, that he can exploit politically? Even if presidents' personal qualities, such as courage or character, were stable and similar from one administration to another, do not the ever-changing situations or circumstances make it most difficult to compare the leadership of presidents? Thus, FDR had both a depression and a war to propel him to greatness, while Theodore Roosevelt had neither. Oh, how he would have loved a little war during his presidency, just a little war, like the one in Cuba that built his reputation.

But sometimes agency, in the form of leadership, trumps situation. TR didn't have a crisis, but he was a kind of a walking crisis, in himself, because of his sheer drive, forcefulness, and, above all, his conviction. On this score alone perhaps he deserves a slightly higher rating than most scholars give him. But a far more common situation facing presidents, as scholars know so well, are intractable circumstances that perhaps no president could overcome. How do we compare the border-state problems facing Lincoln, the Republican Senate confronting Wilson, the Vietnam War confounding Lyndon Johnson? And as situations vary so much, and presidential responses to situations vary so much, how, again, do we compare presidents in terms of greatness?

So, in view of the above four problems, and others, why do we continue to play the game of ranking presidents? First, because everybody does it, especially the voters at election time. And at least scholars bring empirical knowledge, historical experience, and scholarly perspective and disinterest to this endeavor, as well as awareness of the kinds of shortcomings of the rating game that I've mentioned.

Secondly, we do it because it's fun. And to join the fun, I'm now going to reverse direction and offer my own ratings of the qualities necessary to presidential greatness. They are character, competence, courage, conviction, commitment, in rising order of importance. So at least I'm meeting my own demand for prioritizing, though I expect most of you would differ in that particular series of qualities.

Arthur M. Schlesinger, Jr.

My father invented the game of rating the presidents, and his first ranking came in *Life* magazine in November 1948, based on responses from 55 historians. He repeated the experiment in the *New York Times Magazine* of July 1962, this on the basis of replies from 75 historians, political scientists, and occasional people who were neither professional historians nor political scientists but had occasion to understand the problems of the presidency.

The rating game caught on, I think, because it explored scholarly values in the measurement of presidential performance, tested various theories, various criteria, of presidential performance, and also because, as Jim Burns reminded us, it was great fun as a parlor game. My father proposed a simple method of dividing presidents into five categories: Great, Near-Great, Average, Below-Average, and Failure.

As to how presidential performance should be judged, my father, instead of proposing specific criteria, specific yardsticks, left it to scholars to offer their own overall judgments. Some subsequent scholars have regarded such overall judgments as unduly subjective and impressionistic. Also, as political scientists joined the game, with their faith in typologies and models, that too introduced an effort to try to formalize and make objective the judgment of presidential performance. Would not ranking polls be more objective, more scientific, if presidents were given numerical scores against stated criteria?

Scholars, therefore, tried to make the judgments more precise, more objective, by breaking them down to a group of categories, but as Jim Burns has reminded us, these categories are themselves subjective in the sense that they represent the view of the historian as to the hierarchy of values [against] which presidents should be judged—such categories as success in the attaining of objectives, the relationship of those objectives to the general welfare, personal trustworthiness and integrity, impact on history, and so on.

Fred Greenstein, in his interesting new book, *The Presidential Difference*, proposes six criteria: public communication, organizational capacity, political skill, vision, cognitive style, emotional intelligence. Tom Bailey of Stanford, who semi-jocularly regarded the Schlesinger polls as a Harvard, Eastern-elitist Democratic Party plot, came up with no less than 43 yardsticks. The University of Illinois in Chicago and the Chicago *Sun-Times* recently developed a survey on the American presidency, asking respondents to rank each president in each category on a one-to-five scale. And the categories are political leadership, foreign policy, domestic policy, character, and impact on history.

I found I could not comfortably rate presidents in this manner. I am a holist rather than a mechanist when it comes to judgment of presidential performance. The notion that presidential greatness or presidential failure is a sum of designated categories seems to me misleading. The breakdown into a set of standards, a set of criteria, does not allow for the accommodation of presidents to the character of the problems that confronted them, nor for the values that the presidents embody.

This is related, of course, to one of Jim Burns' anomalies. And I think it's also related to an occupational difference between historians and political scientists. Historians tend to focus on the uniqueness of things; political scientists try to abstract from the welter of concrete circumstances certain generalizations of larger applicability. So I think the formalist approach is more congenial to political scientists: the more specific approach—and that is the overall judgment rather than a breakdown into categories—is more congenial to historians. And, for that matter, it should be added that the use of standards, the use of the mechanical rather than the holistic approach, does not make much difference in the end to the results. Even Tom Bailey's complex set of standards, with his 43 yardsticks, ended up with much the same ranking as the Schlesinger polls.

Over the years, it had been suggested that I replicate my father's polls, but the difficulty of making overall judgments about the presidents after Eisenhower stumped me. In the cases of Kennedy and Ford, because of the brevity of their time in office; in the cases of LBJ, Nixon, and Bush, because their foreign policy and domestic policy records were so discordant. Scholars might be inclined, for example, to rate LBJ high in domestic affairs but a failure in foreign affairs, and might be inclined to do the reverse for Nixon and Bush.

Then in 1996, the *Times Magazine* persuaded me to do a poll, in which only 32 scholars out of a much longer list participated. However, I doubt that the longer list would have produced a much different result.

I would like to add a point about failures. Most polls inevitably end up with Grant and Harding as the two conspicuous failures among American presidents. I wonder whether Grant and Harding really deserve this. They're stigmatized because of the scandal and corruption that disgraced their administrations, but they were careless and negligent rather than villainous; their sin was excessive loyalty to crooked friends. Grant, for example, had not a bad record on civil rights; Harding commuted the prison sentence of Eugene Victor Debs, the Socialist leader whom the Wilson administration had sent to prison.

Scandal and corruption are indeed indefensible, but they may injure the general welfare less than misconceived or errant public policies. I think it is reasonable to suggest that James Buchanan, Andrew Johnson, Herbert Hoover, and Richard Nixon damaged the republic a good deal more than did the hapless Grant and the feckless Harding. They are, it seems to me, the true failures in the White House.

Consequences of the ranking? I can report President Kennedy's reaction. In 1962, my father included in the list of historians and political scientists who were to be polled the historian who had written *Profiles in Courage* and *A Nation of Immigrants*. JFK started to fill out my father's questionnaire, and then changed his mind. As he wrote my father, "A year ago I would have responded with confidence, but now I am not so sure. After being in the office for a year, I feel that a good deal more study is required to make the judgment sufficiently informed. There is a tendency to mark the obvious names. I would like to subject those not so well known to a long scrutiny after I have left this office."

President Kennedy said to me, "How the hell can you tell? Only the president himself knows what his real pressures and real alternatives are. If you don't know that, how can you judge performance?" Some of his greatest predecessors, President Kennedy went on, were given credit for doing things when they could have done nothing else. Only a detailed inquiry could disclose what difference a president made by his individual contribution. "War," Kennedy observed, "made it easier for presidents to achieve greatness. But would Lincoln have been judged so great a president if he had to face the almost-insoluble questions of Reconstruction?"

For all this skepticism, JFK read the results of my father's 1962 poll with fascination. He was greatly pleased that Truman came out as a "Near-Great," nor was he displeased that Eisenhower came in 22nd, near the bottom of the "Averages." Later, jokingly (or half-jokingly) he blamed Eisenhower's vigorous entry into the 1962 congressional campaign on the historians. He said to me, "It's all your father's poll. Ike has been going along for years basking in the glow of applause that he has always had. Then he saw the poll and realized how he stood before the cold eye of history way below Truman, even below Hoover. Now he's mad to save his reputation." This is the only evidence I know to suggest that scholars' ratings of presidents have much practical impact.

Of course, there remains the impalpable power of example—what Harold Bloom of Yale calls "the anxiety of influence." Presidents in the present may draw inspiration from the top ranking presidents of the past. When confronted by hard decisions, it might be appropriate for presidents to ask, "What would Lincoln do? What would FDR do?" As Emerson said, "We feed on genius. Great men exist that there may be greater men."

Fred I. Greenstein

I have come here determined to be a lion in a Daniel's den and assail the very practice of rating presidents. The title of my remarks is "Don't Rate Presidents, Heed Their Lessons." My thesis is that the presidential rating game is a distraction from what can be most valuably accomplished by a close examination of the nation's past presidents, culling lessons from their character and performance.

These may be positive lessons, as in those that can be derived from Harry Truman's success in persuading a conservative, isolationist-leaning Republican Congress to enact the Marshall Plan. They may be negative lessons, as in those that can be derived from the Kennedy administration's abortive effort to land a brigade of anti-Castro rebels at Cuba's Bay of Pigs. Positive lessons sometimes can be taken from presidents who are typically ranked low in the ratings scale, for example, Richard Nixon's impressive first-term foreign policy successes. And negative lessons can be derived from so called "great" presidents, as in Franklin Roosevelt's counterproductive effort to "pack" the Supreme Court. My remarks derive from the book that my two predecessors have kindly referred to: *The Presidential Difference: Leadership Style from FDR to Clinton.*

All of the nation's chief executives from George Washington to the present incumbent are potential sources of positive and negative insight, but the eleven presidents I examine in *The Presidential Difference* are particularly worthy of contemporary attention. Beginning with FDR, there was a transformation of the presidential job. Almost from the moment he assumed office, the president began to displace Congress as the principal agenda-setter of the political system. During the Roosevelt years, the United States and therefore its chief executive began to play a central role in the international arena. In the same period, the nation acquired a massive federal government, greatly augmenting the responsibilities of its chief executive. The Roosevelt years also saw the creation of the Executive Office of the President, which provides the occupant of the Oval Office with a support system that makes it possible to carry out his expanded responsibilities.

Let me now provide illustrations of how negative, as well as positive, presidential experience can be instructive, doing so in terms of the six categories I use to assess presidential performance in *The Presidential Difference*—public communication, organizational capacity, political skill, policy vision, cognitive style, and emotional intelligence.

In the realm of public communication, I am struck by how few of the modern presidents perform at the level of a high proportion of the professionals in such spheres as the mass media, academia, and the church. This, despite the critical importance of public communication in presidential leadership. George Herbert Walker Bush is a case in point. As we know from the 1997 Hofstra conference on his presidency, Bush went out of his way not to emulate the gifted presidential communicator whose vice president he had been. Reminding his speech writers that he was no Ronald Reagan, he insisted that they provide him with rhetorically unadorned texts. His preference was to address the nation from the White House briefing room rather than from the Oval Office. His was a conception of the presidency in which there was little room for the bully pulpit.

Bush's minimalist approach to public communication was unproblematic as long as the going was good. He had high levels of public support in 1989 and 1990, when the Soviet empire in Eastern Europe collapsed and the economy prospered. Early in 1991, his public approval reached the highest level in the history of presidential polling after his administration's dramatic victory in the Gulf War. Then the economy took a nosedive, in the crucial fourth year of his presidency. Bush failed to communicate a persuasive message about how he would restore prosperity, and he was swept from office garnering a mere 38 percent of the popular vote.

John F. Kennedy provides the contrasting example of a president who was able to surmount political difficulties by dint of his communication abilities. Kennedy's response to the fiasco of the Bay of Pigs was of a piece with the larger focus on rhetoric in his leadership style. Convening a press conference, he addressed the assembled reporters gravely, but with confidence, declaring that he assumed full responsibility for what had occurred. He then wryly remarked that "victory has a hundred fathers and defeat is an orphan," and moved on to a discussion of his administration's plans for the future. The next Gallup Poll registered an increase in his public approval, rather than the plunge that might have been expected.

My second category, that of organizational capacity, may seem pedantic, but it is of crucial importance. The debacle of the Bay of Pigs is again informative, because it was the product of flawed decision-making. The disorganization of Kennedy's presidency was such that the member of his administration who had the most to contribute to the Cuban deliberations was out of the loop. That member was Treasury Secretary Douglas Dillon, who had been second in command in the Eisenhower State Department and in charge of the contingency plan Kennedy inherited from his predecessor. The precise effect Dillon would have had on the outcome of Kennedy's deliberations cannot be known, but his participation would have made for a better informed and wiser decision-making process.

Just as Kennedy provides an object lesson on how not to organize the presidency, Eisenhower is a font of constructive insight. No American president had richer and more demanding pre-presidential organizational experience than the architect of the Normandy invasion. One of the first tasks Eisenhower set for himself on taking office was that of providing the White House with a more rational and systematic structure. His efforts resulted in a set of organizational arrangements that commend themselves to any future chief executive.

My third category, political skill, is the ability to engage effectively in the art of the possible. Here again there is an illuminating negative example. Jimmy Carter displayed impressive skill in coming out of political obscurity and winning the presidency. However, he and his fellow Georgians came to Washington bent on not engaging in politics as usual. Even before Carter took the oath of office, his chief political aide had offended Speaker of the House Tip O'Neill by refusing his party favorable seats at the inaugural ceremony. Carter barely got in the White House when he canceled water projects in the congressional districts of key members of Congress.

The most conspicuous failure of Carter's presidency was of his signature policy proposal, an ambitious plan to reform the way the nation produces and consumes energy. Carter placed a politically insensitive official in charge of hatching the bill, which was framed in secret without consulting the legislators whose backing would be needed to enact it. It reached Capitol Hill in the form of a lengthy and complex document that was ill-suited for processing by the Congressional committee structure. Congress did eventually enact energy legislation, but well after Carter's deadline for passage and in a highly diluted form.

Carter's mishandled energy reform proposal should have provided an object lesson for his successors, but it did not. Bill Clinton was the next president to propose a major legislative departure—a comprehensive reform of the nation's health care system. Clinton also put the planning of his proposal in the charge of a controversial figure (his wife). His proposal also was drafted in secret without consulting Congress. And it too emerged in the form of an unwieldy bill that did not lend itself to Congressional deliberation. Not surprisingly, it failed to be passed.

I now turn to policy vision. By this I refer to the possession of a realistic sense of direction. The case of Lyndon Johnson is telling. Johnson may well have been the most skilled presidential politician in the nation's history, but his skill was not wed to a capacity to forge workable policies. During his first two years in office, Johnson's political prowess led to such landmark legislative breakthroughs as Medicare, the voting rights bill, and the first effective civil rights law since Reconstruction. In 1965, however, Johnson entered into an open-ended military intervention in Vietnam, never asking such critical questions as the following: How many troops will it require? How much will it cost? What impact will it have on the administration's political support? By 1968, a half-million American troops were mired in Southeast Asia. The war had become so unpopular that Johnson felt compelled to halt the escalation, enter into negotiations with the Vietnamese communists, and withdraw from running for reelection.

My fifth category, that of cognitive style, has many facets, including the sheer ability to process and analyze information. There can be no doubt of the importance of that capacity. Kennedy proceeded with a high degree of caution in the Cuban missile crisis in part because he had been reading a book on the accidental origins of World War I. Still, a president need not be a book worm or a mental giant to turn in a creditable performance. Ronald Reagan, for example, was far from conversant with the details of most of his administration's policies, but he had compensatory strengths. He was a superlative public communicator, he excelled in face-to-face negotiations, and he had the quality that Professor Burns ranks second highest in his list of desirable presidential traits—conviction. All of this contributed to Reagan's success in bringing about a major first-year economic enactment and working effectively with Mikhail Gorbachev in the negotiations that spelled an end to the Cold War.

Finally, there is the category of emotional intelligence, a notion that refers to an individual's capacity to turn his or her emotions to constructive purposes and avoid being dominated by them. Bill Clinton was the only Rhodes Scholar to have made it to the White House. Yet it was not necessary to have studied at Oxford to realize there would be political repercussions over a dalliance with an emotionally volatile White House intern. The Monica Lewinsky affair was a single episode in the presidency of a chief executive whose defective impulse control contributed to his administration's lack of consistent direction.

The modern president who most compellingly illustrates the importance of emotional intelligence is Richard M. Nixon. Everyone associated with Nixon was awed by his political skill and strategic intelligence. This, after all, was a president who entered office with the highly demanding foreign policy goals of getting out of Vietnam, arriving at an accommodation with the Soviet Union, and establishing a constructive relationship with China, and succeeded in all three. But Nixon also was notable for his dark suspiciousness and simmering anger, and in the same period he embarked on the politically unnecessary covert campaign of political espionage and sabotage that was to destroy his presidency.

I conclude by returning to my initial assertion. We derive more from the presidential record if we mine all of it. In ranking presidents, we are likely to focus only on the positive and fail to derive lessons from the low-ranking presidents. Here is my advice for those who persist in the presidential rating game. Stamp your reports with the political equivalent of a Surgeon General's warning: "Beware. The contents may be hazardous."

APPENDIX: C-SPAN Survey of Presidential Leadership, 1999

Historian Survey Results Category:
Total Score/Overall Ranking

President's Name	Final Score	Overall Ranking
Abraham Lincoln	900	1
Franklin Delano Roosevelt	876	2
George Washington	842	3
Theodore Roosevelt	810	4
Harry S. Truman	753	5
Woodrow Wilson	723	6
Thomas Jefferson	711	7
John F. Kennedy	704	8
Dwight D. Eisenhower	699	9
Lyndon Baines Johnson	655	10
Ronald Reagan	634	11
James K. Polk	632	12
Andrew Jackson	632	13
James Monroe	602	14
William McKinley	601	15
John Adams	598	16
Grover Cleveland	576	17
James Madison	567	18
John Quincy Adams	564	19
George Bush	548	20
Bill Clinton	539	21
Jimmy Carter	518	22
Gerald Ford	495	23
William Howard Taft	491	24
Richard Nixon	477	25
Rutherford B. Hayes	477	26
Calvin Coolidge	451	27
Zachary Taylor	447	28
James Garfield	444	29
Martin Van Buren	429	30
Benjamin Harrison	426	31
Chester Arthur	423	32
Ulysses S. Grant	403	33
Herbert Hoover	400	34
Millard Fillmore	395	35
John Tyler	369	36
William Henry Harrison	329	37
Warren G. Harding	326	38
Franklin Pierce	286	39
Andrew Johnson	280	40
James Buchanan	259	41

Questions for Discussion

1. How do Burns, Schlesinger, and Greenstein differ on the value of rating the presidents?
2. What would the rise of a president in the ratings over time (e.g., Eisenhower) tell us about both the individual president and the nature of the presidency overall?
3. Should we be worried about a president in office thinking about his ultimate place in the rankings? Would that be a positive or a negative as to job performance?

 11.4

Inside the Bush Presidency: Reflections of an Academic Interloper

John J. DiIulio, Jr.

Almost all presidents tap a few academics for prominent positions within the administration. Such selections place scholars in a bind. If they are to succeed, their ideas and initiatives must survive battles over practicality and political viability. And if these professors thought that academic politics was mean-spirited, they must confront a far tougher set of adversaries, both inside and outside the administration. Still, the thought of having the president on your side often convinces scholars that they can play the game of Washington politics. Some can, such as Daniel Patrick Moynihan, who left Harvard to work in Richard Nixon's Department of Labor. Many others have been eaten alive.

In 2001, John DiIulio, an energetic, imaginative, and tough-minded scholar accepted an appointment to direct the White House Office of Faith-Based Initiatives. DiIulio agreed to serve for six months, and he did return to academia (the University of Pennsylvania) at the end of his tour. What makes him different from most scholars who get to the White House is that—while not a presidential scholar—he does write a major American government textbook and has more than a passing familiarity with the professional literature on the presidency. Upon his departure from the White House, DiIulio could write about his inside experience from a scholarly perspective. This selection addresses issues of character and agenda setting, two major elements of the modern presidency. This is no "tell all" article; rather, DiIulio offers a glimpse into the contemporary White House and demonstrates that you may be able to take the academic away from his scholarship, but you can't take the scholarly perspective away from the academic.

During my academic leave in 2001 I had an opportunity that most political scientists who study American government and domestic public policy can only dream about. I served as assistant to the President of the United States and first director of a new Executive Office of the President (EOP) entity, the White House Office of Faith-Based and Community Initiatives (OFBCI). . . .

. . . To be clear, while I was on the senior staff, I purposely did not function as a first-rank advisor. For health reasons, and because I had only just moved to a new university and launched two new programs there, I had publicly agreed to serve only six months, but ended up serving about eight. I entered with a profile as a centrist Democrat public intellectual in a conservative Republican administration. Still, I did attend scores of senior staff meetings, talk routinely to other senior and junior EOP staff as well as cabinet officials, brief the president, organize several presidential trips and events, meet with House and Senate leaders both on Capitol Hill and beyond the Beltway, and help to shape many domestic policy speeches and decisions that were well beyond my purview as "faith czar." . . .

As co-author of an American government textbook, I keep up with the presidential studies literature and did a little writing on the subject early in my academic career. . . . [But] I am by no means a presidency scholar. Nonetheless, on many occasions during my White House tenure—early on when my senior colleagues were organizing the EOP and discussing cabinet appointments; later on when they and "the Hill people" (my term for top House Republican staff) were discussing political strategy; at moments when the president would call, button-hole me in the hall, drop by my building, relay questions, or say "get on my dance card" (i.e., arrange to see him); during weeks when important speeches on "faith-based" or other domestic issues were being vetted and finalized; on days when the daily media barrage or the occasional crisis was being managed; and at other times—I found myself focusing on how what I was witnessing fortified or falsified this or that academic concept or theory about presidents and the presidency. . . .

John DiIulio is the Frederic Fox Leadership Professor of Politics, Religion, and Civil Society at the University of Pennsylvania

Greenstein, Fred T., ed. *The George W. Bush Presidency: An Early Assessment.* pp. 245–257. © 2003 The Johns Hopkins University Press. Reprinted with permission of The John Hopkins University Press.

In what follows, I discuss my White House experiences as they relate to . . . three concepts in presidential studies: presidential character, the modern presidency, and the permanent campaign.

Presidential Character: The Small-*d* Texas Democrat

Little as I expected my time near the Oval Office to bug me with big ideas about the contemporary presidency, I was even more surprised to leave Washington convinced that presidential character is absolutely critical to everything from White House organization and staff relations to military policy decision making. I had never agreed with scholars who insisted that, given the massive growth in the EOP and other institutional factors, the White House is home to a "plural presidency" in which the president is best viewed as "but one of the individuals in the executive." But I was always also deeply skeptical about efforts at "predicting performance in the White House" derived from biographical or psychological insights into how a given president "orients himself toward life," including "how much energy" he invests in the job and "how he feels about what he does."

By the time I left the White House, however, I was converted by experience to the view that presidential character, most especially the sitting president's "worldview"—"his primary, politically relevant beliefs, particularly his conceptions of social causality, human nature, and the central moral conflicts of the time"—probably explains as much or more about everything from domestic agenda setting and legislative-executive relations to foreign policy than does any other single variable.

So, what is the essence of [George W.] Bush's presidential character? Plainly, he is what some scholars, following James David Barber, would term an "active-positive" president: he loves the job and is very energetic and focused. . . .

But to conceive Bush as an active-positive president with a penchant for CEO-style operations is to miss what is, in my view, a far more fundamental aspect of his presidential character. [Political scientist] Fred I. Greenstein notes Bush's disdain for "intellectual snobs." What Bush really dislikes are academic or other elites who, as I heard him phrase it on occasion, "are" or "come off" as "smart without any heart," who are "down on average Americans" who "just believe in this great country" and its "great goodness." Thus, compared to other presidencies since that of Franklin D. Roosevelt, the Bush administration is largely bereft of policy intellectuals.

Ivo H. Daalder and James M. Lindsay [see Chapter 14] explore how September 11 confirmed rather than transformed "Bush's beliefs about the world and America's place in it." But the president's main moral rationale for what they term the "Bush revolution" in foreign policy is democratic. Both in public speeches and in private conversations, Bush has deemed it "presumptuous and insulting to suggest that a whole region of the world—or the one-fifth that is Muslim—is somehow untouched by the most basic aspirations of life". He once said,

> Human cultures can be vastly different. Yet the human heart desires the same good
> things, everywhere on earth. . . . In our desire to care for our children and give them a
> better life, we are the same.

It is, I think, impossible to understand Bush's presidential character without fully appreciating his profoundly small-*d* democratic beliefs and sensibilities. Let me offer a homely example relating to my own experiences with the Texan and the administration's faith-based program proposals.

I first met George W. Bush in February 1999. After declining several invitations to visit with the likely Republican presidential aspirant at the governor's mansion in Texas, several friends, including former Indianapolis mayor Stephen Goldsmith, prevailed upon me to attend a small-group meeting with Bush. The general topic was social policy. Bush greeted me very warmly, singling me out for a hug and repeatedly calling on me to give the final word on the issues that generated disagreements. "I can see you're governor's pet," joked one colleague in a whisper.

Bush became noticeably quite animated when, in reply to his request for "one big new idea on compassion," I suggested a national initiative to match low-income children of prisoners with loving, caring, year-round, life-long adult mentors mobilized from inner-city churches. He seemed genuinely stunned, and stung, to learn that on any given day America was home to over two million children with (as he would later often phrase it) "a mom or dad in jail." He cringed as I rapidly recited the grim statistics on how much more likely these children were than otherwise comparable impoverished urban youth to suffer abuse and neglect, fail in school, abuse drugs, get arrested, and wind up behind bars themselves. At a later one-on-one meeting he smiled broadly when I summarized evidence showing that the vast majority of urban community-serving congregations and grassroots religious groups perform such social services as I had suggested without proselytizing and often work via interfaith, religious-secular, and public-private partnerships. "That's exactly how this ought to go," he exclaimed. . . .

In the months that followed the February 1999 meeting in Austin, Goldsmith, in his role as the campaign's senior domestic policy advisor, faxed me every paper on domestic issues, including but not limited to "faith initiatives," generated by ever-expanding cadres of campaign consultants and would-be advisors. My job, essentially, was to read the papers critically, both as a data-demanding social scientist and as a centrist Democrat with a skeptical but hopeful perspective on "compassionate conservatism." As time went on, I became more skeptical than hopeful. Among the things I wrote in the months before being asked to join the administration were an essay in which I expressed doubt whether "compassionate conservatism" would be translated into effective social policy and another criticizing the court majority in the case of *Bush* v. *Gore*.

Bush was aware of my positions and often kidded me about being the in-house Democrat. My president-bestowed nickname, for the record, was "Big

John," and—as he joked when he surprised me with a visit to my office on my birthday—the "big isn't for tall!" There was, indeed, a quasi-corporate culture to the White House staff, but the "CEO" was, more often than not, warm, relaxed, quick to joke and laugh, and quite respectful of all, including the most junior staff people. Meetings generally ran on time, but only generally. Staff got chewed out if they failed to turn off cell phones or made other irritating mistakes, but no heads ever rolled, at least not publicly. The president's nightly briefing book was prepared with care, but we got scolded every morning for failing to get things in on time.

By the same token, the administration's press communications were tightly controlled, but the weekly message meetings were large and improvisational, and they became so unscripted that they were an issue at the July 9, 2001 six-month senior staff retreat. The staff, like the president, was buttoned-down, but he often functioned more like an academic department chairman than a CEO, inviting brief but free-ranging discussions and hearing diverse views. He was subtle about letting staff know what he knew or suspected, and not infrequently seemed purposely to create circumstances that would test their honesty as well as their diplomacy.

For instance, on the day Bush announced the new drug czar, John Walters, we had an Oval Office pre-briefing before heading to the Rose Garden for the event. The president asked a junior staff person whether he was correct in understanding that as much as two-thirds of all illicit drugs are consumed by less than a quarter of all illicit drug users. The aide was caught off guard and mumbled an affirmative. The president then turned to me and asked, "Big John, that so?" He knew I had helped his father's administration with research on drug policy and that I had once been a fairly active student of criminal justice. He also knew—or so I suspect to this day—that the statistic he had cited was possibly way off. I replied that, while some such statistics are cited in the relevant research literatures, the data on which they are based are dated, so we really cannot say. He gave a little laugh and out we went. As I told one reporter, being on the Bush senior staff was just like being in an academic department, with only three exceptions: the issues were mostly real, the people were usually nice, and the meetings normally started on time. . . .

The Modern President Agenda-Setter-in-Chief

As an in-house policy wonk I might have been expected to covet policy and administrative details more than most; and, after all, one thing that sold me on doing the job I did at all was the chance to help produce a substantive report on the extent to which selected federal agencies were following extant laws governing participation by religious organizations in the grant-making process as well as cognate legislatively mandated protocols for program performance and evaluation. Still, I was struck by how, for example, Medicare reform issues would rapidly give way to a narrower focus on prescription drug plans or arguments favoring a patients' bill of rights. I was not surprised, therefore, when in April 2003 the administration produced an eleven-page Medicare reform blueprint and sent it to Capitol Hill.

After its health care policy debacle the Clinton administration had begun framing issues in the broadest possible terms such that multi-faceted policies on which, in fact, it had detailed plans were nonetheless presented for public consumption as representing one simple proposal (for example, an enormously detailed crime bill sold as "a hundred thousand cops"), and an almost daily series of symbolic initiatives were developed and communicated with gusto (for example, uniforms for public school children). As Klein has argued, some of the Clinton administration's greatest domestic policy victories, most especially increased spending on programs that benefit the working poor, were "invisible, in fact, hidden in the massive, incomprehensible budget 'reconciliation' packages negotiated each fall." A former Bush aide quoted by Charles O. Jones states that the Bush administration was basically "un-Clinton." In many respects, I suppose, it most certainly was and is, but as I have come to believe, no modern presidency can do other than favor agenda setting and flexible public communications over specific legislative and administrative initiatives on most issues.

. . . Most citizens, even among the segment of the public that is attentive, know very little, and care even less, about legislative process. Most news organizations, even the elite ones, do not delve very deeply into the competing perspectives and empirical evidence surrounding any given policy pronouncement, and only a few reporters know a thing about the most basic aspects of intergovernmental relations and public administration. Yet nearly everybody knows and reports whether the president has "said something" about a given topic and whether the administration is "for" a "patients' bill of rights" or whatever. Likewise, hardly anybody knows whether, or how, or why the administration has, in turn, engaged "in detailed negotiations—with the departments, the Hill, and major interest groups—that will produce the administration's proposals and that will clarify the administration's bargaining positions as the proposals move through the legislative process" into public law and administrative action.

The concept that best captures how the presidency has evolved since the days before Franklin Delano Roosevelt (F.D.R.) into the institution Bush leads today is that of the modern presidency. Different presidency scholars have emphasized different features, but most would agree that, by "contrast with the traditional (pre-F.D.R.) presidency, the modern president is expected" to "propose legislation and make budget recommendations to Congress, and secure congressional endorsement of his proposals;" be "active in defending and advancing America's interests abroad;" be "a visible national leader, projecting personality and ideas through the media;" and command "the political and national resources to meet these expectations." . . .

Simply stated, what my EOP tenure dramatized for me was that, in this day of multiple twenty-four-hour-news channels and the Internet, it is truer than ever before that the modern presidency, as Greenstein succinctly states, is about "setting the nation's policy agenda." Modern presidents have fewer and fewer incentives to step beyond symbolic politics and agenda setting to detailed legislative proposals and administrative strategies. Today, "a president cannot wait for the perfect proposal any more than a surfer can wait for the perfect wave." Given the complex realities of intergovernmental relations and the rise of so-called government by proxy, a president cannot, in all but the rarest of cases, have much real impact on how or how well most domestic policies and social programs are administered.

Obviously, while presidents must have ideas and policies for everything, it would be impossible, even in periods of unified party government and relatively minor partisan polarization in Congress, for presidents and their administrations to translate every policy idea into legislative language, every favored bill into law, and all law into effective administrative action. According to John Kingdon, "The president may be able to dominate and even determine the policy agenda, but is unable to dominate the alternatives that are seriously considered, and is unable to determine the final outcome." Precisely because of the polarized, partisan character of [contemporary] legislative politics . . . why would any administration invest scarce White House resources on any save its few very top policy priorities?

Take, for example, the Bush faith initiative. During the 2000 presidential campaign Bush called for expanding and implementing the so-called charitable choice laws that had been enacted under President Clinton. The bipartisan laws were intended to ensure that community-serving religious organizations could apply to administer federal social service delivery programs on exactly the same basis as all other nonprofit organizations. Charitable choice first appeared as a provision . . . of the [1996] . . . federal welfare reform law. A charitable choice provision was added to the Community Services Block Grant program when it was reauthorized in 1998. In 2000 another charitable choice provision was added to the Substance Abuse Prevention and Treatment Block Grant and Projects for Assistance in Transition from Homelessness program.

In nearly two dozen public statements and over a dozen public events during the administration's first eight months, Bush strongly promoted faith initiatives. He called for expanding and implementing charitable choice laws and often explicitly embraced the four key principles of charitable choice. First, faith-based providers that compete for public funds should be subjected to the same accountability standards as all other nonprofit organizations, no more, no less. Second, government may not require a religious provider to remove religious art, icons, scripture, or other symbols in order to compete for public funds. Third, religious organizations operate under the civil rights laws, including Titles VI and VII of the 1964 Civil Rights Act and other laws and court decisions affording faith-based organizations with fewer than fifteen employees a broad but not unlimited right, and those with more than fifteen employees a narrow but not trivial right, to take religion into account in making hiring decisions (the so-called ministerial exemption). Fourth, diverse partnerships between government and religious institutions are permissible, but no government funding can be diverted to any inherently religious activities such as worship, sectarian instruction, and proselytizing.

I had been given ample reason to expect that a charitable choice bill would be crafted by the administration, but only after the aforementioned report on extant federal grant-making processes was completed and only after key Senate Democrats had been persuaded that the administration would not instead endorse measures that would promote proselytizing with public funds, unfettered hiring discrimination, or other constitutionally suspect, administratively unworkable, or politically infeasible ideas. As several published accounts have reported, after House Republicans drafted a bill prominently featuring such measures, any chance of expanding or implementing charitable choice, save by the ultimately unsustainable use of executive orders, was lost.

The bill passed the House on July 19, 2001 on a virtual party line vote (with fifteen Democrats plus all Republicans present voting in favor) and was pronounced dead on arrival by Senate Democrats. On July 26, 2001, we brought Democratic Senator Joseph Lieberman, long a supporter of charitable choice, into the Oval Office. The president and Lieberman, joined by Republican Senator Rick Santorum, another respected leader on the issue, agreed to support a bill that would track closely with the 1996 charitable choice law. My staff and I worked with the two senators' staffs on this effort throughout the summer. But, rather than draft a fresh bipartisan bill unburdened by the more controversial features of the House bill, some senior staff wanted to back off charitable choice legislation altogether in favor of a "communities of character" initiative.

Of course September 11 put almost everything other than the war on terror and homeland security on the back burner for months. From January 2002 through June 2003 Bush made fewer than a dozen statements, and attended only a half-dozen events, promoting faith initiatives. In 2003 Congress passed an administration-backed bill to encourage charitable giving. It was a decent little bill, but a far cry from the president's initial call for making tens of billions of dollars in tax credits available to the over 80 million taxpayers who do not itemize deductions on their tax returns. The bill contained no charitable choice provisions at all. . . .

Viewed from the outside, not the inside, following September 11 the administration faced mounting congressional and public pressures to address homeland security challenges. At first President Bush rebuffed calls by Lieberman and others to create a new "Department of Homeland Defense." Instead, by executive order he created within the EOP a new Office of Homeland Security. By spring 2002 the office had released a homeland security blueprint, and, predictably, Congress began badgering the White House for more details. In particular, congressional leaders insisted that Director Tom Ridge testify before Congress about how homeland security budgetary priorities were to be set by the White House in relation to the Department of Justice and other key agencies. The administration refused, citing Ridge's status as a senior presidential advisor not confirmed by the Senate.

But, as became more obvious with each press conference, even to administer its own general homeland security strategy Ridge's office would need to coordinate personnel and budgets across scores of agencies. The homeland security devil, like the faith initiatives devil, was in the details. After spending nearly nine months defending the position that no new department was necessary, the White House reversed itself on June 6, 2002. It proposed the creation of an umbrella-level cabinet bureaucracy with nearly 170,000 employees (third behind Defense and Veterans Affairs) and a total of about $40 billion in budgets (fourth behind Defense, Health and Human Services, and Education). The proposal passed late in 2002, but nobody, not even Director Ridge himself, pretended that what one report termed "Bush's Swift, Sweeping Plan" could be implemented anytime soon, or that the new department had been conceived with all due regard for limiting, rather than multiplying, administrative problems, both present and future.

In sum, my experiences inside the Bush presidency, in conjunction with reflections on other modern presidencies from F.D.R.'s to Clinton's, caused me to recognize how the political and institutional incentives to spend presidential time, staff, and other scarce administration resources on stepping beyond broad agenda setting to detailed legislation and (last and least) effective administration seem to have grown progressively weaker over the past several decades. Or, to state the same point in the affirmative and in the somewhat more technical language of Bryan Jones and colleagues, early "in the policy process, when proposals struggle to gain agenda access, cognitive costs are high but transaction costs are low. The scheduling of a policy topic for a hearing is indicative that policymakers are taking the topic seriously—the topic has accessed the policy or governmental agenda." Whether what appears to be an important institutional trend is real—whether, alas, the next incumbents of the modern presidency will behave ever more as agenda-setters-in-chief—remains to be seen.

Questions for Discussion

1. Why might academics, even one as action-oriented as DiIulio, have problems working smoothly within the White House?
2. How was DiIulio's experience at the White House shaped by his academic background? What does his perspective on the White House offer us that some other staffers would not?

 Chapter 12

BUREAUCRACY

The terms *bureaucracy* and *bureaucrat* evoke negative images for most Americans. To many, *bureaucracy* is a synonym for red tape, rigidity, insensitivity, and long waiting lines, and *bureaucrat* suggests a faceless government drone sitting at a desk, pushing papers, and stamping forms. In fact, a bureaucracy is any complex organization that operates on the basis of a hierarchical authority structure with job specialization. Corporations are bureaucracies, as are educational institutions. The question is whether a bureaucracy complements democracy. On the one hand, it seems wise to have a government run by professionals whose jobs are not dependent on politics. But we may have created a class of government employees who are beyond the control of the voters.

In recent years, public officials and candidates for public office have nurtured the negative image of the public sector and those employed by it. Bureaucracy-bashing is good politics. Four recent presidents—Nixon, Carter, Reagan, and George W. Bush—were first elected during campaigns that made opposition to the Washington bureaucracy a central theme. Every election year congressional candidates remind the public that the federal government has paid $91 for three-cent screws or $511 for a sixty-cent lightbulb. Contempt for the Washington bureaucracy may have reached a zenith during the Reagan presidency. Attorney General Edwin Meese once came to a cabinet meeting carrying a chubby, faceless, large-bottomed doll and announced that it was a bureaucrat doll—you place it on a stack of papers and it just sits there.

According to one student of American bureaucracy, Barry D. Karl, "the growth of the bureaucratic state may be the single most unintended consequence of the Constitution of 1787." The Constitution says little about the administration of government. It gives the president the appointment power and the obligation "to take care that the laws [are] faithfully executed," which suggests that the framers were well aware of the administrative needs of the new nation. But belief in limited government and fear of centralized power led them to envision a minimal role for the new federal government.

Thus, the administrative apparatus during the first few presidencies was very small. The State Department had only nine employees at its beginning, and the War Department had fewer than one hundred employees until 1801, at the start of the Jefferson presidency. Compared to Western European countries, the U.S.

bureaucracy experienced a rather late development, well after the growth of mass democracy under Andrew Jackson in the 1830s. By 1861, on the eve of the Civil War, roughly 80 percent of all federal personnel still worked for the Post Office Department.

The Civil War contributed substantially to the growth of American bureaucracy. Mobilization for the war effort led to the creation of many new agencies and the hiring of a large number of public employees. The establishment of a national economy and rapid industrialization after the war also had a profound effect on the size and functions of the federal government, which began to pay attention to particular constituencies. "Clientele" agencies such as the Department of Agriculture (1889) and the Department of Commerce and Labor (1903) were created to service increasingly organized interests.

This period also marked the beginning of the development of a professional bureaucratic class. Before 1883, all federal workers were patronage employees, appointed by the president. When presidencies changed hands, many government employees were out of a job. The assassination of President James A. Garfield in 1881 by an unsuccessful patronage applicant provided the impetus for passage of the Pendleton Act (1882), which established the civil service system. Only about 10 percent of government employees were initially covered by the act, but today more than 90 percent are; they receive their jobs on the basis of competitive merit, usually as the result of written examinations. Firing someone for political reasons is illegal.

The New Deal and mobilization for World War II gave the federal bureaucracy the basic form it has today. As the federal government took on an expanded social and economic role, myriad new agencies were created. Today there are more than a hundred federal government agencies, and the government employs almost 5 million people, 2.9 million of whom are civilians.

Despite the widely shared view that the federal bureaucracy has grown rapidly in recent decades, the number of federal employees has been relatively constant since 1945. Most of the growth in the public sector has been at the state and local levels. Nor do most federal bureaucrats work in or around the nation's capital. Only about 12 percent of federal employees work in Washington; 300,000, or 10 percent, work in California. Federal government employment as a percentage of the total work force decreased over the past two decades. "Big government" is more dollars and rules than it is huge numbers of federal bureaucrats. Indeed, political scientist Paul Light has argued that the "true size" of government through outsourcing and privatization is five to six times the actual number of federal employees.

Whatever the size of the bureaucracy, its nature poses a dilemma. We need a bureaucratic organization and professional administrators so that government can carry out its basic functions without political interference. But the growth of a professional bureaucratic class has been considered at odds with American political values. Use of the term *civil servant* is an insistence that government employees serve the public, not their employer or themselves. Although Americans want state services, the fear of strong central government and administrative tyranny remains.

Because the U.S. government is involved in so many activities, almost everyone can view some aspect of bureaucracy as illegitimate and threatening. Conservatives generally disapprove of government's redistribution of income and regulation of business, viewing it as intrusive and at odds with traditional free-market philosophy. Liberals are concerned about the bureaucracy's intelligence-gathering and domestic policing activities; the secrecy and potential violation of civil liberties raise concerns about "Big Brother" watching.

And the federal bureaucracy represents more than the passive administration of laws passed by the elected branches of government. Bureaucrats are given substantial authority: They issue rules, enforce compliance, allocate federal funds, and regulate economic activity. Because of their expertise, they often formulate policy, although the most successful bureaucratic policymakers work closely with Congress.

The American solution to the dilemma posed by the coexistence of bureaucracy and democracy is to keep the bureaucracy accountable through scrutiny by the other branches of government and by the nation's press. Congressional oversight of bureaucratic practices and spending, central direction in policymaking by the president and his staff, and judicial review of administrative processes and rule making are all important restraints on bureaucratic discretion.

The selections in this chapter are intended to convey a sense of the impact of the bureaucracy on American politics, the controversial nature of its activities, and the difficulties facing those who wish to reform it. Over the course of American history, both politicians and professional administrators have found themselves viewed with increasing skepticism, notes E. J. Dionne, Jr., in the first selection here. Ironically, we rely heavily on both political appointees and noncareerist bureaucrats to move policies from law to practice. Dionne expresses the fear that public service will become so costly and unattractive that it will not attract the necessary talent to govern effectively.

The next two selections address how the bureaucratic culture of the National Air and Space Administration (NASA) contributed to the *Challenger* (1986) and *Columbia* (2003) space shuttle disasters. Charles Peters notes how problematic information flows can produce deadly consequences, and Stephen Cass follows up with a brief, but chilling, reprise of Peters's critiques. The shuttle tragedies did flow directly from engineering failures, but more broadly, the NASA bureaucracy bore some real responsibility. Moving to an even more general level, James Q. Wilson focuses on the difficulties faced by managers of public organizations and how these can lead to flawed decisions. Finally, *The Economist* provides a perspective on the creation of the Department of Homeland Security, which must integrate various functions and more than 160,000 workers into a single entity. Only in the wake of a major event—in this instance, the 9/11 attacks—would such a merging of units be considered. And only time will tell how it will work out.

 12.1

"Political Hacks" Versus "Bureaucrats": Can't Public Servants Get Some Respect?

E. J. Dionne, Jr.

American national government has always required citizens to enter into public service to serve the executive, administer laws, and respond to the demands from the electorate. Over the course of our history, two principal approaches to filling governmental jobs have evolved. As parties developed in the nineteenth century, so too did the "spoils system," in which the victorious party (for president, governor, mayor) would provide jobs for loyal partisans. The operating theory here was that any average citizen could handle most governmental jobs, thus party leaders should reward their followers when they won control of the government. This approach dominated much of the nineteenth century, but reformers sought a more professional approach to government after the expansion of the bureaucracy in the Civil War. Progressives and administrative science pioneers argued for a rational, professional approach to administration, freed from political considerations. Over the course of the twentieth century, the political and professional approaches to administration have fomented considerable debate and controversy.

E. J. Dionne, Jr., takes a different tack in his discussion of both politicos and professionals. He argues that neither type receives the respect they have won in the past and almost certainly deserve today. Those who serve—whether as political appointees in the executive branch or as civil servants in the national bureaucracy—often make real sacrifices and generally work hard to produce good public policy. The public, however, has grown more cynical over the past 40 years, and finds it difficult to accept the public sector as either interesting or challenging. Dionne's key point is that we rely on fresh faces—whether young idealists or experienced professionals—to fill demanding governmental positions. Allowing for creativity and real responsibility in these positions may be essential if public service is to remain one hallmark of American democracy.

The most moving moment at either party's national convention in 2000 was a resolutely nonpartisan speech that evoked a moment when taking a job in government was seen as far more than, well, just taking a job. "When my brother John and I were growing up," said Caroline Kennedy

Schlossberg, "hardly a day went by when someone didn't come up to us and say, 'Your father changed my life. I went into public service because he asked me.'"

Note that lovely phrase, "public service." Schlossberg was not exaggerating or being unduly romantic about the spirit of John F. Kennedy's New Frontier, which both shaped its time and reflected it. Serving in a new administration, whether on the White House staff, in the cabinet, or in a less grand post, was not simply an obligation or, in the current ugly phrase, "a ticket to punch." It was also a source of excitement. And so, as Godfrey Hodgson put it in his biography of Daniel Patrick Moynihan, "a varied population of political and intellectual adventurers" descended on Washington in the winter of 1960 and 1961."

"They came," Hodgson writes, "from New York and San Francisco law firms, from state and city politics across the nation, from the growing world of foundations and pressure groups, and of course from the great graduate schools, swollen by the postwar demand for academic manpower." Hodgson understood that this crowd of adventures were not saints, but neither were they mere opportunists: "The mood," he says, "was strangely blended from ambition and idealism, aggressive social climbing and a sense of youthful adventure."

The Diminished Promise of Citizen Service

No doubt many entered the Bush administration in 2001 with that same sense of vigor and adventure. Long lists of Republican office seekers, out of executive power for eight years, testified to the continuing lure of executive positions, from the highest posts to the lowest. Still, it is difficult to hear Schlossberg's speech and to read Hodgson's account and not sense a shift in the spirit of the times. Forty years after that winter of the New Frontier, public service in the executive branch retains its allure, but not quite the same sense of glamour or promise.

. . . [M]ost politicians who have won the presidency over the past quarter century did so by running against "the government in Washington." Bush was no exception. As a result, expressing an open desire to serve in that very government and an open belief that it might accomplish large things flies in the face of what is now deeply ingrained conventional wisdom. Those who want to serve in government in Washington have to bash government to get there.

E. J. Dionne, Jr., is a regular columnist for the *Washington Post* and a Senior Fellow at the Brookings Institution.

E. J. Dionne, Jr., " 'Political Hacks' versus 'Bureaucrats': Can't Public Servants Get Some Respect?" by E. J. Dionne, Jr., in *Innocent Until Nominated: The Breakdown of the Presidential Appointments Process,* edited by G. Calvin Mackenzie (Washington, D.C.: Brookings Institution Press, 2001), 254–264. Reprinted by permission of The Brookings Institution.

That cannot make a life in government service very attractive to those not yet committed to the venture.

Yet no country is as dependent as ours on "citizen service" in its national administration. None relies so heavily on people who might be called amateurs, as against career civil servants, to govern. From the beginning of the republic we have operated on the assumption that a professional ruling class is problematic and to be avoided. Government, according to this view, should be refreshed periodically by tides of new leaders with new ideas and untapped energy—the very spirit captured so well by Hodgson and Schlossberg. The assumption continues to prevail that citizen service is essential to the health of civil society—in this case, citizen service at the very highest levels—because citizen service links the government to the rest of the society in a way a purely professional bureaucracy could not.

Professionalism Versus Politics

That is the theory, anyway. In truth, our attitude toward those citizen servants reflects an odd balance of ideas. Our history is one of ambivalence as between professionalism on the one side and politics on the other. We admire the independence and expertise of professionals, yet we regularly denounce them when they work for the government. It is no accident that the famous Republican campaign commercial of 2000 in which the word "rats" appeared ever so briefly on our television screens—conveying or not conveying a "subliminal" message, depending on whom you believed—was in fact depicting the word "bureaucrats" at that critical and controversial moment. However honored they might occasionally be, the day-to-day civil servants who make the American government run do not enjoy the honor or prestige of their counterparts in France or Germany, Britain or Japan.

Yet if we denounce bureaucrats, we also denounce political appointees. This is obvious from the normal parlance of politics and journalism. We condemn certain agencies of government as patronage dumping grounds. We say we dislike the political spoils system. We insist on praising independent, nonpartisan government. Indeed, this was the impetus behind the civil service reform that, from the 1880s forward, took the awarding of tens of thousands of jobs out of politics. The premise, as James Q. Wilson puts it in his classic work *The Amateur Democrat*, was that "the merit system and open competition should be extended to insure, insofar as is feasible, that general principles rather than private advantage govern the awarding" of government benefits.

These two traditions—a preference for political appointees over bureaucrats and a preference for civil servants over the beneficiaries of political patronage—are deeply rooted in our history. To understand the contradictions in our history is to understand our ambivalence today.

Jacksonian Rotation in Office

It is worth remembering that the idea of wholesale changes in the government following the defeat of an incumbent party in an election was originally seen as a "reform" by the advocates of Jacksonian democracy in the 1820s and 1830s. The followers of Andrew Jackson referred not to a spoils system but to a principle they held up as admirable and called "rotation in office." The Jacksonians believed their political foes had come to regard holding the appointive offices of government as a right that could not be disturbed even by the electorate. That is what Andrew Jackson was against. "Office is considered as a species of property," Jackson declared, "and government rather as a means of promoting individual interests than as an instrument created solely for the service of the people."

As Harry L. Watson summarizes Jackson's views in *Liberty and Power,* his admirable book on Jacksonian democracy, "No one in a republic had an inherent right to public office—so no one could complain if he lost a public job in favor of someone more honest, more competent, or more in agreement with elected officials who carried a popular mandate." Jackson . . . emphatically rejected the views of his former Federalist and soon-to-be Whig foes that "no one except a tiny elite had the training or experience to qualify for public office." As Jackson himself put it, "The duties of all public officers are, or admit to being made, so plain and simple that men of intelligence may readily qualify themselves for their performance." Jackson . . . was not arguing for the hiring of incompetents, but he did demand "that public duties be shared among the large body of qualified citizens to avoid the creation of an entrenched and corrupt bureaucracy."

The notion that rotation in office was a mighty weapon in the larger battle against privilege is nicely captured by historian Robert V. Remini in his study of Martin Van Buren. Remini notes that the Democrats' 1828 campaign placed heavy stress on the words "people" and "reform." "The precise direction all this 'reform' was to take," he writes, "was not explained. There was no need to. The people were simply banding together to take the national government out of the hands of the favored few. They were claiming what belonged to them. They were dispossessing 'the wise, the good, and the well born.' "

"Rotation in office" was more than just an excuse to appoint one's friends. "To Jackson the principle of rotation directly addressed the problem of how and by whom government should be run," Remini writes in *The Revolutionary Age of Andrew Jackson.* "Jackson believed that through rotation the federal government in Washington could be made to respond directly to the changing demands of the American people as expressed by their ballots. Thus, each new administration, elected by the people, should bring in its own corps of supporters to make sure the policies of that administration were honestly and fairly implemented."

Prefiguring, perhaps, the New Left's emphasis on participatory democracy, the Jacksonians thought, as Remini puts it, that "rotation meant that a great many more people would get an opportunity to serve the government. The more people actively involved in the affairs of the nation, the more democratic the system, and the more the problems of the nation get to be widely known and understood." The idea came from Jefferson: "Greater participation by the electorate in government safeguards the nation from arbitrary and dictatorial rule."

In other words, America's tradition of political appointments is rooted in a philosophical view of how democratic government can work best—and become more democratic in the process. If European democracies have a much shallower tradition of political nominations and a larger reverence for a career civil service, it is in part because none of the Western European democracies—many of which were not terribly democratic at the time—went through anything that quite resembled the Jacksonian revolution. Hard as it was for reformers to accept the idea later, the creation of a system of political patronage was originally seen as a way to foil both corruption and elitism. Despite abuses, Watson is correct in seeing rotation in office as "a solidly democratic principle that brought greater openness to government."

Civil Service Reform: Depoliticizing Public Service

But there were, indeed, abuses, and they grew over time. The Jacksonian system was "susceptible to political manipulation," as Watson acknowledges. As Remini, a sympathetic student of the Jacksonian principle, puts it, rotation "can be an easy excuse and justification for political head chopping, for regarding political jobs as 'spoils' won in a war in which enemies are punished and friends rewarded   When rotation is administered by incompetents or thieves, then everyone suffers and the democratic system is dangerously compromised." It is precisely that sense of incompetence and thievery that helped unleash the other great American public service tradition—civil service reform combined with a preference for expertise. It reached high tide between the 1880s and 1920.

The historian Robert H. Wiebe picks up this thread in his excellent study of the period, *The Search for Order*. In contrast with the Jacksonians, the new reformers saw the removal of government jobs from the political realm as "democracy's cure." Wiebe notes that "by denying politicians the spoils of office, the argument ran, civil service would drive out the parasites and leave only a pure frugal government behind. The nonpartisanship inherent in civil service would permeate politics, and as party organizations withered away, the men of quality now excluded by the spoilsmen and unscrupulous businessmen would resume their natural posts of command."

It is also important to see that civil service reform and enhanced faith in a professionalized bureaucracy arose at a moment of growing faith in scientific rationality and a belief in the importance of expertise. The professionals of the period, Wiebe observes, "naturally conceived of science as a method for their disciplines instead of a set of universal principles.". . .

The importance of this view to American public life is described well by Moynihan himself in his famous 1965 essay, "The Professionalization of Reform." Moynihan cites Wesley C. Mitchell, of the National Bureau of Economic Research, who offered an almost perfect statement of [rationalism]: "Our best hope for the future lies in the extension to social organization of the methods that we already employ in our most progressive fields of efforts. In science and industry . . . we do not wait for catastrophe to force new ways upon us. . . . We rely, and with success, upon quantitative analysis to point the way; and we advance because we are constantly improving and applying such analysis."

Still a Healthy Tension?

Alas, it is not so clear how much we have advanced when it comes to making a joy in public service part of our political ethic. Where do our dueling traditions of political appointments and professionalized bureaucracy leave us today?

The professional view suffered body blows during the 1960s from left, right, and center. Moynihan predicted this in his original essay on the professionalization of reform: "a certain price will be paid and a considerable risk will be incurred." The price, said the man who journeyed to the New Frontier with such hope, "will be a decline in the moral exhilaration of public affairs at the domestic level." And so there was.

The rise of the idea of participatory democracy on the New Left suggested that the distant bureaucrat claiming vastly more knowledge than average citizens needed to be taken down a peg or two. The goal of Lyndon Johnson's War on Poverty, "maximum feasible participation," suggested that real expertise could be found only on the streets and in the neighborhoods. On the right, George Wallace's attacks on "pointy-headed bureaucrats with thin briefcases full of guidelines" nicely captured the conservative rebellion against experts— and, in the case of Wallace and his followers, especially those pushing for new programs of racial inclusion. But the resentments could not be explained simply by race.

As if this were not enough, the civil service bureaucracy also came under assault from the political center as a system that no longer worked—that no longer effectively delivered the very expertise and public-regarding ethos the civil service reformers at the turn of the century expected it to provide. Consider this thoughtful critique of the civil service offered in *The Public Interest*. Published in the summer of 1973, it was entitled, "The Civil Service: A Meritless System?" Its authors, E. S. Savas and Sigmund G. Ginsburg, [observe]: "The low productivity of public employees and the malfunctioning of governmental bureaucracies are becoming apparent to an increasing number of frustrated and indignant taxpayers. The problem shows up all over the country in the form of uncivil servants going through preprogrammed motions while awaiting their pensions."

. . . Too often, the result is mindless bureaucracies that appear to function for the convenience of their staffs rather than for the public whom they are supposed to serve. [Moreover,] "It is the system itself . . . rather than the hapless politician who heads it or the minions toiling within it that is basically at fault."

That system, they declare, "prohibits good management, frustrates able employees, inhibits productivity, lacks the confidence of the taxpayers, and fails to respond to the needs of citizens." The "worst feature of the promotion system," they continue, "is that an employee's chance of promotion bears no relationship to his performance on the job." At fault was "the rigor mortis of overdeveloped and regressive civil service systems."

. . . [T]his line of criticism, repeated often in subsequent years, led to what might be seen as a neo-Jacksonian call to replace parts of the civil service with political appointees, especially in city governments. The idea (it does, indeed, sound like rotation in office) was to give politicians more direct control over government—and to make governments more accountable to electorates. . . .

Indeed, this neo-Jacksonian reaction also encompassed a certain informed nostalgia in political science for the old political machine—the very institution upon which the civil service reformers had waged war. The problem with institutionalizing social benefits in national entitlement programs, says Calvin Mackenzie in his appropriately titled book, *The Irony of Reform*, was that doing so allowed their beneficiaries "to be less attentive to politics" and less active at election time. Why? Because "government had taken over control of the benefits that had once inspired so much political activity. What had long been the game of the political machines—the provision of material benefits in exchange for political support—soon became the game of government. And when it did, the machines ran out of fuel and shut down." As a result, "the parties and the traditional politics they represented began to wither." Never has patronage and "rotation in office" played as well among political scientists as it does now—after, of course, the machines (and, yes, their abuses) are gone.

But in truth, the spoils system and the political appointees who might be part of it play no better with the public than does the professional bureaucrat. . . . It is thus striking, and not surprising, that young people devoted to public service tend less than ever to carry out that service through government—in either civil service or political posts. As Paul C. Light has pointed out, the trend among young people oriented toward service is to seek to reform institutions and change society through the nonprofit sector rather than through government itself. Part of the problem . . . is the difficulty government has under current rules and practices in offering the flexibility and work opportunities available in the nonprofit sector. But it is also true that the idea of government service as an adventure . . . is about as fashionable as the now late, lamented Oldsmobile.

Another response to the discrediting of both civil servants and political nominees has been the rise in demands for the "privatization" of public services. As Light has shown, even as the formal numbers in some areas of government employment have fallen, many tasks once performed by government employees are taken on by employees of private companies—hired by the government. The merits of privatization can be debated—in general, government officials tend to make pragmatic rather than ideological judgments about which services should be performed by whom. But what is noticeable in much of the privatization rhetoric is the discrediting of government servants as efficient deliverers of public wants and the elevation of the market as the preferred mechanism for introducing responsiveness and productivity.

At its best, the American tradition of tension between the political and the professional control of government is highly productive. The Jacksonian instinct that elections should matter and that there should be a significant degree of political control—meaning democratic control—over the bureaucracy is correct. But the desire for genuine expertise in the right places is also correct. The president, and the people, need military strategists, research scientists, lawyers, economists, and environmental specialists who will feel free to tell the truth as they see it and inform decisionmaking. A democratic government cannot be effective if it changes capriciously from one administration to another.

The American tradition creates a constant battle between the democratic impulse and the impulse for efficiency and predictability. This tension is not only useful but also necessary. The Jacksonian principle insists that in a democracy, there is not a bright line between "the government" on the one side and "civil society"—the array of communal institutions independent of government—on the other. If a government is not rooted in, and does not draw on, civil society, it can be neither democratic nor effective.

A Plague on Both Your Houses

It is not at all clear that the tension between our traditions is serving us well today. At most points in our history, at least one side of the government (the politicians or the professionals) enjoyed some claim on public esteem. Now it can be argued that neither does—and thus the tendency to want to farm government out as much as possible. The Jacksonians lifted up the political appointee to put a check on the arrogance of expertise. The civil service reformers lifted up expertise to put a check on political abuses. Now putting down both sides is the general rule.

The rise of a specifically presidential bureaucracy has in some ways divided the executive branch itself, aggravating its problems and the problems of those who work for it. As the political scientist Nelson Polsby has argued, one of the most interesting developments of the past half century "is the emergence of a presidential branch of government separate and apart from the executive branch." It is the presidential branch, Polsby writes, "that sits across the table from the executive branch at budgetary hearings, and that imperfectly attempts to coordinate both the executive and legislative branches in its own behalf."

In *The Presidency in a Separated System*, Charles O. Jones makes a parallel point: that "the mix of career ambitions represented by presidential appointees may well bring the outside world to Washington, but there is no guarantee that these officials will cohere into a working government." Jones sees the president as "somewhat in the position of the Olympic basketball coach. He may well have talented players but lack a team."

None of this means that George W. Bush or any future president will have trouble filling his (or, someday, her) government. None of it means that the country lacks the "practical idealists" of whom Al Gore liked to speak. But a government as peculiarly dependent as ours is on the willingness of citizens to interrupt the normal trajectory of their lives to devote themselves to government service needs to worry that it is not nourishing either of our great traditions of public service. When the political tradition has faltered, we have been able to call on our civil service tradition. When expertise falters, the politicos can step in to right the balance. But when both traditions fail, where do we turn?

We can privatize as much as we want, but government will never work if there is not a broadly accepted ethic that sees government service as honorable, productive, and creative—if there is not an ethic that views government service as public service. Nor will government work if young people see the independent sector as dynamic and the government sector as sterile and stolid. And, yes, it would help to have a president who drew people to public service because he asked them to do it and because he made it an adventure in which ambition and democratic idealism could coexist.

Questions for Discussion

1. In a federal work force of about 1.5 million civilians, how many of these positions should be based on political loyalty to the president and the president's party? A hundred? A thousand? Ten thousand? Currently the president can appoint about 3000 so-called Schedule C (political) appointees to full-time jobs. Do you think that is enough, given that the president has won a national election? Too many? What are your criteria for thinking about this?

2. One of Dionne's complaints is that many individuals choose public service to "get their tickets punched" before heading into the private sector to make a lot of money. Do you see anything wrong with this? Does it necessarily demean the idea of public service? What might you do to slow down the revolving door?

 12.2

From Ouagadougou to Cape Canaveral: Why the Bad News Doesn't Travel Up

Charles Peters

On January 28, 1986, seven crew members of the space shuttle Challenger were killed in a midflight explosion. The tragedy was caused by the disintegration of a type of seal called an O-ring, which led to failure in the joint between segments of one of the eight solid booster rockets. It can be argued, however, that the fundamental reason for the shuttle disaster was a communication failure within the hierarchy of the National Aeronautics and Space Administration (NASA). Private engineers on the project were aware of a history of problems with the O-rings and had advised certain mid-level NASA officials not to launch under certain conditions. Had top-level officials known of the problems, the launch might not have taken place.

In this selection, Charles Peters suggests that it is extremely difficult for top managers in a large organization to be aware of problems at various levels of a bureaucratic hierarchy. Officials at NASA were under tremendous political pressure to launch the shuttle, so negative information was suppressed within the chain of command. Peters suggests that this problem is common and can be blamed for a number of the government's recent flawed decisions. The remedies, he suggests, are more direct government oversight and an active press.

Everyone is asking why the top NASA officials who decided to launch the fatal Challenger flight had not been told of the concerns of people down below, like Allan McDonald and the other worried engineers at Morton Thiokol.*

In the first issue of *The Washington Monthly*, Russell Baker and I wrote, "In any reasonably large government organization, there exists an elaborate system of information cutoffs, comparable to that by which city water systems shut off large water-main breaks, closing down, first small feeder pipes, then larger and

---

*Morton Thiokol is the private engineering company that was in charge of the design and construction of the space shuttle booster rocket.
Charles Peters is editor-in-chief of *The Washington Monthly*.

Charles Peters, "From Ouagadougou to Cape Canaveral: Why the Bad News Doesn't Travel Up," *The Washington Monthly* 19 (April 1986): 27–31. Reprinted by permission of *The Washington Monthly*.

larger valves. The object is to prevent information, particularly of an unpleasant character, from rising to the top of the agency, where it may produce results unpleasant to the lower ranks.

"Thus, the executive at or near the top lives in constant danger of not knowing, until he reads it on Page One some morning, that his department is hip-deep in disaster."

This seemed to us to be a serious problem for government, not only because the people at the top didn't know but because the same system of cut-offs operated to keep Congress, the press, and the public in the dark. (Often it also would operate to keep in the dark people within the organization but outside the immediate chain of command—this happened with the astronauts, who were not told about the concern with the O-rings.)

I first became aware of this during the sixties, when I worked at the Peace Corps. Repeatedly I would find that a problem that was well-known by people at lower and middle levels of the organization, whose responsibility it was, would be unknown at the top of the chain of command or by anyone outside.

The most serious problems of the Peace Corps had their origins in Sargent Shriver's desire to get the organization moving.* He did not want it to become mired in feasibility studies, he wanted to get volunteers overseas and into action fast. To fulfill his wishes, corners were cut. Training was usually inadequate in language, culture, and technical skills. Volunteers were selected who were not suited to their assignments. For example, the country then known as Tanganyika asked for surveyors, and we sent them people whose only connection with surveying had been holding the rod and chain while the surveyor sighted through his gizmo. Worse, volunteers were sent to places where no job at all awaited them. These fictitious assignments were motivated sometimes by the host official's desire to please the brother-in-law of the president of the United States and sometimes by the official's ignorance of what was going on at the lower levels of his own bureaucracy.

But subordinates would not tell Shriver about the problems. There were two reasons for this. One was fear. They knew that he wanted action, not excuses, and they suspected that their careers would suffer if he heard too many of the latter. The other reason was that they felt it was their job to solve problems, not burden the boss with them. They and Shriver shared the view expressed by Deke Slayton, the former astronaut, when he was asked about the failure of middle-level managers to tell top NASA officials about the problems they were encountering. "You depend on managers to make a decision based on the information they have. If they had to transmit all the fine detail to the top people, it wouldn't get launched but once every ten years."

The point is not without merit. It is easy for large organizations to fall into "once every ten years" habits. Leaders who want to avoid that danger learn to

*Sargent Shriver—President Kennedy's brother-in-law—was the first director of the Peace Corps. The organization was set up to send American volunteers to help people in Third World countries. In 1972, Shriver was the Democratic vice-presidential candidate.

set goals and communicate a sense of urgency about meeting them. But what many of them never learn is that once you set those goals you have to guard against the tendency of those down below to spare you not only "all the fine detail" but essential facts about significant problems.

For instance, when Jimmy Carter gave the Pentagon the goal of rescuing the Iranian hostages, he relied on the chain of command to tell him if there were any problems. So he did not find out until after the disaster at Desert One that the Delta Commandos thought the Marine pilots assigned to fly the helicopters were incompetent.*

In NASA's case chances have been taken with the shuttle from the beginning—the insulating thermal tiles had not gone through a reentry test before the first shuttle crew risked their lives to try them out—but in recent years the pressure to cut corners has increased markedly. Competition with the European Ariane rocket and the Reagan administration's desire to see agencies like NASA run as if they were private businesses have led to a speedup in the launch schedule, with a goal of 14 this year [1986] and 24 by 1988.

"The game NASA is playing is the maximum tonnage per year at the minimum costs possible," says Paul Cloutier, a professor of space physics. "Some high officials don't want to hear about problems," reports *Newsweek,* "especially if fixing them will cost money."

Under pressures like these, the NASA launch team watched Columbia, after seven delays, fall about a month behind schedule and then saw Challenger delayed, first by bad weather, then by damaged door handles, and then by bad weather again. Little wonder that [NASA's launch chief] Lawrence Mulloy, when he heard the warnings from the Thiokol engineers, burst out: "My God, Thiokol, when do you want me to launch? Next April?"

Mulloy may be one of the villains of this story, but it is important to realize that you need Lawrence Mulloys to get things done. It is also important to realize that, if you have a Lawrence Mulloy, you must protect yourself against what he might fail to do or what he might do wrong in his enthusiastic rush to get the job done.

And you can't just ask him if he has any doubts. If he's a gung-ho type, he's going to suppress the negatives. When Jimmy Carter asked General David Jones to check out the Iran rescue plan, Jones said to Colonel Beckwith: "Charlie, tell me what you really think about the mission. Be straight with me."

"Sir, we're going to do it!" Beckwith replied. "We want to do it, and we're ready."

John Kennedy received similar confident reports from the chain of command about the readiness of the CIA's Cuban Brigade to charge ashore at the Bay of

---

*In the spring of 1980, President Carter made a decision to have a U.S. commando force attempt to rescue the American hostages held in Iran. A number of reasons have been suggested for the failure of the mission. The helicopters chosen for the mission evidently could not operate successfully in the sand and wind of the Iranian desert. One crashed on takeoff, killing a number of soldiers, and the mission was aborted.

Pigs and overthrow Fidel Castro. And Sargent Shriver had every reason to believe that the Peace Corps was getting off to a fabulous start, based on what his chain of command was telling him.

With Shriver, as with NASA's senior officials, the conviction that everything was A-OK was fortified by skillful public relations. Bill Moyers was only one of the geniuses involved in this side of the Peace Corps. At NASA, Julian Scheer began a tradition of inspired PR that endured until Challenger. These were men who could sell air conditioning in Murmansk. The trouble is they also sold their bosses the same air conditioning. Every organization has a tendency to believe its own PR—NASA's walls are lined with glamorizing posters and photographs of the shuttle and other space machines—and usually the top man is the most thoroughly seduced because, after all, it reflects the most glory on him.

Favorable publicity and how to get it is therefore the dominant subject of Washington staff meetings. The minutes of the Nuclear Regulatory Commission show that when the reactor was about to melt down at Three Mile Island,* the commissioners were worried less about what to do to fix the reactor than they were about what they were going to say to the press.

One of the hottest rumors around Washington is that the White House had put pressure on NASA to launch so that the president could point with pride to the teacher in space during his State of the Union speech. The White House denies this story, and my sources tell me the denial is true. But NASA had—and this is fact, not rumor—put pressure on *itself* by asking the president to mention Christa McAuliffe. In a memorandum dated January 8, NASA proposed that the president say: "Tonight while I am speaking to you, a young elementary school teacher from Concord, New Hampshire, is taking us all on the ultimate field trip as she orbits the earth as the first citizen passenger on the space shuttle. Christa McAuliffe's journey is a prelude to the journeys of other Americans living and working together in a permanently manned space station in the mid-1990s. Mrs. McAuliffe's week in space is just one of the achievements in space we have planned for the coming year."

The flight was scheduled for January 23. It was postponed and postponed again. Now it was January 28, the morning of the day the speech was to be delivered, the last chance for the launch to take place in time to have it mentioned by the president. NASA officials must have feared they were about to lose a PR opportunity of stunning magnitude, an opportunity to impress not only the media and the public but the agency's two most important constituencies, the White House and the Congress. Wouldn't you feel pressure to get that launch off this morning so that the president could talk about it tonight?

NASA's sensitivity to the media in regard to the launch schedule was nothing short of unreal. Here is what Richard G. Smith, the director of the

---

*Three Mile Island is the site of a Pennsylvania nuclear plant that experienced a serious accident in which the generator overheated. There were no injuries or deaths. Still, the incident helped contribute to growing public concern over the safety of nuclear power plants.

Kennedy Space Center, had to say about it after the disaster: "Every time there was a delay, the press would say, 'Look, there's another delay . . . here's a bunch of idiots who can't even handle a launch schedule.' You think that doesn't have an impact? If you think it doesn't, you're stupid."

I do not recall seeing a single story like those Smith describes. Perhaps there were a few. The point, however, is to realize how large even a little bit of press criticism loomed in NASA's thinking.

Sargent Shriver liked good press as much as, if not more than, the next man. But he also had an instinct that the ultimate bad press would come if the world found out about your disaster before you had a chance to do something to prevent it. He and an assistant named William Haddad decided to make sure that Shriver got the bad news first. Who was going to find it out for them? Me.

It was July 1961. They decided to call me an evaluator and send me out to our domestic training programs and later overseas to find out what was really going on. My first stop was the University of California at Berkeley where our Ghana project was being trained. Fortunately, except for grossly inadequate language instruction, this program was excellent. But soon I began finding serious deficiencies in other training programs and in our projects abroad.

Shriver was not always delighted by these reports. Indeed, at one point I heard I was going to be fired. I liked my job, and I knew that the reports that I and the other evaluators who had joined me were writing were true. I didn't want to be fired. What could I do?

I knew he was planning to visit our projects in Africa. So I prepared a memorandum that contrasted what the chain of command was saying with what I and my associates were reporting. Shriver left for Africa. I heard nothing for several weeks. Then came a cable from Somalia: "Tell Peters his reports are right." I knew then that, however much Shriver wanted to hear the good news and get good publicity, he could take the bad news. The fact that he could take the bad news meant that the Peace Corps began to face its problems and do something about them before they became a scandal.

NASA did the opposite. A 1983 reorganization shifted the responsibility for monitoring flight safety from the chief engineer in Washington to the field. This may sound good. "We're not going to micromanage," said James M. Beggs, then the NASA administrator. But the catch is that if you decentralize, you must maintain the flow of information from the field to the top so that the organization's leader will know what those decentralized managers are doing. What NASA's reorganization did, according to safety engineers who talked to Mark Tapscott of the *Washington Times,* was to close off "an independent channel with authority to make things happen at the top."

I suspect what happened is that the top NASA administrators, who were pushing employees down below to dramatically increase the number of launches, either consciously or unconsciously did not want to be confronted with the dangers they were thereby risking.

This is what distinguishes the bad leaders from the good. The good leader, realizing that there is a natural human tendency to avoid bad news, traps himself into having to face it. He encourages whistleblowers instead of firing them. He visits the field himself and talks to the privates and lieutenants as well as the generals to find out the real problems. He can use others to do this for him, as Shriver used me. . . . But he must have some independent knowledge of what's going on down below in order to have a feel for whether the chain of command is giving him the straight dope.

What most often happens, of course, is that the boss, if he goes to the field at all, talks only to the colonels and generals. Sometimes he doesn't want to know what the privates know. He may be hoping that the lid can be kept on whatever problems are developing, at least until his watch is over, so that he won't be blamed when they finally surface. Or he may have a very good idea that bad things are being done and simply wants to retain "deniability," meaning that the deed cannot be traced to him. The story of Watergate is filled with "Don't tell me" and "I don't want to know."

When NASA's George Hardy told Thiokol engineers that he was appalled by their verbal recommendation that the launch be postponed and asked Thiokol to reconsider and make another recommendation, Thiokol, which Hardy well knew was worried about losing its shuttle contract, was in effect being told, "Don't tell me" or "Don't tell me officially so I won't have to pass bad news along and my bosses will have deniability."

In addition to the leader himself, others must be concerned with making him face the bad news. This includes subordinates. Their having the courage to speak out about what is wrong is crucial, and people like Bruce Cook of NASA and Allan McDonald of Thiokol deserve great credit for having done so. But it is a fact that none of the subordinates who knew the danger to the shuttle took the next step and resigned in protest so that the public could find out what was going on in time to prevent disaster. The almost universal tendency to place one's own career above one's moral responsibility to take a stand on matters like these has to be one of the most depressing facts about bureaucratic culture today.

Even when the issue was simply providing facts for an internal NASA investigation after the disaster, here is the state of mind Bruce Cook describes in a recent article in the *Washington Post*: "Another [NASA employee] told me to step away from his doorway while he searched for a document in his filing cabinet so that no one would see me in his office and suspect that he'd been the one I'd gotten it from."

It may be illuminating to note here that at the Peace Corps I found my most candid informants were the volunteers. They had no career stake in the organization—they were in for just two years—and thus had no reason to fear the results of their candor. Doesn't this suggest that we might be better off with more short-term employees in the government, people who are planning to leave anyway and thus have no hesitation to blow the whistle when necessary?

Certainly the process of getting bad news from the bottom to the top can be helped by institutionalizing it, as it was in the case of the Peace Corps Evaluation Division, and by hiring to perform it employees who have demonstrated courage and independence as well as the ability to elicit the truth and report it clearly.

Two other institutions that can help this process are the Congress and the White House. But the staff they have to perform this function is tiny. The White House depends on the OMB [Office of Management and Budget] to tell it what the executive branch is doing. Before the Challenger exploded, the OMB had four examiners to cover science and space. The Senate subcommittee on Space, Science and Technology had a staff of three. Needless to say, they had not heard about the O-rings.

Another problem is lack of experience. Too few congressmen and too few of their staff have enough experience serving in the executive branch to have a sense of the right question to ask. OMB examiners usually come aboard straight from graduate school, totally innocent of practical experience in government.

The press shares this innocence. Only a handful of journalists have worked in the bureaucracy. Like the members of Congress, they treat policy formulation as the ultimate reality: Congress passed this bill today; the president signed that bill. That's what the TV reporters on the Capitol steps and the White House lawn tell us about. But suppose the legislation in question concerns coal mine safety. Nobody is going to know what it all adds up to until some members of Congress and some members of the press go down into the coal mine to find out if conditions actually are safer or if only more crazy regulations have been added.

Unfortunately, neither the congressmen nor the press display much enthusiasm for visits to the mines. Yet this is what I found to be the key to getting the real story about the Peace Corps. I had to go to Ouagadougou and talk to the volunteers at their sites before I could really know what the Peace Corps was doing and what its problems were. I wasn't going to find out by asking the public affairs office. . . .

Because the reporters don't know any better, they don't press the Congress to do any better. What journalists could do is make the public aware of how little attention Congress devotes to what is called "oversight," i.e., finding out what the programs it has authorized are actually doing. If the press would publicize the nonperformance of this function, it is at least possible that the public would begin to reward the congressmen who perform it consistently and punish those who ignore it by not reelecting them.

But the press will never do this until it gets itself out of Larry Speakes's office. Woodward and Bernstein didn't get the Watergate story by talking to Ron Ziegler,* or, for that matter, by using other reportorial techniques favored by the media elite, like questioning Richard Nixon at a press conference or interviewing other administration luminaries at fancy restaurants. They had to find lower-level sources like Hugh Sloan, just as the reporters who finally got the NASA story had to find the Richard Cooks and Allan McDonalds.

---

*Larry Speakes was Ronald Reagan's press secretary at the time this article was written. Ron Ziegler was President Nixon's press secretary. Bob Woodward and Carl Bernstein were the two *Washington Post* writers credited with unraveling the Watergate scandal.

Eileen Shanahan, a former reporter for the *New York Times* and a former assistant secretary of HEW, recently wrote "of the many times I tried, during my tenure in the Department of Health, Education and Welfare, to interest distinguished reporters from distinguished publications in the effort the department was making to find out whether its billion-dollar programs actually were reaching the intended beneficiaries and doing any good. Their eyes glazed over."

I have had a similar experience with reporters during my 25 years in Washington. For most of that time they have seemed to think they knew everything about bureaucracy because they had read a Kafka novel and stood in line at the post office. In their ignorance, they adopted a kind of wise-guy, world-weary fatalism that said nothing could be done about bureaucratic problems. They had little or no sense about how to approach organizations with an anthropologist's feel for the interaction of attitudes, values, and institutional pressures.

There are a couple of reasons, however, to hope that the performance of the press will improve. The coverage of business news has become increasingly sophisticated about the way institutional pressures affect executive and corporate behavior, mainly because the comparison of our economy with Japan's made the importance of cultural factors so obvious. And on defense issues, visits to the field are increasingly common as reporters attempt to find out whether this or that weapon works.

But these are mere beachheads. They need to be radically expanded to include the coverage of all the institutions that affect our lives, especially government. This may seem unlikely, but if the press studies the Challenger case, I do not see how it can avoid perceiving the critical role bureaucratic pressure played in bringing about the disaster. What the press must then realize is that similar pressures vitally influence almost everything this government does, and that we will never understand why government fails until we understand those pressures and how human beings in public office react to them.*

Questions for Discussion

1. What factors operate within large organizations to prevent top leaders from learning about organizational difficulties? How might a leader of an organization overcome such factors?
2. According to the author, why don't congressional oversight and press scrutiny of the bureaucracy uncover problems? How could such oversight be improved?

---

*In 1990, NASA experienced another public relations disaster when its $1.5 billion Hubble Space Telescope failed to focus clearly. NASA's investigating panel fixed the blame for the telescope flaw in the same management climate that led to the fatal explosion of the space shuttle Challenger in 1986. As in the shuttle case, the report indicated that engineers working on the telescope as far back as 1980 and 1981 were discouraged from bringing potential problems to the attention of their superiors.

12.3

How to Fix the NASA Disaster

Stephen Cass

To once again quote the overquoted Yogi Berra, both the *Columbia* disaster and its aftermath are examples of "déjà vu all over again." Stephen Cass's brief article follows up from where Charles Peters (selection 12.2) left off. The space shuttle may have fallen out of the sky, but it is the organization of NASA that is broken. At the same time, Cass looks farther afield for those responsible and casts his eye on the White House and Congress, both of whom he sees as having failed to exercise proper oversight of the space agency.

Emphasizing the lack of such oversight opens up both political and professional elements of implementing policy. Most space programs have both scientific and political goals, and the technical nature of the projects makes them difficult to oversee. Cass argues that it is the agency itself that must change the internal culture, especially in regard to safety. Failing to do that may well lead to another tragedy that would grievously wound both the agency and the government whose policy NASA has implemented.

N ASA is broken. That's the fundamental message of the Columbia Accident Investigation Board's 248-page report, released on 26 August [2003]. "The past decisions of national leaders—the White House, Congress, and NASA Headquarters—set the Columbia accident in motion," states the report, which details how decisions in Washington, D.C., played as much a part in the loss of Columbia and her crew as the errant piece of foam that fatally damaged the spacecraft's left wing.

As for the foam, there can be no question that 81.7 seconds after launch, a chunk of foam designed to keep propellants in the shuttle's huge external tank at cryogenic temperatures broke free. With the shuttle still accelerating, the chunk crashed into the fragile leading edge of the left wing two-tenths of a second later, at some 877 km per hour. The resulting hole, approximately 25 cm across, remained undetected throughout the flight.

Stephen Cass writes for the IEEE Spectrum.

But upon reentry, superheated air rushed through the breach like a blow-torch, melting the wing's aluminum frame from within. With the Columbia traveling at Mach 19.5, aerodynamic forces tore the collapsing wing and then the entire shuttle apart.

That this chain of events can be stated with certainty is an amazing technical achievement, pieced together as it was from scattered debris, blurry photography, and radio telemetry. But by pursuing multiple independent lines of inquiry, ranging from studying computer simulations to examining the layers of molten metal found on recovered fragments of Columbia, the board was able to zero in on the foam and eliminate virtually all other possible causes of the shuttle's demise.

Digging Deeper

The 13-member board, led by retired Admiral Harold Gehman, was not content with just identifying the proximate cause of the disaster. In attempting to find out why the foam came off the tank and whether or not the deaths of the crew could have been prevented, it embarked on an investigation that led through a dysfunctional safety culture at NASA to, ultimately, the steps of Congress and the White House.

"NASA's safety culture has become reactive, complacent and dominated by unjustified optimism" is the report's blunt assessment of an agency laboring to meet its toughest schedule since President John F. Kennedy's mandate in 1961 to land on the moon before the decade was out. According to the report, as pressure to meet assembly deadlines for the International Space Station mounted, "engineers found themselves in the unusual position of having to prove that the situation was unsafe—a reversal of the usual requirement to prove that a situation is safe."

This pressure to conform arose because NASA programs had developed a built-in conflict of interest: the same people whose feet were being held to the fire to get projects completed on time and on budget were also made responsible for safety. When safety issues, such as the persistent problem of foam falling off the external tank, threatened to disrupt schedules or budgets, it was all too easy to finesse away problems rather than stop and address them.

In particular, a preference for studying problems with analysis and computer simulations rather than doing more expensive physical testing meant that many apparently reasonable engineering decisions were built on foundations of sand. In determining that the foam strike during Columbia's ascent would result in, at most, a minor ding, NASA relied on computer software that was being used to study "a piece of debris that was 400 times larger" than the biggest sample it had ever been actually tested against, fumed the report.

As time went by and shuttles flew without major incident, finesse hardened into certainty—thus foam loss became not a critical problem outside the shuttle's proven safety envelope, but a familiar issue that meant nothing more than that some minor repairs would be needed after the shuttle returned to Earth.

When engineers—worried about the rosy picture painted by the computer analysis of the foam strike—asked for in-orbit imagery to be taken of Columbia's wing, they were refused because they could not prove that it was absolutely necessary. Bureaucracy triumphed over safety; the board found that "management seemed more concerned about the staff following proper channels [in requesting images] than they were about the analysis."

That NASA allowed a cancerous neglect of safety to metastasize across the agency was a consequence of the reorganizations and large workforce reductions that occurred during the 1990s as the agency struggled with a budget that remained flat, representing a 13 percent loss in actual purchasing power. This parsimonious funding came even as the U.S. government's finances blossomed during that same decade, leaving NASA to struggle with decaying facilities and an aging shuttle fleet.

The extent of the problem is illustrated by the board's description of the installation of netting inside the massive Vehicle Assembly Building at Cape Canaveral "to prevent concrete from the building's ceiling from hitting the [shuttle]. . . . NASA, the White House and Congress alike now face the specter of having to deal with years of infrastructure neglect."

The Buck Stops Here

And so the trail of the Columbia disaster ends with those who have ultimate responsibility for NASA—Congress and the White House. "The White House and Congress must recognize the role of their decisions in this accident," chastised the board. Not only did they fail to adequately fund the agency, but they also failed to provide leadership, leaving NASA without a clear vision of national space policy upon which it could build.

Nor did they provide oversight that could have corrected NASA's dying safety culture despite warning report after warning report from independent panels and task forces. Agency leaders would generally be brought before Congress to testify about budgets and schedules rather than safety—sending a clear signal as to what really counted when NASA's performance was being measured.

. . . [B]oth the Senate and the House have embarked on an extensive series of hearings on the board's findings. Despite current economic difficulties, the board's indictment of 30 years of governmental neglect may finally loosen some purse strings. "There's no question . . . if we wish to continue human space flight, we have to put more resources in," said Congressman Sherwood Boehlert (R-N.Y.), the chair of the House Committee on Science, following the publication of the Columbia report. However, more has to be done than simply throwing money at the problem; if NASA supporters are "expecting us to write a blank check, we're unwilling to do so," he cautioned.

Indeed, it is clear that NASA must transform itself. But it cannot be trusted to do so by itself. "The changes we recommend will be difficult to accomplish—and will be internally resisted," said the board. The most difficult problem will be rooting out NASA's dysfunctional safety culture. "Cultural problems are unlikely to be corrected without top-level leadership," the board continues.

What this will mean in terms of concrete changes at NASA is yet unknown. Administrator Sean O'Keefe will likely stay in his post; the board noted many of the positive organizational changes he was making to get programs back under control before the Columbia disaster. But he must consider himself on probation and immediately set about installing new leaders throughout NASA who can, through personal example and decisive action, exorcise the agency's demons and restore NASA to its former glory. Otherwise, it is only a matter of time before the Columbia and Challenger disaster reports are joined by a third.

Questions for Discussion

1. Go back to Peters article and examine his analysis of the Challenger disaster. What would he likely say about the Columbia tragedy?
2. Can a president or the Congress be held responsible for every major failure of a bureaucratic unit? What are the conditions under which it might be reasonable to hold either the Congress or the president accountable?

12.4

Constraints on Public Managers

James Q. Wilson

Companies like AT&T or McDonald's rival in size and budget some of the largest government organizations and, on paper, are organized similarly, with a hierarchical authority structure and multiple layers of administration. They are bureaucracies in every sense of the term. Critics of government bureaucracy often point to the successes of such private sector organizations as efficient deliverers of services or products, in contrast to public bureaucracies that often are stereotyped as being bound by rules or red tape and staffed by unmotivated and unresponsive workers. Every election sees candidates committed to re-forming government bureaucracies in an attempt to "run government more like a business."

Although government and private bureaucracies share many characteristics, they are different in fundamental ways, creating difficulties for those who aspire to make government agencies more like their private sector counterparts. In this selection, James Q. Wilson argues that all government agencies have certain characteristics that tend to make their management far more difficult than man-aging a business: "Government management tends to be driven by the *con-straints* on the organization, not the *tasks* of the organization." Managerial control is particularly problematic because public managers have relatively little control over revenues, factors of production, and agency goals, which are "all vested to an important degree in entities external to the organization—legisla-tures, courts, politicians, and interest groups." One result is that public managers become "averse to any action that risks violating a significant constraint," rigidly interpreting rules and avoiding innovation.

B y the time the office opens at 8:45 A.M., the line of people waiting to do business at the Registry of Motor Vehicles in Watertown, Massachusetts, often will be twenty-five deep. By midday, especially if it is near the end of the month, the line may extend clear around the building. Inside, motorists wait in slow-moving rows before poorly marked windows to get a driver's li-cense or to register an automobile. When someone gets to the head of the line, he or she is often told by the clerk that it is the wrong line: "Get an application over there and then come back," or "This is only for people getting a new li-cense; if you want to replace one you lost, you have to go to the next window." The customers grumble impatiently. The clerks act harried and sometimes speak brusquely, even rudely. What seems to be a simple transaction may take 45 minutes or even longer. . . .

Not far away, people also wait in line at a McDonald's fast-food restaurant. There are several lines; each is short, each moves quickly. The menu is clearly displayed on attractive signs. The workers behind the counter are invariably polite. If someone's order cannot be filled immediately, he or she is asked to step aside for a moment while the food is prepared and then is brought back to

---

James Q. Wilson is professor of management and public policy at UCLA and past president of the American Political Science Association.

From *Bureaucracy: What Government Agencies Do and Why They Do It* by James Q. Wilson. Copyright © 1989 by Basic Books, Inc. Reprinted by permission of Basic Books, a member of Perseus Books, L.L.C.

the head of the line to receive the order. The atmosphere is friendly and good-natured. The room is immaculately clean.

Many people have noticed the difference between getting a driver's license and ordering a Big Mac. Most will explain it by saying that bureaucracies are different from businesses. "Bureaucracies" behave as they do because they are run by unqualified "bureaucrats" and are enmeshed in "rules" and "red tape."

But business firms are also bureaucracies, and McDonald's is a bureaucracy that regulates virtually every detail of its employees' behavior by a complex and all-encompassing set of rules. Its operations manual is six hundred pages long and weights four pounds.[1] In it one learns that french fries are to be nine-thirty-seconds of an inch thick and that grill workers are to place hamburger patties on the grill from left to right, six to a row for six rows. They are then to flip the third row first, followed by the fourth, fifth, and sixth rows, and finally the first and second. The amount of sauce placed on each bun is precisely specified. Every window must be washed every day. Workers must get down on their hands and knees and pick up litter as soon as it appears. These and countless other rules designed to reduce the workers to interchangeable automata were inculcated in franchise managers at Hamburger University located in a $40 million facility. There are plenty of rules governing the Registry, but they are only a small fraction of the rules that govern every detail of every operation at McDonald's. Indeed, if the DMV manager tried to impose on his employees as demanding a set of rules as those that govern the McDonald's staff, they would probably rebel and he would lose his job.

It is just as hard to explain the differences between the two organizations by reference to the quality or compensation of their employees. The Registry workers are all adults, most with at least a high-school education; the McDonald's employees are mostly teenagers, many still in school. The Registry staff is well-paid compared to the McDonald's workers, most of whom receive only the minimum wage. . . .

Not only are the differences between the two organizations not to be explained by reference to "rules" or "red tape" or "incompetent workers," the differences call into question many of the most frequently mentioned complaints about how government agencies are supposed to behave. For example: "Government agencies are big spenders." The Watertown office of the Registry is in a modest building that can barely handle its clientele. The teletype machine used to check information submitted by people requesting a replacement license was antiquated and prone to errors. Three or four clerks often had to wait in line to use equipment described by the office manager as "personally signed by Thomas Edison." No computers or word processors were available to handle the preparation of licenses and registrations; any error made by a clerk while manually typing a form meant starting over again on another form.

Or: "Government agencies hire people regardless of whether they are really needed." Despite the fact that the citizens of Massachusetts probably have more contact with the Registry than with any other state agency, and despite the fact that these citizens complain more about Registry service than about that of any other bureau, the Watertown branch, like all Registry offices, was seriously understaffed. . . .

Or: "Government agencies are imperialistic, always grasping for new functions." But there is no record of the Registry doing much grasping, even though one could imagine a case being made that the state government could usefully create at Registry offices "one-stop" multi-service centers where people could not only get drivers' licenses but also pay taxes and parking fines, obtain information, and transact other official business. The Registry seemed content to provide one service.

In short, many of the popular stereotypes about government agencies and their members are either questionable or incomplete. To explain why government agencies behave as they do, it is not enough to know that they are "bureaucracies"—that is, it is not enough to know that they are big, or complex, or have rules. What is crucial is that they are *government* bureaucracies. . . . [N]ot all government bureaucracies behave the same way or suffer from the same problems. . . . But all government agencies have in common certain characteristics that tend to make their management far more difficult than managing a McDonald's. These common characteristics are the constraints of public agencies.

The key constraints are three in number. To a much greater extent than is true of private bureaucracies, government agencies (1) cannot lawfully retain and devote to the private benefit of their members the earnings of the organization, (2) cannot allocate the factors of production in accordance with the preferences of the organization's administrators, and (3) must serve goals not of the organization's own choosing. Control over revenues, productive factors, and agency goals is all vested to an important degree in entities external to the organization—legislatures, courts, politicians, and interest groups. Given this, agency managers must attend to the demands of these external entities. As a result, government management tends to be driven by the *constraints* on the organization, not the *tasks* of the organization. To say the same thing in other words, whereas business management focuses on the "bottom line" (that is, profits), government management focuses on the "top line" (that is, constraints). . . .

Revenues and Incentives

In the days leading up to September 30, the federal government is Cinderella, courted by legions of individuals and organizations eager to get grants and contracts from the unexpended funds still at the disposal of each agency. At midnight on September 30, the government's coach turns into a pumpkin. That is the moment—the end of the fiscal year—at which every agency, with a few exceptions, must return all unexpended funds to the Treasury Department. . . .

Because of these fiscal rules agencies do not have a material incentive to economize: Why scrimp and save if you cannot keep the results of your frugality?

... When a private firm has a good year, many of its officers and workers may receive bonuses. Even if no bonus is paid, these employees may buy stock in the firm so that they can profit from any growth in earnings (and, if they sell the stock in a timely manner, profit from a drop in earnings). Should a public bureaucrat be discovered trying to do what private bureaucrats routinely do, he or she would be charged with corruption.

We take it for granted that bureaucrats should not profit from their offices and nod approvingly when a bureaucrat who has so benefited is indicted and put on trial. But why should we take this view? Once a very different view prevailed. In the seventeenth century, a French colonel would buy his commission from the king, take the king's money to run his regiment, and pocket the profit. At one time a European tax collector was paid by keeping a percentage of the taxes he collected. In this country, some prisons were once managed by giving the warden a sum of money based on how many prisoners were under his control and letting him keep the difference between what he received and what it cost him to feed the prisoners. Such behavior today would be grounds for criminal prosecution. Why? What has changed?

Mostly we the citizenry have changed. We are creatures of the Enlightenment: We believe that the nation ought not to be the property of the sovereign; that laws are intended to rationalize society and (if possible) perfect mankind; and that public service ought to be neutral and disinterested. We worry that a prison warden paid in the old way would have a strong incentive to starve his prisoners in order to maximize his income; that a regiment supported by a greedy colonel would not be properly equipped; and that a tax collector paid on a commission basis would extort excessive taxes from us. These changes reflect our desire to eliminate moral hazards—namely, creating incentives for people to act wrongly. But why should this desire rule out more carefully designed compensation plans that would pay government managers for achieving officially approved goals and would allow efficient agencies to keep any unspent part of their budget for use next year?

Part of the answer is obvious. Often we do not know whether a manager or an agency has achieved the goals we want because either the goals are vague or inconsistent, or their attainment cannot be observed, or both. Bureau chiefs in the Department of State would have to go on welfare if their pay depended on their ability to demonstrate convincingly that they had attained their bureaus' objectives.

But many government agencies have reasonably clear goals toward which progress can be measured. The Social Security Administration, the Postal Service, and the General Services Administration all come to mind. Why not let earnings depend importantly on performance? Why not let agencies keep excess revenues?

I am not entirely certain why this does not happen. To some degree it is because of a widespread cultural norm that people should not profit from public service. . . .

But in part it is because we know that even government agencies with clear goals and readily observable behavior only can be evaluated by making political (and thus conflict-ridden) judgments. If the Welfare Department delivers every benefit check within 24 hours after the application is received, Senator Smith may be pleased but Senator Jones will be irritated because this speedy delivery almost surely would require that the standards of eligibility be relaxed so that many ineligible clients would get money. There is no objective standard by which the tradeoff between speed and accuracy in the Welfare Department can be evaluated. . . .

The closest we can come to supplying a nonpolitical, nonarbitrary evaluation of an organization's performance is by its ability to earn from customers revenues in excess of costs. This is how business firms, private colleges, and most hospitals are evaluated. But government agencies cannot be evaluated by this market test because they either supply a service for which there are no willing customers (for example, prisons or the IRS) or are monopoly suppliers of a valued service (for example, the welfare department and the Registry of Motor Vehicles). Neither an organization with unwilling customers nor one with the exclusive right to serve such customers as exist can be evaluated by knowing how many customers they attract. When there is no external, nonpolitical evaluation of agency performance, there is no way to allow the agency to retain earnings that is not subject to agency manipulation. . . .

Critics of government agencies like to describe them as "bloated bureaucracies," defenders of them as "starved for funds." The truth is more complicated. Legislators judge government *programs* differently from how they judge government *bureaus*. Programs, such as Social Security, have constituencies that benefit from them. Constituencies press legislators for increases in program expenditures. If the constituencies are found in many districts, the pressures are felt by many legislators. These pressures ordinarily are not countered by those from any organized group that wants the benefits cut. Bureaucrats may or may not be constituencies. If they are few in number or concentrated in one legislative district they may have little political leverage with which to demand an increase in numbers or benefits. For example, expenditures on Social Security have grown steadily since the program began in 1935, but the offices, pay rates, and perquisites of Social Security administrators have not grown correspondingly.

If the bureaucrats are numerous, well-organized, and found in many districts (for example, letter carriers in the old Post Office Department or sanitation workers in New York City) they may have enough leverage to insure that their benefits increase faster than their workload. But even numerous and organized bureaucrats labor under a strategic disadvantage arising from the fact that legislators find it easier to constrain bureaucratic inputs than bureaucratic outputs. The reasons are partly conceptual, partly political. Conceptually, an office building or pay schedule is a tangible input, easily understood by all; "good health" or a "decent retirement" or an "educated child" are matters of opinion. Politically, legislators face more or less steady pressures to keep tax rates down while allowing program benefits to grow. The conceptual ambiguities combine neatly with the political realities: The rational course of action for a legislator is to appeal to taxpayers by ostentatiously constraining the budget for buildings, pay raises, and managerial benefits while appealing to program beneficiaries by loudly calling for more money to be spent on health, retirement, or education. (Witness the difficulty schoolteachers have in obtaining pay increases without threatening a strike, even at a time when expenditures on education are growing.) As a result, there are many lavish programs in this country administered by modestly paid bureaucrats working on out-of-date equipment in cramped offices.*

The inability of public managers to capture surplus revenues for their own use alters the pattern of incentives at work in government agencies. Beyond a certain point additional effort does not produce additional earnings. (In this country, Congress from time to time has authorized higher salaries for senior bureaucrats but then put a cap on actual payments to them so that the pay increases were never received. This was done to insure that no bureaucrat would earn more than members of Congress at a time when those members were unwilling to accept the political costs of raising their own salaries. As a result, the pay differential between the top bureaucratic rank and those just below it nearly vanished.) If political constraints reduce the marginal effect of money incentives, then the relative importance of other, nonmonetary incentives will increase. . . .

That bureaucratic performance in most government agencies cannot be linked to monetary benefits is not the whole explanation for the difference between public and private management. There are many examples of private organizations whose members cannot appropriate money surpluses for their own benefit. Private schools ordinarily are run on a nonprofit basis. Neither the headmaster nor the teachers share in the profit of these schools; indeed, most such schools earn no profit at all and instead struggle to keep afloat by soliciting contributions from friends and alumni. Nevertheless, the evidence is quite clear that on the average, private schools, both secular and denominational, do a better job than public ones in educating children.[2]

Acquiring and Using the Factors of Production

A business firm acquires capital by retaining earnings, borrowing money, or selling shares of ownership; a government agency (with some exceptions) acquires capital by persuading a legislature to appropriate it. A business firm hires,

---

*Elsewhere, government officials may enjoy generous salaries and lavish offices. Indeed, in some underdeveloped nations, travelers see all about them signs of public munificence and private squalor. The two may be connected.

promotes, demotes, and fires personnel with considerable though not perfect freedom; a federal government agency is told by Congress how many persons it can hire and at what rate of pay, by the Office of Personnel Management (OPM) what rules it must follow in selecting and assigning personnel, by the Office of Management and Budget (OMB) how many persons of each rank it may employ, by the Merit Systems Protection Board (MSPB) what procedures it must follow in demoting or discharging personnel, and by the courts whether it has faithfully followed the rules of Congress, OPM, OMB, and MSPB. A business firm purchases goods and services by internally defined procedures (including those that allow it to buy from someone other than the lowest bidder if a more expensive vendor seems more reliable), or to skip the bidding procedure altogether in favor of direct negotiations; a government agency must purchase much of what it uses by formally advertising for bids, accepting the lowest, and keeping the vendor at arm's length. When a business firm develops a good working relationship with a contractor, it often uses that vendor repeatedly without looking for a new one; when a government agency has a satisfactory relationship with a contractor, ordinarily it cannot use the vendor again without putting a new project out for a fresh set of bids. When a business firm finds that certain offices or factories are no longer economical it will close or combine them; when a government agency wishes to shut down a local office or military base often it must get the permission of the legislature (even when formal permission is not necessary, informal consultation is). When a business firm draws up its annual budget each expenditure item can be reviewed as a discretionary amount (except for legally mandated payments of taxes to government and interest to banks and bondholders); when a government agency makes up its budget many of the detailed expenditure items are mandated by the legislature.

All these complexities of doing business in or with the government are well-known to citizens and firms. These complexities in hiring, purchasing, contracting, and budgeting often are said to be the result of the "bureaucracy's love of red tape." But few, if any, of the rules producing this complexity would have been generated by the bureaucracy if left to its own devices, and many are as cordially disliked by the bureaucrats as by their clients. These rules have been imposed on the agencies by external actors, chiefly the legislature. They are not bureaucratic rules but *political* ones. In principle the legislature could allow the Social Security Administration, the Defense Department, or the New York City public school system to follow the same rules as IBM, General Electric, or Harvard University. In practice they could not. The reason is politics, or more precisely, democratic politics.

The differences are made clear in Steven Kelman's comparison of how government agencies and private firms buy computers. The agency officials he interviewed were much less satisfied with the quality of the computers and support services they purchased than were their private counterparts. The reason is that private firms are free to do what every householder does in buying a dishwasher or an automobile—look at the past performance of the people with whom he or she previously has done business and buy a new product based on these judgments. Contrary to what many people suppose, most firms buying a computer do not write up detailed specifications and then ask for bids, giving the contract to the lowest bidder who meets the specifications. Instead, they hold conversations with a computer manufacturer with whom they, or other firms like them, have had experience. In these discussions they develop a sense of their needs and form a judgment as to the quality and reliability of the people with whom they may do business. When the purchase is finally made, only one firm may be asked to bid, and then on the basis of jointly developed (and sometimes rather general) guidelines.

No government purchasing agent can afford to do business this way. He or she would be accused (by unsuccessful bidders and their congressional allies) of collusion, favoritism, and sweetheart deals. Instead, agencies must either ask for sealed bids or for competitive written responses to detailed (*very* detailed) "requests for proposals" (RFPs). The agencies will not be allowed to take into account past performance or intangible managerial qualities. As a result, the agencies must deny themselves the use of the most important information someone can have—judgment shaped by personal knowledge and past experience. Thus, the government often buys the wrong computers from unreliable suppliers.[3]

Constraints at Work: The Case of the Postal Service

From the founding of the republic until 1971 the Post Office Department was a cabinet agency wholly subordinate to the president and Congress. As such it received its funds from annual appropriations, its personnel from presidential appointments and civil service examinations, and its physical plant from detailed political decisions about the appropriate location of post offices. Postal rates were set by Congress after hearings, dominated by organized interests that mail in bulk (for example, direct-mail advertisers and magazine publishers) and influenced by an awareness of the harmful political effects of raising the rates for first-class letters mailed by individual citizens (most of whom voted). Congress responded to these pressures by keeping rates low. . . . The wages of postal employees were set with an eye on the political power of the unions representing those employees: Congress rarely forgot that there were hundreds of organized letter carriers in every congressional district.

In 1971, the Post Office Department was transformed into the United States Postal Service (USPS), a semiautonomous government corporation. The USPS is headed by an eleven-member board of governors, nine appointed by the president and confirmed by the Senate; these nine then appoint a postmaster general and a deputy postmaster general. It derives its revenues entirely from the prices it charges and the money it borrows rather than from congressional appropriations (though subsidies still were paid to the USPS during a transition period). The postal rates are set not by Congress but by the USPS it-self, guided by a legislative standard. . . . The USPS has its own personnel sys-tem, separate from that of the rest of the federal government, and bargains directly with its own unions.

Having loosened some of the constraints upon it, the Postal Service was able to do things that in the past it could do only with great difficulty if at all. . . . When it was still a regular government department, a small local post office could only be closed after a bitter fight with the member of Congress from the affected district. As a result, few were closed. After the reorganization, the num-ber closed increased: Between 1976 and 1979, the USPS closed about twenty-four a year; between 1983 and 1986, it closed over two hundred a year.[4] . . . When the old Post Office, in the interest of cutting costs, tried to end the cus-tom of delivering mail to each recipient's front door and instead proposed to deliver mail (at least in new suburban communities) either to the curbside or to "cluster boxes,"* intense pressure on Congress forced the department to aban-don the idea. By 1978 the USPS had acquired enough autonomy to implement the idea despite continued congressional grumblings.[5] Because the USPS can raise its own capital by issuing bonds it has been able to forge ahead with the automation of mail-sorting procedures. It now has hundreds of sophisticated optical scanners and bar-code readers that enable employees to sort mail much faster than before. By 1986 optical character readers were processing 90 million pieces of mail a day. Finally, despite political objections, the USPS was slowly expanding the use of the nine-digit zip code.

In short, acquiring greater autonomy increased the ability of the Postal Ser-vice to acquire, allocate, and control the factors of production. More broadly, the whole tone of postal management changed. It began to adopt corporate-style management practices, complete with elaborate "mission statements," glossy annual reports, a tightened organizational structure, and an effort to de-centralize some decisions to local managers.

Though Congress loosened the reins, it did not take them off. On many key issues the phrase *quasi-autonomous* meant hardly autonomous at all. Congress at any time can amend the Postal Reorganization Act to limit the service's free-dom of action; even the threat of such an amendment, made evident by com-mittee hearings, often is enough to alter the service's programs. The nine-digit zip code was finally adopted but its implementation was delayed by Congress for over two years, thus impeding the efforts of the USPS to obtain voluntary compliance from the business community.

When the USPS, in a move designed to save over $400 million and thereby avoid a rate increase, announced in 1977 that it planned to eliminate Saturday mail deliveries, the service was able to produce public opinion data indicating that most people would prefer no Saturday delivery to higher postage rates. No

---

*A cluster box is a metal structure containing from twelve to one hundred mailboxes to which mail for a given neighborhood is delivered.

matter. The House of Representatives by an overwhelming vote passed a resolution opposing the change, and the USPS backed down. It seems the employee unions feared that the elimination of Saturday deliveries would lead to laying off postal workers.[6]

Similarly, when the USPS in 1975–76 sought to close many rural post offices it had as an ally the General Accounting Office.* A GAO study suggested that twelve thousand such offices could be closed at a savings of $100 million per year without reducing service to any appreciable extent (many of the small offices served no more than a dozen families and were located within a few miles of other offices that could provide the same service more economically). The rural postmasters saw matters differently, and they found a sympathetic audience in Congress. Announcing that "the rural post office has always been a uniquely American institution" and that "service" is more important than "profit," senators and representatives joined in amending the Postal Reorganization Act to block such closings temporarily and inhibit them permanently.[7] As John Tierney notes, the year that the USPS timidly closed 72 of its 30,521 offices, the Great Atlantic and Pacific Tea Company closed 174 of its 1,634 stores, and "that was that.[8] . . ."

My argument is not that all the changes the USPS would like to make are desirable, or that every vestige of politics should be removed from its management. . . . Rather, it is that one cannot explain the behavior of government bureaucracies simply by reference to the fact that they are bureaucracies; the central fact is that they are *government* bureaucracies. Nor am I arguing that government (or more broadly, politics) is bad, only that it is inevitably (and to some extent desirably) sensitive to constituency demands. . . . For example, if Congress had been content to ask of the old Post Office Department that it deliver all first-class mail within three days at the lowest possible cost, it could have let the department arrange its delivery system, set its rates, locate its offices, and hire its personnel in whatever way it wished—provided that the mail got delivered within three days and at a price that did not lead mail users to abandon the Post Office in favor of a private delivery service. Managers then would be evaluated on the basis of how well they achieved these goals.

Of course, Congress had many goals, not just one: It wanted to please many different classes of mail users, satisfy constituency demands for having many small post offices rather than a few large ones, cope with union demands for wage increases, and respond to public criticism of mail service. Congress could not provide a consistent rank-ordering of these goals, which is to say that it could not decide on how much of one goal (e.g., keeping prices low) should be

---

*The General Accounting Office (GAO), a research agency of Congress, has the broad mission of overseeing and investigating how executive branch agencies spend appropriated funds. Its activities, often controversial, range from investigating cost overruns in the Department of Defense to assessing the adequacy of environmental regulations. GAO typically initiates its activities at the request of congressional committee leaders.

sacrificed to attain more of another goal (e.g., keeping rural post offices open). This inability to decide is not a reflection on the intelligence of Congress; rather, it is the inevitable consequence of Congress being a representative body whose individual members respond differently to different constituencies.

Neither Congress nor the postal authorities have ever supported an obvious method of allowing the customers to decide the matter for themselves— namely, by letting private firms compete with the Postal Service for the first-class mail business. For over a century the Post Office has had a legal monopoly on the regular delivery of first-class mail. It is a crime to establish any "private express for the conveyance of letters or packets . . . by regular trips or at stated periods over any post route."[9] This is justified by postal executives on the grounds that private competitors would skim away the most profitable business (for example, delivering business mail or utility bills in big cities), leaving the government with the most costly business (for example, delivering a Christmas card from Aunt Annie in Eudora, Kansas, to Uncle Matt in Wakefield, Massachusetts). In time the Post Office began to face competition anyway, from private parcel and express delivery services that did not deliver "by regular trips or at stated periods" (so as not to violate the private express statute) and from electronic mail and fund-transferring systems. But by then it had become USPS, giving it both greater latitude in and incentive for meeting that competition.

Faced with political superiors that find it conceptually easier and politically necessary to focus on inputs, agency managers also tend to focus on inputs. Nowhere is this more evident than in defense procurement programs. The Defense Department, through the Defense Logistics Agency (DLA), each year acquires food, fuel, clothing, and spare parts worth (in 1984) $15 billion, manages a supply system containing over two million items, and administers over $186 billion in government contracts.[10] Congress and the president repeatedly have made clear their desire that this system be run efficiently and make use of off-the-shelf, commercially available products (as opposed to more expensive, "made-to-order" items)[11] Periodically, however, the press reports scandals involving the purchase of $435 hammers and $700 toilet seats. Some of these stories are exaggerated,[12] but there is little doubt that waste and inefficiency occur. Congressional investigations are mounted and presidential commissions are appointed to find ways of solving these problems. Among the solutions offered are demands that tighter rules be imposed, more auditors be hired, and fuller reports be made.

Less dramatic but more common than the stories of scandals and overpriced hammers are the continuing demands of various constituencies for influence over the procurement process. Occasionally this takes the form of requests for special favors, such as preferentially awarding a contract to a politically favored firm. But just as important and more pervasive in their effects are the legal constraints placed on the procurement process to insure that contracts are awarded "fairly"—that is, in ways that allow equal access to the bidding process by all firms and special access by politically significant ones. For example, section 52 of the *Federal Acquisition Regulation* contains dozens of provisions governing the need to give special attention to suppliers that are small business (especially a "small disadvantaged business"), women-owned small businesses, handicapped workers, or disabled and Vietnam-era veterans, or are located in areas with a "labor surplus."*[13] Moreover, only materials produced in the United States can be acquired for public use unless, under the Buy American Act, the government certifies that the cost is "unreasonable" or finds that the supplies are not available in this country in sufficient quantity or adequate quality.[14]

The goal of "fairness" underlies almost every phase of the procurement process, not because the American government is committed heart and soul to fairness as an abstract social good but because if a procurement decision is questioned it is much easier to justify the decision if it can be shown that the decision was "fairly" made on the basis of "objective" criteria. Those criteria are spelled out in the *Federal Acquisition Regulation*, a complex document of over six thousand pages. The essential rules are that all potential suppliers must be offered an equal opportunity to bid on a contract; that the agency's procurement decision must be objectively justifiable on the basis of written specifications; that contracts awarded on the basis of sealed bids must go to the contractor offering the lowest price; and that unsuccessful bidders must be offered a chance to protest decisions with which they disagree.[15] . . .

To understand the bureaucratic significance of these rules, put yourself in the shoes of a Defense Logistics Agency manager. A decision you made is challenged because someone thinks that you gave a contract to an unqualified firm or purchased something of poor quality. What is your response—that in your judgment it was a good buy from a reliable firm? Such a remark is tantamount to inviting yourself to explain to a hostile congressional committee why you think your judgment is any good. A much safer response is "I followed the rules." . . .

If despite all your devotion to the rules Congress uncovers an especially blatant case of paying too much for too little (for example, a $3,000 coffeepot), the prudent response is to suggest that what is needed are more rules, more auditors, and more tightly constrained procedures. The consequence of this may

---

*For example, the law requires that a "fair proportion of the total purchases and contracts" shall be "placed with small-business enterprises" and that "small business concerns owned and controlled by socially and economically disadvantaged individuals, shall have the maximum practicable opportunity to participate in the performance of contracts let by any Federal agency" [15 *U.S. Code* 637(d)(i)]. In pursuance of this law, it is the government's policy "to place a fair proportion" of its acquisitions with small business concerns and small business disadvantaged concerns (*Federal Acquisition Regulation,* 19.201a). A "socially and economically disadvantaged individual" includes, but is not limited to, a black American, Hispanic American, Native American, Asian-Pacific American, or Asian-Indian American (ibid., 52.219.2).

be to prevent the buying of any more $3,000 coffeepots, or it may be to increase the complexity of the procurement process so that fewer good firms will submit bids to supply coffeepots, or it may be to increase the cost of monitoring that process so that the money saved by buying cheaper pots is lost by hiring more pot inspectors. . . .

Public Versus Private Management

The late Professor Wallace Sayre once said that public and private management is alike in all unimportant respects.[16] This view has been disputed vigorously by many people who are convinced that whatever problems beset government agencies also afflict private organizations. The clearest statement of that view can be found in John Kenneth Galbraith's *The New Industrial State*. Galbraith argues that large corporations, like public agencies, are dominated by "technostructures" that are governed by their own bureaucratic logic rather than by the dictates of the market. These corporations have insulated themselves from the market by their ability to control demand (through clever advertising) and set prices (by dominating an industry). The rewards to the technocrats who staff these firms are salaries, not profits, and the goals toward which these technocrats move are the assertion and maintenance of their own managerial autonomy. . . .

Professor Galbraith's book appeared at a time (1967) when American businesses were enjoying such unrivaled success that its beautifully crafted sentences seemed to capture some enduring truth. But the passage of time converted many of those eloquent phrases into hollow ones. Within ten years, it had become painfully obvious to General Motors that it could not, in Galbraith's words, "set prices for automobiles . . . secure in the knowledge that no individual buyer, by withdrawing its custom, can force a change."[17] Competition from Toyota, Nissan, and Honda had given the individual buyer great power; coupled with an economic slowdown, that competition led GM, like all auto manufacturers, to start offering cash rebates, cut-rate financing, and price reductions. And still the U.S. firms lost market share despite the "power" of their advertising and saw profits evaporate despite their "dominance" of the industry.

But Galbraith's analysis had more serious flaws than its inability to predict the future; it led many readers to draw the erroneous conclusion that "all bureaucracies are alike" because all bureaucracies employ salaried workers, are enmeshed in red tape, and strive to insure their own autonomy. The large corporation surely is more bureaucratic than the small entrepreneur, but in becoming bureaucratic it has not become a close relative of a government agency. What distinguishes public from private organizations is neither their size nor their desire to "plan" (that is, control) their environments but rather the rules under which they acquire and use capital and labor. General Motors acquires capital by selling shares, issuing bonds, or retaining earnings; the Department of Defense acquires it from an annual appropriation by Congress. GM opens and closes plants, subject to certain government regulations, at its own discretion; DOD opens and closes military bases under the watchful guidance of Congress. GM pays its managers with salaries it sets and bonuses tied to its earnings; DOD pays its managers with salaries set by Congress and bonuses (if any) that have no connection with organizational performance. The number of workers in GM is determined by its level of production; the number in DOD by legislation and civil-service rules.

What all this means can be seen by returning to the Registry of Motor Vehicles and McDonald's. Suppose you were just appointed head of the Watertown office of the Registry and you wanted to improve service there so that it more nearly approximated the service at McDonald's. Better service might well require spending more money (on clerks, equipment, and buildings). Why should your political superiors give you that money? It is a cost to them if it requires either higher taxes or taking funds from another agency; offsetting these real and immediate costs are dubious and postponed benefits. If lines become shorter and clients become happier, no legislator will benefit. There may be fewer complaints, but complaints are episodic and have little effect on the career of any given legislator. By contrast, shorter lines and faster service at McDonald's means more customers can be served per hour and thus more money can be earned per hour. A McDonald's manager can estimate the marginal product of the last dollar he or she spends on improving service; the Registry manager can generate no tangible return on any expenditure he or she makes and thus cannot easily justify the expenditure.

Improving service at the Registry may require replacing slow or surly workers with quick and pleasant ones. But you, the manager, can neither hire nor fire them at will. You look enviously at the McDonald's manager who regularly and with little notice replaces poor workers with better ones. Alternatively, you may wish to mount an extensive training program (perhaps creating a Registration University to match McDonald's Hamburger University) that would imbue a culture of service in your employees. But unless the Registry were so large an agency that the legislature would neither notice nor care about funds spent for this purpose—and it is not that large—you would have a tough time convincing anybody that this was not a wasteful expenditure on a frill project.

If somehow your efforts succeed in making Registry clients happier, you can take vicarious pleasure in it; in the unlikely event a client seeks you out to thank you for those efforts, you can bask in a moment's worth of glory. Your colleague at McDonald's who manages to make customers happier may also derive some vicarious satisfaction from the improvement but in addition he or she will earn more money owing to an increase in sales.

In time it will dawn on you that if you improve service too much, clients will start coming to the Watertown office instead of going to the Boston office. As a result, the lines you succeeded in shortening will become longer again. If you wish to keep complaints down, you will have to spend even more on the Watertown office. But if it was hard to persuade the legislature to do that in the past, it is impossible now. Why should the taxpayer be asked to spend more on Watertown when the Boston office, fully staffed (naturally, no one was laid off when the clients disappeared), has no lines at all? From the legislature's point of view the correct level of expenditure is not that which makes one office better than another but that which produces an equal amount of discontent in all offices.

Finally, you remember that your clients have no choice: The Registry offers a monopoly service. It and only it supplies drivers' licenses. In the long run all that matters is that there are not "too many" complaints to the legislature about service. Unlike McDonald's, the Registry need not fear that its clients will take their business to Burger King or to Wendy's. Perhaps you should just relax. . . .

Notes

1. John F. Love, *McDonald's: Behind the Arches* (New York: Bantam Books, 1986), 140ff.
2. James S. Coleman, Thomas Hoffer, and Sally Kilgore, *High School Achievement* (New York: Basic Books, 1982).
3. Steven Kelman, *Procurement and Public Management* [Lanham: American Enterprise Institute, 1990].
4. John T. Tierney, *The U.S. Postal Service* (Dover, Mass.: Auburn House, 1988), 101–2.
5. Tierney, *U.S. Postal Service*, 94–97.
6. John T. Tierney, *Postal Reorganization: Managing the Public's Business* (Boston: Auburn House, 1981), 67.
7. Ibid., 68–73.
8. Ibid., 72.
9. 18 *U.S. Code* 1696.
10. General Accounting Office, *Progress and Challenges at the Defense Logistics Agency.* GAO report NSIAD-86-64, Washington, D.C., 1986, p. 2.
11. Wendy T. Kirby, "Expanding the Use of Commercial Products and 'Commercial-Style' Acquisition Techniques in Defense Procurement: A Proposed Legal Framework," Appendix H in President's Blue Ribbon Commission on Defense Management (the "Packard Commission"), *A Quest for Excellence: Final Report,* June 1986.
12. I discuss these matters in chap. 17.
13. Kirby, "Expanding the Use," 106–7.
14. 41 *U.S. Code* 10(a).
15. Kirby, "Expanding the Use," 82–83, 91.
16. Quoted in Graham T. Allison, Jr., "Public and Private Management: Are They Fundamentally Alike in All Unimportant Respects?" in Frederick S. Lane, ed., *Current Issues in Public Administration,* 2d ed. (New York: St. Martin's Press, 1982), 13–33. The academic literature on public-private differences is summarized in Hal G. Rainey, Robert W. Backoff, and Charles H. Levine, "Comparing Public and Private Organizations," *Public Administration Review* 36 (1976): 233–44.
17. Galbraith, *New Industrial State,* 46.

Questions for Discussion

1. According to James Q. Wilson, in what ways is managing a private organization different from managing a public one?
2. Wilson suggests that "red tape" is more often the result of democratic politics than the preferences of bureaucrats. What does he mean by this? Would increasing citizen and group participation in politics lead to more or fewer bureaucratic rules and regulations?

 12.5

Washington's Mega-Merger

The Economist

In the corporate world, large-scale mergers occur frequently, and we know that sometimes they work well (Exxon and Mobil) and that sometimes they don't (AOL and TimeWarner). Rarely, however, do we see large-scale integration through merger in the public sphere. Still, occasionally circumstances dictate such an action. The post–World War II recognition that the United States needed to maintain a strong military, even in peacetime, prompted the creation of the Defense Department, which took several decades to work out.

In this article, the British weekly *The Economist* takes an initial look at the "merger" required to form the U.S. Department of Homeland Security. Prompted by a need for a more rational structure and less duplication among subunits, the Department of Homeland Security filled a need that became evident in the wake of the 9/11 attacks and the country's subsequent evaluation of its domestic security capability. Among the problems noted for the new department are the kinds of organizational transition issues that plagued the Defense Department for years, as the various services strived to work together. Although the article concludes that such a national, top-down strategy is essential, it also argues that starting at the local level—from the bottom up—is equally important and, so far, not an adequate part of the overall strategy.

It will be one of the biggest mergers ever. The newly consolidated business
will have an annual turnover of $37 billion and 169,000 employees. The
chief executive is babbling about synergies, benefits of rationalisation and
economies of scale. The track record of ordinary mergers, involving two companies, is poor—and this one consolidates 22 units from 12 different companies.
Meanwhile, in the background, the shareholders—or their representatives—are
bickering and the unions are suspicious. If this were a real corporate merger,
Wall Street would already be discounting the share price.

So the first question to ask about America's new Department of Homeland
Security is whether the basic design (see [Figure 1]) is the right one. It will
bring most of the main functions of domestic security under one roof. Huge
agencies will be seized from other departments—the Immigration and Naturali-
sation Service (39,500 employees) from Justice, the Coast Guard (43,600) from
Transportation, the Customs Service (21,700) from the Treasury. Other independent entities—like the Federal Emergency Management Agency (5,100)—
will be gobbled up whole. Yet the new department will not be omnivorous: it is
not eating up some 100 departments and agencies that remain on its patch.

There are still people who think it should have been bigger or smaller. In
2001 a commission chaired by former senators Gary Hart and Warren Rudman
proposed an even more sweeping reorganisation that would have also shaken
up the Defence Department and the National Security Council (NSC), which
are both basically untouched by the new entity. George Bush initially did not
want a new department at all, merely a co-ordinating office in the White
House, with the operational divisions left in different departments.

In fact, there is a lot to be said for the compromise agreed upon this week. To
have folded everything into one giant department would have been logical but
administratively impractical. As Richard Falkenrath, the policy director for the
Office of Homeland Security, told a panel at the Brookings Institution, the job
"requires specialisation and expertise. There's also a fair bit going on in the rest
of the world which the NSC needs to stay focused on."

But leaving agencies scattered around would have been no good either. Consider two examples. If there were a chemical or biological attack now, health
advice would come from no fewer than 12 federal agencies, to say nothing of
local government ones. If there were an attack on a nuclear power plant, one
agency would distribute anti-radiation treatment if you live within 10 miles. A
different one distributes it if you live outside that circle. A third controls the
drug stockpile. And a fourth takes over if the attack also happens to be within
10 miles of a nuclear-weapons facility.

The Economist is a British weekly journal of opinion and analysis that enjoys a wide circulation
in the United States.

Figure 1 Organization of the Department of Homeland Security

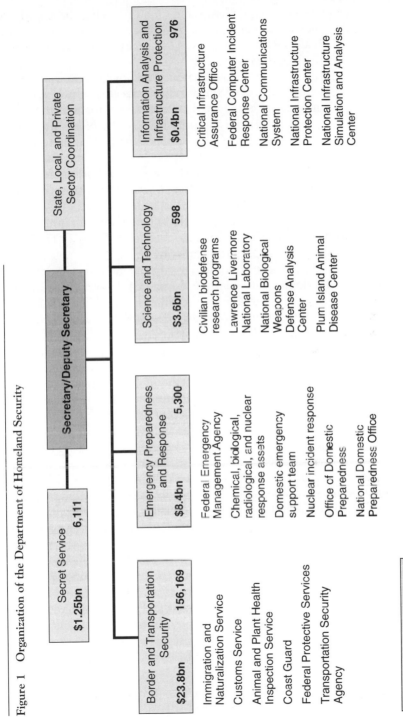

So it is not surprising that the president came round to seeing the benefits of rationalisation. With such an immense job of co-ordination to do, having a single department with budgetary control looked necessary. An advisory White House office could never bang heads together.

The bill approved this week does more than merely move bureaucratic boxes into one place: it vests the powers of the various units in the new secretary (. . . Tom Ridge . . .), in order to eliminate duplication or enforce the adoption of common standards. He can delegate authority back to the bits as he sees fit, and he also has the power to take 5% of the budget of any one bit of his empire and move it around.

In other words, the bill vests a lot of administrative discretion in one person. That may be risky. Democrats also argued that it was unconstitutional, and trampled over employment rights. These were the issues that held up approval of the homeland-security bill for months over the summer and autumn. But it is probably just as well the administration won the fight: much discretionary power will be required to overcome bureaucratic inertia.

Two reforms look particularly promising. First, the new department will gather together all the border and transport agencies into one place. At the moment, people entering America fill in one form for immigration officials and another one for customs, and they may have to see Department of Agriculture officers. That will now be rationalised—a no-brainer, admittedly, but this is by far the largest section of the new department, with 156,200 of the 169,000 employees.

The second reform concerns "information analysis." For the first time, America will have a central clearing house for assessing the vulnerabilities of, and threats to, Americans at home. At present, the Energy Department supervises security at power stations, the Transportation Department looks at roads and bridges, and so on. Bringing these things together will not guarantee better intelligence, but it should be easier to spot trends and connections.

For now, the new department will merely analyse intelligence gathered by others. But several figures, including Richard Shelby, the senior Republican on the Senate Intelligence Committee, and a commission chaired by Jim Gilmore, the former governor of Virginia, have argued that America needs a proper domestic intelligence-gathering operation, like Britain's MI5.* At the moment, the gathering is done by the FBI, whose director, Robert Mueller, vigorously opposes any idea to split off spying from policing, even though most spooks insist that spying and policing are often contradictory things.

That battle is for the future, but similar vested interests are bound to make Mr. Ridge's nice draft design extremely hard to put into practice. One cautionary tale comes from the Transportation Security Administration, the division which supplies the baggage screeners that went to work this week and which, at

---

*MI5 is the British equivalent of parts of both the FBI and the CIA, made famous by James Bond.

full strength, will be the second largest single part of the new department. The TSA was set up last year with congressional goodwill, a tough boss and an ambitious programme. But it lost the confidence of Congress and airport managers. It failed to get baggage-screening devices delivered on time. It could not resolve the competing claims of security and airport efficiency. And its first boss was sacked.

From this perspective, it is worrying that the new department does not really begin with firm political backing. Although the Senate voted 90 to nine this week to set up the department, that was only after months of squabbling. And the new department faces four challenges that may cost it more support.

♦ **The transition.** The new department is supposed to be up and running a year after the president signs the bill. . . . It took 40 years and several congressional interventions to get the last comparable government reorganisation right, the establishment of the Department of Defence. It would be a disaster if the bureaucratic effort to set up the new department distracts from the real job of protecting the homeland.

♦ **Sporadic shortages of money.** Proposed spending on homeland security has roughly doubled since September 11th (though not all the promised money has materialised). Still there are holes. The Coast Guard has one of the oldest fleets in the world and no amount of reorganisation will provide enough money to buy new ships.

♦ **Civil liberties.** Even in its pre-MI5 incarnation, the department's domestic snoops are likely to come into conflict with civil libertarians. Privacy watchdogs are up in arms about a new "office of information awareness" which, they say, could put all e-mails, credit-card transactions, drug prescriptions and every bit of electronic information you generate on to one vast, Orwellian database. This nightmare idea has been floated by the Defence Department, and may come to nothing. But the fracas carries a warning to the Homeland Security Department.

♦ **The private sector.** Many of America's most vulnerable targets, such as chemical factories, are privately owned and guarded. Any Republican government will be reluctant to wade in and impose new federal regulations on private firms. But what if private security is not enough? Mr Ridge could well find himself battling against several huge industries.

In short, the new department is a step forward, but just a step. Eventually, it should make America's borders safer and improve domestic intelligence. But those are only parts of the picture. It is a top-down reform to improve security at a time when the most useful form of protection comes from the bottom up— from a security guard noticing something strange at a power plant, from a customs officer following up a hunch, from passengers overpowering a shoe bomber. Even after the new mega-merger, those are the people who will keep the homeland secure.

Questions for Discussion

1. Would the Department of Homeland Security have ever been created absent the 9/11 terrorist attacks? What are the advantages and pitfalls of creating a major reorganization in the wake of such an unusual and traumatic event?
2. *The Economist* makes a lot of the fact that there will be a single secretary of homeland security, especially given the various tasks that the department will tackle. What are the advantages and disadvantages for assuring the security of the country in such a situation?

 Chapter 13

THE SUPREME COURT

Barely outlined in the Constitution, the Supreme Court and the American judiciary have been forced, almost from the beginning of the republic, to define their own roles within the political system. Historically, this has meant that the Court has engaged in a long-term balancing act, adhering to the rule of law while remaining conscious of the political environment of the times. At the heart of the American court system is a central irony: We rely on a profoundly undemocratic institution to safeguard our democratic state as well as to check the likely excesses of popular rule.

The Court's major tool in its work has been the power of judicial review: The Court determines whether federal laws and regulations and state statutes are in accord with the Constitution and constitutional principles. Although the principle of judicial review was incorporated into American law with Chief Justice John Marshall's 1803 decision in *Marbury* v. *Madison* (see selection 13.2), the Court has not, over the course of two centuries, invalidated many federal laws. Indeed, there was a fifty-four-year gap between *Marbury* and the next such ruling, the 1857 Dred Scott decision, which struck down the Missouri Compromise. Since the New Deal, however, the Court has been somewhat more willing to overturn federal laws, especially when individual rights are at stake (see Chapter 3). State laws have received even more attention; close to a thousand such statutes have been declared unconstitutional. In a federal system, the power to strike down state legislation is essential, whereas the capacity to overrule national laws is less so.

It is surely conceivable that Congress or the executive branch could interpret the Constitution as well as the Court does. Still, the Supreme Court's role provides for a rough balance of power among the three branches. Lacking the authority to enforce its decisions, the Court can scarcely act in an arbitrary or capricious fashion. Nevertheless, it can have a major impact, as indicated by its decisions on subjects such as school desegregation, the rights of the accused, access to executive branch material (the Nixon tapes case), and the separation of powers (the *Chada* case, which invalidated legislative veto sections of approximately two hundred laws). In these and a host of other decisions, the Court clearly has acted in a policymaking role.

Despite the continuing controversy over whether the Supreme Court should make policy or merely interpret the Constitution in light of the framers' intent, the fact remains that it has consistently rendered policy decisions from its earliest days. It can hardly work in any other way. For example, in *Boyle* v. *United Technologies* (1988), conservative justice Antonin Scalia, writing for a five-to-four majority, argued that members of the military service could not sue the manufacturers of possibly defective military equipment (such as a helicopter that crashed). Scalia reasoned that allowing suits would ultimately increase the cost of defense material to the federal government and the American taxpayer. But as dissenting justice William Brennan observed, "the Court lacks both authority and expertise to fashion [a rule that exempts military contractors from civil suits], whether to protect the Treasury of the United States or the coffers of industry. . . . I would leave that exercise of power to Congress, where our Constitution places it." Justice Brennan, however, had previously written a broadly worded ruling that rendered the states almost superfluous in the face of federal power (*Garcia* v. *San Antonio Metropolitan Transit Authority*). In the end, both the conservative Scalia and the liberal Brennan have interpreted the Constitution expansively when doing so has suited their policy preferences. For further discussion of the question of intent and interpretation, see Richard A. Posner's article (selection 13.3) on the problematic notions of original intent and strict construction.

Mechanically, the Court sets its policy agenda by accepting a relatively small number of cases on which to rule. Although Congress and the president seem to have greater flexibility in setting their agendas, the Court can choose from among some 6,000 to 8,000 submitted cases in selecting the fewer than 100 that it will hear in its annual October-through-June session. In fact, its docket often includes controversies from which Congress and the president traditionally have shied away. The most notable example is school desegregation, which the Court addressed in 1954, a full decade before Congress passed a major civil rights bill. (See Chapter 3.)

Reprinted in this chapter, Alexander Hamilton's *The Federalist,* No. 78 (selection 13.1) and John Marshall's opinion in *Marbury* v. *Madison* (selection 13.2) provide the foundations for the Supreme Court's constitutional role. Hamilton articulates the classic formulation of the judiciary as "the least dangerous branch" because it "has no influence over either the sword [the executive] or the purse [the legislature]. . . . It may truly be said to have neither Force nor Will, but merely judgment; and must ultimately depend upon the aid of the executive arm even for the efficacy of its judgments." Marshall demonstrates the accuracy of Hamilton's observations in the *Marbury* decision, which involved a relatively trivial appointment but permitted Marshall to establish the principle of the judicial review of legislation.

In the next selection, Federal Appeals Court Judge Richard A. Posner, a prolific writer on an array of legal issues, addresses the ever-relevant issue of judicial activism. Although Posner is sometimes labeled a conservative, his intellect and range of interests make him difficult to classify. Most important, Posner does not sit as a judge merely to apply the Constitution in some rote manner or to determine what the framers' "original intent" might have been.

Nine justices, appointed for life, sit on the Supreme Court. Each has a single vote, but some exert more power than others. Although this power often flows from the quality of their arguments and thought, it can also derive from one's voting position on the Court. That is, if the justices are frequently divided equally on a set of issues, the one near their mid-point will exercise disproportionate authority. So it has been with Justice Sandra Day O'Connor. A former Arizona state senator, the relatively conservative O'Connor often thinks through major issues on narrow grounds, rarely being willing to break new constitutional ground if she can render a limited ruling. Writing for a conservative audience, in the chapter's final selection (13.4), Ramesh Ponnuru offers a balanced perspective on O'Connor's approach to judicial decision making. Given her cautious approach, O'Connor often blunts the hard-line positions of justices like Antonin Scalia or Clarence Thomas, who would push their conservative agendas far further. At the same time, Ponnuru notes the general approach of the current Court to assert its authority, as it did in *Bush* v. *Gore*. In addition, O'Connor's caution does not prevent her from joining her colleagues in aggressively moving the Court to challenge congressional and executive authority on many of the most important issues of the day.

 13.1

The Federalist, No. 78

Alexander Hamilton

Of the three branches of government, the judiciary is the least fully outlined in the Constitution. To an extent this vagueness reflects the framers' greater concerns with the legislature and the executive, but it also indicates their perception that the judiciary simply did not pose the dangers the other branches did. For Alexander Hamilton, the key problem was to ensure that the judiciary remained independent of the legislature and the executive. One way to provide for this separation was to make court appointments lifetime positions, with removal impossible as long as the incumbents maintained "good behaviour"—a purposefully vague term.

Hamilton also laid out the case for judicial review of legislation. He observed that "no legislative act . . . contrary to the Constitution can be valid." And it is the Supreme Court that makes the final judgment on constitutionality. This seemingly great grant of authority is tempered, however, by the Court's inability to enforce its decisions without cooperation from the executive.

*T*o the People of the State of New York: We proceed now to an examination of the judiciary department of the proposed government.

In unfolding the defects of the existing confederation, the utility and necessity of a federal judicature have been clearly pointed out. It is the less necessary to recapitulate the considerations there urged; as the propriety of the institution in the abstract is not disputed: The only questions which have been raised being relative to the manner of constituting it, and to its extent. To these points therefore our observations shall be confined.

The manner of constituting it seems to embrace these several objects—1st. The mode of appointing the judges. 2d. The tenure by which they are to hold their places. 3d. The partition of the judiciary authority between different courts, and their relations to each other.

First. As to the mode of appointing the judges: This is the same with that of appointing the officers of the union in general, and has been so fully discussed

---

Alexander Hamilton was the first secretary of the treasury and a consistent supporter of strong central government.

in the two last numbers, that nothing can be said here which would not be use-less repetition.

Second. As to the tenure by which the judges are to hold their places: This chiefly concerns their duration in office; the provisions for their support; and the precautions for their responsibility.

According to the plan of the convention, all the judges who may be appointed by the United States are to hold their offices *during good behaviour,* which is conformable to the most approved of the state constitutions; and among the rest, to that of this state. Its propriety having been drawn into question by the adversaries of that plan, is no light symptom of the rage for objection which disorders their imaginations and judgments. The standard of good behaviour for the continuance in office of the judicial magistracy is certainly one of the most valuable of the modern improvements in the practice of government. In a monarchy it is an excellent barrier to the despotism of the prince: In a republic it is a no less excellent barrier to the encroachments and oppressions of the representative body. And it is the best expedient which can be devised in any government, to secure a steady, upright and impartial administration of the laws.

Whoever attentively considers the different departments of power must perceive, that in a government in which they are separated from each other, the judiciary, from the nature of its functions, will always be the least dangerous to the political rights of the constitution; because it will be least in a capacity to annoy or injure them. The executive not only dispenses the honors, but holds the sword of the community. The legislature not only commands the purse, but prescribes the rules by which the duties and rights of every citizen are to be regulated. The judiciary on the contrary has no influence over either the sword or the purse, no direction either of the strength or of the wealth of the society, and can take no active resolution whatever. It may truly be said to have neither Force nor Will, but merely judgment; and must ultimately depend upon the aid of the executive arm even for the efficacy of its judgments.

This simple view of the matter suggests several important consequences It proves incontestibly that the judiciary is beyond comparison the weakest of the three departments of power; that it can never attack with success either of the other two; and that all possible care is requisite to enable it to defend itself against their attacks. It equally proves, that though individual oppression may now and then proceed from the courts of justice, the general liberty of the people can never be endangered from that quarter: I mean, so long as the judiciary remains truly distinct from both the legislative and executive. For I agree that "there is no liberty, if the power of judging be not separated from the legislative and executive powers." And it proves, in the last place, that as liberty can have nothing to fear from the judiciary alone, but would have every thing to fear from its union with either of the other departments; that as all the effects of such an union must ensue from a dependence of the former on the latter, notwithstanding a nominal and apparent separation; that as from the natural feebleness of the judiciary, it is in continual jeopardy of being overpowered, awed or influenced by its coordinate branches; and that as nothing can contribute so much to its firmness and independence, as permanency in office, this quality may therefore be justly regarded as an indispensable ingredient in its constitution; and in a great measure as the citadel of the public justice and the public security.

The complete independence of the courts of justice is peculiarly essential in a limited constitution. By a limited constitution I understand one which contains certain specified exceptions to the legislative authority; such for instance as that it shall pass no bills of attainder, no *ex post facto* laws, and the like.* Limitations of this kind can be preserved in practice no other way than through the medium of the courts of justice; whose duty it must be to declare all acts contrary to the manifest tenor of the constitution void. Without this, all the reservations of particular rights or privileges would amount to nothing.

Some perplexity respecting the right of the courts to pronounce legislative acts void, because contrary to the constitution, has arisen from an imagination that the doctrine would imply a superiority of the judiciary to the legislative power. It is urged that the authority which can declare the acts of another void, must necessarily be superior to the one whose acts may be declared void. As this doctrine is of great importance in all the American constitutions, a brief discussion of the grounds on which it rests cannot be unacceptable.

There is no position which depends on clearer principles, than that every act of a delegated authority, contrary to the tenor of the commission under which it is exercised, is void. No legislative act therefore contrary to the constitution can be valid. To deny this would be to affirm that the deputy is greater than his principal; that the servant is above his master; that the representatives of the people are superior to the people themselves; that men acting by virtue of powers may do not only what their powers do not authorise, but what they forbid.

If it be said that the legislative body are themselves the constitutional judges of their own powers, and that the construction they put upon them is conclusive upon the other departments, it may be answered, that this cannot be the natural presumption, where it is not to be collected from any particular provisions in the constitution. It is not otherwise to be supposed that the constitution could intend to enable the representatives of the people to substitute their *will* to that of their constituents. It is far more rational to suppose that the courts were designed to be an intermediate body between the people and the legislature, in order, among other things, to keep the latter within the limits assigned to their authority. The interpretation of the laws is the proper and peculiar province of the courts. A constitution is in fact, and must be, regarded by

---

*A bill of attainder is a legislative act that inflicts punishment without a judicial trial. Crimes are thus defined by statutes that are general in nature, and the courts interpret those statutes. An *ex post facto* law either makes an act illegal after the fact or removes the legal protection from behavior after that behavior has been performed.

the judges as a fundamental law. It therefore belongs to them to ascertain its meaning as well as the meaning of any particular act proceeding from the legislative body. If there should happen to be an irreconcileable variance between the two, that which has the superior obligation and validity ought of course to be preferred; or in other words, the constitution ought to be preferred to the statute, the intention of the people to the intention of their agents.

Nor does this conclusion by any means suppose a superiority of the judicial to the legislative power. It only supposes that the power of the people is superior to both; and that where the will of the legislature declared in its statutes, stands in opposition to that of the people declared in the constitution, the judges ought to be governed by the latter, rather than the former. They ought to regulate their decisions by the fundamental laws, rather than by those which are not fundamental.

This exercise of judicial discretion in determining between two contradictory laws, is exemplified in a familiar instance. It not uncommonly happens, that there are two statutes existing at one time, clashing in whole or in part with each other, and neither of them containing any repealing clause or expression. In such a case, it is the province of the courts to liquidate and fix their meaning and operation: So far as they can by any fair construction be reconciled to each other; reason and law conspire to dictate that this should be done. Where this is impracticable, it becomes a matter of necessity to give effect to one, in exclusion of the other. The rule which has obtained in the courts for determining their relative validity is that the last in order of time shall be preferred to the first. But this is mere rule of construction, not derived from any positive law, but from the nature and reason of the thing. It is a rule not enjoined upon the courts by legislative provision, but adopted by themselves, as consonant to truth and propriety, for the direction of their conduct as interpreters of the law. They thought it reasonable, that between the interfering acts of an *equal* authority, that which was the last indication of its will, should have the preference.

But in regard to the interfering acts of a superior and subordinate authority, of an original and derivative power, the nature and reason of the thing indicate the converse of that rule as proper to be followed. They teach us that the prior act of a superior ought to be preferred to the subsequent act of an inferior and subordinate authority; and that, accordingly, whenever a particular statute contravenes the constitution, it will be the duty of the judicial tribunals to adhere to the latter, and disregard the former.

It can be of no weight to say, that the courts on the pretence of a repugnancy, may substitute their own pleasure to the constitutional intentions of the legislature. This might as well happen in the case of two contradictory statutes; or it might as well happen in every adjudication upon any single statute. The courts must declare the sense of the law; and if they should be disposed to exercise WILL instead of JUDGMENT, the consequence would equally be the substitution of their pleasure to that of the legislative body. The observation, if it proved any thing, would prove that there ought to be no judges distinct from that body.

If then the courts of justice are to be considered as the bulwarks of a limited constitution against legislative encroachments, this consideration will afford a strong argument for the permanent tenure of judicial offices, since nothing will contribute so much as this to that independent spirit in the judges, which must be essential to the faithful performance of so arduous a duty. . . .

That inflexible and uniform adherence to the rights of the constitution and of individuals, which we perceive to be indispensable in the courts of justice, can certainly not be expected from judges who hold their offices by a temporary commission. Periodical appointments, however regulated, or by whomsoever made, would in some way or other be fatal to their necessary independence. If the power of making them was committed either to the executive or legislature, there would be danger of an improper complaisance to the branch which possessed it; if to both, there would be an unwillingness to hazard the displeasure of either; if to the people, or to persons chosen by them for the special purpose, there would be too great a disposition to consult popularity, to justify a reliance that nothing would be consulted but the constitution and the laws.

There is yet a further and a weighty reason for the permanency of the judicial offices; which is deducible from the nature of the qualifications they require. It has been frequently remarked with great propriety, that a voluminous code of laws is one of the inconveniences necessarily connected with the advantages of a free government. To avoid an arbitrary discretion in the courts, it is indispensable that they should be bound down by strict rules and precedents, which serve to define and point out their duty in every particular case that comes before them; and it will readily be conceived from the variety of controversies which grow out of the folly and wickedness of mankind, that the records of those precedents must unavoidably swell to a very considerable bulk, and must demand long and laborious study to acquire a competent knowledge of them. Hence it is that there can be but few men in the society, who will have sufficient skill in the laws to qualify them for the stations of judges. And making the proper deductions for the ordinary depravity of human nature, the number must be still smaller of those who unite the requisite integrity with the requisite knowledge. These considerations apprise us, that the government can have no great option between fit characters; and that a temporary duration in office, which would naturally discourage such characters from quitting a lucrative line of practice to accept a seat on the bench, would have a tendency to throw the administration of justice into hands less able, and less well qualified to conduct it with utility and dignity. In the present circumstances of this country, and in those in which it is likely to be for a long time to come, the disadvantages on this score would be greater than they may at first sight appear; but it must be confessed that they are far inferior to those which present themselves under the other aspects of the subject.

Upon the whole there can be no room to doubt that the convention acted wisely in copying from the models of those constitutions which have established *good behaviour* as the tenure of their judicial offices in point of duration; and that so far from being blameable on this account, their plan would have been inexcuseably defective if it had wanted this important feature of good government. The experience of Great Britain affords an illustrious comment on the excellence of the institution.

Questions for Discussion

1. Why might a lifetime term for judges and justices be considered a good policy? Why did the framers make officeholding contingent on continued "good behaviour" rather than on some more specific criterion?
2. Why did the framers consider the Supreme Court the weakest of the three branches? How can this be so if the Court has the final say over what the Constitution means?

13.2

Marbury v. Madison (1803)

In March 1801, during the waning hours of his administration, President John Adams appointed William Marbury to be a justice of the peace in Washington, D.C. James Madison, the secretary of state under incoming President Thomas Jefferson, refused to deliver Marbury's commission, following Jefferson's instructions. Marbury subsequently applied to the Supreme Court to obtain the position.

This minor controversy offered a great opportunity to John Marshall, whom Adams had appointed chief justice in the last months of his tenure. Marshall, no friend of Jefferson's, found in this case a way to establish the Court's power to declare a federal law unconstitutional. Although Hamilton argued strenuously in favor of the judicial review of legislation in *The Federalist,* No. 78 (selection 13.1), the Constitution did not speak definitively on the topic. In this case Marshall ruled specifically that Marbury was entitled to his commission but the Court had no legitimate authority to order Madison to deliver it to him because the federal statute providing the Court with the power to provide the appropriate remedy was unconstitutional. In short, this decision answered the open question posed by the Constitution: Who has the authority to declare a statute unconstitutional? In *Marbury* v. *Madison,* Marshall won that power for the Supreme Court.

Mr. Chief Justice Marshall delivered the opinion of the Court. At the last term on the affidavits then read and filed with the clerk, a rule was granted in this case, requiring the secretary of state to show cause why a *mandamus** should not issue, directing him to deliver to William Marbury his commission as a justice of the peace for the county of Washington, in the district of Columbia. . . .

In the order in which the court has viewed this subject, the following questions have been considered and decided.

1st. Has the applicant a right to the commission he demands?

2dly. If he has a right, and that right has been violated, do the laws of his country afford him a remedy?

3dly. If they do afford him a remedy, is it a *mandamus* issuing from this court? . . .

This . . . is a plain case for a *mandamus*, either to deliver the commission, or a copy of it from the record; and it only remains to be inquired,

Whether it can issue from this court.

The act to establish the judicial courts of the United States authorizes the supreme court "to issue writs of *mandamus*, in cases warranted by the principles and usages of law, to any courts appointed, or persons holding office, under the authority of the United States."

The secretary of state, being a person holding an office under the authority of the United States, is precisely within the letter of the description; and if this court is not authorized to issue a writ of *mandamus* to such an officer, it must be because the law is unconstitutional, and therefore absolutely incapable of conferring the authority, and assigning the duties which its words purport to confer and assign.

The constitution vests the whole judicial power of the United States in one supreme court, and such inferior courts as congress shall, from time to time, ordain and establish. This power is expressly extended to all cases arising under the laws of the United States; and, consequently, in some form, may be exercised over the present case; because the right claimed is given by a law of the United States.

In the distribution of this power it is declared that "the supreme court shall have original jurisdiction in all cases affecting ambassadors, other public ministers and consuls, and those in which a state shall be a party. In all other cases, the supreme court shall have appellate jurisdiction."

---

*A writ of *mandamus* is a binding directive, issued to individuals within the executive branch, that requires some action.

It has been insisted, at the bar, that as the original grant of jurisdiction, to the supreme and inferior courts, is general, and the clause, assigning original jurisdiction to the supreme court, contains no negative or restrictive words, the power remains to the legislature, to assign original jurisdiction to that court in other cases than those specified in the article which has been recited; provided those cases belong to the judicial power of the United States.

If it had been intended to leave it in the discretion of the legislature to apportion the judicial power between the supreme and inferior courts according to the will of that body, it would certainly have been useless to have proceeded further than to have defined the judicial power, and the tribunals in which it should be vested. The subsequent part of the section is mere surplusage, is entirely without meaning, if such is to be the construction. If congress remains at liberty to give this court appellate jurisdiction, where the constitution has declared their jurisdiction shall be original; and original jurisdiction where the constitution has declared it shall be appellate; the distribution of jurisdiction, made in the constitution, is form without substance.

Affirmative words are often, in their operations, negative of other objects than those affirmed; and in this case, a negative or exclusive sense must be given to them, or they have no operation at all.

It cannot be presumed that any clause in the constitution is intended to be without effect; and, therefore, such a construction is inadmissible, unless the words require it.

If the solicitude of the convention, respecting our peace with foreign powers, induced a provision that the supreme court should take original jurisdiction in cases which might be supposed to affect them; yet the clause would have proceeded no further than to provide for such cases, if no further restriction on the powers of congress had been intended. That they should have appellate jurisdiction in all other cases, with such exceptions as congress might make, is no restriction; unless the words be deemed exclusive of original jurisdiction. . . .

To enable this Court, then, to issue a *mandamus*, it must be shown to be an exercise of appellate jurisdiction, or to be necessary to enable them to exercise appellate jurisdiction. . . .

It is the essential criterion of appellate jurisdiction, that it revises and corrects the proceedings in a cause already instituted, and does not create that cause. Although, therefore, a *mandamus* may be directed to courts, yet to issue such a writ to an officer for the delivery of a paper, is in effect the same as to sustain an original action for that paper, and, therefore, seems not to belong to appellate, but to original jurisdiction. Neither is it necessary in such a case as this, to enable the court to exercise its appellate jurisdiction.

The authority, therefore, given to the supreme court, by the act establishing the judicial courts of the United States, to issue writs of *mandamus* to public officers, appears not to be warranted by the constitution; and it becomes necessary to inquire whether a jurisdiction so conferred can be exercised.

The question, whether an act, repugnant to the constitution, can become the law of the land, is a question deeply interesting to the United States; but, happily, not of an intricacy proportioned to its interest. It seems only necessary to recognise certain principles, supposed to have been long and well established, to decide it.

That the people have an original right to establish, for their future government, such principles as, in their opinion, shall most conduce to their own happiness is the basis on which the whole American fabric has been erected. The exercise of this original right is a very great exertion; nor can it, nor ought it, to be frequently repeated. The principles, therefore, so established, are deemed fundamental. And as the authority from which they proceed is supreme, and can seldom act, they are designed to be permanent.

This original and supreme will organizes the government, and assigns to different departments their respective powers. It may either stop here, or establish certain limits not to be transcended by those departments.

The government of the United States is of the latter description. The powers of the legislature are defined and limited; and that those limits may not be mistaken, or forgotten, the constitution is written. To what purpose are powers limited, and to what purpose is that limitation committed to writing, if these limits may, at any time, be passed by those intended to be restrained? The distinction between a government with limited and unlimited powers is abolished, if those limits do not confine the persons on whom they are imposed, and if acts prohibited and acts allowed, are of equal obligation. It is a proposition too plain to be contested, that the constitution controls any legislative act repugnant to it; or, that the legislature may alter the constitution by an ordinary act.

Between these alternatives there is no middle ground. The constitution is either a superior paramount law, unchangeable by ordinary means, or it is on a level with ordinary legislative acts, and, like other acts, is alterable when the legislature shall please to alter it.

If the former part of the alternative be true, then a legislative act contrary to the constitution is not law: if the latter part be true, then written constitutions are absurd attempts, on the part of the people, to limit a power in its own nature illimitable.

Certainly all those who have framed written constitutions contemplate them as forming the fundamental and paramount law of the nation, and, consequently, the theory of every such government must be, that an act of the legislature, repugnant to the constitution, is void.

This theory is essentially attached to a written constitution, and, is consequently, to be considered, by this court, as one of the fundamental principles of our society. It is not therefore to be lost sight of in the further consideration of this subject.

If an act of the legislature, repugnant to the constitution, is void, does it, notwithstanding its invalidity, bind the courts, and oblige them to give it ef-

fect? Or, in other words, though it be not law, does it constitute a rule as operative as if it was a law? This would be to overthrow in fact what was established
in theory; and would seem, at first view, an absurdity too gross to be insisted on.
It shall, however, receive a more attentive consideration.

It is emphatically the province and duty of the judicial department to say
what the law is. Those who apply the rule to particular cases, must of necessity
expound and interpret that rule. If two laws conflict with each other, the courts
must decide on the operation of each.

So if a law be in opposition to the constitution; if both the law and the constitution apply to a particular case, so that the court must either decide that
case conformably to the law, disregarding the constitution; or conformably to
the constitution, disregarding the law; the court must determine which of these
conflicting rules governs the case. This is of the very essence of judicial duty.

If, then, the courts are to regard the constitution, and the constitution is superior to any ordinary act of the legislature, the constitution, and not such ordinary act, must govern the case to which they both apply.

Those, then, who controvert the principle that the constitution is to be considered, in court, as a paramount law, are reduced to the necessity of maintaining that courts must close their eyes on the constitution, and see only the law.

This doctrine would subvert the very foundation of all written constitutions.
It would declare that an act which, according to the principles and theory of
our government, is entirely void, is yet, in practice, completely obligatory. It
would declare that if the legislature shall do what is expressly forbidden, such
act, notwithstanding the express prohibition, is in reality effectual. It would be
giving to the legislature a practical and real omnipotence, with the same breath
which professes to restrict their powers within narrow limits. It is prescribing
limits, and declaring that those limits may be passed at pleasure.

That it thus reduces to nothing what we have deemed the greatest improvement on political institutions, a written constitution, would of itself be sufficient, in America, where written constitutions have been viewed with so much
reverence, for rejecting the construction. But the peculiar expressions of the
constitution of the United States furnish additional arguments in favour of its
rejection.

The judicial power of the United States is extended to all cases arising under
the constitution.

Could it be the intention of those who gave this power, to say that in using it
the constitution should not be looked into? That a case arising under the constitution should be decided without examining the instrument under which it
arises?

This is too extravagant to be maintained.

In some cases, then, the constitution must be looked into by the judges. And
if they can open it at all, what part of it are they forbidden to read or to obey?

There are many other parts of the constitution which serve to illustrate this
subject.

It is declared that "no tax or duty shall be laid on articles exported from any state." Suppose a duty on the export of cotton, of tobacco, or of flour; and a suit instituted to recover it. Ought judgment to be rendered in such a case? Ought the judges to close their eyes on the constitution, and only see the law?

The constitution declares "that no bill of attainder or *ex post facto* law shall be passed."

If, however, such a bill should be passed, and a person should be prosecuted under it; must the court condemn to death those victims whom the constitution endeavours to preserve?

"No person," says the constitution, "shall be convicted of treason unless on the testimony of two witnesses to the same overt act, or on confession in open court."

Here the language of the constitution is addressed especially to the courts. It prescribes, directly for them, a rule of evidence not to be departed from. If the legislature should change that rule, and declare *one* witness, or a confession *out* of court, sufficient for conviction, must the constitutional principle yield to the legislative act?

From these, and many other selections which might be made, it is apparent, that the framers of the constitution contemplated that instrument as a rule for the government of *courts*, as well as of the legislature. . . .

It is also not entirely unworthy of observation, that in declaring what shall be the *supreme* law of the land, the *constitution* itself is first mentioned; and not the laws of the United States generally, but those only which shall be made in *pursuance* of the constitution have that rank.

Thus, the particular phraseology of the constitution of the United States confirms and strengthens the principle, supposed to be essential to all written constitutions, that a law repugnant to the constitution is void; and that *courts*, as well as other departments, are bound by that instrument.

Questions for Discussion

1. What was the precise legal issue at the core of *Marbury v. Madison*? Why is this case so important to the ultimate workings of the separation of powers?
2. Is it absolutely imperative that the Constitution be interpreted as the supreme law of the land? Why shouldn't the legislature's interpretation of what is constitutional be weighed equally?

13.3

What Am I? A Potted Plant?

Richard A. Posner

Since the 1960s, there has been a continuing political debate over the appropriate amount of discretion that appeals court judges and Supreme Court justices should exercise in interpreting the Constitution. Liberals have generally argued for substantial leeway, noting that the framers could not have anticipated many key contemporary policy debates, such as those about abortion or the regulation of nuclear plants. By and large, conservatives have made a case for less discretion and a more literal interpretation of the Constitution. Nevertheless, some liberals, such as the late Supreme Court justice Hugo Black, have adopted a literalist position, while some conservatives, such as Court of Appeals judge Richard A. Posner, have taken a more discretionary approach.

Here, Posner reacts to the strict constructionist or "legal formalist" view, labeling it virtually impossible to carry out. "Judges," he notes, "have been entrusted with making policy from the start." Posner endorses this notion in large part because of his tendency to approach legal reasoning from an economic perspective—one that has little, if any, grounding in the Constitution or the ideas of the framers. What is clear from his point of view is that all judges make policy and that both liberals and conservatives can benefit from expanded judicial discretion.

M‌any people, not all of conservative bent, believe that modern American courts are too aggressive, too "activist," too prone to substitute their own policy preferences for those of the elected branches of government. This may well be true. But some who complain of judicial activism espouse a view of law that is too narrow. And a good cause will not hallow a bad argument.

This point of view often is called "strict constructionism." A more precise term would be "legal formalism." A forceful polemic by Walter Berns in the

Richard A. Posner is a judge on the U.S. Court of Appeals for the Seventh Circuit and a senior lecturer at the University of Chicago Law School. He served as a mediator in an unsuccessful attempt to resolve the Justice Department's antitrust lawsuit against Microsoft.

Richard A. Posner, "What Am I? A Potted Plant?" *The New Republic* (September 28, 1997): 23–25. Reprinted by permission of *The New Republic*.

June 1987 issue of *Commentary*—"Government by Lawyers and Judges"—summarizes the formalist view well. Issues of the "public good" can "be decided legitimately only with the consent of the governed." Judges have no legitimate say about these issues. Their business is to address issues of private rights, that is, "to decide whether the right exists—in the Constitution or in a statute—and, if so, what it is; but at that point inquiry ceases." The judge may not use "discretion and the weighing of consequences" to arrive at his decisions and he may not create new rights. The Constitution is a source of rights, but only to the extent that it embodies "fundamental and clearly articulated principles of government." There must be no judicial creativity or "policy-making."

In short, there is a political sphere, where the people rule, and there is a domain of fixed rights, administered but not created or altered by judges. The first is the sphere of discretion, the second of application. Legislators make the law; judges find and apply it.

There has never been a time when the courts of the United States, state or federal, behaved consistently in accordance with this idea. Nor could they, for reasons rooted in the nature of law and legal institutions, in the limitations of human knowledge, and in the character of a political system.

"Questions about the public good" and "questions about private rights" are inseparable. The private right is conferred in order to promote the public good. So in deciding how broadly the right shall be interpreted, the court must consider the implications of its interpretation for the public good. For example, should an heir who murders his benefactor have a right to inherit from his victim? The answer depends, in part anyway, on the public good that results from discouraging murders. Almost the whole of so-called private law, such as property, contract, and tort law, is instrumental to the public end of obtaining the social advantages of free markets. Furthermore, most private law is common law—that is, law made by judges rather than by legislators or by constitution-framers. Judges have been entrusted with making policy from the start.

Often when deciding difficult questions of private rights courts have to weigh policy considerations. If a locomotive spews sparks that set a farmer's crops afire, has the railroad invaded the farmer's property right or does the railroad's ownership of its right of way implicitly include the right to emit sparks? If the railroad has such a right, shall it be conditioned on the railroad's taking reasonable precautions to minimize the danger of fire? If, instead, the farmer has the right, shall it be conditioned on his taking reasonable precautions? Such questions cannot be answered sensibly without considering the social consequences of alternative answers.

A second problem is that when a constitutional convention, a legislature, or a court promulgates a rule of law, it necessarily does so without full knowledge of the circumstances in which the rule might be invoked in the future. When the unforeseen circumstance arises—it might be the advent of the motor vehicle or of electronic surveillance, or a change in attitudes toward religion, race, and sexual propriety—a court asked to apply the rule must decide, in light of information not available to the promulgators of the rule, what the rule should mean in its new setting. That is a creative decision, involving discretion, the weighing of consequences, and, in short, a kind of legislative judgment—though, properly, one more confined than if the decision were being made by a real legislature. A court that decides, say, that copyright protection extends to the coloring of old black-and-white movies is making a creative decision, because the copyright laws do not mention colorization. It is not being lawless or usurpative merely because it is weighing consequences and exercising discretion.

Or if a court decides (as the Supreme Court has done in one of its less controversial modern rulings) that the Fourth Amendment's prohibition against unreasonable searches and seizures shall apply to wiretapping, even though no trespass is committed by wiretapping and hence no property right is invaded, the court is creating a new right and making policy. But in a situation not foreseen and expressly provided for by the Framers of the Constitution, a simple reading out of a policy judgment made by the Framers is impossible.

Even the most carefully drafted legislation has gaps. The Constitution, for example, does not say that the federal government has sovereign immunity—the right, traditionally enjoyed by all sovereign governments, not to be sued without its consent. Nevertheless the Supreme Court held that the federal government has sovereign immunity. Is this interpolation usurpative? The Federal Tort Claims Act, a law waiving sovereign immunity so citizens can sue the government, makes no exception for suits by members of the armed services who are injured through the negligence of their superiors. Nevertheless the Supreme Court has held that the act was not intended to provide soldiers with a remedy. The decision may be right or wrong, but it is not wrong just because it is creative. The 11th Amendment to the Constitution forbids a citizen of one state to sue "another" state in federal court without the consent of the defendant state. Does this mean that you can sue your own state in federal court without the state's consent? That's what the words seem to imply, but the Supreme Court has held that the 11th Amendment was intended to preserve the sovereign immunity of the states more broadly. The Court thought this was implied by the federalist system that the Constitution created. Again the Court may have been right or wrong, but it was not wrong just because it was creative.

Opposite the unrealistic picture of judges who apply law but never make it, Walter Berns hangs an unrealistic picture of a populist legislature that acts only "with the consent of the governed." Speaking for myself, I find that many of the political candidates whom I have voted for have failed to be elected and that those who have been elected have then proceeded to enact much legislation that did not have my consent. Given the effectiveness of interest groups in the political process, much of this legislation probably didn't have the consent of a majority of citizens. Politically, I feel more governed than self-governing. In considering whether to reduce constitutional safeguards to slight dimensions, we should be sure to have a realistic, not an idealized, picture of the legislative and executive branches of government, which would thereby be made more powerful than they are today.

To banish all discretion from the judicial process would indeed reduce the scope of constitutional rights. The framers of a constitution who want to make it a charter of liberties and not just a set of constitutive rules face a difficult choice. They can write specific provisions, and thereby doom their work to rapid obsolescence or irrelevance; or they can write general provisions, thereby delegating substantial discretion to the authoritative interpreters, who in our system are the judges. The U.S. Constitution is a mixture of specific and general provisions. Many of the specific provisions have stood the test of time amazingly well or have been amended without any great fuss. This is especially true of the rules establishing the structure and procedures of Congress. Most of the specific provisions creating rights, however, have fared poorly. Some have proved irksomely anachronistic—for example, the right to a jury trial in federal court in all cases at law if the stakes exceed $20. Others have become dangerously anachronistic, such as the right to bear arms. Some have even turned topsy-turvy, such as the provision for indictment by grand jury. The grand jury has become an instrument of prosecutorial investigation rather than a protection for the criminal suspect. If the Bill of Rights had consisted entirely of specific provisions, it would have aged very rapidly and would no longer be a significant constraint on the behavior of government officials.

Many provisions of the Constitution, however, are drafted in general terms. This creates flexibility in the face of unforeseen changes, but it also creates the possibility of multiple interpretations, and this possibility is an embarrassment for a theory of judicial legitimacy that denies that judges have any right to exercise discretion. A choice among semantically plausible interpretations of a text, in circumstances remote from those contemplated by its drafters, requires the exercise of discretion and the weighing of consequences. Reading is not a form of deduction; understanding requires a consideration of consequences. If I say, "I'll eat my hat," one reason that my listeners will "decode" this in nonliteral fashion is that I couldn't eat a hat if I tried. The broader principle, which applies to the Constitution as much as to a spoken utterance, is that if one possible interpretation of an ambiguous statement would entail absurd or terrible results, that is a good reason to adopt an alternative interpretation.

Even the decision to read the Constitution narrowly, and thereby "restrain" judicial interpretation, is not a decision that can be read directly from the text. The Constitution does not say, "Read me broadly," or, "Read me narrowly." That decision must be made as a matter of political theory, and will depend on such things as one's view of the springs of judicial legitimacy and of the relative competence of courts and legislatures in dealing with particular types of issues.

Consider the provision in the Sixth Amendment that "in all criminal prosecutions, the accused shall enjoy the right . . . to have the Assistance of Counsel for his defense." Read narrowly, this just means that the defendant can't be forbidden to retain counsel; if he can't afford counsel, or competent counsel, he is out of luck. Read broadly, it guarantees even the indigent the effective assistance of counsel; it becomes not just a negative right to be allowed to hire a lawyer but a positive right to demand the help of the government in financing one's defense. Either reading is compatible with the semantics of the provision, but the first better captures the specific intent of the Framers. At the time the Sixth Amendment was written, English law forbade a criminal defendant to have the assistance of counsel unless abstruse questions of law arose in his case. The Framers wanted to do away with this prohibition. But, more broadly, they wanted to give criminal defendants protection against being railroaded. When they wrote, government could not afford, or at least did not think it could afford, to hire lawyers for indigent criminal defendants. Moreover, criminal trials were short and simple, so it was not ridiculous to expect a person to defend himself without a lawyer if he couldn't afford to hire one. Today the situation is different. Not only can the society easily afford to supply lawyers to poor people charged with crimes, but modern criminal law and procedure are so complicated that an unrepresented defendant will usually be at a great disadvantage.

I do not know whether Professor Berns thinks the Supreme Court was usurping legislative power when it held in the *Gideon* case [selection 3.3] that a poor person has a right to the assistance of counsel at the state's expense. But his article does make clear his view that the Supreme Court should not have invalidated racial segregation in public schools. Reading the words of the 14th Amendment in the narrowest possible manner in order to minimize judicial discretion, and noting the absence of evidence that the Framers wanted to eliminate segregation, Berns argues that "equal protection of the laws" just means non-discriminatory enforcement of whatever laws are enacted, even if the laws themselves are discriminatory. He calls the plausible empirical proposition that "separate educational facilities are inherently unequal" "a logical absurdity."

On Berns's reading, the promulgation of the equal protection clause was a trivial gesture at giving the recently freed slaves (and other blacks, whose status at the time was little better than that of serfs) political equality with whites, since the clause in his view forbids the denial of that equality only by executive officers. The state may not withdraw police protection from blacks (unless by legislation?) but it may forbid them to sit next to whites on buses. This is a possible reading of the 14th Amendment but not an inevitable one, unless judges must always interpret the Constitution as denying them the power to exercise judgment.

No one really believes this. Everyone professionally connected with law knows that, in Oliver Wendell Holmes's famous expression, judges legislate "interstitially," which is to say they make law, only more cautiously, more slowly, and in more principled, less partisan, fashion than legislators.* The attempt to deny this truism entangles "strict constructionists" in contradictions. Berns says

---

*Oliver Wendell Holmes (1841–1935) served first on the Massachusetts Supreme Court and then on the U.S. Supreme Court between 1882 and 1932. He was labeled "the Great Dissenter," and many of Holmes's minority opinions became the fodder for subsequent Court majority reasoning.

both that judges can enforce only "clearly articulated principles" and that they may invalidate unconstitutional laws. But the power to do this is not "articulated" in the Constitution; it is merely implicit in it. He believes that the courts have been wrong to interpret the First Amendment as protecting the publication of foul language in school newspapers, yet the words "freedom of speech, or of the press" do not appear to exclude foul language in school newspapers. Berns says he deduces his conclusion from the principle that expression, to be within the scope of the First Amendment, must be related to representative government. Where did he get that principle from? He didn't read it in the Constitution.

The First Amendment also forbids Congress to make laws "respecting an establishment of religion." Berns says this doesn't mean that Congress "must be neutral between religion and irreligion." But the words will bear that meaning, so how does he decide they should be given a different meaning? By appealing to Tocqueville's opinion of the importance of religion in a democratic society. In short, the correct basis for decision is the consequence of the decision for democracy. Yet consequences are not—in the strict constructionist view—a fit thing for courts to consider. Berns even expresses regret that the modern Supreme Court is oblivious to Tocqueville's opinion "of the importance of the woman . . . whose chastity as a young girl is protected not only by religion but by an education that limits her 'imagination.' " A court that took such opinions into account would be engaged in aggressively consequentialist thinking rather than in strict construction.

The liberal judicial activists may be imprudent and misguided in their efforts to enact the liberal political agenda into constitutional law, but it is no use pretending that what they are doing is not interpretation but "deconstruction," not law but politics, because it involves the exercise of discretion and a concern with consequences and because it reaches results not foreseen 200 years ago. It may be bad law because it lacks firm moorings in constitutional text, or structure, or history, or consensus, or other legitimate sources of constitutional law, or because it is reckless of consequences, or because it oversimplifies difficult moral and political questions. But it is not bad law, or no law, just because it violates the tenets of strict construction.

Questions for Discussion

1. Can the notion of "original intent" be defended as a serious legal doctrine according to Posner? Why not?
2. Do all judges make policy at least part of the time?
3. Posner has frequently been mentioned as a prospective Supreme Court nominee. Do you think the sentiments articulated in this selection make his nomination and confirmation more or less likely? Why?

13.4

Sandra's Day: Why the Rehnquist Court Has Been the O'Connor Court, and How to Replace Her (Should It Come to That)

Ramesh Ponnuru

Supreme Court justices can exercise power in any number of ways. They can command powerful majorities, as did Chief Justice Earl Warren in the 1950s and 1960s; they can invent new interpretations of old issues, to the point of creating new "rights," as did William O. Douglas with the unarticulated "right to privacy" (see selection 3.4). Oliver Wendell Holmes gained prominence as the "Great Dissenter" for his opinions as a member of the Court's minority, a role not uncommon to many articulate, if outvoted, justices.

Other justices have power thrust upon them, in that they represent a middle position on a sharply divided Court. So it has been for Sandra Day O'Connor for much of her career. Appointed in 1981 by President Ronald Reagan, the conservative O'Connor has risen to prominence since the early 1990s, when the current conservative-moderate split emerged. There have been no new justices since 1994, so O'Connor's central position has afforded her an extended opportunity to influence the Court. In this article, written for the conservative *National Review*, Ramesh Ponnuru charts O'Connor's course and analyzes her role in the Court's willingness both to take on big issues (federalism) and often move in small increments. In the end, she sees O'Connor's swing vote and fact-based approach to jurisprudence as defining the contemporary Court.

Conservatives have never much cared for Justice Sandra Day O'Connor. They viewed her nomination to the Supreme Court as the result of Ronald Reagan's ill-advised, because gratuitous, 1980 campaign pledge to appoint the first female justice. During her confirmation hearings in 1981, some conservatives argued that her record as a state legislator in Arizona made

Ramesh Ponnuru is a senior editor for *National Review*.

Ramesh Ponnuru, "Sandra's Day: Why the Rehnquist Court Has Been the O'Connor Court, and How to Replace Her (Should It Come to That)," *National Review* (June 30, 2003), 35–37. © 2003 by National Review, Inc., 215 Lexington Avenue, New York, NY 10016. Reprinted by permission.

it unlikely that she would vote against *Roe v. Wade*. Her subsequent votes confirmed that suspicion: She reaffirmed *Roe* in *Planned Parenthood v. Casey* (1992) and even divined a kind of constitutional right to partial-birth abortion in *Stenberg v. Carhart* (2000). Conservative activists tend to regard her as a "moderate," or even "liberal," justice, and say that President Bush should avoid appointing another justice like her.

The standard conservative picture of Justice O'Connor is, at best, an over-simplification. She is, in truth, both better and worse than they think she is. Some conservative Court-watchers fear that the Right's confusion could cost it dearly if there is a nomination fight. . . .

The conservative case for O'Connor is that she has voted reasonably well. While she has become a reliable vote for social liberalism at the Court, she has also sided with conservatives on many occasions. The conservative heroes on the Court have been Clarence Thomas, Antonin Scalia, and, to a lesser extent, the chief justice, William Rehnquist. O'Connor has generally voted with them on racial preferences, the death penalty, criminal procedure, and other issues. She also sided with them in *Bush v. Gore*.

The Rehnquist Court is known for two great doctrinal innovations. Instead of continuing to insist on strict secularism, the Court now merely requires governmental neutrality among religions. The Court has also embarked on a so-called "federalism revolution" that limits the power of Congress while protecting the prerogatives of the states. O'Connor has played a leading role in both areas. Eugene Volokh, a law professor at UCLA who once clerked for her, concludes, "She's a woman of the center-right on a lot of the really important issues that have come before the Supreme Court."

Have conservatives damaged their own cause by taking an excessively negative view of O'Connor? Washington is rife with speculation that Rehnquist, O'Connor, or both will retire [soon]. In one scenario, Rehnquist leaves and Bush elevates O'Connor to chief justice. If O'Connor leaves, however, the conservatives may have lowered the bar for her replacement. Alberto Gonzales, the White House counsel, is often mentioned as a potential Bush nominee. He is a moderate, and possibly to the left of O'Connor on some issues, such as racial preferences. But so hostile are conservatives to O'Connor that the White House could tell them that he is an improvement. If, on the other hand, Bush nominates a true-blue (true-red?)* conservative to replace O'Connor, liberals will say that he is lifting the Court far to the right—and by exaggerating her liberalism, the conservatives will have lent that claim credibility.

The difficulty conservatives have in getting a fix on O'Connor is a function of the bifurcation in their view of the Supreme Court. Conservative lawyers and law professors care a lot about issues such as affirmative action and federal-

---

*The color reference here address the breakdown of the U.S. political map into red (GOP) and blue (Democratic) areas, as presented in television coverage.

ism, on which O'Connor often votes the way they want. But social conservatives are the only mass constituency on the right that pays attention to the Court; and while they are usually allied with the conservative legal community, their priorities are different. The activists tend to disdain O'Connor because of her votes on abortion and, to a lesser extent, gay rights. The conservative lawyers tend to disagree with her decisions on those issues, but are less hostile to her because of her other votes. Another way of saying this is that how happy a conservative is with Justice O'Connor is a reflection on how happy he is with the Rehnquist Court.

Actually, the O'Connor Court might be a better label for it. Justice O'Connor gets her way more often than the chief justice does. As the "swing vote" on the Court, O'Connor is in the majority more often than any of her colleagues. Legal briefs in important cases are written to appeal, above all, to her. As a result of her position at the center of the Court, she can be a powerful voice for conservatives when she is with them. When the Court upheld school choice [in 2002], it was her unqualified endorsement of the decision in a concurring opinion, as much as the majority opinion itself, that conferred solidity to the ruling. But it is disturbing to reflect that, given the power the Supreme Court has assumed, O'Connor has become the most powerful woman in America. Excluding foreign policy, indeed, one could even say that she is the most powerful person in America.

O'Connor's style of judging has increased that power. The justice is famous for issuing narrow rulings that turn on the particular facts of the case rather than rulings that articulate broad principles. Applying this common-law approach to constitutional cases preserves her freedom of action in future cases. But it also, and necessarily, undermines the predictability of the law and aggrandizes the judicial role. This is the principal critique that conservative lawyers—including Justice Scalia, in many opinions—make of O'Connor. She may often vote with Scalia and Thomas, says a former Rehnquist clerk, but "she is not driven by . . . legal arguments in the sense that a conservative jurist should be."

In the 1995 *Adarand* case, for example—concerning racial preferences in federal contracting—O'Connor voted with the conservatives. But she refused to say that racial preferences in federal contracting were always impermissible, or to expound some other rule that made it clear which preferences were okay. Instead she said that such preferences would receive "strict scrutiny" from the Court. [See the discussion of affirmative action in Chapter 3.]

"Strict scrutiny" is the highest degree of scrutiny in the Court's equal-protection jurisprudence; traditionally, a legislative or bureaucratic classification is subjected to strict scrutiny as a prelude to being found impermissible. Justice O'Connor, however, went out of her way to explain that while the program at issue in the case had to go, in future cases strict scrutiny would not necessarily be "fatal in fact." So which preferences should stay and which go? The Clinton administration's response to this uncertain guidance was to preserve all existing federal preference programs except the one at issue and another that fell in court. To this day the Court's position with regard to other contracting preferences remains unclear.

O'Connor has ruled (or rather not ruled) similarly in racial-gerrymandering cases. Jeffrey Rosen, an influential legal commentator, has said that the upshot of those cases is that congressional district lines cannot be drawn with regard to race if the results offend Justice O'Connor's aesthetic sensibilities. Or take abortion. From her earliest days on the Court, O'Connor has argued that restrictions should be upheld so long as they do not impose an "undue burden" on the right to procure abortions. In *Casey*, Justices O'Connor, Anthony Kennedy, and David Souter adopted this standard for the Court. It is a standard, not a rule—in the parlance of the law profs—because its application depends on subjective judgments. In *Stenberg*, Justice O'Connor and four of her colleagues decided that a ban on partial-birth abortion imposed an "undue burden" on the abortion right; Justice Kennedy apparently felt that it was a "due burden," since he dissented from the judgment. Justice Scalia, also in dissent, noted that the only effect of the standard was to turn the Supreme Court into a veto board for abortion regulations.

In *Bush* v. *Gore*, the Court said that the doctrine underlying its decision was "limited to the present circumstances" and would not govern future cases. Critics have seized on the line as the epitome of the decision's lawlessness. But the Court has been making good-for-one-ticket-only decisions for some time, thanks in large part to O'Connor. Volokh, the former clerk for O'Connor, notes that in some areas of the law she has been willing to defend "bright-line rules"* and that other justices also adopt vague, subjective standards on some occasions. This observation should be taken as a qualification, rather than a refutation, of a valid generalization: Justice O'Connor practices "one case at a time" judging more often, and with greater consequence, than her colleagues.

Conservative lawyers consider the federalism revolution the most valuable part of the Rehnquist Court's legacy. O'Connor's record on federalism is not without the ambiguities one would expect from the rest of her jurisprudence. She has sometimes held the revolution back—as in *U.S.* v. *Lopez*, a 1995 case that is something of a landmark. The Constitution gives Congress the power to regulate commerce among the states. In *Lopez*, the Court ruled that the Gun-Free School Zones Act was not a legitimate exercise of this authority. The Court had not imposed a limit on congressional power under the commerce clause in six decades. O'Connor, the swing vote, joined a concurring opinion that appeared to weaken the Court's conclusion and left the law unsettled.

Notwithstanding such episodes, O'Connor can fairly be said to have not only participated in but even led the revolution. Her strong dissent from the federal drinking-age case in 1987 was a harbinger of it. And one of its signal accomplishments was the doctrine, announced by Justice O'Connor in *Gregory* v. *Ashcroft* (1991), that federal law will not be read to compromise the sover-

---

*So-called bright-line rules (or declarative rules) state that something must always be true.

eignty of state governments unless the law includes a clear statement to that effect.

Unfortunately, the Court's federalism revolution isn't all it's cracked up to be by legal conservatives. Michael Greve of the American Enterprise Institute has noted that the Court's federalist decisions partake of romanticism about "states' rights." These decisions contain many references to the "dignity" of states. The Court's assumption is that it can protect federalism by protecting state governments. As a consequence, the Court has been inattentive to the "horizontal" dimension of federalism: to the constitutional provisions that promote competition and accountability among state governments by constraining their power. If Eliot Spitzer wants to nationalize American industries from the New York attorney general's office, the Supreme Court is not going to stop him. The O'Connor Court's federalism is not that of the Founders.

How legal conservatives convinced themselves that federalism could be restored by the federal judiciary is one of the minor mysteries of the age. The O'Connor Court is itself a significant offender against federalism, just as its predecessors, the Warren and Burger courts, were. When the voters of Colorado passed an amendment to the state constitution opposing certain gay-rights laws, the Court's response was to slap them down. On abortion, the Court—O'Connor very much included—is "hysterically nationalist," as Robert Nagel argues in *The Implosion of American Federalism*. When seen against this backdrop, the "federalism revolution" starts to look less like a readjustment of state-federal relations and more like a transfer of power from Congress to the Court.

A highly developed institutional amour propre* may be the most striking feature of the O'Connor Court. It is present in the plurality opinion in *Casey*, which O'Connor joined. The *Casey* Court reaffirmed *Roe* in large part out of a reluctance to give in to the Court's critics. Appearing to capitulate would compromise the Court's ability to "speak before all others" for the nation's constitutional ideals. It is this self-regard that brings together O'Connor's penchant for finicky edicts, the O'Connor Court's marked reluctance to overturn the activist precedents of the Warren and Burger courts, the Court's racial cases, and its intervention in the 2000 election. There is an authoritarian streak in this jurisprudence that Justice O'Connor does not, in all likelihood, perceive.

Should O'Connor either retire or be nominated to chief justice, fixing her position in the conservative-liberal spectrum more precisely may be important in the political battles that follow. But her most important legacy is not as a liberal, moderate, or conservative justice. It might be best expressed in the title of Kenneth Starr's book on the O'Connor Court—*First Among Equals*—except that the title is two words too long. There is little evidence that O'Connor or her Court regards other governmental authorities as equals.

Amour propre means "ego," roughly speaking.

Questions for Discussion

1. How does Justice O'Connor's relative caution and willingness to rule on narrow legal grounds affect the power of the Court in American politics?
2. Justice O'Connor was the presiding officer of the Arizona state senate. Has her background as a legislator contributed to her approach to judicial decision making? How so?

Chapter 14

Policymaking

The policymaking process brings together almost all of the elements in the structure of American politics. We can think of the Constitution as providing a framework within which policies are made—a framework that does not guarantee speedy action or governmental responsiveness to the wishes of the citizens. In addition, public opinion, as expressed through elections or interpreted in the media, is a basic element in policy formulation, yet it is often subject to change and adaptation. After all, presidents and legislators work diligently to generate public support for their own proposals.

The constitutional relationships outlined by the separation of powers and federalism impose serious limitations on policymakers. For example, education has traditionally been a state and local function in the United States; among national institutions, the Supreme Court, with its desegregation rulings, has affected local school districts more than the Congress or the president has.

Beyond these basic rules of the game, contemporary policymaking takes place within the context of a large and growing governmental establishment. Given an annual budget of roughly $2.4 trillion (an almost unimaginable sum), the permanent government of the federal bureaucracy is difficult for elected officials to control. In addition, the government extends its reach by providing guarantees in potentially risky undertakings (the banking industry, student loans, crop damage). The growth of government has produced two other hallmarks of contemporary policymaking: (1) the extensive use of regulation, which has generated substantial debate, and (2) the influence of annual budgetary actions on almost all domestic policy decisions.

Traditionally, students of public policy have focused much of their attention on the legislature and its decisions. But as the reach of government has grown and problems such as environmental pollution have become increasingly complex, Congress has delegated more and more policymaking authority to the bureaucracy and to independent agencies such as the Food and Drug Administration. In terms of the gross number of policies, regulations far outstrip legislation. Both Congress and the president have sought to control this proliferation. Congress has enacted large numbers of legislative veto provisions, which gave it the opportunity to review various regulations, but in 1983 the Supreme Court declared these vetoes an unconstitutional violation of the executive's authority under the separation of powers. The president has had greater success in monitoring regulation. Through the Office of Management and Budget, the executive reviews regulations to determine their consistency with existing policies.

Since the late 1970s, movements toward less new regulation and substantial deregulation have gained ground. Although the Reagan administration generally reduced the number of new regulations, the first moves toward deregulation came in the Carter administration, when economist Alfred Kahn, then chairman of the Civil Aeronautics Board (CAB), began action to curtail regulations within the airline industry. In the end, Kahn succeeded in eliminating the CAB. Increased fare competition among airlines was one short-term result of deregulation, although in the 1990s airline consolidation and higher fares seemed the order of the day. Still, as Pietro S. Nivola argues (in selection 14.2), despite high-profile deregulation, the overall impact of regulation for the society at large has steadily increased, much to the benefit of attorneys and targeted interests.

Although deregulation proved a mixed bag in the 1990s, two major governmental initiatives—eliminating budget deficits and reducing overall federal debt—were more successful. Building on an important 1990 budget deal, President Clinton adopted the elimination of budget deficits as a centerpiece of his economic planning. A second budget deal in 1993 and a strong economy allowed the budget deficit to decrease from $290 billion in 1992 to $200 billion-plus in 2001. Yet, with a post-2000 economic slump, the costs associated with terrorism and the Iraq war, as well as a decline in revenues due to tax cuts, the federal budget *deficit* grew to more than $500 billion in 2004.

No set of readings can adequately capture the diversity of domestic policymaking. In an excerpt from her book *Policy Paradox,* Deborah Stone describes how narratives—essentially stories—can define policy problems and possible solutions (selection 14.1). In a policymaking environment that is complex and filled to the brim with information from various sources, decision makers need stories to understand, and to help the public understand, how policies operate. Ironically, as we are faced with more and more information, the more valuable we will find narratives in allowing us to appear to understand complicated policies that respond to difficult problems like telecommunications reform or the impact of environmental regulations.

Of course, narratives can become obstructions to actual understanding. So it may be with welfare reform, as Christopher Jencks argues in selection 14.3. Few policy debates have been more bitterly fought than welfare reform, which President Bill Clinton first opposed and then signed in 1996. Enacted in the midst of a booming economy, welfare reform—requiring work from recipients, even single mothers—appeared to work. Jencks approaches the early success of the program with caution, yet he offers advice to those liberals who might continue to reject the work provisions out of hand. On occasion, stories must give way to facts, even when they are inconvenient.

The last two selections move into foreign policy, which has received increasing amounts of attention in the wake of 9/11. Journalist Gregg Easterbrook offers in selection 14.4 an optimistic perspective on the impact of past foreign aid and makes the case for even more, as a relatively inexpensive investment for both the improvement of world conditions and the enhanced security of the United States. Finally, Ivo H. Daalder and James M. Lindsay make the argument in selection 14.5 that President George W. Bush, assisted by, but not dominated by, his advisors, has produced a revolution in American foreign policy. In particular, the United States has proven willing to act on its own, and in a preemptive manner, when its safety may be threatened. This major shift will likely define the Bush presidency and will almost certainly alter America's relations with most other countries around the globe.

Stories

Deborah Stone

The context of policymaking in American politics has become increasingly complex over the past forty years. The government and its often overlapping policies have grown steadily; regulations have increased; new rights have been created (by, for example, the Americans with Disabilities Act). And the number of interest groups has kept pace (see Chapter 9). Moreover, legislators, executives, and administrators are deluged with information—from the press, from organized interests, from think tanks, and increasingly from citizens using the Internet. In this "data smog" both decision makers and citizens must try to make sense of an almost incomprehensible world.

Although economists and some political scientists would willingly see the world in simplified economic terms, such simplification does not direct much policymaking (or explanations of policy decisions). Rather, as Deborah Stone points out, we often rely on stories to help us understand broad issues. In this selection, Stone briefly notes two common story lines that are used to justify decisions first to consider a certain problem and then to act on it. These "stories of decline" and "stories of control" are narratives used over and over in the discussion of why a certain issue needs to be addressed by government action. Data and information are included in these stories, but their power comes not from the information but from the construction of the stories themselves. And we may often enact policies in response that make little economic sense or do not improve the quality of societal life. Nevertheless, the narratives create their own realities that virtually demand some governmental response.

D efinitions of policy problems usually have narrative structure; that is, they are stories with a beginning, a middle, and an end, involving some change or transformation. They have heroes and villains and innocent victims, and they pit the forces of evil against the forces of good. The story line in policy writing is often hidden, but one should not be thwarted by the surface

Deborah Stone is the David R. Pokross Professor of Law and Social Policy at Brandeis University.
From *Policy Paradox: The Art of Political Decision Making* by Deborah Stone. Copyright © 1997, 1998 by Deborah Stone. Used by permission of W. W. Norton & Company, Inc.

details from searching for the underlying story. Often what appears as conflict over details is really disagreement about the fundamental story.

Two broad story lines are particularly prevalent in policy politics. One is a *story of decline*, not unlike the biblical story of the expulsion from paradise. It runs like this: "In the beginning, things were pretty good. But they got worse. In fact, right now, they are nearly intolerable. Something must be done." This story usually ends with a prediction of crisis—there will be some kind of breakdown, collapse, or doom—and a proposal for some steps to avoid the crisis. The proposal might even take the form of a warning: Unless such-and-such is done, disaster will follow.

The story of decline almost always begins with a recitation of facts or figures purporting to show that things have gotten worse. Poverty rates are rising, crime rates are higher, import penetration in U.S. markets is greater, environmental quality is worse—you have heard these all before. What gives this story dramatic tension is the assumption, sometimes stated and sometimes implicit, that things were once better than they are now, and that the change for the worse causes or will soon cause suffering. . . .

The story of decline has several variations. The *stymied progress story* runs like this: "In the beginning things were terrible. Then things got better, thanks to a certain someone. But now somebody or something is interfering with our hero, so things are going to get terrible again." This is the story told by every group that wants to resist regulation. In the 1970s and 1980s, the American Medical Association, fighting government cost-containment efforts, reminded us about the days of plagues, tuberculosis, and high infant mortality, and warned that government restrictions on the profession would undo all the progress doctors had brought us. Biotechnology firms, through their trade association known as "BIO," told a very similar story to fight President Clinton's medical cost-containment plans in the 1990s: biotechnology had brought us miracle medicine, but Clinton's planned regulation and price controls threatened the very survival of the nascent industry.[1] Manufacturing concerns, such as automakers, steel companies, and textile firms, tell a story of how minimum wage legislation, mandatory health benefits, and occupational safety regulations threaten to destroy America's once-preeminent position in the world economy. The CIA tells us that restrictions on its operating methods prevent it from maintaining the security it once could provide, and the Pentagon tells how budget constraints have undermined our once-dominant military position.

Another variant of the decline story is the *change-is-only-an-illusion* story. It runs like this: "You always thought things were getting worse (or better). But you were wrong. Let me show you some evidence that things are in fact going in the opposite direction. Decline (or improvement) was an illusion." Examples of the revisionist story are everywhere. Medical researchers tell us that the improved survival rates for cancer patients are really an artifact of measurement; it is only because we can now diagnose cancer at earlier stages that patients appear to live longer.[2] Child abuse (or rape or wife-battering) is not really on the rise; it only appears to have increased because we have more public awareness, more legislation, and more reporting.

The other broad type of narrative in policy analysis is the *story of helplessness and control*. It usually runs like this: "The situation is bad. We have always believed that the situation was out of our control, something we had to accept but could not influence. Now, however, let me show you that in fact we can control things." Stories about control are always gripping because they speak to the fundamental problem of liberty—to what extent do we control our own life conditions and destinies? Stories that purport to tell us of less control are always threatening, and ones that promise more are always heartening.

Much of the analysis in the areas of social policy, health and safety, and environment is a story of control. What had formerly appeared to be "accidental," "random," "a twist of fate," or "natural" is now alleged to be amenable to change through human agency. For example, much modern economic policy—the use of government fiscal and monetary tools to stabilize fluctuations in the economy—is based on a grand story of control. In the 1930s, when national economies had lurched into rampant inflation and disastrous depressions, they seemed to behave more like the weather than like social institutions. Lord Keynes* wrote a highly influential treatise whose central premise was that seemingly random fluctuations in economies are really manageable through government manipulation of spending and money supply.[3] The story of control governs in a vastly different policy area—public health—as well. Cancer, previously thought to strike victims unpredictably, now turns out to be related to diet, smoking, and chemicals—all things humans can control. Increasingly, cancer is linked to mutant genes, and though we cannot control our genes, the knowledge of genetic contributions to cancer can help us target screening and prevention programs, and may eventually help design genetically based therapies. Stories that move us from the realm of fate to the realm of control are always hopeful, and through their hope they invoke our support.

A common twist on the control story is the *conspiracy*. Its plot moves us from the realm of fate to the realm of control, but it claims to show that all along control has been in the hands of a few who have used it to their benefit and concealed it from the rest of us. Ralph Nader's famous crusade against automobile manufacturers was a story that converted car accidents into events controllable through the design of cars, and even willingly accepted by automakers. Advocates of industrial policy tell a story in which unemployment, thought to be intractable, is actually caused by "capital strike" (businessmen refuse to invest in new plants and ventures) and "capital flight" (businesses invest their capital in other regions or other countries). Conspiracy stories always reveal that harm has been deliberately caused or knowingly tolerated, and so evoke

---

*John Maynard Keynes's theories of state intervention in the economy dominated governmental policies and economic theories from the Great Depression until the Reagan-Thatcher era of the 1980s.

horror and moral condemnation. Their ending always takes the form of a call to wrest control from the few who benefit at the expense of the many.

Another variant of the control story is the *blame-the-victim* story.[4] It, too, moves us from the realm of fate to the realm of control, but locates control in the very people who suffer the problem. In one recent analysis of homelessness, "it was the fact that unskilled women not only married less but continued to have children that pushed more of them into the streets."[5] Homelessness, in this view, is the result of women's knowing choice between two alternatives:

> Few unskilled women can earn enough to support a family on their own. For many, therefore, the choices were stark. They could work, refrain from having children and barely avoid poverty, or they could not work, have children, collect welfare and live in extreme poverty. Many became mothers even though this meant extreme poverty.[6]

There are many versions of the blame-the-victim story. The poor are poor because they seek instant pleasures instead of investing in their own futures, or because they choose to live off the dole rather than work. Third World countries are poor because they borrow too eagerly and allow their citizens to live too extravagantly. The sick are sick because they overeat, consume unhealthy foods, smoke, and don't exercise. Women are raped because they "ask for it." Workers succumb to occupational diseases and injuries because they refuse to wear protective gear or to act with caution. Just as the conspiracy story always ends with a call to the many to rise up against the few, the blame-the-victim story always ends with an exhortation to the few (the victims) to reform their own behavior in order to avoid the problem.

What all these stories of control have in common is their assertion that there is choice. The choice may belong to society as a whole, to certain elites, or to victims, but the drama in the story is always achieved by the conversion of a fact of nature into a deliberate human decision. Stories of control offer hope, just as stories of decline foster anxiety and despair. The two stories are often woven together, with the story of decline serving as the stage setting and the impetus for the story of control. The story of decline is meant to warn us of suffering and motivate us to seize control.

Notes

1. "BIO" stands for Biotechnology Industry Organization. See Peter H. Stone, "Lost Cause," *National Journal*, Sept. 17, 1994, p. 2133.
2. Alvan R. Feinstein et al., "The Will Rogers Phenomenon: Stage Migration and New Diagnostic Techniques as a Source of Misleading Statistics for Survival in Cancer," *New England Journal of Medicine* 312, no. 25 (June 20, 1985): 1604–8.
3. John Maynard Keynes, *The General Theory of Employment, Interest and Money* (New York: Harcourt & Brace, 1936).
4. The phrase became a byword in social science after William Ryan's *Blaming the Victim* (New York: Random House, 1971).

5. Christopher Jencks, *The Homeless* (Cambridge, Mass.: Harvard University Press, 1994), p. 58.
6. Christopher Jencks, "The Homeless," *New York Review of Books*, April 21, 1994, p. 25.

Questions for Discussion

1. Relate Deborah Stone's discussion of "stories" to the other selections in this chapter. Why does the use of stories to think through complex issues seem so attractive?

2. Who gets to tell the stories that Stone alludes to: the public, the president, members of Congress, lobbyists, the media? How is the politics of getting our attention different from the politics of affecting decisions?

 14.2

Regulation: The New Pork Barrel

Pietro S. Nivola

Since the deregulation of air travel set off a spate of similar actions in banking, telecommunications, and other fields, the conventional wisdom has been that the United States has become a less highly regulated society. At the same time, although "pork" continues to be distributed in the legislative process, the conventional wisdom holds that there is less governmental "pork" than in years gone by. Regulations continue to be written, however, as legislators and administrators attack social ills ranging from toxic waste to deaths in automobile accidents. What has gone largely unnoticed, at least by the general public, is that many regulations confer benefits on particular groups (and costs on many others). In other words, "pork" lurking under the cover of "good policy" decisions may lessen the cost-effectiveness of policies.

Pietro S. Nivola is a senior fellow in the Brookings Governmental Studies program.

"Regulation: The New Pork Barrell" by Pietro S. Nivola, from *The Brookings Review,* Winter 1998, pp. 6–9. Reprinted by permission from The Brookings Institution.

In this selection, Brookings Institution scholar Pietro S. Nivola argues that many regulatory policies cost the government little or nothing but cost society at large a great deal, and he points out that these dispersed costs often funnel specific benefits to particular interests within society. The Superfund law, for example, has generated huge costs and substantial profits without doing much for the environment. Nivola recommends following the money to see who wins and who loses when the government decides to regulate an activity or require that certain standards be met. Not always, but often, the costs to society are substantial, and particular groups benefit from the regulatory requirements. The source of this type of "pork" may not be the old pork barrel from which legislators distributed benefits to their friends and supporters, but it does reflect a kind of politics that benefits organized interests (such as the waste disposal community) but does little for society at large (such as to improve environmental quality).

A s the federal government's discretionary spending in the 1990s has become less lavish, so has the supply of old-fashioned lard in the U.S. budget. But if you think this means the era of big government is over, think again. Another pork barrel is burgeoning. Along with preferential micromanagement of the tax code, the bacon these days takes the form of unfunded mandates and regulatory programs and of public facilitation of private lawsuits.

Figure 1 tells most of the story. Led by robust military budgets during the late 1970s and the 1980s, discretionary spending increased. Until 1988 the estimated costs associated with federal regulatory activities declined in constant dollars as the economy realized tens of billions in savings from deregulation of the transportation and energy industries and from the Reagan administration's concerted efforts to curb costly new regulations. Afterward, however, regulatory costs turned up sharply and have been on the rise ever since. A profusion of new rules and legal liabilities increasingly bore down on business decisions about products, payrolls, and personnel practices. By the mid-1990s these costs were approaching $700 billion annually—a sum greater than the entire national output of Canada.

Explanations

Whatever else explains this trend, surely it demonstrates that fiscal constraints have not limited the ingenuity of politicians and their clients. Policies that are barely visible on the budget books can still intervene massively on behalf of special interests—and can do so, conveniently, without worsening the deficit or imposing transparent tax increases.

For instance, rules that have encouraged the use of ethanol (a fuel made from corn) are a kind of pork for corn farmers, only less obvious than, say, appropriating millions for irrigation projects in Corn Belt states. Often costing billions of dollars per cancer prevented, the Superfund law to remove carcinogenic toxins from waste dumps is charging society a small fortune. But Superfund's congressional appropriation is suitably modest, and the program is a gravy train for particular groups, like the thousands of lawyers engaged in cleanup litigation. Similarly, antidumping provisions in the trade laws, devised to regulate "unfair" foreign price competition, require small budgetary outlays to administer. At times, however, these regulations force consumers to pay markedly higher prices to protect a handful of domestic companies. The practice of crafting protections and preferences for selected groups in the name of civil rights is a relatively low-budget operation too. But this regulatory regime nonetheless reaches deep into the private sector, dispensing rewards to the regime's extensive vested interests. There is no shortage of examples of Washington's off-budget spoils system.

Though the regulatory pork barrel frequently serves well-organized constituencies, its scope tends to be broader than the traditional treats (a new post office here, a new road or sewer there) that members of Congress offered to their districts. In contemporary American politics, this difference is an added

Figure 1

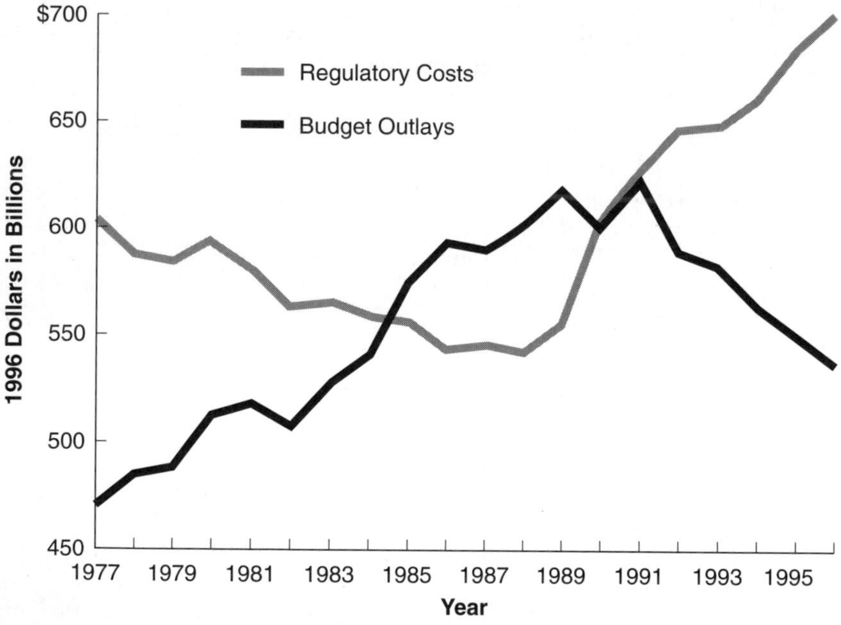

Comparison of Federal Regulatory Costs and Discretionary Budget Outlays, 1977–1996

advantage for members of Congress who need increasingly to curry favor with *national* lobbies and pressure groups that provide valuable political backing. The pattern of influence and obligations is reflected in congressional campaign finance. Whereas candidates in House elections, for example, used to rely for support almost entirely on local constituents and state parties, now the winners draw almost 40 percent of their contributions from political action committees, that is, from the funding arms of national interest groups. Prosaic projects, reaching only hometown folks, do not satisfy many of these hungry organizations; they expect, instead, a diet rich in ubiquitous social mandates: more safety devices in *all* motor vehicles, pure water in *any* river, equality of athletic programs within virtually *every* university, prohibition of smoking from sea to shining sea, and so on.

The number and cost of such commandments also keep mounting because of the extraordinary legitimacy they are accorded. In part, this situation reflects the skill of their advocates and patrons at marshaling notions of fairness or rights. Thus, the trump card played by champions of rigid antipollution regulations is that all citizens have "an inherent right" to a pristine environment. The mandating of benefits for each new class of disadvantaged people reflexively summons the Fourteenth Amendment, rather than a plainspoken demand for government funding. The clinching argument in many product injury verdicts seems to be that buyers should bear no responsibility for the risks they run since consumers are entitled to be absolutely safe. The time-honored defense of antidumping regulations is that they uphold the economic rights of firms and workers victimized by foreign predators who employ "pauper labor."

Because regulatory pork barreling is presented not as a system of special favors, but as a means of honoring solemn legal claims, the claimants are often given a direct hand in enforcement. Many regulatory activities, in other words, gain momentum because they deputize vigilantes. Most environmental statutes and consumer protection laws invite citizen suits to ensure compliance. Of late, the employment laws have induced a surge of job-bias class actions. Various interests are parties to these lawsuits or become beneficiaries of them. Besides awarding significant sums to nonprofit advocacy groups, settlements have ordered a bevy of purchasing contracts and franchises to designated for-profit organizations and produced a billable hours bonanza for the contingency lawyers and for a cottage industry of diversity management consultants.

Concerns

Does all this pose a problem? A prosperous, civilized country should be expected to regulate harmful types of economic fraud and abuse, to reduce socially corrosive inequities, to bar morally repugnant forms of discrimination, and to protect the health and safety of its citizens. Despite the soaring costs of the policies produced by these exertions, their net worth is sometimes impossible to measure. Even though many of them advantage certain groups while disadvantaging others, society may have decided that such uneven outcomes are virtuous and just. And the fact that politicians pull in campaign funds and votes with the decisions does not, in itself, invalidate them. Pork, courtesy of other people's tax payments or of regulatory exactions, is a staple of politics. Without it, democratic government would lose some muscle as well as flab.

What is unsettling, however, is the seeming ease or insouciance with which current political arrangements seem to crank out expensive directives that invoke high principle to conduct . . . "public affairs for private advantage." The old pork barrel, stuffed as it was with federal bricks, mortar, and macadam, at least had to be paid for with tax dollars or with deficit spending. The favoritism was explicit, concrete (often literally), and visibly priced. Even the subtler fiscal delicacy, targeted tax relief, has had reasonably obvious budgetary implications, which sooner or later would alarm deficit hawks. Wasteful as these expenditures and tax measures frequently are, at least they have borne clearly the signatures of elected officials, who occasionally might be asked to answer for the consequences of their actions.

The new system is murkier. Its contents extend far beyond earmarked appropriations or tax breaks to a stack of selective legal strictures that appear budget-neutral and "tax free," and that are partly in the custody, so to speak, of unaccountable private attorneys general. In contrast to honest spending and tax bills, no consistent effort is made to score the economic impacts of the voluminous mandates, especially those that emanate from the executive branch. Hence, as [economists] Robert Hahn and Robert Litan recently reported, approximately half the federal government's social regulations issued between 1982 and mid-1996 generated costs plainly in excess of social benefits, yet remained unchallenged.

The rise of legal and regulatory burdens may seem of trivial consequence to America's formidable economy, but in fact the productivity and incomes of Americans would have grown more rapidly if the nation's cost-oblivious penchant for regulatory sanctions and suits had been brought under better control. As a conservative estimate, just ridding the *Federal Register* of the manifold rules since 1982 that flagrantly flunked an elementary cost-benefit test would have increased the size of the economic pie by almost $300 billion. Fixing countless other programs whose net benefits are not being maximized would "grow the economy" further. The penalty for not seizing these opportunities now while the going is good is likely to worsen substantially in the years ahead. In the next millennium, the competitive heat of the global marketplace will intensify and so will the incentives for firms to outsource across borders. Especially if encumbered by too many injudicious laws and lawsuits, more U.S. businesses will simply off-load more of their operations. In the course of this industrial upheaval, millions of American workers are likely to be sacked or, at a minimum, to see their wages stagnate.

Prudent Corrections

Not unaware of this prospect, the [1995–1996] 104th Congress made some tentative progress toward redressing abuses of the regulatory state. Legislation was passed requiring federal agencies to weigh the costs and benefits of major new mandates and to submit their studies to Congress for review. Narrower statutes were enacted eliminating zero-tolerance standards for health risks in some consumer goods (processed foods, for example) or at least requiring regulators to publish cost justifications for safety standards (as for drinking water). In an attempt to curb the excesses of what might be called privatized social regulation—in particular, the rampant civil litigation that purports to protect consumers—Congress succeeded in setting minimal limits on the rewards to shareholders and plaintiffs' attorneys for suing companies frivolously.

To call such steps anything but a bare beginning, however, would be a delusion. The shareholder "strike" suits bill should have, but didn't, clear the way for a broader legal reform proposal that would have restricted punitive damages in product liability cases generally. (President Clinton vetoed both bills, but only one of his vetoes was overridden.) So far, the new procedural requirements for the formulation of executive rules, in turn, have proved mostly exhortatory. In only one case, the Pipeline Safety and Partnership Act of 1995, is an executive bureau expressly enjoined from promulgating standards whose costs are unjustified by benefits. In the rest, administrators are only asked to consider and report their cost-benefit assessments and to explain any rulemaking that discards them. The provisions for congressional oversight of proposed rules are constrained by tight statutory time-frames, presidential veto power over resolutions of disapproval, and too limited a role for the legislative branch's top economic analysts. (The 1995 Unfunded Mandates Reform Act authorizes the Congressional Budget Office to "score" regulatory acts of Congress, but not those of the executive. The latter's rules, according to the Small Business Regulatory Enforcement Fairness Act of 1996, are to be examined by the General Accounting Office, arguably under unrealistic deadlines.) Perhaps least satisfactory is the grandfathering* of existing laws and rulings. With a few notable exceptions—such as the Delaney clause, which barred any level of risk in food additives—old regulations, no matter how questionable, remain on the books.

Some of these deficiencies might be partially remedied by more fine-tuning. A pending bill, the so-called Regulatory Improvement Act authored by Senators Fred Thompson (R-TN) and Carl Levin (D-MI), would try to ensure, for instance, that agencies take seriously their evaluations and risk assessments of new rules by introducing a process of independent peer review. The bill would also extend methodically a similar review process to extant regulations.

---

*To "grandfather" a policy into law means that a current policy will be exempted from the impact of a newly enacted statute.

Even these corrections, however, will not suffice to sharpen the lines of political accountability for regulatory pork. A proliferation of agency analyses,
peer committees, and reporting requirements is no substitute for democratic
choice. Ultimately, the buck ought to stop with Congress itself, where members
should have to cast transparent up or down votes on all the government's off-
budget activism, just as votes are recorded on other important taxes and expenditures. But unless these decisions are well-informed, legislators will render
them meaningless, if they render them at all. One way to minimize evasion
might be to expand the capacity of the Congressional Budget Office to delin-
eate for the legislature society's gains and losses from every major regulatory initiative, much as CBO performs this annual service with every big budgetary
item. A joint report by the American Enterprise Institute and the Brookings
Institution published last July suggested experimenting along these lines.

Beyond these institutional adjustments lie larger priorities. Sooner or later,
policymakers in the United States will have to face the fact that inordinate
legal contestation pervades the way this society seeks to regulate itself. Much of
this punitive "adversarial legalism" . . . lines the pockets of lawyers and professional litigants while accomplishing little else. The resulting drag on American
economic performance, though little noticed at the moment, may become considerably less affordable in time. Part and parcel of serious regulatory reform,
therefore, has to be a reasonable contraction of federal enactments that stimulate, indeed sometimes sponsor, our seemingly insatiable appetite for litigation.
This won't be easy, for it will mean rolling back an oversupply of suits everywhere, from the workplace to the doctor's office, as well as entertaining fewer
complaints about sagging stock quotations, risky products, and many of life's
hazards, misfortunes, and disappointments.

Questions for Discussion

1. The essence of traditional pork barrel politics has been the distribution of
   favors for political support (including, but not limited to, campaign contributions). What is the difference between what Nivola terms "regulatory
   pork" and traditional spending on roads, the military, or public works
   projects?
2. Implementing policy is a difficult and frequently unrewarding task. Does the
   new pork barrel regulation suffer from an absence of attention to how policies are implemented? How could oversight of such policies be improved?

14.3

Liberal Lessons from Welfare Reform

Christopher Jencks

Major policy reforms are often enacted in an atmosphere of great expectations, major uncertainty, and substantial skepticism. Advocates script a "rosy scenario" (a term drawn from the optimistic projections for the initial Reagan tax cuts in 1981), while opponents foresee doom and the end of the world as we know it. Rarely does either version play out. Rather, both partisans and objective analysts assess the results and use them to address the new policy situation that has emerged. Debates over policies are neverending, and only occasionally do partisans give much ground. Still, from time to time, clear-headed analysis replaces advocacy, as occurs in the following selection by Christopher Jencks.

Few recent policy debates have been more hotly contested than welfare reform which by the 1990s had come to mean requiring recipients, even single mothers, to work in order to receive benefits. Noting the partisan environment in which President Bill Clinton signed 1996 legislation with substantial work requirements, Jencks analyzes the impact of the welfare reform law and concludes that liberals should acknowledge some of the positive aspects of its implementation. Jencks takes account of preliminary research results to make the case that critics of welfare reform should build on its successes, such as focusing more attention on low-wage workers and allowing states greater leeway, in order to produce more program options and more understanding of how both the federal and state governments can further reduce a reliance on welfare.

When Congress passed the Personal Responsibility and Work Opportunity Reconciliation Act (PRWORA) in 1996, the liberal community was almost unanimous in urging President Clinton to veto it. Even people like myself, who had supported Clinton's earlier efforts to "end welfare as we know it," thought that PRWORA went too far. Fortunately for the poor,

Christopher Jencks is the Malcolm Wiener Professor at Harvard's John F. Kennedy School of Government.

Christopher Jencks, "Liberal Lessons from Welfare Reform." Reprinted with permission from *The American Prospect,* Volume 13, Number 13, July 15, 2002. Online at www.prospect.org/print-friendly/print/V13/13/jencks-c.html. The American Prospect, 11 Beacon Street, Suite 1120, Boston, MA 02108. All rights reserved.

the first five years of welfare reform inflicted far less economic pain than we had expected.

Now the Bush administration wants even tougher work requirements. Once again, most liberal Democrats think it is a mistake to worry about making every last single mother work when we have not yet ensured that those who already work can provide for their children. Once again, I agree: The administration's proposals are dreadful. But the people who claimed that PRWORA would cause a lot of suffering no longer have much credibility with middle-of-the-road legislators, who see welfare reform as an extraordinary success. If we want to regain credibility, we need to admit that welfare reform turned out better than we expected and figure out why that was the case. The usual explanation is simply that the economy did better than anyone expected, but that is only part of the story.

The traditional liberal position on single mothers was always "more is always better." More meant not only that the government should provide more resources but also that it should impose fewer restrictions on the recipients. The electorate has never accepted this view. Most Americans favor generous programs for people who are doing their best to help themselves. But when the government helps people who seem lazy or irresponsible, Americans tend to see this as rewarding vice. So the less a program asks of its beneficiaries, the less likely Americans are to support it. America's pre-1996 welfare program, Aid to Families with Dependent Children (AFDC), was a perfect example of how this logic plays out politically. It asked almost nothing of single mothers, and it gave them almost no money in return. As a result, everyone hated it.

Nonetheless, welfare-reform efforts achieved relatively little during the 1970s and 1980s. Welfare-rights groups were against requiring single mothers to work, and the liberal wing of the Democratic Party was reluctant to offend these groups, partly for fear of seeming racist. The labor market was soft, centrists feared that single mothers would not be able to find work in the private sector, and the right was against spending public money to provide jobs. Ambitious politicians came to see welfare reform as the Vietnam of domestic policy: a quagmire to be avoided at almost any cost. And because the welfare rolls were roughly constant from 1975 to 1989, the problem just simmered.

In 1991, with the welfare rolls rising rapidly, Bill Clinton decided that running against AFDC would be a good way to position himself as a "new" Democrat. As president, he set up a task force to propose a new system. By then the Democratic Party was deeply divided on welfare. Some supported a fundamental change, usually because they thought the only way to get more support for single mothers was to insist that the mother go to work. But many traditional liberals remained skeptical about serious work requirements. They saw the least-competent recipients as incapable of doing almost anything, and they could not imagine a system that drew a clear line between those who could work and those who could not. Clinton's 1994 proposals therefore needed Republican support to pass. By then the Republicans were more interested in humiliating Clinton than in reforming welfare, so his relatively generous version of welfare reform was stillborn.

After the Republicans gained control of Congress, they crafted a series of more draconian welfare-reform bills, which most liberals opposed. But after vetoing two such bills, Clinton signed the third. PRWORA replaced AFDC with Temporary Assistance for Needy Families (TANF). Under TANF, states could redesign welfare in almost any way they wanted, setting their own eligibility rules, work requirements, and time limits. TANF did establish federal time limits, but if states wanted to get around those limits they could do so by shuffling funds between programs.

The 1996 legislation was also a powerful symbolic statement. It made clear that America was no longer committed, even in principle, to supporting women who wanted to be full-time mothers. Anyone who wants to have children must either work or find a partner who will work. (The disabled are an exception, but "disability" is quite narrowly defined.) Single mothers judged capable of working can get short-term cash assistance from the government, but they cannot expect long-term assistance unless they have a job, and they cannot expect the government to find them one.

When this legislation was adopted, its opponents made four predictions:

♦ Many mothers would not be able to find jobs when they hit their TANF time limit;
♦ Even mothers who found jobs would seldom earn enough to support their family;
♦ Forcing unmarried mothers to work would not reduce unwed motherhood or discourage divorce; and
♦ There would not be enough good child care, so more children would be neglected.

What actually happened was rather different.

Work

When PRWORA passed, skeptics argued that there would not be enough jobs to go around. The proportion of single mothers who had worked at some point during the year rose from 73 percent in 1995 to 84 percent in 2000, while the proportion who had worked throughout the year rose from 48 percent to 60 percent. These were unprecedented increases: Nothing similar had happened during any earlier boom, and nothing similar happened among married mothers in the late 1990s.

PRWORA's critics often attribute these gains to the unusually tight labor market between mid-1997 and mid-2001. Some have suggested that unemployment among single mothers will rise sharply now that the labor market has gone soft. Some rise is inevitable in a recession, but the proportion of single mothers with jobs will not return to its 1995 level unless the recession gets much, much worse.

The unemployment rate for single mothers is normally about twice the rate for the labor force as a whole. In March 2001, for example, the overall unemployment rate was 4.3 percent but the rate for single mothers was 8.1 percent. The overall unemployment rate reached 6 percent in April 2002, so the rate for single mothers was probably just under 12 percent. That is surely causing a lot of suffering. But the fraction of single mothers with jobs is still far higher than it was before PRWORA.

The critics were right when they said that not all those who leave welfare would find work. Between 1994 and 2000, welfare receipt among single mothers fell from 32 percent to 15 percent, a 17-point drop; employment among single mothers, meanwhile, rose only 11 or 12 points. The question, though, is how many single mothers who wanted jobs failed to find them. . . . [T]he unemployment rate for single mothers fell between 1995 and 2000, which hardly suggests that the labor market was awash in single mothers unable to find work. Of course, workers only get counted as unemployed if they say they are currently looking for work. Some who left welfare presumably had looked earlier, found nothing, grown discouraged, and stopped looking.

Income

When PRWORA was being debated, its opponents often argued that even if single mothers found work they would seldom earn enough to support themselves. If single mothers had to depend entirely on their own wages, this would often have been true. But most single mothers have multiple sources of income, and their economic status has clearly improved since 1996.

The official federal poverty rate among single mothers was 43 percent at the end of the 1980s expansion, 42 percent when PRWORA passed, and 33 percent in 2000. The drop among black single mothers was even larger. Poverty has probably risen over the past 18 months, but the rate for 2001 is almost certain to be lower than the rate for 1996. If the overall unemployment rate stays near 6 percent, single mothers are unlikely to experience as much material hardship in this recession as they did in the last one. A severe recession could be another story.

Even before the current recession began, the Center on Budget and Policy Priorities had reported that the poorest single mothers were doing worse than they had before PRWORA passed. But census data on the poorest of the poor are problematic for a variety of technical reasons. Such data should never be trusted unless they are consistent with other evidence. If deep poverty had really increased between 1995 and 2000, for example, one would have expected more single mothers to move in with relatives. Census surveys showed no such increase. Likewise, an increase in deep poverty should have meant that more single mothers had trouble feeding their families. Yet the Agriculture Department's annual reports on its food-security surveys showed a fairly steady decline in the proportion of single mothers reporting food shortages, hunger, and related problems. My own work with Joseph Swingle and Scott Winship shows the same thing.

So why were the prophets of doom wrong? One answer is that almost everyone underestimated the extent to which government support for the poor was being redirected to people with jobs. Soon after Clinton took office in 1993, he persuaded Congress to expand the Earned Income Tax Credit (EITC). Today the EITC distributes more money to working parents than AFDC ever gave to mothers who stayed at home. For a minimum-wage worker with two children, the EITC means a 40 percent increase in annual earnings. More aggressive child-support enforcement has increased some working mothers' incomes even further. Extending Medicaid coverage to some of the working poor has also reduced some mothers' out-of-pocket medical spending, although much remains to be done in this regard.

TANF also gave states block grants that did not shrink as the welfare rolls shrank and allowed states to use these grants for child-care subsidies, which made it much easier for single mothers to survive on what they earned in low-wage jobs. Unfortunately, these subsidies are now in jeopardy, partly because the recession is putting pressure on state budgets and partly because the administration wants to force states to use their TANF money in other ways.

The net result of these changes is that the old "welfare state" is becoming what one might call a "wage-subsidy state," in which government assistance is tied to employment. By asking more of those who get government largesse, the new wage-subsidy system has substantially reduced political hostility to public spending on the poor. This is especially true at the state level. (In Washington the hard right is still riding high, and the Democrats remain reluctant to oppose the Bush administration even when it tries to limit states' ability to run welfare.)

But what about mothers who left welfare and did not find regular work? Many of these women are clearly struggling, but they are doing better than most of PRWORA's critics expected. They have not benefited from welfare reform, but it has been hard to find much evidence that their position deteriorated, at least prior to last September [2002].

One reason PRWORA's critics were too pessimistic about such mothers' prospects may have been that they were fooled by their own linguistic conventions. When we describe people as welfare mothers, we inevitably begin to see them mainly as people who get a check from the government every month. In reality, however, this check is hardly ever large enough to support the recipient's family. In their book *Making Ends Meet*, Kathryn Edin and Laura Lein reported that welfare checks typically covered about 40 percent of the recipient's expenses. Some of the rest came from food stamps; most of it came from relatives, boyfriends, and working off the books. Edin and Lein's data were gathered in the early 1990s, but the same pattern probably holds today.

When times are good, family members can be more generous and a mother has a better chance of finding off-the-books work. Boyfriends also earn more in good times, which may be one reason why more single mothers reported live-in boyfriends during the late 1990s. The value of an economic boom to a single mother depends, however, on current norms about how money should be spent. When incomes rose in the late 1980s, a lot of the money that flowed into poor neighborhoods ended up in drug dealers' pockets. When incomes rose in the late 1990s, expenditures on drugs were apparently falling, so more of the new money was available for food, rent, and fixing the TV.

Marriage

The idea that sending checks to unmarried mothers will encourage unwed motherhood and divorce has always seemed self-evident to most Americans. But back in 1996 it was hard to find much statistical evidence for this view. Single parenthood was becoming more common in all rich countries, regardless of how they organized their welfare system. And while welfare benefits varied a lot from one American state to the next, neither the proportion of children born out of wedlock nor the proportion of older children living with an unmarried mother appeared to correlate with benefit levels. When welfare reform was being debated in the mid-1990s, I do not recall hearing a single reputable scholar argue that changing the welfare system was likely to have much effect on marriage rates. I certainly expected no such effect. Even Charles Murray,* who believed that welfare had played a role in the spread of single-parent families, felt that something more draconian than PRWORA would be needed to reverse the trend.

Since 1996 both the scholarly consensus and the facts on the ground have changed. Recent research suggests that welfare policy may, in fact, exert some effect on family structure. Furthermore, the spread of single-parent families has stopped. The proportion of mothers raising children without a husband had increased steadily between 1960 and 1996 (from 11 percent to 28 percent). But after March 1997, the proportion began to fall. By March 2001 it was down to 26.6 percent. That was hardly a revolution, but it cut the number of single mothers by half a million.

The proportion of children born to unmarried mothers is still inching up, but the increase since 1995 has been tiny. A study by Richard Bavier of the U.S. Office of Management and Budget suggests that women who have children out

---

*Charles Murray is a social scientist well known for his contrarian writings on social issues, most notably race. Among his books are *Losing Ground* on welfare reform and *The Bell Curve* on race and intelligence.

of wedlock are now marrying in greater numbers. We do not know whether these mothers are marrying their child's father or someone else. That is important, because children who grow up with a stepfather fare no better in adolescence or early adulthood than children who grow up with a single mother, even though the stepfather's presence substantially increases their family's income.

Children

When PRWORA passed, its critics (including me) worried about how it would affect children. In material terms, children are now a little better off than they were in 1996. Children's psychological well-being is probably more important, but it is also harder to measure. A single mother who works full time obviously has less time for her children, and exhaustion may make her more irritable or more punitive. But the long-term effects of a single mother working remain uncertain and controversial. A lot probably depends on what the mother's job is really like, what it pays, and how flexible it is to family needs.

When mothers enter the labor market, however, their children's child-care arrangements become less stable. Government subsidies appear and disappear unpredictably. The women who provide child care for unskilled working mothers are often unreliable. Mothers often have to take either temporary jobs or jobs with unpredictable hours, and they usually have to change their child-care arrangements when their hours change. Children hate this kind of instability. Whether it causes long-term damage, however, remains unclear.

On balance, welfare reform has turned out far better than most liberals expected. Most Americans now see it as one of the great successes of the 1990s. Instead of remaining wedded to the idea that PRWORA was a bad idea because it was supported by the lunatic right, liberals need to rethink. My own conclusions are three:

♦ Telling prospective parents that they would have to take primary responsibility for supporting themselves and their children was a good idea, because 60 years of experience showed that no other approach to reducing family poverty could win broad political support in America.

♦ Shifting government largesse toward those who work was a good idea, because it helped erase the stigma of single motherhood and made more resources available to single mothers and their children.

♦ Turning welfare over to the states was a really good idea, because most states currently take a less ideological view of single mothers' problems than does Congress.

Someday, of course, Congress may also show renewed interest in problem solving. At the moment, however, most states' approach to helping poor families is more pragmatic than Washington's, and the new emphasis on helping low-wage workers has created a significantly better system than we had in 1996.

Questions for Discussion

1. Why are critics of a policy so difficult to convince of its success? What does this tell us about policymaking and—especially—policy evaluation in Washington?
2. To what extent does the very complexity of a policy like welfare reform (or, more recently, Bush's "No Child Left Behind" educational reform) lead to difficulties in understanding and interpreting its impact?
3. How do you think Jencks's article was received by critics of welfare reform? By supporters?

☆ 14.4

Safe Deposit: The Case for Foreign Aid

Gregg Easterbrook

In the aftermath of World War II, American aid to Europe through the Marshall Plan speeded the economic recovery of that war-torn continent. The economic stability of European countries subsequently strengthened the West during the Cold War. In short, the United States "did good" with its financial assistance, but it also "did well" by creating a strengthened set of countries. Although the Marshall Plan received high marks from most political quarters, foreign aid has lost much of its support over the past forty years. The general critiques include high costs, waste, corruption, and the ingratitude of many recipient countries. Moreover, foreign aid has often served the political purposes of American politicians; for example, Israel has received far more assistance than any other nation, in large part due to its strong support from American Jews, who are disproportionately active in politics.

In this selection, journalist Gregg Easterbrook, who often takes a contrarian perspective on public policy issues, makes the argument that foreign aid—even in modest amounts—has served the world, and American interests, admirably. He acknowledges the existence of waste, misdirection, and corruption, but concludes that aid has succeeded in bettering the lives of many nations and literally billions of people. He takes on the American left's assumptions that aid channeled through international institutions such as the World Bank has been too restrictive. Add to this the neo-isolationism of many conservatives, and he notes that the U.S. backing for more aid has shrunk, just at the time it should be increasing. Beyond the political problems faced by those (including President Bush) who have argued for more aid are the escalating demands for additional defense spending. Against this backdrop, Easterbrook remains confident that more aid, even with waste and theft, will benefit its intended recipients and—more profoundly—represents the right thing for the greatest power in the world to do.

PAUL O'NEILL AND BONO'S* [2002] Africa trip—during which the odd couple wore fun clothes and inspected village wells—made headlines across the United States. But lost in the celebrity-induced excitement was a more significant development in the debate over foreign aid: George W. Bush and other prominent Republicans suddenly want to increase it. "I am here today," Bush told a United Nations conference last March, "to reaffirm the commitment of the United States to bring hope and opportunity to the world's poorest people and to call for a new compact for development defined by greater accountability for rich and poor nations alike." The president adroitly avoided the phrase "foreign aid," but everyone knew what he was talking about. Around the same time, Jesse Helms, long the Senate's determined roadblock to international assistance, announced that he too thought aid spending should rise. Bush pledged the United States to its first foreign aid increase in many a moon—a small one but significant for a nation where political discourse generally, and Republican discourse specifically, has been anti-foreign-aid for decades.

Bush's speech and Helms's conversion suggest that the politics of foreign aid may be changing. But they won't change enough as long as most Americans in both parties—think foreign aid doesn't work. One reason many Americans think so is that they expect foreign aid to banish developing-world poverty and to build liberal democracies across the globe; by that standard, aid indeed has failed. But that's the wrong standard. The realistic benchmark is whether international assistance has made the world better than it would otherwise have been. And by that standard, foreign aid has not only been a success; it has been a triumph. In most developing nations, living standards are rising, and health care and education are improving, in part because of foreign aid. Billions of people are better off today thanks to Western help, however inconsistent and snafu-prone that help has often been. "On a world scale, the risk, intensity and

---

*Then Secretary of the Treasury Department, and the lead singer of U2.
Journalist Gregg Easterbrook is a senior editor at *The New Republic* and writes regularly on Easterblogg (http://www.tnr.com/easterbrook.mhtml).
Gregg Easterbrook. "Safe Deposit: The Case for Foreign Aid." *The New Republic* (July 29, 2002), pp. 16–20. Reprinted by permission of The Brookings Institution.

severity of poverty has fallen more sharply in the past fifty years than in the preceding thousand," in part owing to aid from the West, Michael Lipton, a professor at the University of Sussex, has written. If the Bush administration spearheaded an ambitious new commitment to more accountable foreign aid, the cost to the United States would be small, but the benefits to humanity could be remarkable.

Some years ago I had a free day in Dar Es Salaam, Tanzania. I decided to walk around—walking being safer than boarding the perpetually overcrowded buses, off of which passengers often fell. Dotting the city were large structures—office buildings, high-rises—that appeared to be under construction but on closer inspection had been abandoned in the midst of assembly, their exposed beams rusting. Western money funded the building starts, but the aid ran out, or the loans were embezzled; and there the structures sat, worse than useless considering that the resources could have been spent on something simpler, like modest housing. Beat-up old cars, many 1950s-vintage models imported from the United States, bounced along cratered roads that lacked even the simplest maintenance. According to a 1998 World Bank study, Tanzania has received $2 billion from the West in road-maintenance aid since the late '70s, and during that period the condition of its roads has declined. Outside the city stood the hulk of a steel mill, built mainly with Western aid. It was modern, impressive-looking, and it didn't run.

Tanzania is not alone. World Bank officer William Easterly calculates in his 2001 book *The Elusive Quest for Growth* that based on the billions it has received in aid, the Zambian economy could by now have grown to a Western-like $20,000 per capita income. Instead Zambia's per capita income is $600, down in real terms since the '50s. Corruption explains some of this. Jeffrey Winters of Northwestern University estimates that of the $8 billion in World Bank funds channeled to Indonesia since about 1960, one-third has been stolen. In Congo (then Zaire) the late dictator Mobutu Sese Seko siphoned off enough foreign aid to enjoy Nero-level opulence amid the desperation of his people. And though the World Bank and most Western donor nations have worked diligently in the last decade to reduce aid theft (Nobel Prize-winning economist Joseph Stiglitz has said one of the best arguments for international aid is that the corruption problem is finally being resolved), misappropriation is ongoing. A recent bribery scandal, for instance, marred the World Bank-funded Lesotho Highlands Water Project, a water-supply effort in South Africa. Estimates vary, but it is widely believed corruption has claimed at least 10 percent of global aid.

Combine that with the endless depressing statistics about life in the impoverished world, and you can understand why so many Americans consider foreign aid a failure. Some 1.2 billion people now live on $1 or less per day, and every year that quotient of misery increases by another million. Since World War II the West has allocated roughly $1 trillion to foreign aid, yet inequality is "accelerating everywhere on Earth," proclaims the leftist International Forum on Globalization. The gap between the developing and developed countries has grown so wide that the world's three richest individuals are now worth more than the 48 poorest nations.

But these depressing statistics obscure more than they reveal. In fact, much has improved in the developing world during the era of foreign aid. In 1975 the average income in developing nations was $1,300 (in 1985 dollars) per capita; today it is $2,500. In 1974 one-third of the world's nations regularly held genuine multiparty elections; today two-thirds do. In 1975 1.6 billion people lived at what the United Nations classifies as "medium development," meaning with reasonably decent living standards, education, and health care; today 3.5 billion people do—a stunning increase in the sheer number of human beings who are *not* destitute. Global adult literacy was 47 percent in 1970 and is 73 percent today, while school enrollment for girls has skyrocketed. Infant mortality has declined and life expectancy has risen in almost every developing nation. The world's population is growing not because of more births—fertility is down almost everywhere—but because of fewer deaths. Even in developing nations, it is becoming the norm for a person to survive to old age. At the beginning of the twentieth century, average life expectancy in the United States was 47 years; today it is 66 years—*for the world.*

Yes, each year brings more people living on $1 per day, but this is mainly because each year brings more people; the *percentage* of the global population living in such hardship is in steady decline. An estimated 800 million people in the world today are malnourished, but the *percentage* of people who are malnourished is dropping, and the world's average daily caloric intake continues to rise—so much so that for the first time in history, there are roughly as many people on Earth who are overweight as are underweight. A few decades ago the Stanford University population theorist Paul Ehrlich was predicting global famine, projecting that by now hundreds of millions would have died of hunger while Middle Ages-style plagues swept the globe. Respectable opinion echoed this view with a presidential report commissioned by Jimmy Carter, *Global 2000*, forecasting in 1980 that by the year 2000 vast numbers would starve or die of uncontrollable plagues while entire ecosystems collapsed. Not even the awfulness of the African AIDS epidemic comes close to what experts were expecting. Instead, for all the problems poor countries continue to experience—especially in Africa—for most people in most developing nations, life is mostly getting better.

In some ways this is the great story of the developing world over the last half-century: Things have not fallen apart. And one of the reasons is international assistance. Sure, many Third World countries have not enjoyed sustained economic growth. But asking whether foreign aid has brought growth is the wrong question, since Western governments often do poorly in picking and choosing winners in their own economies, too. The morally realistic standard is whether foreign aid brings humanitarian gains. And by that standard, it has been a success.

Consider some of foreign aid's accomplishments. First are the health care initiatives. Smallpox has been eradicated globally via a U.N.-run, Western-financed campaign that completed its work in 1977, the heyday of aid money. River blindness, a scourge of Africa, which once infected hundreds of thousands of people, has been nearly eradicated by Western-backed health initiatives. Fully 80 percent of the world's children are today vaccinated against polio, diphtheria, and other diseases, compared with almost no vaccinations in the developing world when foreign aid began roughly a generation ago. Most of those immunizations were paid for by the World Health Organization (WHO) or by the contractor agencies it dispatches to small villages across the globe; WHO draws most of its money from donor countries in the West. It took about 150 years, from 1800 to 1950, for typical European life expectancy to advance from four decades to six. In most of the developing world, it has taken just 40 years, from 1930 to 1970. Helping most of the world achieve, in 40 years, the life-span improvement that took Europe 150 years is a spectacular achievement—partly attributable to the advent of antibiotics and partly to international aid.

Next, aid has brought birth control and reproductive-health care to the world's impoverished. The International Planned Parenthood Federation, funded mainly by Western aid, has established family-planning clinics throughout the developing world. Its work, and that of other groups with Western support (including about $300 million annually from the United States), is a primary reason the global population runaway, predicted as recently as the '70s, has not come to pass. In the '50s developing-world women averaged six live births; now the figure is three and still declining.

Or consider agriculture. In the mid-'60s India and Pakistan experienced wrenching national famines; Ehrlich predicted that hundreds of millions in the subcontinent would starve to death. A doomsday book called *Famine 1975!*, by Paul and William Paddock, forecasting imminent global starvation, was a bestseller in the late '60s. International aid organizations—some government, some private (mainly the Rockefeller and Ford Foundations)—launched an ambitious initiative to introduce high-yield crops into Pakistan and India, shipping trucks of high-yield seeds from a research institute in Mexico to the subcontinent on an emergency basis. In two years in the mid-'60s conversion to these high-yield crop strains stopped the famines that had been widespread in India and Pakistan for several years. Rather than starving as predicted, Pakistan and India have used these high-yield crops to become self-sufficient in food production despite population growth. Pakistan, which harvested roughly 3.4 million tons of wheat annually in the early '60s, was harvesting 18 million tons by the late '90s; India went from 11 million tons to about 60 million.

Would the Green Revolution have come to developing nations regardless of aid? Perhaps eventually, but many millions would have died needlessly in the interim. China researched high-yield rice strains on its own and dramatically increased rice production without Western help. But the increase did not become significant until the '80s, almost two decades after productivity rose dramatically in the subcontinent, with huge numbers of Chinese suffering malnourishment as their nation went it alone in adopting Green Revolution farming. As Norman Borlaug, the Nobel Peace Prize-winning Iowa plant breeder who oversaw the effort in Pakistan and India, puts it: "What was accomplished in India and Pakistan could not have happened without aid support money."

Foreign aid's success in promoting macroeconomic—as opposed to social and agricultural—development is decidedly mixed. But for every Tanzania, Zambia, and Congo, there is a South Korea. Destitute after Japanese occupation and the Korean War, South Korea has lifted its per capita GDP [gross domestic product] to $16,000 since the '50s. Of course, Seoul's export-led economic model played a major role in that success. But developmental aid was also an important part—particularly in improving the country's infrastructure and educational system. In their book about foreign aid, *A Half Penny on the Federal Dollar*, Brookings Institution analysts Michael O'Hanlon and Carol Graham cite South Korea as a prime example of development aid translating directly into development.

And South Korea isn't alone. Ideologically charged debates often center around whether aid or trade conquers poverty. But in countries that have followed the "Tiger" model of export growth—Indonesia, Bolivia, Ghana, Vietnam, Chile, Botswana—foreign aid has often buttressed market-oriented development strategies. Indeed, foreign aid is one of the levers donors have used in recent years to push developing-world governments to liberalize their economies. Donors, for instance, have helped Vietnam start a thriving coffee-export trade; Chad is on the verge of tapping its petroleum reserves via an oil pipeline built with World Bank support.

Uganda, another African country that has opened itself to market economics, owes about half of its national budget to Western aid. Progress there has been remarkable: Poverty has declined by one-third in the last decade; spiraling inflation has been stopped; the percentage of children in school is sharply increasing; and Uganda also leads Africa in progress against AIDS. Americans spent about 29 cents each on Uganda last year and, for that tiny amount, made a palpable difference in people's lives.

It is true, of course, that not all foreign aid has been this successful. In the '60s and '70s, for instance, European donors pushed on developing countries a statist, socialism-lite that mirrored their own domestic economic organization. And the United States often funneled aid as a reward to corrupt and repressive cold war allies like Mobutu. But there is at least some reason to believe foreign aid is becoming more effective—that we will see more Ugandas and fewer Tanzanias. A group of World Bank analysts concluded in their 1998 study *Assessing Aid* that the main thread running through positive foreign aid projects was association with positive social trends. Give money to entrenched, anti-reform governments, and you shouldn't expect much; fund new or reformist regimes, and good things might happen. Worry less about exactly which project to pick—no one can ever be sure what will work—and more about whether the governments being supported are progressive and accountable. Easterly, in *Elusive Quest for Growth*, adds that it is essential that all aid projects contain incentives. On the local level, individuals in the project area must participate or otherwise get something tangible, however small, granting them an incentive to cooperate. At the national level, only reformist governments should be funded, giving leaders the right incentive. Those principles now form the basis of most International Monetary Fund (IMF) and World Bank aid—and they were the basis for Bush's March speech as well. Foreign aid, which for all its foibles has done tremendous good, may do even more good in the years to come.

But for all its merits, foreign aid lacks a stable, powerful American political constituency. Long scorned by the libertarian right, it is now increasingly scorned by the anti-globalization left as well.

Conservative opposition to foreign aid is nothing new. Some of it is based on stinginess; some on distaste for developing-world anti-Americanism; and some on the view, best elucidated by the late British economist Peter Bauer, that aid actively backfires by keeping corrupt, incompetent developing-world elites in power. But to view foreign aid with disdain, as many conservatives do, deprives the West of credit for one of its signal contributions to the world. It also dishonors America's spiritual heritage, as all the monotheistic faiths impose on the favored an obligation to help the less-well-off. After declaring that the United States should fund a crash program to stop African AIDS, the 81-year-old Jesse Helms gave the suggestion that he had dropped his long-standing opposition to increased foreign aid because he is aware that he will soon meet God. This is clear thinking.

Traditional conservative objections to foreign aid have been joined in recent years by left-wing complaints, via the anti-globalization movement—leaving foreign aid politically stranded. Anti-globalizers don't oppose assistance per se; they oppose aid that comes with reformist strings, such as IMF loans with "structural adjustment" clauses that require recipient governments to adopt free-market and free-trade policies. The leftish Institute for Policy Studies protests that IMF requirements mean the bank "holds virtual neocolonial control over developing nations." Yet though anti-globalizers don't want Western governments imposing terms on aid, *they* are happy to do so. One is that money be spent only on projects deemed "sustainable." In recent years anti-globalizers and various foundation-grant trendies have so barraged the World Bank and similar organizations with the buzz term "sustainability" that donors are increasingly leery about funding anything much beyond village solar projects or similar ideas that sound small-scale and low-input.

Very little in Western economies meets the left's shaky definition of "sustainability," which more or less translates as no fossil fuels, no built structures, and no packaging. Indeed, foisting this standard on the developing world is a formula for keeping living standards low. Even the environmental rationale for "sustainability" doesn't make much sense: No current resource is in short supply, not even petroleum, and no important resource—other than groundwater in China and freshwater in a few other regions—seems likely to fall into short supply in the near future, based on present information. In turn, some industries that could be sustained indefinitely—like logging—are amongst the ones anti-globalizers hate most.

The anti-globalization movement may be politically marginal, but its street protests have proved effective means of political pressure. The movement, for example, has successfully mau-maued the World Bank and other donor institutions into withdrawing essentially all support for the construction of hydro dams, such as the Narmada River complex that India is now struggling to complete without Western financing. To be sure, dam construction in the developing world often displaces the poor, usually on rough terms, and this is a serious problem; the West should not support developing-world dam construction without ensuring fair treatment of the displaced. But the dams themselves provide pollution-free energy, clean drinking water, and irrigation for agriculture. Not only do nearly all developing nations need more electricity generation to improve living standards—India currently has 6 percent as much electric power per capita as the United States—but to improve human health. The number of children in developing nations who die each year from respiratory diseases caused by *indoor* air pollution, mainly from indoor fires for cooking and heating, exceeds the number of Americans of all ages who die of all causes. Anti-globalizers oppose the dams, power plants, water reservoirs, and other big aid-backed projects that could change that, and their views have gained surprising influence among the Western donor institutions that now live in terror of PC [politically correct] criticism.

Similar pressure inhibits Western donors from exporting high-yield agricultural techniques to Africa, the one part of the world where subsistence farming remains ubiquitous. Environmentalists and anti-globalizers have, for example, fought Western proposals to send fertilizer to Africa, which struggles with some of the world's poorest soils. Anti-globalizers romanticize farming with animal-drawn plows as "appropriate," but most wouldn't last a day at the dehumanizing toil this form of existence imposes and rewards only with meager survival. The United States could do its next great service to the world by teaching Africa our granary-filling methods of farming. Instead, trendy complaints from well-fed anti-globalizers and enviros keep donor institutions from supporting an African Green Revolution. It is a strange and terrible irony that the left's influence over the World Bank and IMF, and the American right's influence in Congress, are conspiring to deny needed and worthwhile foreign aid at the very moment, as Stiglitz notes, that such aid is becoming more honest and effective.

As a result, the United States today gives shockingly little to the world's poor. In the years immediately after World War II, when the United States was funding the successful reconstruction of Western Europe under the Marshall Plan, 15 percent of the federal budget went to foreign aid. Today polls show that most Americans *think* 15 percent of the federal budget goes to foreign aid—and they consider that too much. According to polls, most Americans think foreign aid should consume between 1 percent and 5 percent of the federal budget.

If only it did. In fact, the United States devotes about half of 1 percent of federal spending to foreign aid. The roughly $11 billion for foreign aid in Bush's latest budget request is only about one-seventh as much, in inflation-adjusted dollars, as the United States spent on foreign aid during the Marshall Plan years, when the United States had many more domestic problems that required government money. The aid total in Bush's current fiscal year budget is lower in absolute dollars—not inflation-adjusted—than was spent on aid during most years of the Ronald Reagan administration. And the real figure is even smaller than that, since about $4 billion of the $11 billion goes to Israel and Egypt in what is officially called development aid but is for all intents and purposes an annual payment to ensure observation of the treaty that ended the 1973 Israel-Egypt war. By contrast, all of Africa—excluding Egypt—wracked by poor public health, illiteracy, and malnutrition, receives a mere $1.3 billion annually in U.S. development support, a small fraction of the annual amount Congress just added to U.S. agriculture subsidies.

All industrial nations have reduced aid over the last decade, as "donor fatigue" has set in and rising social-welfare obligations to retirees have increasingly dominated the balance sheets of Western governments. But America's reduction has been the most stark, with the country now spending just 0.1 percent of GDP on aid—less a share of national income than that spent by *Portugal*—versus an average of 0.24 percent for the OECD [Organization for Economic Cooperation and Development] nations. True, other OECD nations—like Japan, usually the world leader in total international development assistance, and Denmark, the world leader in assistance as a share of GDP—do not have significant military obligations, mainly because the United States shields them. But while the United States must protect the globe, the United States is also the wealthiest nation on Earth. To trail Portugal in an important measure of moral responsibility to the world should keep even foreign aid skeptics awake at night.

Before the O'Neill-Bono road show, Bush pledged the United States to a roughly $1.5 billion per year increase in foreign aid. That is admirable but would still leave the country well behind what it was spending in the '50s, when the United States was far less affluent. The administration has proposed that the defense budget rise by $48 billion this year, and the increase is justified. But various estimates, including those from WHO and from Columbia University aid advocate Jeffrey Sachs, hold that increasing America's spending against international AIDS by around merely $2.5 billion per year could dramatically improve African public health, perhaps saving millions of lives. Two and a half billion dollars is about what it costs to build a new attack submarine. Can anyone seriously argue that the same amount to help stop a continent-wide epidemic wouldn't be money well spent?

In the aftermath of September 11 some have suggested the United States should increase foreign aid to improve its image abroad and thus make us safer. This would probably not work—after all, most of the 9/11 murderers came from Saudi Arabia, a wealthy nation that receives no aid; and in any case all were fanatics. But most of the men and women of the developing world mean no harm to anyone. They are struggling to survive and appeal to us for aid. Aid we must send them even though we know some will be stolen or wasted. We must do this because it is right.

Questions for Discussion

1. Easterbrook acknowledges that some foreign aid will be stolen or wasted. Yet he continues to advocate for increasing such assistance. On what bases does he make this argument? How might one go about selling this position to American voters?
2. What percentage of its budget does the United States spend on foreign aid? Is this more, less, or much less than the population thinks it is?
3. From a sense of pure self-interest, does foreign aid seem like a good investment? Why or why not?

 14.5

America Unbound: The Bush Revolution in Foreign Policy

Ivo H. Daalder and James M. Lindsay

Without a doubt the terrorist attacks of September 11, 2001, changed the United States policy toward the rest of the world, especially toward nations and forces we deemed dangerous. The Afghan and Iraq invasions demonstrate our new-found aggressiveness, even as we struggle to bring stability and democracy to those countries. One persistent question addresses whether our post-9/11 behavior has largely flowed out of a reaction to the attacks, or if there exists a more coherent, deeper set of policies, based on a coherent philosophy, which underlies our actions.

In this selection, Ivo H. Daalder and James M. Lindsay argue that just such a set of principles does exist and that it has been in place from the beginning of the Bush administration in 2001. Two basic tenets stand at the base of Bush's revolutionary approach to world affairs. First, America would not be constrained by other nations or by international agreements, as it sought to address the dangers in the world. Second, America should *use* its strength to change the status quo. Most observers would agree with these two basic points, but the authors go on to argue that changes in policy direction have come from President Bush himself, not his hawkish policy advisors. Such an interpretation downgrades the importance of his "neoconservative" advisors and offers a distinctive view of George W. Bush as a "revolutionary" leader, whose success will be determined long after he has left office.

When George W. Bush peered out the window of Air Force One as it flew over Baghdad in early June [2003], he had reason to be pleased. He had just completed a successful visit to Europe and the Middle East. The trip began in Warsaw, where he had the opportunity to personally thank Poland for being one of the two European countries to contribute troops to the Iraq War effort. He then traveled to Russia to celebrate the 300th birthday of St. Petersburg. He flew on to Evian, a city in the French Alps, to attend a summit meeting of the heads of the world's major economies. He next stopped in Sharm el Sheik, Egypt, for a meeting with moderate Arab leaders, before heading to Aqaba, Jordan, on the shore of the Red Sea to discuss the road map for peace with the Israeli and Palestinian prime ministers. He made his final stop in Doha, Qatar, where troops at U.S. Central Command greeted him with thunderous applause. Now Bush looked down on the city that American troops had seized only weeks before.

Bush's seven-day, six-nation trip was in many ways a victory lap to celebrate America's triumph in the Iraq War—a war that many of the leaders Bush met on his trip had opposed. But in a larger sense he and his advisers saw it as a vindication of his leadership. During his first 30 months in office, the man from Midland had started a foreign policy revolution. He had discarded many of the constraints that had bound the United States to its allies and redefined key principles that had governed American engagement in the world for more than

---

Ivo H. Daalder is a senior fellow in the Brookings Foreign Policy Studies Program. James M. Lindsay is vice president and director of studies at the Council on Foreign Relations.

Ivo H. Daalder and James M. Lindsay. "America Unbound: The Bush Revolution in Foreign Policy." *The Brookings Review,* Vol. 21, No. 4 (Fall 2003): pp. 2–6. Reprinted by permission of The Brookings Institution.

half a century. Like most revolutions, Bush's had numerous critics. Yet he now traveled through Europe and the Middle East not as a penitent making amends but as a leader commanding respect. America unbound was remaking the course of international politics. Bush was the rare revolutionary who had succeeded. Or had he?

The Bush Revolution

What precisely was the Bush revolution in foreign policy? At its broadest level, it rested on two beliefs. The first was that in a dangerous world the best—if not the only—way to ensure America's security was to shed the constraints imposed by friends, allies, and international institutions. Maximizing America's freedom to act was essential because the unique position of the United States made it the most likely target for any country or group hostile to the West. Americans could not count on others to protect them; countries inevitably ignored threats that did not involve them. Moreover, formal arrangements would inevitably constrain the ability of the United States to make the most of its unrivaled power. Gulliver must shed the constraints that he helped the Lilliputians weave.

The second belief was that an America unbound should use its strength to change the status quo in the world. Bush did not argue that the United States keep its powder dry while it waited for dangers to gather. Whereas John Quincy Adams—the only other son of a president later to occupy the White House—had held that the United States should not go abroad "in search of monsters to destroy," Bush argued that America would be imperiled if it failed to do just that. "Time is not on our side," he warned in the "Axis of Evil" speech, his 2002 State of the Union address. "I will not wait on events, while dangers gather. I will not stand by, as peril draws closer and closer. The United States of America will not permit the world's most dangerous regimes to threaten us with the world's most destructive weapons." That logic guided the Iraq War, and it animated Bush's efforts to deal with other rogue states.

These fundamental beliefs had important consequences for the practice of American foreign policy. One was a disdain for the sorts of multinational institutions and arrangements developed by presidents from Truman through Clinton and a decided preference for the unilateral exercise of American power. Unilateralism was appealing to Bush and his advisers because it was often easier and more efficient, at least in the short term, than multilateralism. In the Kosovo war, for example, Bush and his advisers believed that the task of coordinating the views of all NATO members greatly complicated the military effort. But in the Afghanistan war, Pentagon planners did not need to subject any of their decisions to foreign approval. This is not to say that Bush flatly ruled out working with others. Rather, his preferred form of multilateralism—to be indulged when unilateral action is impossible or unwise—involved building ad hoc coalitions of the willing, or what Richard Haass, a former adviser to Colin Powell, has called "multilateralism à la carte."

Second, preemption was no longer a last resort of American foreign policy. In a world in which weapons of mass destruction were spreading and terrorists and rogue states were readying to attack in unconventional ways, Bush argued in a report laying out his administration's national security strategy, "the United States can no longer solely rely on a reactive posture as we have in the past. . . . We cannot let our enemies strike first." Indeed, the United States should be prepared to act not just preemptively against imminent threats, but also preventively against potential threats. Vice President Dick Cheney was emphatic on this point in justifying the overthrow of Saddam Hussein on the eve of the Iraq War. "There's no question about who is going to prevail if there is military action. And there's no question but what it is going to be cheaper and less costly to do now than it will be to wait a year or two years or three years until he's developed even more deadly weapons, perhaps nuclear weapons."

Third, the United States should use its unprecedented power to change the regimes in rogue states. The idea of regime change was not new to American foreign policy. The Eisenhower administration engineered the overthrow of Iranian Prime Minister Mohammed Mossadegh; the CIA trained Cuban exiles in a botched bid to oust Fidel Castro; Ronald Reagan channeled aid to the Nicaraguan contras to overthrow the Sandinistas; and Bill Clinton helped Serb opposition forces get rid of Slobodan Milosevic. What was different in the Bush presidency was the willingness, even in the absence of a direct attack on the United States, to use U.S. military forces for the express purpose of toppling other governments. This was the gist of both the Afghanistan and the Iraq wars. It rested on the belief that if the United States pushed, nobody could push back.

September 11

The Bush revolution did not start, as many have suggested, on September 11. The worldview that drove it existed long before jet planes plowed into the Twin Towers and the Pentagon. Bush outlined his philosophy while he was on the campaign trail. Most commentators failed to notice what he was saying because they were concerned more with how much he knew about the world than with what he believed. Bush began implementing his ideas as soon as he took the oath of office. His belief in the need for an America unbound was behind his pursuit of missile defense. It was also behind his rejection of the Kyoto Protocol on climate change, the International Criminal Court, and a host of other multilateral agreements he criticized or abandoned during the first eight months of his presidency.

What September 11 provided was the motive to enact the Bush revolution rapidly and without hesitation. Foreign policy went from being a secondary priority of his presidency to being its defining mission. "I'm here for a reason," Bush told his chief political adviser, Karl Rove, shortly after the attacks, "and this is going to be how we're going to be judged." He told Japanese Prime Minister Junichiro Koizumi something similar. "History will be the judge, but it won't judge well somebody who doesn't act, somebody who just bides time here." The war on terrorism became an issue that boiled in his blood, and he intended to fight it in his fashion.

September 11 also gave Bush the opportunity to enact his revolution without fear of being challenged at home. Congressional displeasure with Bush's handling of foreign policy had grown throughout the summer of 2001. Some Democrats even thought it could be a winning issue for them in the midterm elections. In the wake of the attacks, however, congressional resistance to Bush's national security policies evaporated. Congress's deference partly reflected the enormity of the attacks and a principled belief that lawmakers should defer to strong presidential leadership in times of national crisis. But it also reflected a healthy dose of politics. Rather than blame the president for failing to anticipate the attacks, Americans rallied around him. Bush's newfound popularity translated into political power. Lawmakers may ignore the pleadings of an unpopular president, but they usually heed the demands of a popular one.

The Neoconservative Myth

By the end of the Iraq War, most commentators acknowledged that Bush had presided over a revolution in American foreign policy. They were doubtful, however, that the president was responsible for it. They instead gave the credit (or blame) to "neoconservative" thinkers within the administration, led by Deputy Secretary of Defense Paul Wolfowitz, who they said were determined to use America's great power to transform despotic regimes into liberal democracies.* One writer alleged that Bush was "the callow instrument of neoconservative ideologues." Another remarked on the "neoconservative coup" in Washington and wondered if "George W. fully understands the grand strategy that Wolfowitz and other aides are unfolding." A third thought the neoconservatives' victory was obvious. "Unless you live at the bottom of a well, you've probably noticed that 9/11 and Iraq have a transforming effect on the American Right. The short formulation is that so-called neoconservatism has triumphed."

This conventional wisdom was wrong on at least two counts. First, it fundamentally misunderstood the intellectual currents within the Bush administration and the Republican party more generally. Neoconservatives were more

---

*Neoconservativism is a conservative movement with roots in the traditional left of mid-century America. It has supported hawkish foreign policy positions.

prominent outside the administration, particularly in the pages of Commentary and the Weekly Standard and in the television studios of Fox News, than they were inside it. The bulk of Bush's advisers, including most notably Dick Cheney and Defense Secretary Donald Rumsfeld, were not neocons. They were instead assertive nationalists—traditional hard-line conservatives willing to use American military power to defeat threats to U.S. security but reluctant as a general rule to use American primacy to remake the world in its image. Whereas neoconservatives talked of lengthy and expensive military occupation in Iraq, assertive nationalists spoke of a quick transition and leaving "Iraq for the Iraqis."

Although neoconservatives and assertive nationalists differed on whether the United States should actively spread its values abroad, both were deeply skeptical of the cold war consensus on the importance of the rule of law and the relevance of international institutions to American foreign policy. They placed their faith not in diplomacy and treaties, but in power and resolve. Agreement on this key point allowed neoconservatives and assertive nationalists to form a marriage of convenience in overthrowing the cold war approach to foreign policy even as they disagreed about what kind of commitment the United States should make to rebuilding Iraq and remaking the rest of the world.

The second and more important flaw with the neoconservative coup theory was that it grossly underestimated George W. Bush. The man from Midland was not a figurehead in someone else's revolution. He may have entered the Oval Office not knowing which general ran Pakistan, but during his first 30 months in office he was the puppeteer, not the puppet. He actively solicited the counsel of his seasoned advisers, and he tolerated if not encouraged vigorous disagreement among them. When necessary, he overruled them. George W. Bush led his own revolution.

Whither the Revolution?

Not all revolutions succeed. As Air Force One tipped its wings over Baghdad in a gesture of triumph, there were troubling signs of things to come for an America unbound. U.S. troops in Iraq found themselves embroiled in a guerrilla war with remnants of Saddam Hussein's regime. Anger overseas at what was seen as an arrogant and hypocritical America had swelled. Close allies spoke openly not of how best to work with the United States, but of how to constrain its ability to act. Washington was beginning to confront a new question: were the costs of the Bush revolution in foreign policy about to swamp the benefits?

Part of the problem with the Bush revolution lay in how Bush and his advisers conducted it. They declined to cloak the iron fist of American power in the velvet glove of diplomacy, preferring instead to express contempt for opinions different from their own. Donald Rumsfeld, as his dismissal of France and Germany as "old Europe" attested, had a particular zeal for insulting friends and allies. Not surprisingly, this attitude struck many outside the United States—and more than a few within it—as an arrogance born of power, not principle. They resented it profoundly.

The deeper problem, however, was that the fundamental premise of the Bush revolution—that America's security rested on an America unbound—was mistaken. For all the talk at the start of the 21st century of the United States being a hyperpower, the world was beyond the ability of any one country to control. Many of the most important challenges America faced overseas could be met only with the active cooperation of others. The question was how best to secure that cooperation.

Bush maintained that if America led, friends and allies would follow. True, they might grumble because they disliked how Washington intended to lead. Some might even decide to wait until they saw the benefits of American action. In the end, however, they would join forces with the United States in combating threats such as terrorism and weapons proliferation because they trusted America's motives and they shared its interests. Countries would not cut off their nose to spite their face.

Iraq exposed the flaw in this thinking. Most countries, including all members of the UN Security Council, shared a major interest in making sure Iraq did not possess weapons of mass destruction, especially nuclear weapons. But that common interest did not automatically translate into active cooperation in a war to oust Saddam Hussein—or even into support for such a war. A few countries actively tried to stop the march to war, and many others simply sat on the sidelines. Little changed after the toppling of Saddam Hussein's statue in Firdos Square. Although many countries believed that stabilizing postwar Iraq was vitally important—for regional stability, international security, and their own national safety—they did not rush to join the reconstruction effort. In July 2003, American troops constituted more than 90 percent of all forces supporting the Iraq operation—at an annual cost to the American taxpayer of $50 billion. Britain provided most of the other forces. The remaining foreign contributions were insignificant. Hungary, for instance, agreed to provide 133 truck drivers but no trucks, mechanics, or anything else. In other cases, countries agreed to contribute troops only after Washington agreed to pay for them—giving a whole new meaning to the concept of burden sharing.

The lesson of Iraq, then, was that sometimes when America leads, few follow. This ultimately was the real danger of the Bush revolution. America's friends and allies seldom could stop Washington from doing as it wished, no matter how much some commentators opined to the contrary. However, America's friends and allies did not need to resist American policy to make Washington pay a price for its desire to play unbound by any rules. They could simply refuse to come to its aid when their help was most needed or desired. That, in turn, risked undermining not only what America could achieve abroad but also domestic support at home for engaging the world. Americans could rightly ask:

if others are unwilling to bear the burdens of meeting tough challenges, why should we? In that respect, an America unbound could ultimately lead to a America that is less secure.

Questions for Discussion

1. Bush's "revolutionary" foreign policy disdains the use of multilateral institutions (such as the United Nations), according to Daalder and Lindsay. If that is so, what are the advantages for the United States? The disadvantages? Can this be effective as a long-term strategy?
2. What was the role of September 11 in the evolution of Bush's new foreign policy? Could that policy have been carried out absent the terrorist attacks?